Python Network Programming

Conquer all your networking challenges with the powerful Python language

Abhishek Ratan
Eric Chou
Pradeeban Kathiravelu
Dr. M. O. Faruque Sarker

BIRMINGHAM - MUMBAI

Python Network Programming

Copyright © 2019 Packt Publishing

All rights reserved. No part of this book may be reproduced, stored in a retrieval system, or transmitted in any form or by any means, without the prior written permission of the publisher, except in the case of brief quotations embedded in critical articles or reviews.

Every effort has been made in the preparation of this book to ensure the accuracy of the information presented. However, the information contained in this book is sold without warranty, either express or implied. Neither the authors, nor Packt Publishing or its dealers and distributors, will be held liable for any damages caused or alleged to have been caused directly or indirectly by this book.

Packt Publishing has endeavored to provide trademark information about all of the companies and products mentioned in this book by the appropriate use of capitals. However, Packt Publishing cannot guarantee the accuracy of this information.

First published: January 2019

Production reference: 1300119

Published by Packt Publishing Ltd.
Livery Place
35 Livery Street
Birmingham
B3 2PB, UK.

ISBN 978-1-78883-546-6

www.packtpub.com

mapt.io

Mapt is an online digital library that gives you full access to over 5,000 books and videos, as well as industry leading tools to help you plan your personal development and advance your career. For more information, please visit our website.

Why subscribe?

- Spend less time learning and more time coding with practical eBooks and Videos from over 4,000 industry professionals
- Improve your learning with Skill Plans built especially for you
- Get a free eBook or video every month
- Mapt is fully searchable
- Copy and paste, print, and bookmark content

Packt.com

Did you know that Packt offers eBook versions of every book published, with PDF and ePub files available? You can upgrade to the eBook version at www.packt.com and as a print book customer, you are entitled to a discount on the eBook copy. Get in touch with us at customercare@packtpub.com for more details.

At www.packt.com, you can also read a collection of free technical articles, sign up for a range of free newsletters, and receive exclusive discounts and offers on Packt books and eBooks.

Contributors

About the authors

Abhishek Ratan has around 15 years of technical experience in networking, automation, and various ITIL processes, and has worked in various roles in different organizations. As a network engineer, security engineer, automation engineer, TAC engineer, tech lead, and content writer, he has gained a wealth of experience during the 15 years of his career. Abhishek also has a deep interest in strategy game playing, and if he is not working on technical stuff, he is busy spending time on his strategy games.

He is currently working as a Sr. Automation Engineer at ServiceNow, learning, and expanding his automation skills in the ServiceNow platform. His earlier experience includes working for companies such as Microsoft, Symantec, and Navisite,which has given him exposure to various environments.

Eric Chou is a seasoned technologist with an industry experience of over 18 years. He has worked on and helped managed some of the largest networks in the industry while working at Amazon AWS, Microsoft Azure, and other companies. Eric is passionate about network automation, Python, and helping companies build better security postures. Eric is the author of several books and online classes on networking with Python and network security. He is the proud inventor of two patents in IP telephony. Eric shares his deep interest in technology through his books, classes, and his blog, and contributes to some of the popular Python open source projects.

Pradeeban Kathiravelu is an open source evangelist. He is a Ph.D. researcher at INESC-ID Lisboa/Instituto Superior Tecnico, Universidade de Lisboa, Portugal, and Universite Catholique de Louvain, Belgium. He is a fellow of Erasmus Mundus Joint Degree in Distributed Computing (EMJD-DC), researching a software-defined approach to quality of service and data quality in multi-tenant clouds. Pradeeban holds a bachelor's degree in engineering, from the University of Moratuwa, Sri Lanka and a master's degree in science, Erasmus Mundus European Master in Distributed Computing (EMDC), from Instituto Superior Tecnico, Portugal and KTH Royal Institute of Technology, Sweden. His research interests include software-defined networking, distributed systems, cloud computing, web services, big data in biomedical informatics, network functions virtualization, and data mining. He is interested in open source software development and has been an active participant in the Google Summer of Code (GSoC) program since 2009, as a student and as a mentor. Pradeeban has published several conference papers and co-authored a few book chapters. He has also worked on the OpenDaylight Cookbook and the Learning OpenDaylight as a technical reviewer. Python Network Programming Cookbook, Second Edition (2017) is his first book as an author.

Dr. M. O. Faruque Sarker is a software architect, who received his Ph.D. in multi-robot systems from the University of South Wales. Currently, he works at the University College London, where he shapes various Linux and open source software solutions, mainly on cloud computing platforms, for commercial companies, educational institutions, and multinational consultancies. Over the past 10 years, he has led several Python software development and cloud infrastructure automation projects. In 2009, when he started using Python, he was responsible for shepherding a fleet of miniature E-puck robots at the University of South Wales, Newport, UK. Later, he honed his Python skills and was invited to work on the Google Summer of Code (2009/2010) programs for contributing to the BlueZ and Tahoe-LAFS open source projects. He is the author of Python Network Programming Cookbook and Learning Python Network Programming books both by Packt Publishing.

Packt is searching for authors like you

If you're interested in becoming an author for Packt, please visit `authors.packtpub.com` and apply today. We have worked with thousands of developers and tech professionals, just like you, to help them share their insight with the global tech community. You can make a general application, apply for a specific hot topic that we are recruiting an author for, or submit your own idea.

Table of Contents

Preface

Python Network Programming reviews the core elements of Python and the TCP/IP protocol suite. It highlights major aspects of Python network programming such as writing simple networking clients, creating and deploying SDN and NFV systems, and extending your network with Mininet. You'll also learn how to automate legacy and the latest network devices. As you progress through the chapters, you'll use Python for DevOps and open source tools to test, secure, and analyze your network. This Learning Path will guide you in configuring the Linux Foundation networking ecosystem and deploying automated networks in the cloud. You will gain experience in retrieving network information with flow-based monitoring, a polling mechanism, and data visualization. Toward the end, you'll develop client-side applications, such as web API clients, email clients, SSH, and FTP, using socket programming and multithreaded or event-driven architectures.

By the end of this Learning Path, you will have learned how to analyze a network's security vulnerabilities using advanced network packet capture and analysis techniques.

This Learning Path includes content from the following Packt products:

- Practical Network Automation by Abhishek Ratan
- Mastering Python Networking by Eric Chou
- Python Network Programming Cookbook, Second Edition by Pradeeban Kathiravelu, Dr. M. O. Faruque Sarker

Who this book is for

If you are a Python developer or a system administrator who wants to start network programming, this Learning Path gets you a step closer to your goal. IT professionals and DevOps engineers who are new to managing network devices or those with minimal experience looking to expand their knowledge and skills in Python will also find this Learning Path useful. Although prior knowledge of networking is not required, some experience in Python programming will be helpful for a better understanding of the concepts in the Learning Path.

What this book covers

`Chapter 1`, *Fundamental Concepts*, introduces how to get started with automation.

`Chapter 2`, *Python for Network Engineers*, introduces to Python as a scripting language, and samples to explain usage of Python in accessing network devices and data parsing from the device outputs.

`Chapter 3`, *Continuous Integration for Network Engineers*, gives an overview of integration principles for network engineers to manage rapid growth with high availability and rapid disaster recovery.

`Chapter 4`, *SDN Concepts in Network Automation*, talks about moving your enterprise Java applications to virtualized x86 platforms to better utilize resources with easier life cycle and scalability management.

`Chapter 5`, *Low-Level Network Device Interactions*, uses practical examples to illustrate how to use Python to execute commands on a network device. It will also discuss the challenges of having a CLI-only interface in automation. The chapter will use the Pexpect and Paramiko libraries for the examples.

`Chapter 6`, *APIs and Intent-Driven Networking*, discusses the newer network devices that support **Application Programming Interfaces** (**APIs**) and other high-level interaction methods. It also illustrates tools that allow abstraction of low-level tasks while focusing on the intent of the network engineers. A discussion about and examples of Cisco NX-API, Juniper PyEZ, and Arista Pyeapi will be used in the chapter.

`Chapter 7`, *The Python Automation Framework – Ansible Basics*, discusses the basics of Ansible, an open source, Python-based automation framework. Ansible moves one step further from APIs and focuses on declarative task intent. In this chapter, we will cover the advantages of using Ansible, its high-level architecture, and see some practical examples of Ansible with Cisco, Juniper, and Arista devices.

`Chapter 8`, *The Python Automation Framework – Beyond Basics*, builds on the knowledge in the previous chapter and covers the more advanced Ansible topics. We will cover conditionals, loops, templates, variables, Ansible Vault, and roles. It will also cover the basics of writing custom modules.

`Chapter 9`, *AWS Cloud Networking*, shows how we can use AWS to build a virtual network that is functional and resilient. We will cover virtual private cloud technologies such as CloudFormation, VPC routing table, access-list, Elastic IP, NAT Gateway, Direct Connect, and other related topics.

`Chapter 10`, *Working with Git*, we will illustrate how we can leverage Git for collaboration and code version control. Practical examples of using Git for network operations will be used in this chapter.

`Chapter 11`, *Sockets, IPv4, and Simple Client/Server Programming*, introduces you to Python's core networking library with various small tasks and enables you to create your first clientserver application.

`Chapter 12`, *Multiplexing Socket I/O for Better Performance*, discusses various useful techniques for scaling your client/server applications with default and third-party libraries.

`Chapter 13`, *IPv6, Unix Domain Sockets, and Network Interfaces*, focuses more on administering your local machine and looking after your local area network.

`Chapter 14`, *Programming with HTTP for the Internet*, enables you to create a mini commandline browser with various features such as submitting web forms, handling cookies, managing partial downloads, compressing data, and serving secure content over HTTPS.

`Chapter 15`, *Email Protocols, FTP, and CGI Programming*, brings you the joy of automating your FTP and e-mail tasks such as manipulating your Gmail account, and reading or sending emails from a script or creating a guest book for your web application. We learn to write email clients with SMTP and POP3.

`Chapter 16`, *Programming Across Machine Boundaries*, gives you a taste of automating your system administration and deployment tasks over SSH. You can run commands, install packages, or set up new websites remotely from your laptop.

`Chapter 17`, *Working with Web Services – XML-RPC, SOAP, and REST*, introduces you to various API protocols such as XML-RPC, SOAP, and REST. You can programmatically ask any website or web service for information and interact with them. For example, you can search for products on Amazon or Google.

`Chapter 18`, *Network Monitoring and Security*, introduces you to various techniques for capturing, storing, analyzing, and manipulating network packets. This encourages you to go further to investigate your network security issues using concise Python scripts.

`Chapter 19`, *Network Modeling*, introduces you to the world of network simulations and emulations. You learn to simulate networks with NS-3, and emulate networking systems with Mininet and its extensions.

`Chapter 20`, *Authentication, Authorization, and Accounting (AAA)*, introduces how the networks are secured, and discusses configuring LDAP clients with Python, accounting aspects of the network, and authentication and access of network services.

`Chapter 21`, *Open and Proprietary Networking Solutions*, discusses in detail, configuring largescale enterprise networking projects, including a few projects from Cisco, Juniper, VMware, and the Linux Foundation.

`Chapter 22`, *NFV and Orchestration – A Larger Ecosystem*, discusses configuring complex NFV and orchestration systems of the Linux Foundation, such as OPNFV, DPDK, SNAS.io, Dronekit, and PNDA. We elaborate the use of Python in these complex systems.

`Chapter 23`, *Programming the Internet*, presents you various Python libraries for BGP protocol and implementations developed for the internet scale. We learn to use and benchmark libraries such as exabgp and yabgp, and also discuss the looking glass implementations with Python.

To get the most out of this book

To get the most out of this book, some basic hands-on network operation knowledge and Python is recommended. Most of the chapters can be read in any order, with the exceptions of chapters 7 and 8, which should be read in sequence. Besides the basic software and hardware tools introduced at the beginning of the book, new tools relevant to each of the chapters will be introduced.

The hardware and software requirements for this book are Python (3.5 onward), Windows, Linux, an Ansible installation, and GNS3 (for testing) or real routers.

You need an internet connection for downloading the Python libraries. Also, basic knowledge of Python and networking is required.

Download the example code files

You can download the example code files for this book from your account at `www.packt.com`. If you purchased this book elsewhere, you can visit `www.packt.com/support` and register to have the files emailed directly to you.

You can download the code files by following these steps:

1. Log in or register at `www.packt.com`.
2. Select the **SUPPORT** tab.
3. Click on **Code Downloads & Errata**.
4. Enter the name of the book in the **Search** box and follow the onscreen instructions.

Once the file is downloaded, please make sure that you unzip or extract the folder using the latest version of:

- WinRAR/7-Zip for Windows
- Zipeg/iZip/UnRarX for Mac
- 7-Zip/PeaZip for Linux

The code bundle for the book is also hosted on GitHub at `https://github.com/PacktPublishing/Python-Network-Programming`. In case there's an update to the code, it will be updated on the existing GitHub repository.

We also have other code bundles from our rich catalog of books and videos available at `https://github.com/PacktPublishing/`. Check them out!

Download the color images

We also provide a PDF file that has color images of the screenshots/diagrams used in this book. You can download it here: `https://www.packtpub.com/sites/default/files/downloads/9781788835466_ColorImages.pdf`.

Conventions used

There are a number of text conventions used throughout this book.

`CodeInText`: Indicates code words in text, database table names, folder names, filenames, file extensions, pathnames, dummy URLs, user input, and Twitter handles. Here is an example: "The `input()` method is used to get an input from the user."

A block of code is set as follows:

```
#PowerShell sample code:
$countries="India","UK","USA","France"
foreach ($country in $countries)
{
write-host ($country+" is good")
}
```

Any command-line input or output is written as follows:

```
easy_install <name of module>
```

Bold: Indicates a new term, an important word, or words that you see onscreen. For example, words in menus or dialog boxes appear in the text like this. Here is an example: "If you need something different, click on the **DOWNLOADS** link in the header for all possible downloads: "

Warnings or important notes appear like this.

Tips and tricks appear like this.

Get in touch

Feedback from our readers is always welcome.

General feedback: If you have questions about any aspect of this book, mention the book title in the subject of your message and email us at `customercare@packtpub.com`.

Errata: Although we have taken every care to ensure the accuracy of our content, mistakes do happen. If you have found a mistake in this book, we would be grateful if you would report this to us. Please visit `www.packt.com/submit-errata`, selecting your book, clicking on the Errata Submission Form link, and entering the details.

Piracy: If you come across any illegal copies of our works in any form on the Internet, we would be grateful if you would provide us with the location address or website name. Please contact us at `copyright@packt.com` with a link to the material.

If you are interested in becoming an author: If there is a topic that you have expertise in and you are interested in either writing or contributing to a book, please visit `authors.packtpub.com`.

Reviews

Please leave a review. Once you have read and used this book, why not leave a review on the site that you purchased it from? Potential readers can then see and use your unbiased opinion to make purchase decisions, we at Packt can understand what you think about our products, and our authors can see your feedback on their book. Thank you!

For more information about Packt, please visit `packt.com`.

1
Fundamental Concepts

This chapter introduces the concept of network automation and familiarizes you with the keywords that are part of the automation framework. Before we dive into the details of network automation, it is important to understand why we need network automation and what we can achieve if we embrace the automation concepts and framework. This chapter also provides an insight into the traditional model of engineer and support operations, and shows how network automation can help bridge that gap for better efficiency and reliability.

Some of the topics covered in this chapter are as follows:

- What is network automation?
- DevOps
- Software-defined networking
- Basics of OpenFlow
- Basic programming concepts
- Programming language choices for automation
- Introduction to REST framework

Network automation

Automation, as the word suggests, is a framework of automating a particular task by understanding, interpreting, and creating logic. This includes enhancing the current capabilities of the tasks that are done manually and reducing the error rate of those tasks while focusing on scaling the task with reduced effort.

As an example, imagine we need to upgrade the IOS image of a Cisco router. This can involve multiple tasks, such as loading the image on the router, validating the checksum of the image, offloading traffic (if it's a production router), modifying the boot variable, and finally, reloading the router with the new image.

All of this is feasible if we have only one router to upgrade. Now take a similar scenario and try to implement it for around 1,000 routers.

Let's say we take 30 minutes getting each router to perform the aforementioned tasks. It's an easy calculation of 1000*30=30,000 minutes of manual effort.

Also, if we are performing tasks on each router manually, think of the errors that can creep in.

Network automation would be helpful in this scenario, as it can take care of all the preceding aspects and perform the tasks in parallel. Hence, if it takes 30 minutes of manual effort for one router, and in the worst case scenario the same 30 minutes for automation to perform the same task, then parallel execution would result in all 1,000 routers being upgraded within the same 30 minutes.

Hence, final amount of time will be only 30 minutes, irrespective of the number of routers you throw at the automation framework. This also drastically reduces the need for manual work, and an engineer can focus on any failures in the 1,000 network devices.

In the upcoming sections, I will introduce you to some of the concepts, tools, and examples that will get you started with building automation frameworks and effectively using them in network scenarios to perform network-related activities.

This also assumes that you have an idea of network concepts and common terminology used in networking.

Some of the examples that I will provide assume familiarity with syslog, TACACS, basic router configs such as hostnames, iOS image loading, basic routing and switching concepts, and **Simple Network Management Protocol** (**SNMP**).

DevOps

Historically, there have been two specific teams in every networking department. One of the teams is the engineering team, which is responsible for conceiving new ideas to improve the network and designing, deploying, and optimizing the current infrastructure. This team is primarily responsible for performing tasks such as configuration and cabling from scratch.

The other team is the support team. This team, also known as the operations team, ensures the current deployed infrastructure is up and running and focuses on performing day-to-day activities such as upgrades, quick fixes, and support to any consumers of that network infrastructure. In a traditional model, there are hand-offs and knowledge transfers from the engineering team to the operations team for support of the current deployed infrastructure. Because of the segregation of the two teams, the engineer team members do not focus on writing clear documentation, or sometimes do not even provide adequate information to operations team members, causing delays in troubleshooting and fixing issues. This could even lead to a simple solution scaling to a bigger problem because of the different approach that a engineering team member would take compared to an operations team member.

Nowadays, to solve this problem, the DevOps model was conceived, which brings the best from both teams. Rather than being a fancy designation, a DevOps model is a culture that needs to be created among the current teams. In a DevOps model, an engineer from any team is responsible for the complete life cycle of a specific project. This includes creating part of the infrastructure and supporting it by themselves. A big benefit of this model is that because a person has created a part of the system and supports it, they know all the aspects of that part and can work on it again to make it better by understanding the challenges that arise from customer or user experiences. A DevOps engineer should understand the engineering and operations for the part of the infrastructure that they have created. By adding an automation skill set to the DevOps experience, an engineer can manage complex tasks with ease and focus on reliability and scalability in a better manner than engineers who are distributed in different domains in the traditional model.

Software-defined networking

As you may be aware, there have been multiple proprietary networking devices, such as firewalls, switches, and routers, that were made by different network vendors. However, owing to the proprietary information from each different vendor, multiple network devices might not exist in a single network infrastructure environment. Even if they exist together, network engineers have to focus their effort on ensuring that each vendor device can exist in a network path without any hiccups. There might be times when one routing protocol might not be compatible with all the network devices in a multi-vendor environment, and a lot of time is wasted ensuring either the removal of that protocol, or the removal of the vendor which that does not support that protocol. This can waste effort and time, which could be better spent improving the infrastructure.

To solve this type of issue, **software-defined networking** (**SDN**) has been introduced. In an SDN scenario, a packet flow is defined from a central controller that in turn interacts with multi-vendor equipment to create/define rules based upon the required packet flow. This shifts the focus of a network engineer entirely to how the traffic flows, which path the packet takes, to even responding to link down situations through automated routing of packets by configuring some rules or policies on the controllers. Another advantage of SDN is that the multi-vendor equipment is now not the center piece of infrastructure. The focus shifts to how optimally the routing and traffic shaping (the process to identify the optimal path of traffic flow) is occurring. As part of Software driven tasks, there are pieces of code that are specifically written to control a specific task or goal (similar to functions or methods in programming). This piece of code is triggered by controller decisions or rules, which in turn adds, modifies, or deletes configs on the multi-vendor device to ensure the rule set on the controller is adhered to. SDN even has the ability to completely isolate a failure domain, through the identification of a physical link down or even a total device failure without affecting the flow of traffic in real time. For example, a switch can issue a request to the controller if it gets a packet destined for a network that it does not know. This would be a packet drop or route not found in a traditional network model, but with SDN, it is the task of a controller to provide the destination or path information to the switches to correctly route the packet.

This ensures the troubleshooting becomes much easier, since a network engineer now has full control of each path/packet flow, irrespective of the vendor-specific protocol or technology support. Additionally, since now we are following a standard set of protocols, we can even lower our costs by removing more expensive proprietary network devices and replacing them with open standards network gear.

OpenFlow

OpenFlow is a communication protocol that is used for communication between different vendor's equipment for the packet flow. This standard is maintained by a group called **Open Network Foundation** (**ONF**). OpenFlow, as the name suggests, is used to control the flow of packets in a network layer through a mix of **Access Control Lists** (**ACLs**) and routing protocols.

OpenFlow primarily has two components—controllers and switches. Controllers are used to take decisions in terms of creating a path for the packet to flow across the different connected devices, and switches (or network equipment) are dynamically configured from the controller based upon the path that a packet needs to take.

Going a little more in-depth, OpenFlow controllers control the routing of packets in OpenFlow switch forwarding tables through the modification, addition, or deletion of packet matching rules as decided by the controller.

As OpenFlow is another protocol, it runs over TCP and works on port `6653` on controllers. At the time of writing, OpenFlow standard 1.4 is currently active and being widely used in the SDN framework. OpenFlow is an additional service that proprietary network vendors run alongside their custom software. This, in general, ensures that the data forwarding or data packet handling is still part of proprietary switch, but the data flow or control plane tasks is now taken over by OpenFlow controllers. As part of SDN framework, if a participating switch receives a packet and does not know where to send it, it communicates with the OpenFlow controller for an answer. The controller, based upon its preconfigured logic, decides what action to take for that unknown packet and can get switches that it is controlling to create a separate or a specific path for that packet to flow across the network. Because of this behavior, this is the protocol that is currently being deployed across all deployments where SDN is being introduced.

Program concepts

Now, as we start working upon our practical approach to automation, we need to understand the basics of what a program is and how to write one.

Simply explained, a program is a set of instructions that is passed to the system to perform a specific task. This set of instructions is based upon real-life challenges and tasks that need to be accomplished in an automated method. Small sets of programs can be combined to create an application that can be installed, deployed, and configured for individual or organizational requirements. Some of the key concepts and programming techniques that we will discuss from this point onward will be PowerShell and Python. These are the two most popular scripting languages that are used to create quick, effective, and result-oriented automation.

These are some of the key concepts that I would like to introduce while creating a program:

- Variables
- Data types
- Decision makers
- Loops
- Arrays

- Functions
- Best practices

Variables

These are predefined, human-readable, and understandable words or letters that are used to store some values. At the very basis of writing a program we need a variable in which we will store the data or information, and based upon the variables, we can further enhance the programming logic. As we can see in the first line, an important part of creating a variable is that it should be human-readable and understandable.

Let us take an example: Suppose I want to store a number `2` in a variable. We can choose any name for a variable and define it:

```
Option 1: x=2
Option 2: number=2
```

The correct answer will be `Option 2`, as we know by the variable name (`number`) that this variable contains a specific number. As we can see in the preceding example, if we keep on using random ways of defining variables as we would when creating a big program, the complexity would be increased substantially because of the unclear meanings of the variables.

Different programming languages have different ways to define a variable, but the underlying concept of ensuring a variable is human-readable should be the top-most priority of the programmer or program author.

Data types

As the name suggests, these are the classifications of the values that we pass on to the variable. A variable can be defined to store a specific type of value that can be declared based upon the data type.

There are multiple data types, but for our initial discussion there are primarily four data types that need to be understood:

- **String**: This is a catch-all data type. Any value defined as a string is as simple as saying the value is plain English with characters, alphabets, special characters, and so on. I have referred to it as a catch-all data type because nearly all other data types can be converted to string format keeping the same values intact during conversion to string.

Consider the following example:

```
number=2
```

This defines that a variable named `number` has a value of `2`.
Similarly, if we declare:

```
string_value="2"
```

This is same as saying that a value of `2` has been now defined as string and stored in a variable named `string_value`.

- **Integer**: This specifies that any value that is a number needs to be defined with this data type. The key thing to note here is that an integer value will contain a whole number and not a decimal value:

Consider an example as follows:

```
integernumber=2
```

This defines that a variable named as `integernumber` has a value of the number `2`.
An incorrect assignation here would be something like:

```
integernumber=2.4
```

This would give an error in some programming languages as an integer needs to be interpreted as a whole number and not a decimal value.

- **Float**: This data type removes the restriction that we saw earlier with integer. It simply means we can have a decimal number and can perform mathematical calculations and storage of decimal values in a float data type.
- **Datetime**: This is an extended data type found in a lot of modern scripting languages. This data type ensures that the values that are being stored or retrieved are in date format. This is typically useful if we need to create a program that uses some time or date calculations. As an example, perhaps we need to find out how many syslogs were generated from a router in the last seven days. The last seven days will be stored by this data type.

Decision makers

These are one of the very critical components of a program and they can define the flow of the program. As the name suggests, a decision maker decides a certain action based upon a certain condition.

Simply put, if you wanted to buy an ice cream you would go to an ice-cream shop, but for a coffee you would go to a coffee shop. In this case, the condition was whether you wanted ice cream or coffee. The action was based upon the result of the condition: you went to that specific shop.

These decision makers, also called **conditions**, are defined in a different manner in different scripting languages, but the result of each of the conditions decides the future flow of the program.

Generally, in a condition, two or more values are compared and either a true or a false is returned. Depending on the value returned, a specific set of instructions are executed.

Consider the following example:

```
Condition:
if (2 is greater than 3), then
Proceed to perform Option 1
else
Proceed to perform Option 2
```

As we see in the preceding example, a condition is evaluated and if `2 is greater than 3`, then the flow of program will be performed based upon `Option 1`, and in case of a false (which means 2 is not greater than 3), `Option 2` would be chosen.

If we want a bit more complexity, we can add multiple decision-making statements or conditions to granulize the flow of a program.

Let us take an example:

```
if (Car is of red color), then
  if (Car is Automatic), then
    if (Car is a sedan), then
      Option 1 (Purchase the car)
    else (Option 2, ask for a sedan car from dealer)
  else (Option 3, ask for an Automatic car from dealer)
else (Option 4, ask for a red car from dealer)
```

As we can see in this complex condition, we can easily decide the flow of a program based upon additional checks. In this case, I only want to buy a `Car` that is `red`, `Automatic`, and a `sedan`. If any of those conditions are not met, then I ask the dealer to meet that specific condition.

Another thing to notice in the preceding example is that the conditions are nested within each other, hence they are shown as nested with spaces deciding the sub-conditions from its parent condition. This is usually depicted within brackets or with simple indentation based upon the scripting language used.

Sometimes, it is necessary to evaluate a value against multiple conditions and perform an action if it matches any of the conditions. This is called a **switch case** in programming.

Consider an example as follows:

```
Carcolor="Red" (Here we define a variable if the value of string as
Red)
switch (Carcolor)
Case (Red) (Perform Option 1)
Case (Blue) (Perform Option 2)
Case (Green) (Perform Option 3)
```

Here we see that depending upon the variable's value, a certain type of action can be performed. In this case, option 1 will be performed. If we change the value of the `Carcolor` variable to `Blue`, then option 2 will be performed.

An important component of conditions are the comparison operators that we use to compare two values for the result. Some example operators are equal to, greater than, less than, and not equal to. Depending on which comparison operator we use, the results can vary.

Let us take an example:

```
greaternumber=5
lessernumber=6

if (greaternumber 'greater than' lessernumber)
Perform Option 1
else
Perform Option 2
```

We declare two variables named `greaternumber` and `lessernumber` and compare them in a condition. The conditional operator we use is `greater than`, which would result in option 1 if the condition is true (`greaternumber` is greater than `lessernumber`), or would result in option 2 if the condition is false (`greaternumber` is not greater than `lessernumber`).

Additionally, we also have operators that are called logical operators, such as `AND`, `OR`, or `NOT`. We can combine more than one condition by using these logical operators. They have a similar meaning in English, which means that if, for example, we use the `AND` operator, we want condition 1 `AND` condition 2 both to be true before we perform an action.

Consider an example: I want to buy a car only when the `car` is `red`, `automatic`, and a `sedan`:

```
if (car is 'red') AND (car is 'automatic') AND (car is 'sedan')
Perform action 'buy car'
else
Perform action 'do not buy'
```

This simply means I would evaluate all the three conditions and only if all of them are true, then I would perform the action `buy car`. In this case, if any of the conditions do not meet the values, such as the car is blue, then the `do not buy` action will be performed.

Loops

A loop, as we know in common language, is circling the same path over and over again. In other words, if I am asked to fetch five ice creams from the ice cream store, and I can carry only one ice cream at a time, I will repeat the process of going to the ice cream shop to purchase ice cream five times. Correlating this with programming, if the same set of instructions need to be performed multiple times, then we put those instructions inside a loop.

A very basic loop is generally depicted as an iteration of a variable as many times as we want the instructions to be carried out.

Let's take an example:

```
Start the loop from one, until the loop has been repeated sixty times,
adding a value of 1 to the loop:
Perform action
```

If you see the instructions being passed, there are three separate segments that are depicted in a loop:

1. `Start the loop from one`: This means that the loop should start with a value of one.
2. `until the loop has been repeated sixty times`: This means perform the same set of tasks until the loop has completed sixty turns of execution.
3. `adding a value of 1 to the loop`: This means that we dictate that after completion of each round of loop, increment the loop count by 1.

The result will be the same action performed sixty times, until the loop count reaches sixty. Additionally, a loop can used to iterate through multiple values stored in a variable irrespective of whether it is an integer, string, or any other data type.

Arrays

An array (or list in some scripting languages) is used to store a similar set of multiple values inside a single variable. This helps to ensure all data types with similar meanings are stored in a single variable, and also we can easily loop through these array objects to fetch the values stored in an array.

Consider the following example:

```
countries=["India","China","USA","UK"]
for specific country in countries
 Perform action
```

As we can see in the variable declaration, now we are declaring a similar data type with a similar context or meaning by grouping them together and assigning them into a single variable. In our example, it's the country names all assigned to an array variable named `countries`. In the next line, we are now iterating using the loop method, and for every `specific country` in the list or array of `countries`, we will perform the action. In this case, the loop will be executed to perform the action for each country, from the country name `India` to the end of the country name `UK`.

Each value stored in an array is referred to as an element of the array. Additionally, an array can be easily sorted, which means irrespective of the order of the elements in the array, we can get a sorted list or array by calling some additional programming tasks.

Let's consider an example:

```
countries=["India", "China", "USA","UK"]
Sort (countries)
```

The result will be as follows:

```
countries=["China","India","UK",USA"]
```

The sort functionality ensured that all the elements inside the array are sorted alphabetically and stored in the sorted order.

Functions

Functions or methods are a pre-written small set of instructions that result in a specific task being performed when they are called. The functions can also be defined as a single name for a group of programming instructions written together to achieve a common task.

Taking an example, think of driving as a function. In driving, there are multiple things that need to be taken care of, such as understanding traffic signals, running a car, and driving the car in traffic and on the road.

All these tasks are grouped in a function named `driving`. Now, let's say we have two people, example 1 and example 2, who want to learn to drive. From a programming perspective, once we define a function, we need to call it whenever we want to perform the same set of tasks. Hence, we would call `driving(example 1)` and then `driving (example 2)`, which would ensure that both people would become a driver after going through the set of instructions in the `driving` function.

Let us look at another example:

```
countries=["India","China","USA","UK"]

function hellocountry(countryname)
 Return "hello " countryname

for each country in countries:
     hellocountry(each country)
```

In the first line, we declare an array with country names as elements. Next, we define a function named `hellocountry` that accepts an input of `countryname`. In the function itself, we simply return the value of the `countryname` that was passed to the function as input, preceding by the work `hello`.

Now all that remains is to iterate through all the elements of countries and pass each `countryname` as input to the `hellocountry` function. As we can see, we called the same function for each element, and based upon the instructions declared inside the function, that specific task was now performed for each element in the array.

Best practices

As we have now looked at the basics of some of the key components of a program, there is another important aspect of how to write a good program that we will consider.

From a machine's perspective, there is no understanding of how a program is written, as long as the instructions given in the program are in the right format or syntax and the machine is able to interpret each of the instructions correctly. For an end user, again the way the program is written might not be important as long as the end user gets the desired result. The person concerned with how a program is written is a programmer who is writing their own program, or a programmer or developer who needs to interpret another programmer's program.

There may be multiple reasons why a programmer might need to interpret a program that's not been written by them. It may be to support the program while the programmer who wrote the program is not available, or to enhance the program by adding their own piece of code or programming instructions. Another reason for code readability is fixing bugs. Any program or set of instructions may malfunction due to incorrect input or incorrect logic, which can result in unexpected behavior or unexpected results. This is called a bug, and bugs need to be fixed to ensure the program does what it was written for originally.

Every programmer has their own set of best practices, but some of the key aspects of a program are readability, support information, and indentation.

Readability of a program

This is one of the most important aspects of writing a good program. A program needs to be written in such a way that even a layman or a first-time reader of the program should be able to interpret the basics of what is happening.

Variables need to be declared properly so that each variable makes it clear what it stores:

```
x="India"
y="France"
```

could have been written better like this:

```
asiancountry="India"
europecountry="France"
```

Here's another example:

```
x=5
y=2
```

It could be written like this:

```
biggernumber=5
smallernumber=2
```

As we can see in the preceding example, if we write a two- or three-line program, we can easily declare the variables in a random way, but things become much more complex, even for a programmer writing their own program, when these random variables are used in a longer program. Just imagine if you have declared the variables as `a`, `b`, `c`, and so on, and later, after using even 10 or 15 more variables, you need to go back to each line of the program to understand what value was declared in `a`, `b`, or `c`.

Another aspect of writing a good program is commenting. Different scripting languages provide different ways of commenting a program. Comments are necessary to ensure we break the flow of each program into sections, with each section having a comment explaining the use of that section. A very good example is if you declare a function. A function named `Cooking`, for example, and another function named `CookingPractice` might sound confusing because of their names. Now, if we add a comment to the `Cooking` method saying *this function is to master the art of cooking when you have learned how to cook,* and add a comment to `CookingPractice` saying *this method is to learn cooking,* this can make things very easy for someone reading through the program.

A programmer now can easily interpret that whenever he wants to learn to cook, he has to call `CookingPractice` and not the `Cooking` method. Comments don't have any special meaning in any programming language, and they are ignored when the machine is trying to convert the programming language to machine instructions. Hence, comments are only for programmers and to make readers aware of what is happening in a program. A comment should also be placed with every complex condition, loop, and so on, to clarify the usage of that specific condition or loop.

Support information

This, as the name suggests, is additional information, preferably added as comments, containing details about the program and author. As a suggestion, at the minimum a program should have the author info (that is, the person who created the program), contact details such as phone number and email address, basic usage of the program or the purpose of the program, and the version of the program.

The version is specific such as starting from 1.0 and as and when we enhance the program or add new features, we can change it to version 1.1 (for minor changes) or a newer version such as version 2.0 (for major changes).

Consider an example:

```
Program start
Comment: Author: Myself
Comment: Contact: myemail@emailaddress.com
Comment: Phone: 12345
Comment: Version: 1.0
Comment: Purpose: This program is to demo the comments for support
info
Comment: Execution method: Open the Command Prompt and run this
program by calling this program.
Comment: Any extra additional info (if needed)

Program end
```

This approach ensures that everyone knows which is the latest version of the script and how to execute the program or script. Also, this has info about the contact details of the author, so if anything breaks in production, the author can be easily reached to rectify or fix the scripts in production.

Indentation

This is similar to what we do when we write in plain English. Indenting a program is mandatory in some scripting languages, but as a best practice it should be followed for any program that we write in any programming language. Indentation improves the readability of a program because it helps the programmer or someone else reading the program to quickly understand the flow of the program.

Let's see an example where we have a nested condition in which we check if a `Car` is `Red` and if it is a `Sedan` and if it is `Automatic`.
A bad way of writing this would be as follows:

```
if (Car is 'Red')
if (Car is 'Sedan')
if (Car is 'Automatic')
do something
```

Now, think of adding multiple lines like this to a long program, and you will get easily confused by the flow of program as you read through it.
A better and recommended way to write this is as follows:

```
if (Car is 'Red')
    if (Car is 'Sedan')
        if (Car is 'Automatic')
           do something
```

This provides a clear flow of the program. Only check the other conditions if the `Car` is `Red`; otherwise, don't check for the other conditions. This is where we say we are nesting the conditions inside each other, which is also called **nested conditions**.

This also clears a lot of confusion while troubleshooting a complex program. We can easily identify the problematic code or instructions by quickly parsing through the program and understanding the flow for each segment of the program.

Sample best practice example

This example summarizes the best practices using all the elements that we have learned so far, by creating a basic program.

Problem statement: Parse all the countries declared in an array and only print the names of those countries that contain the letter `I` or letter `U` in their names:

```
Program begin:

Comment: This is a sample program to explain best practice
Comment: Author name: Programmer
Comment: Email: Programmer@programming.com
Version: 1.0

Comment: The following section declares the list of countries in array
countrylist
countrylist=['India','US','UK','France','China','Japan']

function validatecountryname(countryname)
   Comment: This function takes the input of countryname, checks if it
contains I or U and returns value based upon the result.
   if ((countryname contains 'I') OR (countryname contains 'U')
         return "Countryname contains I or U"
   else
        return "Countryname does not contain I our U"

Comment: This is a loop that parses each countryname from the
countrylist one by one and sends the variable 'countryname' as input
to function validatecoutryname

foreach countryname in countrylist
     validatecountryname (countryname)

Comment: Program ends here
```

The program is self-explanatory, but it is worth noting the support comments such as author, email, and so on. The indentation ensures that any reader has a clear idea of the flow of program.

Additionally, another thing to observe is the use of names that clearly depict the usage of the variable or name. Each variable and function name clearly specifies what it is being used for. The additional comment lines in between add clarity on what each segment is doing and the purpose of the statement or function.

Language choices (Python/PowerShell)

Moving ahead, armed with the knowledge of how to write a program and an understanding best practices, we will now look at some scripting languages that suffice for our automation scripts. A basic difference between a scripting language and a programming language (such as C and C++) is that a scripting language is not compiled but interpreted through the underlying environment in which it is executed (in other words, a converter is required to convert the commands written in human-readable format to machine format by parsing one line at a time), whereas the programming language is primarily compiled and hence can be executed in multiple environments without the use of any specific underlying environment or requirements.

What this means is if I write a script in Python, PowerShell, or even Perl, I need to install that specific language in order to run the program or script that I have written. C or C++ code can be compiled to make an executable file (`.exe`), and can run independently without the installation of any language. Additionally, a scripting language is less code-intensive, which means that it can automatically interpret some of the code written in a program depending on how it is called.

Let's consider an example. Here's how we declare a variable in scripting language:

```
x=5
```

OR

```
x="author"
```

OR

```
x=3.5
```

Whereas in a programming language, the same type of declaration would be made like this:

```
integer x=5
String x="author"
Float x=3.5
```

This states that depending on the value we assign to the variable, the variable type is automatically identified in an scripting language, whereas in a programming language the declarations are tightly controlled. In this case, if we declare a variable as a `String`, this clearly means that we cannot declare any other type of value in that variable unless we explicitly change the data type of that variable.

We have primarily three types of scripting language that are popular for creating programs and are mainly used for automation scripting or programming. These are Perl, Python, and PowerShell.

With support for the oldest language, Perl, diminishing, the focus is now on Python because of its open source support and on PowerShell because of its Microsoft, or .NET environment. Comparing both languages is not ideal because it's up to the reader which programming language they use to write their programs. As we have more than 70% of computers running Windows, and with a growing market of Microsoft Azure as a cloud operating system from Microsoft, PowerShell is the preferred language owing to the underlying .NET environment. As we create a program in PowerShell, it is easy to port that program and execute it on another machine running Windows without any special settings.

Python, on the other hand, is growing in popularity because of its open source approach. There are thousands of developers who contribute to enhancing Python by adding special functions for specific tasks. For example, there is a function or sub-program, called `Paramiko`, that is used to log into network routers. Another one is `Netmiko`, which is an enhanced version of `Paramiko` that is used to log into network devices based upon network hardware vendor and operating systems (such as Cisco iOS or Cisco NXOS). Python needs to be installed before writing a Python program and successfully executing it.

Going forward, our focus will be on Python, with additional tips and tricks on how to perform the same tasks using PowerShell instead of Python.

Writing your first program

Now, because we are starting from fresh, we need to understand how to write our first program and execute it. PowerShell comes pre-installed on a Windows machine. But we need to install Python by downloading it from the web (`https://www.python.org`) and choosing the right version for your operating system. Once downloaded, it can installed just like any other application that is installed on a Windows machine.

On a Linux machine, the same holds true, but because of the .NET requirement, PowerShell will not be supported on Linux or Unix environments. Hence, if we are using a Unix or Linux environment, Python or Perl remain our preferences for scripting.

There are multiple **Integrated Development Environments** (**IDEs**) for both Python and PowerShell, but the default ones that come with these languages are also pretty helpful.

There are multiple versions of PowerShell and Python being used. When writing programs in higher versions, generally the backwards support is not very good, so make sure you note the users and environment before choosing a version.
In our case, we will be using PowerShell 4 and Python 3 onwards for writing programs. Some commands might not run in older versions of PowerShell and Python, and some syntax or commands are different in older versions.

PowerShell IDE

This can be invoked by clicking on the **Start** button and searching for **Windows PowerShell ISE**. Once invoked, the initial screen will look like this:

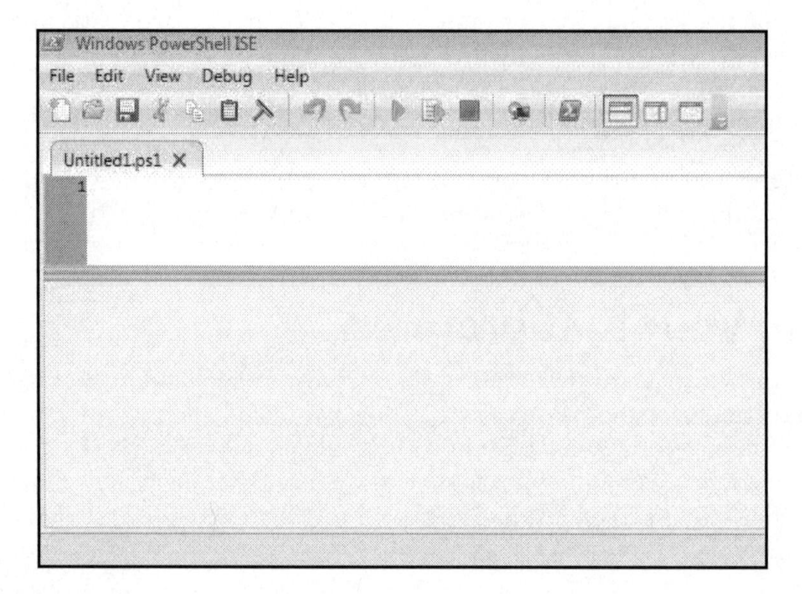

As we can see in the preceding screenshot, a PowerShell script is saved with a `.ps1` extension. Once we write something in the IDE (or ISE, as it is called with PowerShell), it needs to be saved as `somefilename.ps1` and then executed to see the result.

Let's take write a program called `Hello World`:

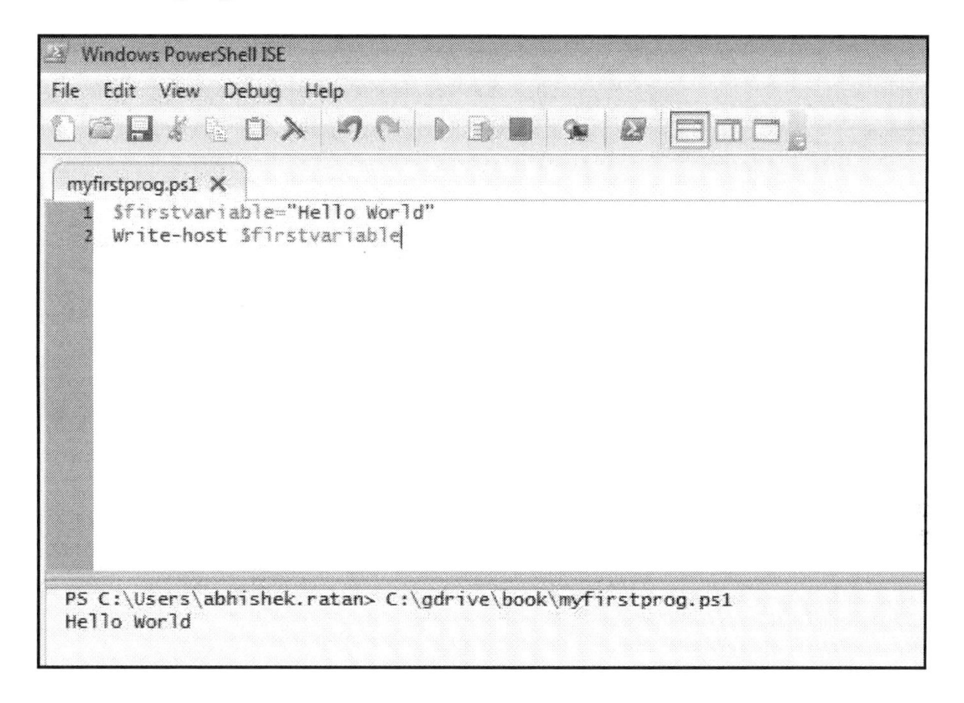

- As we can see in our first program, we write two lines to print `Hello World`. In the ISE, we pass the commands to declare a variable (a variable is denoted by a dollar sign, `$`, in front of the variable in PowerShell), assigning the value `Hello World` to it. The next line is simply printing that variable by calling a method or function called `Write-host`, which is used to print values onscreen in PowerShell.
- Once we write the program and save it, the next step is execution to see our result.
- The green button at the top of the ISE is used to execute the script, and the result of the script is shown at the bottom of the screen. In this case, it was a simple `Hello World` output.

PowerShell scripts can also be invoked directly by the command line. As PowerShell is a scripting language and needs to be installed on a machine, we can directly call PowerShell from the Windows Command Prompt and execute the scripts and individual scripting commands from the PowerShell console itself.

This is how we can find out the version of PowerShell:

```
C:\Windows\system32\cmd.exe - powershell

C:\>powershell
Windows PowerShell
Copyright (C) 2009 Microsoft Corporation. All rights reserved.

PS C:\> $psversiontable

Name                           Value
----                           -----
CLRVersion                     2.0.50727.8669
BuildVersion                   6.1.7601.17514
PSVersion                      2.0
WSManStackVersion              2.0
PSCompatibleVersions           {1.0, 2.0}
SerializationVersion           1.1.0.1
PSRemotingProtocolVersion      2.1


PS C:\>
```

As we can see in the preceding screenshot, PowerShell is invoked by calling `powershell` directly from the Command Prompt in Windows. When PowerShell is invoked, we see `PS` before the command line, which confirms that we are now inside the PowerShell console. To see the version, we call a system variable, `$psversiontable`, which shows the version of PowerShell.

We can see that this is version 2.x (as shown in `CLRVersion`). System variables are special variables that have predefined values based upon the installation types. These special variables can be called at any time in our script to fetch their values and perform actions based upon the returned values.

The following example shows that we are using a higher version of PowerShell:

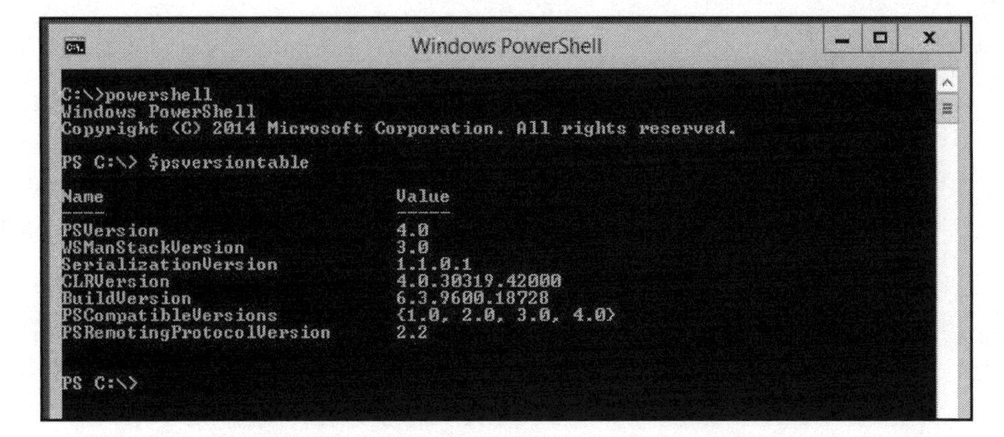

As we can see, the same variable now returns a value of `4.0` for `PSVersion`, which confirms that this is version 4 of PowerShell.

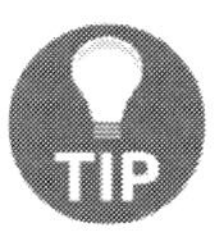

PowerShell 4.0 is the default installation from Windows 8.1 onwards on client operating system, and Windows Server 2012 R2 in a Server environment.

Python IDE

Similar to PowerShell, once Python is installed, it has its own IDE. It can be invoked by typing or calling IDLE (Python) from the **Start** menu:

```
Python 3.6.1 Shell
File  Edit  Shell  Debug  Options  Window  Help
Python 3.6.1 (v3.6.1:69c0db5, Mar 21 2017, 17:54:52) [MSC v.1900 32 bit (Intel)]
 on win32
Type "copyright", "credits" or "license()" for more information.
>>> |
```

The Python IDE, called IDLE, looks similar to the preceding screenshot when it is opened. The heading bar depicts the version of Python (which is 3.6.1 in this case) and the three greater than signs (>>>) show the command line, which is ready to accept Python commands and execute them. To write a program, we click on **File | New File**, which opens up a notepad in which we can write the program.

Lets see a similar `hello world` program in Python:

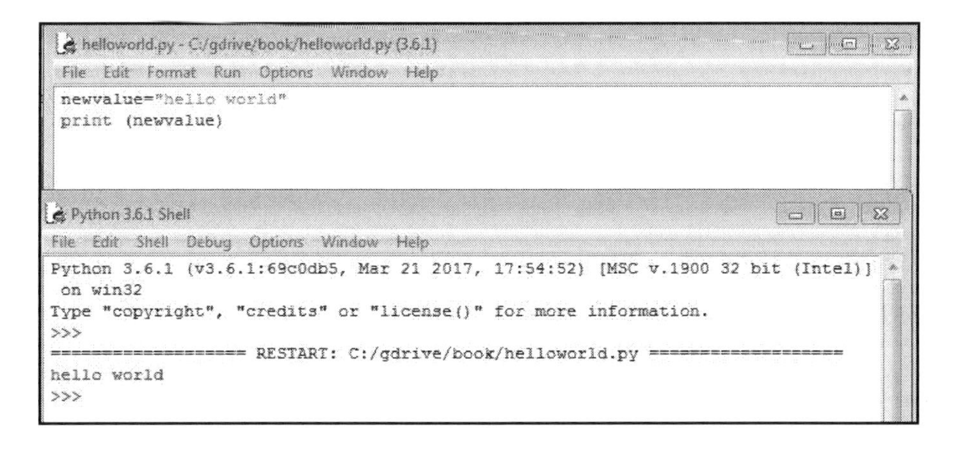

As we write a new program, the variable used is `newvalue`, and the value assigned to it is `hello world`. The next line is simply calling Python's `print` function to print the value inside the variable during the execution of the script.

Once we have written the program, we click on **File** | **Save As** in the window where we wrote the program, and save the script. The script is saved as `filename.py`, with the `.py` extension denoting a Python script. Once it is saved, we can press the *F5* button on the keyboard or select **Run** | **Run Module** in the script window to run that specific script. The following window is the same window that was invoked when we first called the IDLE application from the **Start** menu, but now it has the output of that script that we wrote.

The output of `hello world` is now seen in the IDLE window. Once we are done with writing the script or Python commands, we can simply close the open command windows to close the application or Python interpreter.

Similar to PowerShell, we can also call `python` from the command line, as follows:

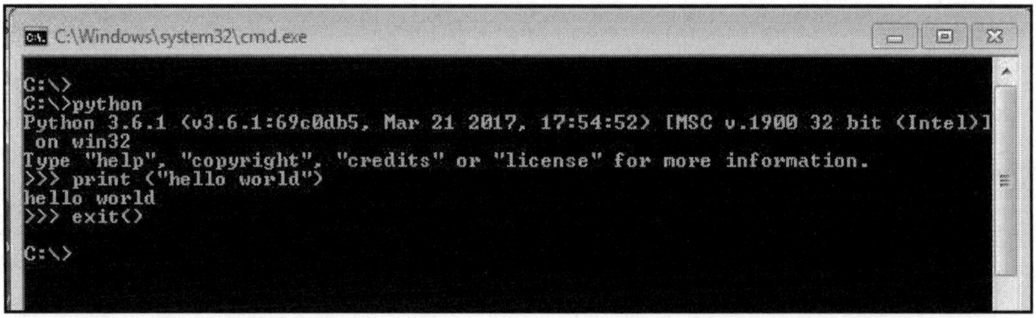

```
C:\Windows\system32\cmd.exe

C:\>
C:\>python
Python 3.6.1 (v3.6.1:69c0db5, Mar 21 2017, 17:54:52) [MSC v.1900 32 bit (Intel)]
 on win32
Type "help", "copyright", "credits" or "license" for more information.
>>> print ("hello world")
hello world
>>> exit()

C:\>
```

One additional thing to notice here is that to exit the Python interpreter, we call the `exit()` function. This tells Python to stop the execution and exit to the Command Prompt in Windows.

Representational State Transfer (REST) framework

One of the most important aspects of network automation is to understand and leverage tools that are currently available for specific tasks. For example, this could be Splunk for data mining, SolarWinds for network monitoring, syslog servers, or even any custom applications to perform various tasks.

Another important aspect of writing an application is how we can utilize the same application for additional tasks without altering the application itself. In other words, let's say we buy a car for our personal use, but an enhancement of this would be using the same car as a taxi or in some other role.

This is we introduce the **Application Program Interface (API)**. APIs are used to expose some aspect of an already written application to merge with the programs that we are writing so that we can easily call that specific task using a specific API. For example, as SolarWinds is a specialized application that is used for network monitoring and other purposes, we can call the API of SolarWinds to get the network device list in our script. Hence, we leave the specialized task of discovering the network devices on the network to SolarWinds, but we utilize its expertise in our script through the API of that application.

Getting a bit deeper, the API is nothing more than a function (similar to the functions that we write in our scripts); the only difference is what values those functions return. An API function generally returns the values in **Extended Markup Language (XML)** or **JavaScript Object Notation (JSON)** format, which are industry standards of cross-environment and cross-machine information exchange. Think of this as similar to how we communicate with each other using English as a common language. Although we may have been born in different cultures, in different countries, we can use English to communicate with each other effectively, since English is the industry standard of human interaction. Similarly, irrespective of how a program is written, in whatever language (such as C, C++, Java, VB, C#, and so on), each program can talk to another program by calling its APIs and the results come in either XML or JSON.

XML is a standard way of encoding results and sending them across to the requestor and, using the same standard, the requestor can decode the results. JSON is another way in which data interactions can happen across applications.

Here is sample XML:

```
<?xml version="1.0" encoding="UTF-8"?>
<note>
  <to>Readers</to>
  <from>JAuthor</from>
  <heading>Reminder</heading>
  <body>Read this for more knowledge</body>
 </note>
```

The first line in the preceding content depicts that whatever follows after that line is in XML format. The XML files are saved with extension of `.xml`.

Now as we can see, if we count the number of characters returned from an XML result, if we add the characters, such as `<heading>Reminder</heading>`, it returns results within the starting tag and ending tag of `<heading>`. This means that the size of an XML file is greatly increased owing to the overhead character counts of additional closing tags.

Here's the same example in JSON:

```
{
"note": {
"to": "Tove",
"from": "Jani",
"heading": "Reminder",
"body": "Don't forget me this weekend!"
}
}
```

As we can see, we have got rid of those extra bulky opening and closing tags that we saw earlier in XML. What this means is if we are calling an API to return a huge amount of data in XML format, it would certainly take a longer time to fetch that data from the application and more consumption of resources such as memory and storage to temporarily or permanently store that data. To overcome this situation, the JSON format is now preferred to XML to exchange data through APIs. JSON is lightweight and less resource-intensive than XML because of differences in the way the data is returned. JSON files are saved with the extension `.json`.

This functionality of working with APIs, back end methods, and functions written in a particular programming language to be called APIs, and functions returning values in XML or JSON format, all of which is running over web protocols such as HTTP or HTTPS, is cumulatively called the REST framework. The REST framework is the same industry standard of interacting using XML or JSON that were referenced earlier, with the addition of GET, POST, and other interactions happening over the web protocols. The HTTP requests to APIs can be GET or POST requests that the REST framework recognizes and, similar to HTTP GET and POST requests, interacts with underlying applications to perform the requested actions.

Scripting languages rely heavily on API calls, and applications that need to provide the API's functionality adhere to REST framework requirements to ensure they extend their capabilities to the scripts that are called to fetch or save data in their choice of scripting language. A big benefit of this is that cross-platform communication is now happening with neither party (the caller of API or the application providing the API's functionality) knowing which language or environment the other are running. Hence, a Windows application can easily work with a Unix environment and vice versa using this approach, with HTTP being the standard communication language for calling APIs, and parsing the results with industry standard XML or JSON formats.

The sample API REST call in PowerShell is as follows:

```
Windows PowerShell
PS C:\> Invoke-RestMethod -Uri https://blogs.msdn.microsoft.com/powershell/feed/
| format-table -property title

title
-----
PowerShell Documentation Migration
PowerShell 6.0 Roadmap: CoreCLR, Backwards Compatibility, and More!
DSC Resource Kit Release July 2017
Getting Started with PowerShell Core on Windows, Mac, and Linux
DSC Resource Kit Release May 2017
Coming Soon - PowerShell in Azure Cloud Shell
Windows 10 Creators Update and PowerShell DSC
Announcing PowerShell for Visual Studio Code 1.0!
PowerShell Core 6 Beta.1 Release
OpenSSH Security Testing Kick Off

PS C:\> _
```

As we can see in the preceding screenshot, we call the `Invoke-RestMethod` function in PowerShell, which is used to call the API method of the application with the default communication and interactions using JSON.

The application called is in a REST framework, with access to the API with the URL `https://blogs.msdn.microsoft.com/powershell/feed/`. This uses the HTTPS protocol to communicate with the application.

`format-table` is a function of PowerShell that specifies that however the result comes, display the `title` property of each record/result returned from the API call. If we had not used that command, the display would have shown all the properties returned for each record.

Here's an example REST call in Python:

```
Python 3.6.1 Shell
File  Edit  Shell  Debug  Options  Window  Help
Python 3.6.1 (v3.6.1:69c0db5, Mar 21 2017, 17:54:52) [MSC v.1900 32 bit (Intel)] on win32
Type "copyright", "credits" or "license()" for more information.
>>> import requests
>>> r=requests.get('http://maps.googleapis.com/maps/api/geocode/json?address=google')
>>> r.json()
{'results': [{'address_components': [{'long_name': '111', 'short_name': '111', 'types': ['street_number']}, {
'long_name': '8th Avenue', 'short_name': '8th Ave', 'types': ['route']}, {'long_name': 'Manhattan', 'short_na
me': 'Manhattan', 'types': ['political', 'sublocality', 'sublocality_level_1']}, {'long_name': 'New York', 's
hort_name': 'New York', 'types': ['locality', 'political']}, {'long_name': 'New York County', 'short_name': '
New York County', 'types': ['administrative_area_level_2', 'political']}, {'long_name': 'New York', 'short_na
me': 'NY', 'types': ['administrative_area_level_1', 'political']}, {'long_name': 'United States', 'short_name
': 'US', 'types': ['country', 'political']}, {'long_name': '10011', 'short_name': '10011', 'types': ['postal_
code']}], 'formatted_address': '111 8th Ave, New York, NY 10011, USA', 'geometry': {'location': {'lat': 40.74
06375, 'lng': -74.0020388}, 'location_type': 'ROOFTOP', 'viewport': {'northeast': {'lat': 40.7419864802915, '
lng': -74.00068981970848}, 'southwest': {'lat': 40.7392885197085, 'lng': -74.00338778029149}}}, 'place_id': '
ChIJH_XxFL9ZwokR8F3XW7NaG8w', 'types': ['establishment', 'point_of_interest']}], 'status': 'OK'}
>>>
```

In this example, we call a standard function called `requests`. The first line, `import requests`, means that we are referencing the `requests` function or library to call in our Python script. On the next line, we are calling the Google Map API with JSON using a `requests.get` method. In other words, we are ensuring a HTTP GET call to the Google API URL. Once we get the result, we call the `json()` method to store the value in the variable `r`.

Sometimes, when we call a custom function or library of Python using `import`, it may give an error stating that the module has not been found. This means that it does not come with the standard Python installation and needs to be installed separately. To fix this, we can install the module manually using the `pip` or `easy_install` commands, which we will see in detail in upcoming chapters.

Summary

In this chapter, we covered the basics of various terminology that we will use while performing network automation. This chapter also introduced the readers to some basic aspects of programming to help build the logic of a program.

This chapter also explained why to write a good program and how to write one, along with some reference points for scripting languages. There was also a brief discussion about the current scripting languages, their basic usage, and writing a very basic program in two of the most popular scripting languages (Python and PowerShell).

Finally, we summed it all up by introducing the REST framework, which included a discussion about APIs, how to call them, and an explanation of XML and JSON as inter-platform data exchange languages.

The next chapter will go deeper into how to write scripts using Python, with relevant examples in PowerShell to ensure the reader becomes familiar with both Python and PowerShell. There will be tips and best practices as well.

2
Python for Network Engineers

As we are now familiar with how to write a program using the concepts used in programming languages, as well as best practices, now let's dig deep into writing an actual Python program or script. Keeping the primary focus on how to write a program in Python, we will also see how to write the same program in PowerShell, since there might be times where we would need to use PowerShell to achieve the results that we are looking for. We will cover various aspects of creating a program with some explanations of each of the statements and provide some tips and tricks to get through those tricky situations.

In this chapter, we will cover the following topics:

- Python interpreter and data types
- Writing Python scripts using conditional loops
- Functions
- Installing new modules/libraries
- Passing arguments from command line for scripts
- Using Netmiko to interact with network devices
- Multithreading

Python interpreter and data types

An interpreter, as the name suggests, is used to interpret instructions so that they are understandable by others. In our case, it is used to convert our Python language to a machine-understandable format that governs the flow of instructions that we gave to the machine.

It is also used to convert the set of values and messages given by a machine to a human-readable format in order to give us insights into how our program is being executed.

As mentioned in `Chapter 1`, *Fundamental Concepts*, the interpreter that we are focusing on is Python 3.6. I will be using it on the Windows platform, but the site has clear instructions on how to download and install the same on other OS like Unix or Linux machines. Once we install it by downloading it from the Python community which can be found at URL `https://www.python.org/downloads`, we can simply click on the setup file to install it. From the installation directory we just need to invoke `python.exe`, which will invoke the Python interpreter.

In order to call Python from anywhere in your Command Prompt, just add the Python installation folder in your PATH variable. Here's an example: `set path=%path%;C:\python36`. This is going to add the Python36 path in the current path. Once this is done, `python.exe` can be called from anywhere in the Command Prompt.

Once we invoke the interpreter, the first step to take is to create a variable and assign a value to it.

Python, as with any other programming language, supports various data types for the variables. A data type typically defines the type of value that can be stored in a variable, but Python and PowerShell have the ability to auto-evaluate the type of variable based upon the value. Python supports a large number of data types, but typically in our daily usage we refer to native data types multiple times.

The Python data type supports:

- **Numbers**: These are integer types, such as 1, 2, 100, and 1,000.
- **String**: These are single or multiple characters and possibly every letter of ASCII, such as Python, network, age123, and India. Additionally, a string needs to be stored inside a double quote (`"`) or a single quote (`'`) to specify that a value is a string. Hence, `1` and `'1'` would be interpreted differently by Python.
- **Boolean**: This can be either a true or a false value.

- **Byte**: These are typically binary values.
- **Lists**: These are an ordered sequence of values.
- **Tuples**: These are similar to lists, but the values or length cannot be altered.
- **Sets**: These are similar to lists, but not ordered.
- **Dictionary** or **hash values**: These are key-value pairs, like a telephone directory in which one primary value (name) is attached with both phone numbers and addresses.

An example on data types is as follows:

```
Python 3.6.1 Shell
File Edit Shell Debug Options Window Help
Python 3.6.1 (v3.6.1:69c0db5, Mar 21 2017, 17:54:52) [MSC v.1900 32 bit (Intel)]
 on win32
Type "copyright", "credits" or "license()" for more information.
>>> intvalue=2
>>> intvalue
2
>>> stringvalue='this is a test'
>>> stringvalue
'this is a test'
>>> booleanvalue=True
>>> booleanvalue
True
>>> bytevalue=bytes(3)
>>> bytevalue
b'\x00\x00\x00'
>>>
```

As we can see in the preceding example, we declared the variables with various values, and based upon the value, Python automatically interprets the specific data type. If we just type the variable name again, it prints out the value stored in the variable based upon its data type.

Similarly, the following example specifies other native data types:

```
Python 3.6.1 Shell
File Edit Shell Debug Options Window Help
Python 3.6.1 (v3.6.1:69c0db5, Mar 21 2017, 17:54:52) [MSC v.1900 32 bit (Intel)]
 on win32
Type "copyright", "credits" or "license()" for more information.
>>> listvalue = [1, 2, 3, 4, 5 ]
>>> listvalue
[1, 2, 3, 4, 5]
>>> tuplevalue = ("one", "two")
>>> tuplevalue
('one', 'two')
>>> setvalue = set(["India", "US", "UK"])
>>> setvalue
{'India', 'UK', 'US'}
>>> dictvalue = {'Country': 'India', 'Currency': 'Rupee', 'Capital': 'Delhi'}
>>> dictvalue
{'Country': 'India', 'Currency': 'Rupee', 'Capital': 'Delhi'}
>>> |
```

Additionally, to see the data type we can use the `type()` function, which returns the type of a variable based upon the value we gave. The variable is passed as an argument to the `type()` function to get the data type value:

```
>>> type(listvalue)
<class 'list'>
>>> type(setvalue)
<class 'set'>
>>> type(dictvalue)
<class 'dict'>
>>> type(tuplevalue)
<class 'tuple'>
>>> |
```

A PowerShell example of the same Python code is as follows:

```
#PowerShell code
$value=5
$value="hello"
write-host $value
write-host $value.gettype()
#This is remark
#A variable in powershell is declared with '$' sign in front.
# The gettype() function in powershell is used to get the type of
variable.
```

There are operations, such as addition (+), for specific variables with particular data types. We have to be sure what types of variable we are adding. If we have an incompatible data type variable being added to another one, Python would throw an error stating the reason.

Here in the following code, we see the result of adding two string variables:

```
Python 3.6.1 Shell
File Edit Shell Debug Options Window Help
Python 3.6.1 (v3.6.1:69c0db5, Mar 21 2017, 17:54:52) [MSC v.1900 32 bit (Intel)]
 on win32
Type "copyright", "credits" or "license()" for more information.
>>> stringval="1"
>>> stringval
'1'
>>> stringval2="2"
>>> stringval2
'2'
>>> stringval3 =stringval+stringval2
>>> stringval3
'12'
>>>
```

Similarly, observe the difference if we use the same addition on integer variables:

```
Python 3.6.1 Shell
File Edit Shell Debug Options Window Help
Python 3.6.1 (v3.6.1:69c0db5, Mar 21 2017, 17:54:52) [MSC v.1900 32 bit (Intel)]
 on win32
Type "copyright", "credits" or "license()" for more information.
>>> intvalue=1
>>> intvalue
1
>>> intvalue2=2
>>> intvalue3=intvalue+intvalue2
>>> intvalue3
3
>>>
```

As mentioned, let's see what happens when we try to add a string and an integer variable together:

```
Python 3.6.1 Shell
File  Edit  Shell  Debug  Options  Window  Help
Python 3.6.1 (v3.6.1:69c0db5, Mar 21 2017, 17:54:52) [MSC v.1900 32 bit (Intel)]
 on win32
Type "copyright", "credits" or "license()" for more information.
>>> stringvalue='1'
>>> intvalue=2
>>> mixedvalue=stringvalue+intvalue
Traceback (most recent call last):
  File "<pyshell#2>", line 1, in <module>
    mixedvalue=stringvalue+intvalue
TypeError: must be str, not int
>>> |
```

The error clearly specifies that we cannot add two different data types because the interpreter cannot recognize which data type needs to be assigned to the mixed value variable.

Sometimes, if necessary, we can convert the values from one data type to another by calling specific functions that convert the data type to another. For example, `int("1")` will convert the string value 1 to integer value 1, or `str(1)` will convert the integer value 1 to the string value 1.

We will be extensively using the various data types depending upon the logic and requirements of the scripts, and also, if necessary, converting one data type to another to achieve certain results.

Conditions and loops

Conditions are checked using a left and right value comparison. The evaluation returns either true or false, and a specific action is performed depending on the result.

There are certain condition operators that are used to evaluate the left and right value comparisons:

Operators	Meaning
==	If both values are equal
!=	If both values are NOT equal

>	If the left value is greater than the right value
<	If the left value is smaller than the right value
>=	If the left value is greater than or equal to the right value
<=	If the left value is lesser than or equal to the right value
`in`	If the left value is part of the right value

An example of the condition evaluation is as follows:

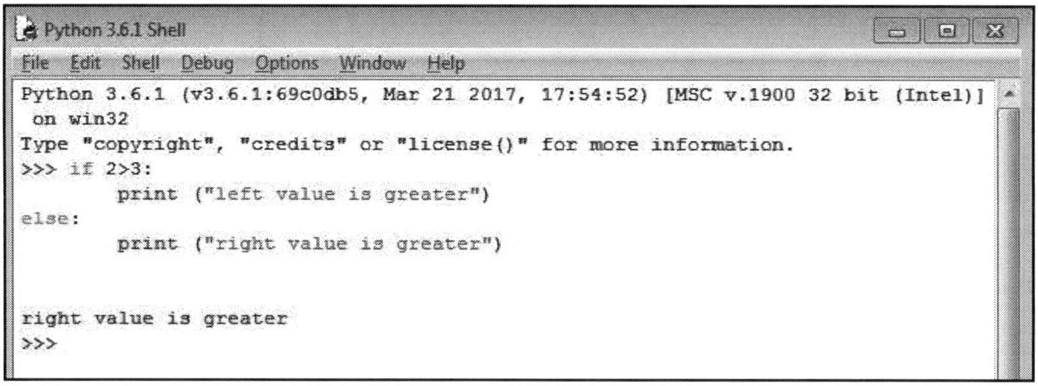

```
Python 3.6.1 Shell
File Edit Shell Debug Options Window Help
Python 3.6.1 (v3.6.1:69c0db5, Mar 21 2017, 17:54:52) [MSC v.1900 32 bit (Intel)]
 on win32
Type "copyright", "credits" or "license()" for more information.
>>> if 2>3:
	print ("left value is greater")
else:
	print ("right value is greater")


right value is greater
>>>
```

As we can see, we are checking whether `2>3` (2 is greater that 3). Of course, this would result in false, so the action in the `else` section is executed. If we reverse the check, `3>2`, then the output would have been `left value is greater`.

In the preceding example, we used the `if` condition block, which consists of the following:

```
if <condition>:
perform action
else:
perform action2
```

Notice the indentation, which is compulsory in Python. If we had not intended it, Python would not interpret what action to execute in which condition, and hence would have thrown an error of incorrect indentation.

Nested and multiple conditions

Sometimes we need to check multiple conditions in a single `if` condition.

Let's see an example of this:

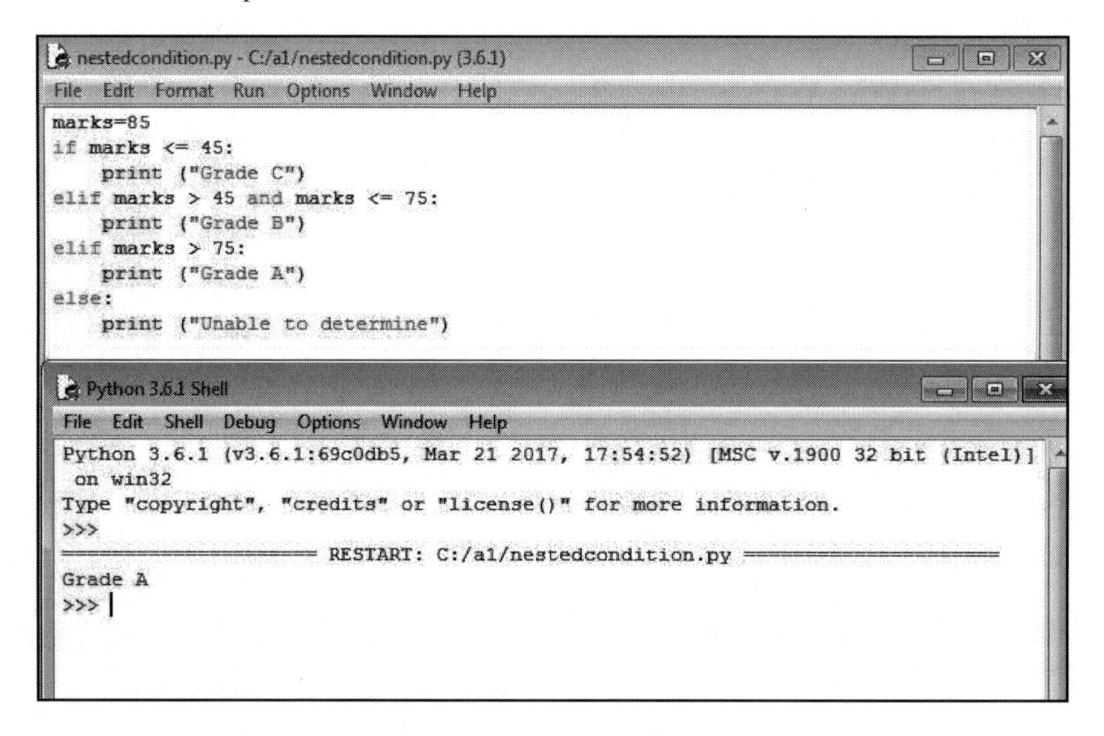

Here, we are checking the range of the marks. The flow of the program is as follows:

Assign a value of `85` to the `marks` variable. If `marks` is less than or equal to `45`, print `Grade C`, else if `marks` is greater than `45` and less than equal to `75`, print `Grade B`, else if `marks` is greater than `75`, print `Grade A`, else if none of the preceding conditions match, then print `Unable to determine`.

The PowerShell sample code for the preceding Python task is as follows:

```
#PowerShell sample code:
$marks=85
if ($marks -le 45)
{
    write-host "Grade C"
}
elseif (($marks -gt 45) -and ($marks -le 75))
```

```
{
    write-host "Grade B"
}
elseif ($marks -gt 75)
{
    write-host "Grade A"
}
else
{
    write-host "Unable to determine"
}
```

Similarly, here is an example of a nested condition (note the indentation that differentiates it from the earlier example of multiple conditions):

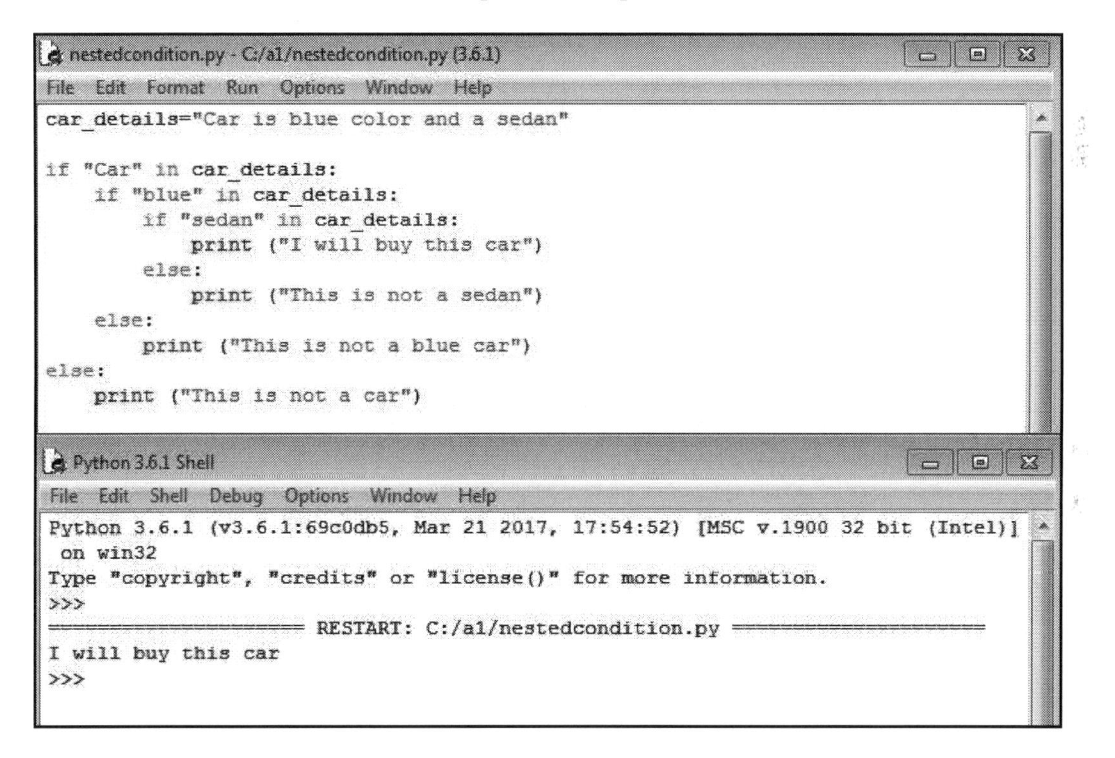

As we can see in the condition, the internal conditions will only be executed if its parent condition evaluates to true. If there is a false, the corresponding `else` action will be taken. In the example, if the `car_details` variable contains `Car`, contains `blue`, and it contains `sedan`, only then will the action `I will buy this car` be performed. If any of those conditions are not met, the relevant else action will be performed.

Loops

A loop is used to repeat a set of instructions until a specific condition is fulfilled. There are two common ways of creating a loop in Python, which are discussed as follows:

For next loop

This type of loop checks for a condition and repeats the instructions inside the loop until the condition is met:

```
for <incremental variable> in final value:
  statements
```

Here's an example of printing numbers from 1 to 10 in a for loop:

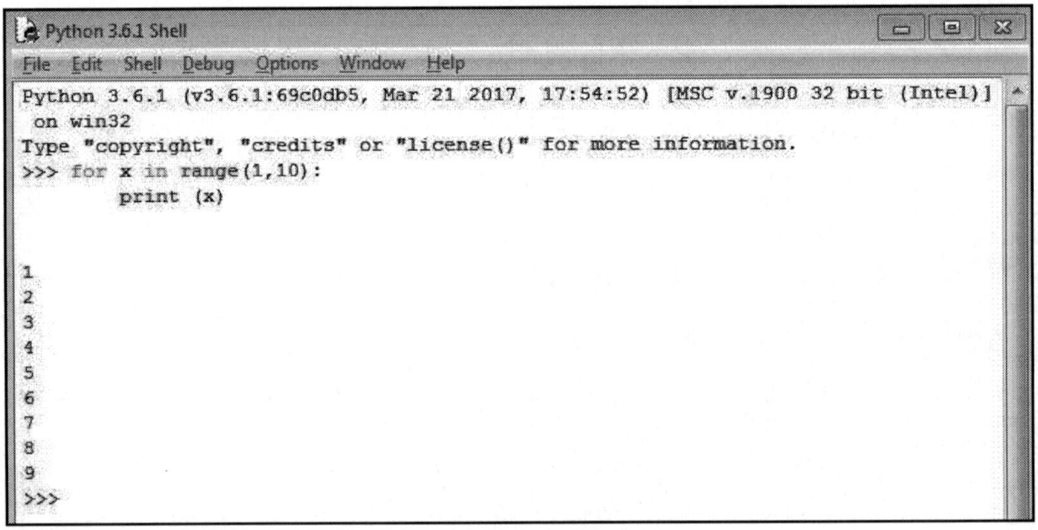

```
Python 3.6.1 Shell
File Edit Shell Debug Options Window Help
Python 3.6.1 (v3.6.1:69c0db5, Mar 21 2017, 17:54:52) [MSC v.1900 32 bit (Intel)]
 on win32
Type "copyright", "credits" or "license()" for more information.
>>> for x in range(1,10):
        print (x)


1
2
3
4
5
6
7
8
9
>>>
```

As we can see, we use a built-in `range(starting value, max value)` function, which specifies the loop to repeat from the starting value until the incremental value reaches the maximum value. In this case, the variable `x` is incremented by 1 and in each loop, the value is printed out. This is repeated until the value of `x` reaches `10`, where the `for` loop terminates.

In a similar way, we can also iterate through the items in a given list:

```
Python 3.6.1 Shell
File Edit Shell Debug Options Window Help
Python 3.6.1 (v3.6.1:69c0db5, Mar 21 2017, 17:54:52) [MSC v.1900 32 bit (Intel)]
 on win32
Type "copyright", "credits" or "license()" for more information.
>>> countries=['India','UK','USA','France']
>>> for country in countries:
        print (country + " is good")


India is good
UK is good
USA is good
France is good
>>>
```

PowerShell sample for the preceding Python code is as follows:

```
#PowerShell sample code:
$countries="India","UK","USA","France"
foreach ($country in $countries)
{
    write-host ($country+" is good")
}
```

Here, we can see that the values are assigned to the countries variable as a list. The `for` loop now iterates through each item in the list, and the print statement adds the string value to another string value and prints the result. This loop is repeated until all the items in the list are printed.

There might be times when we do not want to parse through an entire `for` loop. To break from the loop while it is iterating, we use a `break` statement. Here's an example in which we want to stop printing after `UK` in the `country` list:

```
for country in countries:
    if 'UK' in country:
        break
    else:
        print (country)
```

While loop

`While` loop is different from `for` loop, as no new variable is needed in this loop, and any current variable can be used to perform the tasks inside the `while` loop. An example is as follows:

```
while True:
     perform instructions
     if condition():
       break
```

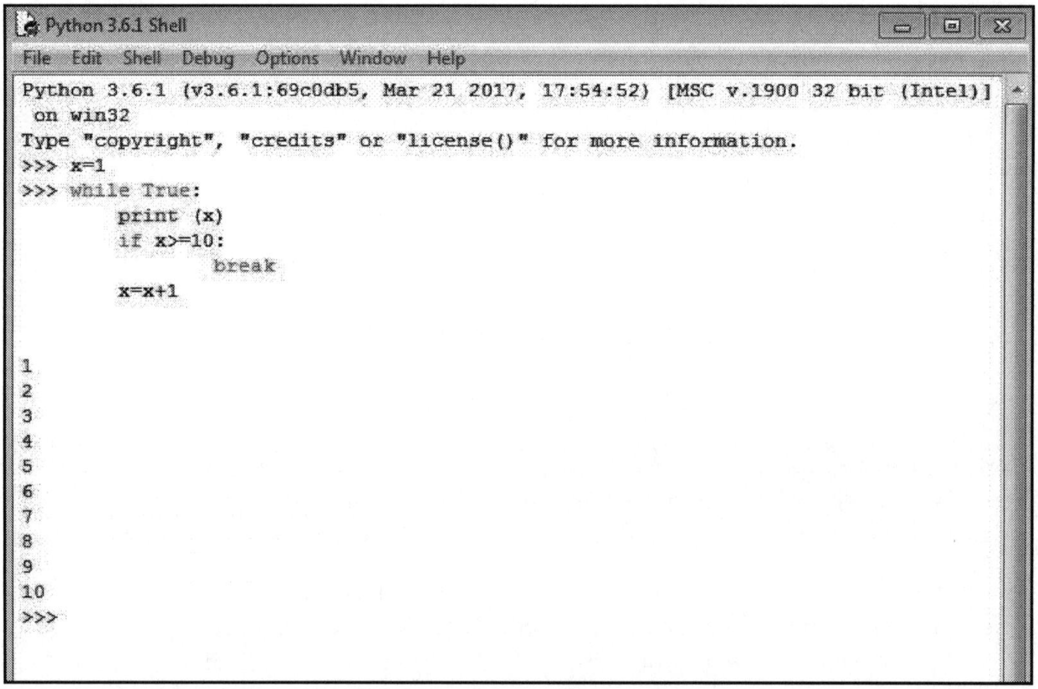

```
Python 3.6.1 Shell
File Edit Shell Debug Options Window Help
Python 3.6.1 (v3.6.1:69c0db5, Mar 21 2017, 17:54:52) [MSC v.1900 32 bit (Intel)]
 on win32
Type "copyright", "credits" or "license()" for more information.
>>> x=1
>>> while True:
        print (x)
        if x>=10:
                break
        x=x+1


1
2
3
4
5
6
7
8
9
10
>>>
```

This is similar to `for`, but in this case the actions are performed first, and then the condition is checked. In the preceding example, the value of `x` is printed first, and we repeat the same set of instructions until the value of `x` reaches `10` or greater. Once the `if` condition is met, we break out of the loop. If we do not specify a `break` condition, we will go into an infinite loop with a increment of 1 for each `x` value.

Writing Python scripts

We are now familiar with the basic concepts of Python. Now we will write an actual program or script in Python.

Ask for the input of a country name, and check whether the last character of the country is a vowel:

```
countryname=input("Enter country name:")
countryname=countryname.lower()
lastcharacter=countryname.strip()[-1]
if 'a' in lastcharacter:
    print ("Vowel found")
elif 'e' in lastcharacter:
    print ("Vowel found")
elif 'i' in lastcharacter:
    print ("Vowel found")
elif 'o' in lastcharacter:
    print ("Vowel found")
elif 'u' in lastcharacter:
    print ("Vowel found")
else:
    print ("No vowel found")
```

Output of the preceding code is as follows:

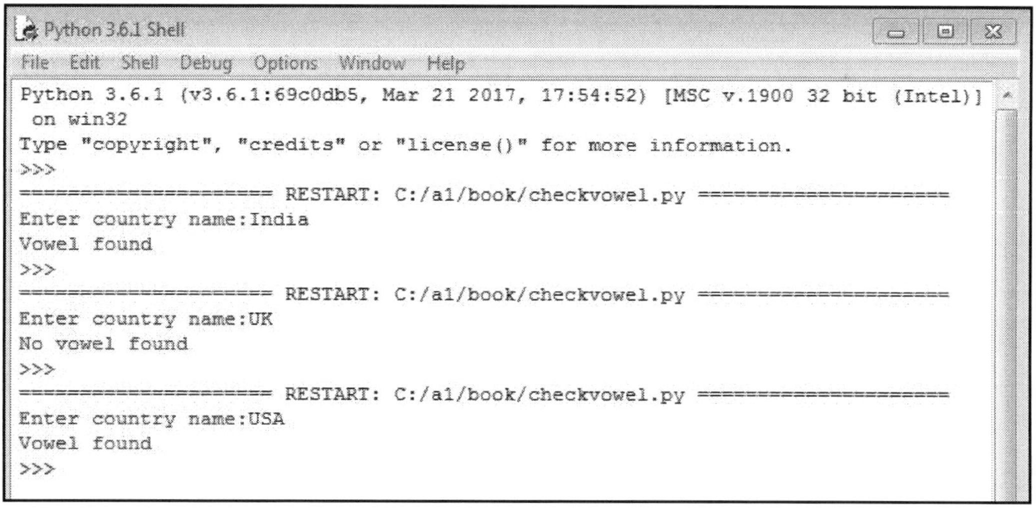

```
Python 3.6.1 Shell
File Edit Shell Debug Options Window Help
Python 3.6.1 (v3.6.1:69c0db5, Mar 21 2017, 17:54:52) [MSC v.1900 32 bit (Intel)]
 on win32
Type "copyright", "credits" or "license()" for more information.
>>>
===================== RESTART: C:/a1/book/checkvowel.py =====================
Enter country name:India
Vowel found
>>>
===================== RESTART: C:/a1/book/checkvowel.py =====================
Enter country name:UK
No vowel found
>>>
===================== RESTART: C:/a1/book/checkvowel.py =====================
Enter country name:USA
Vowel found
>>>
```

1. We ask for the input of a country name. The `input()` method is used to get an input from the user. The value entered is in the string format, and in our case the `countryname` variable has been assigned the input value.
2. In the next line, `countryname.lower()` specifies that the input that we receive needs to converted into all lowercase and stored in the same `countryname` variable. This effectively will have the same value that we entered earlier but in lowercase.
3. In the next line, `countryname.strip()[-1]` specifies two actions in one statement:

    - `countryname.strip()` ensures that the variable has all the leading and trailing extra values removed, such as new line or tab characters.
    - Once we get the clean variable, remove the last character of the string, which in our case is the last character of the country name. The `-1` denotes the character from right to left or end to start, whereas `+1` would denote from left to right.

4. Once we have the last character stored in the `lastcharacter` variable, all that is needed is a nested condition check and, based upon the result, print the value.

To save this program, we need to save this file as `somename.py`, which will specify that this program needs to be executed in Python:

The PowerShell sample code for the preceding Python task is as follows:

```
#PowerShell sample code
$countryname=read-host "Enter country name"
$countryname=$countryname.tolower()
$lastcharacter=$countryname[-1]
if ($lastcharacter -contains 'a')
{
    write-host "Vowel found"
}
elseif ($lastcharacter -contains 'e')
{
    write-host "Vowel found"
}
elseif ($lastcharacter -contains 'i')
{
    write-host "Vowel found"
}
elseif ($lastcharacter -contains 'O')
```

```
{
    write-host "Vowel found"
}
elseif ($lastcharacter -contains 'u')
{
    write-host "Vowel found"
}
else
{
write-host "No vowel found"
}
```

Python is very strict in terms of indentation. As we can see in the example, if we change the indentations or tabs even by a space, Python will spit out an error stating the indentation is not correct and the compilation will fail. This will result in an error and unless the indentation is fixed, the execution will not be performed.

Functions

For any recurring set of instructions, we can define a function. In other words, a function is a closed set of instructions to perform a specific logic or task. Depending upon the input provided, a function has the ability to return the results or parse the input with specific instructions to get results without any return values.

A function is defined by the `def` keyword, which specifies that we need to define a function and provide a set of instructions related to that function.

In this task we will print the greater of two input numbers:

```
def checkgreaternumber(number1,number2):
    if number1 > number2:
      print ("Greater number is ",number1)
    else:
     print ("Greater number is",number2)
checkgreaternumber(2,4)
checkgreaternumber(3,1)
```

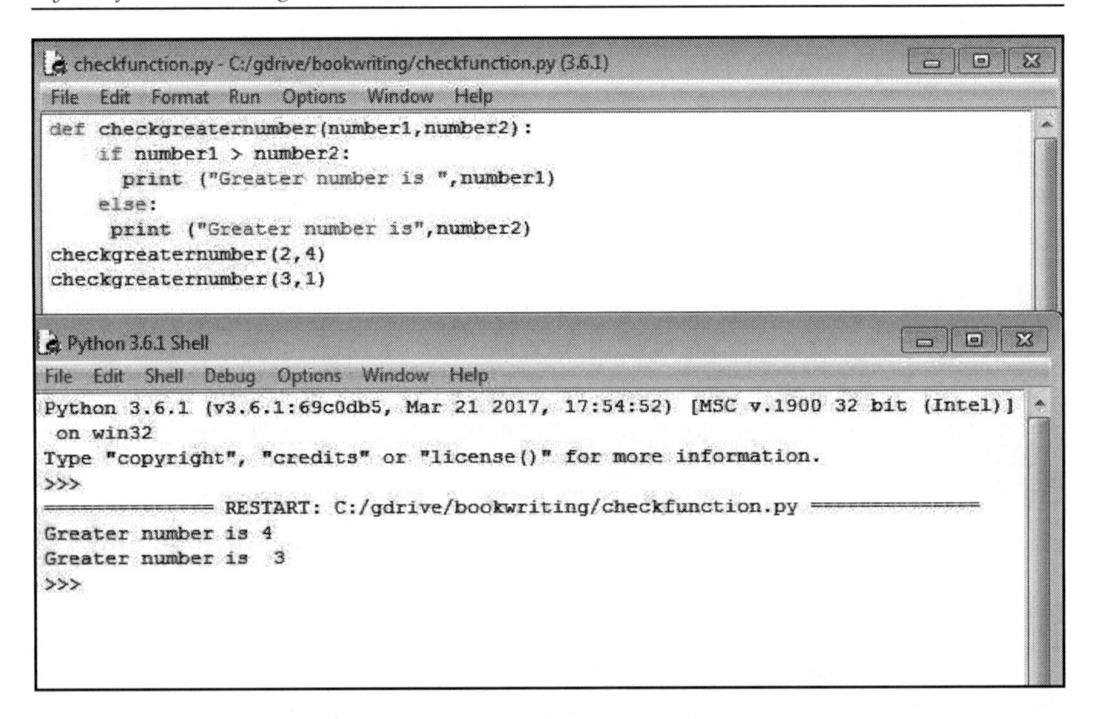

As we can see in the preceding output, the first time we call the `checkgreaternumber(2,4)` function, the function prints the greater value as `4`, and the second time we call the function with different numbers, the function prints the greater value as `3`.

The PowerShell sample code for the preceding task is as follows:

```
#PowerShell sample code
function checkgreaternumber($number1,$number2)
{
    if ($number1 -gt $number2)
    {
        write-host ("Greater number is "+$number1)
    }
    else
    {
        write-host ("Greater number is "+$number2)
    }
}

checkgreaternumber 2 4
checkgreaternumber 3 1
```

We can rewrite the same function, but rather than printing the value inside the function, it should return the greater number:

```
def checkgreaternumber(number1,number2):
    if number1 > number2:
      return number1
    else:
     return number2

print ("My greater number in 2 and 4 is ",checkgreaternumber(2,4))
print ("My greater number in 3 and 1 is ",checkgreaternumber(3,1))
```

In this case, as we can see, the function returns the value, and the result is returned on the line where the function was called. In this case, as it was called inside the `print` function, it evaluates the input and returns the value, which also gets printed out inside the same `print` function.

```
#PowerShell sample code
function checkgreaternumber($number1,$number2)
{
    if ($number1 -gt $number2)
    {
        return $number1
    }
    else
    {
        return $number2
    }
}

write-host ("My greater number in 2 and 4 is ",(checkgreaternumber 2
4))
write-host ("My greater number in 3 and 1 is ",(checkgreaternumber 3
1))
```

Another important aspect of a function is the default values that we can provide in a function. Sometimes we need to write functions that might take multiple, say 4, 5, or more, values as inputs. Since it becomes hard to know what values we need and in which order for the function, we can ensure that the default value is taken into consideration if any value is not provided when calling that specific function:

```
def checkgreaternumber(number1,number2=5):
    if number1 > number2:
      return number1
    else:
     return number2
print ("Greater value is",checkgreaternumber(3))
```

```
print ("Greater value is",checkgreaternumber(6))
print ("Greater value is",checkgreaternumber(1,4))
```

The output of the code execution is given as:

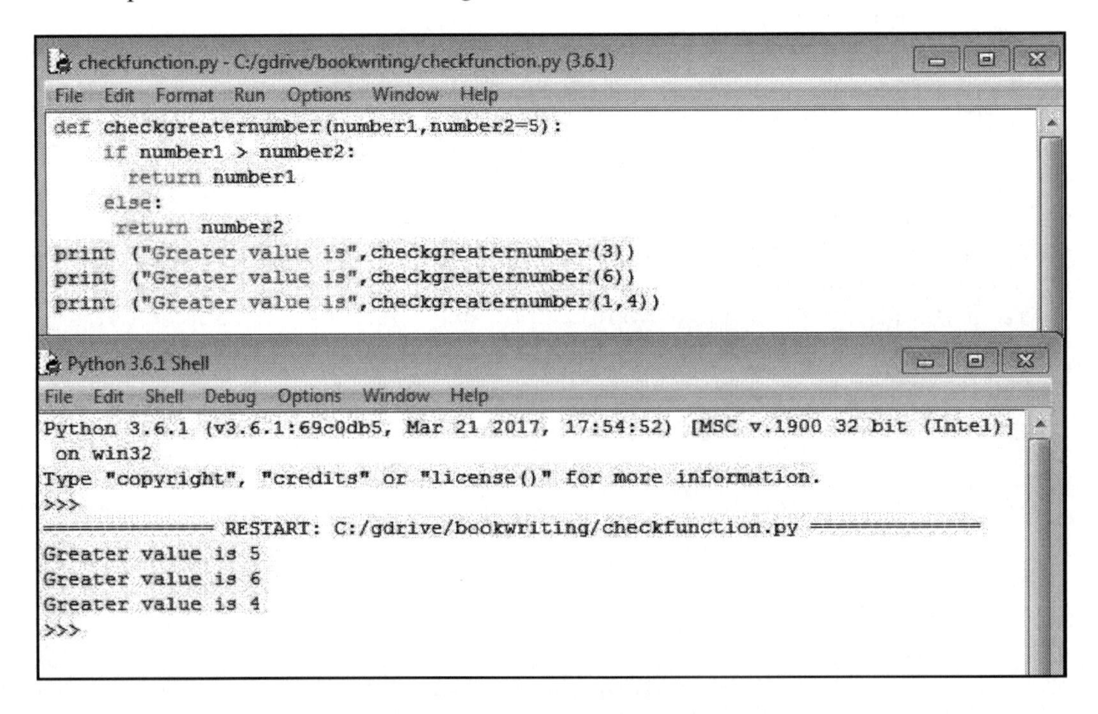

```
def checkgreaternumber(number1,number2=5):
    if number1 > number2:
      return number1
    else:
      return number2
print ("Greater value is",checkgreaternumber(3))
print ("Greater value is",checkgreaternumber(6))
print ("Greater value is",checkgreaternumber(1,4))
```

```
Python 3.6.1 (v3.6.1:69c0db5, Mar 21 2017, 17:54:52) [MSC v.1900 32 bit (Intel)]
 on win32
Type "copyright", "credits" or "license()" for more information.
>>>
============= RESTART: C:/gdrive/bookwriting/checkfunction.py =============
Greater value is 5
Greater value is 6
Greater value is 4
>>>
```

1. As we can see in the preceding output, we specified the default value of `number2` as `5`. Now, as we can see in the first call to the function, we only give the value `3`. Now, as the function needs two inputs or parameters, but we provided only one, the second value for the function is taken from the default one, which is `5` in this case. Hence, a comparison will be done between `3` and `5` to get the greater number.
2. In the second call to the function, a similar call is made with `6`, and since no other value was provided, the comparison was between `6` and `5`, and result returned was the greater value, which is `6`.
3. In the third call, we provide both values, which overrides any default value, so a comparison was done between `1` and `4`. The result was evaluated and the output of `4` was returned.

Another important consideration is the localization of a variable in a function:

```
globalval=6

def checkglobalvalue():
    return globalval

def localvariablevalue():
    globalval=8
    return globalval

print ("This is global value",checkglobalvalue())
print ("This is global value",globalval)
print ("This is local value",localvariablevalue())
print ("This is global value",globalval)
```

The output of the preceding code is as follows:

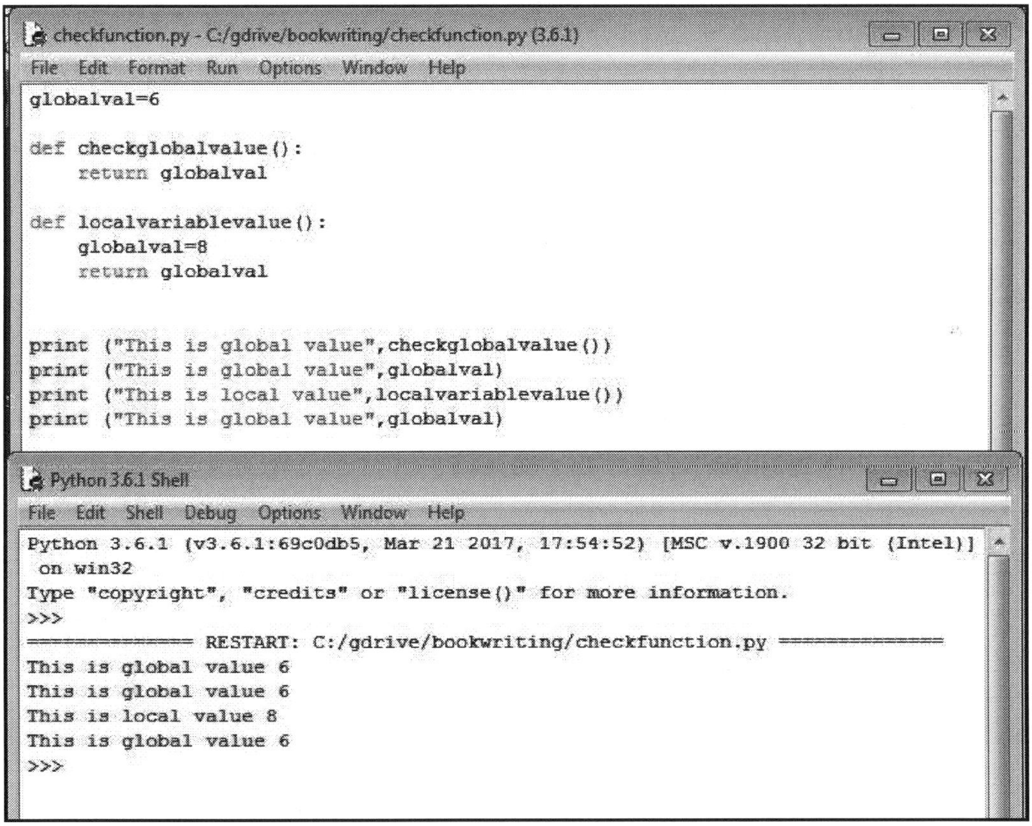

```
checkfunction.py - C:/gdrive/bookwriting/checkfunction.py (3.6.1)
File Edit Format Run Options Window Help
globalval=6

def checkglobalvalue():
    return globalval

def localvariablevalue():
    globalval=8
    return globalval


print ("This is global value",checkglobalvalue())
print ("This is global value",globalval)
print ("This is local value",localvariablevalue())
print ("This is global value",globalval)
```

```
Python 3.6.1 Shell
File Edit Shell Debug Options Window Help
Python 3.6.1 (v3.6.1:69c0db5, Mar 21 2017, 17:54:52) [MSC v.1900 32 bit (Intel)]
 on win32
Type "copyright", "credits" or "license()" for more information.
>>>
============= RESTART: C:/gdrive/bookwriting/checkfunction.py =============
This is global value 6
This is global value 6
This is local value 8
This is global value 6
>>>
```

1. In the preceding output, we define a variable named as `globalval` with a value of `6`. In the `checkglobalvalue` function, we just return the value of the `globalvalvariable`, which prints a value of `6` as we call the first `print` function.
2. The second `print` function just prints the value of the same variable, which also prints `6`.
3. Now, in the third `print` function, `localvariablevalue`, we call the same `globalval`, but give it a value of `8` and return the value of `globalval`. In the print value of local, it prints the result as value 8. It is not assumed that the `globalval` variable has a value of `8` now. But, as we can see in the last `print` function, it still prints a value of `6`, when we call the `print` function to print the value of `globalval`.

This clearly shows that any variable inside a function is locally effective, or is localized, but does not have any impact on any variables outside the function. We need to use the `global` command to reference the global variable and remove the localization impact of it.

Here is the same example before using the `global` command:

```
checkfunction.py - C:\gdrive\bookwriting\checkfunction.py (3.6.1)
File Edit Format Run Options Window Help
globalval=6

def checkglobalvalue():
    global globalval
    return globalval

def localvariablevalue():
    global globalval
    globalval=8
    return globalval


print ("This is global value",checkglobalvalue())
print ("This is global value",globalval)
print ("This is local value",localvariablevalue())
print ("This is global value",globalval)
```

```
Python 3.6.1 Shell
File Edit Shell Debug Options Window Help
Python 3.6.1 (v3.6.1:69c0db5, Mar 21 2017, 17:54:52) [MSC v.1900 32 bit (Intel)]
 on win32
Type "copyright", "credits" or "license()" for more information.
>>>
============== RESTART: C:\gdrive\bookwriting\checkfunction.py ==============
This is global value 6
This is global value 6
This is local value 8
This is global value 8
>>>
```

As can we see in the preceding output, if we change the value of the `globalval` global variable inside the `localvariablevalue` function, we see the effect on the global variable with a new value of `8`.

Passing arguments from the command line

Sometimes it is necessary to pass arguments to the script from the command line. This is generally needed when we need to perform some quick actions in our script, rather than the script asking us for the inputs.

Consider the following lines of code where we pass two numbers as arguments to scripts, and print the sum of them:

```
import sys
print ("Total output is ")
print (int(sys.argv[1])+int(sys.argv[2]))
```

When we run this script, say it's saved as `checkargs.py`, and execute it as follows:

```
python checkargs.py 5 6
```

The output returned is as follows:

```
Total output is
11
```

The key here is the import of the `sys` module, which is a predefined module in Python to handle any system-related tasks of Python. The values that we pass as arguments are stored in `sys.argv[1]` onwards, since `sys.argv[0]` is the name of actual script being run. In this case, `sys.argv[0]` will be `checkargs.py`, `sys.argv[1]` will be `5`, and `sys.argv[2]` will be `6`.

The PowerShell code for the preceding task is as follows:

```
#PowerShell sample code
$myvalue=$args[0]
write-host ("Argument passed to PowerShell is "+$myvalue)
```

The arguments passed in a Python script are in string format, so we need to explicitly convert them to the right type for the expected output. In the preceding script, if we had not converted it to the integer type by using the `int()` function, then the output would have been `56` instead of `int(5)` + `int(6)` = `11`.

Python modules and packages

Because Python is the most popular open source coding language, there are many developers who contribute their expertise by creating specific modules and sharing them for others to use. These modules are a specific set of functions or instructions that are used to perform specialized tasks and can be called easily in our programs. The modules can be easily called using the `import` command inside the scripts. Python has many built-in modules that are directly called using `import`, but for specialized modules, an external installation is needed. Luckily, Python provides a very easy way to download and install these modules.

As an example, let's install a module named `Netmiko` that can help us work on logging into network devices more efficiently. Python provides a well-documented reference for each of the modules, and for our module, the documentation can be found at `https://pypi.python.org/pypi/netmiko`. For installation, all we have to do is go into the folder from the command line where `python.exe` is installed or is present. There is a sub folder in that location called `scripts`.

Inside that folder, we have two options that can be used for installing modules, `easy_install.exe` or `pip.exe`.

Installing the library for Python, can be done in two ways:

- The syntax of `easy_install` is as follows:

  ```
  easy_install <name of module>
  ```

  For example:

  ```
  easy_install netmiko
  ```

- The syntax of `pip install` is as follows:

  ```
  pip install <name of module>
  ```

  For example:

  ```
  pip install netmiko
  ```

Once we install the required module, we need to restart Python by closing all open sessions and invoking IDLE again so the modules can be loaded. More information on modules can be gathered from `https://docs.python.org/2/tutorial/modules.html`.

Multithreading for parallel processing

As we are now focusing on writing our scripts efficiently, a major aspect of this is how efficiently, quickly, and correctly we fetch the information. When we use the `for` loop, we parse through each item one by one, which is fine if we get results quickly.

Now, if each item in a `for` loop is a router from which we need to get the output of show version, and if each router takes around 10 seconds to log in, gather the output, and log out, and we have around 30 routers that we need to get this information from, we would need 10*30 = 300 seconds for the program to complete the execution. If we are looking for more advanced or complex calculations on each output, which might take up to a minute, then it will take 30 minutes for just 30 routers.

This starts becoming very inefficient when our complexity and scalability grows. To help with this, we need to add parallelism to our programs. What this simply means is, we log in simultaneously on all 30 routers, and perform the same task to fetch the output at the same time. Effectively, this means that we now get the output on all 30 routers in 10 seconds, because we have 30 parallel threads being called.

A thread is nothing but another instance of the same function being called, and calling it 30 times means we are invoking 30 threads at the same time to perform the same tasks.

Here's an example:

```
import datetime
from threading import Thread

def checksequential():
    for x in range(1,10):
        print (datetime.datetime.now().time())

def checkparallel():
    print (str(datetime.datetime.now().time())+"\n")

checksequential()
print ("\nNow printing parallel threads\n")
threads = []
for x in range(1,10):
    t = Thread(target=checkparallel)
    t.start()
    threads.append(t)

for t in threads:
    t.join()
```

The output of the multi-threading code is as follows:

1. As we can see in the preceding example, we created two functions, named `checksequential` and `checkparallel`, to print the system's date time. The `datetime` module is used to get the system's date time in this case. In the `for` loop, a sequential run was done that shows the increment time in the output when the function was called.

2. For the threading, we use a blank array named `threads`. Each of the instances that is created has a unique thread number or value, which is stored in this empty thread array each time the `checkparallel` method is spawned. This unique number or reference for each thread identifies each thread as and when its executed. The `start()` method is used to get the thread to perform the function called in the thread.
3. The last loop is important in the thread. What it signifies is that the program will wait for all the threads to complete before moving forward. The `join()` method specifies that until all the threads are complete, the program will not proceed to the next step.

Now, as we can see in the output of the thread, some of the timestamps are the same, which means that all those instances were invoked and executed at the same time in parallel rather than sequentially.

The output in the program is not in order for parallel threads, because the moment any thread is completed, the output is printed, irrespective of the order. This is different to sequential execution, since parallel threads do not wait for any previous thread to complete before executing another. So, any thread that completes will print its value and end.

PowerShell sample code for the preceding task is as follows:

```
#PowerShell sample code
Get-Job  #This get the current running threads or Jobs in PowerShell
Remove-Job -Force * # This commands closes forcible all the previous
threads

$Scriptblock = {
      Param (
         [string]$ipaddress
      )
    if (Test-Connection $ipaddress -quiet)
    {
        return ("Ping for "+$ipaddress+" is successful")
     }
    else
    {
       return ("Ping for "+$ipaddress+" FAILED")
    }
  }

$iplist="4.4.4.4","8.8.8.8","10.10.10.10","20.20.20.20","4.2.2.2"
```

```
foreach ($ip in $iplist)
{
    Start-Job -ScriptBlock $Scriptblock -ArgumentList $ip | Out-Null
    #The above command is used to invoke the $scriptblock in a
multithread
}

#Following logic waits for all the threads or Jobs to get completed
While (@(Get-Job | Where { $_.State -eq "Running" }).Count -ne 0)
  { # Write-Host "Waiting for background jobs..."
     Start-Sleep -Seconds 1
  }

#Following logic is used to print all the values that are returned by
each thread and then remove the thread # #or job from memory
ForEach ($Job in (Get-Job)) {
  Receive-Job $Job
  Remove-Job $Job
  }
```

Using Netmiko for SSH and network device interaction

Netmiko (`https://github.com/ktbyers/netmiko`) is a library in Python that is used extensively an interaction with network devices. This is a multi-vendor library with support for Cisco IOS, NXOS, firewalls, and many other devices. The underlying library of this is Paramiko, which is again used extensively for SSH into various devices.

Netmiko extends the Paramiko ability of SSH to add enhancements, such as going into configuration mode in network routers, sending commands, receiving output based upon the commands, adding enhancements to wait for certain commands to finish executing, and also taking care of yes/no prompts during command execution.

Here's an example of a simple script to log in to the router and show the version:

```
from netmiko import ConnectHandler

device = ConnectHandler(device_type='cisco_ios', ip='192.168.255.249',
username='cisco', password='cisco')
output = device.send_command("show version")
print (output)
device.disconnect()
```

The output of the execution of code against a router is as follows:

As we can see in the sample code, we call the `ConnectHandler` function from the Netmiko library, which takes four inputs (`platform type`, `IP address of device`, `username`, and `password`):

Netmiko works with a variety of vendors. Some of the supported platform types and their abbreviations to be called in Netmiko are:

'a10': A10SSH,
'accedian': AccedianSSH,
'alcatel_aos': AlcatelAosSSH,
'alcatel_sros': AlcatelSrosSSH,
'arista_eos': AristaSSH,
'aruba_os': ArubaSSH,
'avaya_ers': AvayaErsSSH,
'avaya_vsp': AvayaVspSSH,
'brocade_fastiron': BrocadeFastironSSH,
'brocade_netiron': BrocadeNetironSSH,
'brocade_nos': BrocadeNosSSH,
'brocade_vdx': BrocadeNosSSH,
'brocade_vyos': VyOSSSH,
'checkpoint_gaia': CheckPointGaiaSSH,
'ciena_saos': CienaSaosSSH,
'cisco_asa': CiscoAsaSSH,
'cisco_ios': CiscoIosBase,
'cisco_nxos': CiscoNxosSSH,
'cisco_s300': CiscoS300SSH,
'cisco_tp': CiscoTpTcCeSSH,
'cisco_wlc': CiscoWlcSSH,
'cisco_xe': CiscoIosBase,
'cisco_xr': CiscoXrSSH,
'dell_force10': DellForce10SSH,
'dell_powerconnect': DellPowerConnectSSH,
'eltex': EltexSSH,
'enterasys': EnterasysSSH,
'extreme': ExtremeSSH,
'extreme_wing': ExtremeWingSSH,
'f5_ltm': F5LtmSSH,
'fortinet': FortinetSSH,
'generic_termserver': TerminalServerSSH,
'hp_comware': HPComwareSSH,
'hp_procurve': HPProcurveSSH,
'huawei': HuaweiSSH,

> 'juniper': JuniperSSH,
> 'juniper_junos': JuniperSSH,
> 'linux': LinuxSSH,
> 'mellanox_ssh': MellanoxSSH,
> 'mrv_optiswitch': MrvOptiswitchSSH,
> 'ovs_linux': OvsLinuxSSH,
> 'paloalto_panos': PaloAltoPanosSSH,
> 'pluribus': PluribusSSH,
> 'quanta_mesh': QuantaMeshSSH,
> 'ubiquiti_edge': UbiquitiEdgeSSH,
> 'vyatta_vyos': VyOSSSH,
> 'vyos': VyOSSSH,

Depending upon the selection of the platform type, Netmiko can understand the returned prompt and the correct way to SSH to the specific device. Once the connection is made, we can send commands to the device using the `send` method.

Once we get the return value, the value stored in the `output` variable is displayed, which is the string output of the command that we sent to the device. The last line, which uses the `disconnect` function, ensures that the connection is terminated cleanly once we are done with our task.

For configuration (example: We need to provide a description to the router interface `FastEthernet 0/0`), we use Netmiko as shown in the following example:

```
from netmiko import ConnectHandler

print ("Before config push")
device = ConnectHandler(device_type='cisco_ios', ip='192.168.255.249',
username='cisco', password='cisco')
output = device.send_command("show running-config interface
fastEthernet 0/0")
print (output)

configcmds=["interface fastEthernet 0/0", "description my test"]
device.send_config_set(configcmds)

print ("After config push")
output = device.send_command("show running-config interface
fastEthernet 0/0")
print (output)

device.disconnect()
```

The output of the execution of the preceding code is as follows:

```
Python 3.6.1 Shell
File Edit Shell Debug Options Window Help
Python 3.6.1 (v3.6.1:69c0db5, Mar 21 2017, 17:54:52) [MSC v.1900 32 bit (Intel)]
 on win32
Type "copyright", "credits" or "license()" for more information.
>>>
===================== RESTART: C:/a1/checknetmiko.py =====================
Before config push
Building configuration...

Current configuration : 102 bytes
!
interface FastEthernet0/0
 ip address 192.168.255.249 255.255.255.252
 duplex auto
 speed auto
end

After config push
Building configuration...

Current configuration : 123 bytes
!
interface FastEthernet0/0
 description my test
 ip address 192.168.255.249 255.255.255.252
 duplex auto
 speed auto
end

>>>
```

- As we can see, for `config push` we do not have to perform any additional configs but just specify the commands in the same order as we will send them manually to the router in a list, and pass that list as an argument to the `send_config_set` function.
- The output in `Before config push` is a simple output of the `FastEthernet0/0` interface, but the output under `After config push` is now with the description that we configured using the list of commands.

In a similar way, we can pass multiple commands to the router, and Netmiko will go into configuration mode, write those commands to the router, and exit config mode.

If we want to save the configuration, we use the following command after the `send_config_set` command:

```
device.send_command("write memory")
```

This ensures that the router writes the newly pushed config in memory.

Network automation use case

As we have now interacted with multiple sections of Python and device interaction, let's create a use case to incorporate what we have learned so far. The use case is as follows:

Log into the router and fetch some information:

1. `task1()`: Show the version, show the IP in brief, show the clock, and show the configured usernames on the router.
2. `task2()`: Create another username on the `test` router with the password `test` and check whether we can log in successfully with the newly created username.
3. `task3()`: Log in with the newly created username `test`, and delete all the other usernames from the `running-config`. Once this is done, return all the current usernames configured on the router to confirm whether only the `test` username is configured on the router.

Let's build a script to tackle these tasks one by one:

```
from netmiko import ConnectHandler

device = ConnectHandler(device_type='cisco_ios', ip='192.168.255.249',
username='cisco', password='cisco')

def task1():
    output = device.send_command("show version")
    print (output)
    output= device.send_command("show ip int brief")
    print (output)
    output= device.send_command("show clock")
    print (output)
    output= device.send_command("show running-config | in username")
    output=output.splitlines()
    for item in output:
        if ("username" in item):
```

```
            item=item.split(" ")
            print ("username configured: ",item[1])

def task2():
    global device
    configcmds=["username test privilege 15 secret test"]
    device.send_config_set(configcmds)
    output= device.send_command("show running-config | in username")
    output=output.splitlines()
    for item in output:
        if ("username" in item):
            item=item.split(" ")
            print ("username configured: ",item[1])
    device.disconnect()
    try:
        device = ConnectHandler(device_type='cisco_ios',
ip='192.168.255.249', username='test', password='test')
        print ("Authenticated successfully with username test")
        device.disconnect()
    except:
        print ("Unable to authenticate with username test")

def task3():
    device = ConnectHandler(device_type='cisco_ios',
ip='192.168.255.249', username='test', password='test')
    output= device.send_command("show running-config | in username")
    output=output.splitlines()
    for item in output:
        if ("username" in item):
            if ("test" not in item):
                item=item.split(" ")
                cmd="no username "+item[1]
                outputnew=device.send_config_set(cmd)
    output= device.send_command("show running-config | in username")
    output=output.splitlines()
    for item in output:
        if ("username" in item):
            item=item.split(" ")
            print ("username configured: ",item[1])
    device.disconnect()
#Call task1 by writing task1()
#task1()
#Call task2 by writing task2()
#task2()
#Call task3 by writing task3()
#task3()
```

As we can see, the three tasks given are defined as three different functions:

1. The first line indicates that we have imported the Netmiko library, and in the second line we are connecting to our `test` router with the Cisco credentials.
2. In the `task1()` function, we are fetching the outputs of all show commands. Additionally, since we do not want to expose the passwords of the current usernames we have added an extra logic wherein the returned output for `show running-config | in username` will be parsed by each line for every username, and each line will be split by a space character `" "`. Also, since the Cisco device returns the actual username in the second position in the output (for example, username `test` privilege 15 secret 5), we print the value of the second item after we split the output string, which is our actual username.

   Here's the output for the `task1()` method:

```
This product contains cryptographic features and is subject to United
States and local country laws governing import, export, transfer and
use. Delivery of Cisco cryptographic products does not imply
third-party authority to import, export, distribute or use encryption.
Importers, exporters, distributors and users are responsible for
compliance with U.S. and local country laws. By using this product you
agree to comply with applicable laws and regulations. If you are unable
to comply with U.S. and local laws, return this product immediately.

A summary of U.S. laws governing Cisco cryptographic products may be found at:
http://www.cisco.com/wwl/export/crypto/tool/stqrg.html

If you require further assistance please contact us by sending email to
export@cisco.com.

Cisco 3745 (R7000) processor (revision 2.0) with 249856K/12288K bytes of memory.
Processor board ID FTX0945W0MY
R7000 CPU at 350MHz, Implementation 39, Rev 2.1, 256KB L2, 512KB L3 Cache
3 FastEthernet interfaces
1 Serial(sync/async) interface
DRAM configuration is 64 bits wide with parity enabled.
151K bytes of NVRAM.

Configuration register is 0x2102

Interface                  IP-Address      OK? Method Status                Protocol
FastEthernet0/0            192.168.255.249 YES NVRAM  up                    up
Serial0/0                  unassigned      YES NVRAM  administratively down down
FastEthernet0/1            unassigned      YES NVRAM  administratively down down
FastEthernet1/0            unassigned      YES NVRAM  administratively down down
*00:26:48.907 UTC Fri Mar 1 2002
username configured:  cisco
>>>
```

3. In the `task2()` method, we are going to create a username `test` with the password `test`, and authenticate with the new username. We have added a `try:` exception block in this method, which checks for any errors/exceptions for all the statements in the `try:` section, and if there are any exceptions, rather than breaking the script, it runs the code that is given in the exception section (under the `except:` keyword). If there are no errors, it continues with the statements in the `try:` section.

   Here's the output for `task2()`:

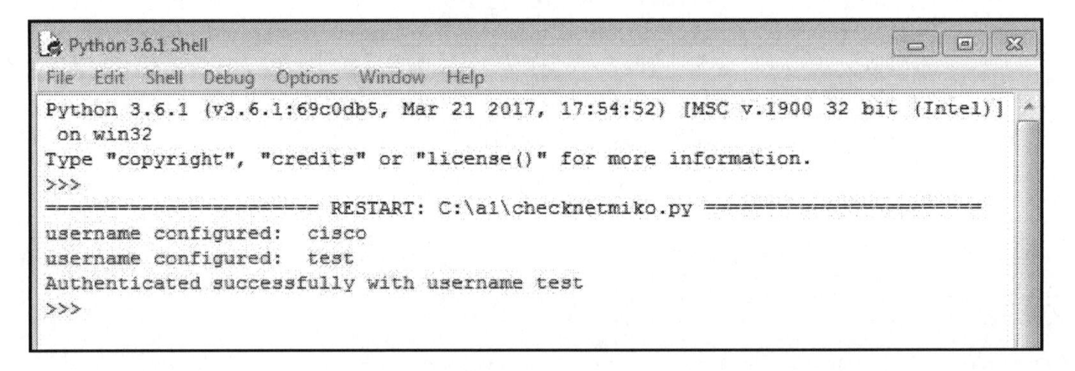

   We can see that we now have two usernames configured, and the router is also now successfully responding to authentication with the `test` username.

4. In `task3()` function, this will first fetch all the usernames that are in `running-config`, and if there are any usernames that are not `test`, it will create a dynamic command with no username `<username>` and send it to the router. Once it is done with all the usernames, it will go ahead and recheck and list out all the usernames not on the router. A success criteria is only the configured username as `test` should be available on the router.

Here's the output of `task3()`:

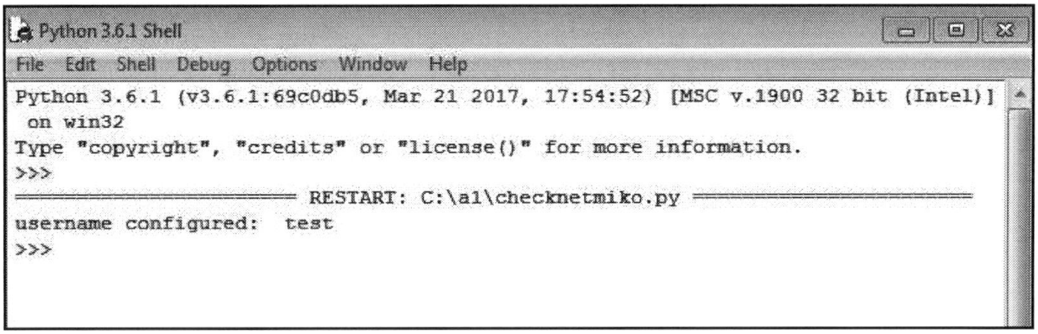

```
Python 3.6.1 Shell
File  Edit  Shell  Debug  Options  Window  Help
Python 3.6.1 (v3.6.1:69c0db5, Mar 21 2017, 17:54:52) [MSC v.1900 32 bit (Intel)]
 on win32
Type "copyright", "credits" or "license()" for more information.
>>>
====================== RESTART: C:\a1\checknetmiko.py ======================
username configured:  test
>>>
```

The result of `task3()` is the result of all configured usernames, which in this case is now only test.

Summary

In this chapter, we learned some advanced techniques for writing scripts by using functions, conditions, and loops; we covered multi-threading our scripts for faster and parallel execution, we got familiar with using Netmiko to interact with network devices, and looked at a real-world example of achieving a certain set of tasks using a single script.

3
Continuous Integration for Network Engineers

In this chapter, we will see some of the tools that help us in working on planning our automation projects, and some examples to interact with some increasingly complex scenarios related to various devices or network technologies.

Some of the aspects that we will be working on are:

- Interaction with Splunk
- BGP and routing table
- Wireless client to AP to switchport
- Phone to switchport
- WLAN and IPAM
- Useful best practices and use cases

Interaction with Splunk

Splunk is one of the most widely used data mining tools. With its data mining and digging capabilities, engineers can take actions based upon decisions. While it is useful in various aspects, here we will see an example of Splunk being used as a Syslog server, with our test router sending a message (as syslog) to this server, and how from automation we can query results from Splunk for these syslogs and take actions.

This is an important part of automation, since based upon certain events (alerts and syslogs), engineers need to perform automated tasks, like self healing, or even triggering emails or using third-party tools to create tickets for various teams to work on.

Here we will see the basic implementation and configuration of Splunk as a Syslog server:

1. After downloading and installing Splunk , it can be accessed from the URL `http://localhost:8000/en-US/account/login?return_to=%2Fen-US%2F` as we can see in the following screenshot:

2. Once we login, we create a listener listed to syslogs (in our case we use the `TCP` protocol and keep the default port `514` open):

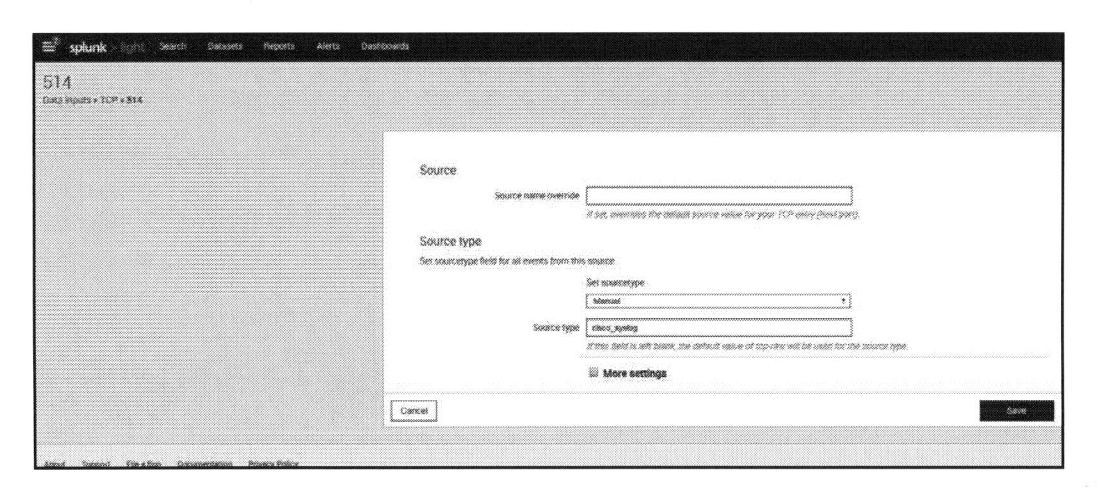

Once the configuration is done for TCP port `514` on Splunk (listening for syslog messages), ensure any local firewall on the server is allowing inbound packets to TCP port `514`, and our machine is ready to access syslogs from network devices on TCP port `514`).

3. Configure the router to send syslogs. We apply the following commands on the router to enable logging (In our case the IP for the Syslog server is `192.168.255.250`):

```
config t
logging host 192.168.255.250 transport tcp port 514
logging buffered informational
exit
```

This configures the router to send syslogs to the given IP address on TCP protocol over port `514`. Additionally, we are also stating to log only information syslog messages on the router.

4. Once done, for confirmation we can try to perform a shutdown and no shutdown of any interface (`Loopback0` in our case), and see the log using the `show logging` command on the router:

```
R2#show logging
Syslog logging: enabled (11 messages dropped, 0 messages
rate-limited,
                0 flushes, 0 overruns, xml disabled,
filtering disabled)
    Console logging: level debugging, 26 messages logged,
xml disabled,
                     filtering disabled
    Monitor logging: level debugging, 0 messages logged,
xml disabled,
                     filtering disabled
    Buffer logging: level informational, 7 messages
logged, xml disabled,
                    filtering disabled
    Logging Exception size (4096 bytes)
    Count and timestamp logging messages: disabled
No active filter modules.
    Trap logging: level informational, 30 message lines
logged
        Logging to 192.168.255.250(global) (tcp port
514,audit disabled, link up), 30 message lines logged, xml
disabled,
               filtering disabled
Log Buffer (4096 bytes):
*Mar  1 01:02:04.223: %SYS-5-CONFIG_I: Configured from
console by console
*Mar  1 01:02:10.275: %SYS-6-LOGGINGHOST_STARTSTOP:
Logging to host 192.168.255.250 started - reconnection
*Mar  1 01:02:32.179: %LINK-5-CHANGED: Interface
Loopback0, changed state to administratively down
*Mar  1 01:02:33.179: %LINEPROTO-5-UPDOWN: Line protocol
on Interface Loopback0, changed state to down
*Mar  1 01:02:39.303: %SYS-5-CONFIG_I: Configured from
console by console
*Mar  1 01:02:39.647: %LINK-3-UPDOWN: Interface Loopback0,
changed state to up
*Mar  1 01:02:40.647: %LINEPROTO-5-UPDOWN: Line protocol
on Interface Loopback0, changed state to up
```

An important aspect to confirm if the router is sending syslogs is the line `tcp port 514, audit disabled, link up`, which confirms that the router is sending syslog traffic to the Syslog server.

5. Here is the raw output on Splunk for the syslog that is generated:

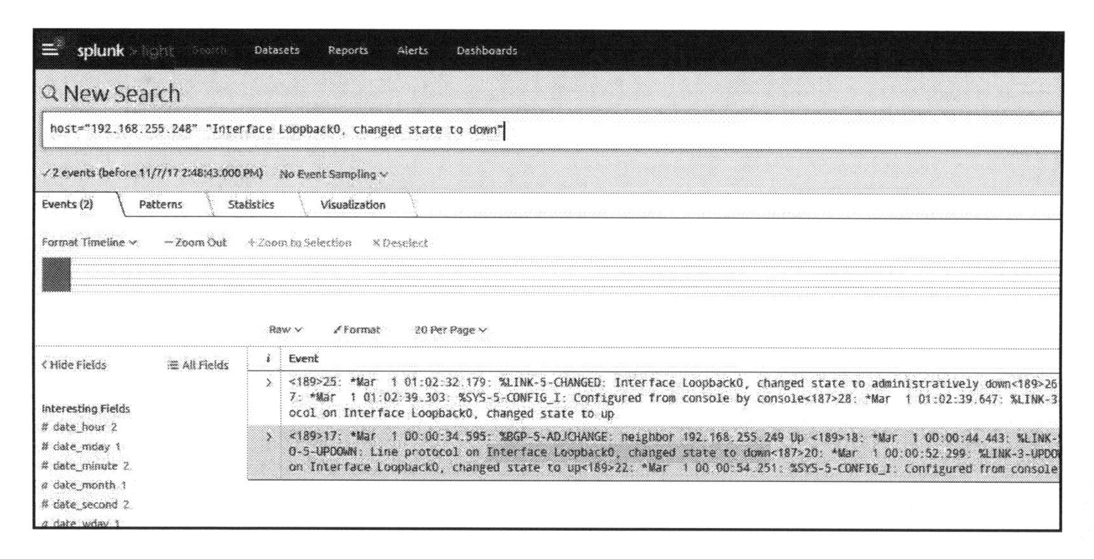

As we see in the **New Search** section we can write queries to fetch the exact data that we want. In our case we wanted to see only the log from our router with the `Interface Loopback0` down messages, hence we wrote the query:

```
host="192.168.255.248" "Interface Loopback0, changed state
to down"
```

6. Now let us see the code from Python that we can write to fetch the same information using a script:

```
import requests
import json
from xml.dom import minidom

username="admin"
password="admin"

### For generating the session key ####
url = 'https://localhost:8089/services/auth/login'
headers = {'Content-Type': 'application/json'}
data={"username":username,"password":password}
requests.packages.urllib3.disable_warnings()
r = requests.get(url, auth=(username, password),
data=data, headers=headers,verify=False)
sessionkey =
```

```
minidom.parseString(r.text).getElementsByTagName('sessionK
ey')[0].childNodes[0].nodeValue

#### For executing the query using the generated
sessionkey
headers={"Authorization":"Splunk "+sessionkey}
data={"search":'search host="192.168.255.248" "Interface
Loopback0, changed state to down"',"output_mode":"json"}
r=requests.post('https://localhost:8089/servicesNS/admin/s
earch/search/jobs/export',data=data ,
headers=headers,verify=False);
print (r.text)
```

In the first section, we query the API of Splunk to fetch the authentication session key (or token) to run our queries and get results. Once we have the session key (extracted from the XML output), we create a header and using `requests.post` we execute our query. The data variable contains our query in the following format:

```
{"search":'search host="192.168.255.248" "Interface
Loopback0, changed state to down"'}
```

In other words, if we take this in a variable (named `Search`), and provide the result as a value to that variable, it would look like below:

```
Search='search host="192.168.255.248" "Interface
Loopback0, changed state to down"'
```

Additionally we also send another option of `output_mode` as JSON , since we want the output in JSON (some other values can be CSV or XML).

Executing the same will get the following output:

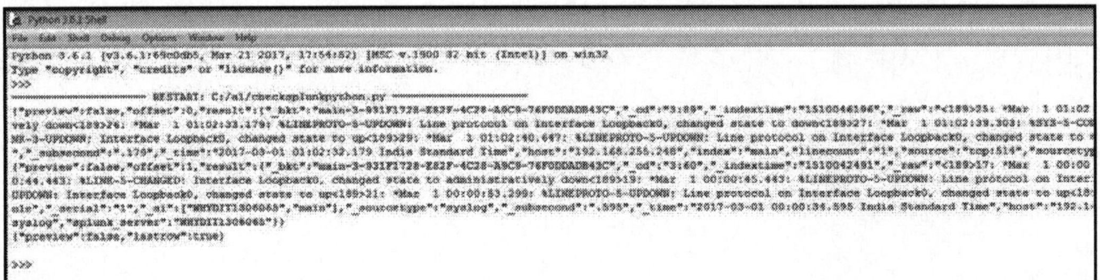

As we see in the preceding output, we are now retrieving and displaying the value in JSON format.

We will stop our example here, but to enhance this script, this result can now become a trigger on which we can add additional methods or logic to decide on the trigger for further actions. By this logic, we can have self-healing scripts that find out the data (as a trigger), evaluate the trigger (identify it actionable), and take actions based upon further logic.

Automation examples on various technology domains

With the familiarity and understanding of automation with the interaction of devices, APIs, controllers, let's see some examples of how to interact with other network domain devices and tackle some complex scenarios using automation frameworks.

Some of these examples will be a small project in themselves, but will help you understand additional ways of performing automation tasks in depth.

BGP and routing table

Let's take an example in which we need to configure BGP, validate if a session is up, and report the details for the same. In our example, we would take two routers (as a prerequisite, both routers are able to ping each other) as follows:

As we see `R2` and `testrouter` are able to ping each other using an IP address of the `FastEthernet0/0` interface of each other.

The next step is a very basic configuration of BGP (in our case, we use the **Autonomous System** (**AS**) number `200`). The code is as follows:

```
from netmiko import ConnectHandler
import time

def
pushbgpconfig(routerip,remoteip,localas,remoteas,newconfig="false"):
    uname="cisco"
    passwd="cisco"
    device = ConnectHandler(device_type='cisco_ios', ip=routerip,
username=uname, password=passwd)
    cmds=""
    cmds="router bgp "+localas
    cmds=cmds+"\n neighbor "+remoteip+" remote-as "+remoteas
    xcheck=device.send_config_set(cmds)
    print (xcheck)
    outputx=device.send_command("wr mem")
    print (outputx)
    device.disconnect()


def validatebgp(routerip,remoteip):
    uname="cisco"
    passwd="cisco"
    device = ConnectHandler(device_type='cisco_ios', ip=routerip,
username=uname, password=passwd)
    cmds="show ip bgp neighbors "+remoteip+" | include BGP state"
    outputx=device.send_command(cmds)
    if ("Established" in outputx):
        print ("Remote IP "+remoteip+" on local router "+routerip+" is
in ESTABLISHED state")
    else:
        print ("Remote IP "+remoteip+" on local router "+routerip+" is
NOT IN ESTABLISHED state")
    device.disconnect()
pushbgpconfig("192.168.255.249","192.168.255.248","200","200")
### we give some time for bgp to establish
print ("Now sleeping for 5 seconds....")
time.sleep(5) # 5 seconds
validatebgp("192.168.255.249","192.168.255.248")
```

The output is as follows:

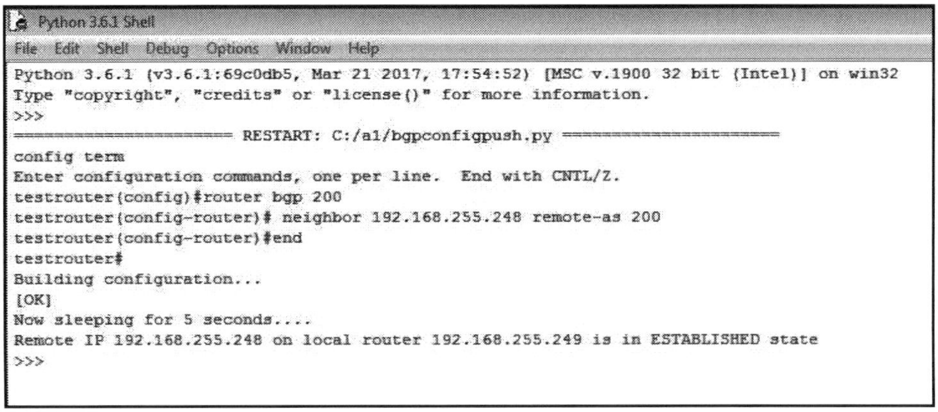

```
Python 3.6.1 Shell
File Edit Shell Debug Options Window Help
Python 3.6.1 (v3.6.1:69c0db5, Mar 21 2017, 17:54:52) [MSC v.1900 32 bit (Intel)] on win32
Type "copyright", "credits" or "license()" for more information.
>>>
===================== RESTART: C:/a1/bgpconfigpush.py =====================
config term
Enter configuration commands, one per line.  End with CNTL/Z.
testrouter(config)#router bgp 200
testrouter(config-router)# neighbor 192.168.255.248 remote-as 200
testrouter(config-router)#end
testrouter#
Building configuration...
[OK]
Now sleeping for 5 seconds....
Remote IP 192.168.255.248 on local router 192.168.255.249 is in ESTABLISHED state
>>>
```

As we see, we push the neighbor config (BGP config) to the router. Once the config is pushed, the script waits for 5 seconds and validates the state of BGP if it is in the `ESTABLISHED state`. This validation confirms that the config that we pushed has all the sessions that are newly configured as established.

Let's push an incorrect config as follows:

```
from netmiko import ConnectHandler
import time
def
pushbgpconfig(routerip,remoteip,localas,remoteas,newconfig="false"):
 uname="cisco"
 passwd="cisco"
 device = ConnectHandler(device_type='cisco_ios', ip=routerip,
username=uname, password=passwd)
 cmds=""
 cmds="router bgp "+localas
 cmds=cmds+"\n neighbor "+remoteip+" remote-as "+remoteas
 xcheck=device.send_config_set(cmds)
 print (xcheck)
 outputx=device.send_command("wr mem")
 print (outputx)
 device.disconnect()
def validatebgp(routerip,remoteip):
 uname="cisco"
 passwd="cisco"
 device = ConnectHandler(device_type='cisco_ios', ip=routerip,
username=uname, password=passwd)
 cmds="show ip bgp neighbors "+remoteip+" | include BGP state"
 outputx=device.send_command(cmds)
```

```
 if ("Established" in outputx):
 print ("Remote IP "+remoteip+" on local router "+routerip+" is in
ESTABLISHED state")
 else:
 print ("Remote IP "+remoteip+" on local router "+routerip+" is NOT IN
ESTABLISHED state")
 device.disconnect()

pushbgpconfig("192.168.255.249","192.168.255.248","200","400")
### we give some time for bgp to establish
print ("Now sleeping for 5 seconds....")
time.sleep(5) # 5 seconds
validatebgp("192.168.255.249","192.168.255.248")
```

The output of the preceding code is as follows:

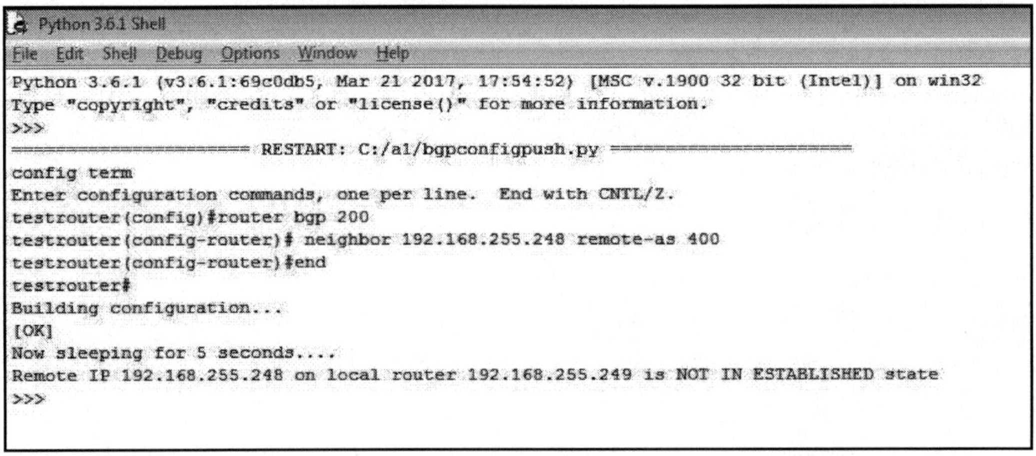

```
Python 3.6.1 Shell
File Edit Shell Debug Options Window Help
Python 3.6.1 (v3.6.1:69c0db5, Mar 21 2017, 17:54:52) [MSC v.1900 32 bit (Intel)] on win32
Type "copyright", "credits" or "license()" for more information.
>>>
===================== RESTART: C:/a1/bgpconfigpush.py =====================
config term
Enter configuration commands, one per line.  End with CNTL/Z.
testrouter(config)#router bgp 200
testrouter(config-router)# neighbor 192.168.255.248 remote-as 400
testrouter(config-router)#end
testrouter#
Building configuration...
[OK]
Now sleeping for 5 seconds....
Remote IP 192.168.255.248 on local router 192.168.255.249 is NOT IN ESTABLISHED state
>>>
```

As we see in the preceding output, now we are pushing the config with an incorrect remote (`400` in this case). Of course, since the config is not correct, we get a non-established message, which confirms that the config that we pushed was not correct. In a similar way, we can push the bulk of the configs by calling the methods as many times as we want for each of the remote neighbors to be configured. Additionally, sometimes we need to get specific information under certain config sections from a running config.

As an example, the following code will give out a list for each section of the running config:

```
from netmiko import ConnectHandler
import itertools

class linecheck:
    def __init__(self):
        self.state = 0
    def __call__(self, line):
        if line and not line[0].isspace():
            self.state += 1
        return self.state

def getbgpipaddress(routerip):
    uname="cisco"
    passwd="cisco"
    device = ConnectHandler(device_type='cisco_ios', ip=routerip,
username=uname, password=passwd)
    cmds="show running-config"
    outputx=device.send_command(cmds)
    device.disconnect()
    for _, group in itertools.groupby(outputx.splitlines(),
key=linecheck()):
        templist=list(group)
        if (len(templist) == 1):
            if "!" in str(templist):
                continue
        print(templist)


getbgpipaddress("192.168.255.249")
```

The output is as follows:

```
Python 3.6.1 Shell
File Edit Shell Debug Options Window Help
Python 3.6.1 (v3.6.1:69c0db5, Mar 21 2017, 17:54:52) [MSC v.1900 32 bit (Intel)] on win32
Type "copyright", "credits" or "license()" for more information.
>>>
===================== RESTART: C:/a1/bgpipaddressiter.py =====================
['Building configuration...', '']
['Current configuration : 1514 bytes']
['version 12.4']
['service timestamps debug datetime msec']
['service timestamps log datetime msec']
['no service password-encryption']
['hostname testrouter']
['boot-start-marker']
['boot-end-marker']
['no aaa new-model']
['no ip icmp rate-limit unreachable']
['ip cef']
['no ip domain lookup']
['ip domain name mycheck.com']
['multilink bundle-name authenticated']
['username test privilege 15 secret 5 $1$TMpC$DCmseRSyR7AOyzMMDYPKp.']
['username cisco privilege 15 secret 5 $1$jOrL$9176BjgDfV1Y80A1hJILf1']
['username checkme password 0 checkme']
['archive', ' log config', '  hidekeys']
['ip tcp synwait-time 5']
['ip ssh version 2']
['interface FastEthernet0/0', ' description my test', ' ip address 192.168.255.249 255.255.255.0', ' duplex auto', ' speed auto']
['interface Serial0/0', ' no ip address', ' shutdown', ' clock rate 2000000']
['interface FastEthernet0/1', ' description this is checkme', ' no ip address', ' shutdown', ' duplex auto', ' speed auto']
['interface FastEthernet1/0', ' no ip address', ' shutdown', ' duplex auto', ' speed auto']
['router bgp 200', ' no synchronization', ' bgp log-neighbor-changes', ' neighbor 192.168.255.248 remote-as 200', ' no auto-summary']
['ip forward-protocol nd']
['no ip http server']
['no ip http secure-server']
['snmp-server community public RO']
['no cdp log mismatch duplex']
['control-plane']
['line con 0', ' exec-timeout 0 0', ' privilege level 15', ' logging synchronous']
['line aux 0', ' exec-timeout 0 0', ' privilege level 15', ' logging synchronous']
['line vty 0 4', ' exec-timeout 5 0', ' login local', ' transport input ssh']
['end']
>>>
```

As we see in the preceding output, we got all the sections of the running config, except the exclamation mark `!` that we see in a running config (executing the router command `show running-config` on router). The focus of this output is that we have a config that is now parsed for each section in running config grouped in a single list, or in other words, a specific set of configs meant for a specific section (such as an interface or BGP) is grouped in a single list.

Lets enhance this code. As an example, we only want to see what BGP remote IPs are configured in our router:

```
from netmiko import ConnectHandler
import itertools
import re

class linecheck:
    def __init__(self):
        self.state = 0
    def __call__(self, line):
        if line and not line[0].isspace():
```

```
            self.state += 1
        return self.state

def getbgpipaddress(routerip):
    uname="cisco"
    passwd="cisco"
    device = ConnectHandler(device_type='cisco_ios', ip=routerip,
username=uname, password=passwd)
    cmds="show running-config"
    outputx=device.send_command(cmds)
    device.disconnect()
    for _, group in itertools.groupby(outputx.splitlines(),
key=linecheck()):
        templist=list(group)
        if (len(templist) == 1):
            if "!" in str(templist):
                continue
        if "router bgp" in str(templist):
            for line in templist:
                if ("neighbor " in line):
                    remoteip=re.search("\d+.\d+.\d+.\d+",line)
                    print ("Remote ip: "+remoteip.group(0))


getbgpipaddress("192.168.255.249")
```

The output is as follows:

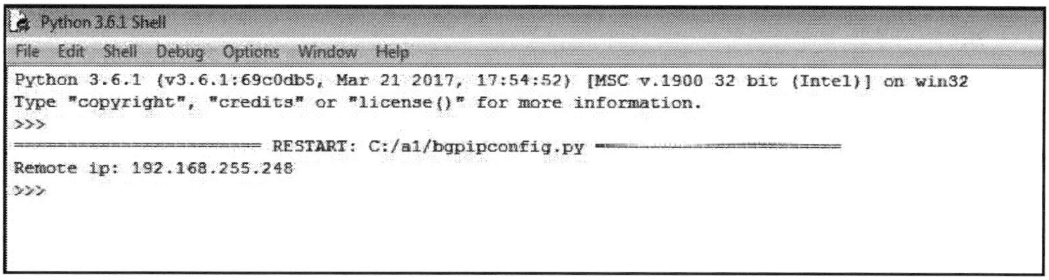

```
Python 3.6.1 Shell
File Edit Shell Debug Options Window Help
Python 3.6.1 (v3.6.1:69c0db5, Mar 21 2017, 17:54:52) [MSC v.1900 32 bit (Intel)] on win32
Type "copyright", "credits" or "license()" for more information.
>>>
======================== RESTART: C:/a1/bgpipconfig.py ========================
Remote ip: 192.168.255.248
>>>
```

In this case, first we parse the running config and focus on the section which has the `router bgp` config. Once we get to that particular list, we parse the list and fetch the remote IP using the regex on the specific command that contains the string `neighbor`. The result values would be the remote IPs under the BGP section.

As we are working with BGP, the AS numbers, being an integral part of BGP, need to be parsed or validated. Using the preceding strategies, we can get the AS numbers for BGP routes/prefixes, but in addition to that, there is a Python library `pyasn` that can easily find out AS number information for a given public IP address.

Again, as mentioned earlier, we need to install the following library before we can call it in the code, by using:

```
pip install cymruwhois
```

The code is as follows:

```
import socket

def getfromhostname(hostname):
    print ("AS info for hostname :"+hostname)
    ip = socket.gethostbyname(hostname)
    from cymruwhois import Client
    c=Client()
    r=c.lookup(ip)
    print (r.asn)
    print (r.owner)

def getfromip(ip):
    print ("AS info for IP : "+ip)
    from cymruwhois import Client
    c=Client()
    r=c.lookup(ip)
    print (r.asn)
    print (r.owner)


getfromhostname("google.com")
getfromip("107.155.8.0")
```

The output is as follows:

```
Python 3.6.1 Shell
File Edit Shell Debug Options Window Help
Python 3.6.1 (v3.6.1:69c0db5, Mar 21 2017, 17:54:52) [MSC v.1900 32 bit (Intel)] on
Type "copyright", "credits" or "license()" for more information.
>>>
======================== RESTART: C:/a1/bgpwhois.py ========================
AS info for hostname :google.com
15169
GOOGLE - Google Inc., US
AS info for IP : 107.155.8.0
3356
LEVEL3 - Level 3 Communications, Inc., US
>>>
```

As we see, the first method `getfromhostname` is used to fetch information for a given hostname. The other method `getfromip` is used to fetch the same information by using an IP address instead of any hostname.

Configuring Cisco switchport for access point

When working with a multi-device environment, along with routers and switches we need to interact with other network gear(s) like wireless devices. This example will show how to configure a switch with specific ports to be connected to **Access Point** (**AP**) as trunk.

In our test case, assuming the VLANs configured on AP are `vlan 100` and `vlan 200` for users, and the native VLAN is `vlan 10`, and the code is as follows:

```
from netmiko import ConnectHandler
import time

def apvlanpush(routerip,switchport):
    uname="cisco"
    passwd="cisco"
    device = ConnectHandler(device_type='cisco_ios', ip=routerip,
username=uname, password=passwd)
    cmds="interface "+switchport
    cmds=cmds+"\nswitchport mode trunk\nswitchport trunk encapsulation
dot1q\n"
    cmds=cmds+ "switchport trunk native vlan 10\nswitchport trunk
allowed vlan add 10,100,200\nno shut\n"
    xcheck=device.send_config_set(cmds)
    print (xcheck)
```

```
    device.disconnect()

def validateswitchport(routerip,switchport):
    uname="cisco"
    passwd="cisco"
    device = ConnectHandler(device_type='cisco_ios', ip=routerip,
username=uname, password=passwd)
    cmds="show interface "+switchport+" switchport "
    outputx=device.send_command(cmds)
    print (outputx)
    device.disconnect()
apvlanpush("192.168.255.245","FastEthernet2/0")
time.sleep(5) # 5 seconds
validateswitchport("192.168.255.245","FastEthernet2/0")
```

The output is as follows:

```
Python 3.6.1 Shell
File Edit Shell Debug Options Window Help
Python 3.6.1 (v3.6.1:69c0db5, Mar 21 2017, 17:54:52) [MSC v.1900 32 bit (Intel)] on win32
Type "copyright", "credits" or "license()" for more information.
>>>
======================== RESTART: C:/a1/apvlanpush.py ========================
config term
Enter configuration commands, one per line.  End with CNTL/Z.
R3(config)#interface FastEthernet2/0
R3(config-if)#switchport mode trunk
R3(config-if)#switchport trunk encapsulation dot1q
R3(config-if)#switchport trunk native vlan 10
R3(config-if)#switchport trunk allowed vlan add 10,100,200
R3(config-if)#no shut
R3(config-if)#end
R3#
Name: Fa2/0
Switchport: Enabled
Administrative Mode: trunk
Operational Mode: down
Administrative Trunking Encapsulation: dot1q
Negotiation of Trunking: Disabled
Access Mode VLAN: 0 ((Inactive))
Trunking Native Mode VLAN: 10 ((Inactive))
Trunking VLANs Enabled: ALL
Trunking VLANs Active: none
Priority for untagged frames: 0
Override vlan tag priority: FALSE
Voice VLAN: none
Appliance trust: none
>>>
```

As we see, the AP needs to be connected to our switchport, which needs to be a trunk, with certain access VLANs to be allowed; hence we create two methods, the first of which passes router/switch name and the interfaces that needs to be configured.

Once the configuration is successfully pushed on the switch, we execute the validateswitchport method to validate if the same port is now in trunk mode. The output of the validateswitchport method spills out the output of the command, on which we can further introduce the regex and splits to get any specific information we want from that output (such as the Administrative Mode or Operational Mode).

As an enhancement, we can also use the outputs from the validation method to call other methods that would perform some additional configs (if required), based on the result that we got earlier. (For example, changing the Trunking Native Mode VLAN to 20).

Let's see the new code with the additional enhancement of changing the native VLAN to 20. The code is as follows:

```
from netmiko import ConnectHandler
import time

def apvlanpush(routerip,switchport):
    uname="cisco"
    passwd="cisco"
    device = ConnectHandler(device_type='cisco_ios', ip=routerip,
username=uname, password=passwd)
    cmds="interface "+switchport
    cmds=cmds+"\nswitchport mode trunk\nswitchport trunk encapsulation
dot1q\n"
    cmds=cmds+ "switchport trunk native vlan 10\nswitchport trunk
allowed vlan add 10,100,200\nno shut\n"
    xcheck=device.send_config_set(cmds)
    print (xcheck)
    device.disconnect()

def validateswitchport(routerip,switchport):
    print ("\nValidating switchport...."+switchport)
    uname="cisco"
    passwd="cisco"
    device = ConnectHandler(device_type='cisco_ios', ip=routerip,
username=uname, password=passwd)
    cmds="show interface "+switchport+" switchport "
    outputx=device.send_command(cmds)
    print (outputx)
    outputx=outputx.split("\n")
    for line in outputx:
        if ("Trunking Native Mode VLAN: 10" in line):
            changenativevlan(routerip,switchport,"20")
    device.disconnect()
```

```
def changenativevlan(routerip,switchport,nativevlan):
    print ("\nNow changing native VLAN on switchport",switchport)
    uname="cisco"
    passwd="cisco"
    device = ConnectHandler(device_type='cisco_ios', ip=routerip,
username=uname, password=passwd)
    cmds="interface "+switchport
    cmds=cmds+"\nswitchport trunk native vlan "+nativevlan+"\n"
    xcheck=device.send_config_set(cmds)
    print (xcheck)
    validateswitchport(routerip,switchport)
    device.disconnect()
apvlanpush("192.168.255.245","FastEthernet2/0")
time.sleep(5) # 5 seconds
validateswitchport("192.168.255.245","FastEthernet2/0")
```

The output is explained in two sections as follows:

- Validating and changing the native VLAN to `20`:

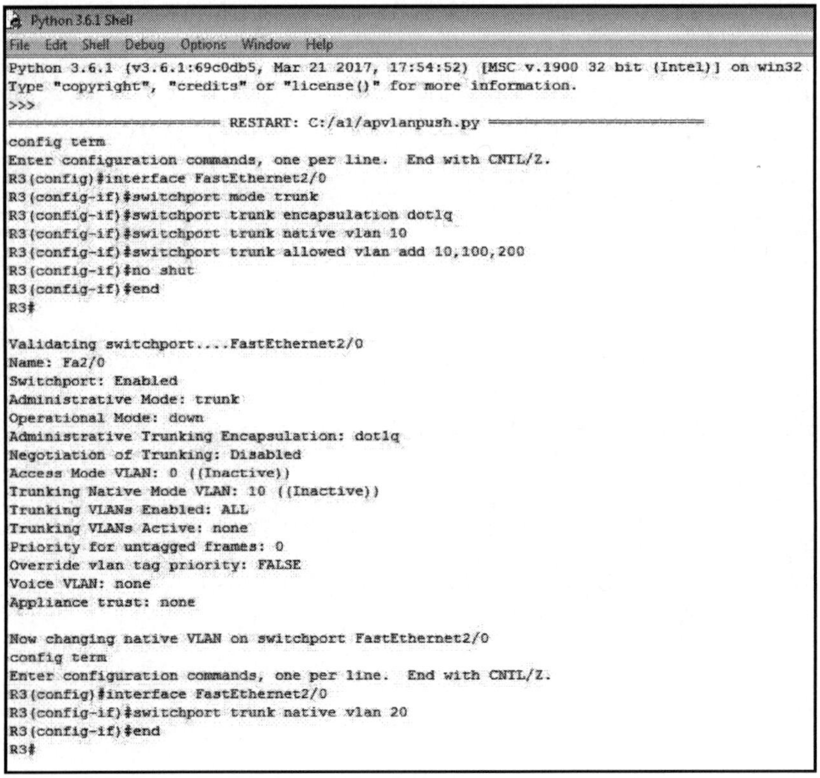

```
Python 3.6.1 Shell
File Edit Shell Debug Options Window Help
Python 3.6.1 (v3.6.1:69c0db5, Mar 21 2017, 17:54:52) [MSC v.1900 32 bit (Intel)] on win32
Type "copyright", "credits" or "license()" for more information.
>>>
======================== RESTART: C:/a1/apvlanpush.py ========================
config term
Enter configuration commands, one per line.  End with CNTL/Z.
R3(config)#interface FastEthernet2/0
R3(config-if)#switchport mode trunk
R3(config-if)#switchport trunk encapsulation dot1q
R3(config-if)#switchport trunk native vlan 10
R3(config-if)#switchport trunk allowed vlan add 10,100,200
R3(config-if)#no shut
R3(config-if)#end
R3#

Validating switchport....FastEthernet2/0
Name: Fa2/0
Switchport: Enabled
Administrative Mode: trunk
Operational Mode: down
Administrative Trunking Encapsulation: dot1q
Negotiation of Trunking: Disabled
Access Mode VLAN: 0 ((Inactive))
Trunking Native Mode VLAN: 10 ((Inactive))
Trunking VLANs Enabled: ALL
Trunking VLANs Active: none
Priority for untagged frames: 0
Override vlan tag priority: FALSE
Voice VLAN: none
Appliance trust: none

Now changing native VLAN on switchport FastEthernet2/0
config term
Enter configuration commands, one per line.  End with CNTL/Z.
R3(config)#interface FastEthernet2/0
R3(config-if)#switchport trunk native vlan 20
R3(config-if)#end
R3#
```

- Revalidating with the new native VLAN number:

```
Validating switchport....FastEthernet2/0
Name: Fa2/0
Switchport: Enabled
Administrative Mode: trunk
Operational Mode: down
Administrative Trunking Encapsulation: dot1q
Negotiation of Trunking: Disabled
Access Mode VLAN: 0 ((Inactive))
Trunking Native Mode VLAN: 20 ((Inactive))
Trunking VLANs Enabled: ALL
Trunking VLANs Active: none
Priority for untagged frames: 0
Override vlan tag priority: FALSE
Voice VLAN: none
Appliance trust: none
>>>
```

As we see in the final validation, now we have a native VLAN 20, instead of the earlier `10`. This is also a good troubleshooting technique as in multiple scenarios there are requirements of a **what if analysis** (to take decisions based upon the evaluation of a certain condition) in which we need to take some actions based on the dynamic results received. Since, here in our code we validated that the native VLAN needs to be `20`, hence we performed another action to correct that earlier config.

Configuring Cisco switchport for IP Phone

Similar to the earlier scenario, where we want a switchport as a trunk port for AP, we can configure the switchport to work with IP Phones. An additional task for configuring a port to be used as IP Phone is that another end machine or data machine can be connected to the IP Phone for data transfer. In other words, a single switchport of a Cisco router can act as both a voice and data port when used with IP Phone.

Let's see an example of configuring a switchport to act as an IP Phone port:

```
from netmiko import ConnectHandler
import time

def ipphoneconfig(routerip,switchport):
    uname="cisco"
    passwd="cisco"
    device = ConnectHandler(device_type='cisco_ios', ip=routerip,
username=uname, password=passwd)
    cmds="interface "+switchport
    cmds=cmds+"\nswitchport mode access\nswitchport access vlan 100\n"
    cmds=cmds+ "switchport voice vlan 200\nspanning-tree portfast\nno
shut\n"
    xcheck=device.send_config_set(cmds)
    print (xcheck)
    device.disconnect()

def validateswitchport(routerip,switchport):
    print ("\nValidating switchport...."+switchport)
    uname="cisco"
    passwd="cisco"
    device = ConnectHandler(device_type='cisco_ios', ip=routerip,
username=uname, password=passwd)
    cmds="show interface "+switchport+" switchport "
    outputx=device.send_command(cmds)
    print (outputx)
    outputx=outputx.split("\n")
    for line in outputx:
        if ("Trunking Native Mode VLAN: 10" in line):
            changenativevlan(routerip,switchport,"20")
    device.disconnect()
ipphoneconfig("192.168.255.245","FastEthernet2/5")
time.sleep(5) # 5 seconds
validateswitchport("192.168.255.245","FastEthernet2/5")
```

The output is as follows:

```
Python 3.6.1 Shell
File Edit Shell Debug Options Window Help
Python 3.6.1 (v3.6.1:69c0db5, Mar 21 2017, 17:54:52) [MSC v.1900 32 bit (Intel)] on win32
Type "copyright", "credits" or "license()" for more information.
>>>
===================== RESTART: C:/a1/ipphonepush.py =====================
config term
Enter configuration commands, one per line.  End with CNTL/Z.
R3(config)#interface FastEthernet2/5
R3(config-if)#switchport mode access
R3(config-if)#switchport access vlan 100
R3(config-if)#switchport voice vlan 200
R3(config-if)#spanning-tree portfast
%Warning: portfast should only be enabled on ports connected to a single host.
 Connecting hubs, concentrators, switches,  bridges, etc.to this interface
 when portfast is enabled, can cause temporary spanning tree loops.
 Use with CAUTION

%Portfast has been configured on FastEthernet2/5 but will only
 have effect when the interface is in a non-trunking mode.
R3(config-if)#no shut
R3(config-if)#end
R3#

Validating switchport....FastEthernet2/5
Name: Fa2/5
Switchport: Enabled
Administrative Mode: static access
Operational Mode: down
Administrative Trunking Encapsulation: dot1q
Negotiation of Trunking: Disabled
Access Mode VLAN: 100 (VLAN0100)
Trunking Native Mode VLAN: 1 (default)
Trunking VLANs Enabled: ALL
Trunking VLANs Active: none
Priority for untagged frames: 0
Override vlan tag priority: FALSE
Voice VLAN: 200
Appliance trust: none
>>>
```

As we see now, the port configured (`FastEthernet 2/5`) has been assigned a `Voice VLAN` of `200` and a data/access VLAN of `100` (from the preceding output, notice the line `Access Mode VLAN: 100 (VLAN0100)`. Any IP Phone connecting to this port will have access to both the VLANs for its voice and data usage. Again, going by previous examples, we can perform additional validations and checks on the ports and trigger some actions in case of any incorrect or missing configs.

Wireless LAN (WLAN)

There are many vendors that have backend APIs that can be controlled or called using Python to perform certain wireless tasks. A commonly used vendor in wireless is `Netgear`. Python has a library `pynetgear` that helps us achieve some of the automation to control our locally connected devices.

Let's see an example of fetching the current network devices connected to the local wireless Netgear router in our network:

```
>>> from pynetgear import Netgear, Device
>>> netgear = Netgear("myrouterpassword",
"192.168.100.1","admin","80")
>>> for i in netgear.get_attached_devices():
  print (i)
```

The `Netgear` method accepts four arguments in the following order (`routerpassword`, `routerip`, `routerusername`, and `routerport`). As we see in the current example, the router is reachable using `http://192.168.100.1` with the username `admin` and password as `myrouterpassword`. Hence, we call the method with these parameters.

The output is shown as follows:

```
>>> netgear.get_attached_devices()
[Device(signal=3, ip='192.168.100.4', name='ANDROID-12345',
mac='xx:xx:xx:xx:xx:xx', type='wireless', link_rate=72),
Device(signal=None, ip='192.168.100.55', name='ANDROID-678910',
mac='yy:yy:yy:yy:yy:yy', type='wireless', link_rate=72),
Device(signal=None, ip='192.168.100.10', name='mylaptop',
mac='zz:zz:zz:zz:zz:zz', type='wireless', link_rate=520)]
```

As we see, the method `get_attached_devices()` returned a list of all the IPs, their MAC addresses (hidden in this example), signal (or wireless band being used), and the link rate for the connection in Mbps.

We can use similar type of methods to manipulate bandwidth, block any user, or perform other tasks that are exposed by the APIs of the specific hardware manufacturer.

Access of IP Address Management (IPAM)

Another requirement in networking is to use the IPAM database for IPAM. It is provided by different vendors, and as an example here, we would refer to SolarWind's IPAM. SolarWinds is again an industry standard tool for monitoring and performing various functionalities on a network, and it has a good set of APIs to interact with using its ORION SDK toolkit.

In Python, we can install the library `orionsdk` to achieve interaction with SolarWinds. Let's see an example in which we fetch the next available IP address from the IPAM module in SolarWinds:

```
from orionsdk import SwisClient

npm_server = 'mysolarwindsserver'
username = "test"
password = "test"

verify = False
if not verify:
    from requests.packages.urllib3.exceptions import
InsecureRequestWarning
    requests.packages.urllib3.disable_warnings(InsecureRequestWarning)

swis = SwisClient(npm_server, username, password)

print("My IPAM test:")
results=swis.query("SELECT TOP 1 Status, DisplayName FROM IPAM.IPNode
WHERE Status=2")
print (results)

### for a formatted printing
for row in results['results']:
 print("Avaliable: {DisplayName}".format(**row))
```

The output is as follows:

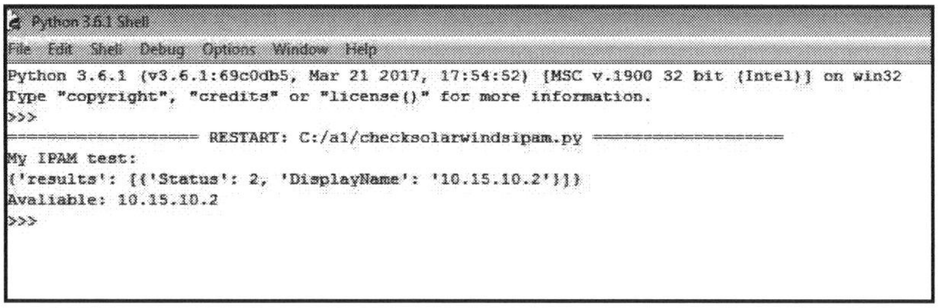

```
Python 3.6.1 Shell
File Edit Shell Debug Options Window Help
Python 3.6.1 (v3.6.1:69c0db5, Mar 21 2017, 17:54:52) [MSC v.1900 32 bit (Intel)] on win32
Type "copyright", "credits" or "license()" for more information.
>>>
================== RESTART: C:/a1/checksolarwindsipam.py ==================
My IPAM test:
{'results': [{'Status': 2, 'DisplayName': '10.15.10.2'}]}
Avaliable: 10.15.10.2
>>>
```

As we see in the preceding code, we use the `orionsdk` library to call the API for SolarWinds from the `mysolarwindsserver` server. The username and password needed for the SolarWinds are passed in script, and we use a simple SQL query (which is understandable by SolarWinds) which is as follows:

```
SELECT TOP 1 Status, DisplayName FROM IPAM.IPNode  WHERE Status=2
```

This query fetches the next available IP address (denoted by `Status=2` in SolarWinds) and prints it. The first print is the raw print and the one in `for` loop; it prints out the value in a better understandable format as shown in the preceding output.

Example and use case

Here, we will see a detailed example that is common to most network engineers, and how to automate it using Python. Also, we will create it as a web based tool, enabling it to run from any environment or machine, using only a browser.

Create a web-based pre and post check tool for validations

In the following example, we will see how we can perform a pre and post check on any network maintenance that we do. This is generally required by every network engineer while performing activities on production devices to ensure that once the maintenance activity is complete, an engineer has not missed out anything that could cause an issue later on. It is also required to validate if our changes and maintenance have been completed successfully, or if we need to perform additional fixes and rollbacks in case of validations that have failed.

The following are the steps to create and execute the tool:

Step 1 – Create the main HTML file

We will design a web-based form to select certain show commands that we will call for performing checks. These commands, when executed, will act as a precheck; once our maintenance activity is complete, we will act again as a postcheck.

Any difference between the same command outputs in precheck or postcheck scenarios will be highlighted and the engineer will be in a good position to make decisions on calling the maintenance a success or failure, based on the outputs.

The HTML code (`prepostcheck.html`) is as follows:

```
<!DOCTYPE html>

<html xmlns="http://www.w3.org/1999/xhtml">
<head>
         <script>
             function checkme() {
        var a=document.forms["search"]["cmds"].value;
        var b=document.forms["search"]["searchbox"].value;
        var c=document.forms["search"]["prepost"].value;
        var d=document.forms["search"]["changeid"].value;
        if (a==null || a=="")
        {
          alert("Please Fill All Fields");
          return false;
        }
        if (b==null || b=="")
        {
          alert("Please Fill All Fields");
          return false;
        }
        if (c==null || c=="")
        {
          alert("Please Fill All Fields");
          return false;
        }
        if (d==null || d=="")
        {
          alert("Please Fill All Fields");
          return false;
        }
document.getElementById("mypoint").style.display = "inline";
             }
```

```
</script>
</head>
<body>
<h2> Pre/Post check selection </h2>
<form name="search" action="checks.py" method="post"
onsubmit="return checkme()">
Host IP: (Multiple IPs seperated by comma)<br><input
type="text" name="searchbox" size='80' required>
<p></p>
Commands (Select):
<br>
<select name="cmds" multiple style="width:200px;height:200px;"
required>
  <option value="show version">show version</option>
  <option value="show ip int brief">show ip int brief</option>
  <option value="show interface description">show interface
description</option>
  <option value="show clock">show clock</option>
  <option value="show log">show log (last 100)</option>
  <option value="show run">show run</option>
  <option value="show ip bgp summary">show ip bgp
summary</option>
  <option value="show ip route">show ip route</option>
  <option value="show ip route summary">show ip route
summary</option>
  <option value="show ip ospf">show ip ospf</option>
  <option value="show interfaces status">show interfaces
status</option>
</select>
<p></p>
Mantainence ID: <input type="text" name="changeid" required>
<p></p>
Pre/Post: <br>
<input type="radio" name="prepost" value="pre" checked>
Precheck<br>
<input type="radio" name="prepost" value="post"> Postcheck<br>
<p></p>
<input type="submit" value="Submit">
<br><br><br>
</form>
<p><label id="mypoint" style="display: none;background-color:
yellow;"><b>Please be Patient.... Gathering
results!!!</b></label></p>
</body>
</html>
```

This will create the main page on which we select our initial options (set of commands and if we need to perform a precheck or a postcheck). The output is as follows:

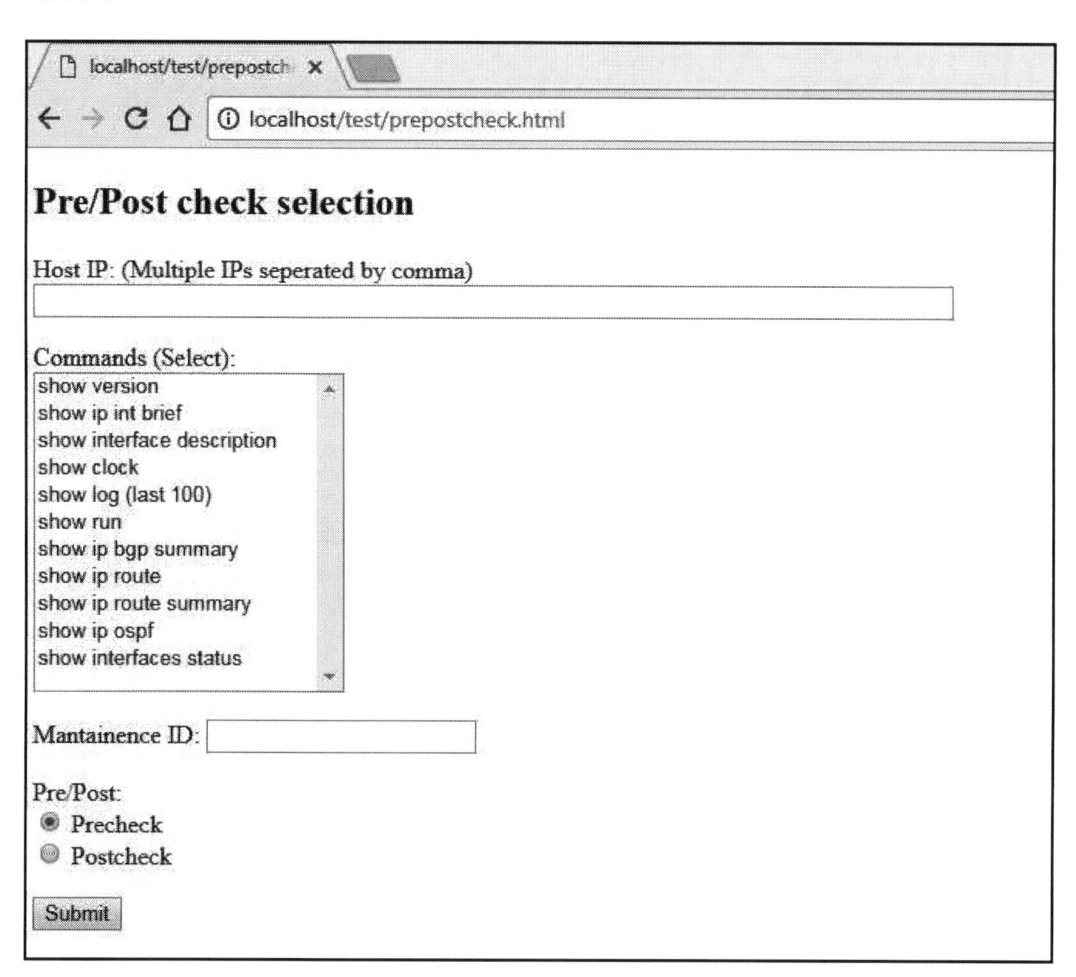

Main page

An additional JavaScript code in HTML ensures that the `Submit` button will not send any data until all the selections are made. There is no point sending data which is not completed; for example, if we do not fill out entire fields the `Submit` option will not proceed, giving out the message that we see in the following screenshot:

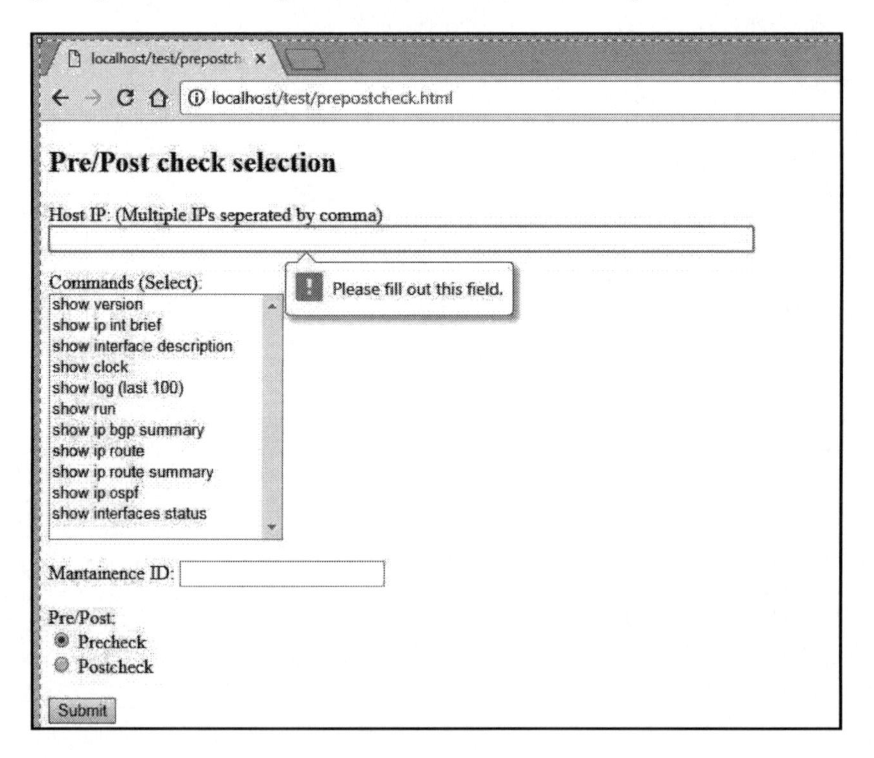

Unless all the fields are not filled, hitting the `Submit` button will spill out this message and the code will not continue. Additionally, as we see in the code, the `Submit` button is tied to the Python script, with `checks.py` as a POST method. In other words, the selections we will make will be sent to `checks.py` as a POST method.

Step 2 – Create the backend Python code

Now, let's see the back end Python code (`checks.py`) that will accept these inputs from HTML form and perform its task. The code is as follows:

```
#!/usr/bin/env python
import cgi
import paramiko
```

```
import time
import re
import sys
import os
import requests
import urllib
import datetime
from datetime import datetime
from threading import Thread
from random import randrange

form = cgi.FieldStorage()
searchterm = form.getvalue('searchbox')
cmds = form.getvalue('cmds')
changeid = form.getvalue('changeid')
prepost=form.getvalue('prepost')
searchterm=searchterm.split(",")
xval=""
xval=datetime.now().strftime("%Y-%m-%d_%H_%M_%S")

returns = {}
def getoutput(devip,cmd):
    try:
        output=""
        mpath="C:/iistest/logs/"
        fname=changeid+"_"+devip+"_"+prepost+"_"+xval+".txt"
        fopen=open(mpath+fname,"w")
        remote_conn_pre = paramiko.SSHClient()
remote_conn_pre.set_missing_host_key_policy(paramiko.AutoAddPolicy())
        remote_conn_pre.connect(devip, username='cisco',
password='cisco', look_for_keys=False, allow_agent=False)
        remote_conn = remote_conn_pre.invoke_shell()
        remote_conn.settimeout(60)
        command=cmd
        remote_conn.send(command+"\n")
        time.sleep(15)
        output=(remote_conn.recv(250000)).decode()
        fopen.write(output)
        remote_conn.close()
        fopen.close()
        returns[devip]=("Success: <a
href='http://localhost/test/logs/"+fname+"' target='_blank'>"+fname
+"</a> Created")
    except:
        returns[devip]="Error. Unable to fetch details"

try:
    xtmp=""
```

```
    cmdval="terminal length 0\n"
    if (str(cmds).count("show") > 1):
        for cmdvalue in cmds:
            if ("show" in cmdvalue):
                if ("show log" in cmdvalue):
                    cmdvalue="terminal shell\nshow log | tail 100"
                cmdval=cmdval+cmdvalue+"\n\n"
    else:
        if ("show" in cmds):
            if ("show log" in cmds):
                cmds="terminal shell\nshow log | tail 100"
            cmdval=cmdval+cmds+"\n\n"
    threads_imagex= []
    for devip in searchterm:
        devip=devip.strip()
        t = Thread(target=getoutput, args=(devip,cmdval,))
        t.start()
        time.sleep(randrange(1,2,1)/20)
        threads_imagex.append(t)
    for t in threads_imagex:
        t.join()
    print("Content-type: text/html")
    print()
    xval=""
    for key in returns:
        print ("<b>"+key+"</b>:"+returns[key]+"<br>")
    print ("<br>Next step: <a
href='http://localhost/test/selectfiles.aspx'> Click here to compare
files </a>")
    print ("<br>Next step: <a
href='http://localhost/test/prepostcheck.html'> Click here to perform
pre/post check </a>")

except:
    print("Content-type: text/html")
    print()
    print("Error fetching details. Need manual validation")
    print ("<br>Next step: <a
href='http://localhost/test/selectfiles.aspx'> Click here to compare
files </a>")
    print ("<br>Next step: <a
href='http://localhost/test/prepostcheck.html'> Click here to perform
pre/post check </a>")
```

This code accepts input from a web page using the CGI parameter. Various values from the web page are parsed into the variables using the following code snippet:

```
form = cgi.FieldStorage()
searchterm = form.getvalue('searchbox')
cmds = form.getvalue('cmds')
changeid = form.getvalue('changeid')
prepost=form.getvalue('prepost')
```

Once we have these values, the additional logic is to log in into the given device(s) using the `paramiko` library, fetch the output of the show commands, and save it in a file under the `logs` folder with the output. An important aspect to note here is the way we are constructing the filename:

```
#xval=datetime.now().strftime("%Y-%m-%d_%H_%M_%S")
#and
#fname=changeid+"_"+devip+"_"+prepost+"_"+xval+".txt"
```

The `fname` is the filename into which we would write the output, but the filename is built dynamically with the inputs provided by the maintenance ID, device IP, pre/post status, and the time the file was created. This is to ensure that we know the device for which we are performing a pre or a post check, and at what time the file was created, to ensure we have a correct pre and post check combination.

The function `getoutput()` is invoked from a thread (in a multi-threaded function call) to fetch the output and store it in the newly created file. A multi-threading process is called, because if we want to perform pre or post checks in multiple devices, we can provide a comma separated IP address list in web, and Python script will in parallel invoke the show commands on all devices and create multiple pre or post check files, based on hostnames.

Let's create a `precheck` file for some commands in our example, where we fill in some values and click on the `Submit` button:

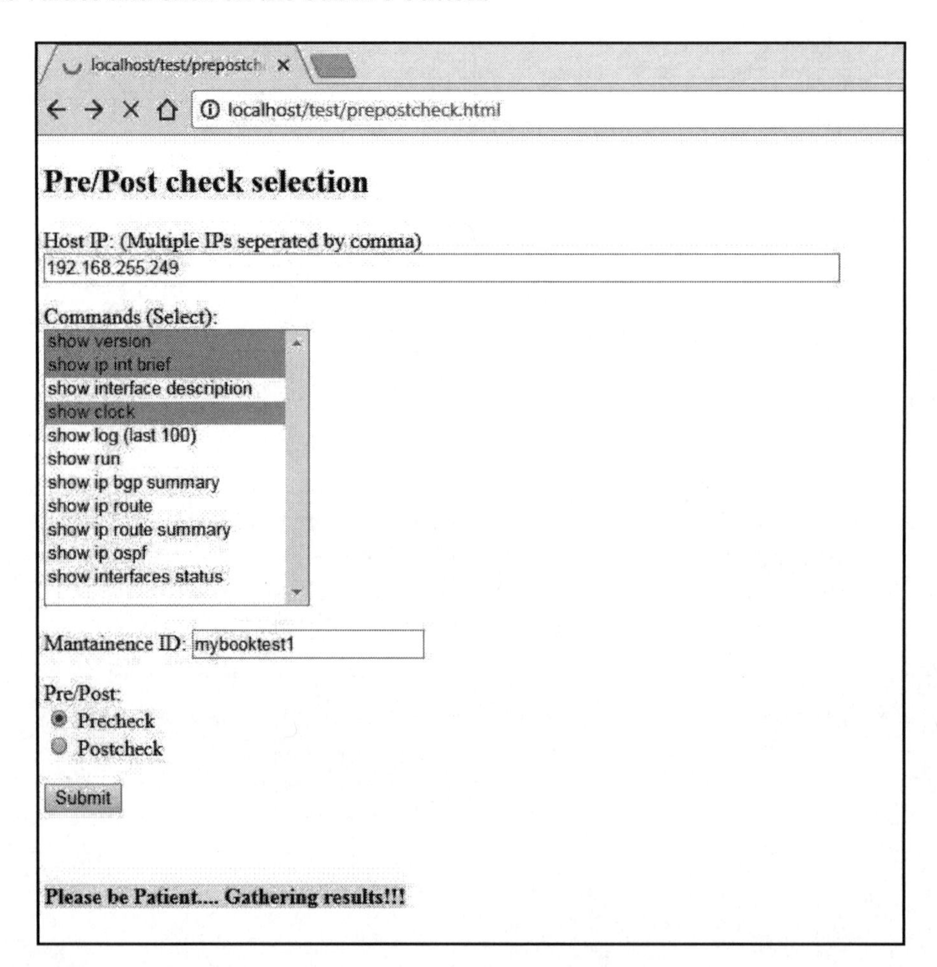

While the gathering of data is in progress, the yellow message will be displayed to confirm that the back end work is going on.

Once the task is completed, this is what we see (as returned from the Python code):

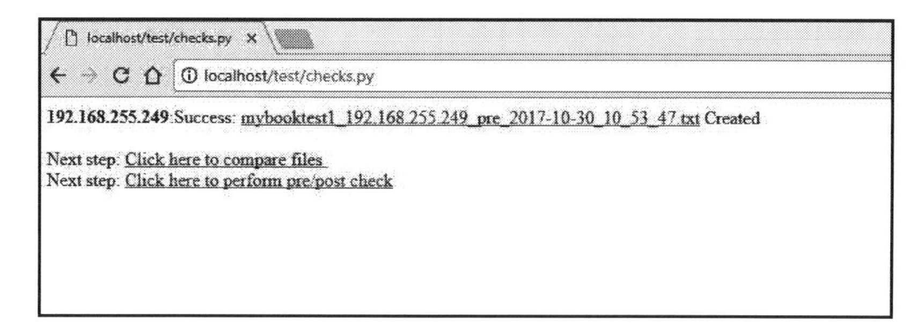

As we see, the code returns a success, which means that it was able to fetch the output of the commands that we want to validate. The filename is dynamically created, based on our selection on the main page.

A click on the `.txt` filename that is generated as a clickable URL (which can be used to reconfirm if we got the correct output of commands we selected earlier), shows the following output:

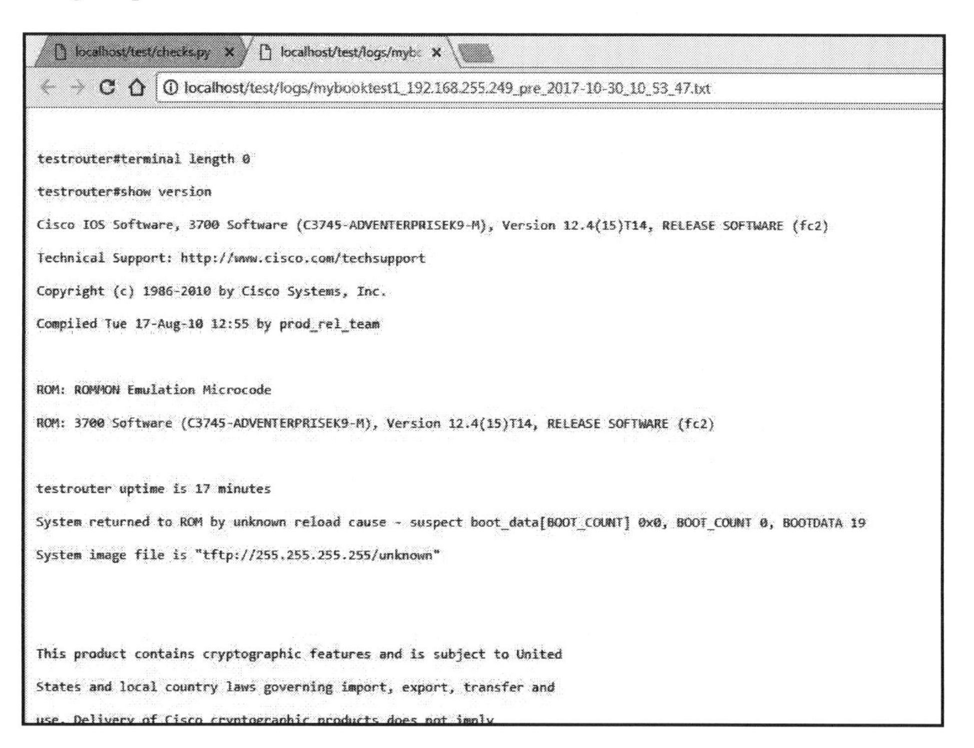

Now, let's perform the same steps and create a `postcheck` file.

We go back to the main page, and keeping the other values the same, we just select the radio button to `Postcheck` instead of `Precheck`. Do ensure that we select the same set of commands, since a pre and post check only make sense if we have the same data to work with:

In a similar way, once the backend execution completes, we have a `postcheck` file created as follows:

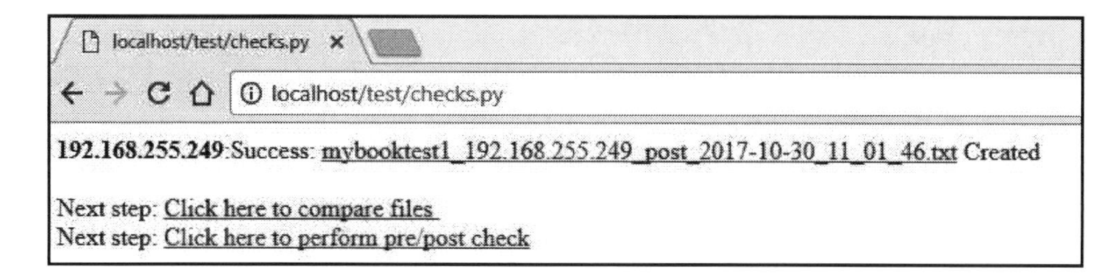

Notice the filename, the timestamp, and the `post` word changes based on our selection.

Step 3 – Create web server based files for the tool

Now with the both pre and post check files created, let's create a web framework to perform web-based pre/post check for the files. We need to create a web page in which our current log files are visible as pre and post files, and we can select the `precheck` file and its relevant `postcheck` file for comparison. As we know that we cannot use HTML or browser languages to fetch information about any files from the server, we need to use some backed web language to perform this function for us. We take advantage of ASP and VB.NET to create the web page to display the already created log files for selection and comparison.

The backend code for `selectfiles.aspx` is as follows (this is to display the files from the log directory on a browser):

```
<%@ Page Language="VB" AutoEventWireup="false"
CodeFile="selectfiles.aspx.vb" Inherits="selectfiles" %>

<!DOCTYPE html>

<html xmlns="http://www.w3.org/1999/xhtml">
<head runat="server">
    <title></title>
</head>
<body>
    <form id="form1" method="post" action="comparefiles.aspx" >
    <div>
    <%response.write(xmystring.tostring())%>
    </div>
         <input type="submit" value="Submit">
    </form>
  <br><br><br>
</body>
</html>
```

The VB.NET backend code, to fill in the values on the preceding `.aspx` page `selectfiles.aspx.vb`, is as follows:

```
Imports System.IO
Partial Class selectfiles
    Inherits System.Web.UI.Page
    Public xmystring As New StringBuilder()
  Public tableval As New Hashtable
    Protected Sub Page_Load(sender As Object, e As EventArgs) Handles
Me.Load
        Dim precheck As New List(Of String)
        Dim postcheck As New List(Of String)
        Dim prename = New SortedList
        Dim postname = New SortedList
        Dim infoReader As System.IO.FileInfo
    Dim rval as Integer
    rval=0
        xmystring.Clear()
        Dim xval As String
    Dim di As New DirectoryInfo("C:\iistest\logs\")
    Dim lFiles As FileInfo() = di.GetFiles("*.txt")
    Dim fi As System.IO.FileSystemInfo
    Dim files() As String = IO.Directory.GetFiles("C:\iistest\logs\",
"*.txt", SearchOption.TopDirectoryOnly)
    xmystring.Append("<head><style
type='text/css'>a:hover{background:blue;color:yellow;}</style></head>"
)
        xmystring.Append("<fieldset style='float: left;width:
49%;display: inline-block;box-sizing: border-box;'>")
        xmystring.Append("<legend>Pre check files (Sorted by Last
Modified Date)</legend>")

         For Each fi In lFiles
      rval=rval+1
tableval.add(fi.LastWriteTime.ToString()+rval.tostring(),fi.Name)
            'infoReader = My.Computer.FileSystem.GetFileInfo(file)
            If (fi.Name.Contains("pre")) Then
precheck.Add(fi.LastWriteTime.ToString()+rval.tostring())
            Else
postcheck.Add(fi.LastWriteTime.ToString()+rval.tostring())
            End If
        Next
        precheck.Sort()
        postcheck.Sort()

        xval = ""
        Dim prekey As ICollection = prename.Keys
        Dim postkey As ICollection = postname.Keys
```

```
        Dim dev As String
    Dim fnameval as String
        For Each dev In precheck
            infoReader =
My.Computer.FileSystem.GetFileInfo(tableval(dev))
fnameval="http://localhost/test/logs/"+Path.GetFileName(tableval(dev))
            xval = "<input type = 'radio' name='prechecklist'
value='C:\iistest\logs\" + tableval(dev) + "' required><a href='" &
fnameval & "' target='blank'>" & tableval(dev) & "</a> ( <b>" &
dev.Substring(0,dev.LastIndexOf("M")).Trim() + "M</b>)<br>"
      xmystring.Append(xval)
        Next
    xmystring.Append("</fieldset>")
           xmystring.Append("<fieldset style='float: right;width:
49%;display: inline-block;box-sizing: border-box;'>")
        xmystring.Append("<legend>Post check files (Sorted by Last
Modified Date)</legend>")
              For Each dev In postcheck
      fnameval="http://localhost/test/logs/"+tableval(dev)
            xval = "<input type = 'radio' name='postchecklist'
value='C:\iistest\logs\" + tableval(dev) + "' required><a href='" &
fnameval & "' target='blank'>" & tableval(dev) & "</a> ( <b>" &
dev.Substring(0,dev.LastIndexOf("M")).Trim() + "M</b>)<br>"
            xmystring.Append(xval)
        Next
        xmystring.Append("</fieldset>")

    End Sub
End Class
```

This code is used to fetch the files from the log directory, and based on their filenames, they are divided into either `precheck` files or `postcheck` files. Also, the files are ordered in chronological order for easy selection during the comparison process.

Let's see the output of this page now:

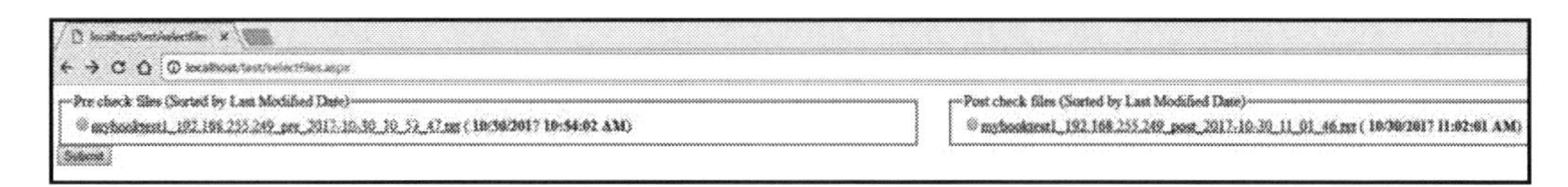

Step 4 – Create server based files for pre and post files comparison

The final step is to create a web page that retrieves the text from these files and also provides frontend (or a web-based tool) for easy comparison. For our purpose, we use a JScript library called `diffview`. To call this dependency, we need to download `diffview.js`, `difflib.js`, and `diffview.css` which available here: `https://github.com/cemerick/jsdifflib`, and copy the files into our web server folder. Once done, in the similar way as accessing the files, we would again create a `.aspx` page to get the content of the selected files and display it for comparison.

The following is the code of the main page `comparefiles.aspx`:

```
<%@ Page Language="VB" AutoEventWireup="false"
CodeFile="comparefiles.aspx.vb" Inherits="comparefiles" %>

<!DOCTYPE html>

<html xmlns="http://www.w3.org/1999/xhtml">
<head>
  <meta charset="utf-8"/>
  <meta http-equiv="X-UA-Compatible" content="IE=Edge,chrome=1"/>
  <link rel="stylesheet" type="text/css" href="diffview.css"/>
  <script type="text/javascript" src="diffview.js"></script>
  <script type="text/javascript" src="difflib.js"></script>
<style type="text/css">
body {
  font-size: 12px;
  font-family: Sans-Serif;
}
h2 {
  margin: 0.5em 0 0.1em;
  text-align: center;
}
.top {
  text-align: center;
}
.textInput {
  display: block;
  width: 49%;
  float: left;
}
textarea {
  width:100%;
  height:300px;
}
```

```
label:hover {
  text-decoration: underline;
  cursor: pointer;
}
.spacer {
  margin-left: 10px;
}
.viewType {
  font-size: 16px;
  clear: both;
  text-align: center;
  padding: 1em;
}
#diffoutput {
  width: 100%;
}
</style>

<script type="text/javascript">

function diffUsingJS(viewType) {
  "use strict";
  var byId = function (id) { return document.getElementById(id); },
    base = difflib.stringAsLines(byId("baseText").value),
    newtxt = difflib.stringAsLines(byId("newText").value),
    sm = new difflib.SequenceMatcher(base, newtxt),
    opcodes = sm.get_opcodes(),
    diffoutputdiv = byId("diffoutput"),
    contextSize = byId("contextSize").value;

  diffoutputdiv.innerHTML = "";
  contextSize = contextSize || null;

  diffoutputdiv.appendChild(diffview.buildView({
    baseTextLines: base,
    newTextLines: newtxt,
    opcodes: opcodes,
    baseTextName: "Base Text",
    newTextName: "New Text",
    contextSize: contextSize,
    viewType: viewType
  }));
}

</script>
</head>
<body>
  <div class="top">
```

```
    <strong>Context size (optional):</strong> <input type="text"
id="contextSize" value="" />
  </div>
  <div class="textInput">
    <h2>Pre check</h2>
    <textarea id="baseText" runat="server" readonly></textarea>
  </div>
  <div class="textInput spacer">
    <h2>Post check</h2>
    <textarea id="newText" runat="server" readonly></textarea>
  </div>
    <% Response.Write(xmystring.ToString()) %>
  <div class="viewType">
    <input type="radio" name="_viewtype" id="sidebyside"
onclick="diffUsingJS(0);" /> <label for="sidebyside">Side by Side
Diff</label>
      &amp;amp;amp;nbsp;
    <input type="radio" name="_viewtype" id="inline"
onclick="diffUsingJS(1);" /> <label for="inline">Inline Diff</label>
  </div>
  <div id="diffoutput"> </div>

</body>
</html>
```

The backend code for the main page, to get the contents of the file (`comparefiles.aspx.vb`), is as follows:

```
Imports System.IO

Partial Class comparefiles
    Inherits System.Web.UI.Page
    Public xmystring As New StringBuilder()

    Protected Sub Page_Load(sender As Object, e As EventArgs) Handles
Me.Load
        Dim fp As StreamReader
        Dim precheck As New List(Of String)
        Dim postcheck As New List(Of String)
        xmystring.Clear()
        Dim prefile As String
        Dim postfile As String
        prefile = Request.Form("prechecklist")
        postfile = Request.Form("postchecklist")
        fp = File.OpenText(prefile)
        baseText.InnerText = fp.ReadToEnd()
        fp = File.OpenText(postfile)
        newText.InnerText = fp.ReadToEnd()
```

```
        fp.Close()

    End Sub

End Class
```

With this ready, let's compare the files and see the results. We select the pre and post check files and click on `Submit`:

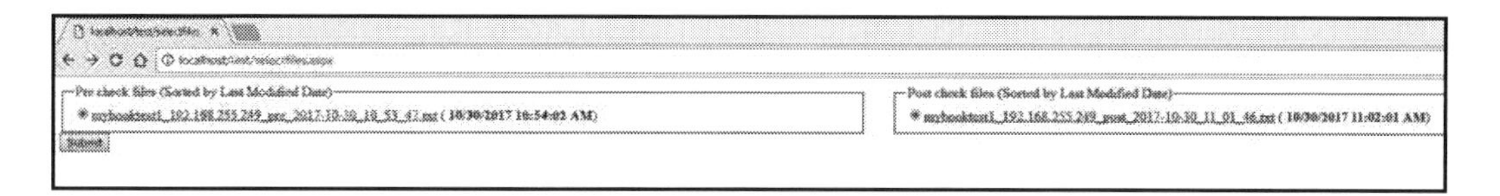

The next page takes us to the content and comparison:

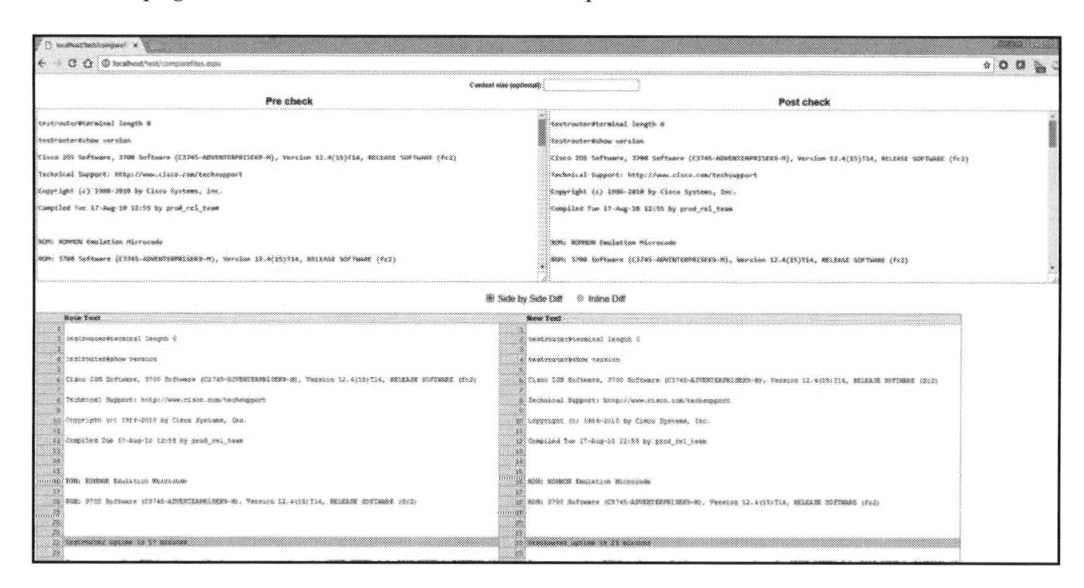

As we see in the preceding screenshot, on the left, we have the `precheck` file, and on the right, we have the `postcheck` file. Both can be read on the page itself through slides on both windows. The bottom window appears when we select either `Side by Side Diff` or `Inline Diff`.

On a `Side by Side Diff`, anything that is different will be highlighted. In our case it was uptime that was different. For everything else in common, no color highlighting will be in place and an engineer can safely assume the same states for non highlighted colors.

Let's see the same example with a `Inline Diff` comparison selection:

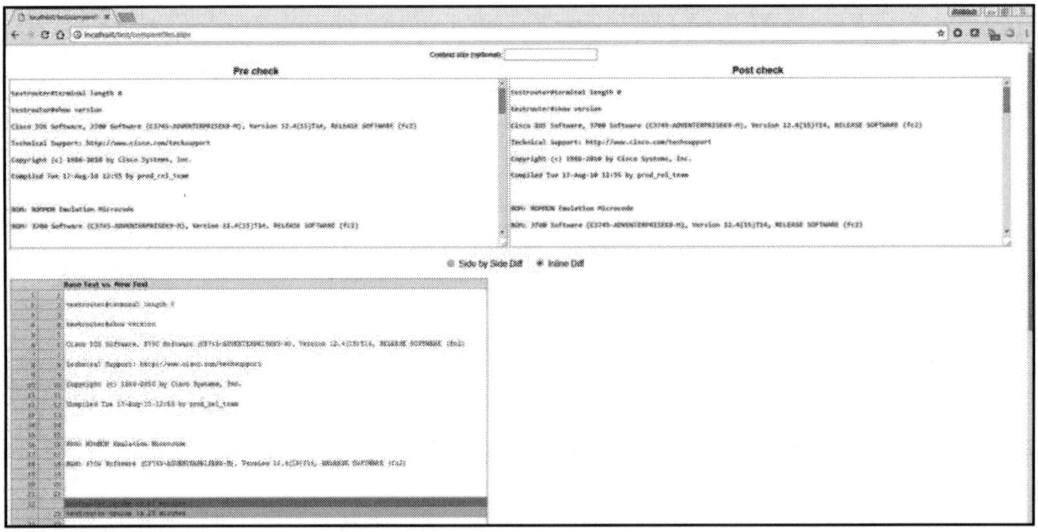

It is the same result; different lines are highlighted in different colors to confirm the pre and post check differences. With this tool now, an engineer can quickly parse through the entire log files, and based on the highlighted differences (a mismatch between `precheck` file content and `postcheck` file content), can make the decision to call the task a success or a failure.

Summary

In this chapter, we saw various concepts related to the usage of automation in daily network scenarios. We got familiar with examples of performing various tasks related to additional devices such as wireless AP and IP Phones. Additionally, we also got introduced to IPAM of SolarWinds and how to work on the API using Python.

We also saw a real-world example of creating a pre and post validation tool to help engineers make quick maintenance validation decisions, and also ported to the web so that the tool can be used from anywhere, instead of running from individual machines with Python installed as a prerequisite.

Finally, in our concluding chapter, we will look at some additional aspects of SDN to understand better usage and how and where to automate, with respect to SDN scenarios.

4
SDN Concepts in Network Automation

As we have seen on our journey so far, there are numerous scenarios where we can automate a network, from daily or routine tasks, to managing infrastructure from a single controller-based architecture. Building upon those concepts, we will now gain some additional insights for working in **software-defined networks** (**SDNs**) and look at some examples of working with cloud platforms.

Some of the key components we are going to cover are:

- Cloud platform automation
- Network automation tools
- Controller-based network fabric
- Programmable network devices

Managing cloud platforms

We can use network automation techniques through Python to work on various cloud providers. From working on cloud instances, to spinning up new VMs, controlling full access like ACLs, and creating specific network layer tasks like VPNs, and network configurations of each instance, we can automate just about anything using available connectors or APIs in Python. Let's see some basic configuration and connections on the most popular cloud platform, **Amazon Web Services** (**AWS**) using Python.

AWS provides an extensive API through its SDK called Boto 3. Boto 3 provides two types of APIs to be used, a low-level API set that is used to interact with direct AWS services, and a high-layer Python friendly API set for quick interactions with AWS. Along with Boto 3, we also would need to have the AWS CLI that is used as a **command-line interface** (**CLI**) to interact with AWS from the local machine. Think of this as a CLI based tool that is equally like DOS is to Windows from a CLI perspective.

The installation of both the AWS CLI and Boto 3 is done using `pip`:

- To install from AWS CLI, use the following command:

```
pip install awscli
```

- To install from Boto 3, use the following command:

```
pip install boto3
```

Once installed, the packages are ready to use. However, we need to configure an access key in the AWS Web Management Console which will have a certain level of restrictions (that we will define while creating the access key).

Let's quickly set up a new access key to manage the AWS in Python from our local machine:

1. Log in to the AWS web console and select **IAM** as the option:

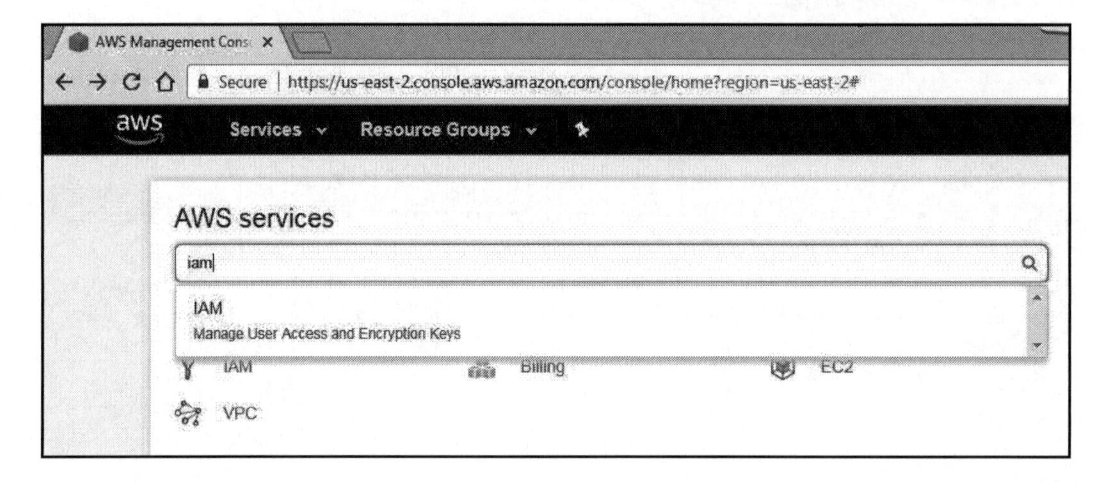

2. Click on **Add user** to create a username and password pair shown as follows:

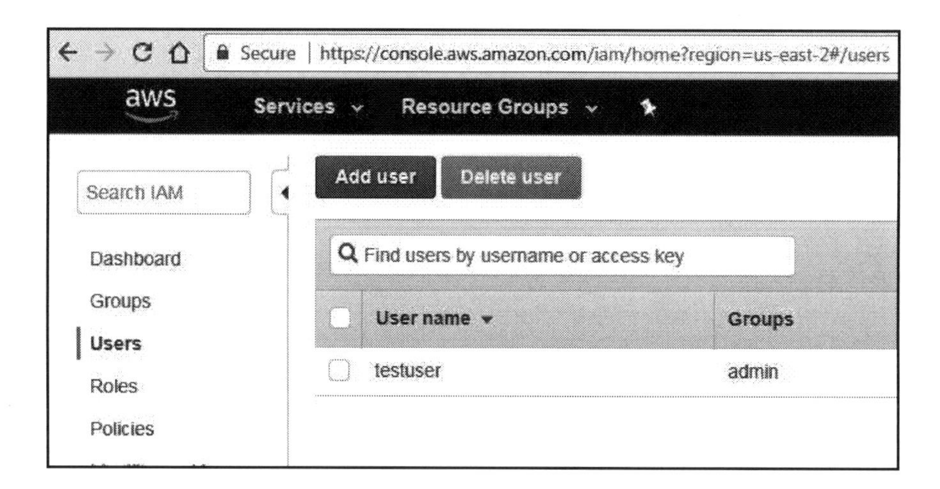

3. Select username and ensure to check **Programmatic access** to get the access ID and secret key to be used in our Python calls:

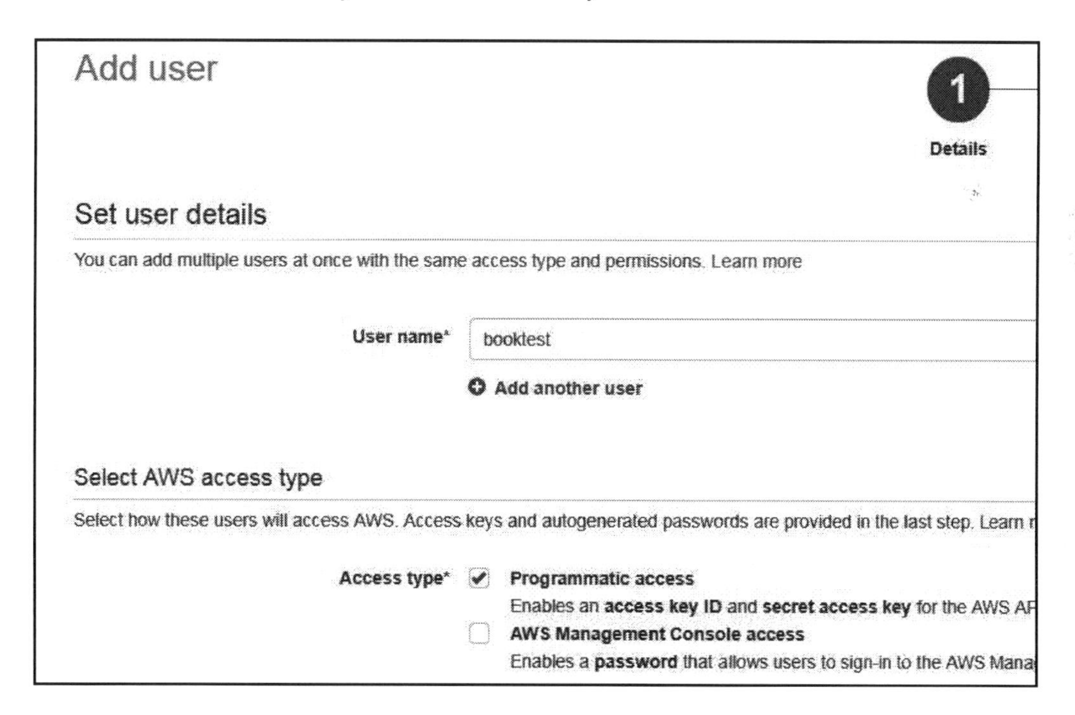

4. We also need the user to be part of a certain group (for security restrictions). In our case we make it part of the admin group which has full rights on the AWS instance:

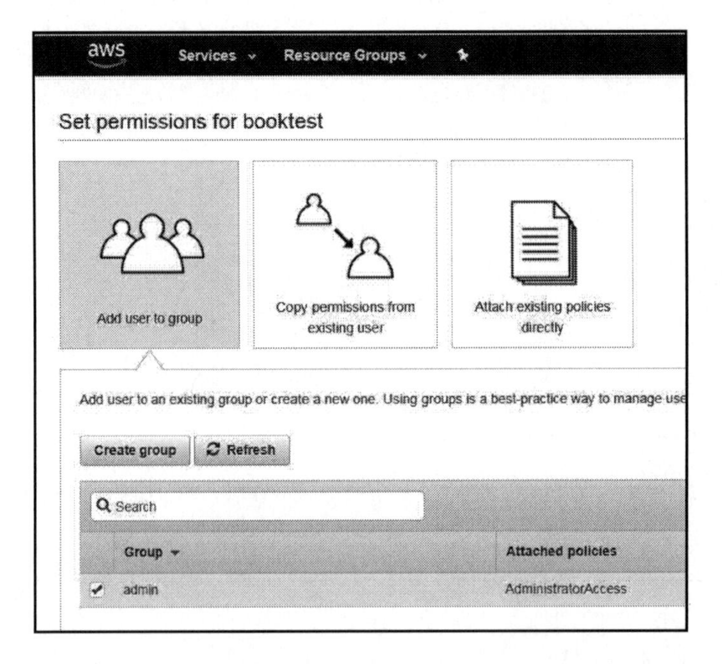

5. If we made our selections correctly, a user is created with the username we selected (`booktest`) with an access key and a secret access key:

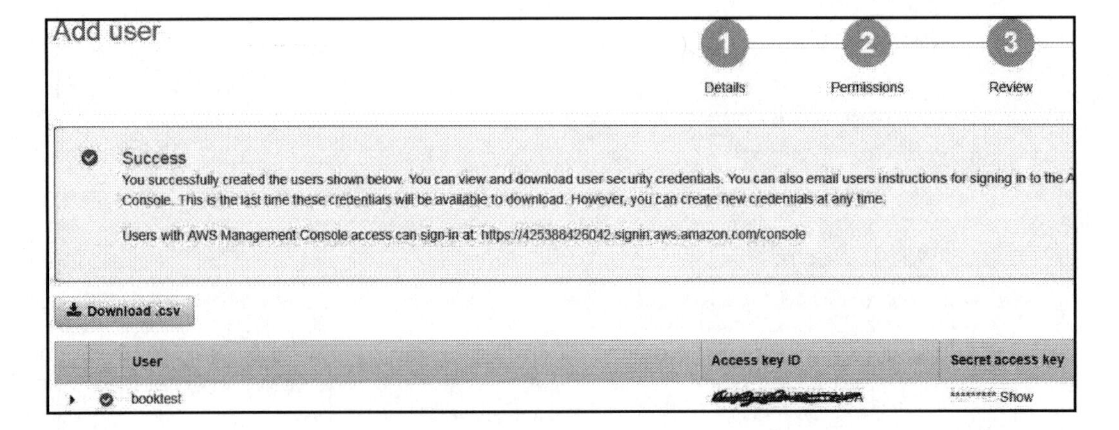

6. Once we have this key, we go back to our Python installation and on the Command Prompt, call the AWS CLI command `aws configure`:

```
C:\Windows\system32\cmd.exe
Microsoft Windows [Version 6.1.7601]
Copyright (c) 2009 Microsoft Corporation.  All rights reserved.

C:\Users\abhishek.ratan>aws configure
AWS Access Key ID [****************GC4A]:
AWS Secret Access Key [****************UmSm]:
Default region name [us-east-2]:
Default output format [json]:

C:\Users\abhishek.ratan>
```

7. As per the questions asked, we fetch the values from the AWS web console and paste them in the CLI. The final question of `Default output format` can be `text` or `json`. However, for our purpose of automation and working with Python, we would select `json` instead of `text`.

Once we are done with this backend configuration, we are ready to test our scripts by calling the Boto 3 API in Python.

Let's see an example of getting all running instances on the current AWS account for which we have the key:

```
import boto3
ec2 = boto3.resource('ec2')
for instance in ec2.instances.all():
    print (instance)
    print (instance.id, instance.state)
```

Since we have already configured the backend credentials and key with the `aws configure` CLI command, we do not need to specify any credentials in our scripts.

The output of the preceding code is as follows:

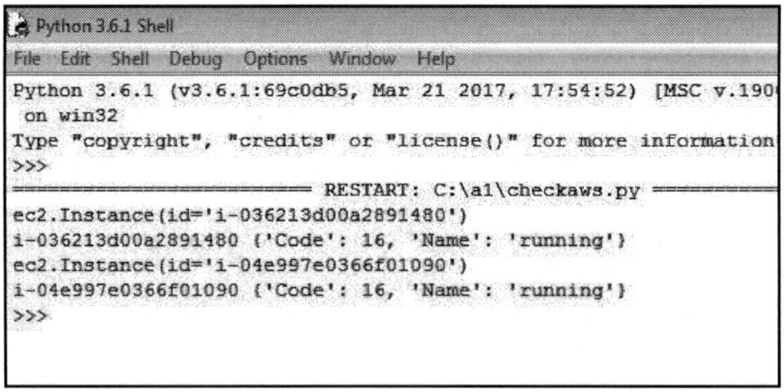

```
Python 3.6.1 Shell
File  Edit  Shell  Debug  Options  Window  Help
Python 3.6.1 (v3.6.1:69c0db5, Mar 21 2017, 17:54:52) [MSC v.190
 on win32
Type "copyright", "credits" or "license()" for more information
>>>
======================= RESTART: C:\a1\checkaws.py =========
ec2.Instance(id='i-036213d00a2891480')
i-036213d00a2891480 {'Code': 16, 'Name': 'running'}
ec2.Instance(id='i-04e997e0366f01090')
i-04e997e0366f01090 {'Code': 16, 'Name': 'running'}
>>>
```

As we see in the preceding output, we get back two instances which are EC2 instances with their instance IDs. Additionally, we also get some other parameters for the currently configured instances. In some cases, if we do not want to use the current preconfigured keys, we can call the Python program by passing the values directly into Boto 3 functions as follows:

```
import boto3

aws_access_key_id = 'accesskey'
aws_secret_access_key = 'secretaccesskey'
region_name = 'us-east-2'

ec2 =
boto3.client('ec2',aws_access_key_id=aws_access_key_id,aws_secret_acce
ss_key=aws_secret_access_key,region_name=region_name)
```

Let's see another example of fetching the private IP address and instance ID for each of the instances:

```
import boto3

ec2 = boto3.client('ec2')
response = ec2.describe_instances()
for item in response['Reservations']:
    for eachinstance in item['Instances']:
        print
(eachinstance['InstanceId'],eachinstance['PrivateIpAddress'])
```

The preceding code gives the following output:

```
Python 3.6.1 (v3.6.1:69c0db5, Mar 21 2017, 17:54:52) [MSC v.1900 32 bi
 on win32
Type "copyright", "credits" or "license()" for more information.
>>>
========================= RESTART: C:\a1\checkaws.py ==================
i-036213d00a2891480 172.31.47.84
i-04e997e0366f01090 172.31.33.197
>>>
```

Using the Boto 3 API, we can also spin up new instances in our subscription. Let's see a final example of spinning up a new **Virtual Machine(VM)** with EC2 using Boto 3.

Before we call the Python to spin a new VM, we need to select which **Amazon Machine Image** (**AMI**) image to use for the instance. To find out the AMI image value, we need to open AMI in the AWS web console shown as follows:

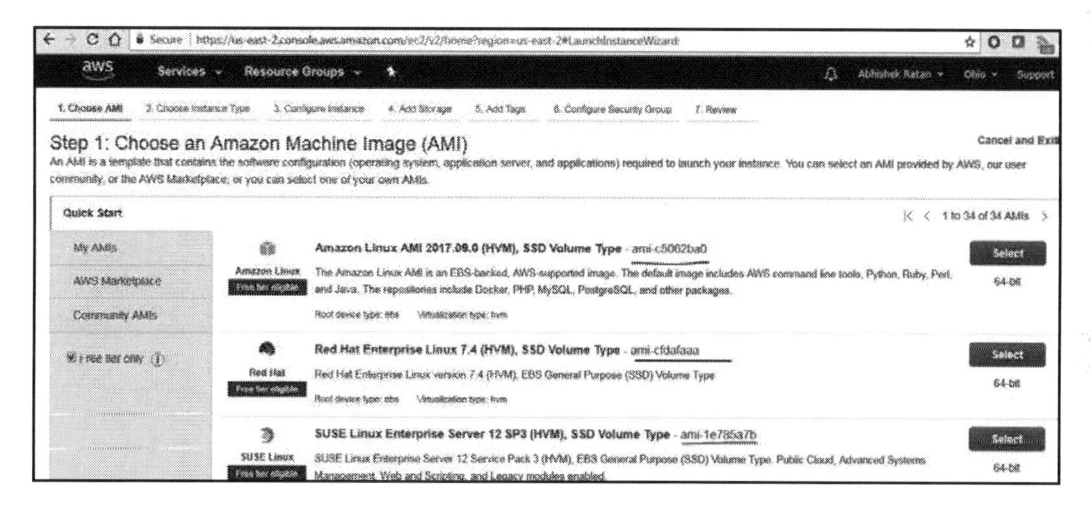

Once we have finalized the AMI, we call the easy part, spinning the new VM:

```
import boto3
ec2 = boto3.resource('ec2')
ec2.create_instances(ImageId='amid-imageid', MinCount=1, MaxCount=5)
```

It will take some time for the script to execute, and the result value would be the instance with all its configured parameters based upon the AMI image ID selected. Similarly, we can spin up various type of instances or even new security filters using Boto 3 and ensure we have cloud controlling automation in place.

Programmable network devices

Looking back at historic implementations, we had a fixed set of hardware or networks geared for catering services to the end users. End users also had a limited set of connection options to access a limited set of networks or connected resources. As the number of users increased, a simple solution was to add additional hardware or network gear. However, with the surge of different end user devices, such as mobile phones, and high data demand and up time requirements for end users, managing the increasing amount of hardware and additional connections becomes a complex task.

A simple device failure or cable failure might impact the entire set of connected hardware or network gears, which would create a widespread downtime for end users, resulting in a loss of man hours both in terms of productivity and trust. Think of a large **internet service provider** (**ISP**) with recurring outages, with each outage affecting a large set of both enterprise and home users. If a new ISP were to enter the market with reliability as its unique selling point, people would not think twice before jumping to the new provider. Effectively, this could result in a loss of business and ultimately, a closure situation for the earlier provider because of the decreasing reliability and trust among its current set of users.

To handle this type of situation, one solution that has emerged is the usability of the same set of devices or network hardware to perform different functions using the same hardware platform. This has been made possible through a combination of SDN and **programmable networks** (**PNs**).

SDN takes care of control plane configurations for data to automatically reroute to a path that is the best available for a specific source to the destination. For example, let's say we need to reach destination D from source A. The best path to reach D is A -> C -> D.

Now, in the case of legacy traffic flow, unless C is down or practically shut, the traffic will not flow from A -> B -> D (unless special complex configurations are done on each network gear/device). In an SDN environment, using OpenFlow as the underlying protocol, the controller will detect any issues in the path of A -> C -> D, and based upon certain issues (like packet drop or congestion in the path), would make an intelligent decision to ensure there is a new path for the data to flow from A -> B -> D.

As we see in this case, even with no physical issues on C, SDN already takes care of identifying the best path for the data to flow on, which effectively results in the best achievable performance for end users with reliability.

PN is an addition which is a collection of hardware devices in the network layer that can be programmed to behave in a different way based upon the requirements. Think of a switch acting as a router by changing its functionality through a written piece of code. Let's say we get an influx of new end users and we need to have a high switching capacity in the network layer. Some of the devices can now act as a switch rather than a router. This ensures a two-fold benefit:

- Using the same set of hardware based upon the demand and requirements, the hardware can be reused to handle new scenarios without introducing more complexity into the network by adding an additional set of hardware.
- Better control over the flow of traffic with the additional capability of securing traffic through the same set of devices. This is introduced by adding ACLs for traffic to flow from a certain set of devices, and even ensuring that a device handles only a particular type of traffic and sends the remaining traffic to other devices that are specifically programmed to handle that particular traffic. Think of it, as video with voice traffic going from a different set of devices to ensure optimal performance and load on specific devices using the same set of hardware that we currently have.

A major component of PNs (the collective name for programmable network devices), is the use of APIs that are provided by various network vendors like Cisco, Arista, and Juniper. By calling these APIs we can ensure that each of the devices from specific vendors can easily talk to each other (exchange information is a unified format), and can change the behavior of a specific hardware based upon the API calls. One example that is common in today's market is Cisco Nexus 9000 series devices. These are modular or fixed switches (with different variations), and by using OpenFlow gives us the ability to programmatically alter their behavior based upon dynamic requirements.

Taking this switch as an example, direct access to **application-specific integrated circuit** (**ASIC**) chip-level programming is also exposed, which ensures that the ASICs can also be programmed based upon the requirement along with the software-level variations. With SDN in place, controllers can take advantage of OpenFlow and the APIs exposed on these switches to control the role of these switches.

Cisco also provides a **Power on Auto Provisioning** (**PoAP**) feature to multiple devices (primarily on the Nexus platform) that helps achieve auto provisioning and commissioning as soon as a new device boots. A basic overview of this process is, if a Nexus device with the PoAP feature enabled boots and is unable to find any startup config, it locates a **Dynamic Host Configuration Protocol** (**DHCP**) server in the network and bootstraps using the IP address and DNS information obtained from that DHCP server. It also fetches a customized script that is executed on the device that has instructions to download and install the relevant software image files and specific configurations for that device.

A big advantage of this type of feature is that we can spin up new devices within one to two minutes by just powering it up and connecting it to a network which has DHCP functionality to fetch relevant information to new devices in the network. Think of the legacy way of bringing a router live with multiple hours of human intervention versus the current way of booting up a router, and the router taking care of itself without any human intervention.

Similarly, using the APIs (**NX-API** is the underlying terminology used for **Nexus API**), better visibility in terms of packet flow and monitoring is also being exposed from Cisco, and, using simple scripts written in any language (like Python), the path and flow of traffic can be modified based upon the results returned back through the call of those APIs.

Taking another example, we have network device vendor Arista. Arista has introduced Arista **Extensible Operating System** (**EOS**), which is a highly modular and Linux-based network OS. Using Arista EOS, managing multiple devices becomes easy as it has the ability to provide extensive APIs (Linux kernel-based and additional ones related to Arista), and call APIs for various vendors to configure and deploy numerous end nodes. A feature introduced by Arista called **Smart System Upgrade** (**SSU**), ensures that as we perform OS upgrades on Arista devices, it restarts its services with the upgraded OS versions but without rebooting to ensure minimal traffic interruption during upgrades. These features ensure that we have resiliency and up time even when we have new patches and OS upgrades rolled out on the data centers or multiple devices at once.

Arista EOS provides extended functionality for the devices to be managed through APIs by providing a set of APIs call **eAPI**. eAPI can be used to configure Arista devices by calling the eAPI framework from any scripting or programmable language. Let's see a very basic example of how to manage an Arista switch using eAPI.

We need to configure eAPI on the Arista switch:

```
Arista> enable
Arista# configure terminal
Arista(config)# management api http-commands
Arista(config-mgmt-api-http-cmds)# no shutdown
Arista(config-mgmt-api-http-cmds)# protocol http
Arista(config-mgmt-api-http-cmds)#end
```

This ensures that the Arista eAPI functionality is enabled on the router, and we can use HTTP protocol to interact with the API. We can also switch between the options of eAPI available over HTTPS, by using the command `protocol https`.

To verify if our configuration is correct, we use the command `show management api http-commands`, as follows:

```
Arista# show management api http-commands
Enabled: Yes
HTTPS server: shutdown, set to use port 443
HTTP server: running, set to use port 80
```

We can check if the eAPI framework is now accessible using the browser command `http://<ip of router>`.

A couple of examples from Arista depict the output that we get using the URL (in this case we have HTTPS enabled instead of HTTP):

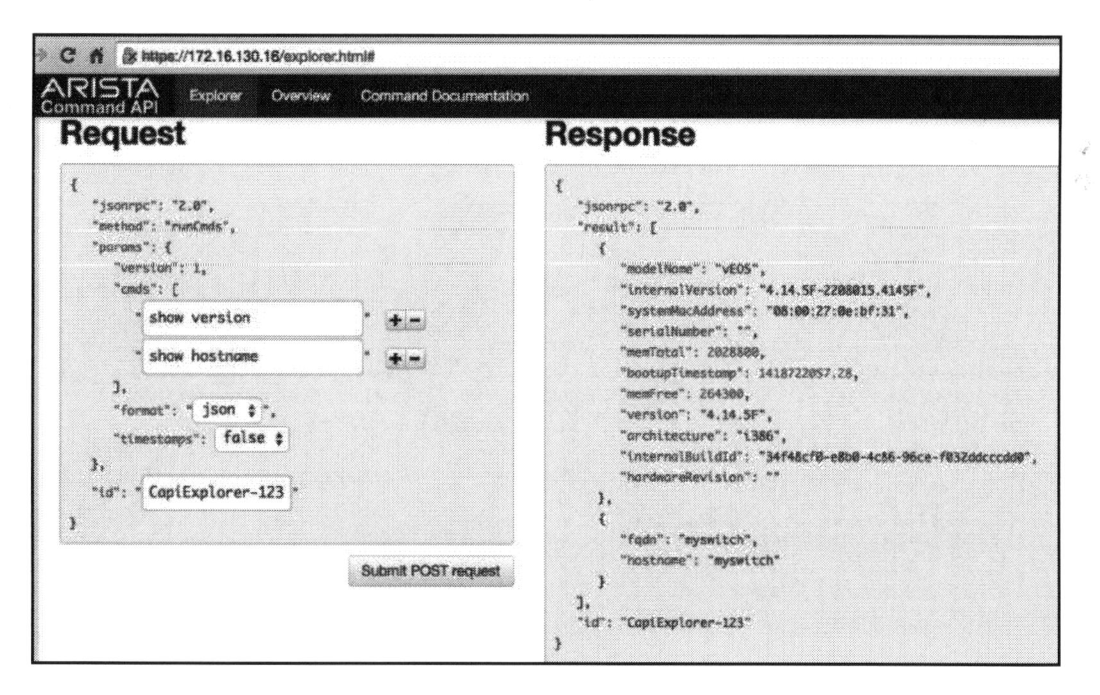

Here we see a set of commands passed (`show version` and `show hostname`), and the response from the API confirms the result set. Additionally, the **Command Response Documentation** tab shows us the available APIs that can be used for reference:

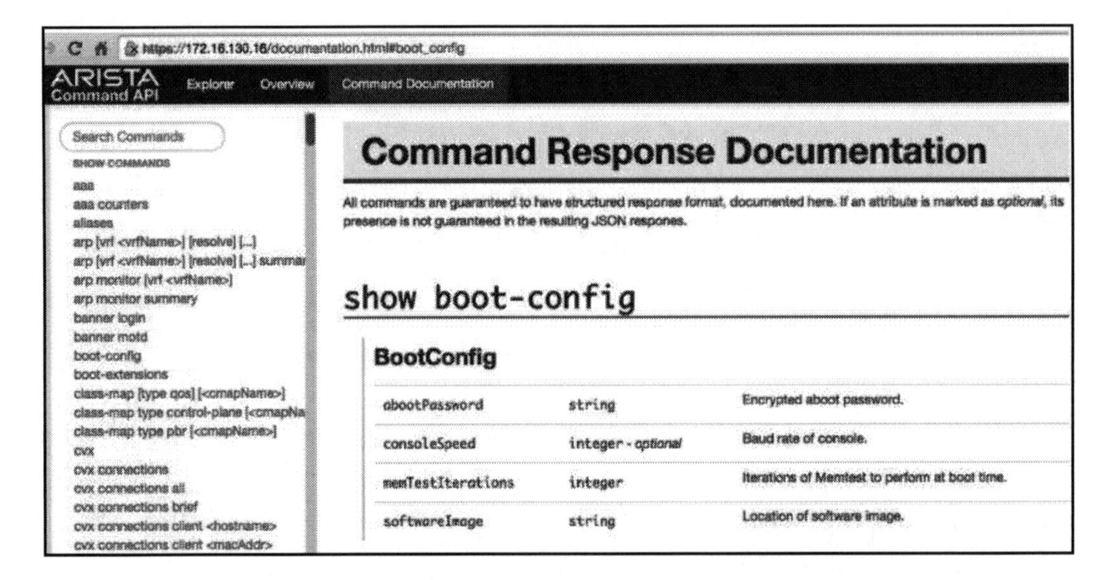

Let's see how to call the same in Python:

As a prerequisite we need to install `jsonrpclib`, which can be found at URL `https://pypi.python.org/pypi/jsonrpclib`. This is used to parse the **remote procedure call** (**RPC**) in JSON format. Once done, the following code will result in the same set of values that we got using the browser:

```
from jsonrpclib import Server
switch = Server( "https://admin:admin@172.16.130.16/command-api" )
response = switch.runCmds( 1, [ "show hostname" ] )
print ("Hello, my name is: ", response[0][ "hostname" ] )
response = switch.runCmds( 1, [ "show version" ] )
print ("My MAC address is: ", response[0][ "systemMacAddress" ] )
print ("My version is: ", response[0][ "version" ])
```

The preceding code gives the following output:

```
Hello, my name is: Arista
My MAC address is: 08:00:27:0e:bf:31
My version is: 4.14.5F
```

In a similar way, Arista has also introduced a library for Python that can be used as an alternate to `jsonrpclib`. The library `pyeapi`, which can be found at URL `https://pypi.python.org/pypi/pyeapi`, is a Python wrapper for the Arista EOS eAPI. Going by the example, here is how we can access the same set of devices using `pyeapi`.

From the developer page, here is an example that depicts how we can use `pyeapi` for API handling on Arista:

```
>>> from pprint import pprint as pp
>>> node = pyeapi.connect(transport='https', host='veos03',
username='eapi', password='secret', return_node=True)
>>> pp(node.enable('show version'))
[{'command': 'show version',
  'encoding': 'json',
  'result': {u'architecture': u'i386',
             u'bootupTimestamp': 1421765066.11,
             u'hardwareRevision': u'',
             u'internalBuildId': u'f590eed4-1e66-43c6-8943-
cee0390fbafe',
             u'internalVersion': u'4.14.5F-2209869.4145F',
             u'memFree': 115496,
             u'memTotal': 2028008,
             u'modelName': u'vEOS',
             u'serialNumber': u'',
             u'systemMacAddress': u'00:0c:29:f5:d2:7d',
             u'version': u'4.14.5F'}}]
```

Looking at both Cisco and Arista (which are two major players in the cloud and SDN marketplace), we can combine both Arista eAPI and Cisco NX-API to manage our entire data center inventory, and work on some tasks like the provisioning of new devices or upgrading of current devices with no or minimal impact, which in turn ensures scalability, reliability, and uptime in the business processes.

Controller-based network fabric

As we come out of the legacy hardware era in which each physical path was connected and designed to take traffic from one point to another, and where a packet had limited availability to reach from one device to another, SDN is ensuring that we have a network fabric for our data to reach between different sources and destinations.

A **network fabric** is a collection of different network devices connected to each other by a common controller ensuring that each component in the network is optimized to send traffic among each of the nodes. The underlying switch fabric, which is a physical switchboard with ports (like Ethernet, ATM, and DSL), is also controlled and programmed by a controller which can ensure (by creating a path or specific port(s)) that a particular type of data can traverse through to reach its destinations.

In a typical network design we have Layer 2 (or switching domains) and Layer 3 (or routing domains). If we do not have a controller-based approach, each network component can learn the behavior of traffic from its next connected component (like **Spanning Tree Protocol** (**STP**) for Layer 2) or some routing protocol (like OSPF for Layer 3). In this case, each device acts as its own controller and only has limited visibility to devices that it is directly connected to (also termed **neighbor devices**). There is no single view of the entire network on any device, and additionally, each component (or individual controller) acts as a single point of failure for its neighbor devices. A failure on any component would result in its neighbor devices reconverging or even getting isolated owing to the failure of their connected component.

Comparing that to a controller-based environment, theoretically each device has as many connections as it has number of ports connected. Hence, if we think of even three devices connected in a controller-based environment, we have multiple connections between each device owing to their physical connectivity to each other. In case of the failure of a component (or device), the controller can quickly make an intelligent decision to reconfigure a new path and alter the behavior of the other two network devices to ensure minimal disruption to traffic, keeping the same throughput and distributed load on all the other available links. A controller in theory eliminates the control plane behavior of each device and ensures an optimized forwarding table (to forward data to specific destinations) is updated on each device the controller is managing. This is because the controller starts acting as the main component which has the visibility of every device, with every entry and exit point of each device and the granularity of the data type that is flowing from each managed network device.

Going by the vendors, major players such as Cisco (with its open network environment), Juniper (with its QFabric switch), and Avaya (with its VENA switch), have provided the ability to act as controllers or be configured to be managed by a controller. Additionally, with the introduction of controller-to-manager network components, each network device can now virtually become a dump client with the controller making all the intelligent decisions, from learning to forwarding tables.

A controller acts as an abstraction layer between multi-vendor network devices and network tasks. As an end user, someone can configure specific tasks to be performed by the controller, and, using the underlying API model from different vendors (using JSON or XML), the controller can convert those specific tasks into various vendor-specific API calls, and devices can be configured by sending those specific instructions using those APIs to each of the vendor devices. The **Application Policy Infrastructure Controller** (**APIC**) component is responsible for controlling and programming the fabric on each network device component.

Let's see an example of Cisco APIC and some basics on how we can use it. Cisco APIC is used to manage, automate, monitor, and program **Application Centric Infrastructure** (**ACI**). ACI is a collection of objects with each object representing a tenant. A tenant can be called a group of specific customers, groups, or business units based upon the business classifications. As an example, a single organization may covert its entire infrastructure into a single tenant, whereas an organization can separate out its tenants based upon its functions like HR and Finance. Tenants can further be divided into contexts, with each context as a separate forwarding plane, hence the same set of IP addresses can be used in each context as each set of IP addresses will be treated differently in each context.

Contexts contain **Endpoints (EPs)** and **Endpoint Groups (EPGs)**. These EPs are physical components like hardware NICs, and EPGs are collections of items like DNSs, IP addresses, and so on, that dictate a similar functionality for a specific application (like a web application).

For programming with APIC, the major components required are as follows:

- **APIC Rest Python Adaptor** (**ARYA**)

  This is a tool created by Cisco to convert the APIC object returned in XML or JSON to direct Python code. Underlying, this leverages the COBRA SDK to perform this task. This can be installed in Python using `pip install arya`.

- **ACI SDK**

  This is the SDK that contains the API to directly call the APIs of the controller. We need to install `acicobra`, which can be found at `https://www.cisco.com/c/en/us/td/docs/switches/datacenter/aci/apic/sw/1-x/api/python/install/b_Install_Cisco_APIC_Python_SDK_Standalone.html`, from Cisco to be able to call it into Python.

Once we have this installed, here are some examples from Cisco which can be found at the URL `https://github.com/CiscoDevNet/python_code_samples_network/blob/master/acitoolkit_show_tenants/aci-show-tenants.py`. This can help us understand creating an object:

```
#!/usr/bin/env python
"""
Simple application that logs on to the APIC and displays all
of the Tenants.
Leverages the DevNet Sandbox - APIC Simulator Always On
    Information at
https://developer.cisco.com/site/devnet/sandbox/available-labs/data-ce
nter/index.gsp
Code sample based off the ACI-Toolkit Code sample
https://github.com/datacenter/acitoolkit/blob/master/samples/aci-show-
tenants.py
"""

import sys
import acitoolkit.acitoolkit as ACI

# Credentials and information for the DevNet ACI Simulator Always-On
Sandbox
APIC_URL = "https://sandboxapicdc.cisco.com/"
APIC_USER = "admin"
APIC_PASSWORD = "C1sco12345"

def main():
    """
    Main execution routine
    :return: None
    """

    # Login to APIC
    session = ACI.Session(APIC_URL, APIC_USER, APIC_PASSWORD)
    resp = session.login()
    if not resp.ok:
        print('%% Could not login to APIC')
        sys.exit(0)

    # Download all of the tenants
    print("TENANT")
    print("------")
    tenants = ACI.Tenant.get(session)
    for tenant in tenants:
        print(tenant.name)
```

```
if __name__ == '__main__':
    main()
```

Looking at the preceding concepts, we can enhance and ensure that our managed nodes in the controller can be controlled based on the application requirements rather than hardware limitations. This also ensures that the infrastructure is now tweaked as per application, and not vice versa, with the application performance restricted by hardware.

Network automation tools

As we have seen throughout the previous chapters, we have multiple choices regarding automating a network. From a basic configuration for any device using Netmiko to deploying and creating configurations across various devices in a network using Ansible, there are many options for engineers to automate networks based upon various needs.

Python is extensively used in creating automation scenarios, owing to its open community support for various vendors and protocols. Nearly every major player in the industry has support for Python programming, tweaking their own tools or any supporting technology that they have. Another major aspect of network automation are the custom-based solutions that could be made for organization requirements. The self-service API model is a good start to ensuring that some of the tasks that are done manually can be converted to APIs, which can then be leveraged into any language based upon the automation needs.

Let's see an example that can be used as a basic guide to understand the advantage of self or custom-created automation tools. The output of `show ip bgp summary` in Cisco is the same as `show bgp summary` in Juniper. Now, as an engineer who needs to validate the BGP on both the vendors, I need to understand both the commands and interpret the output.

Think of this situation by adding more vendors which have their own unique way of fetching BGP output. This becomes complex and a network engineer needs to be trained on a multi-vendor environment to be able to fetch the same type of output from each vendor.

Now, let's say we create an API (for example, `getbgpstatus`), which takes the input as some hostname. The API at the backend is intelligent enough to fetch the vendor model using SNMP, and based upon the vendor sends a specific command (like `show ip bgp summary` for Cisco or `show ip summary` for Juniper), and parses that output to a human-readable format, like only the IP address and status of that BGP neighbor.

For example, instead of printing the raw output of `show ip bgp summary` or `show bgp summary`, it parses the output like this:

```
IPaddress1 : Status is UP
IPaddress2 : Status is Down (Active)
```

This output can be returned as a JSON value back to the call of the API.

Hence, let's say we can call the API as `http://localhost/networkdevices/getbgpstatus?device=devicex` and the API from the backend will identify if `devicex` is Juniper or Cisco or any other vendor, and based upon this the vendor will fetch and parse the output relevant to that vendor. A return of that API call will be JSON text as we saw in the preceding example, that we can parse in our automation language.

Let us see a basic example of another popular tool, SolarWinds. There are many aspects of SolarWinds; it can auto-discover a device (based upon MIBs and SNMP), identify the vendor, and fetch relevant information from the device.

Let's see some of the following screenshots for basic SolarWinds device management. SolarWinds is freely available as a trial download.

The prerequisite for SolarWinds device management is as follows:

1. We need to add a device in SolarWinds, shown as below:

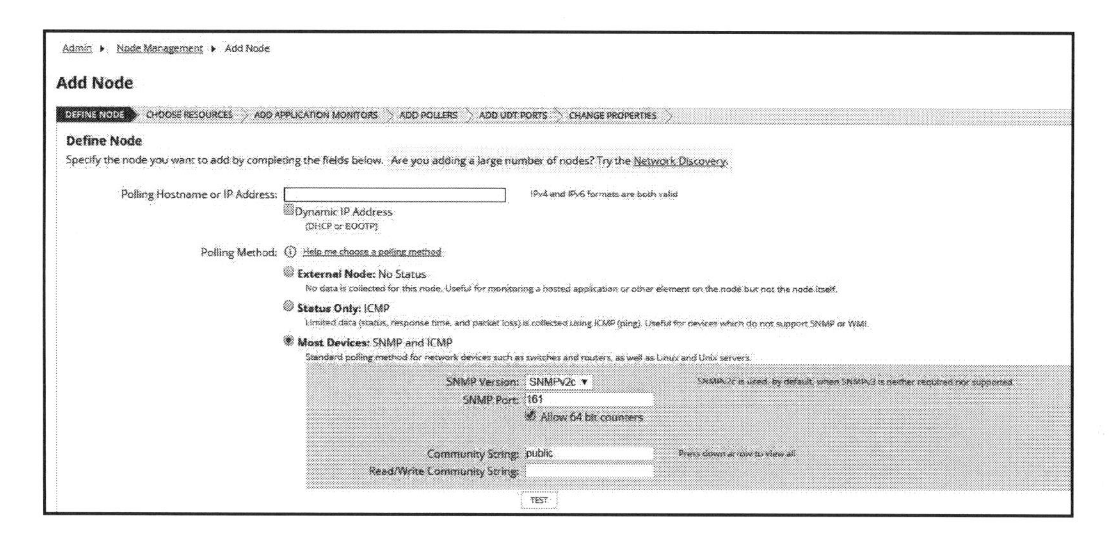

As we can see, SolarWinds has the ability to discover devices (using network discovery), or we can add a specific IP address/hostname with the correct SNMP string for SolarWinds to detect the device.

2. Once the device is detected it will show as the monitored node, as in the below screenshot:

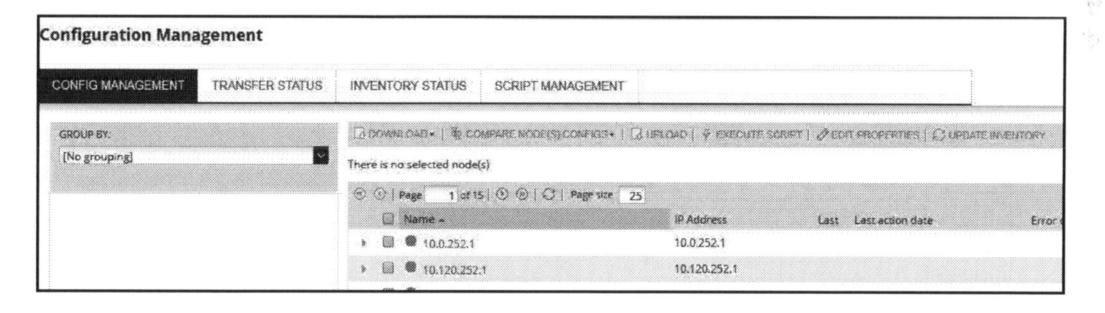

Notice the green dot next to the IP address (or hostname). This signifies that the node is alive (reachable) and SolarWinds can interact with the node correctly.

Additional task(s) that can be performed post device discovery is as follows:

Once we have the node available or detected in SolarWinds, here are some of the additional tasks that can be performed in SolarWinds (as shown in screenshot below):

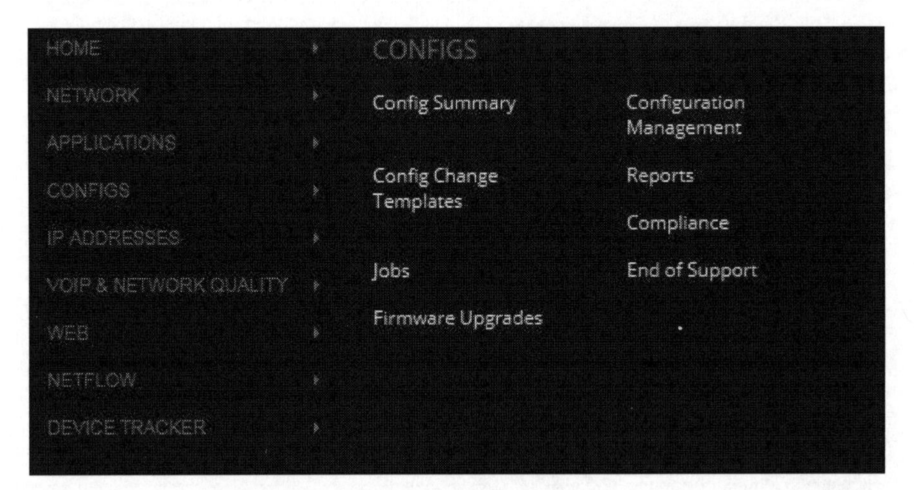

We have selected the **CONFIGS** menu, under which we can perform config management for the devices. Additionally, as we can see in the following screenshot, we have the ability to create small scripts, (like we did here to `show running config`), which we can use to execute against a certain set of devices from SolarWinds itself (as in screenshot below):

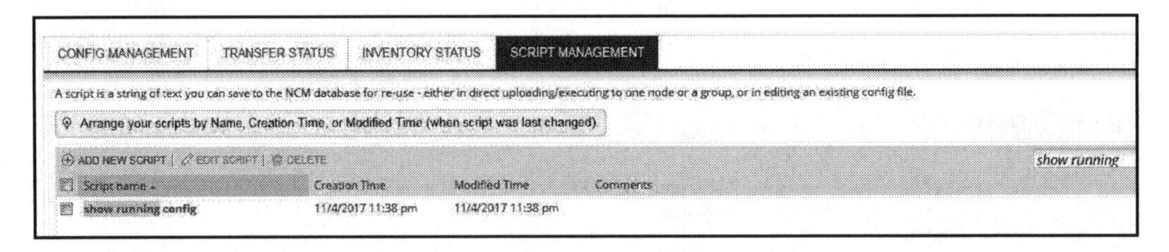

The result is retrieved and can be stored as a text file, or can even be sent as a report back to any email client if configured. Similarly, there are certain tasks (called **jobs** in SolarWinds), that can be done on a scheduled basis, as we can see in the following screenshot:

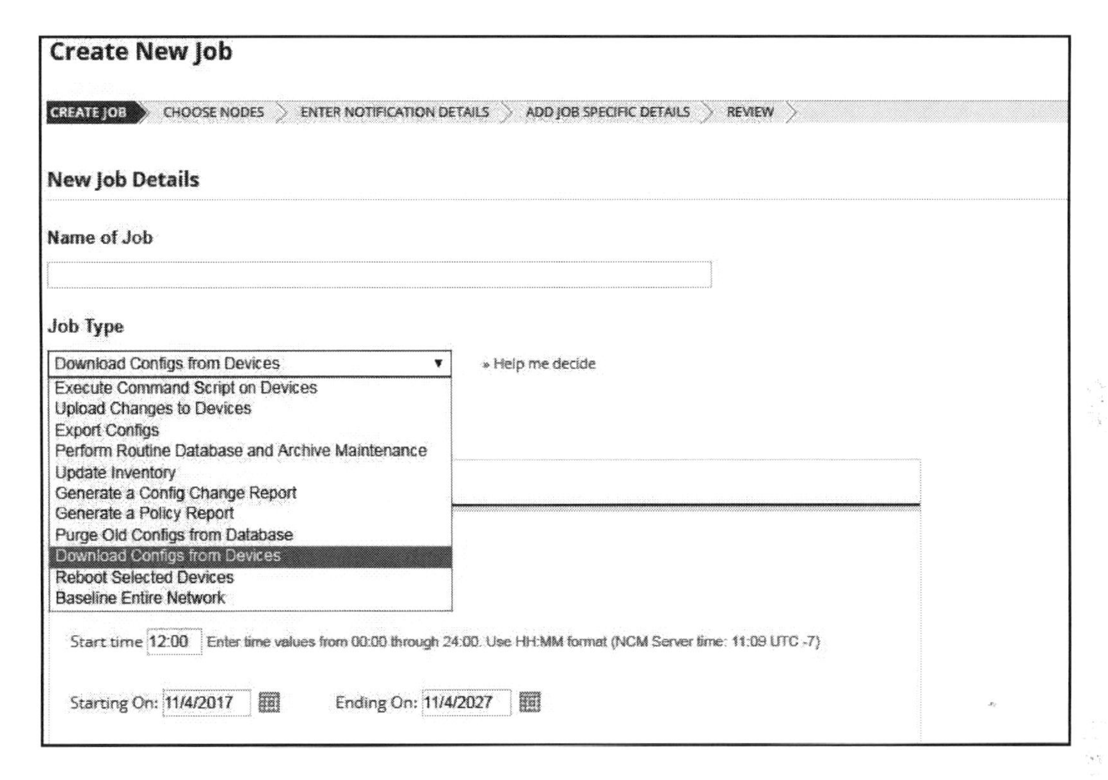

As we can see in the preceding screenshot, we can **Download Configs from Devices**, and then select all or certain devices in the next step and schedule the job. This is very useful in terms of fetching a config from a previous date or in case a rollback is needed to a last known good config scenario. Also, there are times when auditing needs to be performed regarding who changed what and what was changed in configurations, and SolarWinds can extend this ability by sending reports and alerts. Programmatically, we have the additional ability to call the SolarWinds API to fetch the results from Python.

It is assumed that OrionSDK is already installed in Python. If not, we can install it using `pip install orionsdk`.

Consider the following example:

```
from orionsdk import SwisClient
import requests

npm_server = 'myserver'
username = "username"
password = "password"

verify = False
if not verify:
    from requests.packages.urllib3.exceptions import
InsecureRequestWarning
    requests.packages.urllib3.disable_warnings(InsecureRequestWarning)

swis = SwisClient(npm_server, username, password)

results = swis.query("SELECT NodeID, DisplayName FROM Orion.Nodes
Where Vendor= 'Cisco'")

for row in results['results']:
    print("{NodeID:<5}: {DisplayName}".format(**row))
```

Since SolarWinds supports a direct SQL query, we use the query:

```
SELECT NodeID, DisplayName FROM Orion.Nodes Where Vendor= 'Cisco'
```

We are trying to fetch the `NodeID` and `DisplayName` (or the device name) for all the devices which have the vendor Cisco. Once we have the result, we print the result in a formatted way. In our case, the output will be (let's assume our Cisco devices in SolarWinds are added as `mytestrouter1` and `mytestrouter2`):

```
>>>
===================== RESTART: C:\a1\checksolarwinds.py
=====================
101 : mytestrouter1
102 : mytestrouter2
>>>
```

Using some of these automation tools and APIs, we can ensure that our tasks are focused on actual work with some of the basic or core tasks (like fetching values from devices and so on) being offloaded to the tools or APIs to take care of.

Let's now create a basic automation tool from scratch that monitors the reachability of any node that is part of that monitoring tool, using a ping test. We can call it PingMesh or PingMatrix, as the tool will generate a web-based matrix to show the reachability of the routers.

The topology that we would be using is as follows:

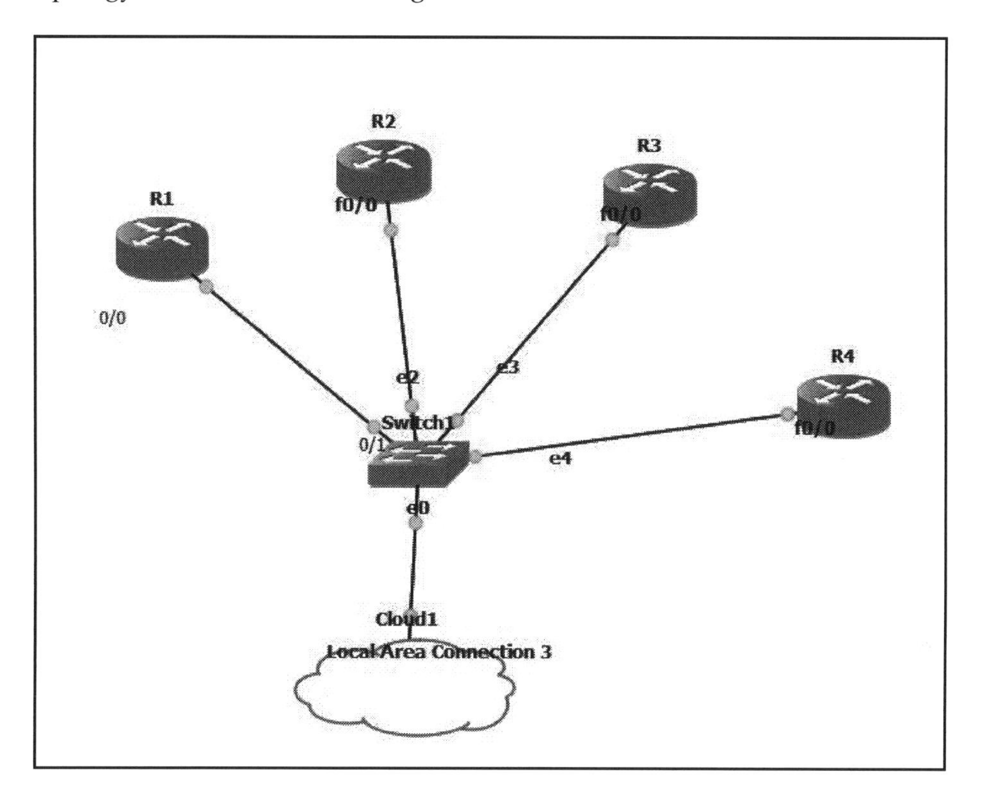

Here, we would be using four routers (`R1` to `R4`), and the `Cloud1` as our monitoring source. Each of the routers will try to reach each other through ping, and will report back to the script running on `Cloud1` which will interpret the results and display the web-based matrix through a web-based URL.

The explanation of the preceding topology is as follows:

1. What we are trying to do is log in to each router (preferably in parallel), ping each destination from each source, and report back the reachability status of each destination.

2. As an example, if we want to do the task manually, we would log in to `R1` and try to ping `R2`, `R3`, and `R4` from the source to check the reachability of each router from `R1`. The main script on `Cloud1` (acting as the controller) will interpret the result and update the web matrix accordingly.
3. In our case all the routers (and the controller) are residing in `192.168.255.x` subnet, hence they are reachable to each other using a simple ping.

We are going to create two separate Python programs (one to be called as the library for invoking the commands on various nodes, fetching the results from the nodes, interpreting the results, and sending the parsed data to the main program). The main program will be responsible for calling the library, and will use the results we get back to create the HTML web matrix.

Let's create the library or the program to be called in the main program first (we called it `getmeshvalues.py`):

```
#!/usr/bin/env python
import re
import sys
import os
import time
from netmiko import ConnectHandler
from threading import Thread
from random import randrange
username="cisco"
password="cisco"

splitlist = lambda lst, sz: [lst[i:i+sz] for i in range(0, len(lst),
sz)]

returns = {}
resultoutput={}
devlist=[]
cmdlist=""
def fetchallvalues(sourceip,sourcelist,delay,cmddelay):
    print ("checking for....."+sourceip)
    cmdend=" repeat 10" # this is to ensure that we ping for 10
packets
    splitsublist=splitlist(sourcelist,6) # this is to ensure we open
not more than 6 sessions on router at a time
    threads_imagex= []
    for item in splitsublist:
        t = Thread(target=fetchpingvalues,
args=(sourceip,item,cmdend,delay,cmddelay,))
        t.start()
```

```
        time.sleep(randrange(1,2,1)/20)
        threads_imagex.append(t)

    for t in threads_imagex:
        t.join()
def fetchpingvalues(devip,destips,cmdend,delay,cmddelay):
    global resultoutput
    ttl="0"
    destip="none"
    command=""
    try:
        output=""
        device = ConnectHandler(device_type='cisco_ios', ip=devip,
username=username, password=password, global_delay_factor=cmddelay)
        time.sleep(delay)
        device.clear_buffer()
        for destip in destips:
            command="ping "+destip+" source "+devip+cmdend
            output =
device.send_command_timing(command,delay_factor=cmddelay)
            if ("round-trip" in output):
                resultoutput[devip+":"+destip]="True"
            elif ("Success rate is 0 percent" in output):
                resultoutput[devip+":"+destip]="False"
        device.disconnect()
    except:
        print ("Error connecting to ..."+devip)
        for destip in destips:
            resultoutput[devip+":"+destip]="False"

def getallvalues(allips):
    global resultoutput
    threads_imagex= []
    for item in allips:
        #print ("calling "+item)
        t = Thread(target=fetchallvalues, args=(item,allips,2,1,))
        t.start()
        time.sleep(randrange(1,2,1)/30)
        threads_imagex.append(t)
    for t in threads_imagex:
        t.join()
    dnew=sorted(resultoutput.items())
    return dnew

#print
(getallvalues(["192.168.255.240","192.168.255.245","192.168.255.248","
192.168.255.249","4.2.2.2"]))
```

In the preceding code, we have created three main functions that we call in a thread (for parallel execution). The `getallvalues()` contains the list of IP addresses that we want to get the data from. It then passes this information to `fetchallvalues()` with specific device information to fetch the ping values again in parallel execution. For executing the command on the router and fetching the results, we call the `fetchpingvalues()` function.

Let's see the result of this code (by removing the remark on the code that calls the function). We need to pass the device IPs that we want to validate as a list. In our case, we have all the valid routers in the `192.168.255.x` range, and `4.2.2.2` is taken as an example of a non-reachable router:

```
print(getallvalues(["192.168.255.240","192.168.255.245","192.168.255.2
48","192.168.255.249","4.2.2.2"]))
```

The preceding code gives the following output:

```
Python 3.6.1 Shell
File Edit Shell Debug Options Window Help
Python 3.6.1 (v3.6.1:69c0db5, Mar 21 2017, 17:54:52) [MSC v.1900 32 bit (Intel)]
 on win32
Type "copyright", "credits" or "license()" for more information.
>>>
=================== RESTART: C:\pingmesh\getmeshvalue2.py ==================
checking for.....192.168.255.240
checking for.....192.168.255.245
checking for.....192.168.255.248
checking for.....192.168.255.249
checking for.....4.2.2.2
Error connecting to ...4.2.2.2
[('192.168.255.240:192.168.255.240', 'True'), ('192.168.255.240:192.168.255.245'
, 'True'), ('192.168.255.240:192.168.255.248', 'True'), ('192.168.255.240:192.16
8.255.249', 'True'), ('192.168.255.240:4.2.2.2', 'False'), ('192.168.255.245:192
.168.255.240', 'True'), ('192.168.255.245:192.168.255.245', 'True'), ('192.168.2
55.245:192.168.255.248', 'True'), ('192.168.255.245:192.168.255.249', 'True'), (
'192.168.255.245:4.2.2.2', 'False'), ('192.168.255.248:192.168.255.240', 'True')
, ('192.168.255.248:192.168.255.245', 'True'), ('192.168.255.248:192.168.255.248
', 'True'), ('192.168.255.248:192.168.255.249', 'True'), ('192.168.255.248:4.2.2
.2', 'False'), ('192.168.255.249:192.168.255.240', 'True'), ('192.168.255.249:19
2.168.255.245', 'True'), ('192.168.255.249:192.168.255.248', 'True'), ('192.168.
255.249:192.168.255.249', 'True'), ('192.168.255.249:4.2.2.2', 'False'), ('4.2.2
.2:192.168.255.240', 'False'), ('4.2.2.2:192.168.255.245', 'False'), ('4.2.2.2:1
92.168.255.248', 'False'), ('4.2.2.2:192.168.255.249', 'False'), ('4.2.2.2:4.2.2
.2', 'False')]
>>>
```

As we can see in the result, we get the reachability in terms of `True` or `False` from each node to the other node.

For example, the first item in the list `('192.168.255.240:192.168.255.240','True')` interprets that from the source `192.168.255.240` to destination `192.168.255.240` (which is the same self IP) is reachable. Similarly, the next item in the same list `('192.168.255.240:192.168.255.245','True')` confirms that from source IP `192.168.255.240` the destination `192.168.255.245` we have reachability from ping. This information is required to create a matrix based upon the results. Next we see the main code where we fetch these results and create a web-based matrix page.

Next, we need to create the main file (we're calling it `pingmesh.py`):

```
import getmeshvalue
from getmeshvalue import getallvalues

getdevinformation={}
devicenamemapping={}
arraydeviceglobal=[]
pingmeshvalues={}

arraydeviceglobal=["192.168.255.240","192.168.255.245","192.168.255.24
8","192.168.255.249","4.2.2.2"]

devicenamemapping['192.168.255.240']="R1"
devicenamemapping['192.168.255.245']="R2"
devicenamemapping['192.168.255.248']="R3"
devicenamemapping['192.168.255.249']="R4"
devicenamemapping['4.2.2.2']="Random"

def getmeshvalues():
        global arraydeviceglobal
        global pingmeshvalues
        arraydeviceglobal=sorted(set(arraydeviceglobal))
        tval=getallvalues(arraydeviceglobal)
        pingmeshvalues = dict(tval)

getmeshvalues()

def createhtml():
    global arraydeviceglobal
    fopen=open("C:\pingmesh\pingmesh.html","w") ### this needs to be
changed as web path of the html location

    head="""<html><head><meta http-equiv="refresh" content="60"
></head>"""
    head=head+"""<script type="text/javascript">
function updatetime() {
    var x = new Date(document.lastModified);
```

```
    document.getElementById("modified").innerHTML = "Last Modified:
"+x+" ";
}
</script>"""+"<body onLoad='updatetime();'>"
    head=head+"<div style='display: inline-block;float: right;font-
size: 80%'><h4><h4><p id='modified'></p></div>"
    head=head+"<div style='display: inline-block;float: left;font-
size: 90%'></h4><center><h2>Network Health Dashboard<h2></div>"
    head=head+"<br><div><table border='1'
align='center'><caption><b>Ping Matrix</b></caption>"
    head=head+"<center><br><br><br><br><br><br><br><br>"
    fopen.write(head)
    dval=""
    fopen.write("<tr><td>Devices</td>")
    for fromdevice in arraydeviceglobal:
fopen.write("<td><b>"+devicenamemapping[fromdevice]+"</b></td>")
    fopen.write("</tr>")
    for fromdevice in arraydeviceglobal:
        fopen.write("<tr>")
fopen.write("<td><b>"+devicenamemapping[fromdevice]+"</b></td>")
        for todevice in arraydeviceglobal:
            askvalue=fromdevice+":"+todevice
            if (askvalue in pingmeshvalues):
                getallvalues=pingmeshvalues.get(askvalue)
                bgcolor='lime'
                if (getallvalues == "False"):
                    bgcolor='salmon'
            fopen.write("<td align='center' font size='2' height='2'
width='2' bgcolor='"+bgcolor+"'title='"+askvalue+"'>"+"<font
color='white'><b>"+getallvalues+"</b></font></td>")
        fopen.write("</tr>\n")
    fopen.write("</table></div>")
    fopen.close()
createhtml()


print("All done!!!!")
```

In this case, we have the following mappings in place:

```
devicenamemapping['192.168.255.240']="R1"
devicenamemapping['192.168.255.245']="R2"
devicenamemapping['192.168.255.248']="R3"
devicenamemapping['192.168.255.249']="R4"
devicenamemapping['4.2.2.2']="Random"
```

The last device named `Random`, is a test device which is not in our network and is non-reachable for test purposes. Once executed, it creates a file named `pingmesh.html` with standard HTML formats and a last-refreshed clock (from JavaScript) to confirm when the last refresh occurred. This is required if we want the script to be executed from the task scheduler (Let's say every five minutes), and anybody opening the HTML page will know when the probe occurred. The HTML file needs to be placed or saved in a folder which is mapped to a web folder so that it can be accessed using the URL `http://<server>/pingmesh.html`.

When executed, here is the output from the Python script:

```
Python 3.6.1 Shell
File Edit Shell Debug Options Window Help
Python 3.6.1 (v3.6.1:69c0db5, Mar 21 2017, 17:54:52) [MSC v.1900 32 bit (Intel)] on win32
Type "copyright", "credits" or "license()" for more information.
>>>
===================== RESTART: C:\pingmesh\pingmesh.py =====================
checking for.....192.168.255.240
checking for.....192.168.255.245
checking for.....192.168.255.248
checking for.....192.168.255.249
checking for.....4.2.2.2
Error connecting to ...4.2.2.2
All done!!!!
>>>
```

The HTML file, when placed in the web-mapped URL and called, looks like this:

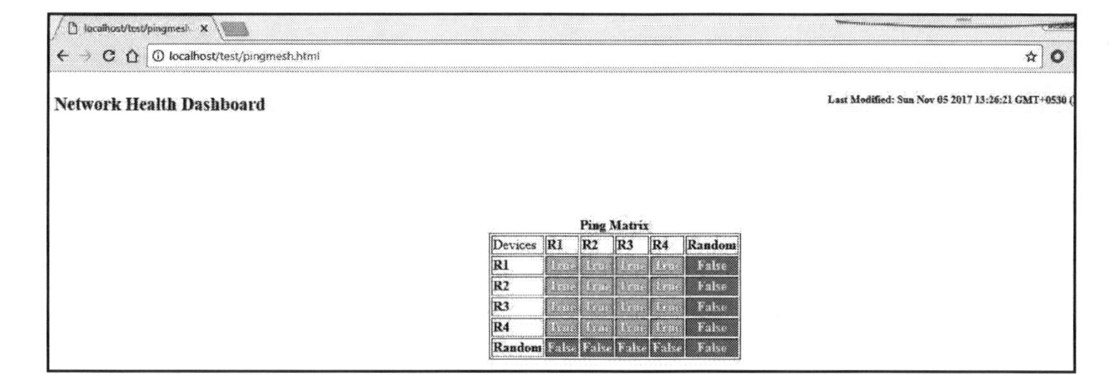

Devices	R1	R2	R3	R4	Random
R1	True	True	True	True	False
R2	True	True	True	True	False
R3	True	True	True	True	False
R4	True	True	True	True	False
Random	False	False	False	False	False

As we can see, in the PingMatrix there is an entire red row and column, which means that any connectivity between any router to the random router and from the random router to any router is not there. Green means that all the connectivity between all other routers is fine.

Additionally, we have also configured a tooltip on each cell, and hovering the mouse over that specific cell would also show the source and destination IP address mapping for that particular cell, as shown in the following screenshot:

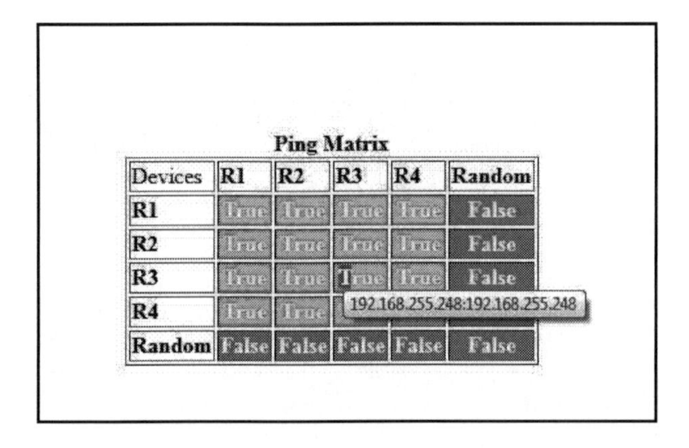
Ping Matrix

Devices	R1	R2	R3	R4	Random
R1	True	True	True	True	False
R2	True	True	True	True	False
R3	True	True	True	True	False
R4	True	True			
Random	False	False	False	False	False

Let's see another screenshot, in which we shut down R2 to make it unreachable:

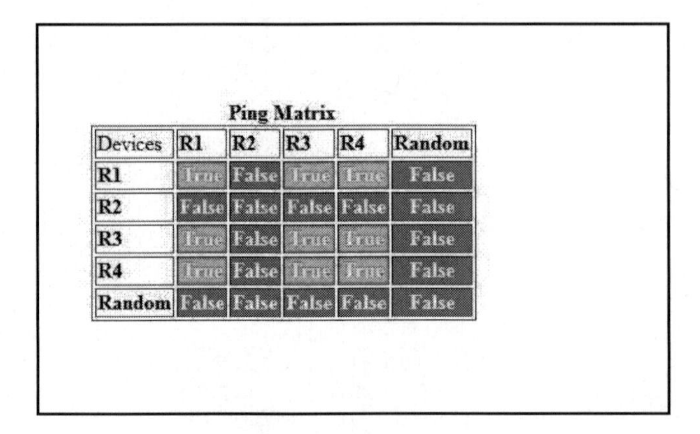
Ping Matrix

Devices	R1	R2	R3	R4	Random
R1	True	False	True	True	False
R2	False	False	False	False	False
R3	True	False	True	True	False
R4	True	False	True	True	False
Random	False	False	False	False	False

Now, as we can see, the entire row and column of `R2` is red, and hence the PingMatrix shows that `R2` is now unreachable from everywhere else, and `R2` also cannot reach anyone else in the network.

Let's see a final example, in which for test purposes we intentionally block the ping traffic from `R2` to `R4` (and vice versa) using an extended Cisco ACL, which in turn reports that `R4` and `R2` have reachability issues in the PingMatrix:

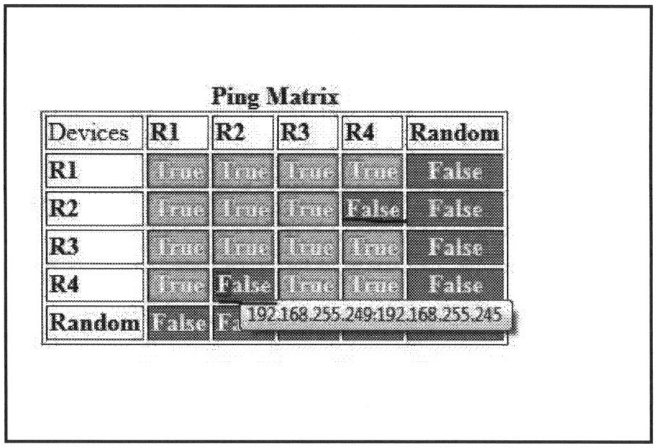

Ping Matrix

Devices	R1	R2	R3	R4	Random
R1	True	True	True	True	False
R2	True	True	True	False	False
R3	True	True	True	True	False
R4	True	False	True	True	False
Random	False	F[illegible]	[illegible]	[illegible]	[illegible]

192.168.255.249:192.168.255.245

As we see can in the preceding screenshot, the Random router is still a red or false, since it is not in our network, but now it is showing red/false between `R2` and `R4` and also between `R4` and `R2`. This gives us a quick view that even with multiple paths to reach each node with another node, we have a connectivity issue between the two nodes.

Going by the preceding examples, we can enhance the tool to easily monitor and understand any routing/reachability issues, or even link down connectivity problems using a holistic view of all of the connections in our network. PingMesh/Matrix can be extended to check latency, and even packet drops in each connection between various nodes. Additionally, using syslog or email functionality (specific Python libraries are available for sending syslog messages from Python or even emails from Python code), alerts or tickets can also be generated in case of failures detected or high latency observed from the Python script itself.

This tool can easily become a central monitoring tool in any organization, and based upon patterns (such as green or red, and other color codes if needed), engineers can make decisions on the actual issues and take proactive actions instead of reactive actions to ensure the high reliability and uptime of the network.

Summary

In this chapter, we learned about the basic functionality of SDN controllers, programmable fabric, and some network automation tools. We have also seen how to work with cloud platforms and, with reference to a live example of managing AWS Cloud from Python, understood how we can control cloud operations using automation.

We gained a deep understanding about the role of controllers, and with some examples of Cisco controllers, went into details on how a controller can be programmed or called in programs/scripts to perform certain tasks. We also saw the basics of some popular network automation tools, such as SolarWinds, and created an in-house web-based automation tool for monitoring our network, called PingMatrix or PingMesh.

5
Low-Level Network Device Interactions

In this chapter, we will start to dive deeper into the management of network devices using Python. In particular, we will examine the different ways in which we can use Python to programmatically communicate with legacy network routers and switches.

What do I mean by legacy network routers and switches? While it is hard to imagine any networking device coming out today without an **Application Program Interface (API)** for programmatic communication, it is a known fact that many of the network devices deployed in previous years did not contain API interfaces. The intended method of management for those devices was through **Command Line Interfaces (CLIs)** using terminal programs, which were originally developed with a human engineer in mind. The management relied on the engineer's interpretation of the data returned from the device for appropriate action. As the number of network devices and the complexity of the network grew, it became increasingly difficult to manually manage them one by one.

Python has two great libraries that can help with these tasks, Pexpect and Paramiko, as well as other libraries derived from them. This chapter will cover Pexpect first, then move on with examples from Paramiko. Once you understand the basics of Paramiko, it is easy to branch out to expanded libraries such as Netmiko. It is also worth mentioning that Ansible (covered in `Chapters 7`, *The Python Automation Framework – Ansible Basics*, and `Chapter 8`, *The Python Automation Framework – Beyond Basics*) relies heavily on Paramiko for its network modules. In this chapter, we will take a look at the following topics:

- The challenges of the CLI
- Constructing a virtual lab
- The Python Pexpect library

- The Python Paramiko library
- The downsides of Pexpect and Paramiko

Let's get started!

The challenges of the CLI

At the Interop expo in Las Vegas in 2014, *BigSwitch Networks'* CEO Douglas Murray displayed the following slide to illustrate what had changed in **Data Center Networking (DCN)** in the 20 years between 1993 to 2013:

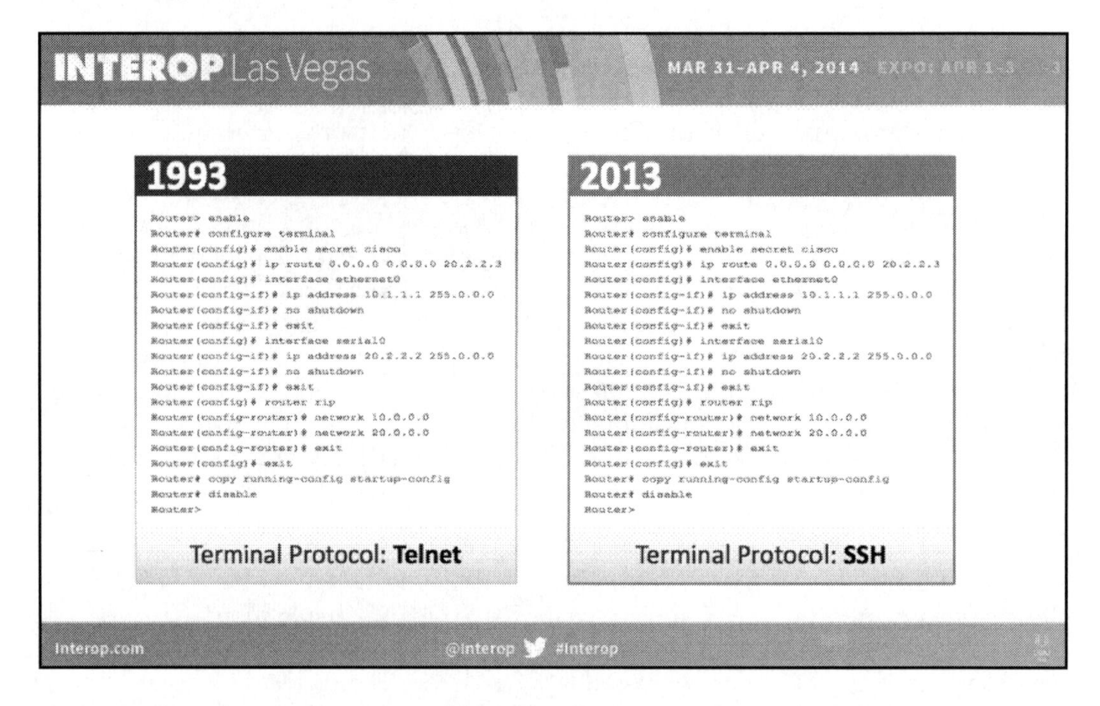

Data center networking changes (source: `https://www.bigswitch.com/sites/default/files/presentations/murraydouglasstartuphotseatpanel.pdf`)

His point was apparent: not much had changed in those 20 years in the way we manage network devices. While he might have been negatively biased toward the incumbent vendors when displaying this slide, his point is well taken. In his opinion, the only thing that had changed about managing routers and switches in 20 years was the protocol changing from the less secure Telnet to the more secure SSH.

It was right around the same time in 2014 that we started to see the industry coming to a consensus about the clear need to move away from manual, human-driven CLI toward an automatic, computer-centric automation API. Make no mistake, we still need to directly communicate with the device when making network designs, bringing up initial proof of concepts, and deploying the topology for the first time. However, once we have moved beyond the initial deployment, the requirement is to consistently make the same changes reliably, to make them error-free, and to repeat them over and over again without the engineer being distracted or feeling tired. This requirement sounds like an ideal job for computers and our favorite language, Python.

Referring back to the slide, the main challenge is the interaction between the router and the administrator. The router will output a series of information and will expect the administrator to enter a series of manual commands from the engineer's interpretation of the output. For example, you have to type in `enable` to get into a privileged mode, and upon receiving the returned prompt with the `#` sign, you then type in `configure terminal` in order to go into the configuration mode. The same process can further be expanded into the interface configuration mode and routing protocol configuration mode. This is in sharp contrast to a computer-driven, programmatic mindset. When the computer wants to accomplish a single task, say, put an IP address on an interface, it wants to structurally give all the information to the router at once, and it would expect a single `yes` or `no` answer from the router to indicate the success or failure of the task.

The solution, as implemented by both Pexpect and Paramiko, is to treat the interactive process as a child process and watch over the interaction between the process and the destination device. Based on the returned value, the parent process will decide the subsequent action, if any.

Constructing a virtual lab

Before we dive into the packages, let's examine the options of putting together a lab for the benefit of learning. As the old saying goes, *practice makes perfect*: we need an isolated sandbox to safely make mistakes, try out new ways of doing things, and repeat some of the steps to reinforce concepts that were not clear in the first try. It is easy enough to install Python and the necessary packages for the management host, but what about those routers and switches that we want to simulate?

To put together a network lab, we basically have two options, each with its advantages and disadvantages:

- **Physical device**: This option consists of physical devices that you can see and touch. If you are lucky enough, you might be able to put together a lab that is an exact replication of your production environment:
    - **Advantages**: It is an easy transition from lab to production, easier to understand by managers and fellow engineers who can look at and touch the devices. In short, the comfort level with physical devices is extremely high because of familiarity.
    - **Disadvantages**: It is relatively expensive to pay for a device that is only used in the lab. Devices require engineering hours to rack and stack and are not very flexible once constructed.
- **Virtual devices**: These are emulations or simulations of actual network devices. They are either provided by the vendors or by the open source community:
    - **Advantages**: Virtual devices are easier to set up, relatively cheap, and can make changes to the topology quickly.
    - **Disadvantages**: They are usually a scaled-down version of their physical counterpart. Sometimes there are feature gaps between the virtual and the physical device.

Of course, deciding on a virtual or physical lab is a personal decision derived from a trade-off between the cost, ease of implementation, and the risk of having a gap between lab and production. In some of the environments I have worked on, the virtual lab is used when doing an initial proof-of-concept while the physical lab is used when we move closer to the final design.

In my opinion, as more and more vendors decide to produce virtual appliances, the virtual lab is the way to proceed in a learning environment. The feature gap of the virtual appliance is relatively small and specifically documented, especially when the virtual instance is provided by the vendor. The cost of the virtual appliance is relatively small compared to buying physical devices. The time-to-build using virtual devices is quicker because they are usually just software programs.

For this book, I will use a combination of physical and virtual devices for concept demonstration with a preference for virtual devices. For the examples we will see, the differences should be transparent. If there are any known differences between the virtual and physical devices pertaining to our objectives, I will make sure to list them.

On the virtual lab front, besides images from various vendors, I am using a program from Cisco called **Virtual Internet Routing Lab** (**VIRL**), `https://learningnetworkstore.cisco.com/virtual-internet-routing-lab-virl/cisco-personal-edition-pe-20-nodes-virl-20`.

I want to point out that the use of this program is entirely optional for the reader. But it is strongly recommended that the reader have some lab equipment to follow along with the examples in this book.

Cisco VIRL

I remember when I first started to study for my **Cisco Certified Internetwork Expert** (**CCIE**) lab exam, I purchased some used Cisco equipment from eBay to study with. Even at a discount, each router and switch cost hundreds of US dollars, so to save money, I purchased some really outdated Cisco routers from the 1980s (search for Cisco AGS routers in your favorite search engine for a good chuckle), which significantly lacked features and horsepower, even for lab standards. As much as it made for an interesting conversation with family members when I turned them on (they were really loud), putting the physical devices together was not fun. They were heavy and clunky, it was a pain to connect all the cables, and to introduce link failure, I would literally unplug a cable.

Fast-forward a few years. **Dynamip** was created and I fell in love with how easy it was to create different network scenarios. This was especially important when I tried to learn a new concept. All you need is the IOS images from Cisco, a few carefully constructed topology files, and you can easily construct a virtual network that you can test your knowledge on. I had a whole folder of network topologies, pre-saved configurations, and different version of images, as called for by the scenario. The addition of a GNS3 frontend gives the whole setup a beautiful GUI facelift. With GNS3, you can just click and drop your links and devices; you can even just print out the network topology for your manager right out of the GNS3 design panel. The only thing that was lacking was the tool not being officially blessed by the vendor and the perceived lack of credibility because of it.

In 2015, the Cisco community decided to fulfill this need by releasing the Cisco VIRL. If you have a server that meets the requirements and you are willing to pay for the required annual license, this is my preferred method of developing and trying out much of the Python code, both for this book and my own production use.

As of January 1 2017, only the personal edition 20-Node license is available for purchase for USD $199.99 per year.

Even at a monetary cost, in my opinion, the VIRL platform offers a few advantages over other alternatives:

- **Ease of use**: All the images for IOSv, IOS-XRv, CSR100v, NX-OSv, and ASAv are included in a single download.
- **Official (kind of)**: Although support is community-driven, it is a widely used tool internally at Cisco. Because of its popularity, the bugs get fixed quickly, new features are carefully documented, and useful knowledge is widely shared among its users.
- **The cloud migration path**: The project offers a logical migration path when your emulation grows out of the hardware power you have, such as Cisco dCloud (`https://dcloud.cisco.com/`), VIRL on Packet (`http://virl.cisco.com/cloud/`), and Cisco DevNet (`https://developer.cisco.com/`). This is an important feature that sometimes gets overlooked.
- **The link and control-plane simulation**: The tool can simulate latency, jitter, and packet loss on a per-link basis for real-world link characteristics. There is also a control-plane traffic generator for external route injection.
- **Others**: The tool offers some nice features, such as VM Maestro topology design and simulation control, AutoNetkit for automatic config generation, and user workspace management if the server is shared. There are also open source projects such as virlutils (`https://github.com/CiscoDevNet/virlutils`), which are actively worked on by the community to enhance the workability of the tool.

We will not use all of the features in VIRL in this book. But since this is a relatively new tool that is worth your consideration, if you do decide this is the tool you would like to use, I want to offer some of the setups I used.

Again, I want to stress the importance of having a lab, but it does not need to be the Cisco VIRL lab. The code examples provided in this book should work across any lab device, as long as they run the same software type and version.

VIRL tips

The VIRL website (`http://virl.cisco.com/`) offers lots of guidance, preparation, and documentation. I also find that the VIRL user community generally offers quick and accurate help. I will not repeat information already offered in those two places; however, here are some of the setups I use for the lab in this book:

1. VIRL uses two virtual Ethernet interfaces for connections. The first interface is set up as NAT for the host machine's internet connection, and the second is used for local management interface connectivity (VMnet2 in the following example). I use a separate virtual machine with a similar network setup in order to run my Python code, with the first primary Ethernet used for internet connectivity and the second Ethernet connection to Vmnet2 for lab device management network:

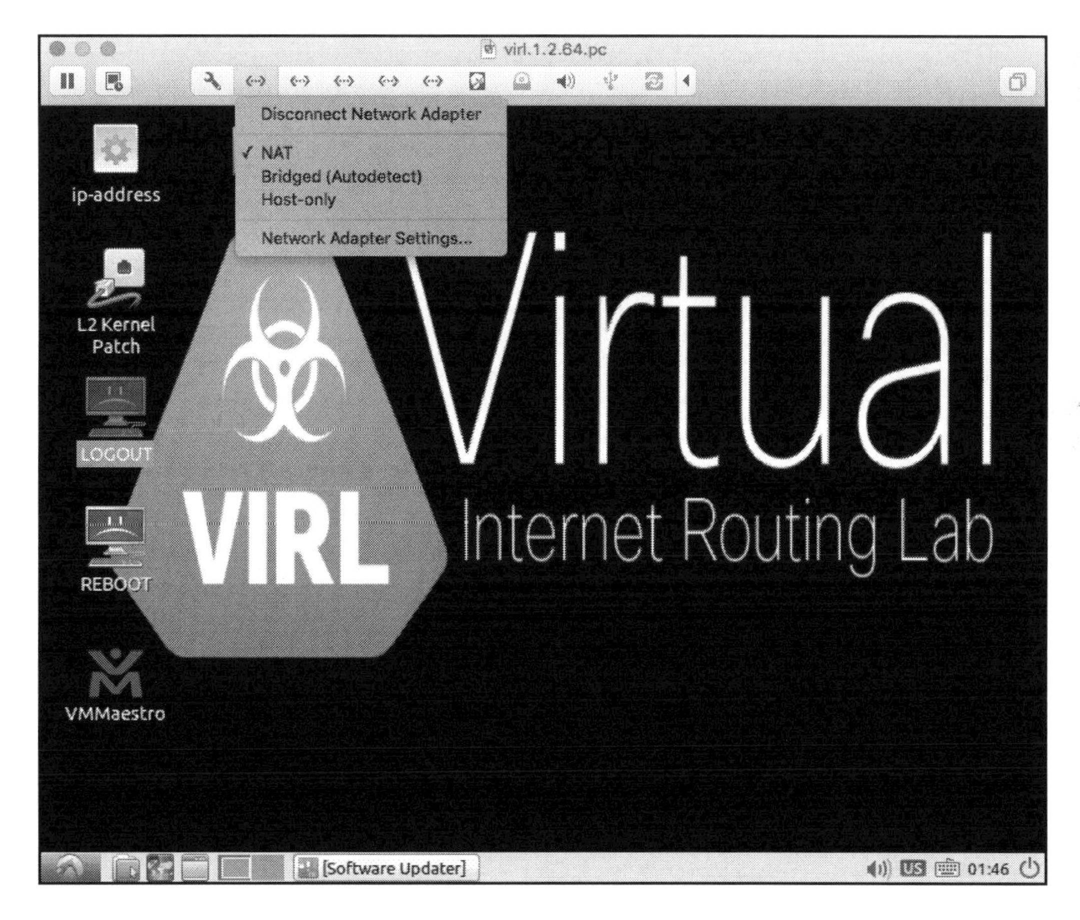

2. VMnet2 is a custom network created to connect the Ubuntu host with the VIRL virtual machine:

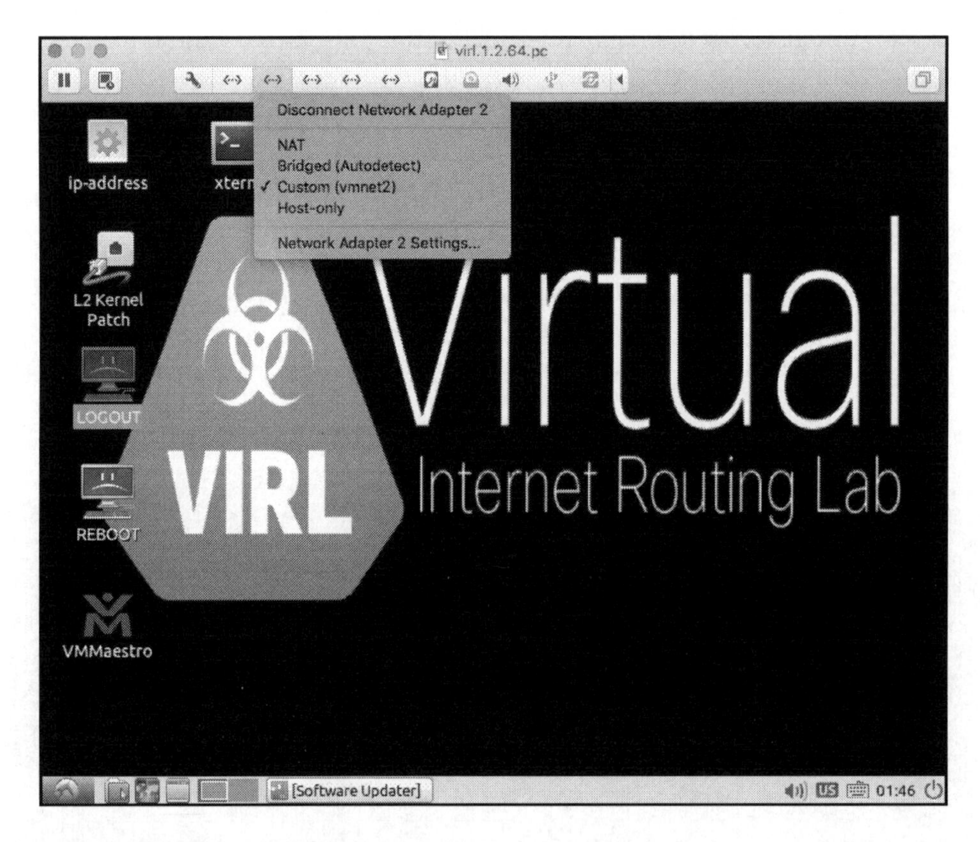

3. In the **Topology Design** option, I set the **Management Network** option to **Shared flat network** in order to use VMnet2 as the management network on the virtual routers:

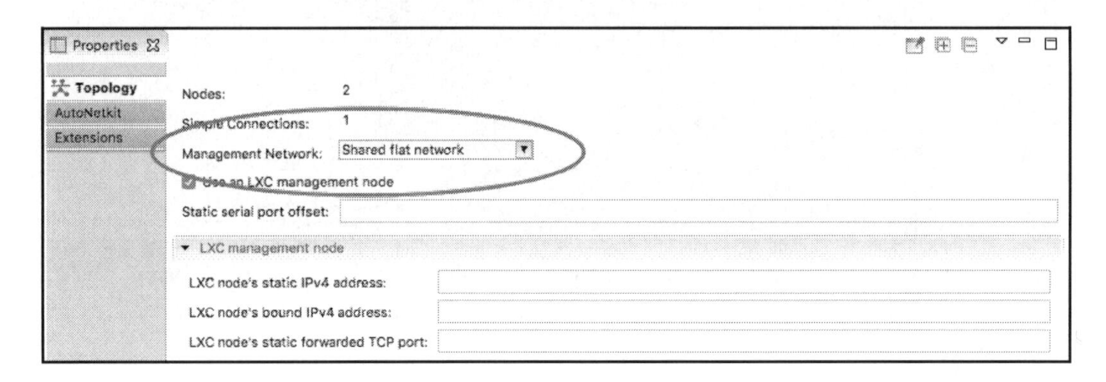

4. Under the node configuration, you have the option to statically configure the management IP. I try to statically set the management IP addresses instead of having them dynamically assigned by the software. This allows for more deterministic accessibility:

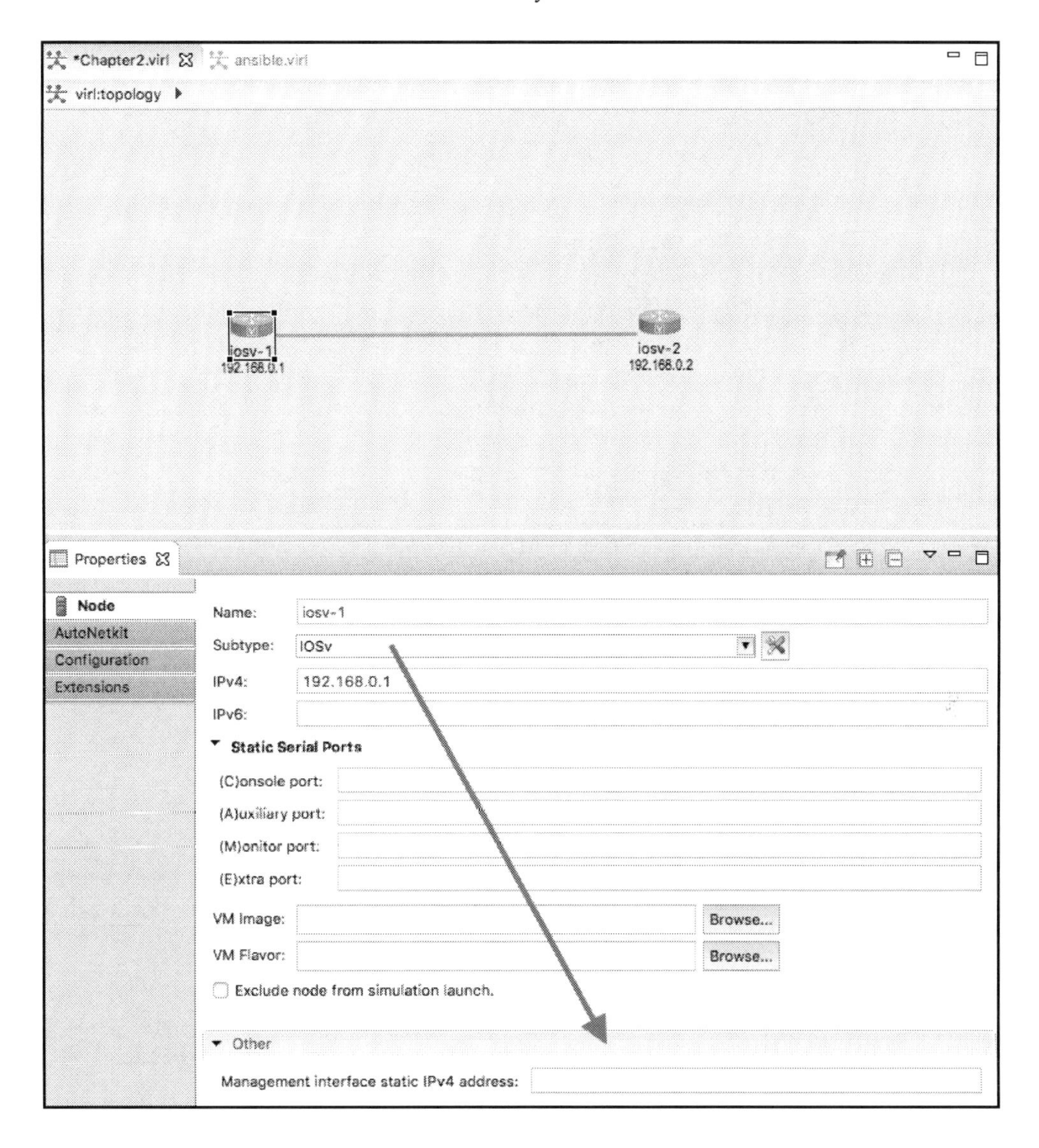

Cisco DevNet and dCloud

Cisco provides two other excellent, and, at the time of writing, free, methods for practicing network automation with various Cisco gears. Both of the tools require a **Cisco Connection Online (CCO)** login. They are both really good, especially for the price point (they are free!). It is hard for me to imagine that these online tools will remain free for long; it is my belief that, at some point, these tools will need to charge money for their usage or be rolled into a bigger initiative that requires a fee. However, we can take advantage of them while they are available at no charge.

The first tool is the Cisco DevNet (`https://developer.cisco.com/`) sandbox, which includes guided learning tracks, complete documentation, and sandbox remote labs, among other benefits. Some of the labs are always on, while others you need to reserve. The lab availability will depend on usage. It is a great alternative if you do not already have a lab at your own disposal. In my experience with DevNet, some of the documentation and links were outdated, but they can be easily retrieved for the most updated version. In a rapidly changing field such as software development, this is somewhat expected. DevNet is certainly a tool that you should take full advantage of, regardless of whether you have a locally run VIRL host or not:

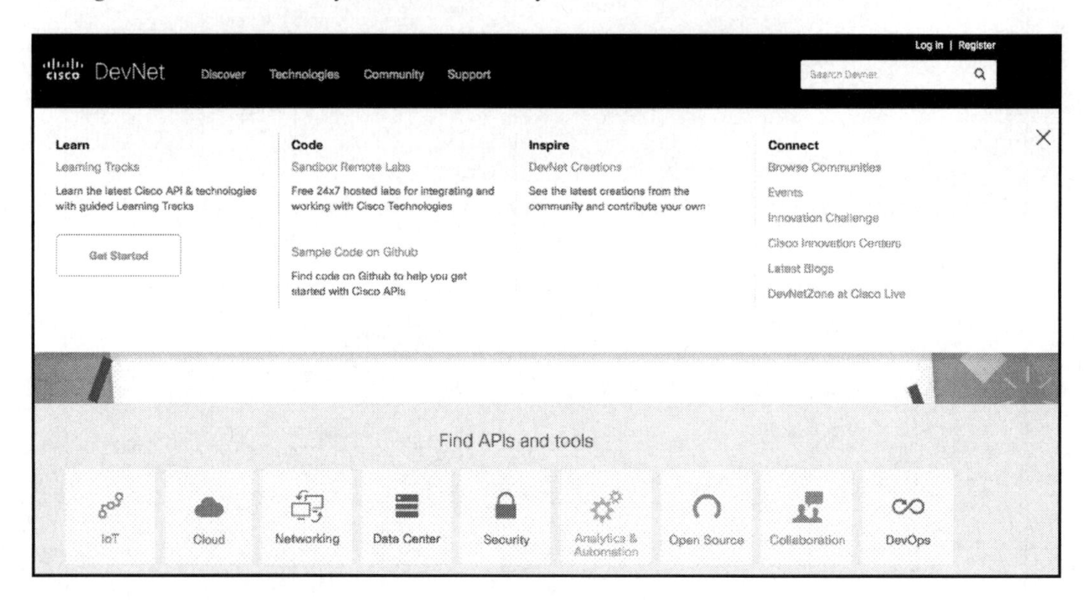

Another online lab option for Cisco is `https://dcloud.cisco.com/`. You can think of dCloud as running VIRL on other people's servers without having to manage or pay for those resources. It seems that Cisco is treating dCloud as both a standalone product as well as an extension to VIRL. For example, in the use case of when you are unable to run more than a few IOX-XR or NX-OS instances locally, you can use dCloud to extend your local lab. It is a relatively new tool, but it is definitely worth a look:

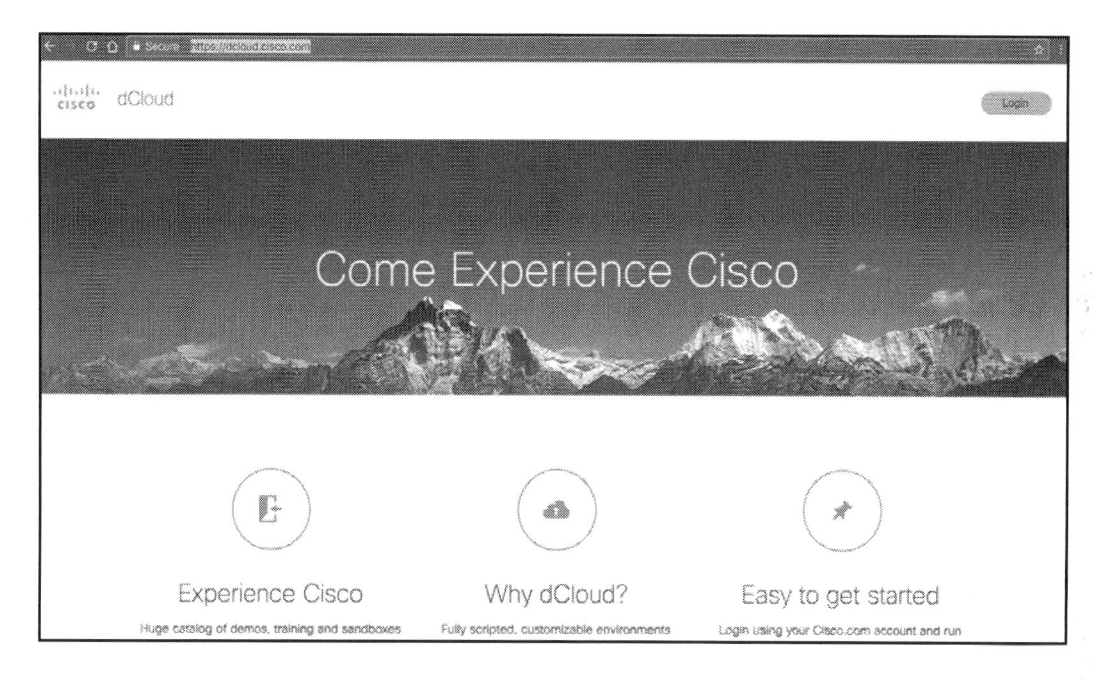

GNS3

There are a few other virtual labs that I use for this book and other purposes. The `GNS3` tool is one of them:

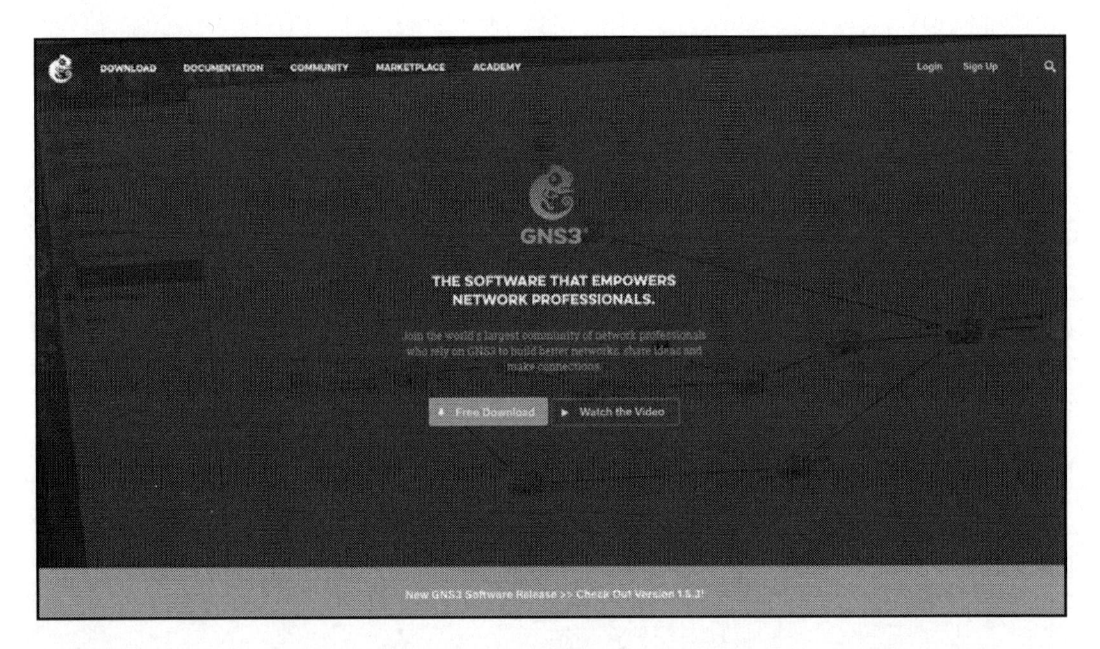

As mentioned previously in this chapter, **GNS3** is what a lot of us used to study for certification tests and to practice for labs. The tool has really grown up from the early days of the simple frontend for Dynamips into a viable commercial product. Cisco-made tools, such as VIRL, DevNet, and dCloud, only contain Cisco technologies. Even though they provide ways for virtual lab devices to communicate with the outside world, they are not as easy as just having multi-vendor virtualized appliances living directly in the simulation environment. **GNS3** is vendor-neutral and can include a multi-vendor virtualized platform directly in the lab. This is typically done either by making a clone of the image (such as Arista vEOS) or by directly launching the network device image via other hypervisors (such as Juniper Olive emulation). Some might argue that GNS3 does not have the breadth and depth of the Cisco VIRL project, but since they can run different variation Cisco technologies, I often use it when I need to incorporate other vendor technologies into the lab.

Another multi-vendor network emulation environment that has gotten a lot of great reviews is the **Emulated Virtual Environment Next Generation (EVE-NG)**, `http://www.eve-ng.net/`. I personally do not have much experience with the tool, but many of my colleagues and friends in the industry use it for their network labs.

There are also other virtualized platforms, such as Arista vEOS (`https://eos.arista.com/tag/veos/`), Juniper vMX (`http://www.juniper.net/us/en/products-services/routing/mx-series/vmx/`), and vSRX (`http://www.juniper.net/us/en/products-services/security/srx-series/vsrx/`), which you can use as a standalone virtual appliance during testing. They are great complementary tools for testing platform-specific features, such as the differences between the API versions on the platform. Many of them are offered as paid products on public cloud provider marketplaces for easier access. They are often offered the identical feature as their physical counterpart.

Python Pexpect library

> *Pexpect is a pure Python module for spawning child applications, controlling them, and responding to expected patterns in their output. Pexpect works like Don Libes' Expect. Pexpct allows your script to spawn a child application and control it as if a human were typing commands. Pexpect, Read the Docs:* `https://pexpect.readthedocs.io/en/stable/index.html`

Let's take a look at the Python Pexpect library. Similar to the original Tcl Expect module by Don Libe, Pexpect launches or spawns another process and watches over it in order to control the interaction. The Expect tool was originally developed to automate interactive processes such as FTP, Telnet, and rlogin, and was later expanded to include network automation. Unlike the original Expect, Pexpect is entirely written in Python, which does not require TCL or C extensions to be compiled. This allows us to use the familiar Python syntax and its rich standard library in our code.

Pexpect installation

Since this is the first package we will install, we will install both the `pip` tool with the `pexpect` package. The process is pretty straightforward:

```
sudo apt-get install python-pip #Python2
sudo apt-get install python3-pip
sudo pip3 install pexpect
sudo pip install pexpect #Python2
```

I am using pip3 to install Python 3 packages, while using pip to install packages in the Python 2 environment.

Do a quick to test to make sure the package is usable:

```
>>> import pexpect
>>> dir(pexpect)
['EOF', 'ExceptionPexpect', 'Expecter', 'PY3',
  'TIMEOUT', '__all__', '__builtins__', '__cached__',
  '__doc__', '__file__', '__loader__', '__name__',
  '__package__', '__path__', '__revision__',
  '__spec__', '__version__', 'exceptions', 'expect',
  'is_executable_file', 'pty_spawn', 'run', 'runu',
  'searcher_re', 'searcher_string', 'spawn',
  'spawnbase', 'spawnu', 'split_command_line', 'sys',
  'utils', 'which']
>>>
```

Pexpect overview

For our first lab, we will construct a simple network with two IOSv devices connected back to back:

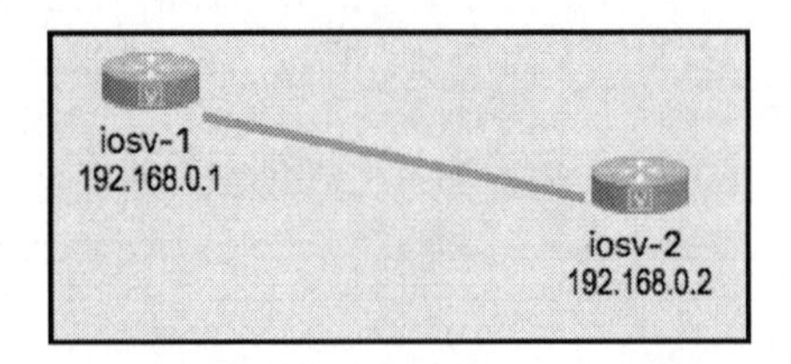

Lab topology

The devices will each have a loopback address in the 192.16.0.x/24 range and the management IP will be in the 172.16.1.x/24 range. The VIRL topology file is included in the accommodated book downloadable files. You can import the topology to your own VIRL software. If you do not have VIRL, you can also view the necessary information by opening the topology file with a text editor. The file is simply an XML file with each node's information under the node element:

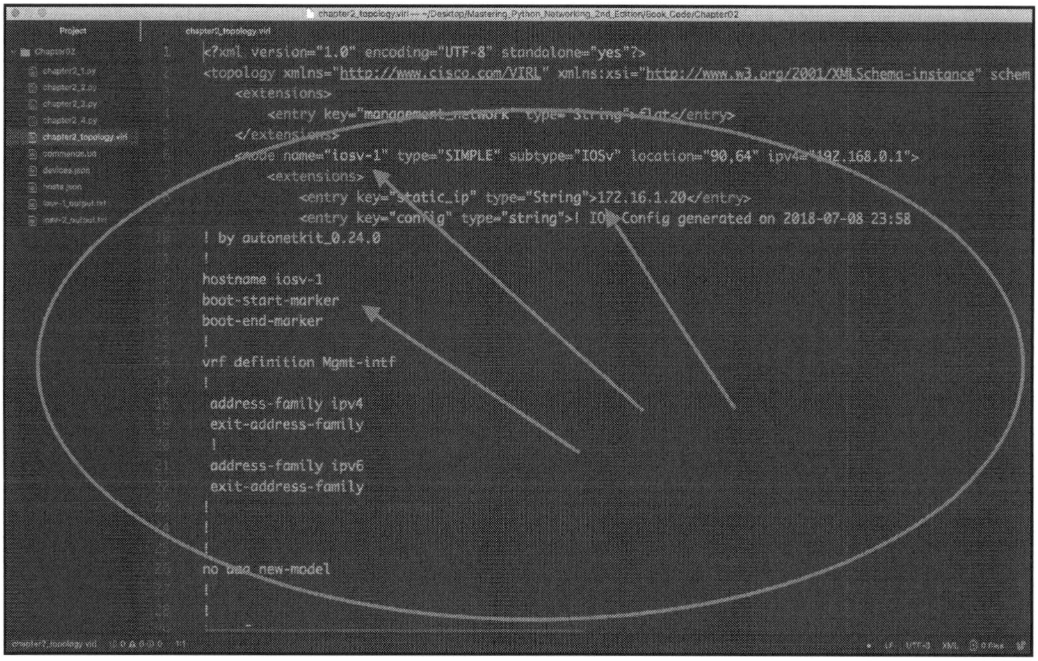

Lab node information

With the devices ready, let's take a look at how you would interact with the router if you were to Telnet into the device:

```
echou@ubuntu:~$ telnet 172.16.1.20
Trying 172.16.1.20...
Connected to 172.16.1.20.
Escape character is '^]'.
<skip>
User Access Verification

Username: cisco
Password:
```

I used VIRL AutoNetkit to automatically generate the initial configuration of the routers, which generated the default username `cisco`, and the password `cisco`. Notice that the user is already in privileged mode because of the privilege assigned in the configuration:

```
iosv-1#sh run | i cisco
enable password cisco
username cisco privilege 15 secret 5 $1$Wiwq$7xt2oE0P9ThdxFS02trFw.
 password cisco
```

```
 password cisco
iosv-1#
```

The auto-config also generated `vty` access for both Telnet and SSH:

```
line vty 0 4
 exec-timeout 720 0
 password cisco
 login local
 transport input telnet ssh
```

Let's see a Pexpect example using the Python interactive shell:

```
Python 3.5.2 (default, Nov 17 2016, 17:05:23)
[GCC 5.4.0 20160609] on linux
Type "help", "copyright", "credits" or "license" for more information.
>>> import pexpect
>>> child = pexpect.spawn('telnet 172.16.1.20')
>>> child.expect('Username')
0
>>> child.sendline('cisco')
6
>>> child.expect('Password')
0
>>> child.sendline('cisco')
6
>>> child.expect('iosv-1#')
0
>>> child.sendline('show version | i V')
19
>>> child.expect('iosv-1#')
0
>>> child.before
b'show version | i VrnCisco IOS Software, IOSv Software (VIOS-
ADVENTERPRISEK9-M), Version 15.6(2)T, RELEASE SOFTWARE
(fc2)rnProcessor board ID 9MM4BI7B0DSWK40KV1IIRrn'
>>> child.sendline('exit')
5
>>> exit()
```

Starting from Pexpect version 4.0, you can run Pexpect on a Windows platform. But, as noted in the Pexpect documentation, running Pexpect on Windows should be considered experimental for now.

In the previous interactive example, Pexpect spawns off a child process and watches over it in an interactive fashion. There are two important methods shown in the example, `expect()` and `sendline()`. The `expect()` line indicates that the string the Pexpect process looks for as an indicator for when the returned string is considered done. This is the expected pattern. In our example, we knew the router had sent us all the information when the hostname prompt (`iosv-1#`) was returned.
The `sendline()` method indicates which words should be sent to the remote device as the command. There is also a method called `send()` but `sendline()` includes a linefeed, which is similar to pressing the *Enter* key at the end of the words you sent in your previous telnet session. From the router's perspective, it is just as if someone typed in the text from a Terminal. In other words, we are tricking the routers into thinking they are interfacing with a human being when they are actually communicating with a computer.

The `before` and `after` properties will be set to the text printed by the child application. The `before` properties will be set to the text printed by the child application up to the expected pattern. The `after` string will contain the text that was matched by the expected pattern. In our case, the `before` text will be set to the output between the two expected matches (`iosv-1#`), including the `show version` command. The `after` text is the router hostname prompt:

```
>>> child.sendline('show version | i V')
19
>>> child.expect('iosv-1#')
0
>>> child.before
b'show version | i VrnCisco IOS Software, IOSv Software (VIOS-
ADVENTERPRISEK9-M), Version 15.6(2)T, RELEASE SOFTWARE
(fc2)rnProcessor board ID 9MM4BI7B0DSWK40KV1IIRrn'
>>> child.after
b'iosv-1#'
```

What would happen if you expected the wrong term? For example, if you typed in `username` instead of `Username` after spawning the child application, then the Pexpect process would look for a string of `username` from the child process. In that case, the Pexpect process would just hang because the word `username` would never be returned by the router. The session would eventually timeout, or you could manually exit out via *Ctrl* + *C*.

The `expect()` method waits for the child application to return a given string, so in the previous example, if you wanted to accommodate both lowercase and uppercase `u`, you could use the following term:

```
>>> child.expect('[Uu]sername')
```

The square bracket serves as an `or` operation that tells the child application to expect a lowercase or uppercase `u` followed by `sername` as the string. What we are telling the process is that we will accept either `Username` or `username` as the expected string.

For more information on Python regular expressions, go to https://docs.python.org/3.5/library/re.html.

The `expect()` method can also contain a list of options instead of just a single string; these options can also be regular expression themselves. Going back to the previous example, you can use the following list of options to accommodate the two different possible strings:

```
>>> child.expect(['Username', 'username'])
```

Generally speaking, use the regular expression for a single `expect` string when you can fit the different hostname in a regular expression, whereas use the possible options if you need to catch completely different responses from the router, such as a password rejection. For example, if you use several different passwords for your login, you want to catch `% Login invalid` as well as the device prompt.

One important difference between Pexpect regular expressions and Python regular expressions is that the Pexpect matching is non-greedy, which means they will match as little as possible when using special characters. Because Pexpect performs regular expression on a stream, you cannot look ahead, as the child process generating the stream may not be finished. This means the special dollar sign character `$` typically matching the end of the line is useless because `.+` will always return no characters, and the `.*` pattern will match as little as possible. In general, just keep this in mind and be as specific as you can be on the `expect` match strings.

Let's consider the following scenario:

```
>>> child.sendline('show run | i hostname')
22
>>> child.expect('iosv-1')
0
```

```
>>> child.before
b'show run | i hostnamernhostname '
>>>
```

Hmm... Something is not quite right here. Compare it to the Terminal output before; the output you expect would be `hostname iosv-1`:

```
iosv-1#show run | i hostname
hostname iosv-1
iosv-1#
```

Taking a closer look at the expected string will reveal the mistake. In this case, we were missing the hash (`#`) sign behind the `iosv-1` hostname. Therefore, the child application treated the second part of the return string as the expected string:

```
>>> child.sendline('show run | i hostname')
22
>>> child.expect('iosv-1#')
0
>>> child.before
b'show run | i hostnamernhostname iosv-1rn'
>>>
```

You can see a pattern emerging from the usage of Pexpect after a few examples. The user maps out the sequence of interactions between the Pexpect process and the child application. With some Python variables and loops, we can start to construct a useful program that will help us gather information and make changes to network devices.

Our first Pexpect program

Our first program, `chapter5_1.py`, extends what we did in the last section with some additional code:

```
    #!/usr/bin/python3

    import pexpect

    devices = {'iosv-1': {'prompt': 'iosv-1#', 'ip': '172.16.1.20'},
'iosv-2': {'prompt': 'iosv-2#', 'ip': '172.16.1.21'}}
    username = 'cisco'
    password = 'cisco'

    for device in devices.keys():
        device_prompt = devices[device]['prompt']
        child = pexpect.spawn('telnet ' + devices[device]['ip'])
```

```
child.expect('Username:')
child.sendline(username)
child.expect('Password:')
child.sendline(password)
child.expect(device_prompt)
child.sendline('show version | i V')
child.expect(device_prompt)
print(child.before)
child.sendline('exit')
```

We use a nested dictionary in line 5:

```
 devices = {'iosv-1': {'prompt': 'iosv-1#', 'ip':
'172.16.1.20'}, 'iosv-2': {'prompt': 'iosv-2#',
'ip': '172.16.1.21'}}
```

The nested dictionary allows us to refer to the same device (such as `iosv-1`) with the appropriate IP address and prompt symbol. We can then use those values for the `expect()` method later on in the loop.

The output prints out the `show version | i V` output on the screen for each of the devices:

```
$ python3 chapter5_1.py
  b'show version | i VrnCisco IOS Software, IOSv
  Software (VIOS-ADVENTERPRISEK9-M), Version 15.6(2)T,
RELEASE SOFTWARE (fc2)rnProcessor board ID
9MM4BI7B0DSWK40KV1IIRrn'
b'show version | i VrnCisco IOS Software, IOSv
Software (VIOS-ADVENTERPRISEK9-M), Version 15.6(2)T,
 RELEASE SOFTWARE (fc2)rn'
```

More Pexpect features

In this section, we will look at more Pexpect features that might come in handy when certain situations arise.

If you have a slow or fast link to your remote device, the default `expect()` method timeout is 30 seconds, which can be increased or decreased via the `timeout` argument:

```
>>> child.expect('Username', timeout=5)
```

You can choose to pass the command back to the user using the `interact()` method. This is useful when you just want to automate certain parts of the initial task:

```
>>> child.sendline('show version | i V')
19
>>> child.expect('iosv-1#')
0
>>> child.before
b'show version | i VrnCisco IOS Software, IOSv Software (VIOS-
ADVENTERPRISEK9-M), Version 15.6(2)T, RELEASE SOFTWARE
(fc2)rnProcessor board ID 9MM4BI7B0DSWK40KV1IIRrn'
>>> child.interact()
iosv-1#show run | i hostname
hostname iosv-1
iosv-1#exit
Connection closed by foreign host.
>>>
```

You can get a lot of information about the `child.spawn` object by printing it out in string format:

```
>>> str(child)
"<pexpect.pty_spawn.spawn object at 0x7fb01e29dba8>ncommand:
/usr/bin/telnetnargs: ['/usr/bin/telnet', '172.16.1.20']nsearcher:
Nonenbuffer (last 100 chars): b''nbefore (last 100 chars):
b'NTERPRISEK9-M), Version 15.6(2)T, RELEASE SOFTWARE (fc2)rnProcessor
board ID 9MM4BI7B0DSWK40KV1IIRrn'nafter: b'iosv-1#'nmatch:
<_sre.SRE_Match object; span=(164, 171),
match=b'iosv-1#'>nmatch_index: 0nexitstatus: 1nflag_eof: Falsenpid:
2807nchild_fd: 5nclosed: Falsentimeout: 30ndelimiter: <class
'pexpect.exceptions.EOF'>nlogfile: Nonenlogfile_read:
Nonenlogfile_send: Nonenmaxread: 2000nignorecase:
Falsensearchwindowsize: Nonendelaybeforesend: 0.05ndelayafterclose:
0.1ndelayafterterminate: 0.1"
>>>
```

The most useful debug tool for Pexpect is to log the output in a file:

```
>>> child = pexpect.spawn('telnet 172.16.1.20')
>>> child.logfile = open('debug', 'wb')
```

Use `child.logfile = open('debug', 'w')` for Python 2. Python 3 uses byte strings by default. For more information on Pexpect features, check out `https://pexpect.readthedocs.io/en/stable/api/index.html`.

Pexpect and SSH

If you try to use the previous Telnet example and plug it into an SSH session instead, you might find yourself pretty frustrated with the experience. You always have to include the username in the session, answering the `ssh` new key question, and much more mundane tasks. There are many ways to make SSH sessions work, but luckily, Pexpect has a subclass called `pxssh`, which specializes in setting up SSH connections. The class adds methods for login, log out, and various tricky things to handle the different situations in the `ssh` login process. The procedures are mostly the same, with the exception of `login()` and `logout()`:

```
>>> from pexpect import pxssh
>>> child = pxssh.pxssh()
>>> child.login('172.16.1.20', 'cisco', 'cisco',
auto_prompt_reset=False)
True
>>> child.sendline('show version | i V')
19
>>> child.expect('iosv-1#')
0
>>> child.before
b'show version | i VrnCisco IOS Software, IOSv Software (VIOS-
ADVENTERPRISEK9-M), Version 15.6(2)T, RELEASE SOFTWARE
(fc2)rnProcessor board ID 9MM4BI7B0DSWK40KV1IIRrn'
>>> child.logout()
>>>
```

Notice the `auto_prompt_reset=False` argument in the `login()` method. By default, `pxssh` uses the Shell prompt to synchronize the output. But since it uses the PS1 option for most of bash or CSH, they will error out on Cisco or other network devices.

Putting things together for Pexpect

As the final step, let's put everything you have learned so far about Pexpect into a script. Putting code into a script makes it easier to use in a production environment, as well as easier to share with your colleagues. We will write our second script, `chapter5_2.py`.

You can download the script from the book GitHub repository, `https://github.com/PacktPublishing/Python-Network-Programming`, as well as looking at the output generated from the script as a result of the commands.

Refer to the following code:

```
#!/usr/bin/python3

import getpass
from pexpect import pxssh

devices = {'iosv-1': {'prompt': 'iosv-1#', 'ip': '172.16.1.20'},
'iosv-2': {'prompt': 'iosv-2#', 'ip': '172.16.1.21'}}
commands = ['term length 0', 'show version', 'show run']

username = input('Username: ')
password = getpass.getpass('Password: ')

# Starts the loop for devices
for device in devices.keys():
    outputFileName = device + '_output.txt'
    device_prompt = devices[device]['prompt']
    child = pxssh.pxssh()
    child.login(devices[device]['ip'], username.strip(),
password.strip(), auto_promp t_reset=False)
    # Starts the loop for commands and write to output
    with open(outputFileName, 'wb') as f:
        for command in commands:
            child.sendline(command)
            child.expect(device_prompt)
            f.write(child.before)

    child.logout()
```

The script further expands from our first Pexpect program with the following additional features:

- It uses SSH instead of Telnet
- It supports multiple commands instead of just one by making the commands into a list (line 8) and loops through the commands (starting at line 20)

- It prompts the user for their username and password instead of hardcoding them in the script
- It writes the output in two files, `iosv-1_output.txt`, and `ios-2_output.txt`, to be further analyzed

For Python 2, use `raw_input()` instead of `input()` for the username prompt. Also, use `w` for the file mode instead of `wb`.

The Python Paramiko library

Paramiko is a Python implementation of the SSHv2 protocol. Just like the `pxssh` subclass of Pexpect, Paramiko simplifies the SSHv2 interaction between the host and the remote device. Unlike `pxssh`, Paramiko focuses only on SSHv2 with no Telnet support. It also provides both client and server operations.

Paramiko is the low-level SSH client behind the high-level automation framework Ansible for its network modules. We will cover Ansible in later chapters. Let's take a look at the Paramiko library.

Installation of Paramiko

Installing Paramiko is pretty straightforward with Python `pip`. However, there is a hard dependency on the cryptography library. The library provides low-level, C-based encryption algorithms for the SSH protocol.

The installation instruction for Windows, Mac, and other flavors of Linux can be found at `https://cryptography.io/en/latest/installation/`.

We will show the Paramiko installation of our Ubuntu 16.04 virtual machine in the following output. The following output shows the installation steps, as well as Paramiko successfully imported into the Python interactive prompt.

If you are using Python 2, please follow the steps below. We will try to import the library in the interactive prompt to make sure the library can be used:

```
sudo apt-get install build-essential libssl-dev libffi-dev python-dev
sudo pip install cryptography
sudo pip install paramiko
$ python
Python 2.7.12 (default, Nov 19 2016, 06:48:10)
[GCC 5.4.0 20160609] on linux2
Type "help", "copyright", "credits" or "license" for more information.
>>> import paramiko
>>> exit()
```

If you are using Python 3, please refer the following command-lines for installing the dependencies. After installation, we will import the library to make sure it is correctly installed:

```
sudo apt-get install build-essential libssl-dev libffi-dev python3-dev
sudo pip3 install cryptography
sudo pip3 install paramiko
$ python3
Python 3.5.2 (default, Nov 17 2016, 17:05:23)
[GCC 5.4.0 20160609] on linux
Type "help", "copyright", "credits" or "license" for more information.
>>> import paramiko
>>>
```

Paramiko overview

Let's look at a quick Paramiko example using the Python 3 interactive shell:

```
>>> import paramiko, time
>>> connection = paramiko.SSHClient()
>>> connection.set_missing_host_key_policy(paramiko.AutoAddPolicy())
>>> connection.connect('172.16.1.20', username='cisco',
password='cisco', look_for_keys=False, allow_agent=False)
>>> new_connection = connection.invoke_shell()
>>> output = new_connection.recv(5000)
>>> print(output)
b"rn*************************************************************
********rn* IOSv is strictly limited to use for evaluation,
demonstration and IOS *rn* education. IOSv is provided as-is and is
```

```
not supported by Cisco's *rn* Technical Advisory Center. Any use or
disclosure, in whole or in part, *rn* of the IOSv Software or
Documentation to any third party for any *rn* purposes is expressly
prohibited except as otherwise authorized by *rn* Cisco in writing.
*rn*****************************************************************
*******rniosv-1#"
>>> new_connection.send("show version | i Vn")
19
>>> time.sleep(3)
>>> output = new_connection.recv(5000)
>>> print(output)
b'show version | i VrnCisco IOS Software, IOSv Software (VIOS-
ADVENTERPRISEK9-M), Version 15.6(2)T, RELEASE SOFTWARE
(fc2)rnProcessor board ID 9MM4BI7B0DSWK40KV1IIRrniosv-1#'
>>> new_connection.close()
>>>
```

The `time.sleep()` function inserts a time delay to ensure that all the outputs were captured. This is particularly useful on a slower network connection or a busy device. This command is not required but is recommended depending on your situation.

Even if you are seeing the Paramiko operation for the first time, the beauty of Python and its clear syntax means that you can make a pretty good educated guess at what the program is trying to do:

```
>>> import paramiko
>>> connection = paramiko.SSHClient()
>>> connection.set_missing_host_key_policy(paramiko.AutoAddPolicy())
>>> connection.connect('172.16.1.20', username='cisco',
password='cisco', look_for_keys=False, allow_agent=False)
```

The first four lines create an instance of the `SSHClient` class from Paramiko. The next line sets the policy that the client should use when the SSH server's hostname; in this case, `iosv-1`, is not present in either the system host keys or the application's keys. In our scenario, we will automatically add the key to the application's `HostKeys` object. At this point, if you log on to the router, you will see the additional login session from Paramiko:

```
iosv-1#who
 Line User Host(s) Idle Location
*578 vty 0 cisco idle 00:00:00 172.16.1.1
 579 vty 1 cisco idle 00:01:30 172.16.1.173
Interface User Mode Idle Peer Address
iosv-1#
```

The next few lines invoke a new interactive shell from the connection and a repeatable pattern of sending a command and retrieving the output. Finally, we close the connection.

Some readers who have used Paramiko before might be familiar with the `exec_command()` method instead of invoking a shell. Why do we need to invoke an interactive shell instead of using `exec_command()` directly? Unfortunately, `exec_command()` on Cisco IOS only allows a single command. Consider the following example with `exec_command()` for the connection:

```
>>> connection.connect('172.16.1.20', username='cisco',
password='cisco', look_for_keys=False, allow_agent=False)
>>> stdin, stdout, stderr = connection.exec_command('show version | i
V')
>>> stdout.read()
b'Cisco IOS Software, IOSv Software (VIOS-ADVENTERPRISEK9-M), Version
15.6(2)T, RELEASE SOFTWARE (fc2)rnProcessor board ID
9MM4BI7B0DSWK40KV1IIRrn'
>>>
```

Everything works great; however, if you look at the number of sessions on the Cisco device, you will notice that the connection is dropped by the Cisco device without you closing the connection:

```
iosv-1#who
 Line User Host(s) Idle Location
*578 vty 0 cisco idle 00:00:00 172.16.1.1
Interface User Mode Idle Peer Address
iosv-1#
```

Because the SSH session is no longer active, `exec_command()` will return an error if you want to send more commands to the remote device:

```
>>> stdin, stdout, stderr = connection.exec_command('show version | i
V')
Traceback (most recent call last):
 File "<stdin>", line 1, in <module>
 File "/usr/local/lib/python3.5/dist-packages/paramiko/client.py",
line 435, in exec_command
 chan = self._transport.open_session(timeout=timeout)
 File "/usr/local/lib/python3.5/dist-packages/paramiko/transport.py",
line 711, in open_session
 timeout=timeout)
```

```
 File "/usr/local/lib/python3.5/dist-packages/paramiko/transport.py",
line 795, in open_channel
 raise SSHException('SSH session not active')
paramiko.ssh_exception.SSHException: SSH session not active
>>>
```

The Netmiko library by Kirk Byers is an open source Python library that simplifies SSH management to network devices. To read about it, check out this article, `https://pynet.twb-tech.com/blog/automation/netmiko.html`, and the source code, `https://github.com/ktbyers/netmiko`.

What would happen if you did not clear out the received buffer? The output would just keep on filling up the buffer and would overwrite it:

```
>>> new_connection.send("show version | i Vn")
19
>>> new_connection.send("show version | i Vn")
19
>>> new_connection.send("show version | i Vn")
19
>>> new_connection.recv(5000)
b'show version | i VrnCisco IOS Software, IOSv Software (VIOS-
ADVENTERPRISEK9-M), Version 15.6(2)T, RELEASE SOFTWARE
(fc2)rnProcessor board ID 9MM4BI7B0DSWK40KV1IIRrniosv-1#show version |
i VrnCisco IOS Software, IOSv Software (VIOS-ADVENTERPRISEK9-M),
Version 15.6(2)T, RELEASE SOFTWARE (fc2)rnProcessor board ID
9MM4BI7B0DSWK40KV1IIRrniosv-1#show version | i VrnCisco IOS Software,
IOSv Software (VIOS-ADVENTERPRISEK9-M), Version 15.6(2)T, RELEASE
SOFTWARE (fc2)rnProcessor board ID 9MM4BI7B0DSWK40KV1IIRrniosv-1#'
>>>
```

For consistency of the deterministic output, we will retrieve the output from the buffer each time we execute a command.

Our first Paramiko program

Our first program will use the same general structure as the Pexpect program we have put together. We will loop over a list of devices and commands while using Paramiko instead of Pexpect. This will give us a good compare and contrast of the differences between Paramiko and Pexpect.

If you have not done so already, you can download the code, `chapter5_3.py`, from the book's GitHub repository, `https://github.com/PacktPublishing/Python-Network-Programming`. I will list the notable differences here:

```
devices = {'iosv-1': {'ip': '172.16.1.20'}, 'iosv-2': {'ip':
'172.16.1.21'}}
```

We no longer need to match the device prompt using Paramiko; therefore, the device dictionary can be simplified:

```
commands = ['show version', 'show run']
```

There is no sendline equivalent in Paramiko; instead, we manually include the newline break in each of the commands:

```
def clear_buffer(connection):
    if connection.recv_ready():
        return connection.recv(max_buffer)
```

We include a new method to clear the buffer for sending commands, such as `terminal length 0` or `enable`, because we do not need the output for those commands. We simply want to clear the buffer and get to the execution prompt. This function will later be used in the loop, such as in line 25 of the script:

```
output = clear_buffer(new_connection)
```

The rest of the program should be pretty self-explanatory, similar to what we have seen in this chapter. The last thing I would like to point out is that since this is an interactive program, we place some buffer and wait for the command to be finished on the remote device before retrieving the output:

```
time.sleep(2)
```

After we clear the buffer, during the time between the execution of commands, we will wait two seconds. This will give the device adequate time to respond if it is busy.

More Paramiko features

We will look at Paramiko a bit later in the book, when we discuss Ansible, as Paramiko is the underlying transport for many of the network modules. In this section, we will take a look at some of the other features of Paramiko.

Paramiko for servers

Paramiko can be used to manage servers through SSHv2 as well. Let's look at an example of how we can use Paramiko to manage servers. We will use key-based authentication for the SSHv2 session.

In this example, I used another Ubuntu virtual machine on the same hypervisor as the destination server. You can also use a server on the VIRL simulator or an instance in one of the public cloud providers, such as Amazon AWS EC2.

We will generate a public-private key pair for our Paramiko host:

```
ssh-keygen -t rsa
```

This command, by default, will generate a public key named `id_rsa.pub`, as the public key under the user home directory `~/.ssh` along with a private key named `id_rsa`. Treat the private key with the same attention as you would private passwords that you do not want to share with anybody else. You can think of the public key as a business card that identifies who you are. Using the private and public keys, the message will be encrypted by your private key locally and decrypted by the remote host using the public key. We should copy the public key to the remote host. In production, we can do this via out-of-band using a USB drive; in our lab, we can simply copy the public key to the remote host's `~/.ssh/authorized_keys` file. Open up a Terminal window for the remote server, so you can paste in the public key.

Copy the content of `~/.ssh/id_rsa` on your management host with Paramiko:

```
<Management Host with Pramiko>$ cat ~/.ssh/id_rsa.pub
ssh-rsa <your public key> echou@pythonicNeteng
```

Then, paste it to the remote host under the `user` directory; in this case, I am using `echou` for both sides:

```
<Remote Host>$ vim ~/.ssh/authorized_keys
ssh-rsa <your public key> echou@pythonicNeteng
```

You are now ready to use Paramiko to manage the remote host. Notice in this example that we will use the private key for authentication as well as the `exec_command()` method for sending commands:

```
Python 3.5.2 (default, Nov 17 2016, 17:05:23)
[GCC 5.4.0 20160609] on linux
Type "help", "copyright", "credits" or "license" for more information.
>>> import paramiko
```

```
>>> key =
paramiko.RSAKey.from_private_key_file('/home/echou/.ssh/id_rsa')
>>> client = paramiko.SSHClient()
>>> client.set_missing_host_key_policy(paramiko.AutoAddPolicy())
>>> client.connect('192.168.199.182', username='echou', pkey=key)
>>> stdin, stdout, stderr = client.exec_command('ls -l')
>>> stdout.read()
b'total 44ndrwxr-xr-x 2 echou echou 4096 Jan 7 10:14 Desktopndrwxr-xr-
x 2 echou echou 4096 Jan 7 10:14 Documentsndrwxr-xr-x 2 echou echou
4096 Jan 7 10:14 Downloadsn-rw-r--r-- 1 echou echou 8980 Jan 7 10:03
examples.desktopndrwxr-xr-x 2 echou echou 4096 Jan 7 10:14
Musicndrwxr-xr-x 2 echou echou 4096 Jan 7 10:14 Picturesndrwxr-xr-x 2
echou echou 4096 Jan 7 10:14 Publicndrwxr-xr-x 2 echou echou 4096 Jan
7 10:14 Templatesndrwxr-xr-x 2 echou echou 4096 Jan 7 10:14 Videosn'
>>> stdin, stdout, stderr = client.exec_command('pwd')
>>> stdout.read()
b'/home/echoun'
>>> client.close()
>>>
```

Notice that in the server example, we do not need to create an interactive session to execute multiple commands. You can now turn off password-based authentication in your remote host's SSHv2 configuration for more secure key-based authentication with automation enabled. Some network devices, such as Cumulus and Vyatta switches, also support key-based authentication.

Putting things together for Paramiko

We are almost at the end of the chapter. In this last section, let's make the Paramiko program more reusable. There is one downside of our existing script: we need to open up the script every time we want to add or delete a host, or whenever we need to change the commands we want to execute on the remote host. This is due to the fact that both the host and command information are statically entered inside of the script. Hardcoding the host and command has a higher chance of making mistakes. Besides, if you were to pass on the script to colleagues, they might not feel comfortable working in Python, Paramiko, or Linux.

By making both the host and command files be read in as parameters for the script, we can eliminate some of these concerns. Users (and a future you) can simply modify these text files when you need to make host or command changes.

We have incorporated the change in the script named `chapter5_4.py`.

Instead of hardcoding the commands, we broke the commands into a separate `commands.txt` file. Up to this point, we have been using show commands; in this example, we will make configuration changes. In particular, we will change the logging buffer size to `30000` bytes:

```
$ cat commands.txt
config t
logging buffered 30000
end
copy run start
```

The device's information is written into a `devices.json` file. We choose JSON format for the device's information because JSON data types can be easily translated into Python dictionary data types:

```
$ cat devices.json
{
     "iosv-1": {"ip": "172.16.1.20"},
     "iosv-2": {"ip": "172.16.1.21"}
}
```

In the script, we made the following changes:

```
with open('devices.json', 'r') as f:
    devices = json.load(f)

with open('commands.txt', 'r') as f:
    commands = [line for line in f.readlines()]
```

Here is an abbreviated output from the script execution:

```
$ python3 chapter5_4.py
Username: cisco
Password:
b'terminal length 0rniosv-2#config trnEnter configuration commands,
one per line. End with CNTL/Z.rniosv-2(config)#'
b'logging buffered 30000rniosv-2(config)#'
...
```

Do a quick check to make sure the change has taken place in both `running-config` and `startup-config`:

```
iosv-1#sh run | i logging
logging buffered 30000
iosv-1#sh start | i logging
```

```
logging buffered 30000
iosv-2#sh run | i logging
logging buffered 30000
iosv-2#sh start | i logging
logging buffered 30000
```

Looking ahead

We have taken a pretty huge leap forward in this chapter as far as automating our network using Python is concerned. However, the method we have used feels like somewhat of a workaround for automation. We attempted to trick the remote devices into thinking they were interacting with a human on the other end.

Downsides of Pexpect and Paramiko compared to other tools

The biggest downside of our method so far is that the remote devices do not return structured data. They return data that is ideal to be fitted on a terminal to be interpreted by a human, not by a computer program. The human eye can easily interpret a space, while a computer only sees a return character.

We will take a look at a better way in the upcoming chapter. As a prelude to `Chapter 6`, *APIs and Intent-Driven Networking*, let's discuss the idea of idempotency.

Idempotent network device interaction

The term **idempotency** has different meanings, depending on its context. But in this book's context, the term means that when a client makes the same call to a remote device, the result should always be the same. I believe we can all agree that this is necessary. Imagine a scenario where each time you execute the same script, you get a different result back. I find that scenario very scary. How can you trust your script if that is the case? It would render our automation effort useless because we need to be prepared to handle different returns.

Since Pexpect and Paramiko are blasting out a series of commands interactively, the chance of having a non-idempotent interaction is higher. Going back to the fact that the return results needed to be screen scraped for useful elements, the risk of difference is much higher. Something on the remote end might have changed between the time we wrote the script and the time when the script is executed for the 100th time. For example, if the vendor makes a screen output change between releases without us updating the script, the script might break.

If we need to rely on the script for production, we need the script to be idempotent as much as possible.

Bad automation speeds bad things up

Bad automation allows you to poke yourself in the eye a lot faster, it is as simple as that. Computers are much faster at executing tasks than us human engineers. If we had the same set of operating procedures executed by a human versus a script, the script would finish faster than humans, sometimes without the benefit of having a solid feedback loop between procedures. The internet is full of horror stories of when someone pressed the *Enter* key and immediately regretted it.

We need to make sure the chances of bad automation scripts screwing things up are as small as possible. We all make mistakes; carefully test your script before any production work and small blast radius are two keys to making sure you can catch your mistake before it comes back and bites you.

Summary

In this chapter, we covered low-level ways to communicate directly with network devices. Without a way to programmatically communicate and make changes to network devices, there is no automation. We looked at two libraries in Python that allow us to manage devices that were meant to be managed by the CLI. Although useful, it is easy to see how the process can be somewhat fragile. This is mostly due to the fact that the network gears in question were meant to be managed by human beings and not computers.

In `Chapter 6`, *APIs and Intent-Driven Networking*, we will look at network devices supporting API and intent-driven networking.

6
APIs and Intent-Driven Networking

In `Chapter 5`, *Low-Level Network Device Interactions*, we looked at ways to interact with the network devices using Pexpect and Paramiko. Both of these tools use a persistent session that simulates a user typing in commands as if they are sitting in front of a Terminal. This works fine up to a point. It is easy enough to send commands over for execution on the device and capture the output. However, when the output becomes more than a few lines of characters, it becomes difficult for a computer program to interpret the output. The returned output from Pexpect and Paramiko is a series of characters meant to be read by a human being. The structure of the output consists of lines and spaces that are human-friendly but difficult to be understood by computer programs.

In order for our computer programs to automate many of the tasks we want to perform, we need to interpret the returned results and make follow-up actions based on the returned results. When we cannot accurately and predictably interpret the returned results, we cannot execute the next command with confidence.

Luckily, this problem was solved by the internet community. Imagine the difference between a computer and a human being when they are both reading a web page. The human sees words, pictures, and spaces interpreted by the browser; the computer sees raw HTML code, Unicode characters, and binary files. What happens when a website needs to become a web service for another computer? The same web resources need to accommodate both human clients and other computer programs. Doesn't this problem sound familiar to the one that we presented before? The answer is the **Application Program Interface** (**API**). It is important to note that an API is a concept and not a particular technology or framework, according to Wikipedia.

> *In computer programming, an* ***Application Programming Interface*** *(**API**) is a set of subroutine definitions, protocols, and tools for building application software. In general terms, it's a set of clearly defined methods of communication between various software components. A good API makes it easier to develop a computer program by providing all the building blocks, which are then put together by the programmer.*

In our use case, the set of clearly defined methods of communication would be between our Python program and the destination device. The APIs from our network devices provide a separate interface for the computer programs. The exact API implementation is vendor specific. One vendor will prefer XML over JSON, some might provide HTTPS as the underlying transport protocol, and others might provide Python libraries as wrappers. Despite the differences, the idea of an API remains the same: it is a separate communication method optimized for other computer programs.

In this chapter, we will look at the following topics:

- Treating infrastructure as code, intent-driven networking, and data modeling
- Cisco NX-API and the application-centric infrastructure
- Juniper NETCONF and PyEZ
- Arista eAPI and PyEAPI

Infrastructure as code

In a perfect world, network engineers and architects who design and manage networks should focus on what they want the network to achieve instead of the device-level interactions. In my first job as an intern for a local ISP, wide-eyed and excited, my first assignment was to install a router on a customer's site to turn up their fractional frame relay link (remember those?). How would I do that? I asked. I was handed a standard operating procedure for turning up frame relay links. I went to the customer site, blindly typed in the commands, and looked at the green lights flashing, then happily packed my bag and patted myself on the back for a job well done. As exciting as that first assignment was, I did not fully understand what I was doing. I was simply following instructions without thinking about the implication of the commands I was typing in. How would I troubleshoot something if the light was red instead of green? I think I would have called back to the office and cried for help (tears optional).

Of course, network engineering is not about typing in commands into a device, but it is about building a way that allows services to be delivered from one point to another with as little friction as possible. The commands we have to use and the output that we have to interpret are merely means to an end. In other words, we should be focused on our intent for the network. What we want our network to achieve is much more important than the command syntax we use to get the device to do what we want it to do. If we further extract that idea of describing our intent as lines of code, we can potentially describe our whole infrastructure as a particular state. The infrastructure will be described in lines of code with the necessary software or framework enforcing that state.

Intent-Driven Networking

Since the publication of the first edition of this book, the term **Intent-Based Networking** has seen an uptick in use after major network vendors chose to use it to describe their next-generation devices. In my opinion, **Intent-Driven Networking** is the idea of defining a state that the network should be in and having software code to enforce that state. As an example, if my goal is to block port 80 from being externally accessible, that is how I should declare it as the intention of the network. The underlying software will be responsible for knowing the syntax of configuring and applying the necessary access-list on the border router to achieve that goal. Of course, Intent-Driven Networking is an idea with no clear answer on the exact implementation. But the idea is simple and clear, I would hereby argue that we should focus as much on the intent of the network and abstract ourselves from the device-level interaction.

In using an API, it is my opinion that it gets us closer to a state of intent-driven networking. In short, because we abstract the layer of a specific command executed on our destination device, we focus on our intent instead of the specific commands. For example, going back to our `block port 80` access-list example, we might use access-list and access-group on a Cisco and filter-list on a Juniper. However, in using an API, our program can start asking the executor for their intent while masking what kind of physical device it is they are talking to. We can even use a higher-level declarative framework, such as Ansible, which we will cover in `Chapter 7`, *The Python Automation Framework – Ansible Basics*. But for now, let's focus on network APIs.

Screen scraping versus API structured output

Imagine a common scenario where we need to log into the network device and make sure all the interfaces on the devices are in an up/up state (both the status and the protocol are showing as `up`). For the human network engineers getting into a Cisco NX-OS device, it is simple enough to issue the `show IP interface brief` command in the Terminal to easily tell from the output which interface is up:

```
nx-osv-2# show ip int brief
IP Interface Status for VRF "default"(1)
Interface IP Address Interface Status
Lo0 192.168.0.2 protocol-up/link-up/admin-up
Eth2/1 10.0.0.6 protocol-up/link-up/admin-up
nx-osv-2#
```

The line break, white spaces, and the first line of the column title are easily distinguished from the human eye. In fact, they are there to help us line up, say, the IP addresses of each interface from line one to line two and three. If we were to put ourselves in the computer's position, all these spaces and line breaks only takes us away from the really important output, which is: which interfaces are in the up/up state? To illustrate this point, we can look at the Paramiko output for the same operation:

```
>>> new_connection.send('sh ip int briefn')
16
>>> output = new_connection.recv(5000)
>>> print(output)
b'sh ip int briefrrnIP Interface Status for VRF
"default"(1)rnInterface IP Address Interface
StatusrnLo0 192.168.0.2 protocol-up/link-up/admin-up
rnEth2/1 10.0.0.6 protocol-up/link-up/admin-up rnrnx-
osv-2# '
>>>
```

If we were to parse out that data, here is what I would do in a pseudo-code fashion (simplified representation of the code I would write):

1. Split each line via the line break.
2. I may or may not need the first line that contains the executed command of `show ip interface brief`. For now, I don't think I need it.
3. Take out everything on the second line up until the VRF, and save it in a variable as we want to know which VRF the output is showing.
4. For the rest of the lines, because we do not know how many interfaces there are, we will use a regular expression statement to search if the line starts with possible interfaces, such as `lo` for loopback and `Eth` for Ethernet interfaces.
5. We will need to split this line into three sections via space, each consisting of the name of the interface, IP address, and then the interface status.
6. The interface status will then be split further using the forward slash (/) to give us the protocol, link, and the admin status.

Whew, that is a lot of work just for something that a human being can tell at a glance! You might be able to optimize the code and the number of lines, but in general this is what we need to do when we need to screen scrap something that is somewhat unstructured. There are many downsides to this method, but some of the bigger problems that I can see are listed as follows:

- **Scalability**: We spent so much time on painstaking details to parse out the outputs from each command. It is hard to imagine how we can do this for the hundreds of commands that we typically run.
- **Predictability**: There is really no guarantee that the output stays the same between different software versions. If the output is changed ever so slightly, it might just render our hard-earned battle of information gathering useless.
- **Vendor and software lock-in**: Perhaps the biggest problem is that once we spend all this time parsing the output for this particular vendor and software version, in this case, Cisco NX-OS, we need to repeat this process for the next vendor that we pick. I don't know about you, but if I were to evaluate a new vendor, the new vendor is at a severe on-boarding disadvantage if I have to rewrite all the screen scrap code again.

Let's compare that with an output from an NX-API call for the same `show IP interface brief` command. We will go over the specifics of getting this output from the device later in this chapter, but what is important here is to compare the following output to the previous screen scraping output:

```
{
 "ins_api":{
 "outputs":{
 "output":{
 "body":{
 "TABLE_intf":[
   {
   "ROW_intf":{
   "admin-state":"up",
   "intf-name":"Lo0",
   "iod":84,
   "ip-disabled":"FALSE",
   "link-state":"up",
   "prefix":"192.168.0.2",
   "proto-state":"up"
   }
   },
 {
 "ROW_intf":{
 "admin-state":"up",
 "intf-name":"Eth2/1",
 "iod":36,
 "ip-disabled":"FALSE",
 "link-state":"up",
 "prefix":"10.0.0.6",
 "proto-state":"up"
 }
 }
 ],
  "TABLE_vrf":[
  {
 "ROW_vrf":{
 "vrf-name-out":"default"
 }
 },
 {
 "ROW_vrf":{
 "vrf-name-out":"default"
 }
 }
 ]
 },
```

```
    "code":"200",
    "input":"show ip int brief",
    "msg":"Success"
    }
    },
    "sid":"eoc",
    "type":"cli_show",
    "version":"1.2"
    }
   }
```

NX-API can return output in XML or JSON, and this is the JSON output that we are looking at. Right away, you can see the output is structured and can be mapped directly to the Python dictionary data structure. There is no parsing required—you can simply pick the key and retrieve the value associated with the key. You can also see from the output that there are various metadata in the output, such as the success or failure of the command. If the command fails, there will be a message telling the sender the reason for the failure. You no longer need to keep track of the command issued, because it is already returned to you in the `input` field. There is also other useful metadata in the output, such as the NX-API version.

This type of exchange makes life easier for both vendors and operators. On the vendor side, they can easily transfer configuration and state information. They can add extra fields when the need to expose additional data arises using the same data structure. On the operator side, they can easily ingest the information and build their infrastructure around it. It is generally agreed on that automation is much needed and a good thing. The questions are usually centered on the format and structure of the automation. As you will see later in this chapter, there are many competing technologies under the umbrella of API. On the transport side alone, we have REST API, NETCONF, and RESTCONF, among others. Ultimately, the overall market might decide about the final data format in the future. In the meantime, each of us can form our own opinions and help drive the industry forward.

Data modeling for infrastructure as code

According to Wikipedia (`https://en.wikipedia.org/wiki/Data_model`), the definition for a data model is as follows:

> *A data model is an abstract model that organizes elements of data and standardizes how they relate to one another and to properties of the real-world entities. For instance, a data model may specify that the data element representing a car be composed of a number of other elements which, in turn, represent the color and size of the car and define its owner.*

The data modeling process can be illustrated in the following diagram:

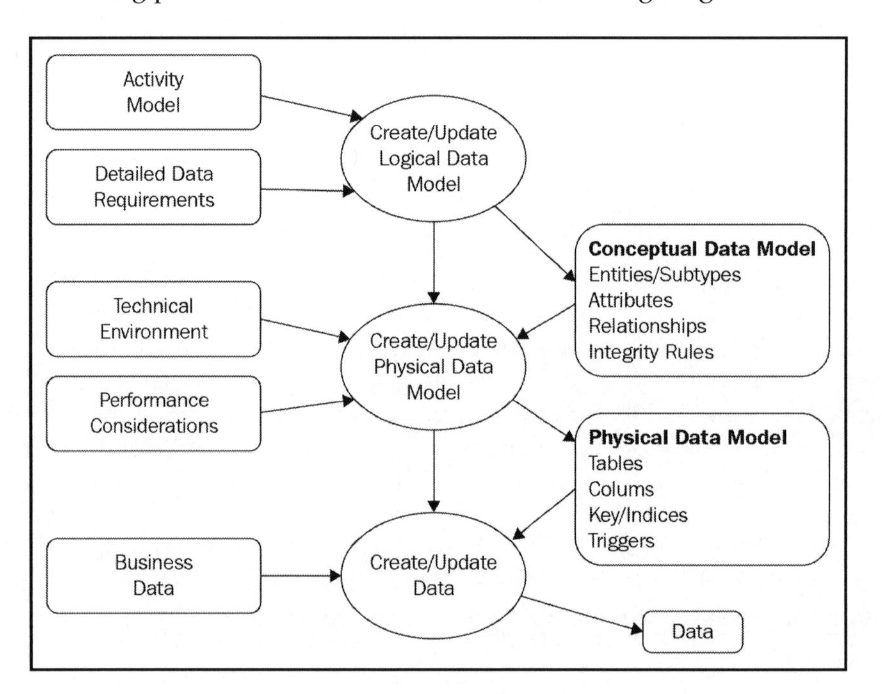

Data modeling process

When applied to the network, we can apply this concept as an abstract model that describes our network, be it a data center, campus, or global wide area network. If we take a closer look at a physical data center, a layer 2 Ethernet switch can be thought of as a device containing a table of MAC addresses mapped to each port. Our switch data model describes how the MAC address should be kept in a table, which includes the keys, additional characteristics (think of VLAN and private VLAN), and more. Similarly, we can move beyond devices and map the whole data center in a model. We can start with the number of devices in each of the access, distribution, and core layers, how they are connected, and how they should behave in a production environment. For example, if we have a fat-tree network, how many links should each of the spine routers have, how many routes they should contain, and how many next-hops should each of the prefixes have? These characteristics can be mapped out in a format that can be referenced against the ideal state that we should always check against.

One of the relatively new network data modeling languages that is gaining traction is **Yet Another Next Generation** (**YANG**) (despite common belief, some of the IETF workgroups do have a sense of humor). It was first published in RFC 6020 in 2010, and has since gained traction among vendors and operators. At the time of writing, the support for YANG has varied greatly from vendors to platforms. The adaptation rate in production is therefore relatively low. However, it is a technology worth keeping an eye out for.

The Cisco API and ACI

Cisco Systems, the 800-pound gorilla in the networking space, have not missed out on the trend of network automation. In their push for network automation, they have made various in-house developments, product enhancements, partnerships, as well as many external acquisitions. However, with product lines spanning routers, switches, firewalls, servers (unified computing), wireless, the collaboration software and hardware, and analytic software, to name a few, it is hard to know where to start.

Since this book focuses on Python and networking, we will scope this section to the main networking products. In particular, we will cover the following:

- Nexus product automation with NX-API
- Cisco NETCONF and YANG examples
- The Cisco application-centric infrastructure for the data center
- The Cisco application-centric infrastructure for the enterprise

For the NX-API and NETCONF examples here, we can either use the Cisco DevNet always-on lab devices or locally run Cisco VIRL. Since ACI is a separate product and is licensed with the physical switches for the following ACI examples, I would recommend using the DevNet labs to get an understanding of the tools. If you are one of the lucky engineers who has a private ACI lab that you can use, please feel free to use it for the relevant examples.

We will use the similar lab topology as we did in `Chapter 5`, *Low-Level Network Device Interactions*, with the exception of one of the devices running **nx-osv**:

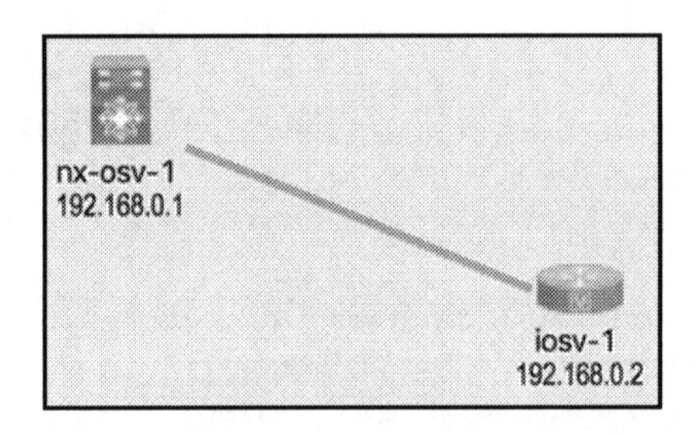

Lab topology

Let's take a look at NX-API.

Cisco NX-API

Nexus is Cisco's primary product line of data center switches. The NX-API (`http://www.cisco.com/c/en/us/td/docs/switches/datacenter/nexus9000/sw/6-x/programmability/guide/b_Cisco_Nexus_9000_Series_NX-OS_Programmability_Guide/b_Cisco_Nexus_9000_Series_NX-OS_Programmability_Guide_chapter_011.html`) allows the engineer to interact with the switch outside of the device via a variety of transports including SSH, HTTP, and HTTPS.

Lab software installation and device preparation

Here are the Ubuntu packages that we will install. You may already have some of the packages such `pip` and `git`:

```
$ sudo apt-get install -y python3-dev libxml2-dev libxslt1-dev libffi-dev libssl-dev zlib1g-dev python3-pip git python3-requests
```

If you are using Python 2, use the following packages instead: `sudo apt-get install -y python-dev libxml2-dev libxslt1-dev libffi-dev libssl-dev zlib1g-dev python-pip git python-requests`.

The `ncclient` (`https://github.com/ncclient/ncclient`) library is a Python library for NETCONF clients. We will install this from the GitHub repository so that we can install the latest version:

```
$ git clone https://github.com/ncclient/ncclient
$ cd ncclient/
$ sudo python3 setup.py install
$ sudo python setup.py install #for Python 2
```

NX-API on Nexus devices is turned off by default, so we will need to turn it on. We can either use the user that is already created (if you are using VIRL auto-config), or create a new user for the NETCONF procedures:

```
feature nxapi
username cisco password 5 $1$Nk7ZkwH0$fyiRmMMfIheqE3BqvcL0C1 role
network-operator
username cisco role network-admin
username cisco passphrase lifetime 99999 warntime 14 gracetime 3
```

For our lab, we will turn on both HTTP and the sandbox configuration, as they should be turned off in production:

```
nx-osv-2(config)# nxapi http port 80
nx-osv-2(config)# nxapi sandbox
```

We are now ready to look at our first NX-API example.

NX-API examples

NX-API sandbox is a great way to play around with various commands, data formats, and even copy the Python script directly from the web page. In the last step, we turned it on for learning purposes. It should be turned off in production. Let's launch a web browser and take a look at the various message formats, requests, and responses based on the CLI commands that we are already familiar with:

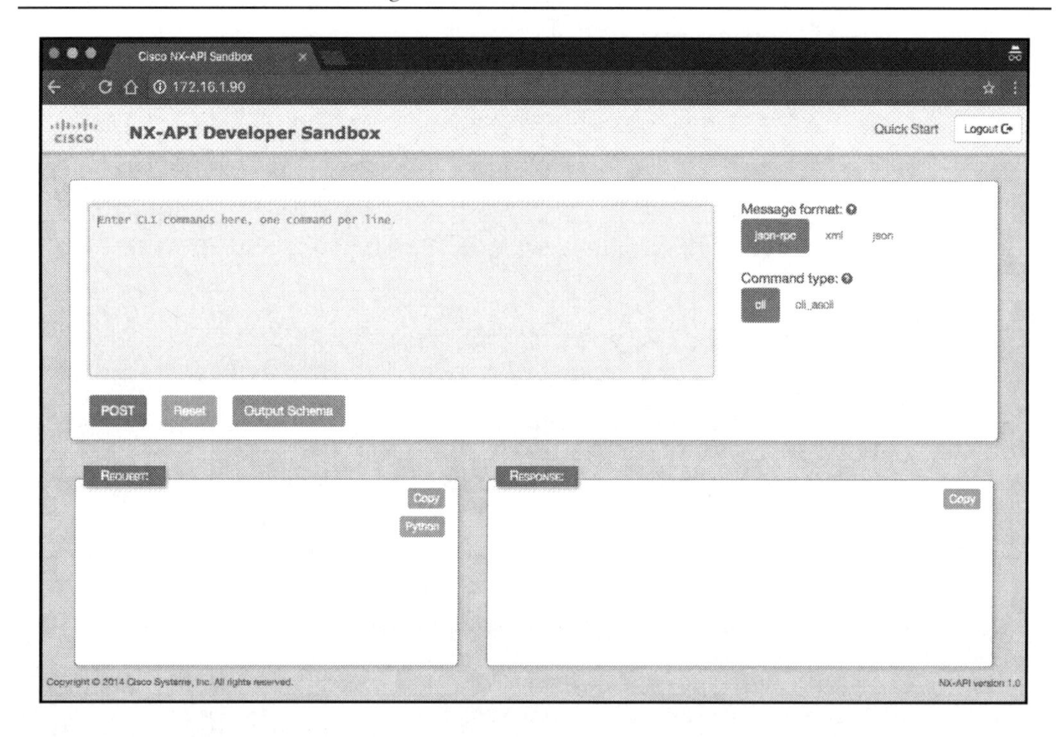

In the following example, I have selected `JSON-RPC` and the `CLI` command type for the `show version` command:

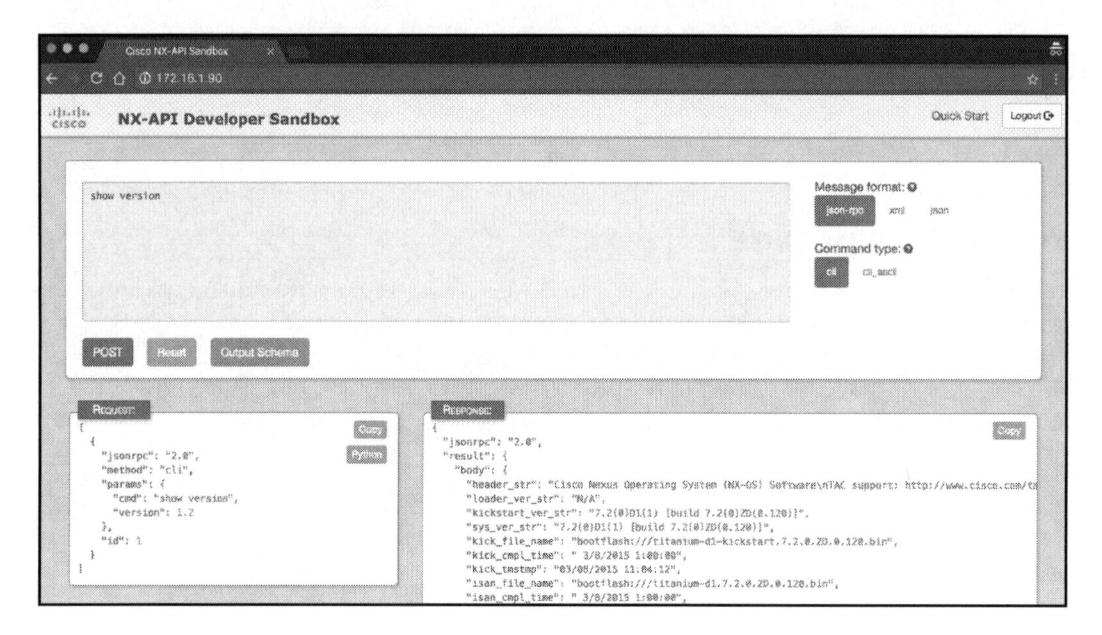

The sandbox comes in handy if you are unsure about the supportability of the message format, or if you have questions about the response data field keys for the value you want to retrieve in your code.

In our first example, we are just going to connect to the Nexus device and print out the capabilities exchanged when the connection was first made:

```
#!/usr/bin/env python3
from ncclient import manager
conn = manager.connect(
        host='172.16.1.90',
        port=22,
        username='cisco',
        password='cisco',
        hostkey_verify=False,
        device_params={'name': 'nexus'},
        look_for_keys=False)
for value in conn.server_capabilities:
    print(value)
conn.close_session()
```

The connection parameters of the host, port, username, and password are pretty self-explanatory. The device parameter specifies the kind of device the client is connecting to. We will see a different response in the Juniper NETCONF sections when using the ncclient library. The `hostkey_verify` bypasses the `known_host` requirement for SSH; if not, the host needs to be listed in the `~/.ssh/known_hosts` file. The `look_for_keys` option disables public-private key authentication, but uses a username and password for authentication.

If you run into an issue with `https://github.com/paramiko/paramiko/issues/748` with Python 3 and Paramiko, please feel free to use Python 2. Hopefully, by the time you read this section, the issue is already fixed.

The output will show the XML and NETCONF supported features by this version of NX-OS:

```
$ python cisco_nxapi_1.py
urn:ietf:params:netconf:capability:writable-running:1.0
urn:ietf:params:netconf:capability:rollback-on-error:1.0
urn:ietf:params:netconf:capability:validate:1.0
urn:ietf:params:netconf:capability:url:1.0?scheme=file
urn:ietf:params:netconf:base:1.0
urn:ietf:params:netconf:capability:candidate:1.0
urn:ietf:params:netconf:capability:confirmed-commit:1.0
urn:ietf:params:xml:ns:netconf:base:1.0
```

Using ncclient and NETCONF over SSH is great because it gets us closer to the native implementation and syntax. We will use the same library later on in this book. For NX-API, it might be easier to deal with HTTPS and JSON-RPC. In the earlier screenshot of **NX-API Developer Sandbox**, if you noticed, in the **Request** box, there is a box labeled **Python**. If you click on it, you will be able to get an automatically converted Python script based on the request library.

The following script uses an external Python library named `requests`. `requests` is a very popular, self-proclaimed HTTP for the human library used by companies like Amazon, Google, NSA, and more. You can find more information about it on the official site (`http://docs.python-requests.org/en/master/`).

For the `show version` example, the following Python script is automatically generated for you. I am pasting in the output without any modification:

```
"""
 NX-API-BOT
"""
import requests
import json

"""
Modify these please
"""
url='http://YOURIP/ins'
switchuser='USERID'
switchpassword='PASSWORD'

myheaders={'content-type':'application/json-rpc'}
payload=[
  {
    "jsonrpc": "2.0",
    "method": "cli",
    "params": {
      "cmd": "show version",
      "version": 1.2
    },
    "id": 1
  }
]
response = requests.post(url,data=json.dumps(payload),
headers=myheaders,auth=(switchuser,switchpassword)).json()
```

In the `cisco_nxapi_2.py` script, you will see that I have only modified the URL, username, and password of the preceding file. The output was parsed to include only the software version. Here is the output:

```
$ python3 cisco_nxapi_2.py
7.2(0)D1(1) [build 7.2(0)ZD(0.120)]
```

The best part about using this method is that the same overall syntax structure works with both configuration commands as well as show commands. This is illustrated in the `cisco_nxapi_3.py` file. For multiline configuration, you can use the ID field to specify the order of operations. In `cisco_nxapi_4.py`, the following payload was listed for changing the description of the interface Ethernet 2/12 in the interface configuration mode:

```
{
  "jsonrpc": "2.0",
  "method": "cli",
  "params": {
    "cmd": "interface ethernet 2/12",
    "version": 1.2
  },
  "id": 1
},
{
  "jsonrpc": "2.0",
  "method": "cli",
  "params": {
    "cmd": "description foo-bar",
    "version": 1.2
  },
  "id": 2
},
{
  "jsonrpc": "2.0",
  "method": "cli",
  "params": {
    "cmd": "end",
    "version": 1.2
  },
  "id": 3
},
{
  "jsonrpc": "2.0",
  "method": "cli",
  "params": {
    "cmd": "copy run start",
    "version": 1.2
```

```
            },
            "id": 4
        }
    ]
```

We can verify the result of the previous configuration script by looking at the running-configuration of the Nexus device:

```
hostname nx-osv-1-new
...
interface Ethernet2/12
description foo-bar
shutdown
no switchport
mac-address 0000.0000.002f
```

In the next section, we will look at some examples for Cisco NETCONF and the YANG model.

The Cisco and YANG models

Earlier in this chapter, we looked at the possibility of expressing the network by using the data modeling language YANG. Let's look into it a little bit more with examples.

First off, we should know that the YANG model only defines the type of data sent over the NETCONF protocol without dictating what the data should be. Secondly, it is worth pointing out that NETCONF exists as a standalone protocol, as we saw in the NX-API section. YANG, being relatively new, has a spotty supportability across vendors and product lines. For example, if we run the same capability exchange script that we have used before for a Cisco 1000v running IOS-XE, this is what we will see:

```
urn:cisco:params:xml:ns:yang:cisco-virtual-service?module=cisco-
virtual-service&revision=2015-04-09
http://tail-f.com/ns/mibs/SNMP-NOTIFICATION-MIB/200210140000Z?
module=SNMP-NOTIFICATION-MIB&revision=2002-10-14
urn:ietf:params:xml:ns:yang:iana-crypt-hash?module=iana-crypt-
hash&revision=2014-04-04&features=crypt-hash-sha-512,crypt-hash-
sha-256,crypt-hash-md5
urn:ietf:params:xml:ns:yang:smiv2:TUNNEL-MIB?module=TUNNEL-
MIB&revision=2005-05-16
urn:ietf:params:xml:ns:yang:smiv2:CISCO-IP-URPF-MIB?module=CISCO-
IP-URPF-MIB&revision=2011-12-29
urn:ietf:params:xml:ns:yang:smiv2:ENTITY-STATE-MIB?module=ENTITY-
STATE-MIB&revision=2005-11-22
urn:ietf:params:xml:ns:yang:smiv2:IANAifType-
```

```
MIB?module=IANAifType-
    MIB&revision=2006-03-31
    <omitted>
```

Compare this to the output that we saw for NX-OS. Clearly, IOS-XE supports the YANG model features more than NX-OS. Industry-wide, network data modeling when supported, is clearly something that can be used across your devices, which is beneficial for network automation. However, given the uneven support of vendors and products, it is not yet mature enough to be used exclusively for the production network, in my opinion. For this book, I have included a script called `cisco_yang_1.py` that shows how to parse out the NETCONF XML output with YANG filters called `urn:ietf:params:xml:ns:yang:ietf-interfaces` as a starting point to see the existing tag overlay.

You can check the latest vendor support on the YANG GitHub project page (`https://github.com/YangModels/yang/tree/master/vendor`).

The Cisco ACI

The Cisco **Application Centric Infrastructure** (**ACI**) is meant to provide a centralized approach to all of the network components. In the data center context, it means that the centralized controller is aware of and manages the spine, leaf, and top of rack switches, as well as all the network service functions. This can be done through GUI, CLI, or API. Some might argue that the ACI is Cisco's answer to the broader controller-based software-defined networking.

One of the somewhat confusing points for ACI is the difference between ACI and APIC-EM. In short, ACI focuses on data center operations while APIC-EM focuses on enterprise modules. Both offer a centralized view and control of the network components, but each has its own focus and share of tool sets. For example, it is rare to see any major data center deploy a customer-facing wireless infrastructure, but a wireless network is a crucial part of enterprises today. Another example would be the different approaches to network security. While security is important in any network, in the data center environment, lots of security policies are pushed to the edge node on the server for scalability. In enterprise security, policies are somewhat shared between the network devices and servers.

Unlike NETCONF RPC, ACI API follows the REST model to use the HTTP verb (`GET`, `POST`, `DELETE`) to specify the operation that's intended.

We can look at the `cisco_apic_em_1.py` file, which is a modified version of the Cisco sample code on `lab2-1-get-network-device-list.py` (`https://github.com/CiscoDevNet/apicem-1.3-LL-sample-codes/blob/master/basic-labs/lab2-1-get-network-device-list.py`).

The abbreviated version without comments and spaces are listed in the following section.

The first function named `getTicket()` uses HTTPS `POST` on the controller with the path of `/api/v1/ticket` with a username and password embedded in the header. This function will return the parsed response for a ticket that is only valid for a limited time:

```
    def getTicket():
        url = "https://" + controller + "/api/v1/ticket"
        payload = {"username":"usernae","password":"password"}
        header = {"content-type": "application/json"}
        response= requests.post(url,data=json.dumps(payload),
headers=header, verify=False)
        r_json=response.json()
        ticket = r_json["response"]["serviceTicket"]
        return ticket
```

The second function then calls another path called `/api/v1/network-devices` with the newly acquired ticket embedded in the header, then parses the results:

```
url = "https://" + controller + "/api/v1/network-device"
header = {"content-type": "application/json", "X-Auth-Token":ticket}
```

This is a pretty common workflow for API interactions. The client will authenticate itself with the server in the first request and receive a time-based token. This token will be used in subsequent requests and will be served as a proof of authentication.

The output displays both the raw JSON response output as well as a parsed table. A partial output when executed against a DevNet lab controller is shown here:

```
Network Devices =
{
 "version": "1.0",
 "response": [
 {
 "reachabilityStatus": "Unreachable",
 "id": "8dbd8068-1091-4cde-8cf5-d1b58dc5c9c7",
 "platformId": "WS-C2960C-8PC-L",
<omitted>
```

```
"lineCardId": null,
"family": "Wireless Controller",
"interfaceCount": "12",
"upTime": "497 days, 2:27:52.95"
}
]
}
8dbd8068-1091-4cde-8cf5-d1b58dc5c9c7 Cisco Catalyst 2960-C Series
 Switches
cd6d9b24-839b-4d58-adfe-3fdf781e1782 Cisco 3500I Series Unified
Access Points
<omitted>
55450140-de19-47b5-ae80-bfd741b23fd9 Cisco 4400 Series Integrated
Services Routers
ae19cd21-1b26-4f58-8ccd-d265deabb6c3 Cisco 5500 Series Wireless
LAN
Controllers
```

As you can see, we only query a single controller device, but we are able to get a high-level view of all the network devices that the controller is aware of. In our output, the Catalyst 2960-C switch, 3500 Access Points, 4400 ISR router, and 5500 Wireless Controller can all be explored further. The downside is, of course, that the ACI controller only supports Cisco devices at this time.

The Python API for Juniper networks

Juniper networks have always been a favorite among the service provider crowd. If we take a step back and look at the service provider vertical, it would make sense that automating network equipment is on the top of their list of requirements. Before the dawn of cloud-scale data centers, service providers were the ones with the most network equipment. A typical enterprise network might have a few redundant internet connections at the corporate headquarter with a few hub-and-spoke remote sites connected back to the HQ using the service provider's private MPLS network. To a service provider, they are the ones who need to build, provision, manage, and troubleshoot the connections and the underlying networks. They make their money by selling the bandwidth along with value-added managed services. It would make sense for the service providers to invest in automation to use the least amount of engineering hours to keep the network humming along. In their use case, network automation is the key to their competitive advantage.

In my opinion, the difference between a service provider's network needs compared to a cloud data center is that, traditionally, service providers aggregate more services into a single device. A good example would be **Multiprotocol Label Switching** (**MPLS**) that almost all major service providers provide but rarely adapt in the enterprise or data center networks. Juniper, as they have been very successful, has identified this need and excel at fulfilling the service provider requirements of automating. Let's take a look at some of Juniper's automation APIs.

Juniper and NETCONF

The **Network Configuration Protocol** (**NETCONF**) is an IETF standard, which was first published in 2006 as `RFC 4741` and later revised in `RFC 6241`. Juniper networks contributed heavily to both of the RFC standards. In fact, Juniper was the sole author for RFC 4741. It makes sense that Juniper devices fully support NETCONF, and it serves as the underlying layer for most of its automation tools and frameworks. Some of the main characteristics of NETCONF include the following:

1. It uses **Extensible Markup Language** (**XML**) for data encoding.
2. It uses **Remote Procedure Calls** (**RPC**), therefore in the case of HTTP(s) as the transport, the URL endpoint is identical while the operation intended is specified in the body of the request.
3. It is conceptually based on layers from top to bottom. The layers include the content, operations, messages, and transport:

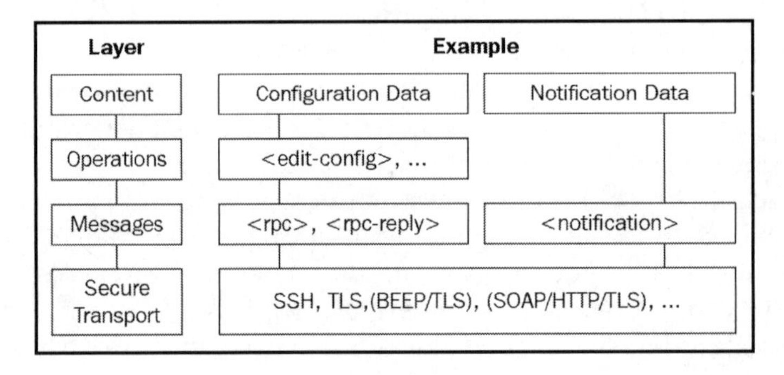

NETCONF model

Juniper networks provide an extensive NETCONF XML management protocol developer guide (`https://www.juniper.net/techpubs/en_US/junos13.2/information-products/pathway-pages/netconf-guide/netconf.html#overview`) in its technical library. Let's take a look at its usage.

Device preparation

In order to start using NETCONF, let's create a separate user as well as turn on the required services:

```
set system login user netconf uid 2001
set system login user netconf class super-user
set system login user netconf authentication encrypted-password
 "$1$0EkA.XVf$cm80A0GC2dgSWJIYWv7Pt1"
set system services ssh
set system services telnet
set system services netconf ssh port 830
```

For the Juniper device lab, I am using an older, unsupported platform called **Juniper Olive**. It is solely used for lab purposes. You can use your favorite search engine to find out some interesting facts and history about Juniper Olive.

On the Juniper device, you can always take a look at the configuration either in a flat file or in XML format. The `flat` file comes in handy when you need to specify a one-liner command to make configuration changes:

```
netconf@foo> show configuration | display set
set version 12.1R1.9
set system host-name foo
set system domain-name bar
<omitted>
```

The XML format comes in handy at times when you need to see the XML structure of the configuration:

```
    netconf@foo> show configuration | display xml
    <rpc-reply
xmlns:junos="http://xml.juniper.net/junos/12.1R1/junos">
     <configuration junos:commit-seconds="1485561328" junos:commit-
    localtime="2017-01-27 23:55:28 UTC" junos:commit-user="netconf">
     <version>12.1R1.9</version>
     <system>
     <host-name>foo</host-name>
    <domain-name>bar</domain-name>
```

We have installed the necessary Linux libraries and the ncclient Python library in the Cisco section. If you have not done so, refer back to that section and install the necessary packages.

We are now ready to look at our first Juniper NETCONF example.

Juniper NETCONF examples

We will use a pretty straightforward example to execute `show version`. We will name this file `junos_netconf_1.py`:

```
#!/usr/bin/env python3

from ncclient import manager

conn = manager.connect(
    host='192.168.24.252',
    port='830',
    username='netconf',
    password='juniper!',
    timeout=10,
    device_params={'name':'junos'},
    hostkey_verify=False)

result = conn.command('show version', format='text')
print(result)
conn.close_session()
```

All the fields in the script should be pretty self-explanatory, with the exception of `device_params`. Starting with ncclient 0.4.1, the device handler was added to specify different vendors or platforms. For example, the name can be juniper, CSR, Nexus, or Huawei. We also added `hostkey_verify=False` because we are using a self-signed certificate from the Juniper device.

The returned output is `rpc-reply` encoded in XML with an `output` element:

```
<rpc-reply message-id="urn:uuid:7d9280eb-1384-45fe-be48-
b7cd14ccf2b7">
<output>
Hostname: foo
Model: olive
JUNOS Base OS boot [12.1R1.9]
JUNOS Base OS Software Suite [12.1R1.9]
<omitted>
```

```
JUNOS Runtime Software Suite [12.1R1.9]
JUNOS Routing Software Suite [12.1R1.9]
</output>
</rpc-reply>
```

We can parse the XML output to just include the output text:

```
print(result.xpath('output')[0].text)
```

In junos_netconf_2.py, we will make configuration changes to the device. We will start with some new imports for constructing new XML elements and the connection manager object:

```
#!/usr/bin/env python3

from ncclient import manager
from ncclient.xml_ import new_ele, sub_ele

conn = manager.connect(host='192.168.24.252', port='830',
username='netconf' , password='juniper!', timeout=10,
device_params={'name':'junos'}, hostkey_v erify=False)
```

We will lock the configuration and make configuration changes:

```
# lock configuration and make configuration changes
conn.lock()

# build configuration
config = new_ele('system')
sub_ele(config, 'host-name').text = 'master'
sub_ele(config, 'domain-name').text = 'python'
```

Under the build configuration section, we create a new element of system with subelements of host-namre and domain-name. If you were wondering about the hierarchy structure, you can see from the XML display that the node structure with system is the parent of host-name and domain-name:

```
<system>
   <host-name>foo</host-name>
   <domain-name>bar</domain-name>
...
</system>
```

After the configuration is built, the script will push the configuration and commit the configuration changes. These are the normal best practice steps (lock, configure, unlock, commit) for Juniper configuration changes:

```
# send, validate, and commit config
conn.load_configuration(config=config)
conn.validate()
commit_config = conn.commit()
print(commit_config.tostring)

# unlock config
conn.unlock()

# close session
conn.close_session()
```

Overall, the NETCONF steps map pretty well to what you would have done in the CLI steps. Please take a look at the `junos_netconf_3.py` script for a more reusable code. The following example combines the step-by-step example with a few Python functions:

```
# make a connection object
def connect(host, port, user, password):
    connection = manager.connect(host=host, port=port, username=user,
            password=password, timeout=10,
device_params={'name':'junos'},
            hostkey_verify=False)
    return connection

# execute show commands
def show_cmds(conn, cmd):
    result = conn.command(cmd, format='text')
    return result

# push out configuration
def config_cmds(conn, config):
    conn.lock()
    conn.load_configuration(config=config)
    commit_config = conn.commit()
    return commit_config.tostring
```

This file can be executed by itself, or it can be imported to be used by other Python scripts.

Juniper also provides a Python library to be used with their devices called PyEZ. We will take a look at a few examples of using the library in the following section.

Juniper PyEZ for developers

PyEZ is a high-level Python implementation that integrates better with your existing Python code. By utilizing the Python API, you can perform common operation and configuration tasks without the extensive knowledge of the Junos CLI.

Juniper maintains a comprehensive Junos PyEZ developer guide at `https://www.juniper.net/techpubs/en_US/junos-pyez1.0/information-products/pathway-pages/junos-pyez-developer-guide.html#configuration` on their technical library. If you are interested in using PyEZ, I would highly recommend at least a glance through the various topics in the guide.

Installation and preparation

The installation instructions for each of the operating systems can be found on the *Installing Junos PyEZ* (`https://www.juniper.net/techpubs/en_US/junos-pyez1.0/topics/task/installation/junos-pyez-server-installing.html`) page. We will show the installation instructions for Ubuntu 16.04.

The following are some dependency packages, many of which should already be on the host from running previous examples:

```
$ sudo apt-get install -y python3-pip python3-dev libxml2-dev
libxslt1-dev libssl-dev libffi-dev
```

`PyEZ` packages can be installed via pip. Here, I have installed for both Python 3 and Python 2:

```
$ sudo pip3 install junos-eznc
$ sudo pip install junos-eznc
```

On the Juniper device, NETCONF needs to be configured as the underlying XML API for PyEZ:

```
set system services netconf ssh port 830
```

For user authentication, we can either use password authentication or an SSH key pair. Creating the local user is straightforward:

```
set system login user netconf uid 2001
set system login user netconf class super-user
set system login user netconf authentication encrypted-password
"$1$0EkA.XVf$cm80A0GC2dgSWJIYWv7Pt1"
```

For the `ssh` key authentication, first, generate the key pair on your host:

```
$ ssh-keygen -t rsa
```

By default, the public key will be called `id_rsa.pub` under `~/.ssh/`, while the private key will be named `id_rsa` under the same directory. Treat the private key like a password that you never share. The public key can be freely distributed. In our use case, we will move the public key to the `/tmp` directory and enable the Python 3 HTTP server module to create a reachable URL:

```
$ mv ~/.ssh/id_rsa.pub /tmp
$ cd /tmp
$ python3 -m http.server
Serving HTTP on 0.0.0.0 port 8000 ...
```

For Python 2, use `python -m SimpleHTTPServer` instead.

From the Juniper device, we can create the user and associate the public key by downloading the public key from the Python 3 web server:

```
netconf@foo# set system login user echou class super-user
authentication load-key-file http://192.168.24.164:8000/id_rsa.pub
/var/home/netconf/...transferring.file........100% of 394 B 2482 kBps
```

Now, if we try to `ssh` with the private key from the management station, the user will be automatically authenticated:

```
$ ssh -i ~/.ssh/id_rsa 192.168.24.252
--- JUNOS 12.1R1.9 built 2012-03-24 12:52:33 UTC
echou@foo>
```

Let's make sure that both of the authentication methods work with PyEZ. Let's try the username and password combination:

```
Python 3.5.2 (default, Nov 17 2016, 17:05:23)
[GCC 5.4.0 20160609] on linux
```

```
Type "help", "copyright", "credits" or "license" for more information.
>>> from jnpr.junos import Device
>>> dev = Device(host='192.168.24.252', user='netconf',
password='juniper!')
>>> dev.open()
Device(192.168.24.252)
>>> dev.facts
{'serialnumber': '', 'personality': 'UNKNOWN', 'model': 'olive',
'ifd_style': 'CLASSIC', '2RE': False, 'HOME': '/var/home/juniper',
'version_info': junos.version_info(major=(12, 1), type=R, minor=1,
build=9), 'switch_style': 'NONE', 'fqdn': 'foo.bar', 'hostname':
'foo', 'version': '12.1R1.9', 'domain': 'bar', 'vc_capable': False}
>>> dev.close()
```

We can also try to use the SSH key authentication:

```
>>> from jnpr.junos import Device
>>> dev1 = Device(host='192.168.24.252', user='echou',
ssh_private_key_file='/home/echou/.ssh/id_rsa')
>>> dev1.open()
Device(192.168.24.252)
>>> dev1.facts
{'HOME': '/var/home/echou', 'model': 'olive', 'hostname': 'foo',
'switch_style': 'NONE', 'personality': 'UNKNOWN', '2RE': False,
'domain': 'bar', 'vc_capable': False, 'version': '12.1R1.9',
'serialnumber': '', 'fqdn': 'foo.bar', 'ifd_style': 'CLASSIC',
'version_info': junos.version_info(major=(12, 1), type=R, minor=1,
build=9)}
>>> dev1.close()
```

Great! We are now ready to look at some examples for PyEZ.

PyEZ examples

In the previous interactive prompt, we already saw that when the device connects, the object automatically retrieves a few facts about the device. In our first example, `junos_pyez_1.py`, we were connecting to the device and executing an RPC call for `show interface em1`:

```
    #!/usr/bin/env python3
    from jnpr.junos import Device
    import xml.etree.ElementTree as ET
    import pprint

    dev = Device(host='192.168.24.252', user='juniper',
passwd='juniper!')
```

```
        try:
            dev.open()
        except Exception as err:
            print(err)
            sys.exit(1)

        result =
      dev.rpc.get_interface_information(interface_name='em1',
terse=True)
        pprint.pprint(ET.tostring(result))

        dev.close()
```

The device class has an `rpc` property that includes all operational commands. This is pretty awesome because there is no slippage between what we can do in CLI versus API. The catch is that we need to find out the `xml rpc` element tag. In our first example, how do we know `show interface em1` equates to `get_interface_information`? We have three ways of finding out this information:

1. We can reference the *Junos XML API Operational Developer Reference*
2. We can use the CLI and display the XML RPC equivalent and replace the dash (-) between the words with an underscore (_)
3. We can also do this programmatically by using the PyEZ library

I typically use the second option to get the output directly:

```
      netconf@foo> show interfaces em1 | display xml rpc
      <rpc-reply
xmlns:junos="http://xml.juniper.net/junos/12.1R1/junos">
       <rpc>
       <get-interface-information>
       <interface-name>em1</interface-name>
       </get-interface-information>
       </rpc>
       <cli>
       <banner></banner>
       </cli>
      </rpc-reply>
```

Here is an example of using PyEZ programmatically (the third option):

```
>>> dev1.display_xml_rpc('show interfaces em1', format='text')
'<get-interface-information>n <interface-name>em1</interface-
name>n</get-interface-information>n'
```

Of course, we will need to make configuration changes as well. In the `junos_pyez_2.py` configuration example, we will import an additional `Config()` method from PyEZ:

```
#!/usr/bin/env python3
from jnpr.junos import Device
from jnpr.junos.utils.config import Config
```

We will utilize the same block for connecting to a device:

```
dev = Device(host='192.168.24.252', user='juniper',
passwd='juniper!')

try:
    dev.open()
except Exception as err:
    print(err)
    sys.exit(1)
```

The new `Config()` method will load the XML data and make the configuration changes:

```
config_change = """
<system>
  <host-name>master</host-name>
  <domain-name>python</domain-name>
</system>
"""

cu = Config(dev)
cu.lock()
cu.load(config_change)
cu.commit()
cu.unlock()

dev.close()
```

The PyEZ examples are simple by design. Hopefully, they demonstrate the ways you can leverage PyEZ for your Junos automation needs.

The Arista Python API

Arista Networks have always been focused on large-scale data center networks. In its corporate profile page (`https://www.arista.com/en/company/company-overview`), it is stated as follows:

> *"Arista Networks was founded to pioneer and deliver software-driven cloud networking solutions for large data center storage and computing environments."*

Notice that the statement specifically called out **large data centers**, which we already know are exploded with servers, databases, and, yes, network equipment. It makes sense that automation has always been one of Arista's leading features. In fact, they have a Linux underpin behind their operating system, allowing many added benefits such as Linux commands and a built-in Python interpreter.

Like other vendors, you can interact with Arista devices directly via eAPI, or you can choose to leverage their `Python` library. We will see examples of both. We will also look at Arista's integration with the Ansible framework in later chapters.

Arista eAPI management

Arista's eAPI was first introduced in EOS 4.12 a few years ago. It transports a list of show or configuration commands over HTTP or HTTPS and responds back in JSON. An important distinction is that it is a **Remote Procedure Call** (**RPC**) and **JSON-RPC**, instead of a pure RESTFul API that's served over HTTP or HTTPS. For our intents and purposes, the difference is that we make the request to the same URL endpoint using the same HTTP method (`POST`). Instead of using HTTP verbs (`GET`, `POST`, `PUT`, `DELETE`) to express our action, we simply state our intended action in the body of the request. In the case of eAPI, we will specify a `method` key with a `runCmds` value for our intention.

For the following examples, I am using a physical Arista switch running EOS 4.16.

The eAPI preparation

The eAPI agent on the Arista device is disabled by default, so we will need to enable it on the device before we can use it:

```
arista1(config)#management api http-commands
arista1(config-mgmt-api-http-cmds)#no shut
arista1(config-mgmt-api-http-cmds)#protocol https port 443
arista1(config-mgmt-api-http-cmds)#no protocol http
arista1(config-mgmt-api-http-cmds)#vrf management
```

As you can see, we have turned off the HTTP server and are using HTTPS as the sole transport instead. Starting from a few EOS versions ago, the management interfaces, by default, reside in a VRF called **management.** In my topology, I am accessing the device via the management interface; therefore, I have specified the VRF for eAPI management. You can check that API management state via the "show management api http-commands" command:

```
arista1#sh management api http-commands
Enabled: Yes
HTTPS server: running, set to use port 443
HTTP server: shutdown, set to use port 80
Local HTTP server: shutdown, no authentication, set to use port 8080
Unix Socket server: shutdown, no authentication
VRF: management
Hits: 64
Last hit: 33 seconds ago
Bytes in: 8250
Bytes out: 29862
Requests: 23
Commands: 42
Duration: 7.086 seconds
SSL Profile: none
QoS DSCP: 0
 User Requests Bytes in Bytes out Last hit
----------- -------------- -------------- --------------- -----------
--
 admin 23 8250 29862 33 seconds ago

URLs
-----------------------------------------
Management1 : https://192.168.199.158:443

arista1#
```

After enabling the agent, you will be able to access the exploration page for eAPI by going to the device's IP address. If you have changed the default port for access, just append it at the end. The authentication is tied into the method of authentication on the switch. We will use the username and password configured locally on the device. By default, a self-signed certificate will be used:

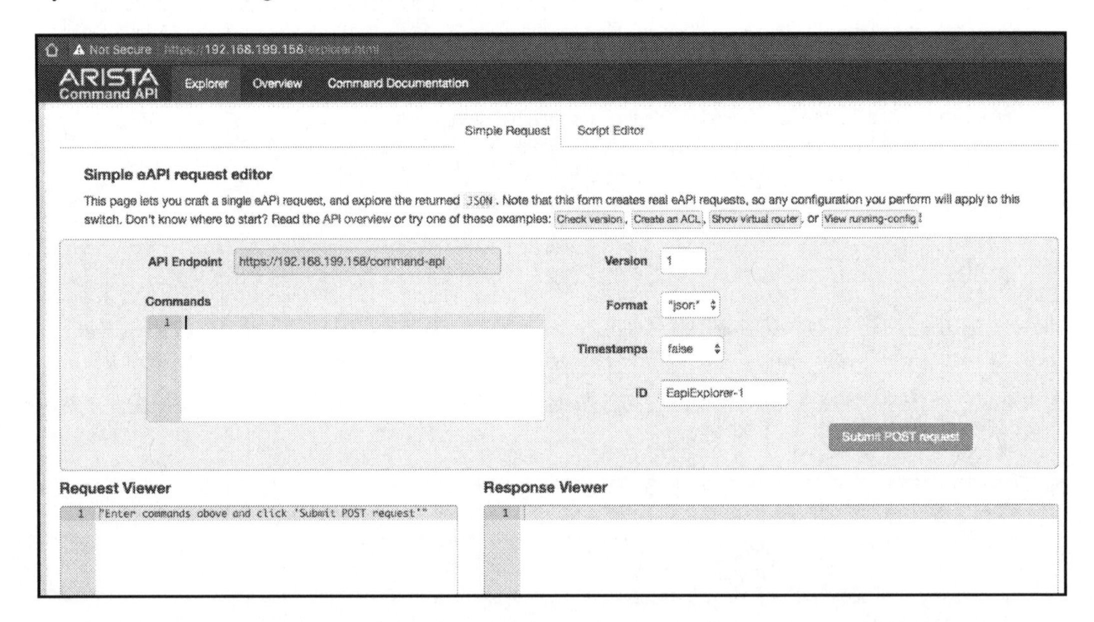

Arista EOS explorer

You will be taken to an explorer page where you can type in the CLI command and get a nice output for the body of your request. For example, if I want to see how to make a request body for `show version`, this is the output I will see from the explorer:

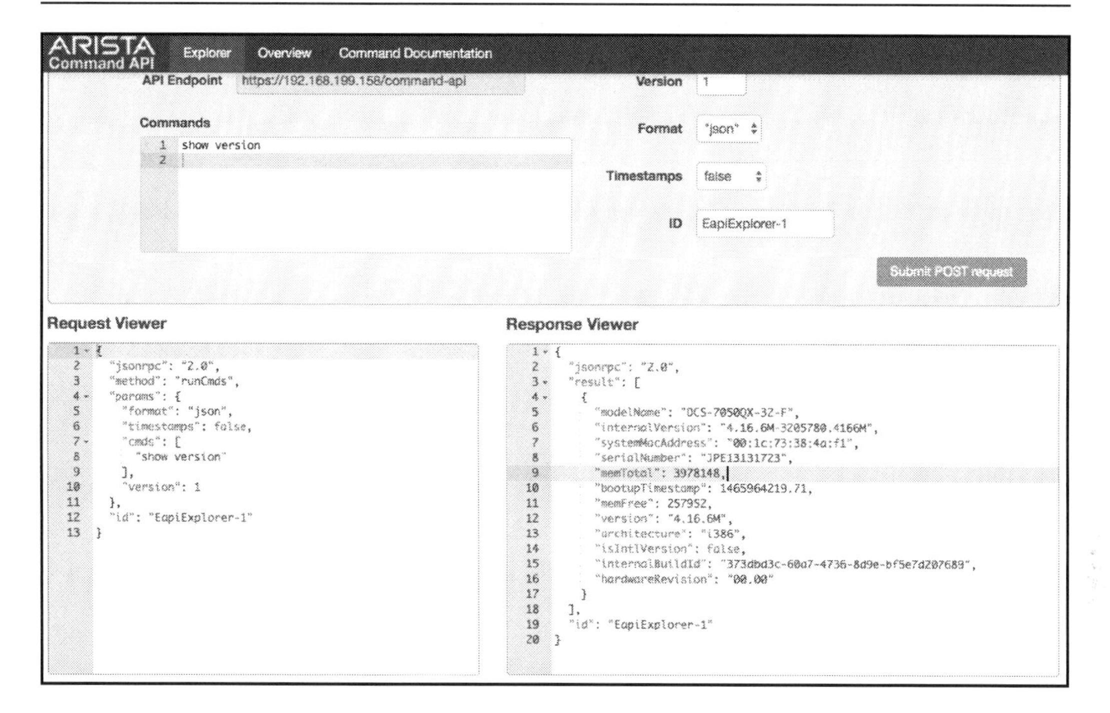

Arista EOS explorer viewer

The overview link will take you to the sample use and background information while the command documentation will serve as reference points for the show commands. Each of the command references will contain the returned value field name, type, and a brief description. The online reference scripts from Arista use jsonrpclib (`https://github.com/joshmarshall/jsonrpclib/`), which is what we will use. However, as of the time of writing this book, it has a dependency of Python 2.6+ and has not yet ported to Python 3; therefore, we will use Python 2.7 for these examples.

By the time you read this book, there might be an updated status. Please read the GitHub pull request (`https://github.com/joshmarshall/jsonrpclib/issues/38`) and the GitHub README (`https://github.com/joshmarshall/jsonrpclib/`) for the latest status.

Installation is straightforward using `easy_install` or `pip`:

```
$ sudo easy_install jsonrpclib
$ sudo pip install jsonrpclib
```

eAPI examples

We can then write a simple program called `eapi_1.py` to look at the response text:

```
    #!/usr/bin/python2

    from __future__ import print_function
    from jsonrpclib import Server
    import ssl

    ssl._create_default_https_context =
ssl._create_unverified_context

    switch =
Server("https://admin:arista@192.168.199.158/command-api")

    response = switch.runCmds( 1, [ "show version" ] )
    print('Serial Number: ' + response[0]['serialNumber'])
```

Note that, since this is Python 2, in the script, I used the `from __future__ import print_function` to make future migration easier. The `ssl`-related lines are for Python version > 2.7.9. For more information, please see `https://www.python.org/dev/peps/pep-0476/`.

This is the response I received from the previous `runCms()` method:


```
  [{u'memTotal': 3978148, u'internalVersion': u'4.16.6M-
  3205780.4166M', u'serialNumber': u'<omitted>',
u'systemMacAddress':
  u'<omitted>', u'bootupTimestamp': 1465964219.71, u'memFree':
  277832, u'version': u'4.16.6M', u'modelName': u'DCS-7050QX-32-F',
  u'isIntlVersion': False, u'internalBuildId': u'373dbd3c-60a7-4736-
  8d9e-bf5e7d207689', u'hardwareRevision': u'00.00', u'architecture':
  u'i386'}]
```


As you can see, the result is a list containing one dictionary item. If we need to grab the serial number, we can simply reference the item number and the key:

```
    print('Serial Number: ' + response[0]['serialNumber'])
```

The output will contain only the serial number:

```
$ python eapi_1.py
Serial Number: <omitted>
```

To be more familiar with the command reference, I recommend that you click on the **Command Documentation** link on the eAPI page, and compare your output with the output of **show version** in the documentation.

As noted earlier, unlike REST, the JSON-RPC client uses the same URL endpoint for calling the server resources. You can see from the previous example that the `runCmds()` method contains a list of commands. For the execution of configuration commands, you can follow the same framework, and configure the device via a list of commands.

Here is an example of configuration commands named `eapi_2.py`. In our example, we wrote a function that takes the switch object and the list of commands as attributes:

```
    #!/usr/bin/python2

    from __future__ import print_function
    from jsonrpclib import Server
    import ssl, pprint

    ssl._create_default_https_context =
ssl._create_unverified_context

    # Run Arista commands thru eAPI
    def runAristaCommands(switch_object, list_of_commands):
        response = switch_object.runCmds(1, list_of_commands)
        return response


    switch = Server("https://admin:arista@192.168.199.158/command-
  api")

    commands = ["enable", "configure", "interface ethernet 1/3",
  "switchport acc ess vlan 100", "end", "write memory"]

   response = runAristaCommands(switch, commands)
   pprint.pprint(response)
```

Here is the output of the command's execution:

```
$ python2 eapi_2.py
[{}, {}, {}, {}, {}, {u'messages': [u'Copy completed successfully.']}]
```

Now, do a quick check on the `switch` to verify the command's execution:

```
arista1#sh run int eth 1/3
interface Ethernet1/3
    switchport access vlan 100
arista1#
```

Overall, eAPI is fairly straightforward and simple to use. Most programming languages have libraries similar to `jsonrpclib`, which abstracts away JSON-RPC internals. With a few commands, you can start integrating Arista EOS automation into your network.

The Arista Pyeapi library

The Python client Pyeapi (`http://pyeapi.readthedocs.io/en/master/index.html`) library is a native Python library wrapper around eAPI. It provides a set of bindings to configure Arista EOS nodes. Why do we need Pyeapi when we already have eAPI? Picking between Pyeapi versus eAPI is mostly a judgment call if you are in a Python environment.

However, if you are in a non-Python environment, eAPI is probably the way to go. From our examples, you can see that the only requirement of eAPI is a JSON-RPC capable client. Thus, it is compatible with most programming languages. When I first started out in the field, Perl was the dominant language for scripting and network automation. There are still many enterprises that rely on Perl scripts as their primary automation tool. If you're in a situation where the company has already invested a ton of resources and the code base is in another language than Python, eAPI with JSON-RPC would be a good bet.

However, for those of us who prefer to code in Python, a native `Python` library means a more natural feeling in writing our code. It certainly makes extending a Python program to support the EOS node easier. It also makes keeping up with the latest changes in Python easier. For example, we can use Python 3 with Pyeapi!

At the time of writing this book, Python 3 (3.4+) support is officially a work-in-progress, as stated in the documentation (`http://pyeapi.readthedocs.io/en/master/requirements.html`). Please check the documentation for more details.

Pyeapi installation

Installation is straightforward with pip:

```
$ sudo pip install pyeapi
$ sudo pip3 install pyeapi
```

Note that pip will also install the netaddr library as it is part of the stated requirements `(http://pyeapi.readthedocs.io/en/master/requirements.html) for Pyeapi.`

By default, the Pyeapi client will look for an INI style hidden (with a period in front) file called `eapi.conf` in your home directory. You can override this behavior by specifying the `eapi.conf` file path, but it is generally a good idea to separate your connection credential and lock it down from the script itself. You can check out the Arista Pyeapi documentation (`http://pyeapi.readthedocs.io/en/master/configfile.html#configfile`) for the fields contained in the file. Here is the file I am using in the lab:

```
cat ~/.eapi.conf
[connection:Arista1]
host: 192.168.199.158
username: admin
password: arista
transport: https
```

The first line, `[connection:Arista1]`, contains the name that we will use in our Pyeapi connection; the rest of the fields should be pretty self-explanatory. You can lock down the file to be read-only for the user using this file:

```
$ chmod 400 ~/.eapi.conf
$ ls -l ~/.eapi.conf
-r-------- 1 echou echou 94 Jan 27 18:15 /home/echou/.eapi.conf
```

Pyeapi examples

Now, we are ready to take a look around the usage. Let's start by connecting to the EOS node by creating an object in the interactive Python shell:

```
Python 3.5.2 (default, Nov 17 2016, 17:05:23)
[GCC 5.4.0 20160609] on linux
Type "help", "copyright", "credits" or "license" for more information.
>>> import pyeapi
>>> arista1 = pyeapi.connect_to('Arista1')
```

We can execute show commands to the node and receive the output:

```
>>> import pprint
>>> pprint.pprint(arista1.enable('show hostname'))
[{'command': 'show hostname',
 'encoding': 'json',
 'result': {'fqdn': 'arista1', 'hostname': 'arista1'}}]
```

The configuration field can be either a single command or a list of commands using the `config()` method:

```
>>> arista1.config('hostname arista1-new')
[{}]
>>> pprint.pprint(arista1.enable('show hostname'))
[{'command': 'show hostname',
 'encoding': 'json',
 'result': {'fqdn': 'arista1-new', 'hostname': 'arista1-new'}}]
>>> arista1.config(['interface ethernet 1/3', 'description my_link'])
[{}, {}]
```

Note that command abbreviation (`show run` versus `show running-config`) and some extensions will not work:

```
>>> pprint.pprint(arista1.enable('show run'))
Traceback (most recent call last):
...
 File "/usr/local/lib/python3.5/dist-packages/pyeapi/eapilib.py", line
396, in send
 raise CommandError(code, msg, command_error=err, output=out)
pyeapi.eapilib.CommandError: Error [1002]: CLI command 2 of 2 'show
run' failed: invalid command [incomplete token (at token 1: 'run')]
>>>
>>> pprint.pprint(arista1.enable('show running-config interface
ethernet 1/3'))
Traceback (most recent call last):
...
pyeapi.eapilib.CommandError: Error [1002]: CLI command 2 of 2 'show
```

```
running-config interface ethernet 1/3' failed: invalid command
[incomplete token (at token 2: 'interface')]
```

However, you can always catch the results and get the desired value:

```
>>> result = arista1.enable('show running-config')
>>> pprint.pprint(result[0]['result']['cmds']['interface
Ethernet1/3'])
{'cmds': {'description my_link': None, 'switchport access vlan 100':
None}, 'comments': []}
```

So far, we have been doing what we have been doing with eAPI for show and configuration commands. Pyeapi offers various APIs to make life easier. In the following example, we will connect to the node, call the VLAN API, and start to operate on the VLAN parameters of the device. Let's take a look:

```
>>> import pyeapi
>>> node = pyeapi.connect_to('Arista1')
>>> vlans = node.api('vlans')
>>> type(vlans)
<class 'pyeapi.api.vlans.Vlans'>
>>> dir(vlans)
[...'command_builder', 'config', 'configure', 'configure_interface',
'configure_vlan', 'create', 'default', 'delete', 'error', 'get',
'get_block', 'getall', 'items', 'keys', 'node', 'remove_trunk_group',
'set_name', 'set_state', 'set_trunk_groups', 'values']
>>> vlans.getall()
{'1': {'vlan_id': '1', 'trunk_groups': [], 'state': 'active', 'name':
'default'}}
>>> vlans.get(1)
{'vlan_id': 1, 'trunk_groups': [], 'state': 'active', 'name':
'default'}
>>> vlans.create(10)
True
>>> vlans.getall()
{'1': {'vlan_id': '1', 'trunk_groups': [], 'state': 'active', 'name':
'default'}, '10': {'vlan_id': '10', 'trunk_groups': [], 'state':
'active', 'name': 'VLAN0010'}}
>>> vlans.set_name(10, 'my_vlan_10')
True
```

Let's verify that VLAN 10 was created on the device:

```
arista1#sh vlan
VLAN Name Status Ports
----- -------------------------------- --------- -------------------
----------
1 default active
10 my_vlan_10 active
```

As you can see, the Python native API on the EOS object is really where Pyeapi excels beyond eAPI. It abstracts the lower-level attributes into the device object and makes the code cleaner and easier to read.

For a full list of ever increasing Pyeapi APIs, check the official documentation (`http://pyeapi.readthedocs.io/en/master/api_modules/_list_of_modules.html`).

To round up this chapter, let's assume that we repeat the previous steps enough times that we would like to write another Python class to save us some work. The `pyeapi_1.py` script is shown as follows:

```
#!/usr/bin/env python3

import pyeapi

class my_switch():

    def __init__(self, config_file_location, device):
        # loads the config file
        pyeapi.client.load_config(config_file_location)
        self.node = pyeapi.connect_to(device)
        self.hostname = self.node.enable('show hostname')[0]
['result']['host name']
       self.running_config = self.node.enable('show running-
config')

    def create_vlan(self, vlan_number, vlan_name):
        vlans = self.node.api('vlans')
        vlans.create(vlan_number)
        vlans.set_name(vlan_number, vlan_name)
```

As you can see from the script, we automatically connect to the node and set the hostname and running_config upon connection. We also create a method to the class that creates VLAN by using the VLAN API. Let's try out the script in an interactive shell:

```
Python 3.5.2 (default, Nov 17 2016, 17:05:23)
[GCC 5.4.0 20160609] on linux
Type "help", "copyright", "credits" or "license" for more information.
>>> import pyeapi_1
>>> s1 = pyeapi_1.my_switch('/tmp/.eapi.conf', 'Arista1')
>>> s1.hostname
'arista1'
>>> s1.running_config
[{'encoding': 'json', 'result': {'cmds': {'interface Ethernet27':
{'cmds': {}, 'comments': []}, 'ip routing': None, 'interface face
Ethernet29': {'cmds': {}, 'comments': []}, 'interface Ethernet26':
{'cmds': {}, 'comments': []}, 'interface Ethernet24/4': h.':
<omitted>
'interface Ethernet3/1': {'cmds': {}, 'comments': []}}, 'comments':
[], 'header': ['! device: arista1 (DCS-7050QX-32, EOS-4.16.6M)n!n']},
'command': 'show running-config'}]
>>> s1.create_vlan(11, 'my_vlan_11')
>>> s1.node.api('vlans').getall()
{'11': {'name': 'my_vlan_11', 'vlan_id': '11', 'trunk_groups': [],
'state': 'active'}, '10': {'name': 'my_vlan_10', 'vlan_id': '10',
'trunk_groups': [], 'state': 'active'}, '1': {'name': 'default',
'vlan_id': '1', 'trunk_groups': [], 'state': 'active'}}
>>>
```

Vendor-neutral libraries

There are several excellent efforts of vendor-neutral libraries such as Netmiko (https://github.com/ktbyers/netmiko) and NAPALM (https://github.com/napalm-automation/napalm). Because these libraries do not come natively from the device vendor, they are sometimes a step slower to support the latest platform or features. However, because the libraries are vendor-neutral, if you do not like vendor lock-in for your tools, then these libraries are a good choice. Another benefit of using these libraries is the fact that they are normally open source, so you can contribute back upstream for new features and bug fixes.

On the other hand, because these libraries are community supported, they are not necessarily the ideal fit if you need to rely on somebody else to fix bugs or implement new features. If you have a relatively small team that still needs to comply with certain service-level assurances for your tools, you might be better off using a vendor-backed library.

Summary

In this chapter, we looked at various ways to communicate and manage network devices from Cisco, Juniper, and Arista. We looked at both direct communication with the likes of NETCONF and REST, as well as using vendor-provided libraries such as PyEZ and Pyeapi. These are different layers of abstractions, meant to provide a way to programmatically manage your network devices without human intervention.

In `Chapter 7`, *The Python Automation Framework – Ansible Basics*, we will take a look at a higher level of vendor-neutral abstraction framework called **Ansible**. Ansible is an open source, general purpose automation tool written in Python. It can be used to automate servers, network devices, load balancers, and much more. Of course, for our purpose, we will focus on using this automation framework for network devices.

7
The Python Automation Framework – Ansible Basics

The previous two chapters incrementally introduced different ways to interact with network devices. In `Chapter 5`, *Low-Level Network Device Interactions*, we discussed Pexpect and Paramiko libraries that manage an interactive session to control the interactions. In `Chapter 6`, *APIs and Intent-Driven Networking*, we started to think of our network in terms of API and intent. We looked at various APIs that contain a well-defined command structure and provide a structured way of getting feedback from the device. As we moved from `Chapter 5`, *Low-Level Network Device Interactions*, to `Chapter 6`, *APIs and Intent-Driven Networking*, we began to think about our intent for the network and gradually expressed our network in terms of code.

Let's expand upon the idea of translating our intention into network requirements. If you have worked on network designs, chances are the most challenging part of the process is not the different pieces of network equipment, but rather qualifying and translating business requirements into the actual network design. Your network design needs to solve business problems. For example, you might be working within a larger infrastructure team that needs to accommodate a thriving online e-commerce site that experiences slow site response times during peak hours.

How do you determine if the network is the problem? If the slow response on the website was indeed due to network congestion, which part of the network should you upgrade? Can the rest of the system take advantage of the bigger speed and feed? The following diagram is an illustration of a simple process of the steps that we might go through when trying to translate our business requirements into a network design:

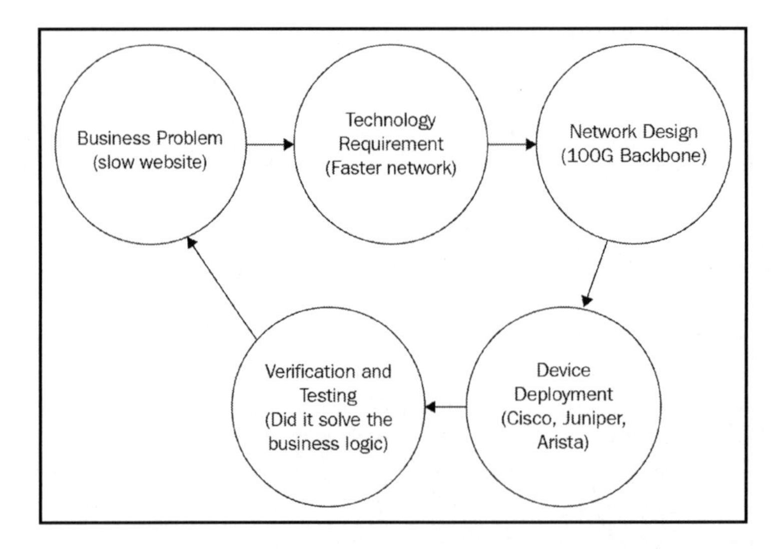

Business logic to network deployment

In my opinion, network automation is not just about faster configuration. It should also be about solving business problems, and accurately and reliably translating our intention into device behavior. These are the goals that we should keep in mind as we march on the network automation journey. In this chapter, we will start to look at a Python-based framework called **Ansible** that allows us to declare our intention for the network and abstract even more from the API and CLI.

A more declarative framework

You woke up one morning in a cold sweat from a nightmare you had about a potential network security breach. You realized that your network contains valuable digital assets that should be protected. You have been doing your job as a network administrator, so it is pretty secure, but you want to put more security measures around your network devices just to be sure.

To start with, you break the objective down into two actionable items:

- Upgrading the devices to the latest version of the software, which requires:
    1. Uploading the image to the device.
    2. Instructing the device to boot from the new image.
    3. Proceeding to reboot the device.
    4. Verifying that the device is running with the new software image.
- Configuring the appropriate access control list on the networking devices, which includes the following:
    1. Constructing the access list on the device.
    2. Configuring the access list on the interface, which in most cases is under the interface configuration section so that it can be applied to the interfaces.

Being an automation-focused network engineer, you want to write scripts to reliably configure the devices and receive feedback from the operations. You begin to research the necessary commands and APIs for each of the steps, validate them in the lab, and finally deploy them in production. Having done a fair amount of work for OS upgrade and ACL deployment, you hope the scripts are transferable to the next generation of devices. Wouldn't it be nice if there was a tool that could shorten this design-develop-deployment cycle?

In this chapter and in `Chapter 8`, *The Python Automation Framework – Beyond Basics*, we will work with an open source automation tool called **Ansible**. It is a framework that can simplify the process of going from business logic to network commands. It can configure systems, deploy software, and orchestrate a combination of tasks. Ansible is written in Python and has emerged as one of the leading automation tools supported by network equipment vendors.

In this chapter, we will take a look at the following topics:

- A quick Ansible example
- The advantages of Ansible

- The Ansible architecture
- Ansible Cisco modules and examples
- Ansible Juniper modules and examples
- Ansible Arista modules and examples

At the time of writing this book, Ansible release 2.5 is compatible with Python 2.6 and 2.7, with Python 3 support recently coming out of the technical review. Just like Python, many of the useful features of Ansible come from the community-driven extension modules. Even with Ansible core module supportability with Python 3, many of the extension modules and production deployments are still in Python 2 mode. It will take some time to bring all the extension modules up from Python 2 to Python 3. Due to this reason, for the rest of this book, we will use Python 2.7 with Ansible 2.2.

Why Ansible 2.2? Ansible 2.5, released in March 2018, offers many new network module features with a new connection method, syntax, and best practices. Given its relatively new features, most of the production deployment is still pre-2.5 release. However, in this chapter, you will also find sections dedicated to Ansible 2.5 examples for those who want to take advantage of the new syntax and features.

For the latest information on Ansible Python 3 support, check out `http://docs.ansible.com/ansible/python_3_support.html`.

As one can tell from the previous chapters, I am a believer in learning by examples. Just like the underlying Python code for Ansible, the syntax for Ansible constructs are easy enough to understand, even if you have not worked with Ansible before. If you have some experience with YAML or Jinja2, you will quickly draw the correlation between the syntax and the intended procedure. Let's take a look at an example first.

A quick Ansible example

As with other automation tools, Ansible started out by managing servers before expanding its ability to manage networking equipment. For the most part, the modules and what Ansible refers to as the playbook are similar between server modules and network modules with subtle differences. In this chapter, we will look at a server task example first and draw comparisons later on with network modules.

The control node installation

First, let's clarify the terminology we will use in the context of Ansible. We will refer to the virtual machine with Ansible installed as the control machine, and the machines being managed as the target machines or managed nodes. Ansible can be installed on most of the Unix systems, with the only dependency of Python 2.6 or 2.7. Currently, the Windows operating system is not officially supported as the control machine. Windows hosts can still be managed by Ansible, as they are just not supported as the control machine.

As Windows 10 starts to adopt the Windows Subsystem for Linux, Ansible might soon be ready to run on Windows as well. For more information, please check the Ansible documentation for Windows (`https://docs.ansible.com/ansible/2.4/intro_windows.html`).

On the managed node requirements, you may notice some documentation mentioning that Python 2.4 or later is a requirement. This is true for managing target nodes with operating systems such as Linux, but obviously not all network equipment supports Python. We will see how this requirement is bypassed for networking modules by local execution on the control node.

For Windows, Ansible modules are implemented in PowerShell. Windows modules in the core and extra repository live in a Windows/subdirectory if you would like to take a look.

We will be installing Ansible on our Ubuntu virtual machine. For instructions on installation on other operating systems, check out the installation documentation (`http://docs.ansible.com/ansible/intro_installation.html`). In the following code block, you will see the steps for installing the software packages:

```
$ sudo apt-get install software-properties-common
$ sudo apt-add-repository ppa:ansible/ansible
$ sudo apt-get update
$ sudo apt-get install ansible
```

We can also use `pip` to install Ansible: `pip install ansible`. My personal preference is to use the operating system's package management system, such as Apt on Ubuntu.

We can now do a quick verification as follows:

```
$ ansible --version
```

```
ansible 2.6.1
  config file = /etc/ansible/ansible.cfg
```

Now, let's see how we can run different versions of Ansible on the same control node. This is a useful feature to adopt if you'd like to try out the latest development features without permanent installation. We can also use this method if we intend on running Ansible on a control node for which we do not have root permissions.

As we saw from the output, at the time of writing this book, the latest release is 2.6.1. Feel free to use this version, but given the relatively new release, we will focus on Ansible version 2.2 in this book.

Running different versions of Ansible from source

You can run Ansible from a source code checkout (we will look at Git as a version control mechanism in `Chapter 10`, *Working with Git*):

```
$ git clone https://github.com/ansible/ansible.git --recursive
$ cd ansible/
$ source ./hacking/env-setup
...
Setting up Ansible to run out of checkout...
$ ansible --version
ansible 2.7.0.dev0 (devel cde3a03b32) last updated 2018/07/11 08:39:39
(GMT -700)
  config file = /etc/ansible/ansible.cfg
...
```

To run different versions, we can simply use `git checkout` for the different branch or tag and perform the environment setup again:

```
$ git branch -a
$ git tag --list
$ git checkout v2.5.6
...
HEAD is now at 0c985fe... New release v2.5.6
$ source ./hacking/env-setup
$ ansible --version
ansible 2.5.6 (detached HEAD 0c985fee8a) last updated 2018/07/11
08:48:20 (GMT -700)
  config file = /etc/ansible/ansible.cfg
```

If the Git commands seem a bit strange to you, we will cover Git in more detail in `Chapter 10`, *Working with Git*.

Once we are at the version you need, such as Ansible 2.2, we can run the update for the core modules for that version:

```
$ ansible --version
ansible 2.2.3.0 (detached HEAD f5be18f409) last updated 2018/07/14
07:40:09 (GMT -700)
...
$ git submodule update --init --recursive
Submodule 'lib/ansible/modules/core'
(https://github.com/ansible/ansible-modules-core) registered for path
'lib/ansible/modules/core'
```

Let's take a look at the lab topology we will use in this chapter and `Chapter 8`, *The Python Automation Framework – Beyond Basics*.

Lab setup

In this chapter and in `Chapter 8`, *The Python Automation Framework – Beyond Basics*, our lab will have an Ubuntu 16.04 control node machine with Ansible installed. This control machine will have reachability for the management network for our VIRL devices, which consist of IOSv and NX-OSv devices. We will also have a separate Ubuntu VM for our playbook example when the target machine is a host:

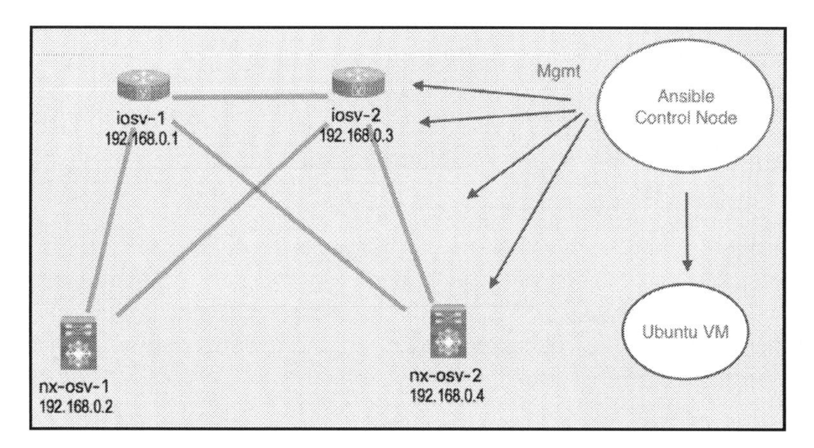

Lab topology

Now, we are ready to see our first Ansible playbook example.

Your first Ansible playbook

Our first playbook will be used between the control node and a remote Ubuntu host. We will take the following steps:

1. Make sure the control node can use key-based authorization.
2. Create an inventory file.
3. Create a playbook.
4. Execute and test it.

The public key authorization

The first thing to do is copy your SSH public key from your control machine to the target machine. A full public key infrastructure tutorial is outside the scope of this book, but here is a quick walkthrough on the control node:

```
$ ssh-keygen -t rsa <<<< generates public-private key pair on the host
machine if you have not done so already
$ cat ~/.ssh/id_rsa.pub <<<< copy the content of the output and paste
it to the ~/.ssh/authorized_keys file on the target host
```

You can read more about PKI at `https://en.wikipedia.org/wiki/Public_key_infrastructure`.

Because we are using key-based authentication, we can turn off password-based authentication on the remote node and be more secure. You will now be able to `ssh` from the control node to the remote node using the private key without being prompted for a password.

Can you automate the initial public key copying? It is possible, but is highly dependent on your use case, regulation, and environment. It is comparable to the initial console setup for network gears to establish initial IP reachability. Do you automate this? Why or why not?

The inventory file

We do not need Ansible if we have no remote target to manage, right? Everything starts with the fact that we need to perform some task on a remote host. In Ansible, the way we specify the potential remote target is with an inventory file. We can have this inventory file as the /etc/ansible/hosts file or use the -i option to specify the file during playbook runtime. Personally, I prefer to have this file in the same directory where my playbook is and use the -i option.

Technically, this file can be named anything you like as long as it is in a valid format. However, the convention is to name this file hosts. You can potentially save yourself and your colleagues some headaches in the future by following this convention.

The inventory file is a simple, plaintext INI-style (https://en.wikipedia.org/wiki/INI_file) file that states your target. By default, the target can either be a DNS FQDN or an IP address:

```
$ cat hosts
192.168.199.170
```

We can now use the command-line option to test Ansible and the hosts file:

```
$ ansible -i hosts 192.168.199.170 -m ping
192.168.199.170 | SUCCESS => {
 "changed": false,
 "ping": "pong"
}
```

By default, Ansible assumes that the same user executing the playbook exists on the remote host. For example, I am executing the playbook as echou locally; the same user also exists on my remote host. If you want to execute as a different user, you can use the -u option when executing, that is, -u REMOTE_USER.

The previous line in the example reads in the host file as the inventory file and executes the ping module on the host called 192.168.199.170. Ping (http://docs.ansible.com/ansible/ping_module.html) is a trivial test module that connects to the remote host, verifies a usable Python installation, and returns the output pong upon success.

You may take a look at the ever-expanding module list (`http://docs.ansible.com/ansible/list_of_all_modules.html`) if you have any questions about the use of existing modules that were shipped with Ansible.

If you get a host key error, it is typically because the host key is not in the `known_hosts` file, and is typically under `~/.ssh/known_hosts`. You can either SSH to the host and answer `yes` when adding the host, or you can disable this by checking on `/etc/ansible/ansible.cfg` or `~/.ansible.cfg` with the following code:

```
[defaults]
host_key_checking = False
```

Now that we have validated the inventory file and Ansible package, we can make our first playbook.

Our first playbook

Playbooks are Ansible's blueprint to describe what you would like to do to the hosts using modules. This is where we will be spending the majority of our time as operators when working with Ansible. If you are building a tree house, the playbook will be your manual, the modules will be your tools, while the inventory will be the components that you will be working on when using the tools.

The playbook is designed to be human readable, and is in YAML format. We will look at the common syntax used in the Ansible architecture section. For now, our focus is to run an example playbook to get the look and feel of Ansible.

Originally, YAML was said to mean Yet Another Markup Language, but now, `http://yaml.org/` has repurposed the acronym to be YAML ain't markup language.

Let's look at this simple 6-line playbook, `df_playbook.yml`:

```
---
- hosts: 192.168.199.170

  tasks:
    - name: check disk usage
      shell: df > df_temp.txt
```

In a playbook, there can be one or more plays. In this case, we have one play (lines two to six). In any play, we can have one or more tasks. In our example play, we have just one task (lines four to six). The `name` field specifies the purpose of the task in a human readable format and the `shell` module was used. The module takes one argument of `df`. The `shell` module reads in the command in the argument and executes it on the remote host. In this case, we execute the `df` command to check the disk usage and copy the output to a file named `df_temp.txt`.

We can execute the playbook via the following code:

```
$ ansible-playbook -i hosts df_playbook.yml
PLAY [192.168.199.170]
*********************************************************

TASK [setup]
*******************************************************************
ok: [192.168.199.170]

TASK [check disk usage]
************************************************
changed: [192.168.199.170]

PLAY RECAP
*********************************************************************
192.168.199.170 : ok=2 changed=1 unreachable=0 failed=0
```

If you log into the managed host (`192.168.199.170`, for me), you will see that the `df_temp.txt` file contains the output of the `df` command. Neat, huh?

You may have noticed that there were actually two tasks executed in our output, even though we only specified one task in the playbook; the setup module is automatically added by default. It is executed by Ansible to gather information about the remote host, which can be used later on in the playbook. For example, one of the facts that the setup module gathers is the operating system. What is the purpose of gathering facts about the remote target? You can use this information as a conditional for additional tasks in the same playbook. For example, the playbook can contain additional tasks to install packages. It can do this specifically to use `apt` for Debian-based hosts and `yum` for Red Hat-based hosts, based on the operation system facts that were gathered in the setup module.

If you are curious about the output of a setup module, you can find out what information Ansible gathers via `$ ansible -i hosts <host> -m setup`.

Underneath the hood, there are actually a few things that have happened for our simple task. The control node copies the Python module to the remote host, executes the module, copies the module output to a temporary file, then captures the output and deletes the temporary file. For now, we can probably safely ignore these underlying details until we need them.

It is important that we fully understand the simple process that we have just gone through because we will be referring back to these elements later in this chapter. I purposely chose a server example to be presented here, because this will make more sense as we dive into the networking modules when we need to deviate from them (remember that we mentioned the Python interpreter is most likely not on the network gear).

Congratulations on executing your first Ansible playbook! We will look more into the Ansible architecture, but for now let's take a look at why Ansible is a good fit for network management. Remember that Ansible modules are written in Python? That is one advantage for a Pythonic network engineer, right?

The advantages of Ansible

There are many infrastructure automation frameworks besides Ansible—namely Chef, Puppet, and SaltStack. Each framework offers its own unique features and models; there is no one right framework that fits all the organizations. In this section, I would like to list some of the advantages of Ansible over other frameworks and why I think this is a good tool for network automation.

I am listing the advantages of Ansible without comparing them to other frameworks. Other frameworks might adopt some of the same philosophy or certain aspects of Ansible, but rarely do they contain all of the features that I will be mentioning. I believe it is the combination of all the following features and philosophy that makes Ansible ideal for network automation.

Agentless

Unlike some of its peers, Ansible does not require a strict master-client model. No software or agent needs to be installed on the client that communicates back to the server. Outside of the Python interpreter, which many platforms have by default, there is no additional software needed.

For network automation modules, instead of relying on remote host agents, Ansible uses SSH or API calls to push the required changes to the remote host. This further reduces the need for the Python interpreter. This is huge for network device management, as network vendors are typically reluctant to put third-party software on their platforms. SSH, on the other hand, already exists on the network equipment. This mentality has changed a bit in the last few years, but overall SSH is the common denominator for all network equipment while configuration management agent support is not. As you will remember from `Chapter 5`, *Low-Level Network Device Interactions*, newer network devices also provide an API layer, which can also be leveraged by Ansible.

Because there is no agent on the remote host, Ansible uses a push model to push the changes to the device, as opposed to the pull model where the agent pulls the information from the master server. The push model, in my opinion, is more deterministic as everything originates from the control machine. In a pull model, the timing of the `pull` might vary from client to client, and therefore results in change timing variance.

Again, the importance of being agentless cannot be stressed enough when it comes to working with the existing network equipment. This is usually one of the major reasons network operators and vendors embrace Ansible.

Idempotent

According to Wikipedia, idempotence is the property of certain operations in mathematics and computer science that can be applied multiple times without changing the result beyond the initial application (`https://en.wikipedia.org/wiki/Idempotence`). In more common terms, it means that running the same procedure over and over again does not change the system after the first time. Ansible aims to be idempotent, which is good for network operations that require a certain order of operations.

The advantage of idempotence is best compared to the Pexpect and Paramiko scripts that we have written. Remember that these scripts were written to push out commands as if an engineer was sitting at the terminal. If you were to execute the script 10 times, the script will make changes 10 times. If we write the same task via the Ansible playbook, the existing device configuration will be checked first, and the playbook will only execute if the changes do not exist. If we execute the playbook 10 times, the change will only be applied during the first run, with the next 9 runs suppressing the configuration change.

Being idempotent means we can repeatedly execute the playbook without worrying that there will be unnecessary changes made. This is important as we need to automatically check for state consistency without any extra overhead.

Simple and extensible

Ansible is written in Python and uses YAML for the playbook language, both of which are considered relatively easy to learn. Remember the Cisco IOS syntax? This is a domain-specific language that is only applicable when you are managing Cisco IOS devices or other similarly structured equipment; it is not a general purpose language beyond its limited scope. Luckily, unlike some other automation tools, there is no extra domain-specific language or DSL to learn for Ansible because YAML and Python are both widely used as general purpose languages.

As you can see from the previous example, even if you have not seen YAML before, it is easy to accurately guess what the playbook is trying to do. Ansible also uses Jinja2 as a template engine, which is a common tool used by Python web frameworks such as Django and Flask, so the knowledge is transferable.

I cannot stress enough the extensibility of Ansible. As illustrated by the preceding example, Ansible starts out with automating server (primarily Linux) workloads in mind. It then branches out to manage Windows machines with PowerShell. As more and more people in the industry started to adapt Ansible, the network became a topic that started to get more attention. The right people and team were hired at Ansible, network professionals started to get involved, and customers started to demand vendors for support. Starting with Ansible 2.0, network automation has become a first-class citizen alongside server management. The ecosystem is alive and well, with continuous improvement in each of the releases.

Just like the Python community, the Ansible community is friendly, and the attitude is inclusive of new members and ideas. I have first-hand experience of being a noob and trying to make sense of contribution procedures and wishing to write modules to be merged upstream. I can testify to the fact that I felt welcomed and respected for my opinions at all times.

The simplicity and extensibility really speak well for future proofing. The technology world is evolving fast, and we are constantly trying to adapt to it. Wouldn't it be great to learn a technology once and continue to use it, regardless of the latest trend? Obviously, nobody has a crystal ball to accurately predict the future, but Ansible's track record speaks well for future technology adaptation.

Network vendor support

Let's face it, we don't live in a vacuum. There is a running joke in the industry that the OSI layer should include a layer 8 (money) and 9 (politics). Every day, we need to work with network equipment made by various vendors.

Take API integration as an example. We saw the difference between the Pexpect and API approach in previous chapters. API clearly has an upper hand in terms of network automation. However, the API interface does not come cheap. Each vendor needs to invest time, money, and engineering resources to make the integration happen. The willingness for the vendor to support a technology matters greatly in our world. Luckily, all the major vendors support Ansible, as clearly indicated by the ever increasingly available network modules (`http://docs.ansible.com/ansible/list_of_network_modules.html`).

Why do vendors support Ansible more than other automation tools? Being agentless certainly helps, since having SSH as the only dependency greatly lowers the bar of entry. Engineers who have been on the vendor side know that the feature request process is usually months long and many hurdles have to be jumped through. Any time a new feature is added, it means more time spent on regression testing, compatibility checking, integration reviews, and many more. Lowering the bar of entry is usually the first step in getting vendor support.

The fact that Ansible is based on Python, a language liked by many networking professionals, is another great propeller for vendor support. For vendors such as Juniper and Arista who already made investments in PyEZ and Pyeapi, they can easily leverage the existing Python modules and quickly integrate their features into Ansible. As you will see in `Chapter 8`, *The Python Automation Framework – Beyond Basics*, we can use our existing Python knowledge to easily write our own modules.

Ansible already had a large number of community-driven modules before it focused on networking. The contribution process is somewhat baked and established, or as baked as an open source project can be. The core Ansible team is familiar with working with the community for submission and contribution.

Another reason for the increased network vendor support also has to do with Ansible's ability to give vendors the ability to express their own strength in the module context. We will see in the coming section that, besides SSH, the Ansible module can also be executed locally and communicate with these devices by using API. This ensures that vendors can express their latest and greatest features as soon as they make them available through the API. In terms of network professionals, this means that you can use the cutting-edge features to select the vendors when you are using Ansible as an automation platform.

We have spent a relatively large portion of space discussing vendor support because I feel that this is often an overlooked part in the Ansible story. Having vendors willing to put their weight behind the tool means you, the network engineer, can sleep at night knowing that the next big thing in networking will have a high chance of Ansible support, and you are not locked into your current vendor as your network needs to grow.

The Ansible architecture

The Ansible architecture consists of playbooks, plays, and tasks. Take a look at `df_playbook.yml` that we used previously:

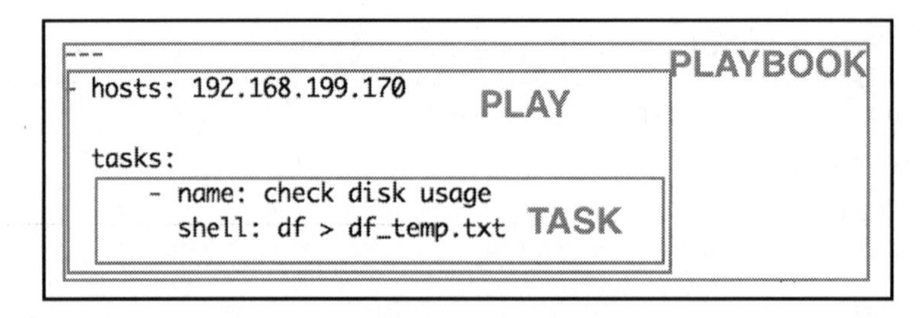

Ansible playbook

The whole file is called a playbook, which contains one or more plays. Each play can consist of one or more tasks. In our simple example, we only have one play, which contains a single task. In this section, we will take a look at the following:

- **YAML**: This format is extensively used in Ansible to express playbooks and variables.
- **Inventory**: The inventory is where you can specify and group hosts in your infrastructure. You can also optionally specify host and group variables in the inventory file.

- **Variables**: Each of the network devices is different. It has a different hostname, IP, neighbor relations, and so on. Variables allow for a standard set of plays while still accommodating these differences.
- **Templates**: Templates are nothing new in networking. In fact, you are probably using one without thinking of it as a template. What do we typically do when we need to provision a new device or replace an RMA (return merchandise authorization)? We copy the old configuration over and replace the differences such as the hostname and the loopback IP addresses. Ansible standardizes the template formatting with Jinja2, which we will dive deeper into later on.

In `Chapter 8`, *The Python Automation Framework – Beyond Basics*, we will cover some more advanced topics such as conditionals, loops, blocks, handlers, playbook roles, and how they can be included with network management.

YAML

YAML is the syntax used for Ansible playbooks and some other files. The official YAML documentation contains the full specifications of the syntax. Here is a compact version as it pertains to the most common usage for Ansible:

- A YAML file starts with three dashes (`---`)
- Whitespace indentation is used to denote structures when they are lined up, just like Python
- Comments begin with the hash (`#`) sign
- List members are denoted by a leading hyphen (`-`), with one member per line
- Lists can also be denoted via square brackets (`[]`), with elements separated by a comma (`,`)
- Dictionaries are denoted by key: value pairs, with a colon for separation
- Dictionaries can be denoted by curly braces, with elements separated by a comma (`,`)
- Strings can be unquoted, but can also be enclosed in double or single quotes

As you can see, YAML maps well into JSON and Python datatypes. If I were to rewrite df_playbook.yml into df_playbook.json, this is what it would look like:

```
[
  {
    "hosts": "192.168.199.170",
    "tasks": [
    "name": "check disk usage",
    "shell": "df > df_temp.txt"
   ]
  }
]
```

This is obviously not a valid playbook, but serves as an aid in helping to understand the YAML formats while using the JSON format as a comparison. Most of the time, comments (#), lists (-), and dictionaries (key: value) are what you will see in a playbook.

Inventories

By default, Ansible looks at the /etc/ansible/hosts file for hosts specified in your playbook. As mentioned previously, I find it more expressive to specify the host file via the -i option. This is what we have been doing up to this point. To expand on our previous example, we can write our inventory host file as follows:

```
[ubuntu]
192.168.199.170

[nexus]
192.168.199.148
192.168.199.149

[nexus:vars]
username=cisco
password=cisco

[nexus_by_name]
switch1 ansible_host=192.168.199.148
switch2 ansible_host=192.168.199.149
```

As you may have guessed, the square bracket headings specify group names, so later on in the playbook we can point to this group. For example, in `cisco_1.yml` and `cisco_2.yml`, I can act on all of the hosts specified under the `nexus` group to the group name of `nexus`:

```
---
- name: Configure SNMP Contact
hosts: "nexus"
gather_facts: false
connection: local
<skip>
```

A host can exist in more than one group. The group can also be nested as `children`:

```
[cisco]
router1
router2

[arista]
switch1
switch2

[datacenter:children]
cisco
arista
```

In the previous example, the datacenter group includes both the `cisco` and `arista` members.

We will discuss variables in the next section. However, you can optionally specify variables belonging to the host and group in the inventory file as well. In our first inventory file example, [`nexus:vars`] specifies variables for the whole nexus group. The `ansible_host` variable declares variables for each of the hosts on the same line.

For more information on the inventory file, check out the official documentation (`http://docs.ansible.com/ansible/intro_inventory.html`).

Variables

We discussed variables a bit in the previous section. Because our managed nodes are not exactly alike, we need to accommodate the differences via variables. Variable names should be letters, numbers, and underscores, and should always start with a letter. Variables are commonly defined in three locations:

- The playbook
- The inventory file
- Separate files to be included in files and roles

Let's look at an example of defining variables in a playbook, `cisco_1.yml`:

```
---
- name: Configure SNMP Contact
hosts: "nexus"
gather_facts: false
connection: local

vars:
cli:
host: "{{ inventory_hostname }}"
username: cisco
password: cisco
transport: cli

tasks:
- name: configure snmp contact
nxos_snmp_contact:
contact: TEST_1
state: present
provider: "{{ cli }}"

register: output

- name: show output
debug:
var: output
```

You can see the `cli` variable declared under the `vars` section, which is being used in the task of `nxos_snmp_contact`.

For more information on the `nxso_snmp_contact` module, check out the online documentation (`http://docs.ansible.com/ansible/nxos_snmp_contact_module.html`).

To reference a variable, you can use the Jinja2 templating system convention of a double curly bracket. You don't need to put quotes around the curly bracket unless you are starting a value with it. I typically find it easier to remember and put a quote around the variable value regardless.

You may have also noticed the `{{ inventory_hostname }}` reference, which is not declared in the playbook. It is one of the default variables that Ansible provides for you automatically, and it is sometimes referred to as the magic variable.

There are not many magic variables, and you can find the list in the documentation (`http://docs.ansible.com/ansible/playbooks_variables.html#magic-variables-and-how-to-access-information-about-other-hosts`).

We have declared variables in an inventory file in the previous section:

```
[nexus:vars]
username=cisco
password=cisco

[nexus_by_name]
switch1 ansible_host=192.168.199.148
switch2 ansible_host=192.168.199.149
```

To use the variables in the inventory file instead of declaring them in the playbook, let's add the group variables for `[nexus_by_name]` in the host file:

```
[nexus_by_name]
switch1 ansible_host=192.168.199.148
switch2 ansible_host=192.168.199.149

[nexus_by_name:vars]
username=cisco
password=cisco
```

Then, modify the playbook to match what we can see here in `cisco_2.yml`, to reference the variables:

```
---
- name: Configure SNMP Contact
hosts: "nexus_by_name"
```

```
gather_facts: false
connection: local

vars:
  cli:
     host: "{{ ansible_host }}"
     username: "{{ username }}"
     password: "{{ password }}"
     transport: cli

tasks:
  - name: configure snmp contact
  nxos_snmp_contact:
    contact: TEST_1
    state: present
    provider: "{{ cli }}"

  register: output

- name: show output
  debug:
    var: output
```

Notice that in this example, we are referring to the `nexus_by_name` group in the inventory file, the `ansible_host` host variable, and the `username` and `password` group variables. This is a good way of hiding the username and password in a write-protected file and publish the playbook without the fear of exposing your sensitive data.

To see more examples of variables, check out the Ansible documentation (`http://docs.ansible.com/ansible/playbooks_variables.html`).

To access complex variable data that's provided in a nested data structure, you can use two different notations. Noted in the `nxos_snmp_contact` task, we registered the output in a variable and displayed it using the debug module. You will see something like the following during playbook execution:

```
TASK [show output]
*************************************************************
ok: [switch1] => {
 "output": {
  "changed": false,
    "end_state": {
      "contact": "TEST_1"
```

```
        },
      "existing": {
         "contact": "TEST_1"
        },
      "proposed": {
        "contact": "TEST_1"
        },
        "updates": []
      }
  }
```

In order to access the nested data, we can use the following notation, as specified in `cisco_3.yml`:

```
msg: '{{ output["end_state"]["contact"] }}'
msg: '{{ output.end_state.contact }}'
```

You will receive just the value indicated:

```
TASK [show output in output["end_state"]["contact"]]
***************************
ok: [switch1] => {
 "msg": "TEST_1"
}
ok: [switch2] => {
 "msg": "TEST_1"
}

TASK [show output in output.end_state.contact]
*********************************
ok: [switch1] => {
 "msg": "TEST_1"
}
ok: [switch2] => {
 "msg": "TEST_1"
}
```

Lastly, we mentioned variables can also be stored in a separate file. To see how we can use variables in a role or included file, we should get a few more examples under our belt, because they are a bit complicated to start with. We will see more examples of roles in `Chapter 8`, *The Python Automation Framework – Beyond Basics*.

Templates with Jinja2

In the previous section, we used variables with the Jinja2 syntax of `{{ variable }}`. While you can do a lot of complex things in Jinja2, luckily, we only need some of the basic things to get started.

Jinja2 (`http://jinja.pocoo.org/`) is a full-featured, powerful template engine that originated in the Python community. It is widely used in Python web frameworks such as Django and Flask.

For now, it is enough to just keep in mind that Ansible utilizes Jinja2 as the template engine. We will revisit the topics of Jinja2 filters, tests, and lookups as the situations call for them. You can find more information on the Ansible Jinja2 template here: `http://docs.ansible.com/ansible/playbooks_templating.html`.

Ansible networking modules

Ansible was originally made for managing nodes with full operating systems such as Linux and Windows before it was extended to support network equipment. You may have already noticed the subtle differences in playbooks that we have used so far for network devices, such as the lines of `gather_facts: false` and `connection: local`; we will take a closer look at the differences in the following sections.

Local connections and facts

Ansible modules are Python code that's executed on the remote host by default. Because of the fact that most network equipment does not expose Python directly, or they simply do not contain Python, we are almost always executing the playbook locally. This means that the playbook is interpreted locally first and commands or configurations are pushed out later on as needed.

Recall that the remote host facts were gathered via the setup module, which was added by default. Since we are executing the playbook locally, the setup module will gather the facts on the localhost instead of the remote host. This is certainly not needed, therefore when the connection is set to local, we can reduce this unnecessary step by setting the fact gathering to false.

Because network modules are executed locally, for those modules that offer a backup option, the files are backed up locally on the control node as well.

One of the most important changes in Ansible 2.5 was the introduction of different communication protocols (`https://docs.ansible.com/ansible/latest/network/getting_started/network_differences.html#multiple-communication-protocols`). The connection method now includes `network_cli`, `netconf`, `httpapi`, and `local`. If the network device uses CLI over SSH, you indicate the connection method as `network_cli` in one of the device variables. However, due to the fact that this is a relatively recent change, you might still see the connection stated as local in many of the existing playbooks.

Provider arguments

As we have seen from `Chapter 5`, *Low-Level Network Device Interactions*, and `Chapter 6`, *APIs and Intent-Driven Networking*, network equipment can be connected via both SSH or API, depending on the platform and software release. All core networking modules implement a `provider` argument, which is a collection of arguments used to define how to connect to the network device. Some modules only support `cli` while some support other values, for example, Arista EAPI and Cisco NXAPI. This is where Ansible's "let the vendor shine" philosophy is demonstrated. The module will have documentation on which transport method they support.

Starting with Ansible 2.5, the recommended way to specify the transport method is by using the `connection` variable. You will start to see the provider parameter being gradually phased out from future Ansible releases. Using the `ios_command` module as an example, `https://docs.ansible.com/ansible/latest/modules/ios_command_module.html#ios-command-module`, the provider parameter still works, but is being labeled as deprecated. We will see an example of this later in this chapter.

Some of the basic arguments supported by the `provider` transport are as follows:

- `host`: This defines the remote host
- `port`: This defines the port to connect to
- `username`: This is the username to be authenticated

- `password`: This is the password to be authenticated
- `transport`: This is the type of transport for the connection
- `authorize`: This enables privilege escalation for devices that require it
- `auth_pass`: This defines the privilege escalation password

As you can see, not all arguments need to be specified. For example, for our previous playbooks, our user is always at the admin privilege when logged in, therefore we do not need to specify the `authorize` or the `auth_pass` arguments.

These arguments are just variables, so they follow the same rules for variable precedence. For example, if I change `cisco_3.yml` to `cisco_4.yml` and observe the following precedence:

```
---
- name: Configure SNMP Contact
  hosts: "nexus_by_name"
  gather_facts: false
  connection: local

  vars:
    cli:
      host: "{{ ansible_host }}"
      username: "{{ username }}"
      password: "{{ password }}"
      transport: cli

  tasks:
    - name: configure snmp contact
      nxos_snmp_contact:
        contact: TEST_1
        state: present
        username: cisco123
        password: cisco123
        provider: "{{ cli }}"

      register: output

    - name: show output in output["end_state"]["contact"]
      debug:
        msg: '{{ output["end_state"]["contact"] }}'

    - name: show output in output.end_state.contact
      debug:
        msg: '{{ output.end_state.contact }}'
```

The username and password defined on the task level will override the username and password at the playbook level. I will receive the following error when trying to connect because the user does not exist on the device:

```
PLAY [Configure SNMP Contact]
**************************************************

TASK [configure snmp contact]
**************************************************
fatal: [switch2]: FAILED! => {"changed": false, "failed": true,
"msg": "failed to connect to 192.168.199.149:22"}
fatal: [switch1]: FAILED! => {"changed": false, "failed": true,
"msg": "failed to connect to 192.168.199.148:22"}
to retry, use: --limit
@/home/echou/Master_Python_Networking/Chapter7/cisco_4.retry

PLAY RECAP
*********************************************************************
switch1 : ok=0 changed=0 unreachable=0 failed=1
switch2 : ok=0 changed=0 unreachable=0 failed=1
```

The Ansible Cisco example

Cisco's support in Ansible is categorized by the operating systems IOS, IOS-XR, and NX-OS. We have already seen a number of NX-OS examples, so in this section let's try to manage IOS-based devices.

Our host file will consist of two hosts, `R1` and `R2`:

```
[ios_devices]
R1 ansible_host=192.168.24.250
R2 ansible_host=192.168.24.251

[ios_devices:vars]
username=cisco
password=cisco
```

Our playbook, `cisco_5.yml`, will use the `ios_command` module to execute arbitrary `show commands`:

```
---
- name: IOS Show Commands
  hosts: "ios_devices"
  gather_facts: false
  connection: local
```

```
  vars:
    cli:
      host: "{{ ansible_host }}"
      username: "{{ username }}"
      password: "{{ password }}"
      transport: cli

  tasks:
    - name: ios show commands
      ios_command:
        commands:
          - show version | i IOS
          - show run | i hostname
        provider: "{{ cli }}"

      register: output

    - name: show output in output["end_state"]["contact"]
      debug:
        var: output
```

The result is what we would expect as the `show version` and `show run` output:

```
$ ansible-playbook -i ios_hosts cisco_5.yml

PLAY [IOS Show Commands]
********************************************************

TASK [ios show commands]
********************************************************
ok: [R1]
ok: [R2]

TASK [show output in output["end_state"]["contact"]]
****************************
ok: [R1] => {
 "output": {
 "changed": false,
 "stdout": [
 "Cisco IOS Software, 7200 Software (C7200-A3JK9S-M), Version
12.4(25g), RELEASE SOFTWARE (fc1)",
 "hostname R1"
 ],
 "stdout_lines": [
 [
 "Cisco IOS Software, 7200 Software (C7200-A3JK9S-M), Version
12.4(25g), RELEASE SOFTWARE (fc1)"
 ],
```

```
 [
 "hostname R1"
 ]
 ]
 }
}
ok: [R2] => {
 "output": {
 "changed": false,
 "stdout": [
 "Cisco IOS Software, 7200 Software (C7200-A3JK9S-M), Version
12.4(25g), RELEASE SOFTWARE (fc1)",
 "hostname R2"
 ],
 "stdout_lines": [
 [
 "Cisco IOS Software, 7200 Software (C7200-A3JK9S-M), Version
12.4(25g), RELEASE SOFTWARE (fc1)"
 ],
 [
 "hostname R2"
 ]
 ]
 }
}

PLAY RECAP
*********************************************************************
R1 : ok=2 changed=0 unreachable=0 failed=0
R2 : ok=2 changed=0 unreachable=0 failed=0
```

I wanted to point out a few things illustrated by this example:

- The playbook between NXOS and IOS is largely identical
- The syntax `nxos_snmp_contact` and `ios_command` modules follow the same pattern, with the only difference being the argument for the modules
- The IOS version of the devices are pretty old with no understanding of API, but the modules still have the same look and feel

As you can see from the preceding example, once we have the basic syntax down for the playbooks, the subtle difference relies on the different modules for the task we would like to perform.

Ansible 2.5 connection example

We have briefly talked about the addition of network connection changes in Ansible playbooks, starting with version 2.5. Along with the changes, Ansible also released a network best practices document, `https://docs.ansible.com/ansible/latest/network/user_guide/network_best_practices_2.5.html`. Let's build an example based on the best practices guide. For our topology, we will reuse the topology in `Chapter 5`, *Low-Level Network Device Interactions*, with two IOSv devices. Since there are multiple files involved in this example, the files are grouped into a subdirectory named `ansible_2-5_example`.

Our inventory file is reduced to the group and the name of the hosts:

```
$ cat hosts
[ios-devices]
iosv-1
iosv-2
```

We have created a `host_vars` directory with two files. Each corresponds to the name specified in the inventory file:

```
$ ls -a host_vars/
. .. iosv-1 iosv-2
```

The variable file for the hosts contains what was previously included in the CLI variable. The additional variable of `ansible_connection` specifies `network_cli` as the transport:

```
$ cat host_vars/iosv-1
---
ansible_host: 172.16.1.20
ansible_user: cisco
ansible_ssh_pass: cisco
ansible_connection: network_cli
ansible_network_os: ios
ansbile_become: yes
ansible_become_method: enable
ansible_become_pass: cisco

$ cat host_vars/iosv-2
---
ansible_host: 172.16.1.21
ansible_user: cisco
ansible_ssh_pass: cisco
ansible_connection: network_cli
ansible_network_os: ios
```

```
ansbile_become: yes
ansible_become_method: enable
ansible_become_pass: cisco
```

Our playbook will use the `ios_config` module with the `backup` option enabled. Notice the use of the `when` condition in this example so that if there are other hosts with a different operating system, this task will not be applied:

```
$ cat my_playbook.yml
---
- name: Chapter 4 Ansible 2.5 Best Practice Demonstration
  connection: network_cli
  gather_facts: false
  hosts: all
  tasks:
    - name: backup
      ios_config:
        backup: yes
      register: backup_ios_location
      when: ansible_network_os == 'ios'
```

When the playbook is run, a new backup folder will be created with the configuration backed up for each of the hosts:

```
$ ansible-playbook -i hosts my_playbook.yml

PLAY [Chapter 4 Ansible 2.5 Best Practice Demonstration]
***********************

TASK [backup]
*******************************************************************
ok: [iosv-2]
ok: [iosv-1]

PLAY RECAP
**********************************************************************
iosv-1 : ok=1 changed=0 unreachable=0 failed=0
iosv-2 : ok=1 changed=0 unreachable=0 failed=0

$ ls -l backup/
total 8
-rw-rw-r-- 1 echou echou 3996 Jul 11 19:01
iosv-1_config.2018-07-11@19:01:55
-rw-rw-r-- 1 echou echou 3996 Jul 11 19:01
iosv-2_config.2018-07-11@19:01:55

$ cat backup/iosv-1_config.2018-07-11@19\:01\:55
Building configuration...
```

```
Current configuration : 3927 bytes
!
! Last configuration change at 01:46:00 UTC Thu Jul 12 2018 by cisco
!
version 15.6
service timestamps debug datetime msec
service timestamps log datetime msec
...
```

This example illustrates the `network_connection` variable and the recommended structure based on network best practices. We will look at offloading variables into the `host_vars` directory and conditionals in `Chapter 8`, *The Python Automation Framework – Beyond Basics*. This structure can also be used for the Juniper and Arista examples in this chapter. For the different devices, we will just use different values for `network_connection`.

The Ansible Juniper example

The Ansible Juniper module requires the Juniper PyEZ package and NETCONF. If you have been following the API example in `Chapter 6`, *APIs and Intent-Driven Networking*, you are good to go. If not, refer back to that section for installation instructions as well as some test script to make sure PyEZ works. The Python package called `jxmlease` is also required:

```
$ sudo pip install jxmlease
```

In the host file, we will specify the device and connection variables:

```
[junos_devices]
J1 ansible_host=192.168.24.252

[junos_devices:vars]
username=juniper
password=juniper!
```

In our Juniper playbook, we will use the `junos_facts` module to gather basic facts for the device. This module is equivalent to the setup module and will come in handy if we need to take action depending on the returned value. Note the different value of transport and port in the example here:

```
---
- name: Get Juniper Device Facts
  hosts: "junos_devices"
  gather_facts: false
```

```
      connection: local

      vars:
        netconf:
          host: "{{ ansible_host }}"
          username: "{{ username }}"
          password: "{{ password }}"
          port: 830
          transport: netconf

      tasks:
        - name: collect default set of facts
          junos_facts:
            provider: "{{ netconf }}"

          register: output

        - name: show output
          debug:
            var: output
```

When executed, you will receive this output from the `Juniper` device:

```
PLAY [Get Juniper Device Facts]
************************************************

TASK [collect default set of facts]
********************************************
ok: [J1]

TASK [show output]
************************************************************
ok: [J1] => {
"output": {
"ansible_facts": {
"HOME": "/var/home/juniper",
"domain": "python",
"fqdn": "master.python",
"has_2RE": false,
"hostname": "master",
"ifd_style": "CLASSIC",
"model": "olive",
"personality": "UNKNOWN",
"serialnumber": "",
"switch_style": "NONE",
"vc_capable": false,
"version": "12.1R1.9",
"version_info": {
```

```
"build": 9,
"major": [
12,
1
],
"minor": "1",
"type": "R"
}
},
"changed": false
 }
}

PLAY RECAP
**********************************************************************
J1 : ok=2 changed=0 unreachable=0 failed=0
```

The Ansible Arista example

The final playbook example we will look at will be the Arista command module. At this point, we are quite familiar with our playbook syntax and structure. The Arista device can be configured to use transport using `cli` or `eapi`, so, in this example, we will use `cli`.

This is the host file:

```
[eos_devices]
A1 ansible_host=192.168.199.158
```

The playbook is also similar to what we have seen previously:

```
    ---
 - name: EOS Show Commands
 hosts: "eos_devices"
 gather_facts: false
 connection: local

 vars:
 cli:
 host: "{{ ansible_host }}"
 username: "arista"
 password: "arista"
 authorize: true
 transport: cli

 tasks:
```

```
- name: eos show commands
eos_command:
commands:
- show version | i Arista
provider: "{{ cli }}"
register: output

- name: show output
debug:
var: output
```

The output will show the standard output as we would expect from the command line:

```
PLAY [EOS Show Commands]
*******************************************************

TASK [eos show commands]
*******************************************************
ok: [A1]

TASK [show output]
*************************************************************
ok: [A1] => {
 "output": {
 "changed": false,
 "stdout": [
 "Arista DCS-7050QX-32-F"
 ],
 "stdout_lines": [
 [
 "Arista DCS-7050QX-32-F"
 ]
 ],
 "warnings": []
 }
}

PLAY RECAP
*********************************************************************
A1 : ok=2 changed=0 unreachable=0 failed=0
```

Summary

In this chapter, we took a grand tour of the open source automation framework Ansible. Unlike Pexpect-based and API-driven network automation scripts, Ansible provides a higher layer of abstraction called the playbook to automate our network devices.

Ansible was originally constructed to manage servers and was later extended to network devices; therefore we took a look at a server example. Then, we compared and contrasted the differences when it came to network management playbooks. Later, we looked at the example playbooks for Cisco IOS, Juniper JUNOS, and Arista EOS devices. We also looked at the best practices recommended by Ansible if you are using Ansible version 2.5 and later.

In `Chapter 8`, *The Python Automation Framework – Beyond Basics,* we will leverage the knowledge we gained in this chapter and start to look at some of the more advanced features of Ansible.

8
The Python Automation Framework – Beyond Basics

In this chapter, we will further build on the knowledge we have gained from the previous chapters and dive deeper into the more advanced topics of Ansible. Many books have been written about Ansible, and there is more to Ansible than we can cover in two chapters. The goal here is to introduce the majority of the features and functions of Ansible that I believe you will need as a network engineer and shorten the learning curve as much as possible.

It is important to point out that if you were not clear on some of the points made in `Chapter 7`, *The Python Automation Framework – Ansible Basics*, now is a good time to go back and review them as they are a prerequisite for this chapter.

In this chapter, we will look into the following topics:

- Ansible conditionals
- Ansible loops
- Templates
- Group and host variables
- The Ansible Vault
- Ansible roles
- Writing your own module

We have a lot of ground to cover, so let's get started!

Ansible conditionals

Ansible conditionals are similar to conditional statements in programming languages. In Ansible, it uses conditional keywords to only run a task when the condition is met. In many cases, the execution of a play or task may depend on the value of a fact, variable, or the previous task result. For example, if you have a play to upgrading router images, you want to include a step to make sure the new router image is on the device before you move on to the next play of rebooting the router.

In this section, we will discuss the `when` clause, which is supported for all modules, as well as unique conditional states that are supported in Ansible networking command modules. Some of the conditions are as follows:

- Equal to (`eq`)
- Not equal to (`neq`)
- Greater than (`gt`)
- Greater than or equal to (`ge`)
- Less than (`lt`)
- Less than or equal to (`le`)
- Contains

The when clause

The `when` clause is useful when you need to check the output of a variable or a play execution result and act accordingly. We saw a quick example of the `when` clause in `Chapter 7`, *The Python Automation Framework – Ansible Basics*, when we looked at the Ansible 2.5 best practices structure. If you recall, the task only ran when the network operating system of the device was the Cisco IOS. Let's look at another example of its use in `chapter8_1.yml`:

```
---
- name: IOS Command Output
  hosts: "iosv-devices"
  gather_facts: false
  connection: local
  vars:
    cli:
      host: "{{ ansible_host }}"
      username: "{{ username }}"
      password: "{{ password }}"
      transport: cli
```

```
tasks:
  - name: show hostname
    ios_command:
      commands:
        - show run | i hostname
          provider: "{{ cli }}"
      register: output
  - name: show output
    when: '"iosv-2" in "{{ output.stdout }}"'
    debug:
      msg: '{{ output }}'
```

We have seen all the elements in this playbook before in `Chapter 7`, *The Python Automation Framework – Ansible Basics,* up to the end of the first task. For the second task in the play, we are using the `when` clause to check if the output contains the `iosv-2` keyword. If true, we will proceed to the task, which is using the debug module to display the output. When the playbook is run, we will see the following output:

```
<skip>
TASK [show output]
*************************************************************
skipping: [ios-r1]
ok: [ios-r2] => {
    "msg": {
        "changed": false,
       "stdout": [
            "hostname iosv-2"
        ],
        "stdout_lines": [
            [
                "hostname iosv-2"
            ]
         ],
         "warnings": []
    }
}
<skip>
```

We can see that the `iosv-r1` device is skipped from the output because the clause did not pass. We can further expand this example in `chapter8_2.yml` to only apply certain configuration changes when the condition is met:

```
<skip>
tasks:
  - name: show hostname
    ios_command:
```

```
        commands:
          - show run | i hostname
        provider: "{{ cli }}"
      register: output
    - name: config example
      when: '"iosv-2" in "{{ output.stdout }}"'
      ios_config:
        lines:
          - logging buffered 30000
        provider: "{{ cli }}"
```

We can see the execution output here:

```
TASK [config example]
**********************************************************
skipping: [ios-r1]
changed: [ios-r2]

PLAY RECAP
***********************************************************
ios-r1 : ok=1 changed=0 unreachable=0 failed=0
ios-r2 : ok=2 changed=1 unreachable=0 failed=0
```

Again, note in the execution output that `ios-r2` was the only change applied while `ios-r1` was skipped. In this case, the logging buffer size was only changed on `ios-r2`.

The `when` clause is also very useful in situations when the setup or facts module is used – you can act based on some of the `facts` that were gathered initially. For example, the following statement will ensure that only the Ubuntu host with major release `16` will be acted upon by placing a conditional statement in the clause:

```
when: ansible_os_family == "Debian" and ansible_lsb.major_release|int
>= 16
```

For more conditionals, check out the Ansible conditionals documentation (`http://docs.ansible.com/ansible/playbooks_conditionals.html`).

Ansible network facts

Prior to 2.5, Ansible networking shipped with a number of network-specific fact modules. The network fact modules exist, but the naming and usage was different between vendors. Starting with version 2.5, Ansible started to standardize its network fact module usage. The Ansible network fact modules gather information from the system and store the results in facts prefixed with `ansible_net_`. The data collected by these modules is documented in the *return values* in the module documentation. This is a pretty big milestone for Ansible networking modules, as it does a lot of the heavy lifting for you to abstract the fact-gathering process by default.

Let's use the same structure we saw in `Chapter 7`, *The Python Automation Framework – Ansible Basics,* Ansible 2.5 best practices, but expand upon it to see how the `ios_facts` module was used to gather facts. As a review, our inventory file contains two iOS hosts with the host variables residing in the `host_vars` directory:

```
$ cat hosts
[ios-devices]
iosv-1
iosv-2

$ cat host_vars/iosv-1
---
ansible_host: 172.16.1.20
ansible_user: cisco
ansible_ssh_pass: cisco
ansible_connection: network_cli
ansible_network_os: ios
ansbile_become: yes
ansible_become_method: enable
ansible_become_pass: cisco
```

Our playbook will have three tasks. The first task will use the `ios_facts` module to gather facts for both of our network devices. The second task will display certain facts gathered and stored for each of the two devices. You will see that the facts we displayed were the default `ansible_net` facts, as opposed to a registered variable from the first task. The third task will display all the facts we collected for the `iosv-1` host:

```
$ cat my_playbook.yml
---
- name: Chapter 5 Ansible 2.5 network facts
  connection: network_cli
  gather_facts: false
  hosts: all
```

```
    tasks:
      - name: Gathering facts via ios_facts module
        ios_facts:
        when: ansible_network_os == 'ios'

      - name: Display certain facts
        debug:
          msg: "The hostname is {{ ansible_net_hostname }} running {{
ansible_net_version }}"

      - name: Display all facts for a host
        debug:
          var: hostvars['iosv-1']
```

When we run the playbook, you can see that the result for the first two tasks were what we would have expected:

```
$ ansible-playbook -i hosts my_playbook.yml

PLAY [Chapter 5 Ansible 2.5 network facts]
*************************************

TASK [Gathering facts via ios_facts module]
************************************
ok: [iosv-2]
ok: [iosv-1]

TASK [Display certain facts]
**************************************************
ok: [iosv-2] => {
    "msg": "The hostname is iosv-2 running 15.6(3)M2"
}
ok: [iosv-1] => {
    "msg": "The hostname is iosv-1 running 15.6(3)M2"
}
```

The third task will display all the network device facts gathered for iOS devices. There is a ton of information that has been gathered for iOS devices that can help with your networking automation needs:

```
TASK [Display all facts for a host]
*******************************************
ok: [iosv-1] => {
    "hostvars['iosv-1']": {
        "ansbile_become": true,
        "ansible_become_method": "enable",
        "ansible_become_pass": "cisco",
        "ansible_check_mode": false,
```

```
        "ansible_connection": "network_cli",
        "ansible_diff_mode": false,
        "ansible_facts": {
            "net_all_ipv4_addresses": [
                "10.0.0.5",
                "172.16.1.20",
                "192.168.0.1"
            ],
            "net_all_ipv6_addresses": [],
            "net_filesystems": [
                "flash0:"
            ],
            "net_gather_subset": [
                "hardware",
                "default",
                "interfaces"
            ],
            "net_hostname": "iosv-1",
            "net_image": "flash0:/vios-adventerprisek9-m",
            "net_interfaces": {
                "GigabitEthernet0/0": {
                    "bandwidth": 1000000,
                    "description": "OOB Management",
                    "duplex": "Full",
                    "ipv4": [
                        {
                            "address": "172.16.1.20",
                            "subnet": "24"
                        }
[skip]
```

The network facts module in Ansible 2.5 was a big step forward in streamlining your workflow and brought it on par with other server modules.

Network module conditional

Let's take a look at another network device conditional example by using the comparison keyword we saw at the beginning of this chapter. We can take advantage of the fact that both IOSv and Arista EOS provide the outputs in JSON format for the `show` commands. For example, we can check the status of the interface:

```
arista1#sh interfaces ethernet 1/3 | json
{
 "interfaces": {
 "Ethernet1/3": {
 "interfaceStatistics": {
```

```
<skip>
 "outPktsRate": 0.0
 },
 "name": "Ethernet1/3",
 "interfaceStatus": "disabled",
 "autoNegotiate": "off",
 <skip>
}
arista1#
```

If we have an operation that we want to perform and it depends on `Ethernet1/3` being disabled in order to have no user impact, such as to ensure no users are actively connected to `Ethernet1/3`, we can use the following tasks in the `chapter8_3.yml` playbook. It uses the `eos_command` module to gather the interface state output, and checks the interface status using the `waitfor` and `eq` keywords before proceeding to the next task:

```
<skip>
 tasks:
    - name: "sh int ethernet 1/3 | json"
      eos_command:
        commands:
          - "show interface ethernet 1/3 | json"
        provider: "{{ cli }}"
        waitfor:
          - "result[0].interfaces.Ethernet1/3.interfaceStatus eq
disabled"
      register: output
    - name: show output
      debug:
        msg: "Interface Disabled, Safe to Proceed"
```

Upon the condition being met, the second task will be executed:

```
TASK [sh int ethernet 1/3 | json]
**********************************************
ok: [arista1]

TASK [show output]
*************************************************************
ok: [arista1] => {
 "msg": "Interface Disabled, Safe to Proceed"
}
```

If the interface is active, an error will be given as follows following the first task:

```
TASK [sh int ethernet 1/3 | json]
```

```
*********************************************
fatal: [arista1]: FAILED! => {"changed": false, "commands": ["show
interface ethernet 1/3 | json | json"], "failed": true, "msg":
"matched error in response: show interface ethernet 1/3 | json |
jsonrn% Invalid input (privileged mode required)rn********1>"}
 to retry, use: --limit
@/home/echou/Master_Python_Networking/chapter8/chapter8_3.retry

PLAY RECAP
******************************************************************
arista1 : ok=0 changed=0 unreachable=0 failed=1
```

Check out the other conditions such as `contains`, `greater than`, and `less than`, as they fit into your situation.

Ansible loops

Ansible provides a number of loops in the playbook, such as standard loops, looping over files, subelements, do-until, and many more. In this section, we will look at two of the most commonly used loop forms: standard loops and looping over hash values.

Standard loops

Standard loops in playbooks are often used to easily perform similar tasks multiple times. The syntax for standard loops is very easy: the `{{ item }}` variable is the placeholder looping over the `with_items` list. For example, take a look at the following section in the `chapter8_4.yml` playbook:

```
tasks:
  - name: echo loop items
    command: echo {{ item }}
    with_items: ['r1', 'r2', 'r3', 'r4', 'r5']
```

It will loop over the five list items with the same `echo` command:

```
TASK [echo loop items]
*********************************************************
changed: [192.168.199.185] => (item=r1)
changed: [192.168.199.185] => (item=r2)
changed: [192.168.199.185] => (item=r3)
changed: [192.168.199.185] => (item=r4)
changed: [192.168.199.185] => (item=r5)
```

We will combine the standard loop with the network command module in the chapter8_5.yml playbook to add multiple VLANs to the device:

```
tasks:
  - name: add vlans
    eos_config:
      lines:
          - vlan {{ item }}
      provider: "{{ cli }}"
    with_items:
        - 100
        - 200
        - 300
```

The with_items list can also be read from a variable, which gives greater flexibility to the structure of your playbook:

```
vars:
  vlan_numbers: [100, 200, 300]
<skip>
tasks:
  - name: add vlans
    eos_config:
      lines:
          - vlan {{ item }}
      provider: "{{ cli }}"
    with_items: "{{ vlan_numbers }}"
```

The standard loop is a great time saver when it comes to performing redundant tasks in a playbook. It also makes the playbook more readable by reducing the lines required for the task.

In the next section, we will take a look at looping over dictionaries.

Looping over dictionaries

Looping over a simple list is nice. However, we often have an entity with more than one attribute associated with it. If you think about the vlan example in the last section, each vlan would have several unique attributes to it, such as the vlan description, the gateway IP address, and possibly others. Oftentimes, we can use a dictionary to represent the entity to incorporate multiple attributes to it.

Let's expand on the `vlan` example in the last section for a dictionary example in `chapter8_6.yml`. We defined the dictionary values for three `vlans`, each with a nested dictionary for the description and the IP address:

```
<skip>
vars:
   cli:
     host: "{{ ansible_host }}"
     username: "{{ username }}"
     password: "{{ password }}"
     transport: cli
   vlans: {
       "100": {"description": "floor_1", "ip": "192.168.10.1"},
       "200": {"description": "floor_2", "ip": "192.168.20.1"}
       "300": {"description": "floor_3", "ip": "192.168.30.1"}
   }
```

We can configure the first task, `add vlans`, by using the key of the each of items as the `vlan` number:

```
tasks:
  - name: add vlans
    nxos_config:
      lines:
        - vlan {{ item.key }}
      provider: "{{ cli }}"
    with_dict: "{{ vlans }}"
```

We can proceed with configuring the `vlan` interfaces. Note that we use the `parents` parameter to uniquely identify the section the commands should be checked against. This is due to the fact that the description and the IP address are both configured under the `interface vlan <number>` subsection in the configuration:

```
- name: configure vlans
  nxos_config:
     lines:
       - description {{ item.value.name }}
       - ip address {{ item.value.ip }}/24
     provider: "{{ cli }}"
     parents: interface vlan {{ item.key }}
  with_dict: "{{ vlans }}"
```

Upon execution, you will see the dictionary being looped through:

```
TASK [configure vlans]
*********************************************************
```

```
changed: [nxos-r1] => (item={'key': u'300', 'value': {u'ip':
u'192.168.30.1', u'name': u'floor_3'}})
changed: [nxos-r1] => (item={'key': u'200', 'value': {u'ip':
u'192.168.20.1', u'name': u'floor_2'}})
changed: [nxos-r1] => (item={'key': u'100', 'value': {u'ip':
u'192.168.10.1', u'name': u'floor_1'}})
```

Let's check if the intended configuration is applied to the device:

```
nx-osv-1# sh run | i vlan
<skip>
vlan 1,10,100,200,300
nx-osv-1#

nx-osv-1# sh run | section "interface Vlan100"
interface Vlan100
  description floor_1
  ip address 192.168.10.1/24
nx-osv-1#
```

For more loop types of Ansible, feel free to check out the documentation (http://docs.ansible.com/ansible/playbooks_loops.html).

Looping over dictionaries takes some practice the first few times you use them. But just like standard loops, looping over dictionaries will be an invaluable tool in your tool belt.

Templates

For as long as I can remember, working as a network engineer, I have always used a kind of network template. In my experience, many of the network devices have sections of the network configuration that are identical, especially if these devices serve the same role in the network.

Most of the time, when we need to provision a new device, we use the same configuration in the form of a template, replace the necessary fields, and copy the file over to the new device. With Ansible, you can automate all of the work by using the template module (http://docs.ansible.com/ansible/template_module.html).

The base template file we are using utilizes the Jinja2 template language (`http://jinja.pocoo.org/docs/`). We briefly discussed the Jinja2 templating language in `Chapter 7`, *The Python Automation Framework – Ansible Basics*, and we will look at it a bit more here. Just like Ansible, Jinja2 has its own syntax and method of doing loops and conditionals; fortunately, we just need to know the very basics of it for our purpose. The Ansible template is an important tool that we will be using in our daily task, and we will spend more of this section exploring it. We will learn the syntax by gradually building up our playbook from simple to more complex.

The basic syntax for template usage is very simple; you just need to specify the source file and the destination location that you want to copy it to.

We will create an empty file for now:

```
$ touch file1
```

Then, we will use the following playbook to copy `file1` to `file2`. Note that the playbook is executed on the control machine only. Next, we will specify the path of both the source and destination files as arguments for the `template` module:

```
---
- name: Template Basic
  hosts: localhost

  tasks:
    - name: copy one file to another
      template:
        src=./file1
        dest=./file2
```

We do not need to specify a host file during playbook execution since the localhost is available by default. However, you will get a warning:

```
$ ansible-playbook chapter8_7.yml
 [WARNING]: provided hosts list is empty, only localhost is available
<skip>
TASK [copy one file to another]
************************************************

changed: [localhost]
<skip>
```

The source file can have any extension, but since they are processed through the Jinja2 template engine, let's create a text file called `nxos.j2` as the template source. The template will follow the Jinja2 convention of using double curly brace to specify the variables:

```
hostname {{ item.value.hostname }}
feature telnet
feature ospf
feature bgp
feature interface-vlan

username {{ item.value.username }} password {{ item.value.password
}} role network-operator
```

The Jinja2 template

Let's also modify the playbook accordingly. In `chapter8_8.yml`, we will make the following changes:

1. Change the source file to `nxos.j2`
2. Change the destination file to be a variable
3. Provide the variable values as a dictionary that we will substitute in the template:

```
---
- name: Template Looping
  hosts: localhost

  vars:
    nexus_devices: {
      "nx-osv-1": {"hostname": "nx-osv-1", "username": "cisco",
"password": "cisco"}
    }

  tasks:
    - name: create router configuration files
      template:
        src=./nxos.j2
        dest=./{{ item.key }}.conf
      with_dict: "{{ nexus_devices }}"
```

After running the playbook, you will find the destination file called `nx-osv-1.conf` with the values filled in and ready to be used:

```
$ cat nx-osv-1.conf
```

```
hostname nx-osv-1

feature telnet
feature ospf
feature bgp
feature interface-vlan

username cisco password cisco role network-operator
```

Jinja2 loops

We can also loop through a list as well as a dictionary in Jinja2. We will use both as loops in `nxos.j2`:

```
{% for vlan_num in item.value.vlans %}
vlan {{ vlan_num }}
{% endfor %}

{% for vlan_interface in item.value.vlan_interfaces %}
interface {{ vlan_interface.int_num }}
  ip address {{ vlan_interface.ip }}/24
{% endfor %}
```

Provide the additional list and dictionary variables in the `chapter8_8.yml` playbook:

```
vars:
  nexus_devices: {
    "nx-osv-1": {
    "hostname": "nx-osv-1",
    "username": "cisco",
    "password": "cisco",
    "vlans": [100, 200, 300],
    "vlan_interfaces": [
       {"int_num": "100", "ip": "192.168.10.1"},
       {"int_num": "200", "ip": "192.168.20.1"},
       {"int_num": "300", "ip": "192.168.30.1"}
     ]
    }
  }
```

Run the playbook, and you will see the configuration for both `vlan` and `vlan_interfaces` filled in on the router config.

The Jinja2 conditional

Jinja2 also supports an `if` conditional check. Let's add this field in for turning on the netflow feature for certain devices. We will add the following to the `nxos.j2` template:

```
{% if item.value.netflow_enable %}
feature netflow
{% endif %}
```

We will list out the difference in the playbook:

```
vars:
  nexus_devices: {
  <skip>
         "netflow_enable": True
  <skip>
 }
```

The last step we will undertake is to make `nxos.j2` more scalable by placing the `vlan` interface section inside of a `true-false` conditional check. In the real world, more often than not, we will have multiple devices with knowledge of the `vlan` information, but only one device as the gateway for client hosts:

```
{% if item.value.l3_vlan_interfaces %}
{% for vlan_interface in item.value.vlan_interfaces %}
interface {{ vlan_interface.int_num }}
 ip address {{ vlan_interface.ip }}/24
{% endfor %}
{% endif %}
```

We will also add a second device, called `nx-osv-2`, in the playbook:

```
vars:
  nexus_devices: {
  <skip>
    "nx-osv-2": {
      "hostname": "nx-osv-2",
      "username": "cisco",
      "password": "cisco",
      "vlans": [100, 200, 300],
      "l3_vlan_interfaces": False,
      "netflow_enable": False
    }
   <skip>
}
```

We are now ready to run our playbook:

```
$ ansible-playbook chapter8_8.yml
 [WARNING]: provided hosts list is empty, only localhost is available.
Note
that the implicit localhost does not match 'all'


PLAY [Template Looping]
*********************************************************

TASK [Gathering Facts]
**********************************************************
ok: [localhost]

TASK [create router configuration files]
****************************************
ok: [localhost] => (item={'value': {u'username': u'cisco',
u'password': u'cisco', u'hostname': u'nx-osv-2', u'netflow_enable':
False, u'vlans': [100, 200, 300], u'l3_vlan_interfaces': False},
'key': u'nx-osv-2'})
ok: [localhost] => (item={'value': {u'username': u'cisco',
u'password': u'cisco', u'hostname': u'nx-osv-1', u'vlan_interfaces':
[{u'int_num': u'100', u'ip': u'192.168.10.1'}, {u'int_num': u'200',
u'ip': u'192.168.20.1'}, {u'int_num': u'300', u'ip':
u'192.168.30.1'}], u'netflow_enable': True, u'vlans': [100, 200, 300],
u'l3_vlan_interfaces': True}, 'key': u'nx-osv-1'})

PLAY RECAP
**********************************************************************
localhost : ok=2 changed=0 unreachable=0 failed=0
```

Let's check the differences in the two configuration files to make sure that the conditional changes are taking place:

```
$ cat nx-osv-1.conf
hostname nx-osv-1

feature telnet
feature ospf
feature bgp
feature interface-vlan

feature netflow

username cisco password cisco role network-operator

vlan 100
```

```
vlan 200
vlan 300

interface 100
  ip address 192.168.10.1/24
interface 200
  ip address 192.168.20.1/24
interface 300
  ip address 192.168.30.1/24

$ cat nx-osv-2.conf
hostname nx-osv-2

feature telnet
feature ospf
feature bgp
feature interface-vlan


username cisco password cisco role network-operator

vlan 100
vlan 200
vlan 300
```

Neat, huh? This can certainly save us a ton of time for something that required repeated copy and paste before. Personally, the template module was a big game changer for me. This module alone was enough to motivate me to learn and use Ansible a few years ago.

Our playbook is getting kind of long. In the next section, we will see how we can optimize the playbook by offloading the variable files into groups and directories.

Group and host variables

Note that, in the previous playbook, `chapter8_8.yml`, we have repeated ourselves in the username and password variables for the two devices under the `nexus_devices` variable:

```
vars:
  nexus_devices: {
    "nx-osv-1": {
      "hostname": "nx-osv-1",
      "username": "cisco",
      "password": "cisco",
```

```
  "vlans": [100, 200, 300],
<skip>
"nx-osv-2": {
  "hostname": "nx-osv-2",
  "username": "cisco",
  "password": "cisco",
  "vlans": [100, 200, 300],
<skip>
```

This is not ideal. If we ever need to update the username and password values, we will need to remember to update at two locations. This increases the management burden as well as the chances of making mistakes. For a best practice, Ansible suggests that we use the `group_vars` and `host_vars` directories to separate out the variables.

For more Ansible best practices, check out `http://docs.ansible.com/ansible/playbooks_best_practices.html`.

Group variables

By default, Ansible will look for group variables in the same directory as the playbook called `group_vars` for variables that can be applied to the group. By default, it will look for the filename that matches the group name in the inventory file. For example, if we have a group called `[nexus-devices]` in the inventory file, we can have a file under `group_vars` named `nexus-devices` to house all the variables that can be applied to the group.

We can also use a special file named `all` to include variables applied to all the groups.

We will utilize this feature for our username and password variables. First, we will create the `group_vars` directory:

```
$ mkdir group_vars
```

Then, we can create a YAML file called `all` to include the username and password:

```
$ cat group_vars/all
---
username: cisco
password: cisco
```

We can then use variables for the playbook:

```
vars:
  nexus_devices: {
   "nx-osv-1": {
      "hostname": "nx-osv-1",
      "username": "{{ username }}",
      "password": "{{ password }}",
      "vlans": [100, 200, 300],
    <skip>
     "nx-osv-2": {
      "hostname": "nx-osv-2",
      "username": "{{ username }}",
      "password": "{{ password }}",
      "vlans": [100, 200, 300],
    <skip>
```

Host variables

We can further separate out the host variables in the same format as the group variables. This was how we were able to apply the variables in the Ansible 2.5 playbook examples in `Chapter 7`, *The Python Automation Framework – Ansible Basics*, and earlier in this chapter:

```
$ mkdir host_vars
```

In our case, we execute the commands on the localhost, and so the file under `host_vars` should be named accordingly, such as `host_vars/localhost`. In our `host_vars/localhost` file, we can also keep the variables declared in `group_vars`:

```
$ cat host_vars/localhost
---
"nexus_devices":
  "nx-osv-1":
    "hostname": "nx-osv-1"
    "username": "{{ username }}"
    "password": "{{ password }}"
    "vlans": [100, 200, 300]
    "l3_vlan_interfaces": True
    "vlan_interfaces": [
        {"int_num": "100", "ip": "192.168.10.1"},
        {"int_num": "200", "ip": "192.168.20.1"},
        {"int_num": "300", "ip": "192.168.30.1"}
     ]
    "netflow_enable": True
```

```
  "nx-osv-2":
    "hostname": "nx-osv-2"
    "username": "{{ username }}"
    "password": "{{ password }}"
    "vlans": [100, 200, 300]
    "l3_vlan_interfaces": False
    "netflow_enable": False
```

After we separate out the variables, the playbook now becomes very lightweight and only consists of the logic of our operation:

```
$ cat chapter8_9.yml
---
- name: Ansible Group and Host Variables
  hosts: localhost

  tasks:
    - name: create router configuration files
      template:
        src=./nxos.j2
        dest=./{{ item.key }}.conf
      with_dict: "{{ nexus_devices }}"
```

The `group_vars` and `host_vars` directories not only decrease our operations overhead, they can also help with securing the files by allowing us to encrypt the sensitive information with Ansible Vault, which we will look at next.

The Ansible Vault

As you can see from the previous section, in most cases, the Ansible variable provides sensitive information such as a username and password. It would be a good idea to put some security measures around the variables so that we can safeguard against them. The Ansible Vault (`https://docs.ansible.com/ansible/2.5/user_guide/vault.html`) provides encryption for files so they appear in plaintext.

All Ansible Vault functions start with the `ansible-vault` command. You can manually create an encrypted file via the create option. You will be asked to enter a password. If you try to view the file, you will find that the file is not in clear text. If you have downloaded the book example, the password I used was just the word *password*:

```
$ ansible-vault create secret.yml
Vault password: <password>

$ cat secret.yml
$ANSIBLE_VAULT;1.1;AES256
336564626462373962326635326361323639323635353630646665656430353261383737623<skip>65353733383738386363653035646462303233343238613930333566326
2
3962
```

To edit or view an encrypted file, we will use the `edit` option for edit or view the file via the `view` option:

```
$ ansible-vault edit secret.yml
Vault password:

$ ansible-vault view secret.yml
Vault password:
```

Let's encrypt the `group_vars/all and host_vars/localhost` variable files:

```
$ ansible-vault encrypt group_vars/all host_vars/localhost
Vault password:
Encryption successful
```

Now, when we run the playbook, we will get a decryption failed error message:

```
ERROR! Decryption failed on
/home/echou/Master_Python_Networking/chapter8/Vaults/group_vars/all
```

We will need to use the `--ask-vault-pass` option when we run the playbook:

```
$ ansible-playbook chapter8_10.yml --ask-vault-pass
Vault password:
```

The decryption will happen in memory for any Vault-encrypted files that are accessed.

Prior to Ansible 2.4, Ansible Vault required all the files to be encrypted with the same password. Since Ansible 2.4 and later, you can use vault ID to supply a different password file (https://docs.ansible.com/ansible/2.5/user_guide/vault.html#multiple-vault-passwords).

We can also save the password in a file and make sure that the specific file has restricted permission:

```
$ chmod 400 ~/.vault_password.txt
$ ls -lia ~/.vault_password.txt
809496 -r-------- 1 echou echou 9 Feb 18 12:17
/home/echou/.vault_password.txt
```

We can then execute the playbook with the `--vault-password-file` option:

```
$ ansible-playbook chapter8_10.yml --vault-password-file
~/.vault_password.txt
```

We can also encrypt just a string and embed the encrypted string inside of the playbook by using the `encrypt_string` option (https://docs.ansible.com/ansible/2.5/user_guide/vault.html#use-encrypt-string-to-create-encrypted-variables-to-embed-in-yaml):

```
$ ansible-vault encrypt_string
New Vault password:
Confirm New Vault password:
Reading plaintext input from stdin. (ctrl-d to end input)
new_user_password
!vault |
          $ANSIBLE_VAULT;1.1;AES256
6163643864383932626231396235616135396566643838346433383239666238363437
37373361326134663232623861313338383534613865303864616364380a6263653936
6531613361646264383165333266326364373436386366663263646463656361626530
3665626364636562316635636462323135663163663331320a62356361326639333165
3939626639623066303037616564356339666334376130303266333364383662646264
64366138323666376239656633623233353832

Encryption successful
```

The string can then be placed in the playbook file as a variable. In the next section, we will optimize our playbook even further with `include` and `roles`.

The Ansible include and roles

The best way to handle complex tasks is to break them down into smaller pieces. Of course, this approach is common in both Python and network engineering. In Python, we break complicated code into functions, classes, modules, and packages. In networking, we also break large networks into sections such as racks, rows, clusters, and datacenters. In Ansible, we can use `roles` and `includes` to segment and organize a large playbook into multiple files. Breaking up a large Ansible playbook simplifies the structure as each of the files focuses on fewer tasks. It also allows the sections of the playbook to be reused.

The Ansible include statement

As the playbook grows in size, it will eventually become obvious that many of the tasks and plays can be shared across different playbooks. The Ansible `include` statement is similar to many Linux configuration files that just tell the machine to extend the file the same way as if the file was directly written in. We can use an `include` statement for both playbooks and tasks. Here, we will look at a simple example of extending our task.

Let's assume that we want to show outputs for two different playbooks. We can make a separate YAML file called `show_output.yml` as an additional task:

```
---
- name: show output
    debug:
      var: output
```

Then, we can reuse this task in multiple playbooks, such as in `chapter8_11_1.yml`, which looks largely identical to the last playbook with the exception of registering the output and the include statement at the end:

```
---
- name: Ansible Group and Host Varibles
  hosts: localhost

  tasks:
    - name: create router configuration files
      template:
        src=./nxos.j2
        dest=./{{ item.key }}.conf
      with_dict: "{{ nexus_devices }}"
```

```
        register: output

      - include: show_output.yml
```

Another playbook, `chapter8_11_2.yml`, can reuse `show_output.yml` in the same way:

```
---
- name: show users
  hosts: localhost

  tasks:
    - name: show local users
      command: who
      register: output

    - include: show_output.yml
```

Note that both playbooks use the same variable name, `output`, because in `show_output.yml`, we hard coded the variable name for simplicity. You can also pass variables into the included file.

Ansible roles

Ansible roles separate the logical function with a physical host to fit your network better. For example, you can construct roles such as spines, leafs, core, as well as Cisco, Juniper, and Arista. The same physical host can belong to multiple roles; for example, a device can belong to both Juniper and the core. This flexibility allows us to perform operations, such as upgrade all Juniper devices, without worrying about the device's location in the layer of the network.

Ansible roles can automatically load certain variables, tasks, and handlers based on a known file infrastructure. The key is that this is a known file structure that we automatically include. In fact, you can think of roles as pre-made `include` statements by Ansible.

The Ansible playbook role documentation (`http://docs.ansible.com/ansible/playbooks_roles.html#roles`) describes a list of role directories that we can configure. We do not need to use all of them. In our example, we will only modify the `tasks and the vars` folders. However, it is good to know all of the available options in the Ansible role directory structure.

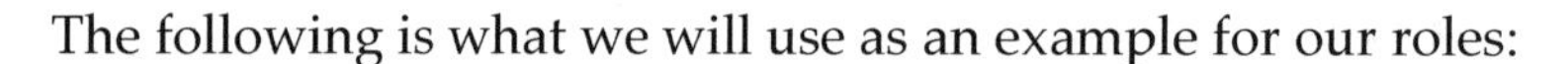

The following is what we will use as an example for our roles:

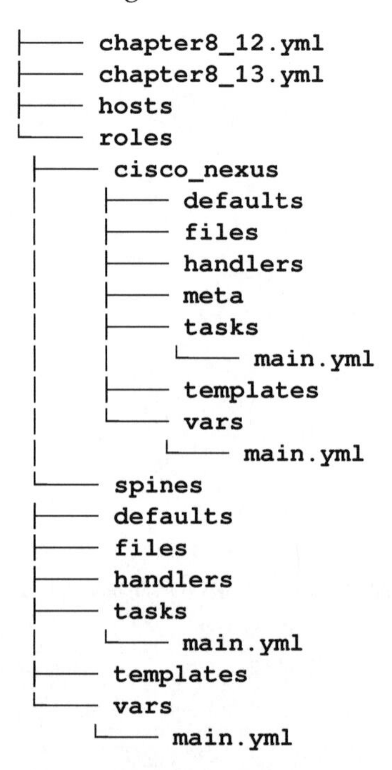

You can see that, at the top level, we have the hosts file as well as the playbooks. We also have a folder named `roles`. Inside the folder, we have two roles defined: `cisco_nexus` and `spines`. Most of the subfolders under the roles were empty, with the exception of the `tasks and vars` folders. There is a file named `main.yml` inside each of them. This is the default behavior: the `main.yml` file is your entry point that is automatically included in the playbook when you specify the role in the playbook. If you need to break out additional files, you can use the include statement in the `main.yml` file.

Here is our scenario:

- We have two Cisco Nexus devices, `nxos-r1` and `nxos-r2`. We will configure the logging server as well as the log link-status for all of them, utilizing the `cisco_nexus` role for them.
- In addition, nxos-r1 is also a spine device, where we will want to configure more verbose logging, perhaps because spines are at a more critical position within our network.

For our cisco_nexus role, we have the following variables in roles/cisco_nexus/vars/main.yml:

```
---
cli:
  host: "{{ ansible_host }}"
  username: cisco
  password: cisco
  transport: cli
```

We have the following configuration tasks in roles/cisco_nexus/tasks/main.yml:

```
---
- name: configure logging parameters
  nxos_config:
    lines:
      - logging server 191.168.1.100
      - logging event link-status default
    provider: "{{ cli }}"
```

Our playbook is extremely simple, as it just needs to specify the hosts that we would like to configure according to cisco_nexus role:

```
---
- name: playbook for cisco_nexus role
  hosts: "cisco_nexus"
  gather_facts: false
  connection: local

  roles:
    - cisco_nexus
```

When you run the playbook, the playbook will include the tasks and variables defined in the cisco_nexus role and configure the devices accordingly.

For our spine role, we will have an additional task of more verbose logging in roles/spines/tasks/mail.yml:

```
---
- name: change logging level
  nxos_config:
    lines:
      - logging level local7 7
    provider: "{{ cli }}"
```

In our playbook, we can specify that it contains both the role of `cisco_nexus` as well as `spines`:

```
---
- name: playbook for spine role
  hosts: "spines"
  gather_facts: false
  connection: local

  roles:
    - cisco_nexus
    - spines
```

When we include both roles in this order, the `cisco_nexus` role tasks will be executed, followed by the spines role:

```
TASK [cisco_nexus : configure logging parameters]
******************************
changed: [nxos-r1]

TASK [spines : change logging level]
*******************************************
ok: [nxos-r1]
```

Ansible roles are flexible and scalable – just like Python functions and classes. Once your code grows beyond a certain level, it is almost always a good idea to break it into smaller pieces for maintainability.

You can find more examples of roles in the Ansible examples Git repository at `https://github.com/ansible/ansible-examples`.

Ansible Galaxy (`https://docs.ansible.com/ansible/latest/reference_appendices/galaxy.html`) is a free community site for finding, sharing, and collaborating on roles. You can see an example of the Juniper networks supplied by the Ansible role on Ansible Galaxy:

JUNOS Role on Ansible Galaxy (`https://galaxy.ansible.com/Juniper/junos`)

In the next section, we will take a look at how to write our own custom Ansible module.

Writing your own custom module

By now, you may get the feeling that network management in Ansible is largely dependent on finding the right module for your task. There is certainly a lot of truth in that logic. Modules provide a way to abstract the interaction between the managed host and the control machine; they allow us to focus on the logic of our operations. Up to this point, we have seen the major vendors providing a wide range of modules for Cisco, Juniper, and Arista.

Use the Cisco Nexus modules as an example, besides specific tasks such as managing the BGP neighbor (`nxos_bgp`) and the aaa server (`nxos_aaa_server`). Most vendors also provide ways to run arbitrary show (`nxos_config`) and configuration commands (`nxos_config`). This generally covers most of our use cases.

Starting with Ansible 2.5, there is also the streamline naming and usage of network facts modules.

What if the device you are using does not currently have the module for the task that you are looking for? In this section, we will look at several ways that we can remedy this situation by writing our own custom module.

The first custom module

Writing a custom module does not need to be complicated; in fact, it doesn't even need to be in Python. But since we are already familiar with Python, we will use Python for our custom modules. We are assuming that the module is what we will be using ourselves and our team without submitting back to Ansible, therefore we will ignore some of the documentation and formatting for the time being.

If you are interested in developing modules that can be submitted upstream to Ansible, please consult the developing modules guide from Ansible (`https://docs.ansible.com/ansible/latest/dev_guide/developing_modules.html`).

By default, if we create a folder named `library` in the same directory as the playbook, Ansible will include the directory in the module search path. Therefore, we can put our custom module in the directory and we will be able to use it in our playbook. The requirement for the custom module is very simple: all the module needs is to return a JSON output to the playbook.

Recall that in `Chapter 6`, *APIs and Intent-Driven Networking*, we used the following NXAPI Python script to communicate to the NX-OS device:

```
import requests
import json

url='http://172.16.1.142/ins'
switchuser='cisco'
switchpassword='cisco'
```

```
myheaders={'content-type':'application/json-rpc'}
payload=[
 {
   "jsonrpc": "2.0",
   "method": "cli",
   "params": {
     "cmd": "show version",
     "version": 1.2
   },
   "id": 1
 }
]
response = requests.post(url,data=json.dumps(payload),
headers=myheaders,auth=(switchuser,switchpassword)).json()

print(response['result']['body']['sys_ver_str'])
```

When we executed it, we simply received the system version. We can simply modify the last line to be a JSON output, as shown in the following code:

```
version = response['result']['body']['sys_ver_str']
print json.dumps({"version": version})
```

We will place this file under the `library` folder:

```
$ ls -a library/
. .. custom_module_1.py
```

In our playbook, we can then use the action plugin (`https://docs.ansible.com/ansible/dev_guide/developing_plugins.html`), `chapter8_14.yml`, to call this custom module:

```
---
- name: Your First Custom Module
  hosts: localhost
  gather_facts: false
  connection: local

  tasks:
    - name: Show Version
      action: custom_module_1
      register: output

    - debug:
        var: output
```

Note that, just like the ssh connection, we are executing the module locally with the module making API calls outbound. When you execute this playbook, you will get the following output:

```
$ ansible-playbook chapter8_14.yml
 [WARNING]: provided hosts list is empty, only localhost is available

PLAY [Your First Custom Module]
**********************************************

TASK [Show Version]
**********************************************************
ok: [localhost]

TASK [debug]
*****************************************************************
ok: [localhost] => {
 "output": {
 "changed": false,
 "version": "7.3(0)D1(1)"
 }
}

PLAY RECAP
*******************************************************************
localhost : ok=2 changed=0 unreachable=0 failed=0
```

As you can see, you can write any module that is supported by API, and Ansible will happily take any returned JSON output.

The second custom module

Building upon the last module, let's utilize the common module boilerplate from Ansible that's stated in the module development documentation (http://docs.ansible.com/ansible/dev_guide/developing_modules_general.html). We will modify the last custom module and create custom_module_2.py to ingest inputs from the playbook.

First, we will import the boilerplate code from ansible.module_utils.basic:

```
from ansible.module_utils.basic import AnsibleModule
if __name__ == '__main__':
    main()
```

From there, we can define the main function where we will house our code. `AnsibleModule`, which we have already imported, provides lots of common code for handling returns and parsing arguments. In the following example, we will parse three arguments for `host`, `username`, and `password`, and make them required fields:

```
def main():
    module = AnsibleModule(
      argument_spec = dict(
      host = dict(required=True),
      username = dict(required=True),
      password = dict(required=True)
  )
)
```

The values can then be retrieved and used in our code:

```
device = module.params.get('host')
username = module.params.get('username')
password = module.params.get('password')

url='http://' + host + '/ins'
switchuser=username
switchpassword=password
```

Finally, we will follow the exit code and return the value:

```
module.exit_json(changed=False, msg=str(data))
```

Our new playbook, `chapter8_15.yml`, will look identical to the last playbook, except now we can pass values for different devices in the playbook:

```
tasks:
  - name: Show Version
    action: custom_module_1 host="172.16.1.142" username="cisco"
password="cisco"
    register: output
```

When executed, this playbook will produce the exact same output as the last playbook. However, because we are using arguments in the custom module, the custom module can now be passed around for other people to use without them knowing the details of our module. They can write in their own username, password, and host IP in the playbook.

Of course, this is a functional but incomplete module. For one, we did not perform any error checking, nor did we provide any documentation for usage. However, it is a good demonstration of how easy it is to build a custom module. The additional benefit is that we saw how we can use an existing script that we already made and turn it into a custom Ansible module.

Summary

In this chapter, we covered a lot of ground. Building from our previous knowledge of Ansible, we expanded into more advanced topics such as conditionals, loops, and templates. We looked at how to make our playbook more scalable with host variables, group variables, include statements, and roles. We also looked at how to secure our playbook with the Ansible Vault. Finally, we used Python to make our own custom modules.

Ansible is a very flexible Python framework that can be used for network automation. It provides another abstraction layer separated from the likes of the Pexpect and API-based scripts. It is declarative in nature in that it is more expressive in terms of matching our intent. Depending on your needs and network environment, it might be the ideal framework that you can use to save time and energy.

9
AWS Cloud Networking

Cloud computing is one of the major trends in computing today. Public cloud providers have transformed the high-tech industry and what it means to launch a service from scratch. We no longer need to build our own infrastructure; we can pay the public cloud providers to rent a portion of their resources for our infrastructure needs. Nowadays, walking around any technology conferences or meetups, we will be hard-pressed to find a person who has not learned about, used, or built services based in the cloud. Cloud computing is here, and we better get used to working with it.

There are several service models of cloud computing, roughly divided into **Software-as-a-Service (SaaS)** (`https://en.wikipedia.org/wiki/Software_as_a_service`), **Platform-as-a-Service (PaaS)** (`https://en.wikipedia.org/wiki/Cloud_computing#Platform_as_a_service_(PaaS)`), and **Infrastructure-as-a-Service (IaaS)** (`https://en.wikipedia.org/wiki/Infrastructure_as_a_service`). Each service model offers a different level of abstraction from the user's perspective. For us, networking is part of the Infrastructure-as-a-Service offering and the focus of this chapter.

Amazon Web Services (AWS—`https://aws.amazon.com/`) is the first company to offer IaaS public cloud services and the clear leader in the space by market share in 2018. If we define the term **Software Defined Networking (SDN)** as a group of software services working together to create network constructs – IP addresses, access lists, Network Address Translation, routers – we can make the argument that AWS is the world's largest implementation of SDN. They utilize their massive scale of the global network, data centers, and hosts to offer an amazing array of networking services.

If you are interested in learning about Amazon's scale and networking, I would highly recommend taking a look at James Hamilton's AWS re:Invent 2014 talk: `https://www.youtube.com/watch?v=JIQETrFC_SQ`. It is a rare insider's view of the scale and innovation at AWS.

In this chapter, we will discuss the networking services offered by the AWS cloud services and how we can use Python to work with them:

- AWS setup and networking overview
- Virtual private cloud
- Direct Connect and VPN
- Networking scaling services
- Other AWS network services

AWS setup

If you do not already have an AWS account and wish to follow along with these examples, please log on to `https://aws.amazon.com/` and sign up. The process is pretty straightforward and simple; you will need a credit card and some form of verification. AWS offers a number of services in a free tier (`https://aws.amazon.com/free/`), where you can use some of the most popular services for free up to a certain level.

Some of the services listed are free for the first year, and others are free up to a certain limit without time restraint. Please check the AWS site for the latest offerings:

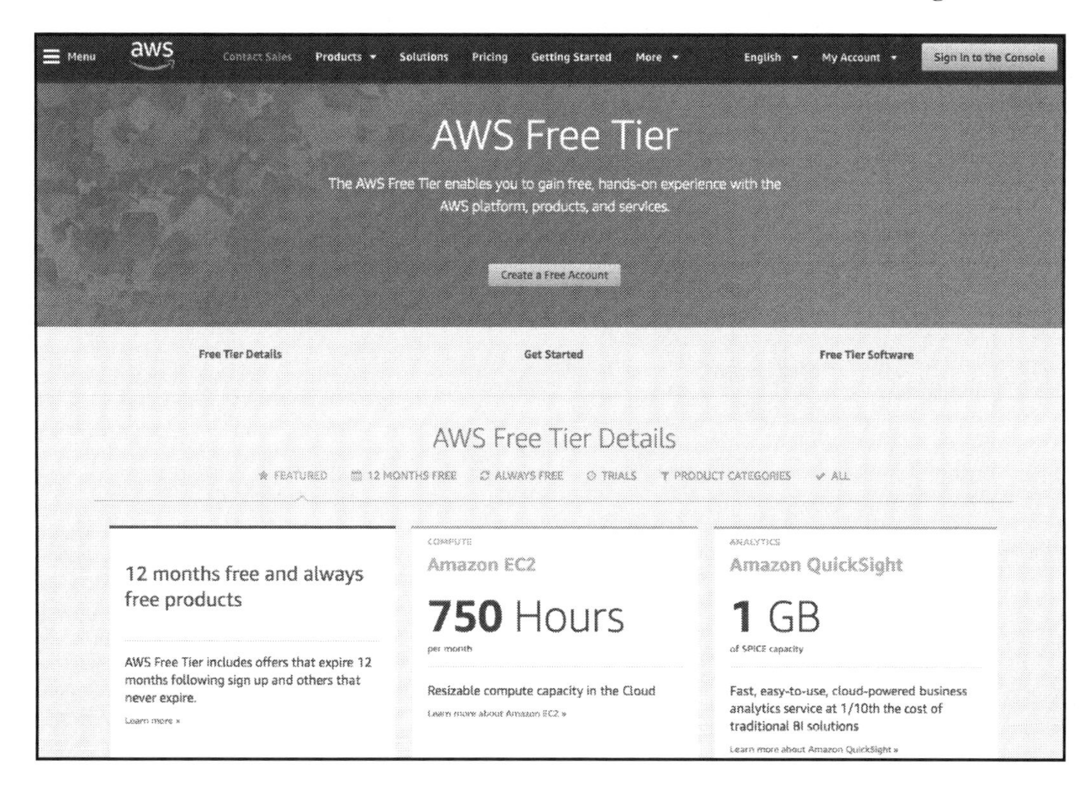

AWS free tier

Once you have an account, you can sign in via the AWS console (`https://console.aws.amazon.com/`) and take a look at the different services offered by AWS. The console is where we can configure all the services and look at our monthly bills:

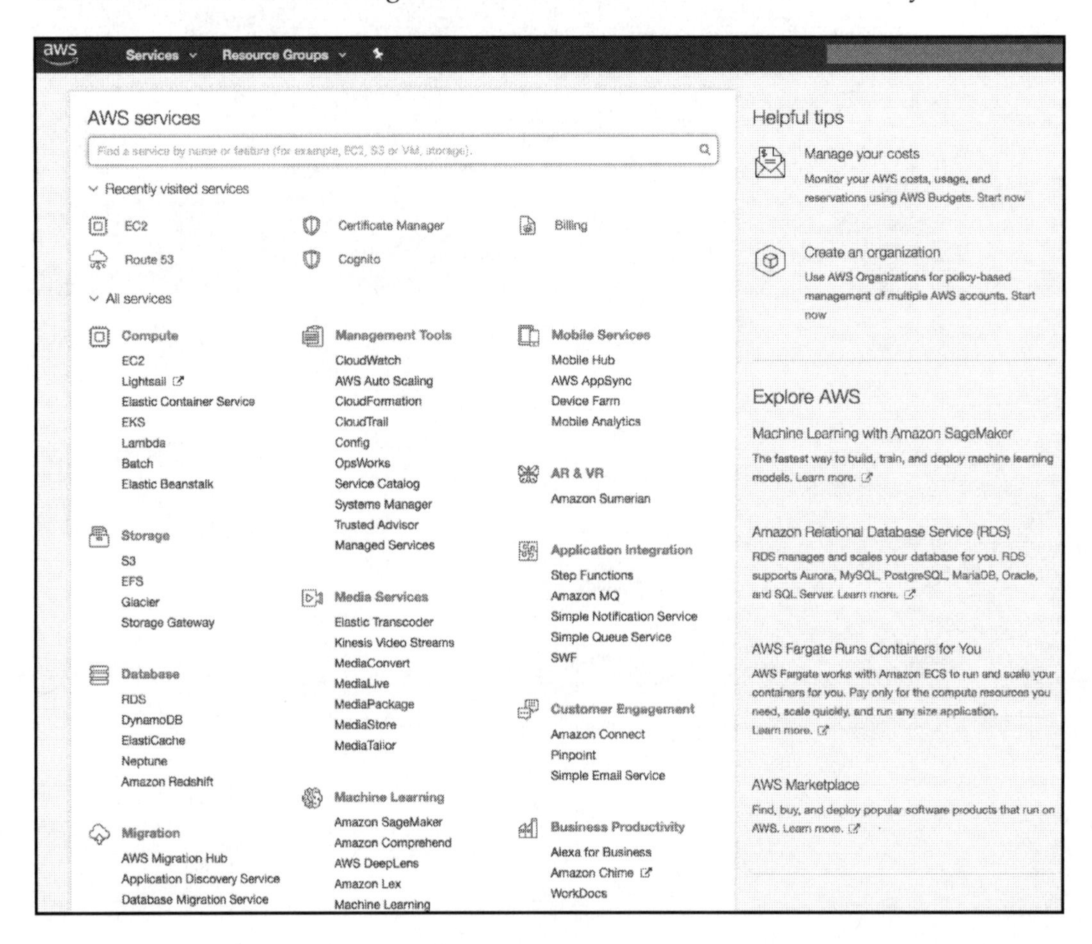

AWS console

AWS CLI and Python SDK

We can also manage the AWS services via the command-line interface. The AWS CLI is a Python package that can be installed via PIP (`https://docs.aws.amazon.com/cli/latest/userguide/installing.html`). Let's install it on our Ubuntu host:

```
$ sudo pip3 install awscli
$ aws --version
aws-cli/1.15.59 Python/3.5.2 Linux/4.15.0-30-generic botocore/1.10.58
```

Once the AWS CLI is installed, for easier and more secure access, we will create a user and configure AWS CLI with the user credentials. Let's go back to the AWS console and select **IAM** for user and access management:

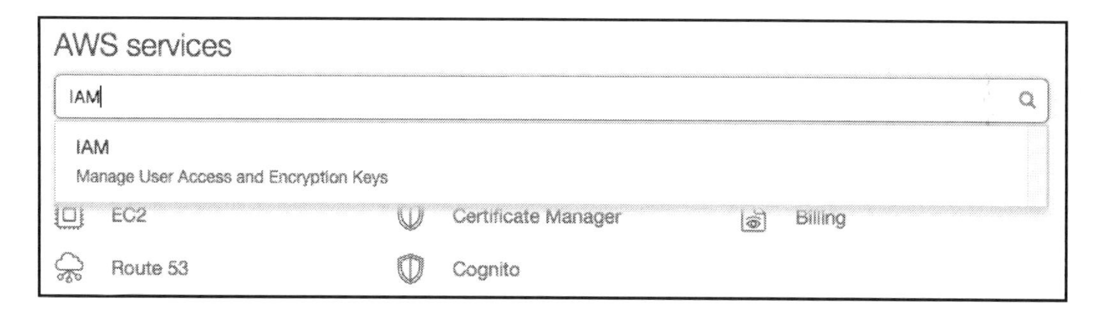

AWS IAM

We can choose `Users` on the left panel to create a user:

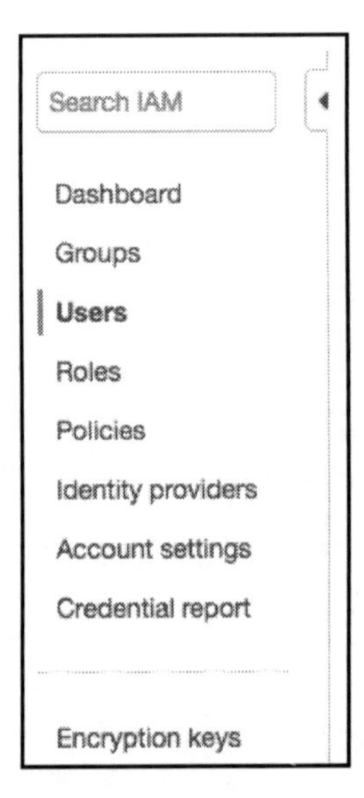

Select programmatic access and assign the user to the default administrator group:

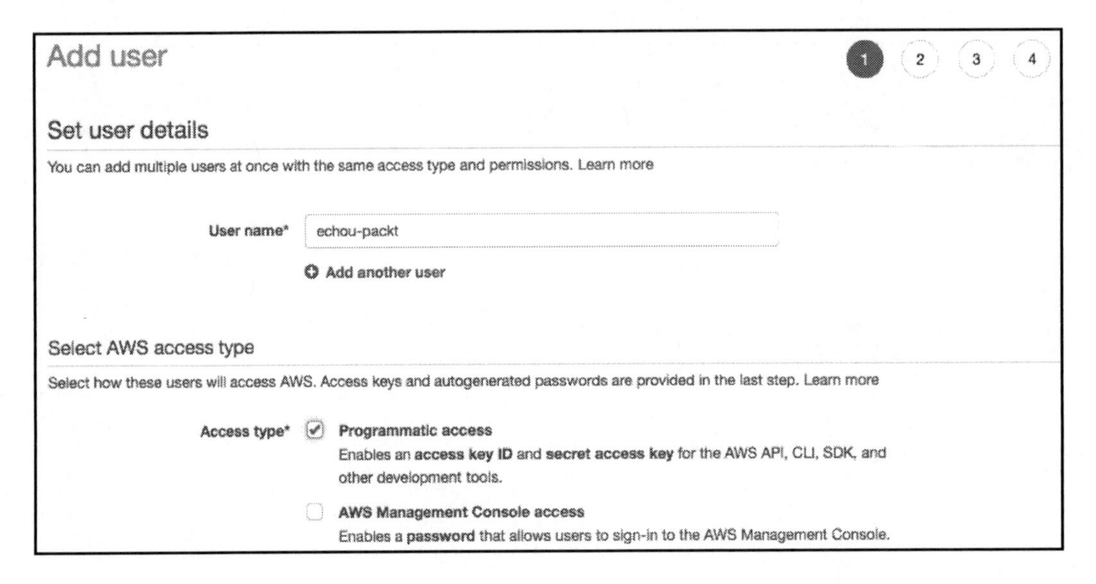

The last step will show an **Access key ID** and a **Secret access key**. Copy them into a text file and keep it in a safe place:

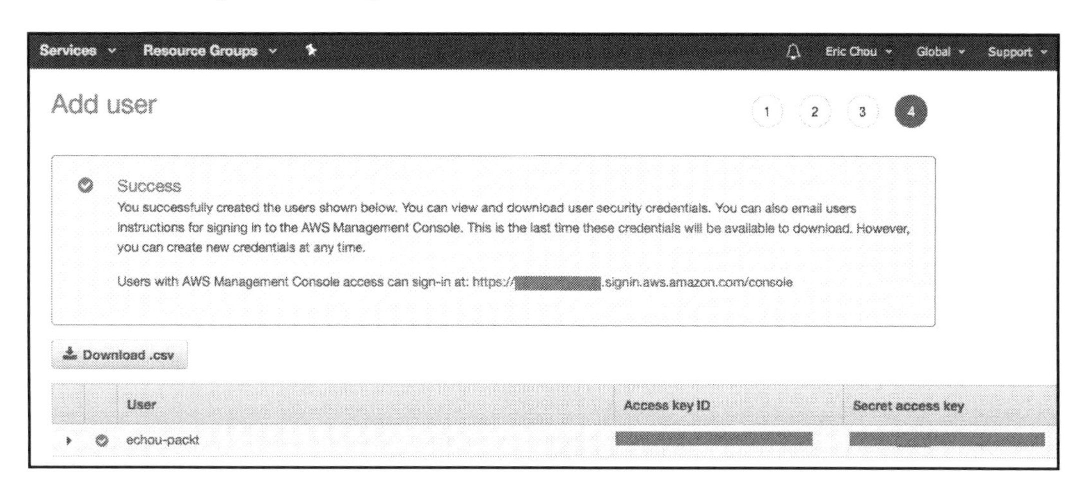

We will complete the AWS CLI authentication credential setup via `aws configure` in the terminal. We will go over AWS regions in the upcoming section; we will use `us-east-1` for now, but feel free to come back and change this value later:

```
$ aws configure
AWS Access Key ID [None]: <key>
AWS Secret Access Key [None]: <secret>
Default region name [None]: us-east-1
Default output format [None]: json
```

We will also install the AWS Python SDK, Boto3 (`https://boto3.readthedocs.io/en/latest/`):

```
$ sudo pip install boto3
$ sudo pip3 install boto3

# verification
$ python3
Python 3.5.2 (default, Nov 23 2017, 16:37:01)
[GCC 5.4.0 20160609] on linux
Type "help", "copyright", "credits" or "license" for more information.
>>> import boto3
>>> exit()
```

We are now ready to move on to the subsequent sections, starting with an introduction to AWS cloud networking services.

AWS network overview

When we discuss AWS services, we need to start at the top with regions and availability zones. They have big implications for all of our services. At the time of writing this book, AWS listed 18 Regions, 55 **Availability Zones** (**AZ**), and one local region around the world. In the words of AWS Global Infrastructure, (`https://aws.amazon.com/about-aws/global-infrastructure/`):

> *"The AWS Cloud infrastructure is built around Regions and Availability Zones (AZs). AWS Regions provide multiple, physically separated and isolated Availability Zones which are connected with low latency, high throughput, and highly redundant networking."*

Some of the services AWS offer are global, but most of the services are region-based. What this means for us is that we should build our infrastructure in a region that is closest to our intended users. This will reduce the latency of the service to our customer. If our users are in the United States east coast, we should pick `us-east-1` (N. Virginia) or `us-east-2` (Ohio) as our region if the service is regional-based:

Region & Number of Availability Zones

US East
N. Virginia (6),
Ohio (3)

US West
N. California (3),
Oregon (3)

Asia Pacific
Mumbai (2),
Seoul (2),
Singapore (3),
Sydney (3),
Tokyo (4),
Osaka-Local (1)[1]

Canada
Central (2)

China
Beijing (2),
Ningxia (3)

Europe
Frankfurt (3),
Ireland (3),
London (3),
Paris (3)

South America
São Paulo (3)

AWS GovCloud (US-West) (3)

New Region (coming soon)

Bahrain

Hong Kong SAR, China

Sweden

AWS GovCloud (US-East)

AWS regions

Not all regions are available to all users, for example, GovCloud and the **China** region are not available to users in the United States by default. You can list the regions available to you via `aws ec2 describe-regions`:

```
$ aws ec2 describe-regions
{
    "Regions": [
        {
            "RegionName": "ap-south-1",
            "Endpoint": "ec2.ap-south-1.amazonaws.com"
        },
        {
            "RegionName": "eu-west-3",
            "Endpoint": "ec2.eu-west-3.amazonaws.com"
        },
...
```

All the regions are completely independent of one another. Most resources are not replicated across regions. If we have multiple regions, say `US-East` and `US-West`, and need redundancy between them, we will need to replicate the necessary resources ourselves. The way you choose a region is on the top right corner of the console:

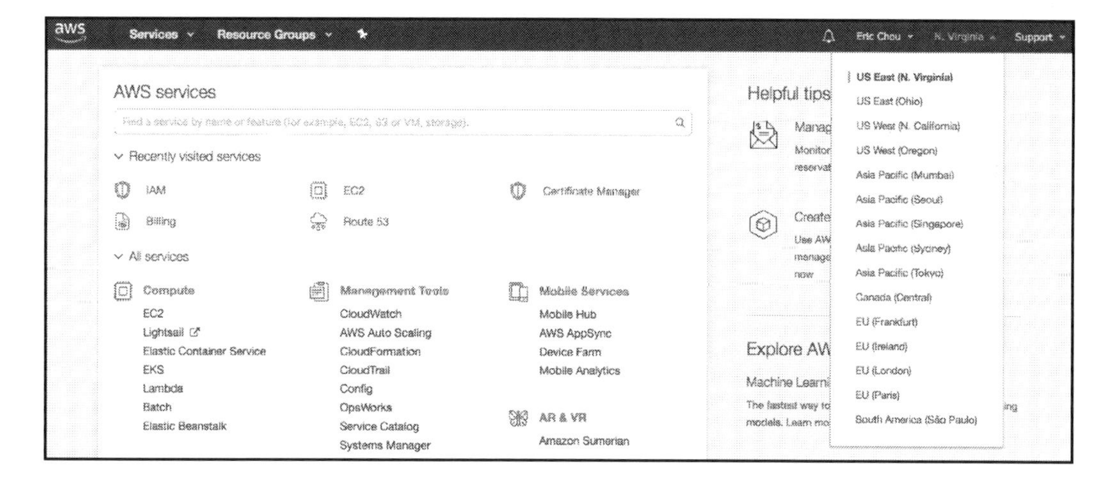

If the service is region-based, for example, EC2, the portal will only show the service when the right region is selected. If our EC2 instances are in `us-east-1` and we are looking at the us-west-1 portal, none of the EC2 instances will show up. I have made this mistake a few times, and wondered where all of my instances went!

The number behind the regions in the preceding AWS regions screenshot represents the number of AZ in each region. Each region has multiple availability zones. Each availability zone is isolated, but the AZs in a region are connected through low-latency fiber connections:

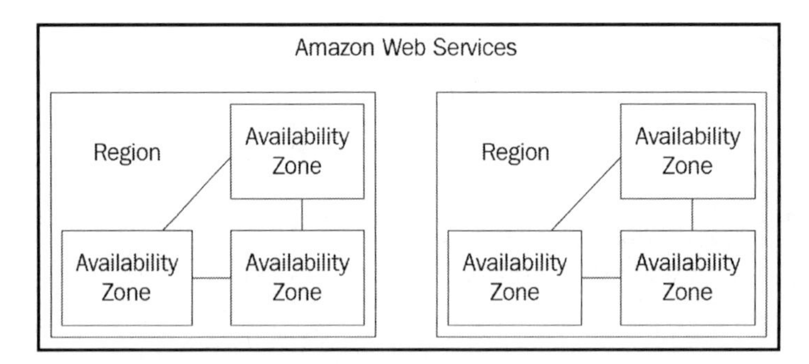

AWS regions and availability zones

Many of the resources we built are copied across availability zones. The concept of AZ is very important, and its constraints are important to us for the network services we will build.

AWS independently maps availability zones to identifiers for each account. For example, my availability zone, us-eas-1a, might not be the same as `us-east-1a` for another account.

We can check the AZs in a region in AWS CLI:

```
$ aws ec2 describe-availability-zones --region us-east-1
{
    "AvailabilityZones": [
        {
            "Messages": [],
            "RegionName": "us-east-1",
            "State": "available",
            "ZoneName": "us-east-1a"
        },
        {
            "Messages": [],
            "RegionName": "us-east-1",
            "State": "available",
            "ZoneName": "us-east-1b"
        },
...
```

Why do we care about regions and availability zones so much? As we will see in the coming few sections, the networking services are usually bound by the region and availability zones. **Virtual Private Cloud (VPC)**, for example, needs to reside entirely in one region, and each subnet needs to reside entirely in one availability zone. On the other hand, **NAT Gateway** is AZ-bound, so we will need to create one per AZ if we needed redundancy. We will go over both services in more detail, but their use cases are offered here as examples of how regions and availability zones are the basis of the AWS network services offering.

AWS Edge locations are part of the **AWS CloudFront** content delivery network in 59 cities across 26 countries. These edge locations are used to distribute content with low latency with a smaller footprint than the full data center Amazon builds for the region and availability zones. Sometimes, people mistook the edge locations' point-of-presence for full AWS regions. If the footprint is listed as an edge location only, the AWS services such as EC2 or S3 will not be offered. We will revisit the edge location in the *AWS CloudFront* section.

AWS Transit Centers is one of the least documented aspects of AWS networks. It was mentioned in James Hamilton's 2014 **AWS re:Invent** keynote (`https://www.youtube.com/watch?v=JIQETrFC_SQ`) as the aggregation points for different AZs in the region. To be fair, we do not know if the transit center still exists and functions the same way after all these years. However, it is fair to make an educated guess about the placement of the transit center and its correlation about the **AWS Direct Connect** service that we will look at later in this chapter.

James Hamilton, a VP and distinguished engineer from AWS, is one of the most influential technologists at AWS. If there is anybody who I would consider authoritative when it comes to AWS networking, it would be him. You can read more about his visions on his blog, Perspectives, at `https://perspectives.mvdirona.com/`.

It is impossible to cover all of the services related to AWS in one chapter. There are some relevant services not directly related to networking that we do not have the space to cover, but we should be familiar with:

- The **Identify and Access Management (IAM)** service, `https://aws.amazon.com/iam/`, is the service that enables us to manage access to AWS services and resources securely.

- **Amazon Resource Names (ARNs)**, `https://docs.aws.amazon.com/general/latest/gr/aws-arns-and-namespaces.html`, uniquely identify AWS resources across all of AWS. This resource name is important when we need to identify a service, such as DynamoDB and API Gateway, that needs access to our VPC resources.
- **Amazon Elastic Compute Cloud (EC2)**, `https://aws.amazon.com/ec2/`, is the service that enables us to obtain and provision compute capacities, such as Linux and Windows instances, via AWS interfaces. We will use EC2 instances throughout this chapter in our examples.

For the sake of learning, we will exclude AWS GovCloud (US) and China, neither of which uses the AWS global infrastructure and have their own limitations.

This was a relatively long introduction to the AWS network overview, but an important one. These concepts and terms will be referred to in the rest of the chapters in this book. In the upcoming section, we will take a look at the most import concept (in my opinion) for AWS networking: the virtual private cloud.

Virtual private cloud

Amazon Virtual Private Cloud (Amazon VPC) enables customers to launch AWS resources into a virtual network dedicated to the customer's account. It is truly a customizable network that allows you to define your own IP address range, add and delete subnets, create routes, add VPN gateways, associate security policies, connect EC2 instances to your own datacenter, and much more. In the early days when VPC was not available, all EC2 instances in the AZ were on a single, flat network that was shared among all customers. How comfortable would the customer be with putting their information in the cloud? Not very, I'd imagine. Between the launch of EC2 in 2007 until the launch of VPC in 2009, VPC functions was one of the most requested features of AWS.

The packets leaving your EC2 host in a VPC are intercepted by the Hypervisor. The Hypervisor will check them with a mapping service which understands our VPC construct. The packets leaving your EC2 hosts are encapsulated with the AWS real servers' source and destination addresses. The encapsulation and mapping service allows for the flexibility of VPC, but also some of the limitations (multicast, sniffing) of VPC. This is, after all, a virtual network.

Since December 2013, all EC2 instances are VPC-only. If we use a launch wizard to create our EC2 instance, it will automatically be put into a default VPC with a virtual internet gateway for public access. In my opinion, all but the most basic use cases should use the default VPC. For most cases, we would need to define our non-default, customized VPC.

Let's create the following VPC using the AWS console in `us-east-1`:

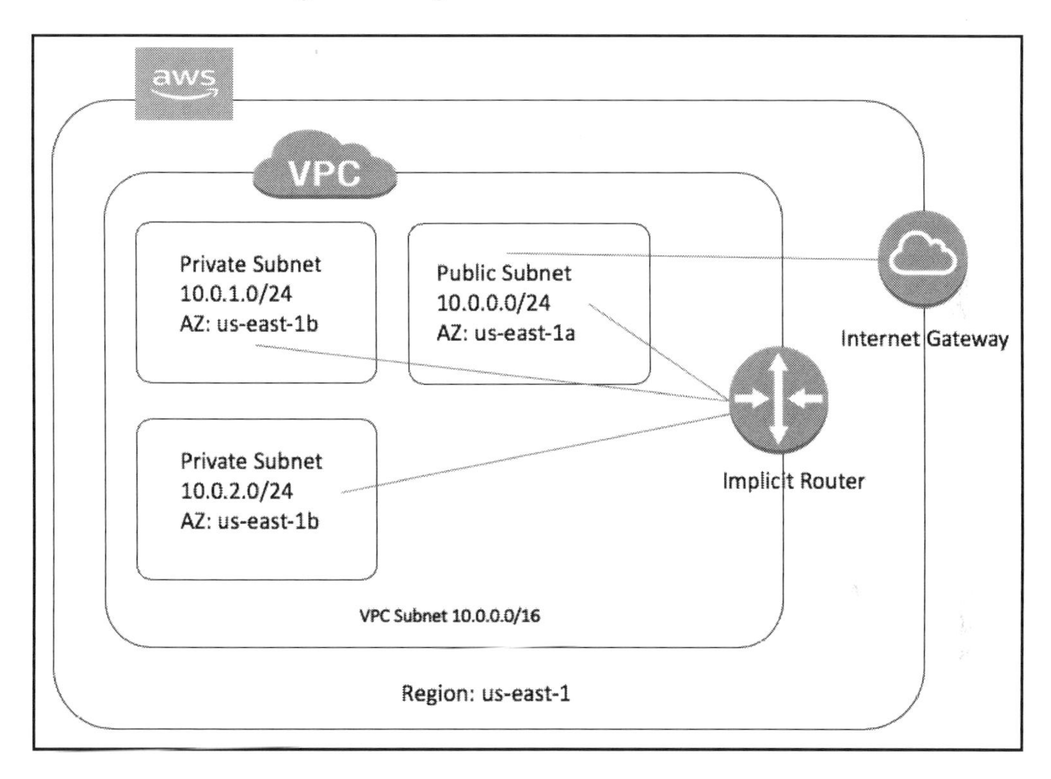

Our first VPC in US-East-1

If you recall, VPC is AWS region-bound, and the subnets are Availability Zone-based. Our first VPC will be based in `us-east-1`; the three subnets will be allocated to three different availability zones in 1a, 1b, and 1c.

Using the AWS console to create the VPC and subnets is pretty straightforward, and AWS provides a number of good tutorials online. I have listed the steps with the associated links on the VPC dashboard:

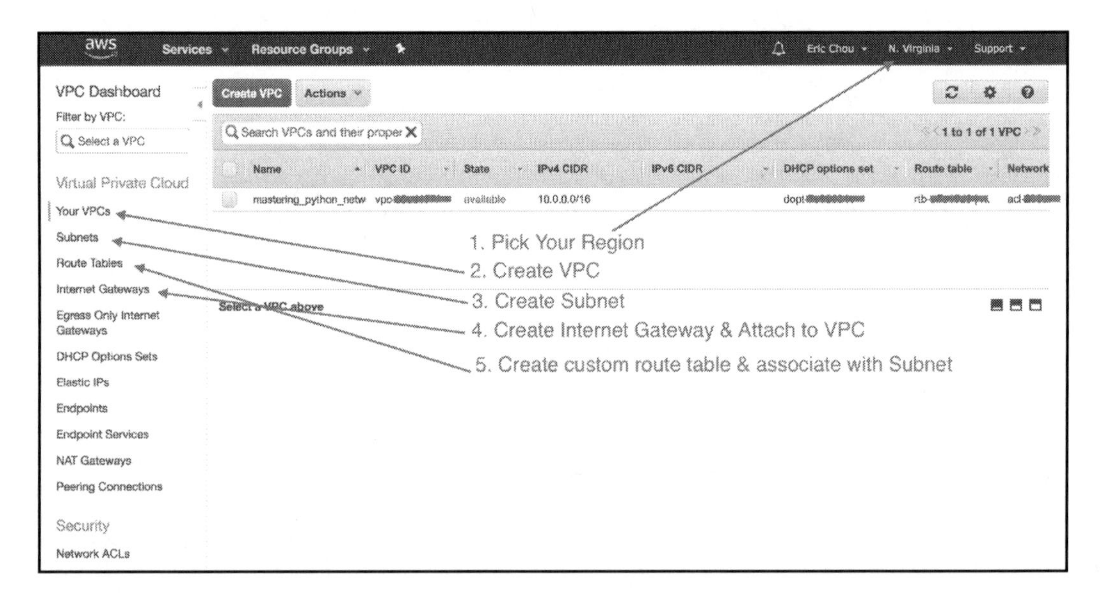

The first two steps are point and click processes that most network engineers can work through, even without prior experience. By default, the VPC only contains the local route, `10.0.0.0/16`. Now, we will create an internet gateway and associate it with the VPC:

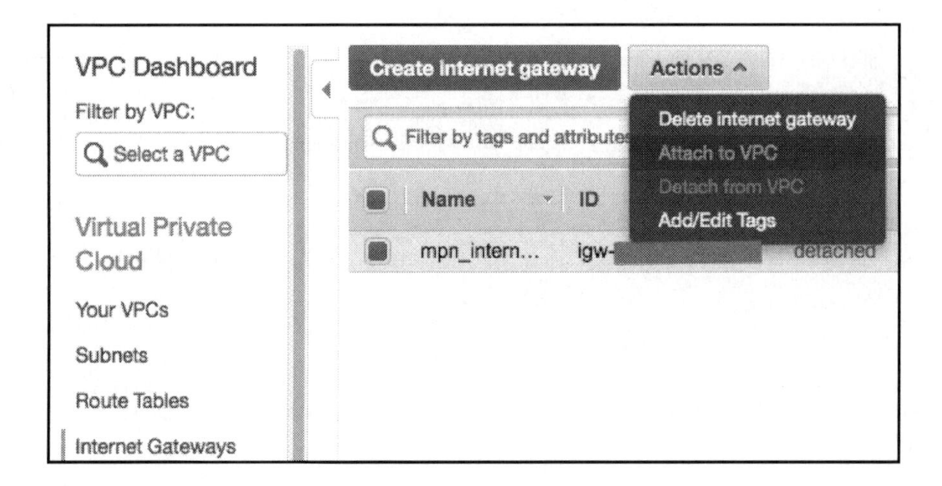

We can then create a custom route table with a default route pointing to the internet gateway. We will associate this route table with our subnet in `us-east-1a`, `10.0.0.0/24`, thus allowing it to be public facing:

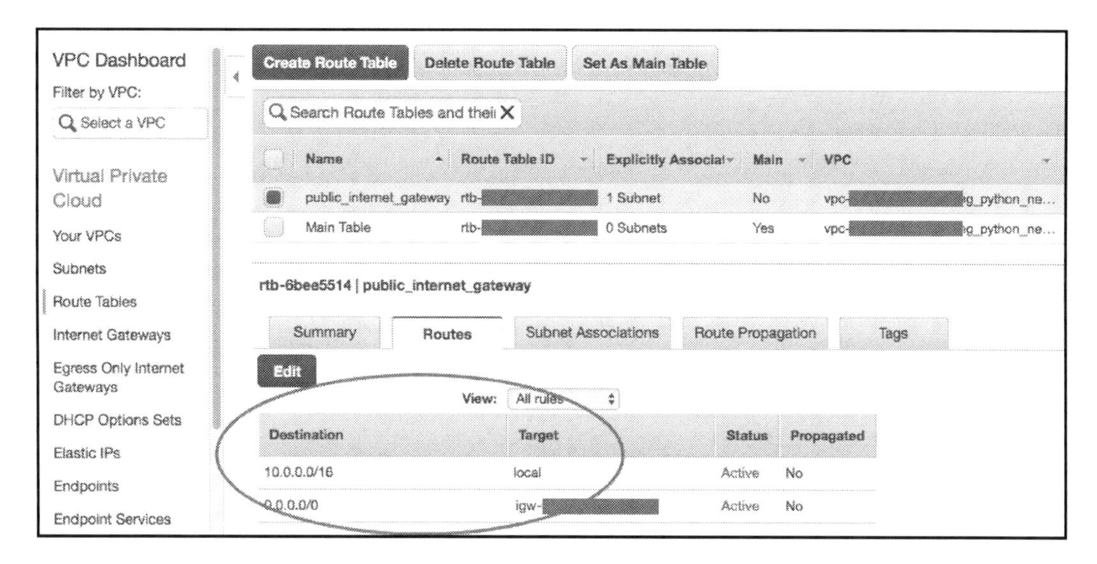

Route table

Let's use Boto3 Python SDK to see what we have created; I used the tag `mastering_python_networking_demo` as the tag for the VPC, which we can use as the filer:

```
$ cat Chapter9_1_query_vpc.py
#!/usr/bin/env python3

import json, boto3

region = 'us-east-1'
vpc_name = 'mastering_python_networking_demo'

ec2 = boto3.resource('ec2', region_name=region)
client = boto3.client('ec2')

filters = [{'Name':'tag:Name', 'Values':[vpc_name]}]

vpcs = list(ec2.vpcs.filter(Filters=filters))
for vpc in vpcs:
    response = client.describe_vpcs(
                 VpcIds=[vpc.id,]
                )
```

```
    print(json.dumps(response, sort_keys=True, indent=4))
```

This script will allow us to programmatically query the region for the VPC we created:

```
$ python3 Chapter9_1_query_vpc.py
{
    "ResponseMetadata": {
        "HTTPHeaders": {
            "content-type": "text/xml;charset=UTF-8",
            ...
        },
        "HTTPStatusCode": 200,
        "RequestId": "48e19be5-01c1-469b-b6ff-9c45f2745483",
        "RetryAttempts": 0
    },
    "Vpcs": [
        {
            "CidrBlock": "10.0.0.0/16",
            "CidrBlockAssociationSet": [
                {
                    "AssociationId": "...",
                    "CidrBlock": "10.0.0.0/16",
                    "CidrBlockState": {
                        "State": "associated"
                    }
                }
            ],
            "DhcpOptionsId": "dopt-....",
            "InstanceTenancy": "default",
            "IsDefault": false,
            "State": "available",
            "Tags": [
                {
                    "Key": "Name",
                    "Value": "mastering_python_networking_demo"
                }
            ],
            "VpcId": "vpc-...."
        }
    ]
}
```

The Boto3 VPC API documentation can be found at `https://boto3.readthedocs.io/en/latest/reference/services/ec2.html#vpc`.

You may be wondering about how the subnets can reach one another within the VPC. In a physical network, the network needs to connect to a router to reach beyond its own local network. It is not so different in VPC, except it is an *implicit router* with a default routing table of the local network, which in our example is `10.0.0.0/16`. This implicit router was created when we created our VPC.

Route tables and route targets

Routing is one of the most important topics in network engineering. It is worth looking at it more closely. We already saw that we had an implicit router and the main routing table when we created the VPC. From the last example, we created an internet gateway, a custom routing table with a default route pointing to the internet gateway, and associated the custom routing table with a subnet.

The concept of the route target is where VPC is a bit different than traditional networking. In summary:

- Each VPC has an implicit router
- Each VPC has the main routing table with the local route populated
- You can create custom-routing tables
- Each subnet can follow a custom-routing table or the default main routing table
- The route table route target can be an internet gateway, NAT gateway, VPC peers, and so on

We can use Boto3 to look at the custom route tables and association with the subnets:

```
$ cat Chapter9_2_query_route_tables.py
#!/usr/bin/env python3

import json, boto3

region = 'us-east-1'
vpc_name = 'mastering_python_networking_demo'

ec2 = boto3.resource('ec2', region_name=region)
client = boto3.client('ec2')

response = client.describe_route_tables()
print(json.dumps(response['RouteTables'][0], sort_keys=True,
indent=4))
```

We only have one custom route table:

```
$ python3 Chapter9_2_query_route_tables.py
{
    "Associations": [
        {
         ....
        }
    ],
    "PropagatingVgws": [],
    "RouteTableId": "rtb-6bee5514",
    "Routes": [
        {
            "DestinationCidrBlock": "10.0.0.0/16",
            "GatewayId": "local",
            "Origin": "CreateRouteTable",
            "State": "active"
        },
        {
            "DestinationCidrBlock": "0.0.0.0/0",
            "GatewayId": "igw-...",
            "Origin": "CreateRoute",
            "State": "active"
        }
    ],
    "Tags": [
        {
            "Key": "Name",
            "Value": "public_internet_gateway"
        }
    ],
    "VpcId": "vpc-..."
}
```

Creating the subnets are straight forward by clicking on the left subnet section and follow the on-screen instruction. For our purpose, we will create three subnets, `10.0.0.0/24` public subnet, `10.0.1.0/24`, and `10.0.2.0/24` private subnets.

We now have a working VPC with three subnets: one public and two private. So far, we have used the AWS CLI and Boto3 library to interact with AWS VPC. Let's take a look at another automation tool, **CloudFormation**.

Automation with CloudFormation

AWS CloudFomation (https://aws.amazon.com/cloudformation/), is one way in which we can use a text file to describe and launch the resource that we need. We can use CloudFormation to provision another VPC in the us-west-1 region:

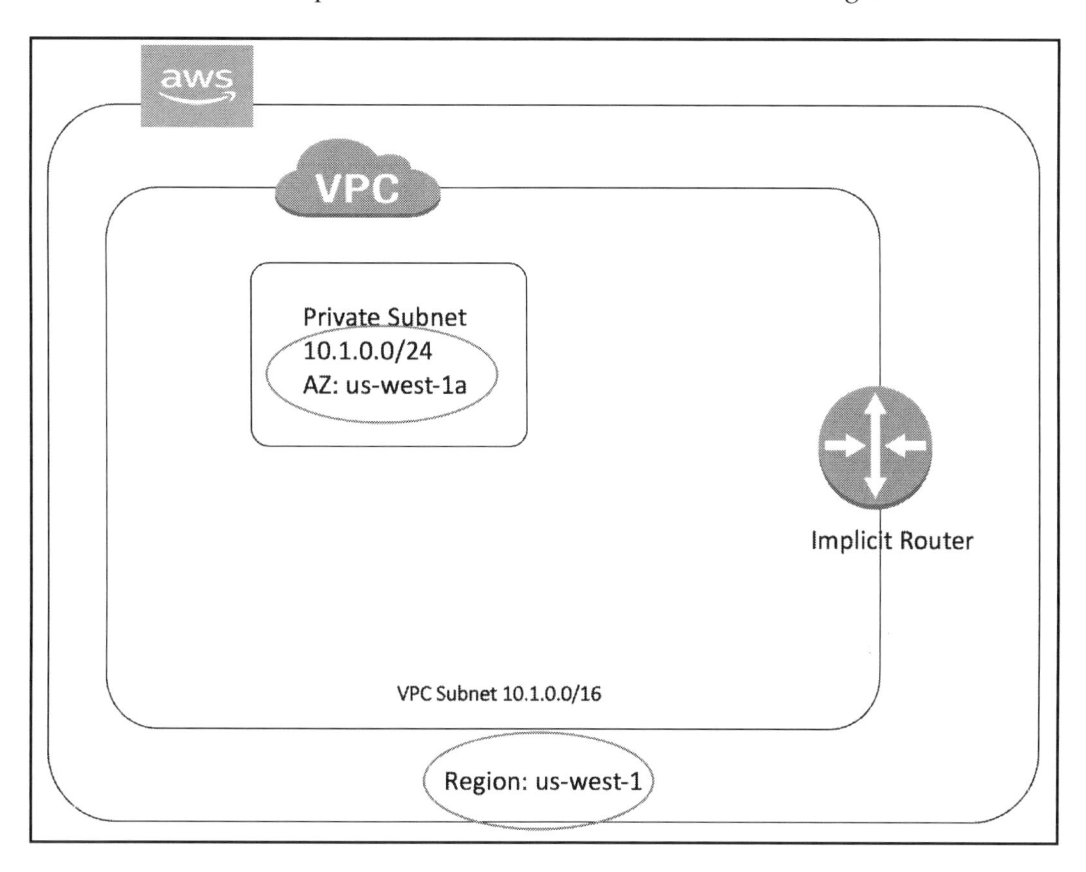

VPC for US-West-1

The CloudFormation template can be in YAML or JSON; we will use YAML for our first template for provisioning:

```
$ cat Chapter9_3_cloud_formation.yml
AWSTemplateFormatVersion: '2010-09-09'
Description: Create VPC in us-west-1
Resources:
  myVPC:
    Type: AWS::EC2::VPC
    Properties:
```

```
        CidrBlock: '10.1.0.0/16'
        EnableDnsSupport: 'false'
        EnableDnsHostnames: 'false'
        Tags:
          - Key: Name
            Value: 'mastering_python_networking_demo_2'
```

We can execute the template via the AWS CLI. Notice that we specify a region of `us-west-1` in our execution:

```
$ aws --region us-west-1 cloudformation create-stack --stack-name
'mpn-ch10-demo' --template-body file://Chapter9_3_cloud_formation.yml
{
    "StackId": "arn:aws:cloudformation:us-west-1:<skip>:stack/mpn-
ch10-demo/<skip>"
}
```

We can verify the status via AWS CLI:

```
$ aws --region us-west-1 cloudformation describe-stacks --stack-name
mpn-ch10-demo
{
    "Stacks": [
        {
            "CreationTime": "2018-07-18T18:45:25.690Z",
            "Description": "Create VPC in us-west-1",
            "DisableRollback": false,
            "StackName": "mpn-ch10-demo",
            "RollbackConfiguration": {},
            "StackStatus": "CREATE_COMPLETE",
            "NotificationARNs": [],
            "Tags": [],
            "EnableTerminationProtection": false,
            "StackId": "arn:aws:cloudformation:us-west-1<skip>"
        }
    ]
}
```

For demonstration purposes, the last CloudFormation template created a VPC without any subnet. Let's delete that VPC and use the following template to create both the VPC as well as the subnet. Notice that we will not have the VPC-id before VPC creation, so we will use a special variable to reference the VPC-id in the subnet creation. This is the same technique we can use for other resources, such as the routing table and internet gateway:

```
$ cat Chapter9_4_cloud_formation_full.yml
AWSTemplateFormatVersion: '2010-09-09'
```

```
Description: Create subnet in us-west-1
Resources:
  myVPC:
    Type: AWS::EC2::VPC
    Properties:
      CidrBlock: '10.1.0.0/16'
      EnableDnsSupport: 'false'
      EnableDnsHostnames: 'false'
      Tags:
        - Key: Name
          Value: 'mastering_python_networking_demo_2'

  mySubnet:
    Type: AWS::EC2::Subnet
    Properties:
      VpcId: !Ref myVPC
      CidrBlock: '10.1.0.0/24'
      AvailabilityZone: 'us-west-1a'
      Tags:
        - Key: Name
          Value: 'mpn_demo_subnet_1'
```

We can execute and verify the creation of the resources as follows:

```
$ aws --region us-west-1 cloudformation create-stack --stack-name mpn-
ch10-demo-2 --template-body file://Chapter9_4_cloud_formation_full.yml
{
    "StackId": "arn:aws:cloudformation:us-west-1:<skip>:stack/mpn-
ch10-demo-2/<skip>"
}

$ aws --region us-west-1 cloudformation describe-stacks --stack-name
mpn-ch10-demo-2
{
    "Stacks": [
        {
            "StackStatus": "CREATE_COMPLETE",
            ...
            "StackName": "mpn-ch10-demo-2",
            "DisableRollback": false
        }
    ]
}
```

We can also verify the VPC and subnet information from the AWS console. We will verify the VPC from the console first:

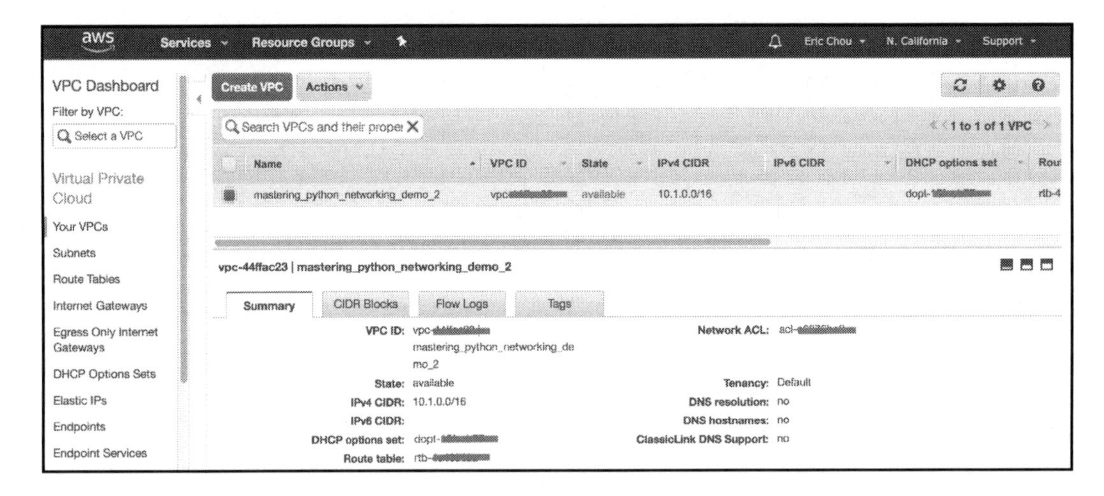

VPC in us-west-1

We can also take a look at the subnet:

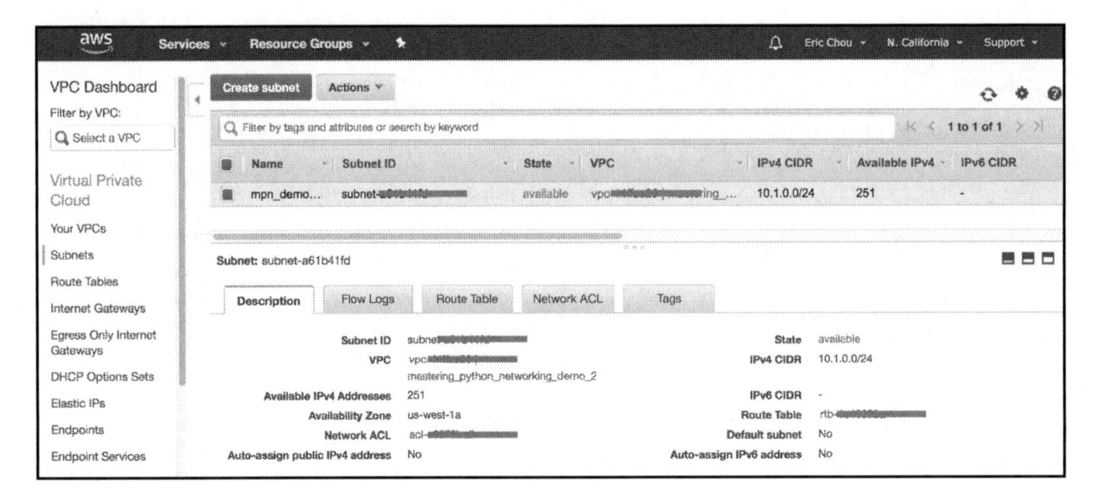

Subnet in us-west-1

We now have two VPCs in the two coasts of the United States. They are currently behaving like two islands, each by themselves. This may or may not be your desired state of operation. If you would like the to VPC to be able to connect them to each other, we can use VPC peering (`https://docs.aws.amazon.com/AmazonVPC/latest/PeeringGuide/vpc-peering-basics.html`) to allow direct communication.

VPC peering is not limited to the same account. You can connect VPCs across different accounts, as long as the request was accepted and the other aspects (security, routing, DNS name) are taken care of.

In the coming section, we will take a look at VPC security groups and the network access control list.

Security groups and the network ACL

AWS **Security Groups** and the **Access Control** list can be found under the **Security** section of your VPC:

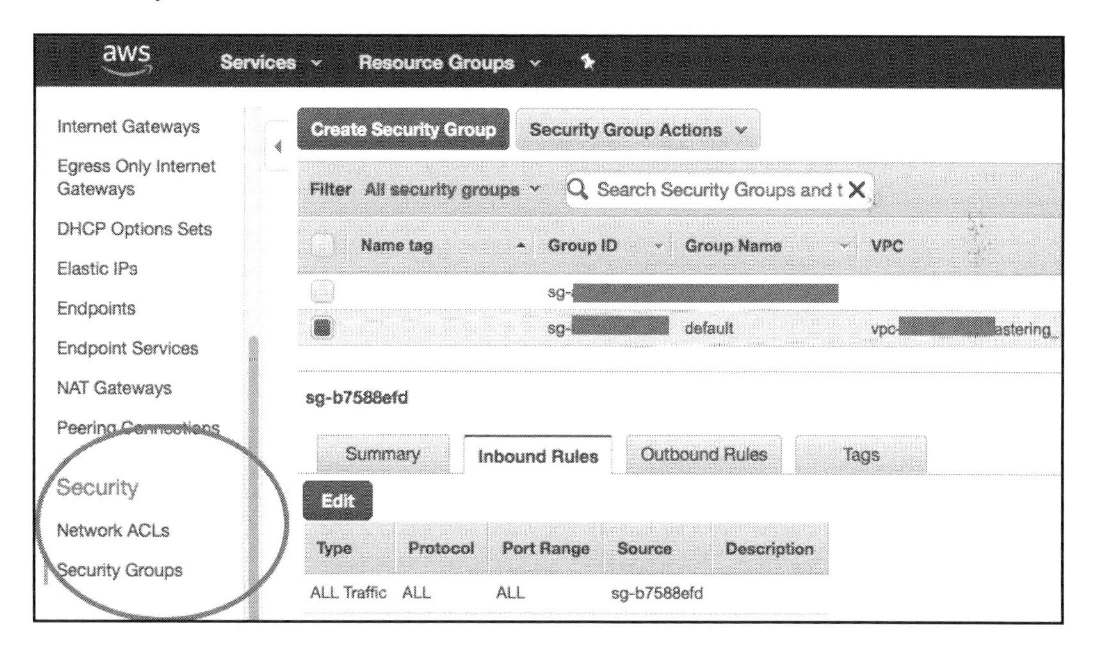

VPC security

A security group is a stateful virtual firewall that controls inbound and outbound access for resources. Most of the time, we will use the security group as a way to limit public access to our EC2 instance. The current limitation is 500 security groups in each VPC. Each security group can contain up to 50 inbound and 50 outbound rules. You can use the following sample script to create a security group and two simple ingress rules:

```
$ cat Chapter9_5_security_group.py
#!/usr/bin/env python3

import boto3

ec2 = boto3.client('ec2')

response = ec2.describe_vpcs()
vpc_id = response.get('Vpcs', [{}])[0].get('VpcId', '')

# Query for security group id
response = ec2.create_security_group(GroupName='mpn_security_group',
                                     Description='mpn_demo_sg',
                                     VpcId=vpc_id)
security_group_id = response['GroupId']
data = ec2.authorize_security_group_ingress(
    GroupId=security_group_id,
    IpPermissions=[
        {'IpProtocol': 'tcp',
         'FromPort': 80,
         'ToPort': 80,
         'IpRanges': [{'CidrIp': '0.0.0.0/0'}]},
        {'IpProtocol': 'tcp',
         'FromPort': 22,
         'ToPort': 22,
         'IpRanges': [{'CidrIp': '0.0.0.0/0'}]}
    ])
print('Ingress Successfully Set %s' % data)

# Describe security group
#response = ec2.describe_security_groups(GroupIds=[security_group_id])
print(security_group_id)
```

We can execute the script and receive confirmation on the creation of the security group that can be associated with other AWS resources:

```
$ python3 Chapter9_5_security_group.py
Ingress Successfully Set {'ResponseMetadata': {'RequestId': '<skip>',
'HTTPStatusCode': 200, 'HTTPHeaders': {'server': 'AmazonEC2',
'content-type': 'text/xml;charset=UTF-8', 'date': 'Wed, 18 Jul 2018
20:51:55 GMT', 'content-length': '259'}, 'RetryAttempts': 0}}
sg-<skip>
```

Network **Access Control Lists** (**ACLs**) is an additional layer of security that is stateless. Each subnet in VPC is associated with a network ACL. Since ACL is stateless, you will need to specify both inbound and outbound rules.

The important differences between the security group and ACLs are as follows:

- The security group operates at the network interface level where ACL operates at the subnet level
- For a security group, we can only specify allow rules but not deny rules, whereas ACL supports both allow and deny rules
- A security group is stateful; return traffic is automatically allowed. Return traffic needs to be specifically allowed in ACL

Let's take a look at one of the coolest feature of AWS networking, Elastic IP. When I initially learned about Elastic IP, I was blown away by the ability of assigning and reassigning IP addresses dynamically.

Elastic IP

Elastic IP (**EIP**) is a way to use a public IPv4 address that's reachable from the internet. It can be dynamically assigned to an EC2 instance, network interface, or other resources. A few characteristics of Elastic IP are as follows:

- The Elastic IP is associated with the account and is region-specific. For example, the EIP in `us-east-1` can only be associated with resources in `us-east-1`.
- You can disassociate an Elastic IP from a resource, and re-associate it with a different resource. This flexibility can sometimes be used to ensure high availability. For example, you can migrate from a smaller EC2 instance to a larger EC2 instance by reassigning the same IP address from the small EC2 instance to the larger one.
- There is a small hourly charge associated with Elastic IP.

You can request **Elastic IP** from the portal. After assignment, you can associate it with the desired resources:

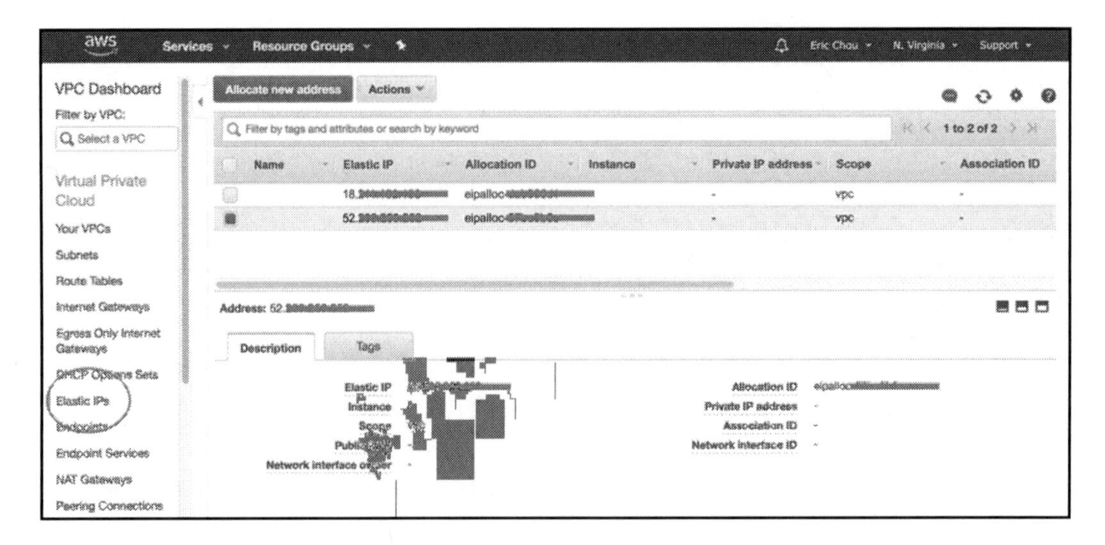

Elastic IP

Unfortunately, Elastic IP has a default limit of five per region, `https://docs.aws.amazon.com/vpc/latest/userguide/amazon-vpc-limits.html`.

In the coming section, we will look at how we can use the NAT Gateway to allow communication for the private subnets to the internet.

NAT Gateway

To allow the hosts in our EC2 public subnet to be accessed from the internet, we can allocate an Elastic IP and associate it with the network interface of the EC2 host. However, at the time of writing this book, there is a limit of five Elastic IPs per EC2-VPC (`https://docs.aws.amazon.com/AmazonVPC/latest/UserGuide/VPC_Appendix_Limits.html#vpc-limits-eips`). Sometimes, it would be nice to allow the host in a private subnet outbound access when needed without creating a permanent one-to-one mapping between the Elastic IP and the EC2 host.

This is where **NAT Gateway** can help, by allowing the hosts in the private subnet temporarily outbound access by performing a **Network Address Translation** (**NAT**). This operation is similar to the **Port Address Translation** (**PAT**) that we normally perform on the corporate firewall. To use a NAT Gateway, we can perform the following steps:

- Create a NAT Gateway in a subnet with access to the internet gateway via the AWS CLI, Boto3 library, or AWS console. The NAT Gateway will need to be assigned with an Elastic IP.
- Point the default route in the private subnet to the NAT Gateway.
- The NAT Gateway will follow the default route to the internet gateway for external access.

This operation can be illustrated in the following diagram:

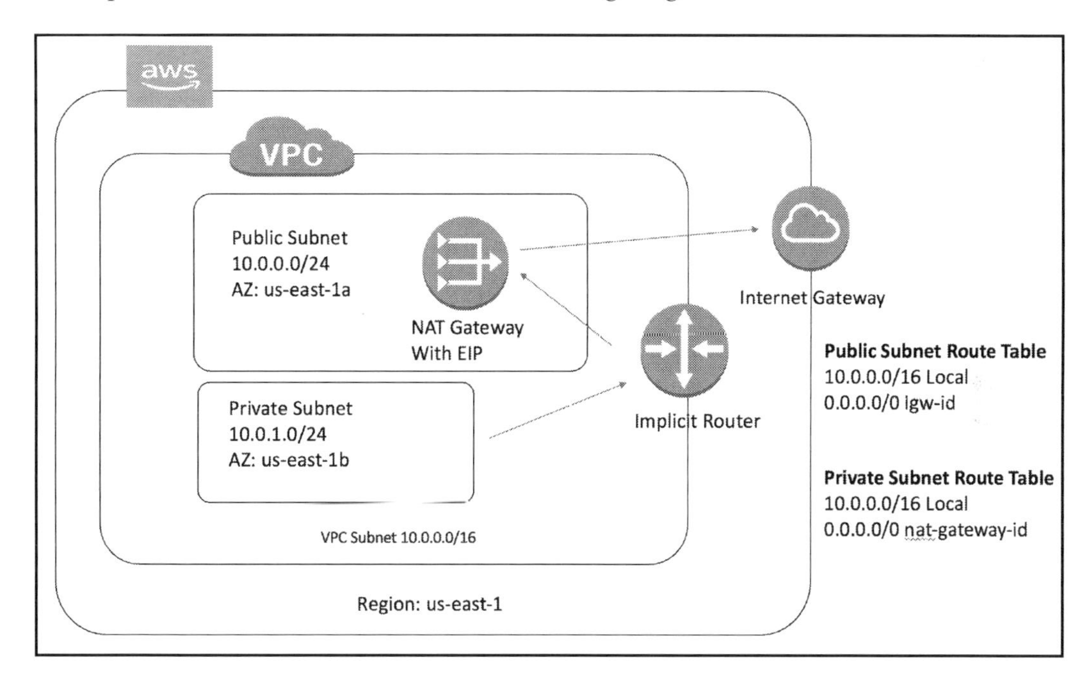

NAT Gateway operations

One of the most common questions for NAT Gateway typically surrounds which subnet the NAT Gateway should reside in. The rule of thumb is to remember that the NAT Gateway needs public access. Therefore, it should be created in the subnet with public internet access with an available Elastic IP to be assigned to it:

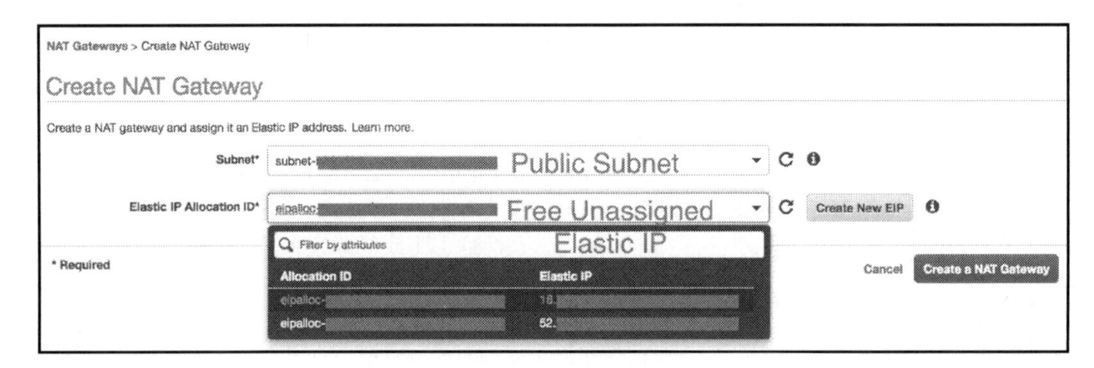

NAT Gateway creation

In the coming section, we will take a look at how to connect our shiny virtual network in AWS to our physical network.

Direct Connect and VPN

Up to this point, our VPC is a self-contained network that resides in the AWS network. It is flexible and functional, but to access the resources inside of the VPC, we will need to access them with their internet-facing services such as SSH and HTTPS.

In this section, we will look at the two ways AWS allow us to connect to the VPC from our private network: IPSec VPN Gateway and Direct Connect.

VPN Gateway

The first way to connect our on-premise network to VPC is with traditional IPSec VPN connections. We will need a publicly accessible device that can establish VPN connections to AWS's VPN device. The customer gateway needs to support route-based IPSec VPNs where the VPN connection is treated as a connection that a routing protocol can run over the virtual link. Currently, AWS recommends using BGP to exchange routes.

On the VPC side, we can follow a similar routing table where we can route a particular subnet toward the **Virtual Private Gateway** target:

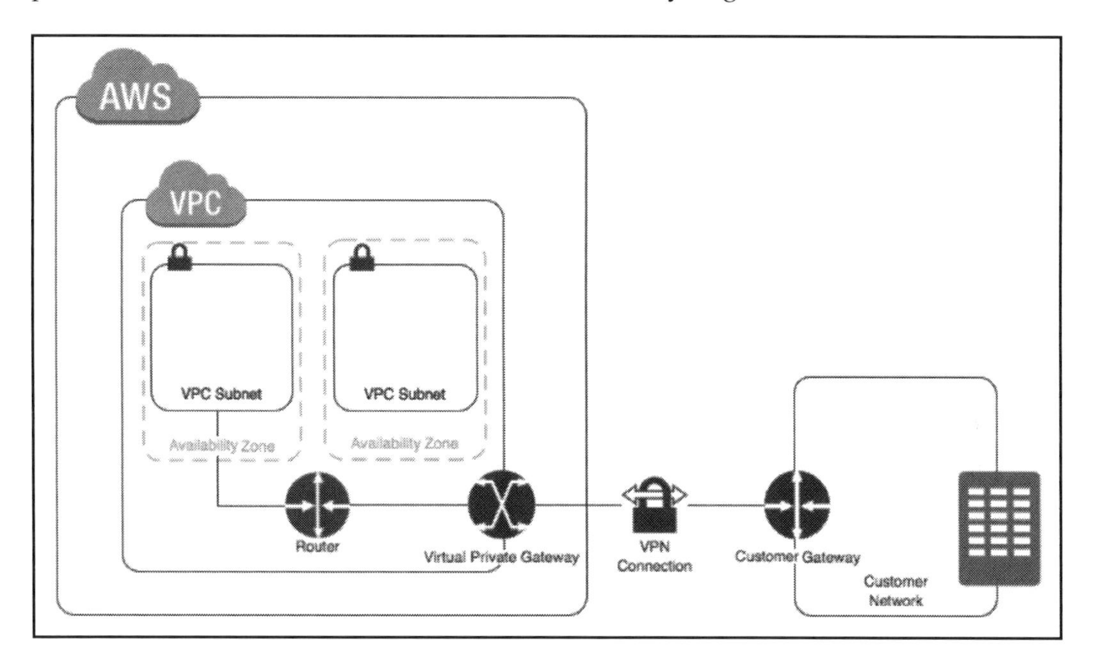

VPC VPN connection (source: https://docs.aws.amazon.com/AmazonVPC/latest/UserGuide/VPC_VPN.html)

Besides IPSec VPN, we can also use a dedicated circuit to connect.

Direct Connect

The IPSec VPN connection we saw is an easy way to provide connectivity for on-premise equipment to the AWS cloud resources. However, it suffers the same faults that IPSec over the internet always does: it is unreliable, and we have very little control over it. There is very little performance monitoring and no **Service-Level Agreement** (**SLA**) until the connection reaches a part of the internet that we can control.

For all of these reasons, any production-level, mission-critical traffic is more likely to traverse through the second option Amazon provides, that is, AWS Direct Connect. AWS Direct Connect allows customers to connect their data center and colocation to their AWS VPC with a dedicated virtual circuit. The somewhat difficult part of this operation is usually bringing our network to where we can connect with AWS physically, typically in a carrier hotel. You can find a list of the AWS Direct Connect locations here: `https://aws.amazon.com/directconnect/details/`. The Direct Connect link is just a fiber patch connection that you can order from the particular carrier hotel to patch the network to a network port and configure the dot1q trunk's connectivity.

There are also increasingly more connectivity options for Direct Connect via a third-party carrier with MPLS circuits and aggregated links. One of the most affordable options that I found and use is the Equinix Cloud Exchange (`https://www.equinix.com/services/interconnection-connectivity/cloud-exchange/`). By using the Equinix Cloud Exchange, we can leverage the same circuit and connect to different cloud providers at a fraction of the cost of dedicated circuits:

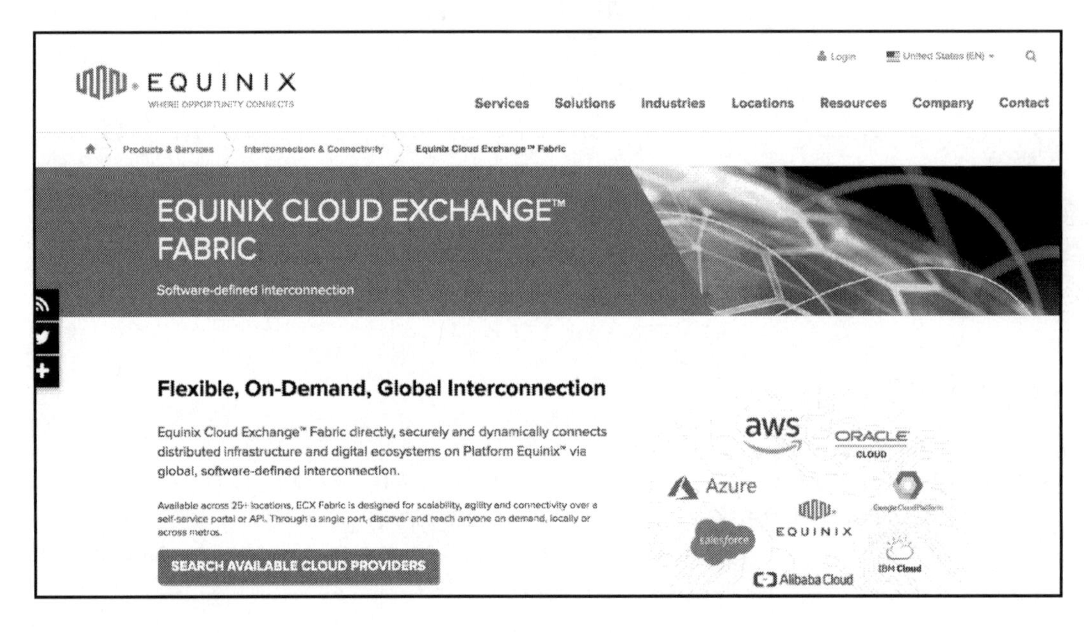

Equinix Cloud Exchange (source: `https://www.equinix.com/services/interconnection-connectivity/cloud-exchange/`)

In the upcoming section, we will take a look at some of the network scaling services AWS offers.

Network scaling services

In this section, we will take a look at some of the network services AWS offers. Many of the services do not have a direct network implication, such as DNS and content distribution network. They are relevant in our discussion due to their close relationship with the network and application's performance.

Elastic Load Balancing

Elastic Load Balancing (**ELB**) allows incoming traffic from the internet to be automatically distributed across multiple EC2 instances. Just like load balancers in the physical world, this allows us to have better redundancy and fault tolerance while reducing the per-server load. ELB comes in two flavors: application and network load balancing.

The application load balancer handles web traffic via HTTP and HTTPS; the network load balancer operates on a TCP level. If your application runs on HTTP or HTTPS, it is generally a good idea to go with the application load balancer. Otherwise, using the network load balancer is a good bet.

A detailed comparison of the application and network load balancer can be found at `https://aws.amazon.com/elasticloadbalancing/details/`:

Comparison of Elastic Load Balancing Products

You can select the appropriate load balancer based on your application needs. If you need flexible application management, we recommend that you use an **Application Load Balancer**. If extreme performance and static IP is needed for your application, we recommend that you use a **Network Load Balancer**. If you have an existing application that was built within the EC2-Classic network, then you should use a **Classic Load Balancer**.

Feature	Application Load Balancer	Network Load Balancer	Classic Load Balancer
Protocols	HTTP, HTTPS	TCP	TCP, SSL, HTTP, HTTPS
Platforms	VPC	VPC	EC2-Classic, VPC
Health checks	✔	✔	✔
CloudWatch metrics	✔	✔	✔
Logging	✔	✔	✔
Zonal fail-over	✔	✔	✔

Elastic Load Balancer Comparison (Source: `https://aws.amazon.com/elasticloadbalancing/details/`)

Elastic Load Balancer offers a way to load balance traffic once it enters the resource in our region. The AWS Route53 DNS service allows geographic load balance between regions.

Route53 DNS service

We all know what domain name services are; Route53 is AWS's DNS service. Route53 is a full-service domain registrar where you can purchase and manage domains directly from AWS. Regarding network services, DNS allows a way to load balance between geographic regions by service domain names in a round-robin fashion between regions.

We need the following items before we can use DNS for load balancing:

- An Elastic Load Balancer in each of the intended load balance regions.
- A registered domain name. We do not need Route53 as the domain registrar.
- Route53 is the DNS service for the domain.

We can then use the Route 53 latency-based routing policy with health-check in an active-active environment between the two Elastic Load Balancers.

CloudFront CDN services

CloudFront is Amazon's **Content Delivery Network** (**CDN**) that reduces the latency for content delivery by physically serving the content closer to the customer. The content can be static web page content, videos, applications, APIs, or most recently, Lambda functions. CloudFront edge locations include the existing AWS regions, but are also in many other locations around the globe. The high-level operation of CloudFront is as follows:

- Users access your website for one or more objects
- DNS routes the request to the Amazon CloudFront edge location closest to the user's request
- The CloudFront edge location will either service the content via the cache or request the object from the origin

AWS CloudFront and CDN services in general are typically handled by application developers or DevOps engineers. However, it is always good to be aware of their operations.

Other AWS network services

There are lots of other AWS Network Services that we do not have the space to cover. Some of the more important ones are listed in this section:

- **AWS Transit VPC** (`https://aws.amazon.com/blogs/aws/aws-solution-transit-vpc/`): This is a way to connect multiple virtual private clouds to a common VPC that serves as a transit center. This is a relatively new service, but it can minimize the connection that you need to set up and manage. This can also serve as a tool when you need to share resources between separate AWS accounts.
- **Amazon GuardDuty** (`https://aws.amazon.com/guardduty/`): This is a managed threat detection service that continuously monitors for malicious or unauthorized behavior to help protect our AWS workloads. It monitors API calls or potentially unauthorized deployments.
- **AWS WAF** (`https://aws.amazon.com/waf/`): This is a web application firewall that helps protect web applications from common exploits. We can define customized web security rules to allow or block web traffic.
- **AWS Shield** (`https://aws.amazon.com/shield/`): This is a managed **Distributed Denial of Service** (**DDoS**) protection service that safeguards applications running on AWS. The protection service is free for all customers at the basic level; the advanced version of AWS Shield is a fee-based service.

Summary

In this chapter, we looked at AWS Cloud Networking services. We went over the AWS network definitions of Region, Availability Zone, Edge Locations, and Transit Center. By understanding the overall AWS network, this gives us a good idea of some of the limitations and contains for the other AWS network services. Throughout this chapter, we used the AWS CLI, the Python Boto3 library, as well as CloudFormation to automate some of the tasks.

We covered the AWS virtual private cloud in depth with the configuration of the route table and route targets. The example on security groups and network ACL controls the security for our VPC. We also looked at Elastic IP and NAT Gateways regarding allowing external access.

There are two ways to connect AWS VPC to on-premise networks: Direct Connect and IPSec VPN. We briefly looked at each and the advantages of using them. Toward the end of this chapter, we looked at network scaling services offered by AWS, including Elastic Load Balancing, Route53 DNS, and CloudFront.

In `Chapter 10`, *Working with Git*, we will take a more in-depth look at the version control system we have been working with: Git.

10
Working with Git

We have worked on various aspects of network automation with Python, Ansible, and many other tools. If you have been following along with the examples, in the first nine chapters of the book, we have used over 150 files containing over 5,300 lines of code. That's pretty good for network engineers who may have been working primarily with the command-line interface! With our new set of scripts and tools, we are now ready to go out and conquer our network tasks, right? Well, not so fast, my fellow network ninjas.

The first task we face with the code files is how to keep them in a location where they can be retrieved and used by us and others. Ideally, this location would be the only place where the latest version of the file is kept. After the initial release, we might add features and fix bugs in the future, so we would like a way to track these changes and keep the latest ones available for download. If the new changes do not work, we would like to rollback the changes and reflect the differences in the history of the file. This would give us a good idea of the evolution of the code files.

The second question is the collaboration process between our team members. If we work with other network engineers, we will need to work collectively on the files. The files can be the Python scripts, Ansible Playbook, Jinja2 templates, INI-style configuration files, and many others. The point is any kind of text-based files should be tracked with multiple input that everybody in the team should be able to see.

The third question is accountability. Once we have a system that allows for multiple inputs and changes, we need to mark these changes with an appropriate track record to reflect the owner of the change. The track record should also include a brief reason for the change so the person reviewing the history can get an understanding of why the change was made.

These are some of the main challenges a version-control (or source-control) system tries to solve. To be fair, version control can exist in forms other than a dedicated system. For example, if I open up my Microsoft Word program, the file constantly saves itself, and I can go back in time to revisit the changes or rollback to a previous version. The version-control system we are focused on here is standalone software tools with the primary purpose of tracking software changes.

There is no shortage of different source-control tools in software engineering, both proprietary and open source. Some of the more popular open source version-control systems are CVS, SVN, Mercurial, and Git. In this chapter, we will focus on the source-control system **Git**, the tool that we have been downloading in many of the `.software` packages we have used in this book. We will be taking a more in-depth look at the tool. Git is the de facto version-control system for many large, open source projects, including Python and the Linux kernel.

As of February 2017, the CPython development process has moved to GitHub. It was a work in progress since January 2015. For more information, check out PEP 512 at `https://www.python.org/dev/peps/pep-0512/`.

Before we dive into the working examples of Git, let's take a look at the history and advantages of the Git system.

Introduction to Git

Git was created by Linus Torvalds, the creator of the Linux kernel, in April 2005. With his dry wit, he has affectionately called the tool the information manager from hell. In an interview with the Linux Foundation, Linus mentioned that he felt source-control management was just about the least interesting thing in the computing world (`https://www.linuxfoundation.org/blog/10-years-of-git-an-interview-with-git-creator-linus-torvalds/`). Nevertheless, he created the tool after a disagreement between the Linux kernel developer community and BitKeeper, the proprietary system they were using at the time.

What does the name Git stand for? In British English slang, a Git is an insult denoting an unpleasant, annoying, childish person. With his dry humor, Linus said he is an egotistical bastard and that he named all of his projects after himself. First Linux, now Git. However, some suggested that the name is short for **Global Information Tracker** (**GIT**). You can be the judge.

The project came together really quickly. About ten days after its creation (yeah, you read that right), Linus felt the basic ideas for Git were right and started to commit the first Linux kernel code with Git. The rest, as they say, is history. More than ten years after its creation, it is still meeting all the expectations of the Linux kernel project. It took over as the version-control system for many other open source projects despite the inherent inertia in switching source-control systems. After many years of hosting the Python code from Mercurial at `https://hg.python.org/`, the project was switched to Git on GitHub in February of 2017.

Benefits of Git

The success of hosting large and distributed open source projects, such as the Linux kernel and Python, speaks to the advantages of Git. This is especially significant given that Git is a relatively new source-control tool and people do not tend to switch to a new tool unless it offers significant advantages over the old tool. Let's look at some of the benefits of Git:

- **Distributed development**: Git supports parallel, independent, and simultaneous development in private repositories offline. Compare this to some other version-control systems that require constant synchronization with a central repository; this allows significantly greater flexibility for the developers.
- **Scale to handle thousands of developers**: The number of developers working on different parts of some of the open source projects is in the thousands. Git supports the integration of their work reliably.
- **Performance**: Linus was determined to make sure Git was fast and efficient. To save space and transfer time for the sheer volume of updates for the Linux kernel code alone, compression and a delta check would be needed to make Git fast and efficient.
- **Accountability and immutability**: Git enforces a change log on every commit that changes a file so that there is a trail for all the changes and the reason behind them. The data objects in Git cannot be modified after they were created and placed in the database, making them immutable. This further enforces accountability.
- **Atomic transactions**: The integrity of the repository is ensured as the different, but related, change is performed either all together or not at all. This will ensure the repository is not left in a partially-changed or corrupted state.

- **Complete repositories**: Each repository has a complete copy of all historical revisions of every file.
- **Free, as in freedom**: The origin of the Git tool was born out of the disagreement between free, as in beer version of the Linux kernel with BitKeeper VCS, it makes sense that the tool has a very liberal usage license.

Let's take a look at some of the terms used in Git.

Git terminology

Here are some Git terminologies we should be familiar with:

- **Ref**: The name that begins with `refs` that point to an object.
- **Repository**: A database that contains all of a project's information, files, metadata, and history. It contains a collection of `ref` for all the collections of objects.
- **Branch**: An active line of development. The most recent commit is the `tip` or the `HEAD` of that branch. A repository can have multiple branches, but your `working tree` or `working directory` can only be associated with one branch. This is sometimes referred to as the current or `checked out` branch.
- **Checkout**: The action of updating all or part of the working tree to a particular point.
- **Commit**: A point in time in Git history, or it can mean to store a new snapshot into the repository.
- **Merge**: The action to bring the content of another branch into the current branch. For example, I am merging the `development` branch with the `master` branch.
- **Fetch**: The action of getting the content from a remote repository.
- **Pull**: Fetching and merging a repository.
- **Tag**: A mark in a point in time in a repository that is significant. In `Chapter 7`, *The Python Automation Framework – Ansible Basics*, we saw the tag used to specify the release points, `v2.5.0a1`.

This is not a complete list; please refer to the Git glossary, `https://git-scm.com/docs/gitglossary`, for more terms and their definitions.

Git and GitHub

Git and GitHub are not the same thing. Sometimes, for engineers who are new to version-control systems, this is confusing. Git is a revision-control system while GitHub, `https://github.com/`, is a centralized hosting service for Git repositories.

Because Git is a decentralized system, GitHub stores a copy of our project's repository, just like any other developer. Often, we just designate the GitHub repository as the project's central repository and all other developers push and pull their changes to and from that repository.

GitHub takes this idea of being the centralized repository in a distributed system further by using the `fork` and `pull requests` mechanisms. For projects hosted on GitHub, encourage developers to `fork` the repository, or make a copy of the repository, and work on that copy as their centralized repository. After making changes, they can send a `pull request` to the main project, and the project maintainers can review the changes and `commit` the changes if they see fit. GitHub also adds the web interface to the repositories besides command line; this makes Git more user-friendly.

Setting up Git

So far, we have been using Git to just download files from GitHub. In this section, we will go a bit further by setting up Git variables so we can start committing our files. I am going to use the same Ubuntu 16.04 host in the example. The installation process is well-documented; if you are using a different version of Linux or other operating systems, a quick search should land you at the right set of instructions.

If you have not done so already, install Git via the `apt` package-management tool:

```
$ sudo apt-get update
$ sudo apt-get install -y git
$ git --version
git version 2.7.4
```

Once `git` is installed, we need to configure a few things so our commit messages can contain the correct information:

```
$ git config --global user.name "Your Name"
$ git config --global user.email "email@domain.com"
$ git config --list
user.name=Your Name
user.email=email@domain.com
```

Alternatively, you can modify the information in the `~/.gitconfig` file:

```
$ cat ~/.gitconfig
[user]
  name = Your Name
  email = email@domain.com
```

There are many other options in Git that we can change, but the name and email are the ones that allow us to commit the change without getting a warning. Personally, I like to use VIM, instead of the default Emac, as my text editor for typing commit messages:

```
(optional)
$ git config --global core.editor "vim"
$ git config --list
user.name=Your Name
user.email=email@domain.com
core.editor=vim
```

Before we move on to using Git, let's go over the idea of a `gitignore` file.

Gitignore

From time to time, there are files you do not want Git to check into GitHub or other repositories. The easiest way to do this is to create `.gitignore` in the `repository` folder; Git will use it to determine which files a directory should ignore before you make a commit. This file should be committed into the repository to share the ignore rules with other users.

This file can include language-specific files, for example, let's exclude the Python `Byte-compiled` files:

```
# Byte-compiled / optimized / DLL files
__pycache__/
*.py[cod]
*$py.class
```

We can also include files that are specific to your operating system:

```
# OSX
# =========================

.DS_Store
.AppleDouble
.LSOverride
```

You can learn more about `.gitignore` on GitHub's help page: `https://help.github.com/articles/ignoring-files/`. Here are some other references:

- Gitignore manual: `https://git-scm.com/docs/gitignore`
- GitHub's collection of `.gitignore` templates: `https://github.com/github/gitignore`
- Python language `.gitignore` example: `https://github.com/github/gitignore/blob/master/Python.gitignore`
- The `.gitignore` file for this book's repository: `https://github.com/PacktPublishing/Python-Network-Programming`

I see the `.gitignore` file as a file that should be created at the same time as any new repository. That is why this concept is introduced as early as possible. We will take a look at some of the Git usage examples in the next section.

Git usage examples

Most of the time, when we work with Git, we will use the command line:

```
$ git --help
usage: git [--version] [--help] [-C <path>] [-c name=value]
           [--exec-path[=<path>]] [--html-path] [--man-path] [--info-
path]
           [-p | --paginate | --no-pager] [--no-replace-objects] [--
bare]
           [--git-dir=<path>] [--work-tree=<path>] [--
namespace=<name>]
           <command> [<args>]
```

We will create a `repository` and create a file inside the repository:

```
$ mkdir TestRepo
$ cd TestRepo/
$ git init
Initialized empty Git repository in
/home/echou/Master_Python_Networking_second_edition/Chapter10/TestRepo
/.git/
$ echo "this is my test file" > myFile.txt
```

When the repository was initialized with Git, a new hidden folder of `.git` was added to the directory. It contains all the Git-related files:

```
$ ls -a
. .. .git myFile.txt

$ ls .git/
branches config description HEAD hooks info objects refs
```

There are several locations Git receives its configurations in a hierarchy format. You can use the `git config -l` command to see the aggregated configuration:

```
$ ls .git/config
.git/config

$ ls ~/.gitconfig
/home/echou/.gitconfig

$ git config -l
user.name=Eric Chou
user.email=<email>
core.editor=vim
core.repositoryformatversion=0
core.filemode=true
core.bare=false
core.logallrefupdates=true
```

When we create a file in the repository, it is not tracked. For `git` to be aware of the file, we need to add the file:

```
$ git status
On branch master

Initial commit

Untracked files:
  (use "git add <file>..." to include in what will be committed)

  myFile.txt

nothing added to commit but untracked files present (use "git add" to
track)

$ git add myFile.txt
$ git status
On branch master

Initial commit

Changes to be committed:
  (use "git rm --cached <file>..." to unstage)

  new file: myFile.txt
```

When you add the file, it is in a staged status. To make the changes official, we will need to commit the change:

```
$ git commit -m "adding myFile.txt"
[master (root-commit) 5f579ab] adding myFile.txt
 1 file changed, 1 insertion(+)
 create mode 100644 myFile.txt

$ git status
On branch master
nothing to commit, working directory clean
```

In the last example, we provided the commit message with the `-m` option when we issue the commit statement. If we did not use the option, we would have been taken to a page to provide the commit message. In our scenario, we configured the text editor to be vim so we will be able to use vim to edit the message.

Let's make some changes to the file and commit it:

```
$ vim myFile.txt
$ cat myFile.txt
this is the second iteration of my test file
$ git status
On branch master
Changes not staged for commit:
  (use "git add <file>..." to update what will be committed)
  (use "git checkout -- <file>..." to discard changes in working
directory)

  modified: myFile.txt
$ git add myFile.txt
$ git commit -m "made modificaitons to myFile.txt"
[master a3dd3ea] made modificaitons to myFile.txt
 1 file changed, 1 insertion(+), 1 deletion(-)
```

The `git commit` number is a `SHA1 hash`, which an important feature. If we had followed the same step on another computer, our `SHA1 hash` value would be the same. This is how Git knows the two repositories are identical even when they are worked on in parallel.

We can show the history of the commits with `git log`. The entries are shown in reverse chronological order; each commit shows the author's name and email address, the date, the log message, as well as the internal identification number of the commit:

```
$ git log
commit a3dd3ea8e6eb15b57d1f390ce0d2c3a03f07a038
Author: Eric Chou <echou@yahoo.com>
Date: Fri Jul 20 09:58:24 2018 -0700

    made modificaitons to myFile.txt

commit 5f579ab1e9a3fae13aa7f1b8092055213157524d
Author: Eric Chou <echou@yahoo.com>
Date: Fri Jul 20 08:05:09 2018 -0700

    adding myFile.txt
```

We can also show more details about the change using the commit ID:

```
$ git show a3dd3ea8e6eb15b57d1f390ce0d2c3a03f07a038
commit a3dd3ea8e6eb15b57d1f390ce0d2c3a03f07a038
Author: Eric Chou <echou@yahoo.com>
Date: Fri Jul 20 09:58:24 2018 -0700

    made modificaitons to myFile.txt

diff --git a/myFile.txt b/myFile.txt
index 6ccb42e..69e7d47 100644
--- a/myFile.txt
+++ b/myFile.txt
@@ -1 +1 @@
-this is my test file
+this is the second iteration of my test file
```

If you need to revert the changes you have made, you can choose between `revert` and `reset`. Revert changes all the file for a specific commit back to their state before the commit:

```
$ git revert a3dd3ea8e6eb15b57d1f390ce0d2c3a03f07a038
[master 9818f29] Revert "made modificaitons to myFile.txt"
 1 file changed, 1 insertion(+), 1 deletion(-)

# Check to verified the file content was before the second change.
$ cat myFile.txt
this is my test file
```

The `revert` command will keep the commit you reverted and make a new commit. You will be able to see all the changes up to that point, including the revert:

```
$ git log
commit 9818f298f477fd880db6cb87112b50edc392f7fa
Author: Eric Chou <echou@yahoo.com>
```

```
Date: Fri Jul 20 13:11:30 2018 -0700

    Revert "made modificaitons to myFile.txt"

    This reverts commit a3dd3ea8e6eb15b57d1f390ce0d2c3a03f07a038.

        modified: reverted the change to myFile.txt

commit a3dd3ea8e6eb15b57d1f390ce0d2c3a03f07a038
Author: Eric Chou <echou@yahoo.com>
Date: Fri Jul 20 09:58:24 2018 -0700

    made modificaitons to myFile.txt

commit 5f579ab1e9a3fae13aa7f1b8092055213157524d
Author: Eric Chou <echou@yahoo.com>
Date: Fri Jul 20 08:05:09 2018 -0700

    adding myFile.txt
```

The `reset` option will reset the status of your repository to an older version and discard all the changes in between:

```
$ git reset --hard a3dd3ea8e6eb15b57d1f390ce0d2c3a03f07a038
HEAD is now at a3dd3ea made modificaitons to myFile.txt

$ git log
commit a3dd3ea8e6eb15b57d1f390ce0d2c3a03f07a038
Author: Eric Chou <echou@yahoo.com>
Date: Fri Jul 20 09:58:24 2018 -0700

    made modificaitons to myFile.txt

commit 5f579ab1e9a3fae13aa7f1b8092055213157524d
Author: Eric Chou <echou@yahoo.com>
Date: Fri Jul 20 08:05:09 2018 -0700

    adding myFile.txt
```

Personally, I like to keep all the history, including any rollbacks that I have done. Therefore, when I need to rollback a change, I usually pick `revert` instead of `reset`.

A `branch` in `git` is a line of development within a repository. Git allows many branches and thus different lines of development within a repository. By default, we have the master branch. There are many reasons for branching, but most of them represent an individual customer release or a development phase, that is, the `dev` branch.

Let's create a `dev` branch within our repository:

```
$ git branch dev
$ git branch
  dev
* master
```

To start working on the branch, we will need to `checkout` the branch:

```
$ git checkout dev
Switched to branch 'dev'
$ git branch
* dev
  master
```

Let's add a second file to the `dev` branch:

```
$ echo "my second file" > mySecondFile.txt
$ git add mySecondFile.txt
$ git commit -m "added mySecondFile.txt to dev branch"
[dev c983730] added mySecondFile.txt to dev branch
 1 file changed, 1 insertion(+)
 create mode 100644 mySecondFile.txt
```

We can go back to the `master` branch and verify that the two lines of development are separate:

```
$ git branch
* dev
  master
$ git checkout master
Switched to branch 'master'
$ ls
myFile.txt
$ git checkout dev
Switched to branch 'dev'
$ ls
myFile.txt mySecondFile.txt
```

To have the contents in the `dev` branch be written into the `master` branch, we will need to `merge` them:

```
$ git branch
* dev
  master
$ git checkout master
$ git merge dev master
Updating a3dd3ea..c983730
```

```
Fast-forward
 mySecondFile.txt | 1 +
 1 file changed, 1 insertion(+)
 create mode 100644 mySecondFile.txt
$ git branch
  dev
* master
$ ls
myFile.txt mySecondFile.txt
```

We can use `git rm` to remove a file. Let's create a third file and remove it:

```
$ touch myThirdFile.txt
$ git add myThirdFile.txt
$ git commit -m "adding myThirdFile.txt"
[master 2ec5f7d] adding myThirdFile.txt
 1 file changed, 0 insertions(+), 0 deletions(-)
 create mode 100644 myThirdFile.txt
$ ls
myFile.txt mySecondFile.txt myThirdFile.txt
$ git rm myThirdFile.txt
rm 'myThirdFile.txt'
$ git status
On branch master
Changes to be committed:
  (use "git reset HEAD <file>..." to unstage)

  deleted: myThirdFile.txt
$ git commit -m "deleted myThirdFile.txt"
[master bc078a9] deleted myThirdFile.txt
 1 file changed, 0 insertions(+), 0 deletions(-)
 delete mode 100644 myThirdFile.txt
```

We will be able to see the last two changes in the log:

```
$ git log
commit bc078a97e41d1614c1ba1f81f72acbcd95c0728c
Author: Eric Chou <echou@yahoo.com>
Date: Fri Jul 20 14:02:02 2018 -0700

    deleted myThirdFile.txt

commit 2ec5f7d1a734b2cc74343ce45075917b79cc7293
Author: Eric Chou <echou@yahoo.com>
Date: Fri Jul 20 14:01:18 2018 -0700

    adding myThirdFile.txt
```

We have gone through most of the basic operations we would use for Git. Let's take a look at how to use GitHub to share our repository.

GitHub example

In this example, we will use GitHub as the centralized location to synchronize our local repository and share with other users.

We will create a repository on GitHub. By default, GitHub has a free public repository; in my case, I pay a small monthly fee to host private repositories. At the time of creation, you can choose to create the license and the `.gitignore` file:

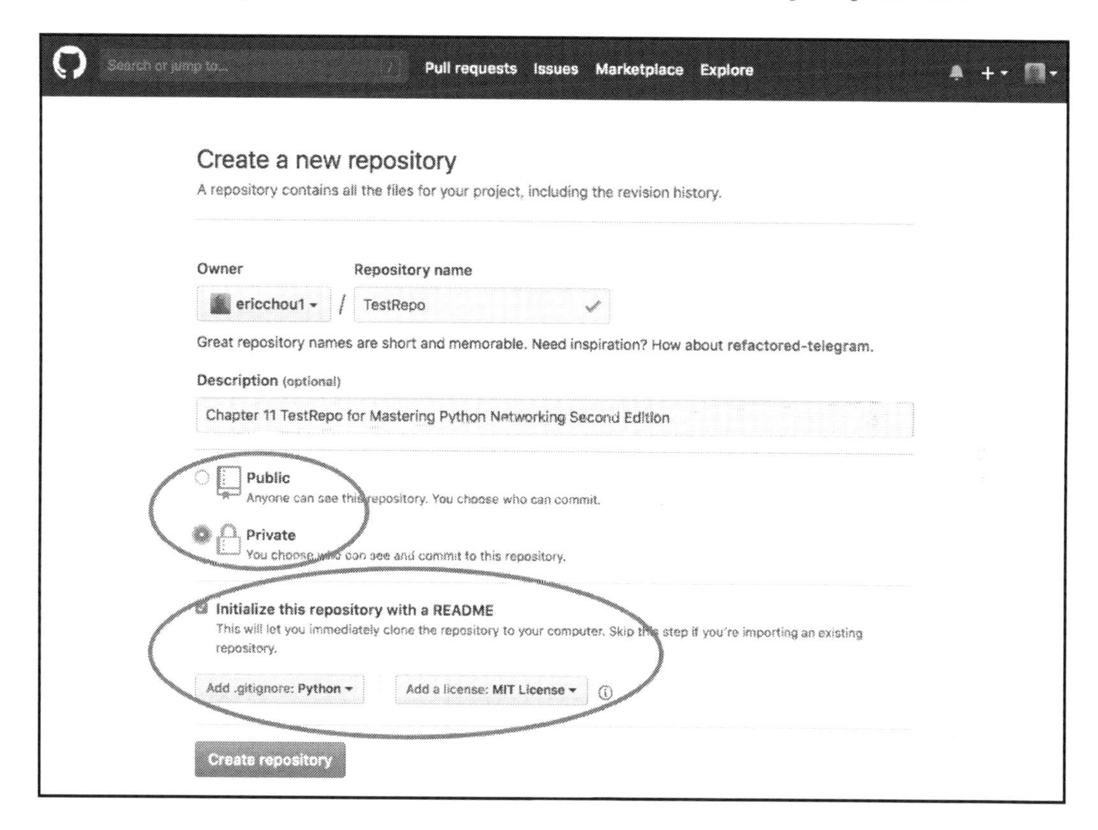

GitHub private repository

Once the repository is created, we can find the URL for this repository:

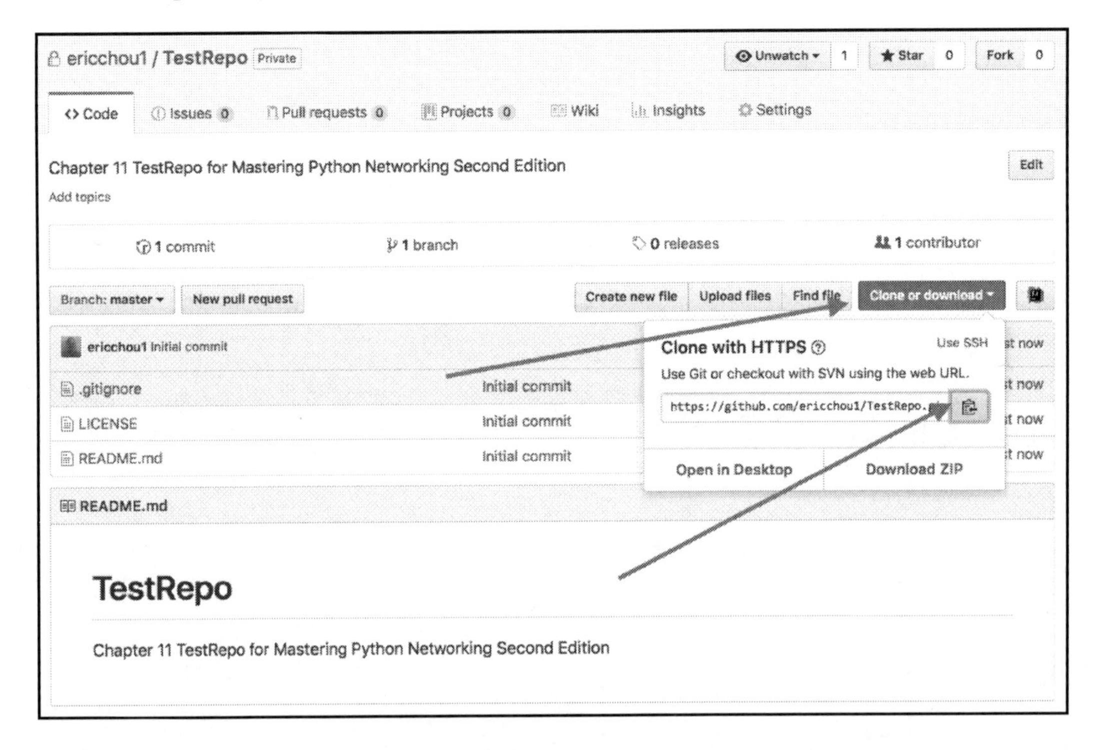

GitHub repository URL

We will use this URL to create a `remote` target; we will name it `gitHubRepo`:

```
$ git remote add gitHubRepo https://github.com/ericchou1/TestRepo.git
$ git remote -v
gitHubRepo https://github.com/ericchou1/TestRepo.git (fetch)
gitHubRepo https://github.com/ericchou1/TestRepo.git (push)
```

Since we chose to create a README.md and LICENSE file during creation, the remote repository and current repository are not the same. If we were to push local changes to the GitHub repository, we would receive the following error:

```
$ git push gitHubRepo master
Username for 'https://github.com': echou@yahoo.com
Password for 'https://echou@yahoo.com@github.com':
To https://github.com/ericchou1/TestRepo.git
 ! [rejected] master -> master (fetch first)
```

We will go ahead and use git pull to get the new files from GitHub:

```
$ git pull gitHubRepo master
Username for 'https://github.com': <username>
Password for 'https://<username>@github.com':
From https://github.com/ericchou1/TestRepo
 * branch master -> FETCH_HEAD
Merge made by the 'recursive' strategy.
 .gitignore | 104
+++++++++++++++++++++++++++++++++++++++++++++++++++++++++++++++
 LICENSE | 21 ++++++++++++
 README.md | 2 ++
 3 files changed, 127 insertions(+)
 create mode 100644 .gitignore
 create mode 100644 LICENSE
 create mode 100644 README.md
```

Now we will be able to push the contents over to GitHub:

```
$ git push gitHubRepo master
Username for 'https://github.com': <username>
Password for 'https://<username>@github.com':
Counting objects: 15, done.
Compressing objects: 100% (9/9), done.
Writing objects: 100% (15/15), 1.51 KiB | 0 bytes/s, done.
Total 15 (delta 1), reused 0 (delta 0)
remote: Resolving deltas: 100% (1/1), done.
To https://github.com/ericchou1/TestRepo.git
   a001b81..0aa362a master -> master
```

We can verify the content of the GitHub repository on the web page:

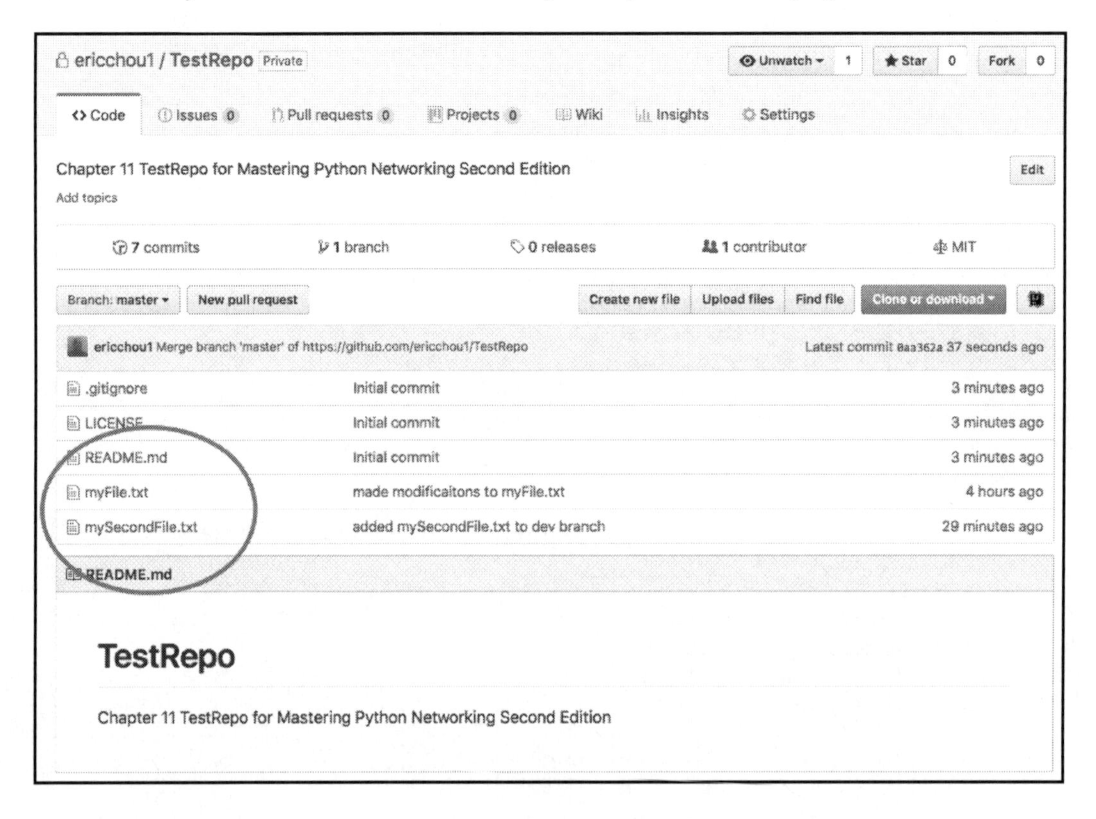

GitHub repository

Now another user can simply make a copy, or `clone`, of the repository:

```
[This is operated from another host]
$ cd /tmp
$ git clone https://github.com/ericchou1/TestRepo.git
Cloning into 'TestRepo'...
remote: Counting objects: 20, done.
remote: Compressing objects: 100% (13/13), done.
remote: Total 20 (delta 2), reused 15 (delta 1), pack-reused 0
Unpacking objects: 100% (20/20), done.
$ cd TestRepo/
$ ls
LICENSE myFile.txt
README.md mySecondFile.txt
```

This copied repository will be the exact copy of my original repository, including all the commit history:

```
$ git log
commit 0aa362a47782e7714ca946ba852f395083116ce5 (HEAD -> master,
origin/master, origin/HEAD)
Merge: bc078a9 a001b81
Author: Eric Chou <echou@yahoo.com>
Date: Fri Jul 20 14:18:58 2018 -0700

    Merge branch 'master' of https://github.com/ericchou1/TestRepo

commit a001b816bb75c63237cbc93067dffcc573c05aa2
Author: Eric Chou <ericchou1@users.noreply.github.com>
Date: Fri Jul 20 14:16:30 2018 -0700

    Initial commit
...
```

I can also invite another person as a collaborator for the project under the repository setting:

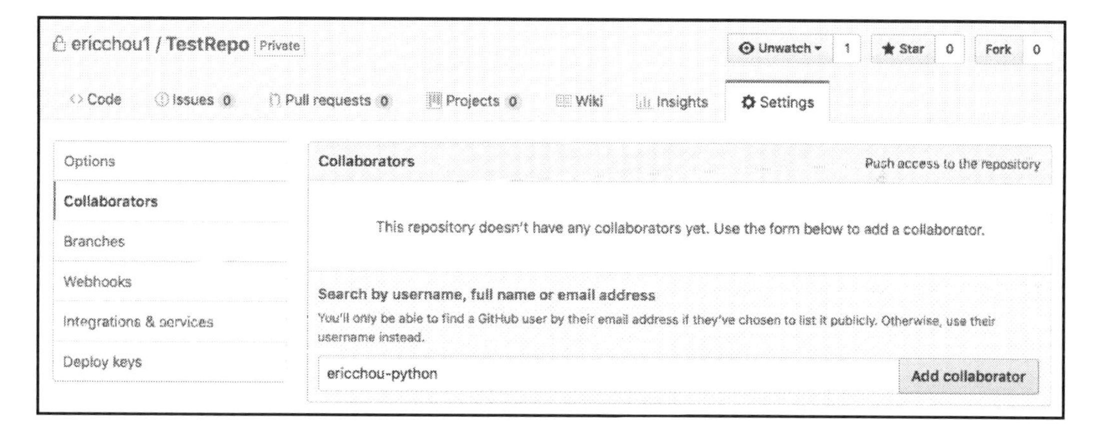

Repository invite

In the next example, we will see how we can fork a repository and perform a pull request for a repository that we do not maintain.

Collaborating with pull requests

As mentioned, Git supports collaboration between developers for a single project. We will take a look at how it is done when the code is hosted on GitHub.

In this case, I am going to take a look at the GitHub repository for this book. I am going to use a different GitHub handle, so I appear as a different user. I will click on the **Fork** bottom to make a copy of the repository in my personal account:

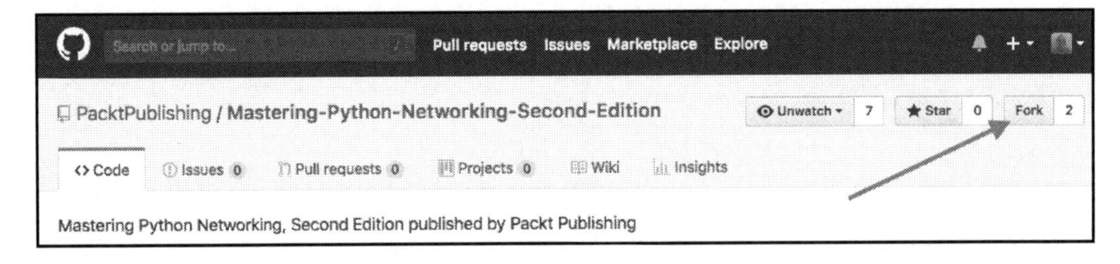

Git fork bottom

It will take a few seconds to make a copy:

Git fork in progress

After it is forked, we will have a copy of the repository in our personal account:

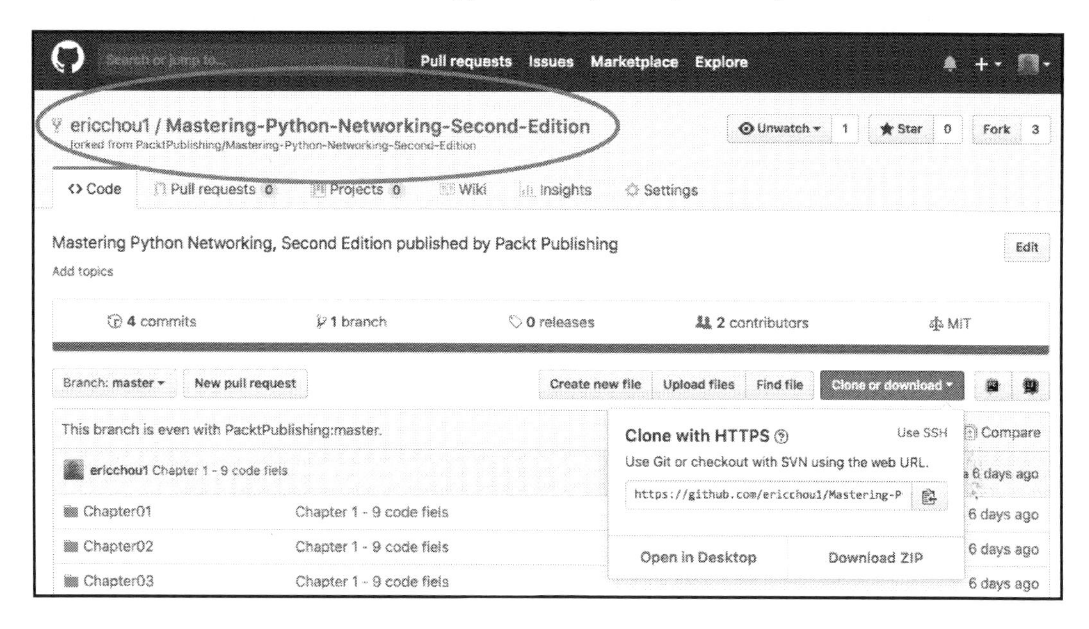

Git fork

We can follow the same steps we have used before to make some modifications to the files. In this case, I will make some changes to the `README.md` file. After the change is made, I can click on the **New pull request** button to create a pull request:

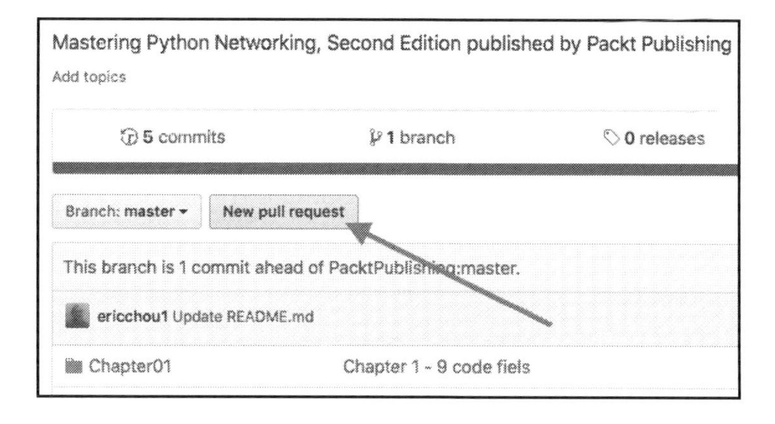

Pull request

When making a pull request, we should fill in as much information as possible to provide justifications for making the change:

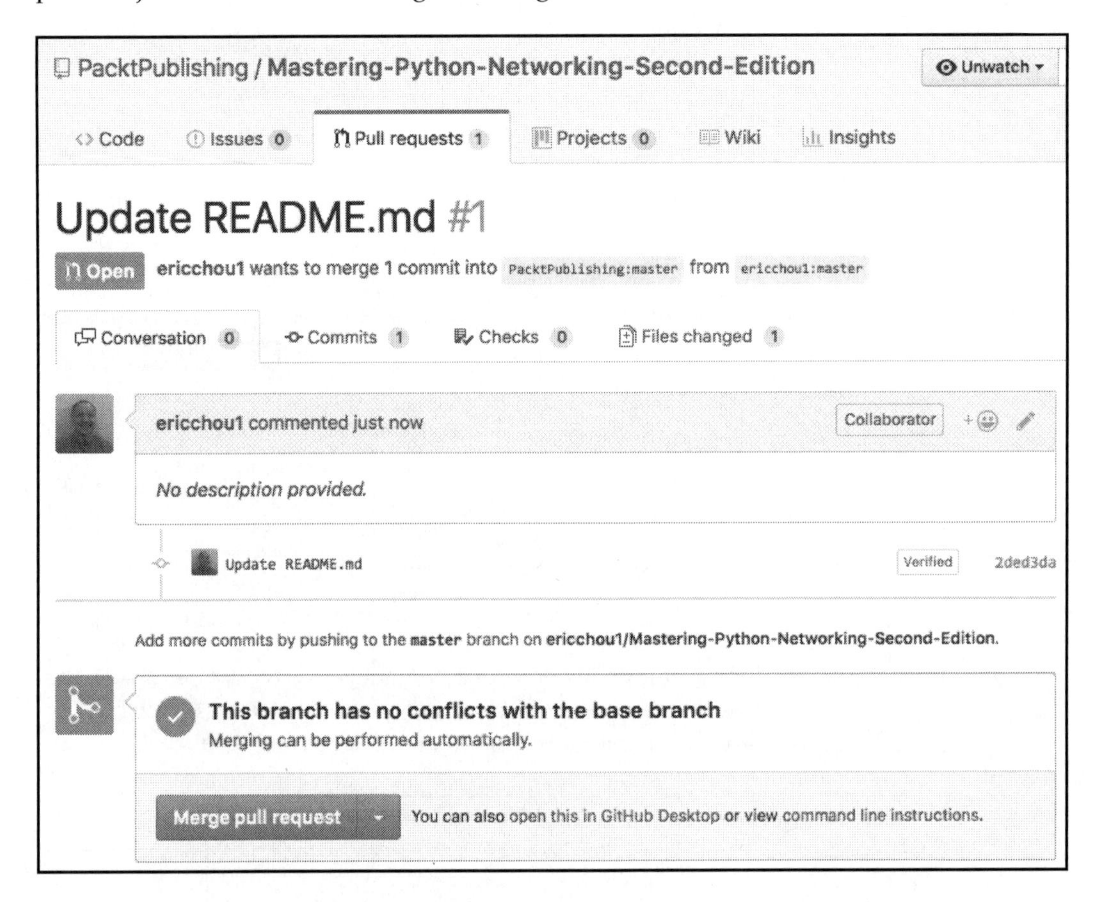

Pull request details

The repository maintainer will receive a notification of the pull request; if accepted, the change will make its way to the original repository:

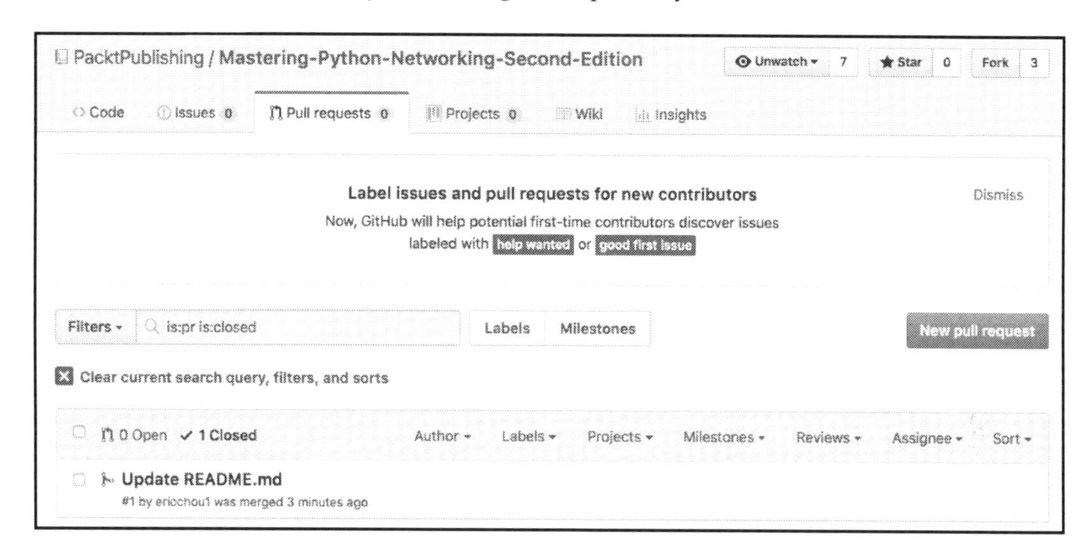

Pull request record

GitHub provides an excellent platform for collaboration with other developers; this is quickly becoming the de facto development choice for many large, open source projects. In the following section, let's take a look at how we can use Git with Python.

Git with Python

There are some Python packages that we can use with Git and GitHub. In this section, we will take a look at the GitPython and PyGithub libraries.

GitPython

We can use the GitPython package, `https://gitpython.readthedocs.io/en/stable/index.html`, to work with our Git repository. We will install the package and use the Python shell to construct a `Repo` object. From there, we can list all the commits in the repository:

```
$ sudo pip3 install gitpython
$ python3
>>> from git import Repo
```

```
>>> repo =
Repo('/home/echou/Master_Python_Networking/Chapter10/TestRepo')
>>> for commits in list(repo.iter_commits('master')):
... print(commits)
...
0aa362a47782e7714ca946ba852f395083116ce5
a001b816bb75c63237cbc93067dffcc573c05aa2
bc078a97e41d1614c1ba1f81f72acbcd95c0728c
2ec5f7d1a734b2cc74343ce45075917b79cc7293
c98373069f27d8b98d1ddacffe51b8fa7a30cf28
a3dd3ea8e6eb15b57d1f390ce0d2c3a03f07a038
5f579ab1e9a3fae13aa7f1b8092055213157524d
```

We can also look at the index entries:

```
>>> for (path, stage), entry in index.entries.items():
... print(path, stage, entry)
...
mySecondFile.txt 0 100644 75d6370ae31008f683cf18ed086098d05bf0e4dc 0
mySecondFile.txt
LICENSE 0 100644 52feb16b34de141a7567e4d18164fe2400e9229a 0 LICENSE
myFile.txt 0 100644 69e7d4728965c885180315c0d4c206637b3f6bad 0
myFile.txt
.gitignore 0 100644 894a44cc066a027465cd26d634948d56d13af9af 0
.gitignore
README.md 0 100644 a29fe688a14d119c20790195a815d078976c3bc6 0
README.md
>>>
```

GitPython offers good integration with all the Git functions. However, it is not the easiest to work with. We need to understand the terms and structure of Git to take full advantage of GitPython. But it is always good to keep it in mind in case we need it for other projects.

PyGitHub

Let's look at using the PyGitHub package, `http://pygithub.readthedocs.io/en/latest/`, to interact with GitHub repositories. The package is a wrapper around GitHub APIv3, `https://developer.github.com/v3/`:

```
$ sudo pip install pygithub
$ sudo pip3 install pygithub
```

Let's use the Python shell to print out the user's current repository:

```
$ python3
>>> from github import Github
>>> g = Github("ericchou1", "<password>")
>>> for repo in g.get_user().get_repos():
...     print(repo.name)
...
ansible
...
-Hands-on-Network-Programming-with-Python
Mastering-Python-Networking
Mastering-Python-Networking-Second-Edition
>>>
```

For more programmatic access, we can also create more granular control using an access token. Github allows a token to be associated with the selected rights:

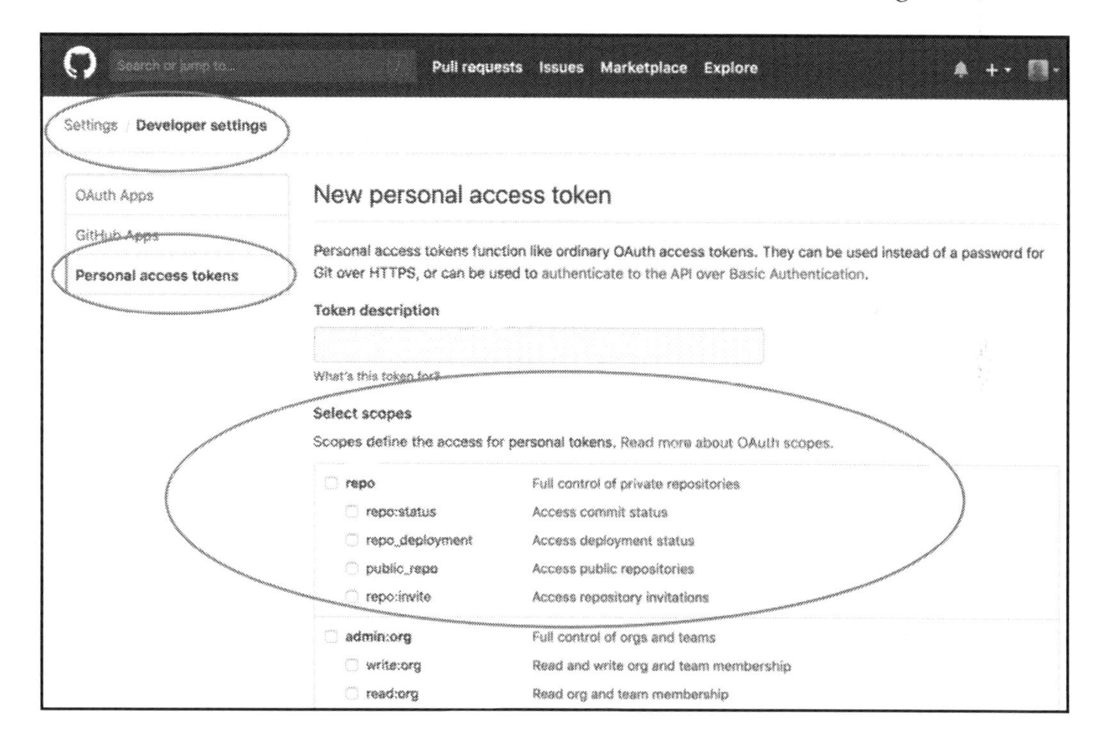

GitHub token generation

The output is a bit different if you use the access token as the authentication mechanism:

```
>>> from github import Github
>>> g = Github("<token>")
>>> for repo in g.get_user().get_repos():
...     print(repo)
...
Repository(full_name="oreillymedia/distributed_denial_of_service_ddos"
)
Repository(full_name="PacktPublishing/-Hands-on-Network-Programming-
with-Python")
Repository(full_name="PacktPublishing/Mastering-Python-Networking")
Repository(full_name="PacktPublishing/Mastering-Python-Networking-
Second-Edition")
...
```

Now that we are familiar with Git, GitHub, and some of the Python packages, we can use them to work with the technology. We will take a look at some practical examples in the coming section.

Automating configuration backup

In this example, we will use PyGithub to back up a directory containing our router configurations. We have seen how we can retrieve the information from our devices with Python or Ansible; we can now check them into GitHub.

We have a subdirectory, named `config`, with our router configs in text format:

```
$ ls configs/
iosv-1 iosv-2

$ cat configs/iosv-1
Building configuration...

Current configuration : 4573 bytes
!
! Last configuration change at 02:50:05 UTC Sat Jun 2 2018 by cisco
!
version 15.6
service timestamps debug datetime msec
...
```

We can use the following script to retrieve the latest index from our GitHub repository, build the content that we need to commit, and automatically commit the configuration:

```
$ cat Chapter10_1.py
#!/usr/bin/env python3
# reference:
https://stackoverflow.com/questions/38594717/how-do-i-push-new-files-t
o-github

from github import Github, InputGitTreeElement
import os

github_token = '<token>'
configs_dir = 'configs'
github_repo = 'TestRepo'

# Retrieve the list of files in configs directory
file_list = []
for dirpath, dirname, filenames in os.walk(configs_dir):
    for f in filenames:
        file_list.append(configs_dir + "/" + f)

g = Github(github_token)
repo = g.get_user().get_repo(github_repo)

commit_message = 'add configs'
master_ref = repo.get_git_ref('heads/master')
master_sha = master_ref.object.sha
base_tree = repo.get_git_tree(master_sha)

element_list = list()

for entry in file_list:
    with open(entry, 'r') as input_file:
        data = input_file.read()
    element = InputGitTreeElement(entry, '100644', 'blob', data)
    element_list.append(element)

# Create tree and commit
tree = repo.create_git_tree(element_list, base_tree)
parent = repo.get_git_commit(master_sha)
commit = repo.create_git_commit(commit_message, tree, [parent])
master_ref.edit(commit.sha)
```

We can see the `configs` directory in the GitHub repository:

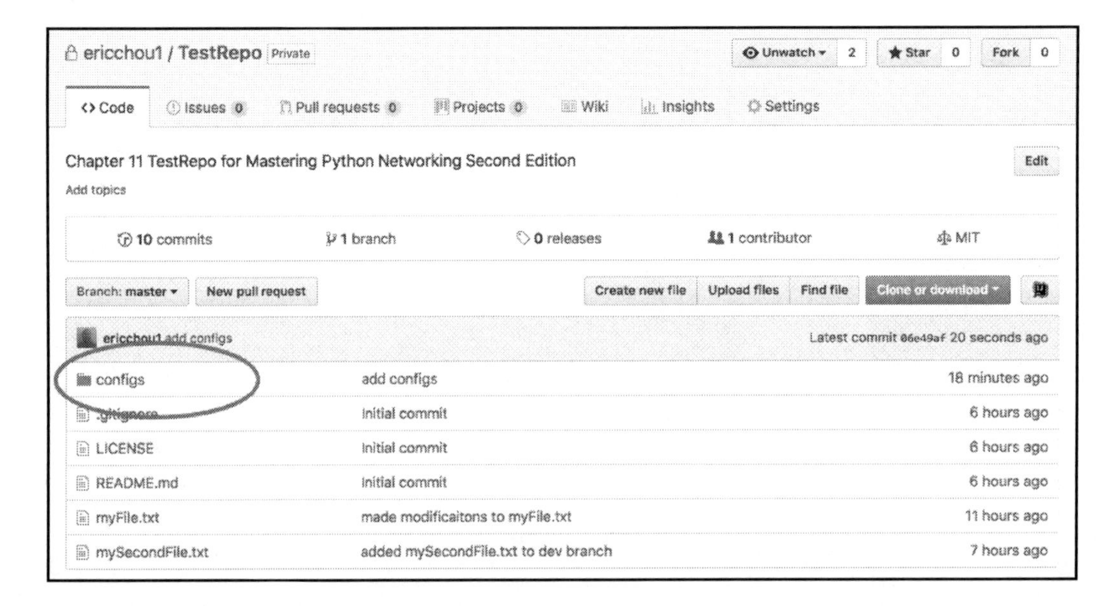

Configs directory

The commit history shows the commit from our script:

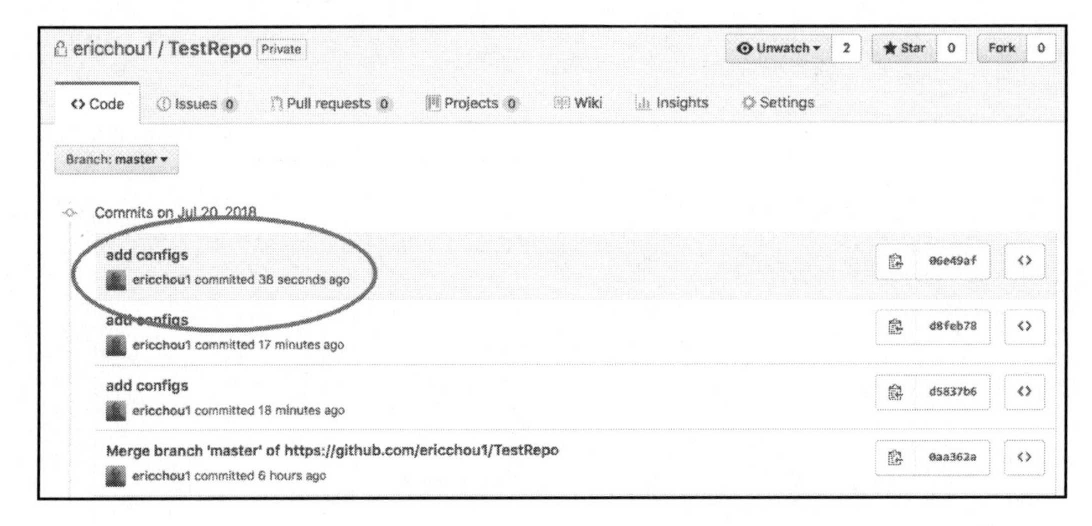

Commit history

In the *GitHub example* section, we saw how we could collaborate with other developers by forking the repository and making pull requests. Let's look at how we can further collaborate with Git.

Collaborating with Git

Git is an awesome collaboration technology, and GitHub is an incredibly effective way to develop projects together. GitHub provides a place for anyone in the world with internet access to share their thoughts and code for free. We know how to use Git and some of the basic collaboration steps using GitHub, but how do we join and contribute to a project? Sure, we would like to give back to these open source projects that have given us so much, but how do we get started?

In this section, we'll look at some of the things to know about software-development collaboration using Git and GitHub:

- **Start small**: One of the most important things to understand is the role we can play within a team. We might be awesome at network engineering but a mediocre Python developer. There are plenty of things we can do that don't involve being a highly-skilled developer. Don't be afraid to start small, documentation and testing are two good ways to get your foot in the door as a contributor.
- **Learn the ecosystem**: With any project, large or small, there is a set of conventions and a culture that has been established. We are all drawn to Python for its easy-to-read syntax and beginner-friendly culture; they also have a development guide that is centered around that ideology (`https://devguide.python.org/`). The Ansible project, on the other hand, also has an extensive community guide (`https://docs.ansible.com/ansible/latest/community/index.html`). It includes the code of conduct, the pull request process, how to report bugs, and the release process. Read these guides and learn the ecosystem for the project of interest.
- **Make a branch**: I have made the mistake of forking a project and making a pull request for the main branch. The main branch should be left alone for the core contributors to make changes to. We should create a separate branch for our contribution and allow the branch to be merged at a later date.

- **Keep forked repository synchronized**: Once you have forked a project, there is no rule that forces the cloned repository to sync with the main repository. We should make a point to regularly do `git pull` (get the code and merge locally) or `git fetch` (get the code with any change locally) to make sure we have the latest copy of the main repository.
- **Be friendly**: Just as in the real world, the virtual world has no place for hostility. When discussing an issue, be civil and friendly, even in disagreements.

Git and GitHub provide a way for any motivated individual to make a difference by making it easy to collaborate on projects. We are all empowered to contribute to any open source or private projects that we find interesting.

Summary

In this chapter, we looked at the version-control system known as Git and its close sibling, GitHub. Git was developed by Linus Torvolds in 2005 to help develop the Linux kernel and later adopted by other open source projects as the source-control system. Git is a fast, distributed, and scalable system. GitHub provides a centralized location to host Git repositories on the internet that allow anybody with an internet connection to collaborate.

We looked at how to use Git in the command line, its various operations, and how they are applied in GitHub. We also studied two of the popular Python libraries for working with Git: GitPython and PyGitHub. We ended the chapter with a configuration backup example and notes about project collaboration.

11
Sockets, IPv4, and Simple Client/Server Programming

In this chapter, we will cover the following recipes:

- Printing your machine's name and IPv4 address
- Retrieving a remote machine's IP address
- Converting an IPv4 address to different formats
- Finding a service name, given the port and protocol
- Converting integers to and from host to network byte order
- Setting and getting the default socket timeout
- Handling socket errors gracefully
- Modifying a socket's send/receive buffer size
- Changing a socket to the blocking/non-blocking mode
- Reusing socket addresses
- Printing the current time from the internet time server
- Writing an SNTP client
- Writing a simple TCP echo client/server application
- Writing a simple UDP echo client/server application

Introduction

This chapter introduces Python's core networking library through some simple recipes. Python's socket module has both class-based and instances-based utilities. The difference between a class-based and instance-based method is that the former doesn't need an instance of a socket object. This is a very intuitive approach. For example, in order to print your machine's IP address, you don't need a socket object. Instead, you can just call the socket's class-based methods. On the other hand, if you need to send some data to a server application, it is more intuitive that you create a socket object to perform that explicit operation. The recipes presented in this chapter can be categorized into three groups as follows:

- In the first few recipes, the class-based utilities have been used in order to extract some useful information about host, network, and any target service.
- After that, some more recipes have been presented using the instance-based utilities. Some common socket tasks, including manipulating the socket timeout, buffer size, and blocking mode has been demonstrated.
- Finally, both class-based and instance-based utilities have been used to construct some clients, which perform some practical tasks, for example, synchronizing the machine time with an internet server or writing a generic client/server script.

You can use these demonstrated approaches to write your own client/server application.

Printing your machine's name and IPv4 address

Sometimes, you need to quickly discover some information about your machine, for example, the hostname, IP address, number of network interfaces, and so on. This is very easy to achieve using Python scripts.

Getting ready

You need to install Python on your machine before you start coding. Python comes preinstalled in most of the Linux distributions. For Microsoft Windows operating systems, you can download binaries from the Python website: `http://www.python.org/download/`.

Currently, Python 3.x is released in addition to Python 2.x. Many of the current Linux distributions and macOS versions are still shipping Python 2 by default. However, some ship both of them.

Download the relevant installer for your operating system and the relevant version based on whether your operating system is 32 bit or 64 bit.

You may consult the documentation of your operating system to check and review your Python setup. After installing Python on your machine, you can try opening the Python interpreter from the command line by typing python. This will show the interpreter prompt, >>>, which should be similar to the following output:

```
~$ python
Python 2.7.12 (default, Nov 19 2016, 06:48:10)
[GCC 5.4.0 20160609] on linux2
Type "help", "copyright", "credits" or "license" for more information.
>>>
```

How to do it...

In the latter versions of Ubuntu since Ubuntu 14.04, Python 3 can be executed by typing python3:

```
~$ python3
Python 3.5.2 (default, Nov 17 2016, 17:05:23)
[GCC 5.4.0 20160609] on linux
Type "help", "copyright", "credits" or
"license" for more information.
>>>
```

Similarly, to be specific about which version you prefer to use, you may type python2 to execute Python 2 as well:

```
~$ python2
Python 2.7.12 (default, Nov 19 2016, 06:48:10)
[GCC 5.4.0 20160609] on linux2
Type "help", "copyright", "credits" or "license" for more information.
>>>
```

There are a few changes in Python 3 that made some code written for Python 2 incompatible with Python 3. When you write network applications, try to follow the Python 3 best practices as these changes and improvements are back ported to the latter versions of Python 2. Thus, you may be fine by running the latest versions of Python 2 such as Python 2.7. However, some code developed focusing on Python 2 may not run on Python 3.

The following recipes in this chapter are written in Python 3. However, please keep in mind that a few network projects and modules may have been developed for Python 2. In that case, you will either have to port the application to Python 3 or use Python 2 depending on your requirements.

As this recipe is very short, you can try this in the Python interpreter interactively.

First, we need to import the Python `socket` library with the following command:

```
>>> import socket
```

Then, we call the `gethostname()` method from the `socket` library and store the result in a variable as follows:

```
>>> host_name = socket.gethostname()
>>> print "Host name: %s" %host_name
Host name: llovizna
>>> print "IP address: %s"
%socket.gethostbyname(host_name)
IP address: 127.0.1.1
```

The entire activity can be wrapped in a free-standing function, `print_machine_info()`, which uses the built-in socket class methods.

We call our function from the usual Python `__main__` block. During runtime, Python assigns values to some internal variables such as `__name__`. In this case, `__name__` refers to the name of the calling process. When running this script from the command line, as shown in the following command, the name will be `__main__`. But it will be different if the module is imported from another script. This means that, when the module is called from the command line, it will automatically run our `print_machine_info` function; however, when imported separately, the user will need to explicitly call the function.

Listing 1.1 shows how to get our machine info, as follows:

```
#!/usr/bin/env python
# This program is optimized for Python 2.7.12
  and Python 3.5.2.
# It may run on any other version with/without
  modifications.
    import socket
    def print_machine_info():
        host_name = socket.gethostname()
        ip_address = socket.gethostbyname(host_name)
        print ("Host name: %s" %host_name)
        print ("IP address: %s" %ip_address)
    if __name__ == '__main__':
        print_machine_info()
```

In order to run this recipe, you can use the provided source file from the command line as follows:

```
$ python 11_1_local_machine_info.py
```

On my machine, the following output is shown:

```
Host name: llovizna
IP address: 127.0.1.1
```

The hostname is what you assigned to your computer when you configured your operating system. This output will be different on your machine depending on the system's host configuration. Here hostname indicates where the Python interpreter is currently executing.

Please note that the programs in this book are run with both versions 2 and 3. We avoid mentioning `python3` and `python2` in commands, as they are too specific to some distributions and assumes that a specific version is installed. You may run any of the programs in either version by using `python2` or `python3` accordingly.

How it works...

The import socket statement imports one of Python's core networking libraries. Then, we use the two utility functions, `gethostname()` and `gethostbyname(host_name)`. You can type `help(socket.gethostname)` to see the online help information from within the command line. Alternatively, you can type the following address in your web browser at `http://docs.python.org/3/library/socket.html`. You can refer to the following code:

```
gethostname(...)
    gethostname() -> string
    Return the current host name.
gethostbyname(...)
    gethostbyname(host) -> address
    Return the IP address (a string of the form
    '255.255.255.255') for a host.
```

The first function takes no parameter and returns the current or localhost name. The second function takes a single `hostname` parameter and returns its IP address.

Retrieving a remote machine's IP address

Sometimes, you need to translate a machine's hostname into its corresponding IP address, for example, a quick domain name lookup. This recipe introduces a simple function to do that.

How to do it...

If you need to know the IP address of a remote machine, you can use a built-in library function, `gethostbyname()`. In this case, you need to pass the remote hostname as its parameter.

In this case, we need to call the `gethostbyname()` class function. Let's have a look at this short code snippet.

Listing 1.2 shows how to get a remote machine's IP address as follows:

```
#!/usr/bin/env python
# This program is optimized for Python 2.7.12 and
  Python 3.5.2.
# It may run on any other version with/without
  modifications.
import socket
def get_remote_machine_info():
    remote_host = 'www.python.org'
    try:
        print ("IP address of %s: %s" %(remote_host,
        socket.gethostbyname(remote_host)))
    except socket.error as err_msg:
        print ("%s: %s" %(remote_host, err_msg))
if __name__ == '__main__':
    get_remote_machine_info()
```

If you run the preceding code it gives the following output:

```
$ python 11_2_remote_machine_info.py
IP address of www.python.org: 151.101.36.223
```

How it works...

This recipe wraps the `gethostbyname()` method inside a user-defined function called `get_remote_machine_info()`. In this recipe, we introduced the notion of exception handling. As you can see, we wrapped the main function call inside a `try-except` block. This means that, if some error occurs during the execution of this function, this error will be dealt with by this `try-except` block.

For example, let's change the `remote_host` value and replace `https://www.python.org/` with something non-existent, for example, `www.pytgo.org`:

```
#!/usr/bin/env python
# This program is optimized for Python 2.7.12 and
  Python 3.5.2.
# It may run on any other version with/without
  modifications.
    import socket
    def get_remote_machine_info():
        remote_host = 'www.pytgo.org'
```

```
        try:
            print ("IP address of %s: %s" %
                   (remote_host,
            socket.gethostbyname(remote_host)))
        except socket.error as err_msg:
            print ("%s: %s" %(remote_host, err_msg))
    if __name__ == '__main__':
        get_remote_machine_info()
```

Now run the following command:

```
$ python 11_2_remote_machine_info.py
www.pytgo.org: [Errno -2] Name or service not known
```

The `try-except` block catches the error and shows the user an error message that there is no IP address associated with the hostname, `www.pytgo.org`.

Converting an IPv4 address to different formats

When you would like to deal with low-level network functions, sometimes, the usual string notation of IP addresses are not very useful. They need to be converted to the packed 32-bit binary formats.

How to do it...

The Python `socket` library has utilities to deal with the various IP address formats. Here, we will use two of them: `inet_aton()` and `inet_ntoa()`.

Let us create the `convert_ip4_address()` function, where `inet_aton()` and `inet_ntoa()` will be used for the IP address conversion. We will use two sample IP addresses, `127.0.0.1` and `192.168.0.1`.

Listing 1.3 shows `ip4_address_conversion` as follows:

```
#!/usr/bin/env python
# This program is optimized for Python 2.7.12 and
  Python 3.5.2.
# It may run on any other version with/without
  modifications.
    import socket
    from binascii import hexlify
```

```
def convert_ip4_address():
    for ip_addr in ['127.0.0.1', '192.168.0.1']:
        packed_ip_addr = socket.
                         inet_aton(ip_addr)
        unpacked_ip_addr = socket.inet_ntoa
                           (packed_ip_addr)
        print ("IP Address: %s => Packed: %s,
                Unpacked: %s" %(ip_addr,
                hexlify(packed_ip_addr),
                unpacked_ip_addr))
if __name__ == '__main__':
    convert_ip4_address()
```

Now, if you run this recipe, you will see the following output:

```
$ python 11_3_ip4_address_conversion.py
IP Address: 127.0.0.1 => Packed: 7f000001, Unpacked:
127.0.0.1
IP Address: 192.168.0.1 => Packed: c0a80001, Unpacked: 192.168.0.1
```

How it works...

In this recipe, the two IP addresses have been converted from a string to a 32-bit packed format using a `for-in` statement. Additionally, the Python `hexlify` function is called from the `binascii` module. This helps to represent the binary data in a hexadecimal format.

Finding a service name, given the port and protocol

If you would like to discover network services, it may be helpful to determine what network services run on which ports using either the TCP or UDP protocol.

Getting ready

If you know the port number of a network service, you can find the service name using the `getservbyport()` socket class function from the socket library. You can optionally give the protocol name when calling this function.

How to do it...

Let us define a `find_service_name()` function, where the `getservbyport()` socket class function will be called with a few ports, for example, `80, 25`. We can use Python's `for-in` loop construct.

Listing 1.4 shows `finding_service_name` as follows:

```
#!/usr/bin/env python
# This program is optimized for Python 2.7.12 and Python 3.5.2.
# It may run on any other version with/without modifications.

import socket

def find_service_name():
    protocolname = 'tcp'
    for port in [80, 25]:
        print ("Port: %s => service name: %s" %(port,
socket.getservbyport(port, protocolname)))
    print ("Port: %s => service name: %s" %(53,
socket.getservbyport(53, 'udp')))
if __name__ == '__main__':
    find_service_name()
```

If you run this script, you will see the following output:

```
$ python 11_4_finding_service_name.py
Port: 80 => service name: http
Port: 25 => service name: smtp
Port: 53 => service name: domain
```

This indicates that `http`, `smtp`, and `domain` services are running on the ports `80`, `25`, and `53` respectively.

How it works...

In this recipe, the `for-in` statement is used to iterate over a sequence of variables. So for each iteration, we use one IP address to convert them in their packed and unpacked format.

Converting integers to and from host to network byte order

If you ever need to write a low-level network application, it may be necessary to handle the low-level data transmission over the wire between two machines. This operation requires some sort of conversion of data from the native host operating system to the network format and vice versa. This is because each one has its own specific representation of data.

How to do it...

Python's `socket` library has utilities for converting from a network byte order to host byte order and vice versa. You may want to become familiar with them, for example, `ntohl()/htonl()`.

Let us define the `convert_integer()` function, where the `ntohl()/htonl()` socket class functions are used to convert IP address formats.

Listing 1.5 shows `integer_conversion` as follows:

```
#!/usr/bin/env python
# This program is optimized for Python 2.7.12 and Python 3.5.2.
# It may run on any other version with/without modifications.

import socket

def convert_integer():
    data = 1234
    # 32-bit
    print ("Original: %s => Long  host byte order: %s, Network byte
order: %s" %(data, socket.ntohl(data), socket.htonl(data)))
    # 16-bit
    print ("Original: %s => Short  host byte order: %s, Network byte
order: %s" %(data, socket.ntohs(data), socket.htons(data)))

if __name__ == '__main__':
    convert_integer()
```

If you run this recipe, you will see the following output:

```
$ python 11_5_integer_conversion.py
Original: 1234 => Long  host byte order: 3523477504,
Network byte order: 3523477504
Original: 1234 => Short  host byte order: 53764,
Network byte order: 53764
```

How it works...

Here, we take an integer and show how to convert it between network and host byte orders. The `ntohl()` socket class function converts from the network byte order to host byte order in a long format. Here, `n` represents network and `h` represents host; `l` represents long and `s` represents short, that is, 16-bit.

Setting and getting the default socket timeout

Sometimes, you need to manipulate the default values of certain properties of a `socket` library, for example, the socket timeout.

How to do it...

You can make an instance of a `socket` object and call a `gettimeout()` method to get the default timeout value and the `settimeout()` method to set a specific timeout value. This is very useful in developing custom server applications.

We first create a `socket` object inside a `test_socket_timeout()` function. Then, we can use the `getter/setter` instance methods to manipulate timeout values.

Listing 1.6 shows `socket_timeout` as follows:

```
#!/usr/bin/env python
# This program is optimized for Python 2.7.12 and Python 3.5.2.
# It may run on any other version with/without modifications.


import socket

def test_socket_timeout():
```

```
        s = socket.socket(socket.AF_INET, socket.SOCK_STREAM)
        print ("Default socket timeout: %s" %s.gettimeout())
        s.settimeout(100)
        print ("Current socket timeout: %s" %s.gettimeout())
    if __name__ == '__main__':
        test_socket_timeout()
```

After running the preceding script, you can see how this modifies the default socket timeout as follows:

```
$ python 11_6_socket_timeout.py
Default socket timeout: None
Current socket timeout: 100.0
```

How it works...

In this code snippet, we have first created a `socket` object by passing the socket family and socket type as the first and second arguments of the socket constructor. Then, you can get the socket timeout value by calling `gettimeout()` and alter the value by calling the `settimeout()` method. The timeout value passed to the `settimeout()` method can be in seconds (non-negative float) or `None`. This method is used for manipulating the blocking-socket operations. Setting a timeout of `None` disables timeouts on socket operations.

Handling socket errors gracefully

In any networking application, it is very common that one end is trying to connect, but the other party is not responding due to networking media failure or any other reason. The Python `socket` library has an elegant method of handing these errors via the `socket.error` exceptions. In this recipe, a few examples are presented.

How to do it...

Let us create a few try-except code blocks and put one potential error type in each block. In order to get a user input, the `argparse` module can be used. This module is more powerful than simply parsing command-line arguments using `sys.argv`. In the try-except blocks, put typical socket operations, for example, create a `socket` object, connect to a server, send data, and wait for a reply.

The following recipe illustrates the concepts in a few lines of code.

Listing 1.7 shows `socket_errors` as follows:

```
#!/usr/bin/env python
# This program is optimized for Python 2.7.12 and Python 3.5.2.
# It may run on any other version with/without modifications.

import sys
import socket
import argparse


def main():
    # setup argument parsing
    parser = argparse.ArgumentParser(description='Socket Error
Examples')
    parser.add_argument('--host', action="store", dest="host",
required=False)
    parser.add_argument('--port', action="store", dest="port",
type=int,
required=False)
    parser.add_argument('--file', action="store", dest="file",
required=False)
    given_args = parser.parse_args()
    host = given_args.host
    port = given_args.port
    filename = given_args.file
    # First try-except block -- create socket
    try:
        s = socket.socket(socket.AF_INET, socket.SOCK_STREAM)
    except socket.error as e:
        print ("Error creating socket: %s" % e)
        sys.exit(1)
    # Second try-except block -- connect to given host/port
    try:
        s.connect((host, port))
    except socket.gaierror as e:
        print ("Address-related error connecting to
```

```
                    server: %s" % e)
            sys.exit(1)
        except socket.error as e:
            print ("Connection error: %s" % e)
            sys.exit(1)
        # Third try-except block -- sending data
        try:
            msg = "GET %s HTTP/1.0\r\n\r\n" % filename
            s.sendall(msg.encode('utf-8'))
        except socket.error as e:
            print ("Error sending data: %s" % e)
            sys.exit(1)
        while 1:
            # Fourth tr-except block -- waiting
               to receive
              data from remote host
            try:
                buf = s.recv(2048)
            except socket.error as e:
                print ("Error receiving data: %s" % e)
                sys.exit(1)
            if not len(buf):
                break
            # write the received data
            sys.stdout.write(buf.decode('utf-8'))
    if __name__ == '__main__':
        main()
```

How it works...

In Python, passing command-line arguments to a script and parsing them in the script can be done using the `argparse` module. This is available in Python 2.7. For earlier versions of Python, this module is available separately in **Python Package Index (PyPI)**. You can install this via `easy_install` or `pip`.

In this recipe, three arguments are set up—a hostname, port number, and filename. The usage of this script is as follows:

```
$ python 11_7_socket_errors.py --host=<HOST>
  --port=<PORT> --file=<FILE>
In the preceding recipe, msg.encode('utf-8')
encodes the message into UTF-8, and
buf.decode('utf-8') decodes the received UTF-8
format.
```

If you try the preceding recipe with a non-existent host, this script will print an address error as follows:

```
$ python 11_7_socket_errors.py
  --host=www.pytgo.org --port=8080
  --file=11_7_socket_errors.py
Address-related error connecting to
server: [Errno -2] Name or service not known
```

If there is no service on a specific port and if you try to connect to that port, then this will throw a connection timeout error as follows:

```
$ python 11_7_socket_errors.py
  --host=www.python.org --port=8080
  --file=11_7_socket_errors.py
```

This will return the following error since the host, `www.python.org`, is not listening on port `8080`:

```
Connection error: [Errno 110] Connection timed out
```

However, if you send an arbitrary request as a correct request to a correct port, the error may not be caught at the application level. For example, running the following script returns no error, but the HTML output tells us what's wrong with this script:

```
$ python 11_7_socket_errors.py
  --host=www.python.org --port=80
  --file=11_7_socket_errors.py
HTTP/1.1 500 Domain Not Found
Server: Varnish
Retry-After: 0
content-type: text/html
Cache-Control: private, no-cache
connection: keep-alive
Content-Length: 179
Accept-Ranges: bytes
Date: Thu, 01 Jun 2017 22:02:24 GMT
Via: 1.1 varnish
Connection: close
<html>
<head>
<title>Fastly error: unknown domain </title>
</head>
<body>
Fastly error: unknown domain: . Please check that this domain has been
added to a service.</body></html>
```

In the preceding example, four try-except blocks have been used. All blocks use `socket.error` except for the second block, which uses `socket.gaierror`. This is used for address-related errors. There are two other types of exceptions—`socket.herror` is used for legacy C API, and if you use the `settimeout()` method in a socket, `socket.timeout` will be raised when a timeout occurs on that socket.

Modifying a socket's send/receive buffer sizes

The default socket buffer size may not be suitable in many circumstances. In such circumstances, you can change the default socket buffer size to a more suitable value.

How to do it...

Let us manipulate the default socket buffer size using a socket object's `setsockopt()` method.

First, define two constants: `SEND_BUF_SIZE`/`RECV_BUF_SIZE` and then wrap a socket instance's call to the `setsockopt()` method in a function. It is also a good idea to check the value of the buffer size before modifying it. Note that we need to set up the send and receive buffer size separately.

Listing 1.8 shows how to modify socket send/receive buffer sizes as follows:

```
#!/usr/bin/env python
# This program is optimized for Python 2.7.12 and Python 3.5.2.
# It may run on any other version with/without modifications.

import socket

SEND_BUF_SIZE = 4096
RECV_BUF_SIZE = 4096

def modify_buff_size():
    sock = socket.socket( socket.AF_INET, socket.SOCK_STREAM )
    # Get the size of the socket's send buffer
    bufsize = sock.getsockopt(socket.SOL_SOCKET, socket.SO_SNDBUF)
    print ("Buffer size [Before]:%d" %bufsize)
    sock.setsockopt(socket.SOL_TCP,
                    socket.TCP_NODELAY, 1)
```

```
    sock.setsockopt(
            socket.SOL_SOCKET,
            socket.SO_SNDBUF,
            SEND_BUF_SIZE)
    sock.setsockopt(
            socket.SOL_SOCKET,
            socket.SO_RCVBUF,
            RECV_BUF_SIZE)
    bufsize = sock.getsockopt(socket.SOL_SOCKET, socket.SO_SNDBUF)
    print ("Buffer size [After]:%d" %bufsize)

if __name__ == '__main__':
    modify_buff_size()
```

If you run the preceding script, it will show the changes in the socket's buffer size. The following output may be different on your machine depending on your operating system's local settings:

```
$ python 11_8_modify_buff_size.py
Buffer size [Before]:16384
Buffer size [After]:8192
```

How it works...

You can call the `getsockopt()` and `setsockopt()` methods on a socket object to retrieve and modify the socket object's properties respectively. The `setsockopt()` method takes three arguments: `level`, `optname`, and `value`. Here, `optname` takes the option name and `value` is the corresponding value of that option. For the first argument, the needed symbolic constants can be found in the socket module (`SO_*etc.`).

Changing a socket to the blocking/non-blocking mode

By default, TCP sockets are placed in a blocking mode. This means the control is not returned to your program until some specific operation is complete. If you call the `connect()` API, the connection blocks your program until the operation is complete. On many occasions, you don't want to keep your program waiting forever, either for a response from the server or for any error to stop the operation. For example, when you write a web browser client that connects to a web server, you should consider a stop functionality that can cancel the connection process in the middle of this operation. This can be achieved by placing the socket in the non-blocking mode.

How to do it...

Let us see what options are available under Python. In Python, a socket can be placed in the blocking or non-blocking mode. In the non-blocking mode, if any call to API, for example, `send()` or `recv()`, encounters any problem, an error will be raised. However, in the blocking mode, this will not stop the operation. We can create a normal TCP socket and experiment with both the blocking and non-blocking operations.

To manipulate the socket's blocking nature, we should create a socket object first.

We can then call `setblocking(1)` to set up blocking or `setblocking(0)` to unset blocking. Finally, we bind the socket to a specific port and listen for incoming connections.

Listing 1.9 shows how the socket changes to blocking or non-blocking mode as follows:

```
#!/usr/bin/env python
# This program is optimized for Python 2.7.12 and Python 3.5.2.
# It may run on any other version with/without modifications.

import socket

def test_socket_modes():
    s = socket.socket(socket.AF_INET,
                      socket.SOCK_STREAM)
    s.setblocking(1)
    s.settimeout(0.5)
    s.bind(("127.0.0.1", 0))
```

```
        socket_address = s.getsockname()
        print ("Trivial Server launched on
                  socket: %s" %str(socket_address))
        while(1):
            s.listen(1)
    if __name__ == '__main__':
        test_socket_modes()
```

If you run this recipe, it will launch a trivial server that has the blocking mode enabled as shown in the following command:

```
$ python 11_9_socket_modes.py
Trivial Server launched on
socket: ('127.0.0.1', 51410)
```

How it works...

In this recipe, we enable blocking on a socket by setting the value `1` in the `setblocking()` method. Similarly, you can unset the value `0` in this method to make it non-blocking.

This feature will be reused in some later recipes, where its real purpose will be elaborated.

Reusing socket addresses

You want to run a socket server always on a specific port even after it is closed intentionally or unexpectedly. This is useful in some cases where your client program always connects to that specific server port. So, you don't need to change the server port.

How to do it...

If you run a Python socket server on a specific port and try to rerun it after closing it once, you won't be able to use the same port. It will usually throw an error like the following command:

```
Traceback (most recent call last):
   File "11_10_reuse_socket_address.py",
   line 40, in <module>
        reuse_socket_addr()
   File "11_10_reuse_socket_address.py",
   line 25, in reuse_socket_addr
        srv.bind( ('', local_port) )
   File "<string>", line 1, in bind
    socket.error: [Errno 98] Address
    already in use
```

The remedy to this problem is to enable the socket reuse option, `SO_REUSEADDR`.

After creating a `socket` object, we can query the state of address reuse, say an old state. Then, we call the `setsockopt()` method to alter the value of its address reuse state. Then, we follow the usual steps of binding to an address and listening for incoming client connections.

In the preceding example, when you close the Python script with *Ctrl* + *C*, you notice an exception:

```
^CTraceback (most recent call last):File "11_9_socket_modes.py", line
20, in <module>
test_socket_modes()
File "11_9_socket_modes.py", line 17, in test_socket_modes
s.listen(1)
KeyboardInterrupt
```

This indicates that there was a keyboard interrupt in the execution.

In this example, we catch the `KeyboardInterrupt` exception so that if you issue *Ctrl* + *C*, then the Python script gets terminated without showing any exception message.

Listing 1.10 shows how to reuse socket addresses as follows:

```
#!/usr/bin/env python
# This program is optimized for Python 2.7.12 and Python 3.5.2.
# It may run on any other version with/without modifications.

import socket
import sys
```

```
def reuse_socket_addr():
    sock = socket.socket( socket.AF_INET, socket.SOCK_STREAM )

    # Get the old state of the SO_REUSEADDR option
    old_state = sock.getsockopt(socket.SOL_SOCKET,
                                socket.SO_REUSEADDR )
    print ("Old sock state: %s" %old_state)

    # Enable the SO_REUSEADDR option
    sock.setsockopt( socket.SOL_SOCKET,
                     socket.SO_REUSEADDR, 1 )
    new_state = sock.getsockopt(
      socket.SOL_SOCKET, socket.SO_REUSEADDR )
    print ("New sock state: %s" %new_state)

    local_port = 8282
    srv = socket.socket(socket.AF_INET,
                        socket.SOCK_STREAM)
    srv.setsockopt(socket.SOL_SOCKET,
                   socket.SO_REUSEADDR, 1)
    srv.bind( ('', local_port) )
    srv.listen(1)
    print ("Listening on port: %s " %local_port)
    while True:
        try:
            connection, addr = srv.accept()
            print ('Connected by %s:%s'
                   % (addr[0], addr[1]))
        except KeyboardInterrupt:
            break
        except socket.error as msg:
            print ('%s' % (msg,))


if __name__ == '__main__':
    reuse_socket_addr()
```

The output from this recipe will be similar to the outcomes produced here, by executing the program:

```
$ python 11_10_reuse_socket_address.py
Old sock state: 0
New sock state: 1
Listening on port: 8282
```

How it works...

You may run this script from one console window and try to connect to this server from another console window by typing `telnet localhost 8282`.

You will see an output printed in the program window as your telnet connects to it:

```
Connected by 127.0.0.1:46584
```

Here the host and port will defer based on the telnet instance that you are sending this request from.

After you close the server program, you can rerun it again on the same port. However, if you comment out the line that sets the `SO_REUSEADDR`, the server will not run for the second time.

Printing the current time from the internet time server

Many programs rely on the accurate machine time, such as the `make` command in UNIX. Your machine time may be different and need synchronizing with another time server in your network.

Getting ready

In order to synchronize your machine time with one of the internet time servers, you can write a Python client for that. For this, `ntplib` will be used. Here, the client/server conversation will be done using **Network Time Protocol** (**NTP**). If `ntplib` is not installed on your machine, you can get it from `PyPI` with the following command using `pip` or `easy_install`:

```
$ pip install ntplib
```

If `pip` is not installed on your computer, first install it before executing the preceding command. In Debian-based Linux distributions such as Ubuntu, this can be installed by:

```
$ sudo apt install python-pip
```

Note that you will need to install `pip` for Python 3 separately if you are running it along side Python 2, as typically Python 2 is set as the default version:

```
$ sudo apt-get install python3-pip
```

Similarly, `ntplib` needs to be installed for `python3-pip` (also called `pip3`) separately:

```
$ pip3 install ntplib
```

It is a good idea to upgrade `pip` to the latest version if you are running an outdated version, by issuing the following command:

```
$ pip install --upgrade pip
```

or:

```
$ pip3 install --upgrade pip
```

If Python 2 and Python 3 are installed alongside in your computer then use `pip3`.

I am using the `pip` version 9.0.1, for both Python 2 and Python 3. This is the latest version at the time of writing.

How to do it...

We create an instance of NTPClient and then we call the request() method on it by passing the NTP server address.

Listing 1.11 shows how to print the current time from the internet time server as follows:

```
#!/usr/bin/env python
# This program is optimized for Python 2.7.12
  and Python 3.5.2.
# It may run on any other version with/without
  modifications.
import ntplib
from time import ctime
def print_time():
    ntp_client = ntplib.NTPClient()
    response = ntp_client.request('pool.ntp.org')
    print (ctime(response.tx_time))
if __name__ == '__main__':
    print_time()
```

In my machine, this recipe shows the following output:

```
$ python 11_11_print_machine_time.py
Fri Jun  2 16:01:35 2017
```

How it works...

Here, an NTP client has been created and an NTP request has been sent to one of the internet NTP servers, pool.ntp.org. The ctime() function is used for printing the response.

Writing an SNTP client

Unlike the previous recipe, sometimes, you don't need to get the precise time from the NTP server. You can use a simpler version of NTP called simple network time protocol.

How to do it...

Let us create a plain SNTP client without using any third-party library.

Let us first define two constants: `NTP_SERVER` and `TIME1970`. `NTP_SERVER` is the server address to which our client will connect, and `TIME1970` is the reference time on January 1, 1970 (also called *Epoch*). You may find the value of the Epoch time or convert to the Epoch time at `http://www.epochconverter.com/`. The actual client creates a UDP socket (`SOCK_DGRAM`) to connect to the server following the UDP protocol. The client then needs to send the SNTP protocol data (`'\x1b' + 47 * '\0'`) in a packet. Our UDP client sends and receives data using the `sendto()` and `recvfrom()` methods.

When the server returns the time information in a packed array, the client needs a specialized `struct` module to unpack the data. The only interesting data is located in the 11th element of the array. Finally, we need to subtract the reference value, `TIME1970`, from the unpacked value to get the actual current time.

Listing 1.12 shows how to write an SNTP client as follows:

```
#!/usr/bin/env python
# This program is optimized for Python 2.7.12
  and Python 3.5.2.
# It may run on any other version with/without
  modifications.
import socket
import struct
import sys
import time
NTP_SERVER = "0.uk.pool.ntp.org"
TIME1970 = 2208988800
def sntp_client():
    client = socket.socket( socket.AF_INET,
                            socket.SOCK_DGRAM )
    data = '\x1b' + 47 * '\0'
    client.sendto( data.encode('utf-8'),
                   ( NTP_SERVER, 123 ))
    data, address = client.recvfrom( 1024 )
    if data:
        print ('Response received
                   from:', address)
    t = struct.unpack( '!12I', data )[10]
    t -= TIME1970
    print ('\tTime=%s' % time.ctime(t))
if __name__ == '__main__':
    sntp_client()
```

This recipe prints the current time from the internet time server received with the SNTP protocol as follows:

```
$ python 11_12_sntp_client.py
('Response received from:',
('192.146.137.13', 123))
     Time=Sat Jun  3 14:45:45 2017
```

How it works...

This SNTP client creates a socket connection and sends the protocol data. After receiving the response from the NTP server (in this case, `0.uk.pool.ntp.org`), it unpacks the data with `struct`. Finally, it subtracts the reference time, which is January 1, 1970, and prints the time using the `ctime()` built-in method in the Python time module.

Writing a simple TCP echo client/server application

After testing with basic socket APIs in Python, let us create a TCP socket server and client now. Here, you will have the chance to utilize your basic knowledge gained in the previous recipes.

How to do it...

In this example, a server will echo whatever it receives from the client. We will use the Python `argparse` module to specify the TCP port from a command line. Both the server and client script will take this argument.

First, we create the server. We start by creating a TCP socket object. Then, we set the reuse address so that we can run the server as many times as we need. We bind the socket to the given port on our local machine. In the listening stage, we make sure we listen to multiple clients in a queue using the backlog argument to the `listen()` method. Finally, we wait for the client to be connected and send some data to the server. When the data is received, the server echoes back the data to the client.

Listing 1.13a shows how to write a simple TCP echo client/server application as follows:

```
#!/usr/bin/env python
# This program is optimized for Python 2.7.12
  and Python 3.5.2.
# It may run on any other version with/without
  modifications.
import socket
import sys
import argparse
host = 'localhost'
data_payload = 2048
backlog = 5
def echo_server(port):
    """ A simple echo server """
    # Create a TCP socket
    sock = socket.socket(socket.AF_INET,
                         socket.SOCK_STREAM)
    # Enable reuse address/port
    sock.setsockopt(socket.SOL_SOCKET,
                     socket.SO_REUSEADDR, 1)
    # Bind the socket to the port
    server_address = (host, port)
    print ("Starting up echo server  on %s
                port %s" % server_address)
    sock.bind(server_address)
    # Listen to clients, backlog argument
      specifies the max no.
      of queued connections
    sock.listen(backlog)
    while True:
        print ("Waiting to receive message
                from client")
        client, address = sock.accept()
        data = client.recv(data_payload)
        if data:
            print ("Data: %s" %data)
            client.send(data)
            print ("sent %s bytes back
                   to %s" % (data, address))
        # end connection
        client.close()
if __name__ == '__main__':
    parser = argparse.ArgumentParser
    (description='Socket Server Example')
    parser.add_argument('--port',
    action="store", dest="port", type=int,
```

```
                            required=True)
        given_args = parser.parse_args()
        port = given_args.port
        echo_server(port)
```

On the client side code, we create a client socket using the port argument and connect to the server. Then, the client sends the message, `Test message. This will be echoed` to the server, and the client immediately receives the message back in a few segments. Here, two try-except blocks are constructed to catch any exception during this interactive session.

Listing 1-13b shows the TCP echo client as follows:

```
#!/usr/bin/env python
# This program is optimized for Python 2.7.12
   and Python 3.5.2.
# It may run on any other version with/without modifications.

import socket
import sys

import argparse

host = 'localhost'

def echo_client(port):
    """ A simple echo client """
    # Create a TCP/IP socket
    sock = socket.socket(socket.AF_INET, socket.SOCK_STREAM)
    # Connect the socket to the server
    server_address = (host, port)
    print ("Connecting to %s port %s" % server_address)
    sock.connect(server_address)
    # Send data
    try:
        # Send data
        message = "Test message. This will be
                   echoed"
        print ("Sending %s" % message)
        sock.sendall(message.encode('utf-8'))
        # Look for the response
        amount_received = 0
        amount_expected = len(message)
        while amount_received < amount_expected:
            data = sock.recv(16)
            amount_received += len(data)
            print ("Received: %s" % data)
```

```
    except socket.error as e:
        print ("Socket error: %s" %str(e))
    except Exception as e:
        print ("Other exception: %s" %str(e))
    finally:
        print ("Closing connection to the server")
        sock.close()
if __name__ == '__main__':
    parser = argparse.ArgumentParser
            (description='Socket Server Example')
    parser.add_argument('--port', action="store",
dest="port", type=int, required=True)
    given_args = parser.parse_args()
    port = given_args.port
    echo_client(port)
```

How it works...

In order to see the client/server interactions, launch the following server script in one console:

```
$ python 11_13a_echo_server.py --port=9900
Starting up echo server  on localhost port 9900
Waiting to receive message from client
```

Now, run the client from another Terminal as follows:

```
$ python 11_13b_echo_client.py --port=9900
Connecting to localhost port 9900
Sending Test message. This will be echoed
Received: Test message. Th
Received: is will be echoe
Received: d
Closing connection to the server
```

Upon receiving the message from the client, the server will also print something similar to the following message:

```
Data: Test message. This will be echoed
sent Test message. This will be echoed
bytes back to ('127.0.0.1', 42961)
Waiting to receive message from client
```

Writing a simple UDP echo client/server application

As we have developed a simple TCP server and client in the previous recipe, we will now look at how to develop the same with UDP.

How to do it...

This recipe is similar to the previous one, except this one is with UDP. The method `recvfrom()` reads the messages from the socket and returns the data and the client address.

Listing 1.14a shows how to write a simple UDP echo client/server application as follows:

```
#!/usr/bin/env python
# This program is optimized for Python 2.7.12
   and Python 3.5.2.
# It may run on any other version with/without
  modifications.

import socket
import sys
import argparse

host = 'localhost'
data_payload = 2048

def echo_server(port):
    """ A simple echo server """
    # Create a UDP socket
    sock = socket.socket(socket.AF_INET,
                         socket.SOCK_DGRAM)

    # Bind the socket to the port
    server_address = (host, port)
    print ("Starting up echo server
            on %s port %s" % server_address)

    sock.bind(server_address)

    while True:
        print ("Waiting to receive message
                 from client")
```

```
            data, address = sock.
                            recvfrom(data_payload)
            print ("received %s bytes
                    from %s" % (len(data), address))
            print ("Data: %s" %data)
            if data:
                sent = sock.sendto(data, address)
                print ("sent %s bytes back
                        to %s" % (sent, address))


if __name__ == '__main__':
    parser = argparse.ArgumentParser
            (description='Socket Server Example')
    parser.add_argument('--port', action="store", dest="port",
type=int, required=True)
    given_args = parser.parse_args()
    port = given_args.port
    echo_server(port)
```

On the client side code, we create a client socket using the port argument and connect to the server, as we did in the previous recipe. Then, the client sends the message, `Test message. This will be echoed`, and the client immediately receives the message back in a few segments.

Listing 1-14b shows the echo client as follows:

```
#!/usr/bin/env python
# This program is optimized for Python 2.7.12 and Python 3.5.2.
# It may run on any other version with/without modifications.

import socket
import sys
import argparse

host = 'localhost'
data_payload = 2048

def echo_client(port):
    """ A simple echo client """
    # Create a UDP socket
    sock = socket.socket(socket.AF_INET,
                         socket.SOCK_DGRAM)

    server_address = (host, port)
    print ("Connecting to %s port %s" % server_address)
    message = 'This is the message.  It will be
              repeated.'
```

```
    try:

        # Send data
        message = "Test message. This will be
                   echoed"
        print ("Sending %s" % message)
        sent = sock.sendto(message.encode
               ('utf-8'), server_address)

        # Receive response
        data, server = sock.recvfrom(data_payload)
        print ("received %s" % data)

    finally:
        print ("Closing connection to the server")
        sock.close()

if __name__ == '__main__':
    parser = argparse.ArgumentParser
             (description='Socket Server Example')
    parser.add_argument('--port', action="store", dest="port",
type=int, required=True)
    given_args = parser.parse_args()
    port = given_args.port
    echo_client(port)
```

Downloading the example code
Detailed steps to download the code bundle are mentioned in the Preface of this book. The code bundle for the book is also hosted on GitHub at: `https://github.com/PacktPublishing/Python-Network-Programming`. We also have other code bundles from our rich catalog of books and videos available at: `https://github.com/PacktPublishing/`. Check them out!

How it works...

In order to see the client/server interactions, launch the following server script in one console:

```
$ python 11_14a_echo_server_udp.py --port=9900
Starting up echo server on localhost port 9900
Waiting to receive message from client
```

Now, run the client from another terminal as follows:

```
$ python 11_14b_echo_client_udp.py --port=9900
Connecting to localhost port 9900
Sending Test message. This will be echoed
received Test message. This will be echoed
Closing connection to the server
```

Upon receiving the message from the client, the server will also print something similar to the following message:

```
received 33 bytes from ('127.0.0.1', 43542)
Data: Test message. This will be echoed
sent 33 bytes back to ('127.0.0.1', 43542)
Waiting to receive message from client
```

12 Multiplexing Socket I/O for Better Performance

In this chapter, we will cover the following recipes:

- Using ForkingMixIn in your socket server applications
- Using ThreadingMixIn in your socket server applications
- Writing a chat server using select.select
- Multiplexing a web server using select.epoll
- Multiplexing an echo server using Diesel concurrent library

Introduction

This chapter focuses on improving the socket server performance using a few useful techniques. Unlike the previous chapter, here we consider multiple clients that will be connected to the server and the communication can be asynchronous. The server does not need to process the request from clients in a blocking manner; this can be done independently of each other. If one client takes more time to receive or process data, the server does not need to wait for that. It can talk to other clients using separate threads or processes.

In this chapter, we will also explore the `select` module that provides the platform-specific I/O monitoring functions. This module is built on top of the select system call of the underlying operating system's kernel. For Linux, the manual page is located at `http://man7.org/linux/man-pages/man2/select.2.html` and can be checked to see the available features of this system call. Since our socket server would like to interact with many clients, `select` can be very helpful to monitor non-blocking sockets. There are some third-party Python libraries that can also help us to deal with multiple clients at the same time. We have included one sample recipe using Diesel concurrent library.

Although, for the sake of brevity, we will be using two or few clients, readers are free to extend the recipes of this chapter and use them with tens and hundreds of clients.

Using ForkingMixIn in your socket server applications

You have decided to write an asynchronous Python socket server application. The server will not block in processing a client request. So the server needs a mechanism to deal with each client independently.

Python `SocketServer` class comes with two utility classes: `ForkingMixIn` and `ThreadingMixIn`. The `ForkingMixIn` class will spawn a new process for each client request. This class is discussed in this section. The `ThreadingMixIn` class will be discussed in the next section. For more information, you can refer to the relevant Python 2 documentation at `http://docs.python.org/2/library/socketserver.html` and Python 3 documentation at `https://docs.python.org/3/library/socketserver.html`.

How to do it...

Let us rewrite our echo server, previously described in `Chapter 11`, *Sockets, IPv4, and Simple Client/Server Programming*. We can utilize the subclasses of the `SocketServer` class family. It has ready-made TCP, UDP, and other protocol servers. We can create a `ForkingServer` class inherited from `TCPServer` and `ForkingMixIn`. The former parent will enable our `ForkingServer` class to do all the necessary server operations that we did manually before, such as creating a socket, binding to an address, and listening for incoming connections. Our server also needs to inherit from `ForkingMixIn` to handle clients asynchronously.

The `ForkingServer` class also needs to set up a request handler that dictates how to handle a client request. Here our server will echo back the text string received from the client. Our request handler class, `ForkingServerRequestHandler`, is inherited from the `BaseRequestHandler` provided with the `SocketServer` library.

We can code the client of our echo server, `ForkingClient`, in an object-oriented fashion. In Python, the constructor method of a class is called `__init__()`. By convention, it takes a self-argument to attach attributes or properties of that particular class. The `ForkingClient` echo server will be initialized at `__init__()` and sends the message to the server at the `run()` method respectively.

If you are not familiar with **object-oriented programming** (**OOP**) at all, it might be helpful to review the basic concepts of OOP while attempting to grasp this recipe.

In order to test our `ForkingServer` class, we can launch multiple echo clients and see how the server responds back to the clients.

Listing 2.1 shows a sample code using `ForkingMixIn` in a socket server application as follows:

```
#!/usr/bin/env python
# Python Network Programming Cookbook, Second Edition -- Chapter - 2
# This program is optimized for Python 3.5.2.
# It may run on any other version with/without modifications.
# To make it run on Python 2.7.x, needs some changes due to API
differences.
# begin with replacing "socketserver" with "SocketServer" throughout
the program.
# See more: http://docs.python.org/2/library/socketserver.html
# See more: http://docs.python.org/3/library/socketserver.html

import os
import socket
import threading
import socketserver


SERVER_HOST = 'localhost'
SERVER_PORT = 0 # tells the kernel to pickup a port dynamically
BUF_SIZE = 1024
ECHO_MSG = 'Hello echo server!'


class ForkedClient():
    """ A client to test forking server"""
    def __init__(self, ip, port):
```

```
        # Create a socket
        self.sock = socket.socket(socket.AF_INET, socket.SOCK_STREAM)
        # Connect to the server
        self.sock.connect((ip, port))
    def run(self):
        """ Client playing with the server"""
        # Send the data to server
        current_process_id = os.getpid()
        print ('PID %s Sending echo message to the server : "%s"' %
                (current_process_id, ECHO_MSG))

        sent_data_length = self.sock.send(bytes(ECHO_MSG, 'utf-8'))

        print ("Sent: %d characters, so far..." %sent_data_length)
        # Display server response
        response = self.sock.recv(BUF_SIZE)
        print ("PID %s received: %s" % (current_process_id,
response[5:]))
    def shutdown(self):
        """ Cleanup the client socket """
        self.sock.close()
class ForkingServerRequestHandler(socketserver.BaseRequestHandler):
    def handle(self):
        # Send the echo back to the client

        #received = str(sock.recv(1024), "utf-8")
        data = str(self.request.recv(BUF_SIZE), 'utf-8')

        current_process_id = os.getpid()
        response = '%s: %s' % (current_process_id, data)
        print ("Server sending response [current_process_id: data] =
[%s]"
               %response)
        self.request.send(bytes(response, 'utf-8'))
        return

class ForkingServer(socketserver.ForkingMixIn,
                    socketserver.TCPServer,
                    ):
    """Nothing to add here, inherited everything necessary from
parents"""
    pass


def main():
    # Launch the server
    server = ForkingServer((SERVER_HOST, SERVER_PORT),
                           ForkingServerRequestHandler)
```

```
    ip, port = server.server_address # Retrieve the port number
    server_thread = threading.Thread(target=server.serve_forever)
    server_thread.setDaemon(True) # don't hang on exit
    server_thread.start()
    print ("Server loop running PID: %s" %os.getpid())
    # Launch the client(s)

    client1 =  ForkedClient(ip, port)
    client1.run()

    print("First client running")
    client2 =  ForkedClient(ip, port)
    client2.run()

    print("Second client running")

    # Clean them up
    server.shutdown()
    client1.shutdown()
    client2.shutdown()
    server.socket.close()


if __name__ == '__main__':
    main()
```

How it works...

An instance of `ForkingServer` is launched in the main thread, which has been daemonized to run in the background. Now, the two clients have started interacting with the server.

If you run the script, it will show the following output:

```
$ python 12_1_forking_mixin_socket_server.py
Server loop running PID: 26479
PID 26479 Sending echo message to the server :
 "Hello echo server!"
Sent: 18 characters, so far...
Server sending response [current_process_id: data] = [26481: Hello
echo server!]
PID 26479 received: b': Hello echo server!'
First client running
PID 26479 Sending echo message to the server : "Hello echo server!"
Sent: 18 characters, so far...
Server sending response [current_process_id: data] = [26482: Hello
```

```
echo server!]
PID 26479 received: b': Hello echo server!'
Second client running
```

The server port number might be different in your machine since this is dynamically chosen by the operating system kernel.

Using ThreadingMixIn in your socket server applications

Perhaps you prefer writing a multi-threaded application over a process-based one due to any particular reason, for example, sharing the states of that application across threads, avoiding the complexity of inter-process communication, or something else. In such a situation, if you want to write an asynchronous network server using `SocketServer` library, you will need `ThreadingMixIn`.

Getting ready

By making a few minor changes to our previous recipe, you can get a working version of socket server using `ThreadingMixIn`.

How to do it...

As seen in the previous socket server based on `ForkingMixIn`, `ThreadingMixIn` socket server will follow the same coding pattern of an echo server except for a few things. First, our `ThreadedTCPServer` will inherit from `TCPServer` and `TheadingMixIn`. This multi-threaded version will launch a new thread when a client connects to it. Some more details can be found at `http://docs.python.org/2/library/socketserver.html`.

The request handler class of our socket server, `ForkingServerRequestHandler`, sends the echo back to the client from a new thread. You can check the thread information here. For the sake of simplicity, we put the client code in a function instead of a class. The client code creates the client socket and sends the message to the server.

Listing 2.2 shows a sample code on the echo socket server using `ThreadingMixIn` as follows:

```
#!/usr/bin/env python
# Python Network Programming Cookbook, Second Edition -- Chapter - 2
# This program is optimized for Python 3.5.2.
# It may run on any other version with/without modifications.
# To make it run on Python 2.7.x, needs some changes due to API
differences.
# begin with replacing "socketserver" with "SocketServer" throughout
the program.
# See more: http://docs.python.org/2/library/socketserver.html
# See more: http://docs.python.org/3/library/socketserver.html

import os
import socket
import threading
import socketserver

SERVER_HOST = 'localhost'
SERVER_PORT = 0 # tells the kernel to pickup a port dynamically
BUF_SIZE = 1024


def client(ip, port, message):
    """ A client to test threading mixin server"""
    # Connect to the server
    sock = socket.socket(socket.AF_INET, socket.SOCK_STREAM)
    sock.connect((ip, port))
    try:
        sock.sendall(bytes(message, 'utf-8'))
        response = sock.recv(BUF_SIZE)
        print ("Client received: %s" %response)
    finally:
        sock.close()


class ThreadedTCPRequestHandler(socketserver.BaseRequestHandler):
    """ An example of threaded TCP request handler """
    def handle(self):
        data = self.request.recv(1024)
        cur_thread = threading.current_thread()
        response = "%s: %s" %(cur_thread.name, data)
        self.request.sendall(bytes(response, 'utf-8'))

class ThreadedTCPServer(socketserver.ThreadingMixIn,
socketserver.TCPServer):
    """Nothing to add here, inherited everything necessary from
```

```
parents"""
    pass


if __name__ == "__main__":
    # Run server
    server = ThreadedTCPServer((SERVER_HOST, SERVER_PORT),
                               ThreadedTCPRequestHandler)
    ip, port = server.server_address # retrieve ip address

    # Start a thread with the server -- one  thread per request
    server_thread = threading.Thread(target=server.serve_forever)
    # Exit the server thread when the main thread exits
    server_thread.daemon = True
    server_thread.start()
    print ("Server loop running on thread: %s"  %server_thread.name)
    # Run clients
    client(ip, port, "Hello from client 1")
    client(ip, port, "Hello from client 2")
    client(ip, port, "Hello from client 3")
    # Server cleanup
    server.shutdown()
```

How it works...

This recipe first creates a server thread and launches it in the background. Then it launches three test clients to send messages to the server. In response, the server echoes back the message to the clients. In the `handle()` method of the server's request handler, you can see that we retrieve the current thread information and print it. This should be different in each client connection.

In this client/server conversation, the `sendall()` method has been used to guarantee the sending of all data without any loss:

```
$ python 12_2_threading_mixin_socket_server.py
Server loop running on thread: Thread-1
Client received: b"Thread-2: b'Hello from client 1'"
Client received: b"Thread-3: b'Hello from client 2'"
Client received: b"Thread-4: b'Hello from client 3'"
```

Writing a chat server using select.select

Launching a separate thread or process per client may not be viable in any larger network server application where several hundred or thousand clients are concurrently connected to the server. Due to the limited available memory and host CPU power, we need a better technique to deal with a large number of clients. Fortunately, Python provides the `select` module to overcome this problem.

How to do it...

We need to write an efficient chat server that can handle several hundred or a large number of client connections. We will use the `select()` method from the `select` module that will enable our chat server and client to do any task without blocking a send or receive a call all the time.

Let us design this recipe such that a single script can launch both client and server with an additional `--name` argument. Only if `--name=server` is passed from the command line, the script will launch the chat server. Any other value passed to the `--name` argument, for example, `client1`, `client2`, will launch a chat client. Let's specify our chat server port number from the command line using the `--port` argument. For a larger application, it may be preferable to write separate modules for the server and client.

Listing 2.3 shows an example of chat application using `select.select` as follows:

```
#!/usr/bin/env python
# Python Network Programming Cookbook, Second Edition -- Chapter - 2
# This program is optimized for Python 2.7.12 and Python 3.5.2.
# It may run on any other version with/without modifications.

import select
import socket
import sys
import signal
import pickle
import struct
import argparse

SERVER_HOST = 'localhost'
CHAT_SERVER_NAME = 'server'

# Some utilities
def send(channel, *args):
```

```
        buffer = pickle.dumps(args)
        value = socket.htonl(len(buffer))
        size = struct.pack("L",value)
        channel.send(size)
        channel.send(buffer)

    def receive(channel):
        size = struct.calcsize("L")
        size = channel.recv(size)
        try:
            size = socket.ntohl(struct.unpack("L", size)[0])
        except struct.error as e:
            return ''
        buf = ""
        while len(buf) < size:
            buf = channel.recv(size - len(buf))
        return pickle.loads(buf)[0]
```

The `send()` method takes one named argument channel and positional argument `*args`. It serializes the data using the `dumps()` method from the `pickle` module. It determines the size of the data using the `struct` module. Similarly, `receive()` takes one named argument `channel`.

Now we can code the `ChatServer` class as follows:

```
    class ChatServer(object):
        """ An example chat server using select """
        def __init__(self, port, backlog=5):
            self.clients = 0
            self.clientmap = {}
            self.outputs = [] # list output sockets
            self.server = socket.socket(socket.AF_INET,
    socket.SOCK_STREAM)
            self.server.setsockopt(socket.SOL_SOCKET, socket.SO_REUSEADDR,
    1)
            self.server.bind((SERVER_HOST, port))
            print ('Server listening to port: %s ...' %port)
            self.server.listen(backlog)
            # Catch keyboard interrupts
            signal.signal(signal.SIGINT, self.sighandler)
        def sighandler(self, signum, frame):
            """ Clean up client outputs"""
            # Close the server
            print ('Shutting down server...')
            # Close existing client sockets
            for output in self.outputs:
                output.close()
```

```
            self.server.close()

    def get_client_name(self, client):
        """ Return the name of the client """
        info = self.clientmap[client]
        host, name = info[0][0], info[1]
        return '@'.join((name, host))
```

Now the main executable method of the `ChatServer` class should look like the following code:

```
    def run(self):
        inputs = [self.server, sys.stdin]
        self.outputs = []
        running = True
        while running:
            try:
                readable, writeable, exceptional = select.
                select(inputs, self.outputs, [])
            except select.error as e:
                break

            for sock in readable:
                if sock == self.server:
                    # handle the server socket
                    client, address = self.server.accept()
                    print ("Chat server: got connection %d from %s" %
                            (client.fileno(), address))
                    # Read the login name
                    cname = receive(client).split('NAME: ')[1]
                    # Compute client name and send back
                    self.clients += 1
                    send(client, 'CLIENT: ' + str(address[0]))
                    inputs.append(client)
                    self.clientmap[client] = (address, cname)
                    # Send joining information to other clients
                    msg = "\n(Connected: New client (%d) from %s)" %
                            (self.clients,
self.get_client_name(client))
                    for output in self.outputs:
                        send(output, msg)
                    self.outputs.append(client)

                elif sock == sys.stdin:
                    # handle standard input
                    junk = sys.stdin.readline()
                    running = False
                else:
```

```
                    # handle all other sockets
                    try:
                        data = receive(sock)
                        if data:
                            # Send as new client's message...
                            msg = '\n#[' + self.get_client_name(sock)
                                      + ']>>' + data
                            # Send data to all except ourself
                            for output in self.outputs:
                                if output != sock:
                                    send(output, msg)
                        else:
                            print ("Chat server: %d hung up"
                                   % sock.fileno())
                            self.clients -= 1
                            sock.close()
                            inputs.remove(sock)
                            self.outputs.remove(sock)

                            # Sending client leaving information to
others
                            msg = "\n(Now hung up: Client from %s)" %
                                    self.get_client_name(sock)
                            for output in self.outputs:
                                send(output, msg)
                    except socket.error as e:
                        # Remove
                        inputs.remove(sock)
                        self.outputs.remove(sock)
        self.server.close()
```

The chat server initializes with a few data attributes. It stores the count of clients, map of each client, and output sockets. The usual server socket creation also sets the option to reuse an address so that there is no problem restarting the server again using the same port. An optional backlog argument to the chat server constructor sets the maximum number of queued connections to listen to the server.

An interesting aspect of this chat server is to catch the user interrupt, usually via keyboard, using the `signal` module. So a signal handler `sighandler` is registered for the interrupt signal (`SIGINT`). This signal handler catches the keyboard interrupt signal and closes all output sockets where data may be waiting to be sent.

The main executive method of our chat server `run()` performs its operation inside a `while` loop. This method registers with a select interface where the input argument is the chat server socket, `stdin`. The output argument is specified by the server's output socket list. In return, `select` provides three lists: readable, writable, and exceptional sockets. The chat server is only interested in readable sockets where some data is ready to be read. If that socket indicates to itself, then that will mean a new client connection has been established. So the server retrieves the client's name and broadcasts this information to other clients. In another case, if anything comes from the input arguments, the chat server exits. Similarly, the chat server deals with the other client's socket inputs. It relays the data received from any client to others and also shares their joining/leaving information.

The chat client code class should contain the following code:

```
class ChatClient(object):
    """ A command line chat client using select """

    def __init__(self, name, port, host=SERVER_HOST):
        self.name = name
        self.connected = False
        self.host = host
        self.port = port
        # Initial prompt
        self.prompt='[' + '@'.join((name,
socket.gethostname().split('.')[0]))
                        + ']> '
        # Connect to server at port
        try:
            self.sock = socket.socket(socket.AF_INET,
socket.SOCK_STREAM)
            self.sock.connect((host, self.port))
            print ("Now connected to chat server@ port %d" %
self.port)
            self.connected = True
            # Send my name...
            send(self.sock,'NAME: ' + self.name)
            data = receive(self.sock)
            # Contains client address, set it
            addr = data.split('CLIENT: ')[1]
            self.prompt = '[' + '@'.join((self.name, addr)) + ']> '
        except socket.error as e:
            print ("Failed to connect to chat server
                    @ port %d" % self.port)
            sys.exit(1)

    def run(self):
```

```
        """ Chat client main loop """
        while self.connected:
            try:
                sys.stdout.write(self.prompt)
                sys.stdout.flush()
                # Wait for input from stdin and socket
                readable, writeable,exceptional = select.select
                                                  ([0, self.sock],
[],[])
                for sock in readable:
                    if sock == 0:
                        data = sys.stdin.readline().strip()
                        if data: send(self.sock, data)
                    elif sock == self.sock:
                        data = receive(self.sock)
                        if not data:
                            print ('Client shutting down.')
                            self.connected = False
                            break
                        else:
                            sys.stdout.write(data + '\n')
                            sys.stdout.flush()
            except KeyboardInterrupt:
                print (" Client interrupted. """)
                self.sock.close()
                break
```

The chat client initializes with a name argument and sends this name to the chat server upon connecting. It also sets up a custom prompt `[ name@host ]>`. The executive method of this client `run()` continues its operation as long as the connection to the server is active. In a manner similar to the chat server, the chat client also registers with `select()`. If anything in readable sockets is ready, it enables the client to receive data. If the sock value is `0` and there's any data available then the data can be sent. The same information is also shown in `stdout` or, in our case, the command-line console. Our main method should now get command-line arguments and call either the server or client as follows:

```
if __name__ == "__main__":
    parser = argparse.ArgumentParser(description='Socket Server
                                                  Example with
Select')
    parser.add_argument('--name', action="store", dest="name",
                                                 required=True)
    parser.add_argument('--port', action="store", dest="port",
                                     type=int, required=True)
    given_args = parser.parse_args()
    port = given_args.port
```

```
    name = given_args.name
    if name == CHAT_SERVER_NAME:
        server = ChatServer(port)
        server.run()
    else:
        client = ChatClient(name=name, port=port)
        client.run()
```

We would like to run this script thrice: once for the chat server and twice for two chat clients. For the server, we pass `-name=server` and `port=8800`. For `client1`, we change the name argument `--name=client1` and for `client2`, we put `--name=client2`. Then from the `client1` value prompt we send the message `"Hello from client 1"`, which is printed in the prompt of the `client2`. Similarly, we send `"hello from client 2"` from the prompt of the `client2`, which is shown in the prompt of the `client1`.

The output for the server is as follows:

```
$ python 12_3_chat_server_with_select.py --name=server --port=8800
Server listening to port: 8800 ...
Chat server: got connection 4 from ('127.0.0.1', 59254)
Chat server: got connection 5 from ('127.0.0.1', 59256)
```

The output for `client1` is as follows:

```
$ python 12_3_chat_server_with_select.py --name=client1 --port=8800
Now connected to chat server@ port 8800
[client1@127.0.0.1]>
(Connected: New client (2) from client2@127.0.0.1)
[client1@127.0.0.1]> Hello from client1
[client1@127.0.0.1]>
#[client2@127.0.0.1]>>hello from client2
[client1@127.0.0.1]>
```

The output for `client2` is as follows:

```
$ python 12_3_chat_server_with_select.py --name=client2 --port=8800
Now connected to chat server@ port 8800
[client2@127.0.0.1]>
#[client1@127.0.0.1]>>Hello from client1
[client2@127.0.0.1]> hello from client2
[client2@127.0.0.1]>
```

The whole interaction is shown in the following screenshot:

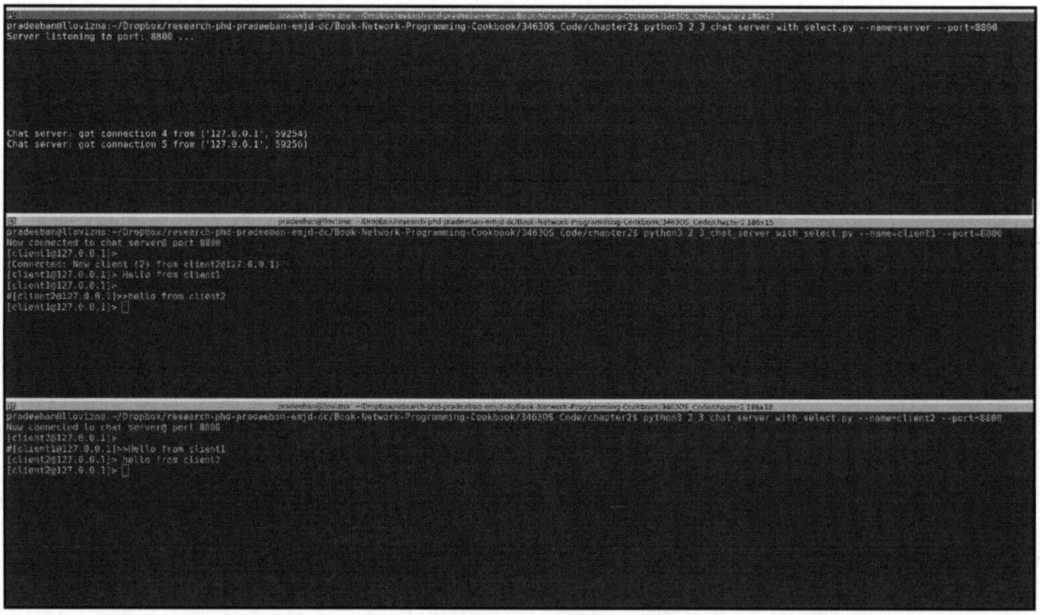

Chat Server and Clients

How it works...

At the top of our module, we defined two utility functions: `send()` and `receive()`.

The chat server and client use these utility functions, which were demonstrated earlier. The details of the chat server and client methods were also discussed earlier.

Multiplexing a web server using select.epoll

Python's `select` module has a few platform-specific, networking event management functions. On a Linux machine, `epoll` is available. This will utilize the operating system kernel that will poll network events and let our script know whenever something happens. This sounds more efficient than the previously mentioned `select.select` approach.

How to do it...

Let's write a simple web server that can return a single line of text to any connected web browser.

The core idea is during the initialization of this web server, we should make a call to `select.epoll()` and register our server's file descriptor for event notifications. In the web server's executive code, the socket event is monitored as follows:

```
Listing 2.4 Simple web server using select.epoll
#!/usr/bin/env python
# Python Network Programming Cookbook, Second Edition -- Chapter - 2
# This program is optimized for Python 2.7.12 and Python 3.5.2.
# It may run on any other version with/without modifications.


import socket
import select
import argparse

SERVER_HOST = 'localhost'

EOL1 = b'\n\n'
EOL2 = b'\n\r\n'
SERVER_RESPONSE  = b"""HTTP/1.1 200 OK\r\nDate: Mon, 1 Apr 2013
01:01:01 GMT\r\nContent-Type: text/plain\r\nContent-Length: 25\r\n\r\n
Hello from Epoll Server!"""


class EpollServer(object):
    """ A socket server using Epoll"""
    def __init__(self, host=SERVER_HOST, port=0):
        self.sock = socket.socket(socket.AF_INET, socket.SOCK_STREAM)
        self.sock.setsockopt(socket.SOL_SOCKET, socket.SO_REUSEADDR,
1)
        self.sock.bind((host, port))
        self.sock.listen(1)
        self.sock.setblocking(0)
        self.sock.setsockopt(socket.IPPROTO_TCP, socket.TCP_NODELAY,
1)
        print ("Started Epoll Server")
        self.epoll = select.epoll()
        self.epoll.register(self.sock.fileno(), select.EPOLLIN)
    def run(self):
        """Executes epoll server operation"""
        try:
            connections = {}; requests = {}; responses = {}
```

```
            while True:
                events = self.epoll.poll(1)
                for fileno, event in events:
                    if fileno == self.sock.fileno():
                        connection, address = self.sock.accept()
                        connection.setblocking(0)
                        self.epoll.register(connection.fileno(),
                        select.EPOLLIN)
                        connections[connection.fileno()] = connection
                        requests[connection.fileno()] = b''
                        responses[connection.fileno()] =
SERVER_RESPONSE
                    elif event & select.EPOLLIN:
                        requests[fileno] +=
connections[fileno].recv(1024)
                        if EOL1 in requests[fileno] or EOL2
                        in requests[fileno]:
                            self.epoll.modify(fileno, select.EPOLLOUT)
                            print('-'*40 + '\n' +
requests[fileno].decode()
                                          [:-2])
                    elif event & select.EPOLLOUT:
                        byteswritten = connections[fileno].
                                       send(responses[fileno])
                        responses[fileno] = responses[fileno]
                                            [byteswritten:]
                        if len(responses[fileno]) == 0:
                            self.epoll.modify(fileno, 0)
connections[fileno].shutdown(socket.SHUT_RDWR)
                    elif event & select.EPOLLHUP:
                        self.epoll.unregister(fileno)
                        connections[fileno].close()
                        del connections[fileno]
        finally:
            self.epoll.unregister(self.sock.fileno())
            self.epoll.close()
            self.sock.close()


if __name__ == '__main__':
    parser = argparse.ArgumentParser(description='Socket Server
                                               Example with Epoll')
    parser.add_argument('--port', action="store", dest="port",
                                          type=int, required=True)
    given_args = parser.parse_args()
    port = given_args.port
    server = EpollServer(host=SERVER_HOST, port=port)
    server.run()
```

If you run this script and access the web server from your browsers, such as Google Chrome or Mozilla Firefox, by entering `http://localhost:8800/`, the following output will be shown in the console:

```
$ python 12_4_simple_web_server_with_epoll.py --port=8800
Started Epoll Server
----------------------------------------
GET / HTTP/1.1
Host: localhost:8800
Connection: keep-alive
Upgrade-Insecure-Requests: 1
User-Agent: Mozilla/5.0 (X11; Linux x86_64) AppleWebKit/537.36 (KHTML,
like Gecko) Chrome/58.0.3029.110 Safari/537.36
Accept:
text/html,application/xhtml+xml,application/xml;q=0.9,image/webp,*/*;q
=0.8
DNT: 1
Accept-Encoding: gzip, deflate, sdch, br
Accept-Language: en-US,en;q=0.8
----------------------------------------
GET /favicon.ico HTTP/1.1
Host: localhost:8800
Connection: keep-alive
User-Agent: Mozilla/5.0 (X11; Linux x86_64) AppleWebKit/537.36 (KHTML,
like Gecko) Chrome/58.0.3029.110 Safari/537.36
Accept: image/webp,image/*,*/*;q=0.8
DNT: 1
Referer: http://localhost:8800/
Accept-Encoding: gzip, deflate, sdch, br
Accept-Language: en-US,en;q=0.8
```

You will also be able to see the following line in your browser:

```
Hello from Epoll Server!
```

The following screenshot shows the scenario:

Simple Web Server: Terminal and Browser

How it works...

In our `EpollServer` web server's constructor, a socket server is created and bound to a localhost at a given port. The server's socket is set to the non-blocking mode (`setblocking(0)`). The `TCP_NODELAY` option is also set so that our server can exchange data without buffering (as in the case of an SSH connection). Next, the `select.epoll()` instance is created and the socket's file descriptor is passed to that instance to help monitoring.

In the `run()` method of the web server, it starts receiving the socket events. These events are denoted as follows:

- `EPOLLIN`: This socket reads events
- `EPOLLOUT`: This socket writes events

In the case of a server socket, it sets up the response SERVER_RESPONSE. When the socket has any connection that wants to write data, it can do that inside the EPOLLOUT event case. The EPOLLHUP event signals an unexpected close to a socket that is due to the internal error conditions.

Multiplexing an echo server using Diesel concurrent library

Sometimes you need to write a large custom networking application that wants to avoid repeated server initialization code that creates a socket, binds to an address, listens, and handles basic errors. There are numerous Python networking libraries out there to help you remove boiler-plate code. Here, we can examine such a library called Diesel.

Getting ready

Diesel uses a non-blocking technique with co-routines to write networking severs efficiently. As stated on the website, Diesel's core is a tight event loop that uses epoll to deliver nearly flat performance out to 10,000 connections and beyond. Here, we introduce Diesel with a simple echo server. You also need Diesel library 3.0 or any later version. You can do that with pip command:

```
$ pip install diesel
```

If you encounter some issues in installing, make sure you have the dependencies installed. The following command should fix most of these errors:

```
$ sudo apt-get install build-essential libssl-dev libffi-dev python-
dev
```

You may need to run as a super-user depending on your operating systems configurations, since diesel installs some critical dependencies such as the cryptography module that requires admin privileges to install.

Diesel has some dependency issues in Python 3. Installing and getting it to work is easier with Python 2.

You may install `diesel` as follows:

```
$ sudo su
# pip install diesel
```

This will display the logs as follows while installing `diesel`:

```
Collecting diesel
Requirement already satisfied: http-parser>=0.7.12 in
/usr/local/lib/python3.5/dist-packages (from diesel)
Requirement already satisfied: flask in /usr/local/lib/python3.5/dist-
packages (from diesel)
Requirement already satisfied: greenlet in
/usr/local/lib/python3.5/dist-packages (from diesel)
Requirement already satisfied: twiggy in
/usr/local/lib/python3.5/dist-packages (from diesel)
Requirement already satisfied: dnspython in
/usr/local/lib/python3.5/dist-packages (from diesel)
Collecting pyopenssl (from diesel)\
Using cached pyOpenSSL-17.0.0-py2.py3-none-any.whl
Requirement already satisfied: Werkzeug>=0.7 in
/usr/local/lib/python3.5/dist-packages (from flask->diesel)
Requirement already satisfied: Jinja2>=2.4 in /usr/lib/python3/dist-
packages (from flask->diesel)
Requirement already satisfied: itsdangerous>=0.21 in
/usr/local/lib/python3.5/dist-packages (from flask->diesel)
Requirement already satisfied: click>=2.0 in
/usr/local/lib/python3.5/dist-packages (from flask->diesel)
Requirement already satisfied: six>=1.5.2 in /usr/lib/python3/dist-
packages (from pyopenssl->diesel)
Collecting cryptography>=1.7 (from pyopenssl->diesel)
Using cached cryptography-1.9.tar.gz
Requirement already satisfied: MarkupSafe in /usr/lib/python3/dist-
packages (from Jinja2>=2.4->flask->diesel)
Requirement already satisfied: idna>=2.1 in
/usr/local/lib/python3.5/dist-packages (from
cryptography>=1.7->pyopenssl->diesel)
Requirement already satisfied: asn1crypto>=0.21.0 in
/usr/local/lib/python3.5/dist-packages (from
cryptography>=1.7->pyopenssl->diesel)
Requirement already satisfied: cffi>=1.7 in
/usr/local/lib/python3.5/dist-packages (from
cryptography>=1.7->pyopenssl->diesel)
Requirement already satisfied: pycparser in
/usr/local/lib/python3.5/dist-packages (from
cffi>=1.7->cryptography>=1.7->pyopenssl->diesel)
Building wheels for collected packages: cryptography
Running setup.py bdist_wheel for cryptography ... done
```

```
Stored in directory:
/root/.cache/pip/wheels/ff/a5/ef/186bb4f6a89ef0bb8373bf53e5c9884b96722
f0857bd3111b8
Successfully built cryptography
Installing collected packages: cryptography, pyopenssl, diesel
Found existing installation: cryptography 1.2.3
Uninstalling cryptography-1.2.3:
Successfully uninstalled cryptography-1.2.3
Successfully installed cryptography-1.9 diesel-3.0.24 pyopenssl-17.0.0
```

How to do it...

In the Python Diesel framework, applications are initialized with an instance of the `Application()` class and an event handler is registered with this instance. Let's see how simple it is to write an echo server.

Listing 2.5 shows the code on the echo server example using Diesel as follows:

```
#!/usr/bin/env python
# Python Network Programming Cookbook, Second Edition -- Chapter - 2
# This program is optimized for Python 2.7.12.
# It will work with Python 3.5.2 once the depedencies for diesel are
sorted out.
# It may run on any other version with/without modifications.
# You also need diesel library 3.0 or a later version.
# Make sure to install the dependencies beforehand.

import diesel
import argparse

class EchoServer(object):
    """ An echo server using diesel"""

    def handler(self, remote_addr):
        """Runs the echo server"""
        host, port = remote_addr[0], remote_addr[1]
        print ("Echo client connected from: %s:%d" %(host, port))
        while True:
            try:
                message = diesel.until_eol()
                your_message = ': '.join(['You said', message])
                diesel.send(your_message)
            except Exception as e:
                print ("Exception:",e)

def main(server_port):
```

```
    app = diesel.Application()
    server = EchoServer()
    app.add_service(diesel.Service(server.handler, server_port))
    app.run()


if __name__ == '__main__':
    parser = argparse.ArgumentParser(description='Echo server
                                        example with Diesel')
    parser.add_argument('--port', action="store", dest="port",
                                      type=int, required=True)
    given_args = parser.parse_args()
    port = given_args.port
    main(port)
```

If you run this script, the server will show the following output:

```
$ python 12_5_echo_server_with_diesel.py --port=8800
[2017/06/04 13:37:36] {diesel} WARNING|Starting diesel <hand-rolled
select.epoll>
Echo client connected from: 127.0.0.1:57506
```

On another console window, another `telnet` client can be launched and the echoing message to our server can be tested as follows:

```
$ telnet localhost 8800
Trying 127.0.0.1...
Connected to localhost.
Escape character is '^]'.
Hello Diesel server ?
You said: Hello Diesel server ?
```

The following screenshot illustrates the interaction of the Diesel chat server:

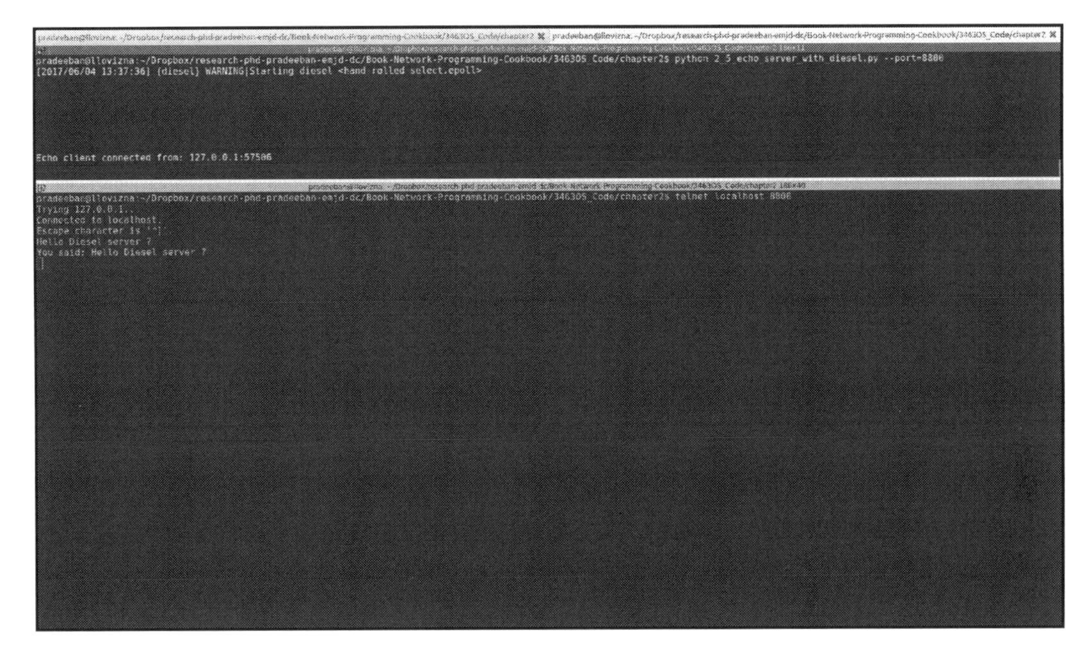

Chat Server and Telnet

How it works...

Our script has taken a command-line argument for `--port` and passed this to the `main()` function where our Diesel application has been initialized and run.

Diesel has a notion of service where an application can be built with many services. `EchoServer` has a `handler()` method. This enables the server to deal with individual client connections. The `Service()` method takes the `handler` method and a port number to run that service.

Inside the `handler()` method, we determine the behavior of the server. In this case, the server is simply returning the message text.

If we compare this code with `Chapter 11`, *Sockets, IPv4, and Simple Client/Server Programming*, in the *Writing a simple echo client/server application* recipe (*listing 1.13a*), it is very clear that we do not need to write any boiler-plate code and hence it's very easy to concentrate on high-level application logic.

13
IPv6, Unix Domain Sockets, and Network Interfaces

In this chapter, we will cover the following topics:

- Forwarding a local port to a remote host
- Pinging hosts on the network with ICMP
- Waiting for a remote network service
- Enumerating interfaces on your machine
- Finding the IP address for a specific interface on your machine
- Finding whether an interface is up on your machine
- Detecting inactive machines on your network
- Performing a basic IPC using connected sockets (socketpair)
- Performing IPC using Unix domain sockets
- Finding out if your Python supports IPv6 sockets
- Extracting an IPv6 prefix from an IPv6 address
- Writing an IPv6 echo client/server

Introduction

This chapter extends the use of Python's `socket` library with a few third-party libraries. It also discusses some advanced techniques, for example, the asynchronous `ayncore` module from the Python standard library. This chapter also touches upon various protocols, ranging from an ICMP ping to an IPv6 client/server.

In this chapter, a few useful Python third-party modules have been introduced by some example recipes. For example, the network packet capture library, `Scapy`, is well known among Python network programmers.

A few recipes have been dedicated to explore the IPv6 utilities in Python including an IPv6 client/server. Some other recipes cover Unix domain sockets.

Forwarding a local port to a remote host

Sometimes, you may need to create a local port forwarder that will redirect all traffic from a local port to a particular remote host. This might be useful to enable proxy users to browse a certain site while preventing them from browsing some others.

How to do it...

Let us create a local port forwarding script that will redirect all traffic received at port `8800` to the Google home page (`http://www.google.com`). We can pass the local and remote host as well as port number to this script. For the sake of simplicity, let's only specify the local port number as we are aware that the web server runs on port `80`.

Listing 3.1 shows a port forwarding example, as follows:

```
#!/usr/bin/env python
# Python Network Programming Cookbook, Second Edition -- Chapter - 3
# This program is optimized for Python 2.7.12 and Python 3.5.2.
# It may run on any other version with/without modifications.


import argparse

LOCAL_SERVER_HOST = 'localhost'
REMOTE_SERVER_HOST = 'www.google.com'
BUFSIZE = 4096

import asyncore
import socket

class PortForwarder(asyncore.dispatcher):
    def __init__(self, ip, port, remoteip,remoteport,backlog=5):
        asyncore.dispatcher.__init__(self)
        self.remoteip=remoteip
        self.remoteport=remoteport
        self.create_socket(socket.AF_INET,socket.SOCK_STREAM)
```

```
        self.set_reuse_addr()
        self.bind((ip,port))
        self.listen(backlog)

    def handle_accept(self):
        conn, addr = self.accept()
        print ("Connected to:",addr)
        Sender(Receiver(conn),self.remoteip,self.remoteport)

class Receiver(asyncore.dispatcher):
    def __init__(self,conn):
        asyncore.dispatcher.__init__(self,conn)
        self.from_remote_buffer=''
        self.to_remote_buffer=''
        self.sender=None

    def handle_connect(self):
        pass

    def handle_read(self):
        read = self.recv(BUFSIZE)
        self.from_remote_buffer += read

    def writable(self):
        return (len(self.to_remote_buffer) > 0)

    def handle_write(self):
        sent = self.send(self.to_remote_buffer)
        self.to_remote_buffer = self.to_remote_buffer[sent:]

    def handle_close(self):
        self.close()
        if self.sender:
            self.sender.close()

class Sender(asyncore.dispatcher):
    def __init__(self, receiver, remoteaddr,remoteport):
        asyncore.dispatcher.__init__(self)
        self.receiver=receiver
        receiver.sender=self
        self.create_socket(socket.AF_INET, socket.SOCK_STREAM)
        self.connect((remoteaddr, remoteport))
    def handle_connect(self):
        pass
    def handle_read(self):
        read = self.recv(BUFSIZE)
        self.receiver.to_remote_buffer += read
    def writable(self):
```

```
            return (len(self.receiver.from_remote_buffer) > 0)
        def handle_write(self):
            sent = self.send(self.receiver.from_remote_buffer)
            self.receiver.from_remote_buffer = self.receiver.
              from_remote_buffer[sent:]
        def handle_close(self):
            self.close()
            self.receiver.close()


    if __name__ == "__main__":
        parser = argparse.ArgumentParser(description='Stackless
                  Socket Server Example')
        parser.add_argument('--local-host', action="store",
        dest="local_host", default=LOCAL_SERVER_HOST)
        parser.add_argument('--local-port', action="store",
        dest="local_port", type=int, required=True)
        parser.add_argument('--remote-host', action="store",
        dest="remote_host",  default=REMOTE_SERVER_HOST)
        parser.add_argument('--remote-port', action="store",
        dest="remote_port", type=int, default=80)
        given_args = parser.parse_args()
        local_host, remote_host = given_args.local_host,
        given_args.remote_host
        local_port, remote_port = given_args.local_port,
        given_args.remote_port
        print ("Starting port forwarding local %s:%s => remote
        %s:%s" % (local_host, local_port, remote_host, remote_port))
        PortForwarder(local_host, local_port, remote_host, remote_port)
        asyncore.loop()
```

If you run this script, it will show the following output:

```
$ python 13_1_port_forwarding.py --local-port=8800
Starting port forwarding local localhost:8800 => remote
www.google.com:80
```

Now, open your browser and visit `http://localhost:8800`. This will take you to the Google home page and the script will print something similar to the following command:

```
('Connected to:', ('127.0.0.1', 37236))
```

The following screenshot shows the forwarding of a local port to a remote host:

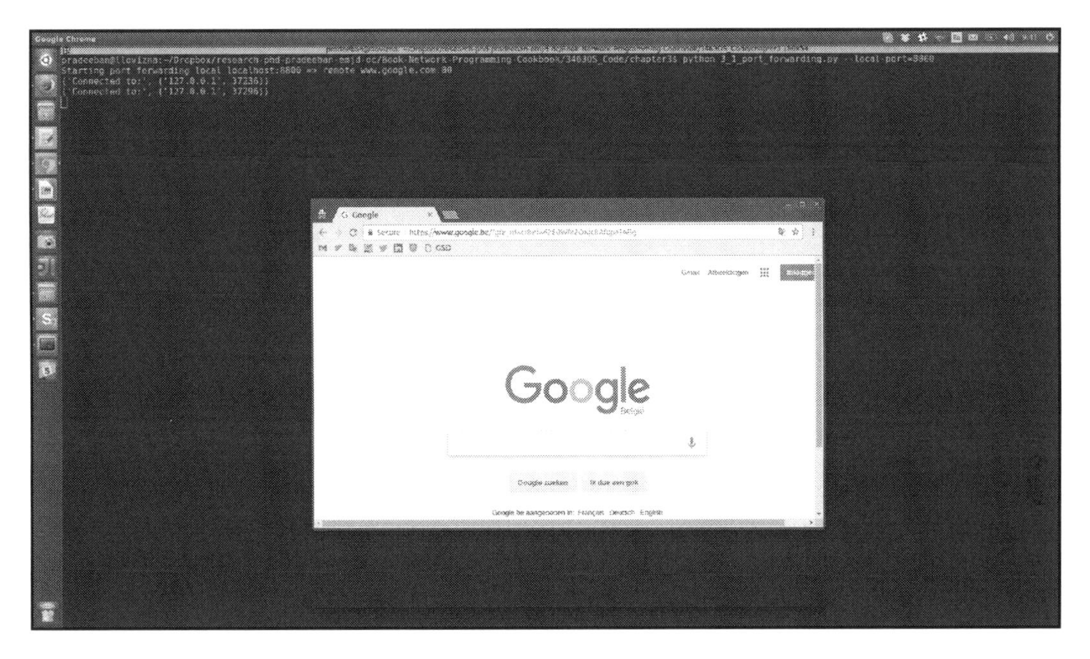

Port Forwarding to Remote Host

How it works...

We created a port forwarding class, `PortForwarder` subclassed, from `asyncore.dispatcher`, which wraps around the `socket` object. It provides a few additional helpful functions when certain events occur, for example, when the connection is successful or a client is connected to a server socket. You have the choice of overriding the set of methods defined in this class. In our case, we only override the `handle_accept()` method.

Two other classes have been derived from `asyncore.dispatcher`. The `Receiver` class handles the incoming client requests and the `Sender` class takes this `Receiver` instance and processes the sent data to the clients. As you can see, these two classes override the `handle_read()`, `handle_write()`, and `writeable()` methods to facilitate the bi-directional communication between the remote host and local client.

In summary, the `PortForwarder` class takes the incoming client request in a local socket and passes this to the `Sender` class instance, which in turn uses the `Receiver` class instance to initiate a bi-directional communication with a remote server in the specified port.

Pinging hosts on the network with ICMP

An ICMP ping is the most common type of network scanning you have ever encountered. It is very easy to open a command-line prompt or Terminal and type `ping www.google.com`. How difficult is that from inside a Python program? This recipe shows you an example of a Python ping.

Getting ready

You need the superuser or administrator privilege to run this recipe on your machine.

How to do it...

You can lazily write a Python script that calls the system ping command-line tool, as follows:

```
import subprocess
import shlex

command_line = "ping -c 1 www.google.com"
args = shlex.split(command_line)
try:
      subprocess.check_call(args,stdout=subprocess.PIPE,\
stderr=subprocess.PIPE)
    print ("Google web server is up!")
except subprocess.CalledProcessError:
    print ("Failed to get ping.")
```

However, in many circumstances, the system's ping executable may not be available or may be inaccessible. In this case, we need a pure Python script to do that ping. Note that this script needs to be run as a superuser or administrator.

Listing 3.2 shows the ICMP ping, as follows:

```
#!/usr/bin/env python
# Python Network Programming Cookbook -- Chapter - 3
```

```
# This program is optimized for Python 3.5.2.
# Instructions to make it run with Python 2.7.x is given below.
# It may run on any other version with/without modifications.

import os
import argparse
import socket
import struct
import select
import time


ICMP_ECHO_REQUEST = 8 # Platform specific
DEFAULT_TIMEOUT = 2
DEFAULT_COUNT = 4


class Pinger(object):
    """ Pings to a host -- the Pythonic way"""
    def __init__(self, target_host, count=DEFAULT_COUNT,
                 timeout=DEFAULT_TIMEOUT):
        self.target_host = target_host
        self.count = count
        self.timeout = timeout


    def do_checksum(self, source_string):
        """  Verify the packet integritity """
        sum = 0
        max_count = (len(source_string)/2)*2
        count = 0
        while count < max_count:

            # To make this program run with Python 2.7.x:
            # val = ord(source_string[count + 1])*256 +
                        ord(source_string[count])
            # ### uncomment the above line, and comment
                  out the below line.
            val = source_string[count + 1]*256 + source_string[count]
            # In Python 3, indexing a bytes object returns an integer.
            # Hence, ord() is redundant.

            sum = sum + val
            sum = sum & 0xffffffff
            count = count + 2
        if max_count<len(source_string):
            sum = sum + ord(source_string[len(source_string) - 1])
            sum = sum & 0xffffffff
```

```
        sum = (sum >> 16)  +  (sum & 0xffff)
        sum = sum + (sum >> 16)
        answer = ~sum
        answer = answer & 0xffff
        answer = answer >> 8 | (answer << 8 & 0xff00)
        return answer
    def receive_pong(self, sock, ID, timeout):
        """
        Receive ping from the socket.
        """
        time_remaining = timeout
        while True:
            start_time = time.time()
            readable = select.select([sock], [], [], time_remaining)
            time_spent = (time.time() - start_time)
            if readable[0] == []: # Timeout
                return
            time_received = time.time()
            recv_packet, addr = sock.recvfrom(1024)
            icmp_header = recv_packet[20:28]
            type, code, checksum, packet_ID, sequence = struct.unpack(
                "bbHHh", icmp_header
            )
            if packet_ID == ID:
                bytes_In_double = struct.calcsize("d")
                time_sent = struct.unpack("d", recv_packet[28:28 +
                                          bytes_In_double])[0]
                return time_received - time_sent
            time_remaining = time_remaining - time_spent
            if time_remaining <= 0:
                return
```

We need a send_ping() method that will send the data of a ping request to the target host. Also, this will call the do_checksum() method for checking the integrity of the ping data, as follows:

```
    def send_ping(self, sock,  ID):
        """
        Send ping to the target host
        """
        target_addr  =  socket.gethostbyname(self.target_host)
        my_checksum = 0
        # Create a dummy heder with a 0 checksum.
        header = struct.pack("bbHHh", ICMP_ECHO_REQUEST, 0,
                             my_checksum, ID, 1)
        bytes_In_double = struct.calcsize("d")
        data = (192 - bytes_In_double) * "Q"
        data = struct.pack("d", time.time()) +
```

```
            bytes(data.encode('utf-8'))
        # Get the checksum on the data and the dummy header.
        my_checksum = self.do_checksum(header + data)
        header = struct.pack(
            "bbHHh", ICMP_ECHO_REQUEST, 0,
            socket.htons(my_checksum), ID, 1
        )
        packet = header + data
        sock.sendto(packet, (target_addr, 1))
```

Let us define another method called `ping_once()` that makes a single ping call to the target host. It creates a raw ICMP socket by passing the ICMP protocol to `socket()`. The exception handling code takes care if the script is not run by a superuser or if any other socket error occurs. Let's take a look at the following code:

```
    def ping_once(self):
        """
        Returns the delay (in seconds) or none on timeout.
        """
        icmp = socket.getprotobyname("icmp")
        try:
            sock = socket.socket(socket.AF_INET,
                                 socket.SOCK_RAW, icmp)
        except socket.error as e:
            if e.errno == 1:
                # Not superuser, so operation not permitted
                e.msg +=  "ICMP messages can only be sent
                           from root user processes"
                raise socket.error(e.msg)
        except Exception as e:
            print ("Exception: %s" %(e))
        my_ID = os.getpid() & 0xFFFF
        self.send_ping(sock, my_ID)
        delay = self.receive_pong(sock, my_ID, self.timeout)
        sock.close()
        return delay
```

The main executive method of this class is `ping()`. It runs a for loop inside, which the `ping_once()` method is called count times and receives a delay in the ping response in seconds. If no delay is returned, that means the ping has failed. Let's take a look at the following code:

```
    def ping(self):
        """
        Run the ping process
        """
        for i in range(self.count):
```

```
            print ("Ping to %s..." % self.target_host,)
            try:
                delay  =  self.ping_once()
            except socket.gaierror as e:
                print ("Ping failed. (socket error: '%s')" % e[1])
                break
            if delay  ==  None:
                print ("Ping failed. (timeout within %ssec.)"
                         % self.timeout)
            else:
                delay  =  delay * 1000
                print ("Get pong in %0.4fms" % delay)

if __name__ == '__main__':
    parser = argparse.ArgumentParser(description='Python ping')
    parser.add_argument('--target-host', action="store",
dest="target_host", required=True)
    given_args = parser.parse_args()
    target_host = given_args.target_host
    pinger = Pinger(target_host=target_host)
    pinger.ping()
```

This script shows the following output. This has been run with the superuser privilege:

```
$ sudo python 13_2_ping_remote_host.py --target-host=www.google.com
Ping to www.google.com...
Get pong in 27.0808ms
Ping to www.google.com...
Get pong in 17.3445ms
Ping to www.google.com...
Get pong in 33.3586ms
Ping to www.google.com...
Get pong in 32.3212ms
```

How it works...

A `Pinger` class has been constructed to define a few useful methods. The class initializes with a few user-defined or default inputs, which are as follows:

- `target_host`: This is the target host to ping
- `count`: This is how many times to do the ping
- `timeout`: This is the value that determines when to end an unfinished ping operation

The `send_ping()` method gets the DNS hostname of the target host and creates an `ICMP_ECHO_REQUEST` packet using the `struct` module. It is necessary to check the data integrity of the method using the `do_checksum()` method. It takes the source string and manipulates it to produce a proper checksum. On the receiving end, the `receive_pong()` method waits for a response until the timeout occurs or receives the response. It captures the ICMP response header and then compares the packet ID and calculates the delay in the request and response cycle.

Waiting for a remote network service

Sometimes, during the recovery of a network service, it might be useful to run a script to check when the server is online again.

How to do it...

We can write a client that will wait for a particular network service forever or for a timeout. In this example, by default, we would like to check when a web server is up in localhost. If you specified some other remote host or port, that information will be used instead.

Listing 3.3 shows waiting for a remote network service, as follows:

```
#!/usr/bin/env python
# Python Network Programming Cookbook, Second Edition -- Chapter - 3
# This program is optimized for Python 2.7.12 and Python 3.5.2.
# It may run on any other version with/without modifications.

import argparse
import socket
import errno
from time import time as now

DEFAULT_TIMEOUT = 120
DEFAULT_SERVER_HOST = 'localhost'
DEFAULT_SERVER_PORT = 80

class NetServiceChecker(object):
    """ Wait for a network service to come online"""
    def __init__(self, host, port, timeout=DEFAULT_TIMEOUT):
        self.host = host
        self.port = port
        self.timeout = timeout
```

```
        self.sock = socket.socket(socket.AF_INET, socket.SOCK_STREAM)
    def end_wait(self):
        self.sock.close()

    def check(self):
        """ Check the service """
        if self.timeout:
            end_time = now() + self.timeout
        while True:
            try:
                if self.timeout:
                    next_timeout = end_time - now()
                    if next_timeout < 0:
                        return False
                    else:
                        print ("setting socket next timeout %ss"
                               %round(next_timeout))
                        self.sock.settimeout(next_timeout)
                self.sock.connect((self.host, self.port))
            # handle exceptions
            except socket.timeout as err:
                if self.timeout:
                    return False
            except socket.error as err:
                print ("Exception: %s" %err)
            else: # if all goes well
                self.end_wait()
                return True

if __name__ == '__main__':
    parser = argparse.ArgumentParser(description='Wait for
             Network Service')
    parser.add_argument('--host', action="store", dest="host",
    default=DEFAULT_SERVER_HOST)
    parser.add_argument('--port', action="store", dest="port",
    type=int, default=DEFAULT_SERVER_PORT)
    parser.add_argument('--timeout', action="store", dest="timeout",
    type=int, default=DEFAULT_TIMEOUT)
    given_args = parser.parse_args()
    host, port, timeout = given_args.host, given_args.port,
                          given_args.timeout
    service_checker = NetServiceChecker(host, port, timeout=timeout)
    print ("Checking for network service %s:%s ..." %(host, port))
    if service_checker.check():
        print ("Service is available again!")
```

If a web server is running on your machine, this script will show the following output:

```
$ python 13_3_wait_for_remote_service.py
Waiting for network service localhost:80 ...
setting socket next timeout 120.0s
Service is available again!
```

If you do not have a web server already running in your computer, make sure to install one such as **Apache 2** web server:

```
$ sudo apt install apache2
```

Now, stop the Apache process:

```
$ sudo /etc/init.d/apache2 stop
```

It will print the below message while stopping the service.

```
[ ok ] Stopping apache2 (via systemctl): apache2.service.
```

Run this script, and start Apache again.

```
$ sudo /etc/init.d/apache2 start
[ ok ] Starting apache2 (via systemctl): apache2.service.
```

The output pattern will be different for a different machine. On my machine, the following output pattern was found:

```
Exception: [Errno 103] Software caused connection abort
setting socket next timeout 119.0s
Exception: [Errno 111] Connection refused
setting socket next timeout 119.0s
Exception: [Errno 103] Software caused connection abort
setting socket next timeout 119.0s
Exception: [Errno 111] Connection refused
setting socket next timeout 119.0s
And finally when Apache2 is up again, the following log is printed:
Service is available again!
```

The following screenshot shows the waiting for an active Apache web server process:

Waiting for Apache2 Process

How it works...

The preceding script uses the `argparse` module to take the user input and process the hostname, port, and timeout, which is how long our script will wait for the desired network service. It launches an instance of the `NetServiceChecker` class and calls the `check()` method. This method calculates the final end time of waiting and uses the socket's `settimeout()` method to control each round's end time, that is `next_timeout`. It then uses the socket's `connect()` method to test if the desired network service is available until the socket timeout occurs. This method also catches the socket timeout error and checks the socket timeout against the timeout values given by the user.

Enumerating interfaces on your machine

If you need to list the network interfaces present on your machine, it is not very complicated in Python. There are a couple of third-party libraries out there that can do this job in a few lines. However, let's see how this is done using a pure socket call.

Getting ready

You need to run this recipe on a Linux box. To get the list of available interfaces, you can execute the following command:

```
$ /sbin/ifconfig
```

How to do it...

Listing 3.4 shows how to list the networking interfaces, as follows:

```
#!/usr/bin/env python
# Python Network Programming Cookbook, Second Edition -- Chapter - 3
# This program is optimized for Python 2.7.12 and Python 3.5.2.
# It may run on any other version with/without modifications.

import sys
import socket
import fcntl
import struct
import array

SIOCGIFCONF = 0x8912 #from C library sockios.h
STUCT_SIZE_32 = 32
STUCT_SIZE_64 = 40
PLATFORM_32_MAX_NUMBER =  2**32
DEFAULT_INTERFACES = 8


def list_interfaces():
    interfaces = []
    max_interfaces = DEFAULT_INTERFACES
    is_64bits = sys.maxsize > PLATFORM_32_MAX_NUMBER
    struct_size = STUCT_SIZE_64 if is_64bits else STUCT_SIZE_32
    sock = socket.socket(socket.AF_INET, socket.SOCK_DGRAM)
    while True:
        bytes = max_interfaces * struct_size
        interface_names = array.array('B', b'\0' * bytes)
```

```
        sock_info = fcntl.ioctl(
            sock.fileno(),
            SIOCGIFCONF,
            struct.pack('iL', bytes, interface_names.buffer_info()[0])
        )
        outbytes = struct.unpack('iL', sock_info)[0]
        if outbytes == bytes:
            max_interfaces *= 2
        else:
            break
    namestr = interface_names.tostring()
    for i in range(0, outbytes, struct_size):
        interfaces.append((namestr[i:i+16].split(b'\0', 1)
                          [0]).decode('ascii', 'ignore'))
    return interfaces


if __name__ == '__main__':
    interfaces = list_interfaces()
    print ("This machine has %s network interfaces: %s."
%(len(interfaces), interfaces))
```

The preceding script will list the network interfaces, as shown in the following output:

```
$ python 13_4_list_network_interfaces.py
This machine has 2 network interfaces: ['lo', 'wlo1'].
```

How it works...

This recipe code uses a low-level socket feature to find out the interfaces present on the system. The single `list_interfaces()` method creates a socket object and finds the network interface information from manipulating this object. It does so by making a call to the `fnctl` module's `ioctl()` method. The `fnctl` module interfaces with some Unix routines, for example, `fnctl()`. This interface performs an I/O control operation on the underlying file descriptor socket, which is obtained by calling the `fileno()` method of the `socket` object.

The additional parameter of the `ioctl()` method includes the `SIOCGIFADDR` constant defined in the C `socket` library and a data structure produced by the `struct` module's `pack()` function. The memory address specified by a data structure is modified as a result of the `ioctl()` call. In this case, the `interface_names` variable holds this information. After unpacking the `sock_info` return value of the `ioctl()` call, the number of network interfaces is increased twice if the size of the data suggests it. This is done in a while loop to discover all interfaces if our initial interface count assumption is not correct.

The names of interfaces are extracted from the string format of the `interface_names` variable. It reads specific fields of that variable and appends the values in the interfaces' list. At the end of the `list_interfaces()` function, this is returned.

Finding the IP address for a specific interface on your machine

Finding the IP address of a particular network interface may be needed from your Python network application.

Getting ready

This recipe is prepared exclusively for a Linux box. There are some Python modules specially designed to bring similar functionalities on Windows and macOS platforms. For example, see `http://sourceforge.net/projects/pywin32/` for Windows-specific implementation.

How to do it...

You can use the `fnctl` module to query the IP address on your machine.

Listing 3.5 shows us how to find the IP address for a specific interface on your machine, as follows:

```
#!/usr/bin/env python
# Python Network Programming Cookbook, Second Edition -- Chapter - 3
# This program is optimized for Python 2.7.12 and Python 3.5.2.
# It may run on any other version with/without modifications.
```

```
import argparse
import sys
import socket
import fcntl
import struct
import array


def get_ip_address(ifname):
    s = socket.socket(socket.AF_INET, socket.SOCK_DGRAM)
    return socket.inet_ntoa(fcntl.ioctl(
        s.fileno(),
        0x8915,  # SIOCGIFADDR
        struct.pack(b'256s', bytes(ifname[:15], 'utf-8'))
    )[20:24])

if __name__ == '__main__':
    parser = argparse.ArgumentParser(description='Python
                                     networking utils')
    parser.add_argument('--ifname', action="store",
                        dest="ifname", required=True)
    given_args = parser.parse_args()
    ifname = given_args.ifname
    print ("Interface [%s] --> IP: %s" %(ifname,
get_ip_address(ifname)))
```

The output of this script is shown in one line, as follows:

```
$ python 13_5_get_interface_ip_address.py --ifname=lo
Interface [lo] --> IP: 127.0.0.1
```

In the preceding execution, make sure to use an existing interface, as printed in the previous recipe. In my computer, I got the output previously for `13_4_list_network_interfaces.py`:

```
This machine has 2 network interfaces: ['lo', 'wlo1'].
```

If you use a non-existing interface, an error will be printed.

For example, I do not have eth0 interface right now. So the output is:

```
$ python3 13_5_get_interface_ip_address.py --ifname=eth0
Traceback (most recent call last):
File "13_5_get_interface_ip_address.py", line 27, in <module>
  print ("Interface [%s] --> IP: %s" %(ifname,
get_ip_address(ifname)))
  File "13_5_get_interface_ip_address.py", line 19, in get_ip_address
  struct.pack(b'256s', bytes(ifname[:15], 'utf-8'))
OSError: [Errno 19] No such device
```

How it works...

This recipe is similar to the previous one. The preceding script takes a command-line argument: the name of the network interface whose IP address is to be known. The `get_ip_address()` function creates a `socket` object and calls the `fnctl.ioctl()` function to query on that object about IP information. Note that the `socket.inet_ntoa()` function converts the binary data to a human-readable string in a dotted format as we are familiar with it.

Finding whether an interface is up on your machine

If you have multiple network interfaces on your machine, before doing any work on a particular interface, you would like to know the status of that network interface, for example, if the interface is actually up. This makes sure that you route your command to active interfaces.

Getting ready

This recipe is written for a Linux machine. So, this script will not run on a Windows or macOS host. In this recipe, we use **Nmap**, a famous network scanning tool. You can find more about Nmap from its website `http://nmap.org/`.

Install Nmap in your computer. For Debian-based systems, the command is:

```
$ sudo apt-get install nmap
```

You also need the `python-nmap` module to run this recipe. This can be installed by pip, as follows:

```
$ pip install python-nmap
```

How to do it...

We can create a `socket` object and get the IP address of that interface. Then, we can use any of the scanning techniques to probe the interface status.

Listing 3.6 shows the detect network interface status, as follows:

```
#!/usr/bin/env python
# Python Network Programming Cookbook, Second Edition -- Chapter - 3
# This program is optimized for Python 2.7.12 and Python 3.5.2.
# It may run on any other version with/without modifications.


import argparse
import socket
import struct
import fcntl
import nmap

SAMPLE_PORTS = '21-23'

def get_interface_status(ifname):
    sock = socket.socket(socket.AF_INET, socket.SOCK_DGRAM)
    ip_address = socket.inet_ntoa(fcntl.ioctl(
        sock.fileno(),
        0x8915, #SIOCGIFADDR, C socket library sockios.h
        struct.pack(b'256s', bytes(ifname[:15], 'utf-8'))
    )[20:24])
    nm = nmap.PortScanner()
    nm.scan(ip_address, SAMPLE_PORTS)
    return nm[ip_address].state()
if  __name__ == '__main__':
    parser = argparse.ArgumentParser(description='Python
                                   networking utils')
    parser.add_argument('--ifname', action="store", dest="ifname",
                         required=True)
    given_args = parser.parse_args()
    ifname = given_args.ifname
    print ("Interface [%s] is: %s" %(ifname,
get_interface_status(ifname)))
```

If you run this script to inquire the status of the eth0 status, it will show something similar to the following output:

```
$ python 13_6_find_network_interface_status.py --ifname=lo
Interface [lo] is: up
```

How it works...

The recipe takes the interface's name from the command line and passes it to the `get_interface_status()` function. This function finds the IP address of that interface by manipulating a UDP `socket` object.

This recipe needs the Nmap third-party module. We can install that PyPI using the `pip install` command. The Nmap scanning instance, `nm`, has been created by calling `PortScanner()`. An initial scan to a local IP address gives us the status of the associated network interface.

Detecting inactive machines on your network

If you have been given a list of IP addresses of a few machines on your network and you are asked to write a script to find out which hosts are inactive periodically, you would want to create a network scanner type program without installing anything on the target host computers.

Getting ready

This recipe requires installing the `Scapy` library (> 2.2), which can be obtained at `http://www.secdev.org/projects/scapy/files/scapy-latest.zip`.

At the time of writing, the default `Scapy` release works with Python 2, and does not support Python 3. You may download the `Scapy` for Python 3 from `https://pypi.python.org/pypi/scapy-python3/0.20`.

How to do it...

We can use `Scapy`, a mature network-analyzing, third-party library, to launch an ICMP scan. Since we would like to do it periodically, we need Python's `sched` module to schedule the scanning tasks.

Listing 3.7 shows us how to detect inactive machines, as follows:

```
#!/usr/bin/env python
# Python Network Programming Cookbook, Second Edition -- Chapter - 3
# This program is optimized for Python 2.7.12 and Python 3.5.2.
# It may run on any other version with/without modifications.
# Requires scapy-2.2.0 or higher for Python 2.7.
# Visit: http://www.secdev.org/projects/scapy/files/scapy-latest.zip
# As of now, requires a separate bundle for Python 3.x.
# Download it from: https://pypi.python.org/pypi/scapy-python3/0.20


import argparse
import time
import sched
from scapy.all import sr, srp, IP, UDP, ICMP, TCP, ARP, Ether

RUN_FREQUENCY = 10

scheduler = sched.scheduler(time.time, time.sleep)


def detect_inactive_hosts(scan_hosts):
    """
    Scans the network to find scan_hosts are live or dead
    scan_hosts can be like 10.0.2.2-4 to cover range.
    See Scapy docs for specifying targets.
    """
    global scheduler
    scheduler.enter(RUN_FREQUENCY, 1, detect_inactive_hosts,
                    (scan_hosts, ))
    inactive_hosts = []
    try:
        ans, unans = sr(IP(dst=scan_hosts)/ICMP(), retry=0, timeout=1)
        ans.summary(lambda r : r.sprintf("%IP.src% is alive"))
        for inactive in unans:
            print ("%s is inactive" %inactive.dst)
            inactive_hosts.append(inactive.dst)
        print ("Total %d hosts are inactive" %(len(inactive_hosts)))
    except KeyboardInterrupt:
        exit(0)
```

```
if __name__ == "__main__":
    parser = argparse.ArgumentParser(description='Python
                                     networking utils')
    parser.add_argument('--scan-hosts', action="store",
    dest="scan_hosts", required=True)
    given_args = parser.parse_args()
    scan_hosts = given_args.scan_hosts
    scheduler.enter(1, 1, detect_inactive_hosts, (scan_hosts, ))
    scheduler.run()
```

The output of this script will be something like the following command:

```
$ sudo python 13_7_detect_inactive_machines.py --scan-hosts=10.0.2.2-4
Begin emission:
.*...Finished to send 3 packets.
.
Received 6 packets, got 1 answers, remaining 2 packets
10.0.2.2 is alive
10.0.2.4 is inactive
10.0.2.3 is inactive
Total 2 hosts are inactive
Begin emission:
*.Finished to send 3 packets.
Received 3 packets, got 1 answers, remaining 2 packets
10.0.2.2 is alive
10.0.2.4 is inactive
10.0.2.3 is inactive
Total 2 hosts are inactive
```

How it works...

The preceding script first takes a list of network hosts, `scan_hosts`, from the command line. It then creates a schedule to launch the `detect_inactive_hosts()` function after a one-second delay. The target function takes the `scan_hosts` argument and calls `Scapy` library's `sr()` function.

This function schedules itself to rerun after every 10 seconds by calling the `schedule.enter()` function once again. This way, we run this scanning task periodically.

The `Scapy` library's `sr()` scanning function takes an IP, protocol, and some scan-control information. In this case, the `IP()` method passes `scan_hosts` as the destination hosts to scan, and the protocol is specified as ICMP. This can also be TCP or UDP. We do not specify a retry and one-second timeout to run this script faster. However, you can experiment with the options that suit you.

The scanning `sr()` function returns the hosts that answer and those that don't as a tuple. We check the hosts that don't answer, build a list, and print that information.

Performing a basic IPC using connected sockets (socketpair)

Sometimes, two scripts need to communicate some information between themselves via two processes. In Unix/Linux, there's a concept of connected socket, of `socketpair`. We can experiment with this here.

Getting ready

This recipe is designed for a Unix/Linux host. Windows/macOS is not suitable for running this one.

How to do it...

We use a `test_socketpair()` function to wrap a few lines that test the socket's `socketpair()` function.

List 3.8 shows an example of `socketpair`, as follows:

```
#!/usr/bin/env python
# Python Network Programming Cookbook, Second Edition -- Chapter - 3
# This program is optimized for Python 3.5.2.
# It may run on any other version with/without modifications.
# To make it run on Python 2.7.x, needs some changes due to API
differences.
# Follow the comments inline to make the program work with Python 2.

import socket
import os

BUFSIZE = 1024

def test_socketpair():
    """ Test Unix socketpair"""
    parent, child = socket.socketpair()
    pid = os.fork()
    try:
        if pid:
            print ("@Parent, sending message...")
            child.close()

            parent.sendall(bytes("Hello from parent!", 'utf-8'))
            # Comment out the above line and uncomment
              the below line for Python 2.7.
            # parent.sendall("Hello from parent!")

            response = parent.recv(BUFSIZE)
            print ("Response from child:", response)
            parent.close()
        else:
            print ("@Child, waiting for message from parent")
            parent.close()
            message = child.recv(BUFSIZE)
            print ("Message from parent:", message)

            child.sendall(bytes("Hello from child!!", 'utf-8'))
            # Comment out the above line and
              uncomment the below line for Python 2.7.
            # child.sendall("Hello from child!!")

            child.close()
    except Exception as err:
        print ("Error: %s" %err)
```

```
if __name__ == '__main__':
    test_socketpair()
```

The output from the preceding script is as follows:

```
$ python 13_8_ipc_using_socketpairs.py
@Parent, sending message...
@Child, waiting for message from parent
Message from parent: b'Hello from parent!'
Response from child: b'Hello from child!!'
```

How it works...

The `socket.socketpair()` function simply returns two connected `socket` objects. In our case, we can say that one is a parent and another is a child. We fork another process via a `os.fork()` call. This returns the process ID of the parent. In each process, the other process' socket is closed first and then a message is exchanged via a `sendall()` method call on the process's socket. The try-except block prints any error in case of any kind of exception.

Performing IPC using Unix domain sockets

Unix domain sockets (UDS) are sometimes used as a convenient way to communicate between two processes. As in Unix, everything is conceptually a file. If you need an example of such an IPC action, this can be useful.

How to do it...

We launch a UDS server that binds to a filesystem path, and a UDS client uses the same path to communicate with the server.

Listing 3.9a shows a Unix domain socket server, as follows:

```
#!/usr/bin/env python
# Python Network Programming Cookbook, Second Edition -- Chapter - 3
# This program is optimized for Python 2.7.12 and Python 3.5.2.
# It may run on any other version with/without modifications.
```

```
import socket
import os
import time

SERVER_PATH = "/tmp/python_unix_socket_server"
def run_unix_domain_socket_server():
    if os.path.exists(SERVER_PATH):
        os.remove( SERVER_PATH )
    print ("starting unix domain socket server.")
    server = socket.socket( socket.AF_UNIX, socket.SOCK_DGRAM )
    server.bind(SERVER_PATH)
    print ("Listening on path: %s" %SERVER_PATH)
    while True:
        datagram = server.recv( 1024 )
        if not datagram:
            break
        else:
            print ("-" * 20)
            print (datagram)
        if "DONE" == datagram:
            break
    print ("-" * 20)
    print ("Server is shutting down now...")
    server.close()
    os.remove(SERVER_PATH)
    print ("Server shutdown and path removed.")

if __name__ == '__main__':
    run_unix_domain_socket_server()
```

Listing 3.9b shows a UDS client, as follows:

```
#!/usr/bin/env python
# Python Network Programming Cookbook, Second Edition -- Chapter - 3
# This program is optimized for Python 3.5.2.
# It may run on any other version with/without modifications.
# To make it run on Python 2.7.x, needs some changes due to API
differences.
# Follow the comments inline to make the program work with Python 2.


import socket
import sys

SERVER_PATH = "/tmp/python_unix_socket_server"

def run_unix_domain_socket_client():
    """ Run "a Unix domain socket client """
```

```
        sock = socket.socket(socket.AF_UNIX, socket.SOCK_DGRAM)
        # Connect the socket to the path where the server is listening
        server_address = SERVER_PATH
        print ("connecting to %s" % server_address)
        try:
            sock.connect(server_address)
        except socket.error as msg:
            print (msg)
            sys.exit(1)
        try:
            message = "This is the message.  This will be echoed back!"
            print  ("Sending [%s]" %message)

            sock.sendall(bytes(message, 'utf-8'))
            # Comment out the above line and uncomment
              the below line for Python 2.7.
            # sock.sendall(message)

            amount_received = 0
            amount_expected = len(message)
            while amount_received < amount_expected:
                data = sock.recv(16)
                amount_received += len(data)
                print ("Received [%s]" % data)
        finally:
            print ("Closing client")
            sock.close()

    if __name__ == '__main__':
        run_unix_domain_socket_client()
```

The server output is as follows:

```
$ python 13_9a_unix_domain_socket_server.py
starting unix domain socket server.
Listening on path: /tmp/python_unix_socket_server
--------------------
This is the message.  This will be echoed back!
```

The client output is as follows:

```
$ python 13_9b_unix_domain_socket_client.py
connecting to /tmp/python_unix_socket_server
Sending [This is the message.  This will be echoed back!]
```

How it works...

A common path is defined for a UDS client/server to interact. Both the client and server use the same path to connect and listen to.

In a server code, we remove the path if it exists from the previous run of this script. It then creates a Unix `datagram` socket and binds it to the specified path. It then listens for incoming connections. In the data processing loop, it uses the `recv()` method to get data from the client and prints that information on screen.

The client-side code simply opens a Unix `datagram` socket and connects to the shared server address. It sends a message to the server using `sendall()`. It then waits for the message to be echoed back to itself and prints that message.

Finding out if your Python supports IPv6 sockets

IP version 6 or IPv6 is increasingly adopted by the industry to build newer applications. In case you would like to write an IPv6 application, the first thing you'd like to know is if your machine supports IPv6. This can be done from the Linux/Unix command line, as follows:

```
$ cat /proc/net/if_inet6
00000000000000000000000000000001 01 80 10 80       lo
fe800000000000000642a57c2e51932a2 03 40 20 80     wlo1
```

From your Python script, you can also check if the IPv6 support is present on your machine, and Python is installed with that support.

Getting ready

For this recipe, use `pip` to install a Python third-party library, `netifaces`, as follows:

```
$ pip install netifaces
```

How to do it...

We can use a third-party library, `netifaces`, to find out if there is IPv6 support on your machine. We can call the `interfaces()` function from this library to list all interfaces present in the system.

Listing 3.10 shows the Python IPv6 support checker, as follows:

```
#!/usr/bin/env python
# Python Network Programming Cookbook, Second Edition -- Chapter - 3
# This program is optimized for Python 2.7.12 and Python 3.5.2.
# It may run on any other version with/without modifications.
# This program depends on Python module netifaces => 0.8

import socket
import argparse
import netifaces as ni


def inspect_ipv6_support():
    """ Find the ipv6 address"""
    print ("IPV6 support built into Python: %s" %socket.has_ipv6)
    ipv6_addr = {}
    for interface in ni.interfaces():
        all_addresses = ni.ifaddresses(interface)
        print ("Interface %s:" %interface)

        for family,addrs in all_addresses.items():
            fam_name = ni.address_families[family]
            print ('  Address family: %s' % fam_name)
            for addr in addrs:
                if fam_name == 'AF_INET6':
                    ipv6_addr[interface] = addr['addr']
                print ('    Address   : %s' % addr['addr'])
                nmask = addr.get('netmask', None)
                if nmask:
                    print ('    Netmask   : %s' % nmask)
                bcast = addr.get('broadcast', None)
                if bcast:
                    print ('    Broadcast: %s' % bcast)
    if ipv6_addr:
        print ("Found IPv6 address: %s" %ipv6_addr)
    else:
        print ("No IPv6 interface found!")

if __name__ == '__main__':
    inspect_ipv6_support()
```

The output from this script will be as follows:

```
$ python 13_10_check_ipv6_support.py
IPV6 support built into Python: True
Interface lo:
  Address family: AF_PACKET
    Address   : 00:00:00:00:00:00
  Address family: AF_INET
    Address   : 127.0.0.1
    Netmask   : 255.0.0.0
  Address family: AF_INET6
    Address   : ::1
    Netmask   : ffff:ffff:ffff:ffff:ffff:ffff:ffff:ffff/128
Interface enp2s0:
  Address family: AF_PACKET
    Address   : 9c:5c:8e:26:a2:48
    Broadcast: ff:ff:ff:ff:ff:ff
  Address family: AF_INET
    Address   : 130.104.228.90
    Netmask   : 255.255.255.128
    Broadcast: 130.104.228.127
  Address family: AF_INET6
    Address   : 2001:6a8:308f:2:88bc:e3ec:ace4:3afb
    Netmask   : ffff:ffff:ffff:ffff::/64
    Address   : 2001:6a8:308f:2:5bef:e3e6:82f8:8cca
    Netmask   : ffff:ffff:ffff:ffff::/64
    Address   : fe80::66a0:7a3f:f8e9:8c03%enp2s0
    Netmask   : ffff:ffff:ffff:ffff::/64
Interface wlp1s0:
  Address family: AF_PACKET
    Address   : c8:ff:28:90:17:d1
    Broadcast: ff:ff:ff:ff:ff:ff
Found IPv6 address: {'lo': '::1', 'enp2s0':
'fe80::66a0:7a3f:f8e9:8c03%enp2s0'}
```

How it works...

The IPv6 support checker function, `inspect_ipv6_support()`, first checks if Python is built with IPv6 using `socket.has_ipv6`. Next, we call the `interfaces()` function from the `netifaces` module. This gives us the list of all interfaces. If we call the `ifaddresses()` method by passing a network interface to it, we can get all the IP addresses of this interface. We then extract various IP-related information, such as protocol family, address, netmask, and broadcast address. Then, the address of a network interface has been added to the `IPv6_address` dictionary if its protocol family matches `AF_INET6`.

Extracting an IPv6 prefix from an IPv6 address

In your IPv6 application, you need to dig out the IPv6 address for getting the prefix information. Note that the upper 64-bits of an IPv6 address are represented from a global routing prefix plus a subnet ID, as defined in RFC 3513. A general prefix (for example, `/48`) holds a short prefix based on which a number of longer, more specific prefixes (for example, `/64`) can be defined. A Python script can be very helpful in generating the prefix information.

How to do it...

We can use the `netifaces` and `netaddr` third-party libraries to find out the IPv6 prefix information for a given IPv6 address.

Make sure to have `netifaces` and `netaddr` installed in your system:

```
$ pip install netaddr
```

The program is as follows:

```
#!/usr/bin/env python
# Python Network Programming Cookbook, Second Edition -- Chapter - 3
# This program is optimized for Python 2.7.12 and Python 3.5.2.
# It may run on any other version with/without modifications.
# This program depends on Python modules netifaces and netaddr.

import socket
import netifaces as ni
import netaddr as na

def extract_ipv6_info():
    """ Extracts IPv6 information"""
    print ("IPv6 support built into Python: %s" %socket.has_ipv6)
    for interface in ni.interfaces():
        all_addresses = ni.ifaddresses(interface)
        print ("Interface %s:" %interface)
        for family,addrs in all_addresses.items():
            fam_name = ni.address_families[family]

            for addr in addrs:
                if fam_name == 'AF_INET6':
                    addr = addr['addr']
                    has_eth_string = addr.split("%eth")
```

```
                if has_eth_string:
                    addr = addr.split("%eth")[0]
                try:
                    print ("    IP Address: %s"
                    %na.IPNetwork(addr))
                    print ("    IP Version: %s"
                    %na.IPNetwork(addr).version)
                    print ("    IP Prefix length: %s"
                    %na.IPNetwork(addr).prefixlen)
                    print ("    Network: %s"
                    %na.IPNetwork(addr).network)
                    print ("    Broadcast: %s"
                    %na.IPNetwork(addr).broadcast)
                except Exception as e:
                    print ("Skip Non-IPv6 Interface")

if __name__ == '__main__':
    extract_ipv6_info()
```

The output from this script is as follows:

```
$ python 13_11_extract_ipv6_prefix.py
IPv6 support built into Python: True
Interface lo:
    IP Address: ::1/128
    IP Version: 6
    IP Prefix length: 128
    Network: ::1
    Broadcast: ::1
Interface enp2s0:
    IP Address: 2001:6a8:308f:2:88bc:e3ec:ace4:3afb/128
    IP Version: 6
    IP Prefix length: 128
    Network: 2001:6a8:308f:2:88bc:e3ec:ace4:3afb
    Broadcast: 2001:6a8:308f:2:88bc:e3ec:ace4:3afb
    IP Address: 2001:6a8:308f:2:5bef:e3e6:82f8:8cca/128
    IP Version: 6
    IP Prefix length: 128
    Network: 2001:6a8:308f:2:5bef:e3e6:82f8:8cca
    Broadcast: 2001:6a8:308f:2:5bef:e3e6:82f8:8cca
Skip Non-IPv6 Interface
Interface wlp1s0:
```

How it works...

Python's `netifaces` module gives us the network interface IPv6 address. It uses the `interfaces()` and `ifaddresses()` functions for doing this. The `netaddr` module is particularly helpful to manipulate a network address. It has a `IPNetwork()` class that provides us with an address, IPv4 or IPv6, and computes the prefix, network, and broadcast addresses. Here, we find this information class instance's `version`, `prefixlen`, and `network` and `broadcast` attributes.

Writing an IPv6 echo client/server

You need to write an IPv6 compliant server or client and wonder what could be the differences between an IPv6 compliant server or client and its IPv4 counterpart.

How to do it...

We use the same approach as writing an echo client/server using IPv6. The only major difference is how the socket is created using IPv6 information.

Listing 12a shows an IPv6 echo server, as follows:

```
#!/usr/bin/env python
# Python Network Programming Cookbook, Second Edition -- Chapter - 3
# This program is optimized for Python 2.7.12 and Python 3.5.2.
# It may run on any other version with/without modifications.

import argparse
import socket
import sys

HOST = 'localhost'

def echo_server(port, host=HOST):
    """Echo server using IPv6 """
    for result in socket.getaddrinfo(host, port, socket.AF_UNSPEC,
socket.SOCK_STREAM, 0, socket.AI_PASSIVE):
        af, socktype, proto, canonname, sa = result
        try:
            sock = socket.socket(af, socktype, proto)
        except socket.error as err:
            print ("Error: %s" %err)
        try:
```

```
            sock.bind(sa)
            sock.listen(1)
            print ("Server lisenting on %s:%s" %(host, port))
        except socket.error as msg:
            sock.close()
            continue
        break
        sys.exit(1)
    conn, addr = sock.accept()
    print ('Connected to', addr)
    while True:
        data = conn.recv(1024)
        print ("Received data from the client: [%s]" %data)
        if not data: break
        conn.send(data)
        print ("Sent data echoed back to the client: [%s]" %data)
    conn.close()

if __name__ == '__main__':
    parser = argparse.ArgumentParser(description='IPv6 Socket
                Server Example')
    parser.add_argument('--port', action="store", dest="port",
                        type=int, required=True)
    given_args = parser.parse_args()
    port = given_args.port
    echo_server(port)
```

Listing 12b shows an IPv6 echo client, as follows:

```
#!/usr/bin/env python
# Python Network Programming Cookbook, Second Edition -- Chapter - 3
# This program is optimized for Python 2.7.12 and Python 3.5.2.
# It may run on any other version with/without modifications.

import argparse
import socket
import sys

HOST = 'localhost'
BUFSIZE = 1024

def ipv6_echo_client(port, host=HOST):
    for res in socket.getaddrinfo(host, port, socket.AF_UNSPEC,
socket.SOCK_STREAM):
        af, socktype, proto, canonname, sa = res
        try:
            sock = socket.socket(af, socktype, proto)
        except socket.error as err:
```

```
                print ("Error:%s" %err)
            try:
                sock.connect(sa)
            except socket.error as msg:
                sock.close()
                continue
        if sock is None:
            print ('Failed to open socket!')
            sys.exit(1)
        msg = "Hello from ipv6 client"
        print ("Send data to server: %s" %msg)
        sock.send(bytes(msg.encode('utf-8')))
        while True:
            data = sock.recv(BUFSIZE)
            print ('Received from server', repr(data))
            if not data:
                break
        sock.close()

    if __name__ == '__main__':
        parser = argparse.ArgumentParser(description='IPv6 socket
                                          client example')
        parser.add_argument('--port', action="store", dest="port",
                            type=int, required=True)
        given_args = parser.parse_args()
        port = given_args.port
        ipv6_echo_client(port)
```

The server output is as follows:

```
$ python 13_12a_ipv6_echo_server.py --port=8800
Server lisenting on localhost:8800
('Connected to', ('127.0.0.1', 56958))
Received data from the client: [Hello from ipv6 client]
Sent data echoed back to the client: [Hello from ipv6 client]
```

The client output is as follows:

```
$ python 13_12b_ipv6_echo_client.py --port=8800
Send data to server: Hello from ipv6 client
('Received from server', "'Hello from ipv6 client'")
```

The following screenshot indicates the server and client output:

IPv6 Echo Server and Client

How it works...

The IPv6 echo server first determines its IPv6 information by calling `socket.getaddrinfo()`. Notice that we passed the `AF_UNSPEC` protocol for creating a TCP socket. The resulting information is a tuple of five values. We use three of them, address family, socket type, and protocol, to create a server socket. Then, this socket is bound with the socket address from the previous tuple. It then listens to the incoming connections and accepts them. After a connection is made, it receives data from the client and echoes it back.

On the client-side code, we create an IPv6-compliant client socket instance and send the data using the `send()` method of that instance. When the data is echoed back, the `recv()` method is used to get it back.

14
Programming with HTTP for the Internet

In this chapter, we will cover the following topics:

- Downloading data from an HTTP server
- Serving HTTP requests from your machine
- Extracting cookie information after visiting a website
- Submitting web forms
- Sending web requests through a proxy server
- Checking whether a web page exists with the HEAD request
- Spoofing Mozilla Firefox in your client code
- Saving bandwidth in web requests with the HTTP compression
- Writing an HTTP fail-over client with resume and partial downloading
- Writing a simple HTTPS server code with Python and OpenSSL
- Building asynchronous network applications with Twisted
- Building asynchronous network applications with Tornado
- Building concurrent applications with Tornado Future

Introduction

This chapter explains Python HTTP networking library functions with a few third-party libraries. For example, the `requests` library deals with the HTTP requests in a nicer and cleaner way. The `OpenSSL` library is used in one of the recipes to create an SSL-enabled web server.

Many common HTTP protocol features have been illustrated in a few recipes, for example, the web form submission with `POST`, manipulating header information, use of compression, and so on.

Downloading data from an HTTP server

You would like to write a simple HTTP client to fetch some data from any web server using the native HTTP protocol. This can be the very first steps towards creating your own HTTP browser.

How to do it...

Let us access `https://www.python.org/` with our *Pythonic minimal browser*.

You may need to install `urllib` module for the relevant Python versions:

```
$ sudo pip2 install urllib
```

Listing 4.1 explains the following code for a simple HTTP client:

```
#!/usr/bin/env python
# Python Network Programming Cookbook -- Chapter - 4
# This program requires Python 3.5.2 or any later version
# It may run on any other version with/without modifications.
#
# Follow the comments inline to make it run on Python 2.7.x.

import argparse

import urllib.request
# Comment out the above line and uncomment the below for Python 2.7.x.
#import urllib2

REMOTE_SERVER_HOST = 'http://www.cnn.com'
```

```
class HTTPClient:

    def __init__(self, host):
        self.host = host

    def fetch(self):
        response = urllib.request.urlopen(self.host)
        # Comment out the above line and uncomment the below for
          Python 2.7.x.
        #response = urllib2.urlopen(self.host)

        data = response.read()
        text = data.decode('utf-8')
        return text

if __name__ == "__main__":
    parser = argparse.ArgumentParser(description='HTTP Client
Example')
    parser.add_argument('--host', action="store",
     dest="host",  default=REMOTE_SERVER_HOST)

    given_args = parser.parse_args()
    host = given_args.host
    client = HTTPClient(host)
    print (client.fetch())
```

This recipe will by default fetch a page from `http://www.cnn.com`. You can run this recipe with or without the `host` argument. You may choose to fetch any specific web page by passing the URL as an argument. If this script is executed, it will show the following output:

```
$  python 14_1_download_data.py --host=http://www.python.org
<!doctype html>
<!--[if lt IE 7]>   <html class="no-js ie6 lt-ie7 lt-ie8 lt-ie9">
<![endif]-->
<!--[if IE 7]>      <html class="no-js ie7 lt-ie8 lt-ie9">
<![endif]-->
<!--[if IE 8]>      <html class="no-js ie8 lt-ie9">
<![endif]-->
<!--[if gt IE 8]><!--><html class="no-js" lang="en" dir="ltr">  <!--
<![endif]-->

<head>
    <meta charset="utf-8">
    <meta http-equiv="X-UA-Compatible" content="IE=edge">

    <link rel="prefetch" href="//ajax.googleapis.com/ajax/libs/
                              jquery/1.8.2/jquery.min.js">
```

```
    <meta name="application-name" content="Python.org">
    <meta name="msapplication-tooltip" content="The official
     home of the Python Programming Language">
    <meta name="apple-mobile-web-app-title" content="Python.org">
    <meta name="apple-mobile-web-app-capable" content="yes">
    <meta name="apple-mobile-web-app-status-bar-style"
content="black">

    <meta name="viewport" content="width=device-width, initial-
scale=1.0">
    <meta name="HandheldFriendly" content="True">
    <meta name="format-detection" content="telephone=no">
    <meta http-equiv="cleartype" content="on">

....
```

The following is the screenshot of the program:

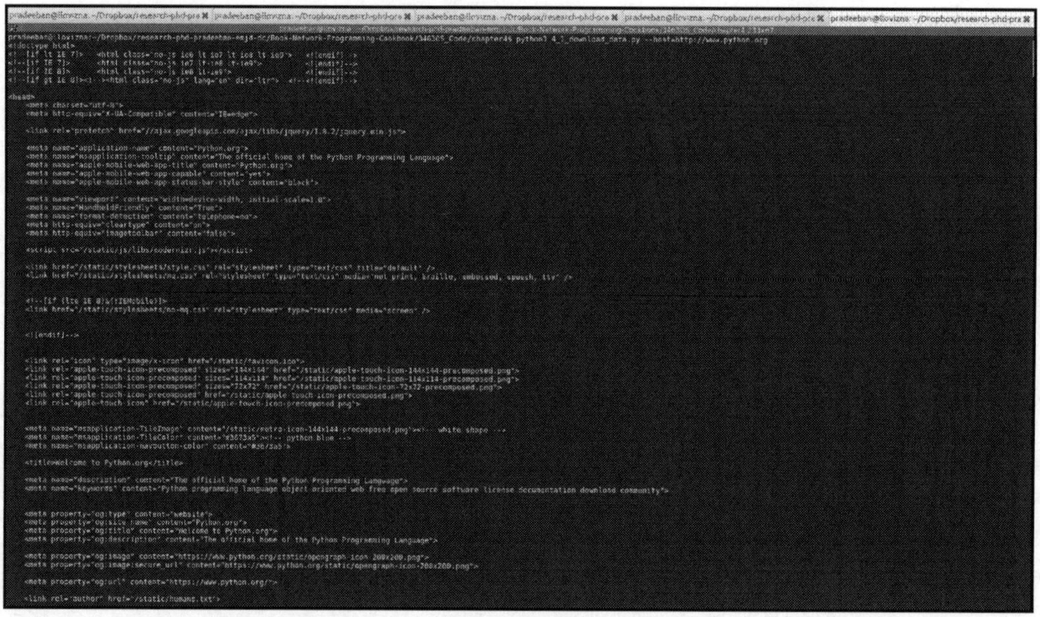

Download Data from an HTTP Server

This recipe will also work for any page in the sites. Not just the home page:

```
$ python 14_1_download_data.py --
host=https://www.python.org/downloads/
<!doctype html>
<!--[if lt IE 7]>   <html class="no-js ie6 lt-ie7 lt-ie8 lt-ie9">
```

```
<![endif]-->
<!--[if IE 7]>      <html class="no-js ie7 lt-ie8 lt-ie9">
<![endif]-->
<!--[if IE 8]>      <html class="no-js ie8 lt-ie9">
<![endif]-->
<!--[if gt IE 8]><!--><html class="no-js" lang="en" dir="ltr">  <!--
<![endif]-->

...
    <title>Download Python | Python.org</title>
....
```

If you run this recipe with an invalid path, it will show the following server response:

```
$ python 14_1_download_data.py --
host=https://www.python.org/downloads222/
Traceback (most recent call last):
File "14_1_download_data.py", line 39, in <module>
print (client.fetch())
File "14_1_download_data.py", line 24, in fetch
response = urllib.request.urlopen(self.host)
File "/usr/lib/python3.5/urllib/request.py", line 163, in urlopen
return opener.open(url, data, timeout)
File "/usr/lib/python3.5/urllib/request.py", line 472, in open
response = meth(req, response)
File "/usr/lib/python3.5/urllib/request.py", line 582, in
http_response
'http', request, response, code, msg, hdrs)
File "/usr/lib/python3.5/urllib/request.py", line 510, in error
return self._call_chain(*args)
File "/usr/lib/python3.5/urllib/request.py", line 444, in _call_chain
result = func(*args)
File "/usr/lib/python3.5/urllib/request.py", line 590, in
http_error_default
raise HTTPError(req.full_url, code, msg, hdrs, fp)
urllib.error.HTTPError: HTTP Error 404: OK
```

How it works...

This recipe defines an `urllib.request` module that fetches data from the remote host. `urllib.request.urlopen()` opens the given web page and fetches it. Since it comes with Python 3, it does not support Python 2. However, you may install and use `urllib` for Python 2 as we elaborated before.

Serving HTTP requests from your machine

You would like to create your own web server. Your web server should handle client requests and send a simple hello message.

How to do it...

Python ships with a very simple web server that can be launched from the command line as follows:

```
$ python -m SimpleHTTPServer 8080
```

This will launch an HTTP web server on port `8080`. You can access this web server from your browser by typing `http://localhost:8080`. This will show the contents of the current directory from where you run the preceding command. If there is any web server index file, for example, `index.html`, inside that directory, your browser will show the contents of `index.html`. However, if you like to have full control over your web server, you need to launch your customized HTTP server.

Listing 4.2 gives the following code for the custom HTTP web server:

```
#!/usr/bin/env python
# Python Network Programming Cookbook -- Chapter - 4
# This program requires Python 3.5.2 or any later version
# It may run on any other version with/without modifications.
#
# Follow the comments inline to make it run on Python 2.7.x.


import argparse
import sys

from http.server import BaseHTTPRequestHandler, HTTPServer
# Comment out the above line and uncomment the below for Python 2.7.x.
#from BaseHTTPServer import BaseHTTPRequestHandler, HTTPServer

DEFAULT_HOST = '127.0.0.1'
DEFAULT_PORT = 8800


class RequestHandler(BaseHTTPRequestHandler):
    """ Custom request handler"""
```

```
    def do_GET(self):
        """ Handler for the GET requests """
        self.send_response(200)
        self.send_header('Content-type','text/html')
        self.end_headers()
        # Send the message to browser
        self.wfile.write("Hello from server!")
        return

class CustomHTTPServer(HTTPServer):
    "A custom HTTP server"
    def __init__(self, host, port):
        server_address = (host, port)
        HTTPServer.__init__(self, server_address, RequestHandler)

def run_server(port):
    try:
        server= CustomHTTPServer(DEFAULT_HOST, port)
        print ("Custom HTTP server started on port: %s" % port)
        server.serve_forever()
    except Exception as err:
        print ("Error:%s" %err)
    except KeyboardInterrupt:
        print ("Server interrupted and is shutting down...")
        server.socket.close()


if __name__ == "__main__":
    parser = argparse.ArgumentParser(description='Simple HTTP Server
              Example')
    parser.add_argument('--port', action="store",
     dest="port", type=int, default=DEFAULT_PORT)
    given_args = parser.parse_args()
    port = given_args.port
    run_server(port)
```

The following screenshot shows a simple HTTP server:

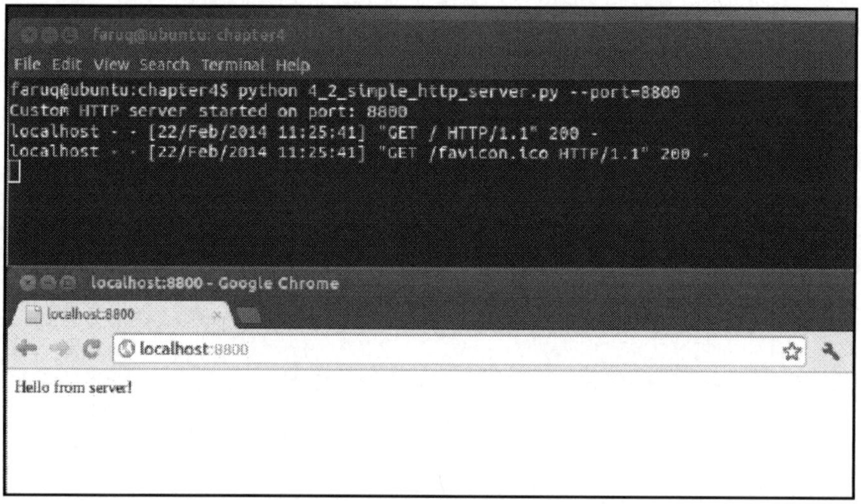

Serving HTTP Request from the Machine

If you run this web server and access the URL from a browser, this will send the one line text **Hello from server!** to the browser, as follows:

```
$ python 14_2_simple_http_server.py --port=8800
Custom HTTP server started on port: 8800
localhost - - [18/Apr/2013 13:39:33] "GET / HTTP/1.1" 200 -
localhost - - [18/Apr/2013 13:39:33] "GET /favicon.ico HTTP/1.1" 200
```

How it works...

In this recipe, we created the `CustomHTTPServer` class inherited from the `HTTPServer` class. In the constructor method, the `CustomHTTPServer` class sets up the server address and port received as a user input. In the constructor, our web server's `RequestHandler` class has been set up. Every time a client is connected, the server handles the request according to this class.

The `RequestHandler` defines the action to handle the client's `GET` request. It sends an HTTP `header` (code `200`) with a success message Hello from server! using the `write()` method.

Extracting cookie information after visiting a website

Many websites use cookies to store their various information on to your local disk. You would like to see this cookie information and perhaps log in to that website automatically using cookies.

How to do it...

Let us try to pretend to log in to a popular code-sharing website, `https://bitbucket.org/`. We would like to submit the login information on the login page, `https://bitbucket.org/account/signin/?next=/`. The following screenshot shows the login page:

Log in to BitBucket

So, we note down the form element IDs and decide which fake values should be submitted. We access this page the first time, and the next time, we access the home page to observe what cookies have been set up.

Listing 4.3 explains extracting cookie information as follows:

```
#!/usr/bin/env python
# Python Network Programming Cookbook -- Chapter - 4
# This program requires Python 3.5.2 or any later version
```

```
# It may run on any other version with/without modifications.
#
# Follow the comments inline to make it run on Python 2.7.x.

import http.cookiejar
# Comment out the above line and uncomment the below for Python 2.7.x.
#import cookielib

import urllib

# Uncomment the below line for Python 2.7.x.
#import urllib2


ID_USERNAME = 'id_username'
ID_PASSWORD = 'id_password'
USERNAME = 'you@email.com'
PASSWORD = 'mypassword'
LOGIN_URL = 'https://bitbucket.org/account/signin/?next=/'
NORMAL_URL = 'https://bitbucket.org/'

def extract_cookie_info():
    """ Fake login to a site with cookie"""
    # setup cookie jar

    cj = http.cookiejar.CookieJar()
    # Comment out the above line and uncomment the below for Python
2.7.x.
    #cj = cookielib.CookieJar()

    login_data = urllib.parse.urlencode({ID_USERNAME : USERNAME,
                  ID_PASSWORD : PASSWORD}).encode("utf-8")
    # Comment out the above line and uncomment the below for Python
2.7.x.
    #login_data = urllib.urlencode({ID_USERNAME : USERNAME,
                                   ID_PASSWORD : PASSWORD})

    # create url opener

    opener = urllib.request.
    build_opener(urllib.request.HTTPCookieProcessor(cj))
    # Comment out the above line and uncomment the below for Python
2.7.x.
    #opener = urllib2.build_opener(urllib2.HTTPCookieProcessor(cj))

    resp = opener.open(LOGIN_URL, login_data)

    # send login info
```

```
    for cookie in cj:
        print ("----First time cookie: %s --> %s"
         %(cookie.name, cookie.value))
    print ("Headers: %s" %resp.headers)

    # now access without any login info
    resp = opener.open(NORMAL_URL)
    for cookie in cj:
        print ("++++Second time cookie: %s --> %s"
                %(cookie.name, cookie.value))
    print ("Headers: %s" %resp.headers)

if __name__ == '__main__':
    extract_cookie_info()
```

Running this recipe results in the following output:

```
$ python 14_3_extract_cookie_information.py
----First time cookie: bb_session --> aed58dde1228571bf60466581790566d
Headers: Server: nginx/1.2.4
Date: Sun, 05 May 2013 15:13:56 GMT
Content-Type: text/html; charset=utf-8
Content-Length: 21167
Connection: close
X-Served-By: bitbucket04
Content-Language: en
X-Static-Version: c67fb01467cf
Expires: Sun, 05 May 2013 15:13:56 GMT
Vary: Accept-Language, Cookie
Last-Modified: Sun, 05 May 2013 15:13:56 GMT
X-Version: 14f9c66ad9db
ETag: "3ba81d9eb350c295a453b5ab6e88935e"
X-Request-Count: 310
Cache-Control: max-age=0
Set-Cookie: bb_session=aed58dde1228571bf60466581790566d; expires=Sun,
19-May-2013 15:13:56 GMT; httponly; Max-Age=1209600; Path=/; secure
Strict-Transport-Security: max-age=2592000
X-Content-Type-Options: nosniff
++++Second time cookie: bb_session -->
aed58dde1228571bf60466581790566d
Headers: Server: nginx/1.2.4
Date: Sun, 05 May 2013 15:13:57 GMT
Content-Type: text/html; charset=utf-8
Content-Length: 36787
Connection: close
X-Served-By: bitbucket02
Content-Language: en
X-Static-Version: c67fb01467cf
```

```
Vary: Accept-Language, Cookie
X-Version: 14f9c66ad9db
X-Request-Count: 97
Strict-Transport-Security: max-age=2592000
X-Content-Type-Options: nosniff
```

How it works...

We have used Python's `cookielib` and set up a `CookieJar` and `cj`. The login data has been encoded using `urllib.urlencode`. `urllib2` has a `build_opener()` method, which takes the predefined `CookieJar` with an instance of `HTTPCookieProcessor()` and returns a URL `opener`. We call this `opener` twice: once for the login page and once for the home page of the website. It seems that only one cookie, `bb_session`, was set with the `set-cookie` directive present in the page header. More information about `cookielib` can be found on the official Python documentation site at `http://docs.python.org/2/library/cookielib.html`. `Cookielib` has been replaced by `http.cookiejar` in Python 3. You may find more information on this at `https://docs.python.org/3/library/http.cookiejar.html`.

Submitting web forms

During web browsing, we submit web forms many times in a day. Now, you would like do that using the Python code.

Getting ready

This recipe uses a third-party Python module called `requests`. You can install the compatible version of this module by following the instructions from `http://docs.python-requests.org/en/latest/user/install/`. For example, you can use `pip` to install requests from the command line as follows:

```
$ pip install requests
```

How to do it...

Let us submit some fake data to register with `https://twitter.com/`. Each form submission has two methods: `GET` and `POST`. The less sensitive data, for example, search queries, are usually submitted by `GET` and the more sensitive data is sent via the `POST` method. Let us try submitting data with both of them.

Listing 4.4 explains the submit web forms, as follows:

```
#!/usr/bin/env python
# Python Network Programming Cookbook -- Chapter - 4
# This program requires Python 3.5.2 or any later version
# It may run on any other version with/without modifications.
#
# Follow the comments inline to make it run on Python 2.7.x.


import requests
import urllib

# Uncomment the below line for Python 2.7.x.
#import urllib2

ID_USERNAME = 'signup-user-name'
ID_EMAIL = 'signup-user-email'
ID_PASSWORD = 'signup-user-password'
USERNAME = 'username'
EMAIL = 'you@email.com'
PASSWORD = 'yourpassword'
SIGNUP_URL = 'https://twitter.com/account/create'


def submit_form():
    """Submit a form"""
    payload = {ID_USERNAME : USERNAME,
               ID_EMAIL    :  EMAIL,
               ID_PASSWORD : PASSWORD,}
    # make a get request
    resp = requests.get(SIGNUP_URL)
    print ("Response to GET request: %s" %resp.content)
    # send POST request
    resp = requests.post(SIGNUP_URL, payload)
    print ("Headers from a POST request response: %s" %resp.headers)


if __name__ == '__main__':
    submit_form()
```

If you run this script, you will see the following output:

```
$ python 14_4_submit_web_form.py
Response to GET request: <?xml version="1.0" encoding="UTF-8"?>
    <hash>
      <error>This method requires a POST.</error>
      <request>/account/create</request>
    </hash>
Headers from a POST request response: {'status': '200 OK', 'content-
length': '21064', 'set-cookie': '_twitter_sess=BAh7CD--
d2865d40d1365eeb2175559dc5e6b99f64ea39ff; domain=.twitter.com;
path=/; HttpOnly', 'expires': 'Tue, 31 Mar 1981 05:00:00 GMT',
'vary': 'Accept-Encoding', 'last-modified': 'Sun, 05 May 2013
15:59:27 GMT', 'pragma': 'no-cache', 'date': 'Sun, 05 May 2013
15:59:27 GMT', 'x-xss-protection': '1; mode=block', 'x-transaction':
'a4b425eda23b5312', 'content-encoding': 'gzip', 'strict-transport-
security': 'max-age=631138519', 'server': 'tfe', 'x-mid':
'f7cde9a3f3d111310427116adc90bf3e8c95e868', 'x-runtime': '0.09969',
'etag': '"7af6f92a7f7b4d37a6454caa6094071d"', 'cache-control': 'no-
cache, no-store, must-revalidate, pre-check=0, post-check=0', 'x-
frame-options': 'SAMEORIGIN', 'content-type': 'text/html;
charset=utf-8'}
```

How it works...

This recipe uses a third-party module, `requests`. It has convenient wrapper methods, `get()` and `post()`, which do the URL encoding of data and submit forms properly.

In this recipe, we created a data payload with a `USERNAME`, `PASSWORD`, and `EMAIL` for creating the Twitter account. When we first submit the form with the `GET` method, the Twitter website returns an error saying that the page only supports `POST`. After we submit the data with `POST`, the page processes it. We can confirm this from the header data.

Sending web requests through a proxy server

You would like to browse web pages through a proxy. If you have configured your browser with a proxy server and that works, you can try this recipe. Otherwise, you can use any of the public proxy servers available on the internet.

Getting ready

You need to have access to a proxy server. You can find a free proxy server by searching on Google or on any other search engine. Here, for the sake of demonstration, we have used `165.24.10.8`.

How to do it...

Let us send our HTTP request through a public domain proxy server.

Listing 4.5 explains proxying web requests across a proxy server as follows:

```
#!/usr/bin/env python
# Python Network Programming Cookbook -- Chapter - 4
# This program requires Python 3.5.2 or any later version
# It may run on any other version with/without modifications.
#
# Follow the comments inline to make it run on Python 2.7.x.

import urllib.request, urllib.parse, urllib.error
# Comment out the above line and uncomment the below for Python 2.7.x.
#import urllib

URL = 'https://www.github.com'
PROXY_ADDRESS = "165.24.10.8:8080" # By Googling free proxy server


if __name__ == '__main__':

    proxy = urllib.request.ProxyHandler({"http" : PROXY_ADDRESS})
    opener = urllib.request.build_opener(proxy)
    urllib.request.install_opener(opener)
    resp = urllib.request.urlopen(URL)
    # Comment out the above 4 lines and uncomment the below
       for Python 2.7.x.
    #resp = urllib.urlopen(URL, proxies = {"http" : PROXY_ADDRESS})

    print ("Proxy server returns response headers: %s " %resp.headers)
```

If you run this script, it will show the following output:

```
$ python 14_5_proxy_web_request.py
Proxy server returns response headers: Server: GitHub.com
Date: Thu, 22 Jun 2017 14:26:52 GMT
Content-Type: text/html; charset=utf-8
Transfer-Encoding: chunked
```

```
Connection: close
Status: 200 OK
Cache-Control: no-cache
Vary: X-PJAX
X-UA-Compatible: IE=Edge,chrome=1
Set-Cookie: logged_in=no; domain=.github.com; path=/; expires=Mon, 22
Jun 2037 14:26:52 -0000; secure; HttpOnly
Set-Cookie:
_gh_sess=eyJzZXNzaW9uX2lkIjoiNzNiODUwNjg1M2M1ZWQ3NjQxZmE2ODI5NTY5Y2UxN
mUiLCJsYXN0X3JlYWRfZnJvbV9yZXBsaWNhcyI6MTQ5ODE0MTYxMjA2NCwiX2NzcmZfdG9
rZW4iOiJmdlM1ME5oUGUyUU1hS0pVQ29EZnlTL1Bab0pZOHM1ZlpBT2JoRUhYL1NRPSJ9-
-9db8c2d5bd3e75a1ec5250192094de38937398f8; path=/; secure; HttpOnly
X-Request-Id: 88704a9ed7378c7d930cdff660739693
X-Runtime: 0.033159
Content-Security-Policy: default-src 'none'; base-uri 'self'; block-
all-mixed-content; child-src render.githubusercontent.com; connect-src
'self' uploads.github.com status.github.com collector.githubapp.com
api.github.com www.google-analytics.com github-cloud.s3.amazonaws.com
github-production-repository-file-5c1aeb.s3.amazonaws.com github-
production-upload-manifest-file-7fdce7.s3.amazonaws.com github-
production-user-asset-6210df.s3.amazonaws.com wss://live.github.com;
font-src assets-cdn.github.com; form-action 'self' github.com
gist.github.com; frame-ancestors 'none'; img-src 'self' data: assets-
cdn.github.com identicons.github.com collector.githubapp.com github-
cloud.s3.amazonaws.com *.githubusercontent.com; media-src 'none';
script-src assets-cdn.github.com; style-src 'unsafe-inline' assets-
cdn.github.com
Strict-Transport-Security: max-age=31536000; includeSubdomains;
preload
Public-Key-Pins: max-age=5184000; pin-
sha256="WoiWRyIOVNa9ihaBciRSC7XHjliYS9VwUGOIud4PB18="; pin-
sha256="RRM1dGqnDFsCJXBTHky16vi1obOlCgFFn/yOhI/y+ho="; pin-
sha256="k2v657xBsOVe1PQRwOsHsw3bsGT2VzIqz5K+59sNQws="; pin-
sha256="K87oWBWM9UZfyddvDfoxL+8lpNyoUB2ptGtn0fv6G2Q="; pin-
sha256="IQBnNBEiFuhj+8x6X8XLgh01V9Ic5/V3IRQLNFFc7v4="; pin-
sha256="iie1VXtL7HzAMF+/PVPR9xzT80kQxdZeJ+zduCB3uj0="; pin-
sha256="LvRiGEjRqfzurezaWuj8Wie2gyHMrW5Q06LspMnox7A=";
includeSubDomains
X-Content-Type-Options: nosniff
X-Frame-Options: deny
X-XSS-Protection: 1; mode=block
X-Runtime-rack: 0.036536
Vary: Accept-Encoding
X-Served-By: 29885c8097c6d503a86029451b2e021c
X-GitHub-Request-Id: 9144:282AF:FE7E37:17F7695:594BD3AB
```

How it works...

This is a short recipe where we access the social code-sharing site, `https://www.github.com`, with a public proxy server found on Google search. The proxy address argument has been passed to the `urlopen()` method of `urllib`. We print the HTTP `header` of the response to show that the proxy settings work here.

Checking whether a web page exists with the HEAD request

You would like to check the existence of a web page without downloading the HTML content. This means that we need to send a get `HEAD` request with a browser client. According to Wikipedia, the `HEAD` request asks for the response identical to the one that would correspond to a `GET` request, but without the response body. This is useful for retrieving meta-information written in response headers, without having to transport the entire content.

How to do it...

We would like to send a `HEAD` request to `http://www.python.org`. This will not download the content of the home page, rather it checks whether the server returns one of the valid responses, for example, `OK`, `FOUND`, `MOVED PERMANENTLY`, and so on.

Listing 4.6 explains checking a web page with the `HEAD` request as follows:

```
#!/usr/bin/env python
# Python Network Programming Cookbook -- Chapter - 4
# This program requires Python 3.5.2 or any later version
# It may run on any other version with/without modifications.
#
# Follow the comments inline to make it run on Python 2.7.x.

import argparse

import http.client
# Comment out the above line and uncomment the below for Python 2.7.x.
#import httplib

import urllib.parse
# Comment out the above line and uncomment the below for Python 2.7.x.
```

```
#import urlparse

import re
import urllib.request, urllib.error
# Comment out the above line and uncomment the below for Python 2.7.x.
#import urllib

DEFAULT_URL = 'http://www.python.org'

HTTP_GOOD_CODES =  [http.client.OK, http.client.FOUND,
http.client.MOVED_PERMANENTLY]
# Comment out the above line and uncomment the below for Python 2.7.x.
#HTTP_GOOD_CODES =  [httplib.OK, httplib.FOUND,
httplib.MOVED_PERMANENTLY]

def get_server_status_code(url):
    """
    Download just the header of a URL and
    return the server's status code.
    """
    host, path = urllib.parse.urlparse(url)[1:3]
    # Comment out the above line and uncomment the below for Python
2.7.x.
    #host, path = urlparse.urlparse(url)[1:3]
    try:
        conn = http.client.HTTPConnection(host)
        # Comment out the above line and uncomment the below for
           Python 2.7.x.
        #conn = httplib.HTTPConnection(host)

        conn.request('HEAD', path)
        return conn.getresponse().status

    except Exception as e:
        print ("Server: %s status is: %s " %(url, e))
        # Comment out the above line and uncomment the below for
           Python 2.7.x.
        #except StandardError:
        return None
if __name__ == '__main__':
    parser = argparse.ArgumentParser(description='Example HEAD
Request')
    parser.add_argument('--url', action="store", dest="url",
                         default=DEFAULT_URL)
    given_args = parser.parse_args()
    url = given_args.url
    if get_server_status_code(url) in HTTP_GOOD_CODES:
        print ("Server: %s status is OK: %s "
```

```
                %(url, get_server_status_code(url)))
    else:
        print ("Server: %s status is NOT OK: %s"
                %(url, get_server_status_code(url)))
```

Executing this script shows the success or error if the page is found by the `HEAD` request as follows:

```
$ python 14_6_checking_webpage_with_HEAD_request.py
Server: http://www.python.org status is OK.
$ python 14_6_checking_webpage_with_HEAD_request.py --
url=http://www.cnn.com
Server: http://www.cnn.com status is OK.
$ python3 14_6_checking_webpage_with_HEAD_request.py --
url=http://www.zytho.org
Server: http://www.zytho.org status is: [Errno -2] Name or service not
known
Server: http://www.zytho.org status is: [Errno -2] Name or service not
known
Server: http://www.zytho.org status is NOT OK: None
```

How it works...

We used the `HTTPConnection()` method of `httplib`, which can make a `HEAD` request to a server. We can specify the path if necessary. Here, the `HTTPConnection()` method checks the home page or path of `http://www.python.org`. However, if the URL is not correct, it can't find the return response inside the accepted list of return codes.

Spoofing Mozilla Firefox in your client code

From your Python code, you would like to pretend to the web server that you are browsing from Mozilla Firefox.

How to do it...

You can send the custom `user-agent` values in the HTTP request `header`.

Listing 4.7 explains spoofing Mozilla Firefox in your client code as follows:

```
#!/usr/bin/env python
# Python Network Programming Cookbook -- Chapter - 4
# This program requires Python 3.5.2 or any later version
# It may run on any other version with/without modifications.
#
# Follow the comments inline to make it run on Python 2.7.x.

import urllib.request, urllib.error, urllib.parse
# Comment out the above line and uncomment the below for Python 2.7.x.
#import urllib2

BROWSER = 'Mozilla/5.0 (Windows NT 5.1; rv:20.0) Gecko/20100101
Firefox/20.0'
URL = 'http://www.python.org'

def spoof_firefox():

    opener = urllib.request.build_opener()
    # Comment out the above line and uncomment the below for Python
2.7.x.
    #opener = urllib2.build_opener()

    opener.addheaders = [('User-agent', BROWSER)]
    result = opener.open(URL)
    print ("Response headers:")

    for header in  result.headers:
    # Comment out the above line and uncomment the below for Python
2.7.x.
    #for header in  result.headers.headers:
        print ("%s: %s" %(header, result.headers.get(header)))
        # Comment out the above line and uncomment the below for
           Python 2.7.x.
        #print (header)
if __name__ == '__main__':
    spoof_firefox()
```

If you execute this script, you will see the following output:

```
$ python 14_7_spoof_mozilla_firefox_in_client_code.py
Response headers:
Server: nginx
Content-Type: text/html; charset=utf-8
X-Frame-Options: SAMEORIGIN
X-Clacks-Overhead: GNU Terry Pratchett
Content-Length: 47755
Accept-Ranges: bytes
Date: Thu, 22 Jun 2017 15:38:39 GMT
Via: 1.1 varnish
Age: 834
Connection: close
X-Served-By: cache-ams4150-AMS
X-Cache: HIT
X-Cache-Hits: 1
X-Timer: S1498145920.740508,VS0,VE2
Vary: Cookie
Strict-Transport-Security: max-age=63072000; includeSubDomains
```

How it works...

We used the `build_opener()` method of `urllib2` to create our custom browser whose `user-agent` string has been set up as `Mozilla/5.0 (Windows NT 5.1; rv:20.0) Gecko/20100101 Firefox/20.0)`.

Saving bandwidth in web requests with the HTTP compression

You would like to give your web server users better performance in downloading web pages. By compressing HTTP data, you can speed up the serving of web contents.

How to do it...

Let us create a web server that serves contents after compressing it to the `gzip` format.

Listing 4.8 explains the HTTP compression as follows:

```
#!/usr/bin/env python
# Python Network Programming Cookbook -- Chapter - 4
# This program requires Python 3.5.2 or any later version
# It may run on any other version with/without modifications.
#
# Follow the comments inline to make it run on Python 2.7.x.

import argparse
import string
import os
import sys
import gzip

import io
# Comment out the above line and uncomment the below for Python 2.7.x.
#import cStringIO

from http.server import BaseHTTPRequestHandler, HTTPServer
# Comment out the above line and uncomment the below for Python 2.7.x.
#from BaseHTTPServer import BaseHTTPRequestHandler, HTTPServer

DEFAULT_HOST = '127.0.0.1'
DEFAULT_PORT = 8800

HTML_CONTENT = b"""<html><body><h1>Compressed Hello
World!</h1></body></html>"""
# Comment out the above line and uncomment the below for Python 2.7.x.
#HTML_CONTENT = b"""<html><body><h1>Compressed Hello
World!</h1></body></html>"""

class RequestHandler(BaseHTTPRequestHandler):
    """ Custom request handler"""
    def do_GET(self):
        """ Handler for the GET requests """
        self.send_response(200)
        self.send_header('Content-type','text/html')
        self.send_header('Content-Encoding','gzip')
        zbuf = self.compress_buffer(HTML_CONTENT)
        sys.stdout.write("Content-Encoding: gzip\r\n")
        self.send_header('Content-Length',len(zbuf))
        self.end_headers()
```

```
        # Send the message to browser
        zbuf = self.compress_buffer(HTML_CONTENT)
        sys.stdout.write("Content-Encoding: gzip\r\n")
        sys.stdout.write("Content-Length: %d\r\n" % (len(zbuf)))
        sys.stdout.write("\r\n")

        self.wfile.write(zbuf)

        return
    def compress_buffer(self, buf):

        zbuf = io.BytesIO()
        # Comment out the above line and uncomment the below for
           Python 2.7.x.
        #zbuf = cStringIO.StringIO()

        zfile = gzip.GzipFile(mode = 'wb',
        fileobj = zbuf, compresslevel = 6)
        zfile.write(buf)
        zfile.close()
        return zbuf.getvalue()

if __name__ == '__main__':
    parser = argparse.ArgumentParser(description='Simple HTTP
     Server Example')
    parser.add_argument('--port', action="store",
     dest="port", type=int, default=DEFAULT_PORT)
    given_args = parser.parse_args()
    port = given_args.port
    server_address =  (DEFAULT_HOST, port)
    server = HTTPServer(server_address, RequestHandler)
    server.serve_forever()
```

You can execute this script and see the **Compressed Hello World!** text (as a result of the HTTP compression) on your browser screen when accessing `http://localhost:8800` as follows:

```
$ python 14_8_http_compression.py
localhost - - [22/Feb/2014 12:01:26] "GET / HTTP/1.1" 200 -
Content-Encoding: gzip
Content-Encoding: gzip
Content-Length: 71
localhost - - [22/Feb/2014 12:01:26] "GET /favicon.ico HTTP/1.1" 200 -
Content-Encoding: gzip
Content-Encoding: gzip
Content-Length: 71
```

The following screenshot illustrates serving compressed content by a web server:

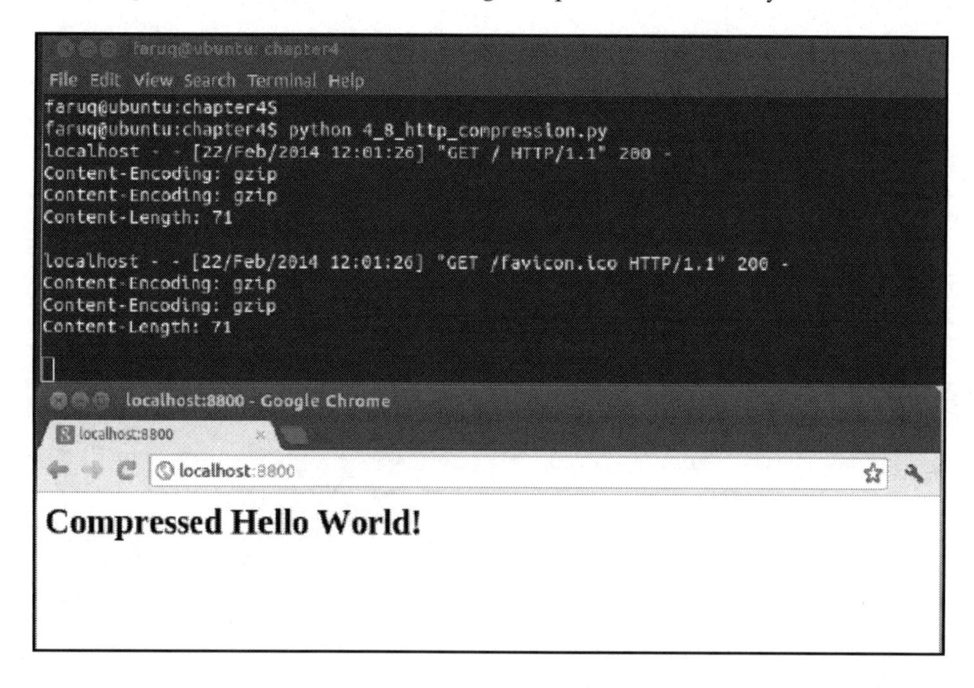

Compressed Content in a Web Server

How it works...

We created a web server by instantiating the `HTTPServer` class from the `BaseHTTPServer` module. We attached a custom request handler to this server instance, which compresses every client response using a `compress_buffer()` method. A predefined HTML content has been supplied to the clients.

Writing an HTTP fail-over client with resume and partial downloading

You would like to create a fail-over client that will resume downloading a file if it fails for any reason in the first instance.

How to do it...

Let us download the Python 2.7 code from `http://www.python.org`. A `resume_download()` file will resume any unfinished download of that file.

Listing 4.9 explains resume downloading as follows:

```
#!/usr/bin/env python
# Python Network Programming Cookbook -- Chapter - 4
# This program requires Python 3.5.2 or any later version
# It may run on any other version with/without modifications.
#
# Follow the comments inline to make it run on Python 2.7.x.

import urllib.request, urllib.parse, urllib.error
# Comment out the above line and uncomment the below for Python 2.7.x.
#import urllib

import os

TARGET_URL = 'http://python.org/ftp/python/2.7.4/'
TARGET_FILE = 'Python-2.7.4.tgz'

class CustomURLOpener(urllib.request.FancyURLopener):
# Comment out the above line and uncomment the below for Python 2.7.x.
#class CustomURLOpener(urllib.FancyURLopener):
    """Override FancyURLopener to skip error 206 (when a
       partial file is being sent)
    """
    def http_error_206(self, url, fp, errcode, errmsg, headers,
data=None):
        pass

def resume_download():
    file_exists = False
    CustomURLClass = CustomURLOpener()
    if os.path.exists(TARGET_FILE):
          out_file = open(TARGET_FILE,"ab")
          file_exists = os.path.getsize(TARGET_FILE)
          #If the file exists, then only download the unfinished part
          CustomURLClass.addheader("range","bytes=%s-" % (file_exists))
    else:
          out_file = open(TARGET_FILE,"wb")

    web_page = CustomURLClass.open(TARGET_URL + TARGET_FILE)

    #Check if last download was OK
    if int(web_page.headers['Content-Length']) == file_exists:
```

```
            loop = 0
            print ("File already downloaded!")

    byte_count = 0
    while True:
            data = web_page.read(8192)
            if not data:
                  break
            out_file.write(data)
            byte_count = byte_count + len(data)

    web_page.close()
    out_file.close()

    for k,v in list(web_page.headers.items()):
     # Comment out the above line and uncomment the below for Python
2.7.x.
    #for k,v in web_page.headers.items():
            print (k, "=",v)
    print ("File copied", byte_count, "bytes from", web_page.url)

if __name__ == '__main__':
    resume_download()
```

Executing this script will result in the following output:

```
$   python 14_9_http_fail_over_client.py
content-length = 14489063
content-encoding = x-gzip
accept-ranges = bytes
connection = close
server = Apache/2.2.16 (Debian)
last-modified = Sat, 06 Apr 2013 14:16:10 GMT
content-range = bytes 0-14489062/14489063
etag = "1748016-dd15e7-4d9b1d8685e80"
date = Tue, 07 May 2013 12:51:31 GMT
content-type = application/x-tar
File copied 14489063 bytes from
http://python.org/ftp/python/2.7.4/Python-2.7.4.tgz
```

How it works...

In this recipe, we created a `CustomURLOpener` class inheriting from the `FancyURLopener` method of `urllib`, but `http_error_206()` is overridden where partial content is downloaded. So, our method checks the existence of the target file and if it is not present, it tries to download with the custom URL opener class.

Writing a simple HTTPS server code with Python and OpenSSL

You need a secure web server code written in Python. You already have your SSL keys and certificate files ready with you.

Getting ready

You need to install the third-party Python module, `pyOpenSSL`. This can be grabbed from PyPI (`https://pypi.python.org/pypi/pyOpenSSL`). Both on Windows and Linux hosts, you may need to install some additional packages, which are documented at `http://pythonhosted.org//pyOpenSSL/`.

How to do it...

After placing a certificate file on the current working folder, we can create a web server that makes use of this certificate to serve encrypted content to the clients.

Listing 4.10 explains the code for a secure HTTP server as follows:

```
#!/usr/bin/env python
# Python Network Programming Cookbook -- Chapter - 4
# This program requires Python 3.5.2 or any later version
# It may run on any other version with/without modifications.
#
# Follow the comments inline to make it run on Python 2.7.x.
# Requires pyOpenSSL and SSL packages installed

import socket, os
from OpenSSL import SSL

from socketserver import BaseServer
from http.server import HTTPServer
from http.server import SimpleHTTPRequestHandler
# Comment out the above 3 lines and uncomment the below 3 lines for
Python 2.7.x.
#from SocketServer import BaseServer
#from BaseHTTPServer import HTTPServer
#from SimpleHTTPServer import SimpleHTTPRequestHandler


class SecureHTTPServer(HTTPServer):
```

```
    def __init__(self, server_address, HandlerClass):
        BaseServer.__init__(self, server_address, HandlerClass)
        ctx = SSL.Context(SSL.SSLv23_METHOD)
        fpem = 'server.pem' # location of the server private
              key and the server certificate
        ctx.use_privatekey_file (fpem)
        ctx.use_certificate_file(fpem)
        self.socket = SSL.Connection(ctx,
        socket.socket(self.address_family, self.socket_type))
        self.server_bind()
        self.server_activate()


class SecureHTTPRequestHandler(SimpleHTTPRequestHandler):
    def setup(self):
        self.connection = self.request
        self.rfile = socket._fileobject(self.request, "rb",
self.rbufsize)
        self.wfile = socket._fileobject(self.request, "wb",
self.wbufsize)


def run_server(HandlerClass = SecureHTTPRequestHandler,
         ServerClass = SecureHTTPServer):
    server_address = ('', 4443) # port needs to be accessible by user
    server = ServerClass(server_address, HandlerClass)
    running_address = server.socket.getsockname()
    print ("Serving HTTPS Server on %s:%s ..." %(running_address[0],
     running_address[1]))
    server.serve_forever()


if __name__ == '__main__':
    run_server()
```

If you execute this script, it will result in the following output:

```
$ python 14_10_https_server.py
Serving HTTPS Server on 0.0.0.0:4443 ...
```

How it works...

If you notice the previous recipes that create the web server, there is not much difference in terms of the basic procedure. The main difference is in applying the SSL `Context()` method with the `SSLv23_METHOD` argument. We have created the SSL socket with the `pyOpenSSL` third-party module's `Connection()` class. This class takes this context object along with the address family and socket type.

The server's certificate file is kept in the current directory, and this has been applied with the context object. Finally, the server has been activated with the `server_activate()` method.

Building asynchronous network applications with Twisted

Twisted is an event-driven network engine written in Python. Twisted can be used to develop asynchronous and publish/subscribe based Python applications.

Getting ready

You need to install the third-party Python module, `twisted`. This can be grabbed from PyPI (`https://pypi.org/project/Twisted/`). Both on Windows and Linux hosts, you may need to install some additional packages. The installation procedure is documented at `https://twistedmatrix.com/trac/`.

Follow the following guidelines to install Twisted in your Debian/Ubuntu based Linux distributions.

Twisted suggests against installing anything into global site-package. It recommends using `virtualenv` to set up isolated publish/subscribe modules. `virtualenv` is a product aimed to create isolated execution environments for Python. While we can indeed make Twisted work by directly installing the bundles using `pip`, we respect the suggestion of Twisted, and follow their installation guidelines for this recipe. Read more on this at `https://hynek.me/articles/virtualenv-lives/`.

You may install `virtualenv` by the following, in Ubuntu:

```
$ sudo apt install virtualenv
```

Now you are ready to initialize the execution environment with Twisted, by following this command:

```
$ virtualenv try-twisted
```

The preceding command uses the current directory to set up the Python test environment under the subdirectory `try-twisted`. You may activate/initialize the environment as indicated here:

```
$ . try-twisted/bin/activate
$ sudo pip install twisted[tls]
```

Once you have installed Twisted (following the preceding instructions or otherwise), you will be able to build asynchronous network applications. To make sure you have installed Twisted successfully, you may execute the following:

```
$ twist --help
Usage: twist [options] plugin [plugin_options]
Options:
      --reactor=     The name of the reactor to use. (options:
"asyncio", "kqueue", "glib2", "win32", "iocp", "default", "cf",
"epoll", "gtk2", "poll", "gtk3", "gi", "wx", "select")
  ..
Commands:
    conch        A Conch SSH service.
    ftp          An FTP server.
    manhole      An interactive remote debugger service accessible via
telnet and ssh and providing syntax coloring and basic line editing
functionality.
    web          A general-purpose web server which can serve from a
filesystem or application resource.
```

How to do it...

We will build a publish-subscribe paradigm based server-client system in this recipe. In this simple application, all the clients are subscribed to all the messages sent by the other clients. This can be configured further to alter the client or server behavior.

Listing 4.11 explains the code for a publish/subscribe server as follows:

```
#!/usr/bin/env python
# Python Network Programming Cookbook, Second Edition -- Chapter - 3
# This program is optimized for Python 2.7.12 and Python 3.5.2.
# It may run on any other version with/without modifications.

import argparse
```

```
from twisted.internet import reactor, protocol, endpoints
from twisted.protocols import basic

class PubProtocol(basic.LineReceiver):
    def __init__(self, factory):
        self.factory = factory

    def connectionMade(self):
        self.factory.clients.add(self)

    def connectionLost(self, reason):
        self.factory.clients.remove(self)

    def lineReceived(self, line):
        for c in self.factory.clients:
            source = u"<{}>
".format(self.transport.getHost()).encode("ascii")
            c.sendLine(source + line)

class PubFactory(protocol.Factory):
    def __init__(self):
        self.clients = set()

    def buildProtocol(self, addr):
        return PubProtocol(self)


if __name__ == '__main__':
    parser = argparse.ArgumentParser(description='Socket Server
    Example with Epoll')
    parser.add_argument('--port', action="store", dest="port",
    type=int, required=True)
    given_args = parser.parse_args()
    port = given_args.port
    endpoints.serverFromString(reactor,
     "tcp:%s" %port).listen(PubFactory())
    reactor.run()
```

Run the following script to start the server in the specified port:

```
$ python 14_11_twisted_async_server.py --port=9999
```

Now, start two or more telnet clients to the same port. Type something from one of those telnet instances, and you will be able to see the same message echoed from all the client (telnet) instances:

```
Sending telnet client:
$ telnet localhost 9999
```

```
Trying 127.0.0.1...
Connected to localhost.
Escape character is '^]'.
zszz
<IPv4Address(TCP, '127.0.0.1', 9999)> zszz
Receiving telnet client:
$ telnet localhost 9999
Trying 127.0.0.1...
Connected to localhost.
Escape character is '^]'.
<IPv4Address(TCP, '127.0.0.1', 9999)> zszz
```

The following screenshot indicates the outputs of the environment: publish/subscribe server along with four telnet clients subscribed to the messages sent to the server by other instances:

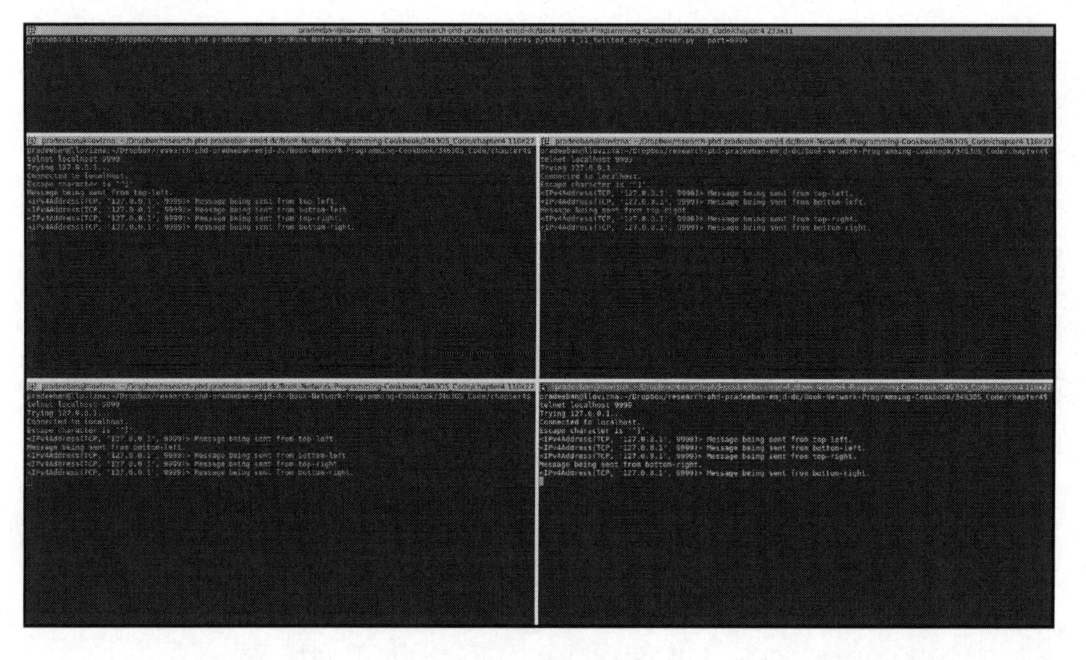

Pub/Sub Server and Telnet Clients

How it works...

Twisted is developed as an asynchronous service development bundle, developed for Python 2. Currently it has also been ported to Python 3.

The system has a server that listens to the messages published to it. The server functions as a broker in the publish/subscribe paradigm. Any of the clients that send messages to the server (in this example, a telnet client), functions as the publisher. All the other instances function as the subscriber. As all the instances in this example listen to each other, each of them function as both publisher and subscriber.

You may use various options and commands of the `twisted` module to achieve various tasks such as SSH and FTP servers effectively.

Building asynchronous network applications with Tornado

Developed in Python, Tornado is a highly-scalable framework to build asynchronous network applications. In this recipe, we will build a simple asynchronous application using Tornado.

Getting ready

Tornado is a web framework that can be considered an alternative to Twisted. In order to execute this recipe, first you need to install Tornado in your computer, which can be done by the following command in Linux environments:

```
$ sudo pip install tornado
```

How to do it...

We will build an asynchronous application to illustrate the functionality of Tornado. In this example, `AsyncHttpClient` of Tornado has been used.

Listing 4.12 explains the code for a simple network application using Tornado:

```
#!/usr/bin/env python
# Python Network Programming Cookbook, Second Edition -- Chapter - 3
# This program is optimized for Python 2.7.12 and Python 3.5.2.
# It may run on any other version with/without modifications.

import argparse
import tornado.ioloop
import tornado.httpclient


class TornadoAsync():
    def handle_request(self,response):
        if response.error:
            print ("Error:", response.error)
        else:
            print (response.body)
        tornado.ioloop.IOLoop.instance().stop()

def run_server(url):
    tornadoAsync = TornadoAsync()
    http_client = tornado.httpclient.AsyncHTTPClient()
    http_client.fetch(url, tornadoAsync.handle_request)
    tornado.ioloop.IOLoop.instance().start()

if __name__ == '__main__':
    parser = argparse.ArgumentParser(description='Async Server
Example')
    parser.add_argument('--url', action="store", dest="url",
     type=str, required=True)
    given_args = parser.parse_args()
    url = given_args.url
    run_server(url)
```

Execute the following script to start the asynchronous application to fetch any web page. We will use it to fetch `http://www.axn.com/` as follows:

```
$ python 14_12_tornado_async_server.py --url="http://www.axn.com/"
```

The following screenshot indicates the output of the execution:

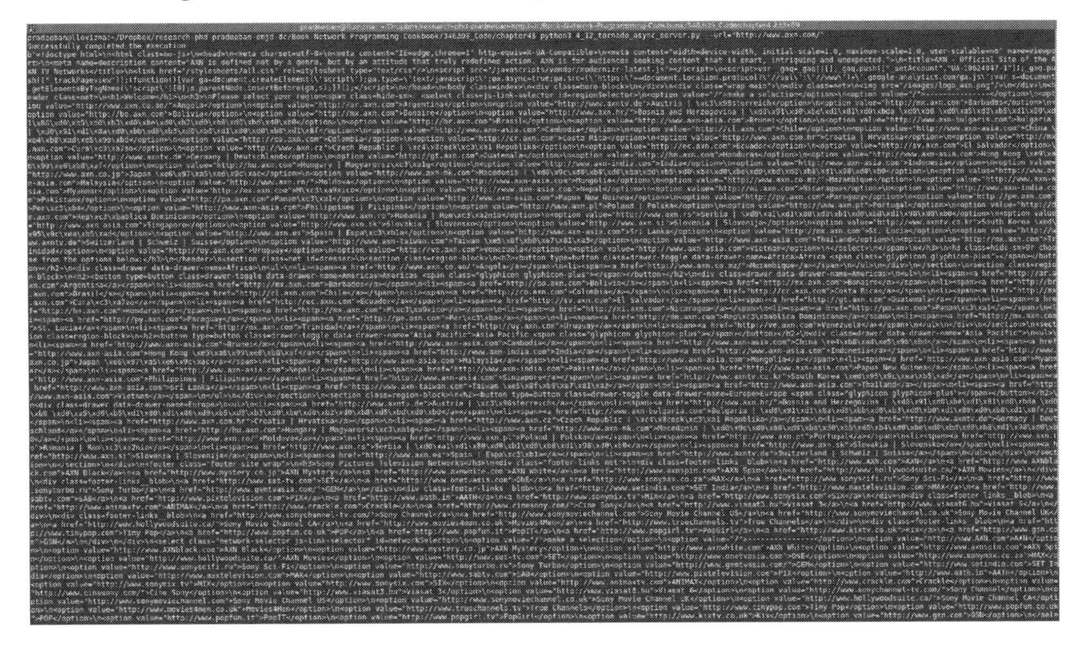

Fetching axn.com Asynchronously

How it works...

Tornado is a framework to build asynchronous network applications. It is developed for Python 2 and Python 3. In the preceding example, `http_client` is an object of the `AsyncHTTPClient` class of Tornado. As it is developed in a non-blocking manner, the execution does not wait until the application to finish fetching the website. It returns even before the method returns the output.

On the other hand, if it was developed as a synchronous blocking manner using the `HTTPClient` class of Tornado, the application will wait for the method to complete before proceeding further.

Building concurrent applications with Tornado Future

Tornado **Future** construct allows us to develop non-blocking and asynchronous calls in a more efficient way. In this recipe, we will develop a simple asynchronous application based on Tornado Future constructs.

To learn more about the concurrent and asynchronous applications in Tornado with Future, please visit: `http://www.tornadoweb.org/en/stable/concurrent.html`.

Getting ready

Tornado is a web framework. In order to execute this recipe, first you need to install Tornado in your computer, which can be done by using the following command in Linux environments:

```
$ sudo pip install tornado
```

How to do it...

We will build a concurrent application to illustrate the functionality of Tornado. In this example, the `tornado.concurrent` module of Tornado has been used.

Listing 4.13 explains the code for a simple concurrent application using Tornado:

```
#!/usr/bin/env python
# Python Network Programming Cookbook, Second Edition -- Chapter - 3
# This program is optimized for Python 3.5.2.
# It may run on any other version with/without modifications.

import argparse
import time
import datetime

import tornado.httpserver
import tornado.ioloop
import tornado.options
import tornado.web

from tornado import gen
```

```
from tornado.concurrent import return_future

class AsyncUser(object):
    @return_future
    def req1(self, callback=None):
        time.sleep(0.1)
        result = datetime.datetime.utcnow()
        callback(result)

    @return_future
    def req2(self, callback=None):
        time.sleep(0.2)
        result = datetime.datetime.utcnow()
        callback(result)



class Application(tornado.web.Application):
    def __init__(self):
        handlers = [
            (r"/", UserHandler),
        ]
        tornado.web.Application.__init__(self, handlers)


class UserHandler(tornado.web.RequestHandler):
    @gen.coroutine
    def get(self):
        user = AsyncUser()
        response1 = yield (user.req1())
        response2 = yield (user.req2())
        print ("response1,2: %s %s" %(response1, response2))
        self.finish()

def main(port):
    http_server = tornado.httpserver.HTTPServer(Application())
    print("Server listening at Port: ", port)
    http_server.listen(port)
    tornado.ioloop.IOLoop.instance().start()
```

```
if __name__ == "__main__":
    parser = argparse.ArgumentParser(description='Async Server
Example')
    parser.add_argument('--port', action="store",
     dest="port", type=int, required=True)
    given_args = parser.parse_args()
    port = given_args.port
    main(port)
```

Execute the following script to start the concurrent application:

```
$ python 14_13_tornado_conc_future.py --port=3333
```

The following screenshot indicates the output of the execution:

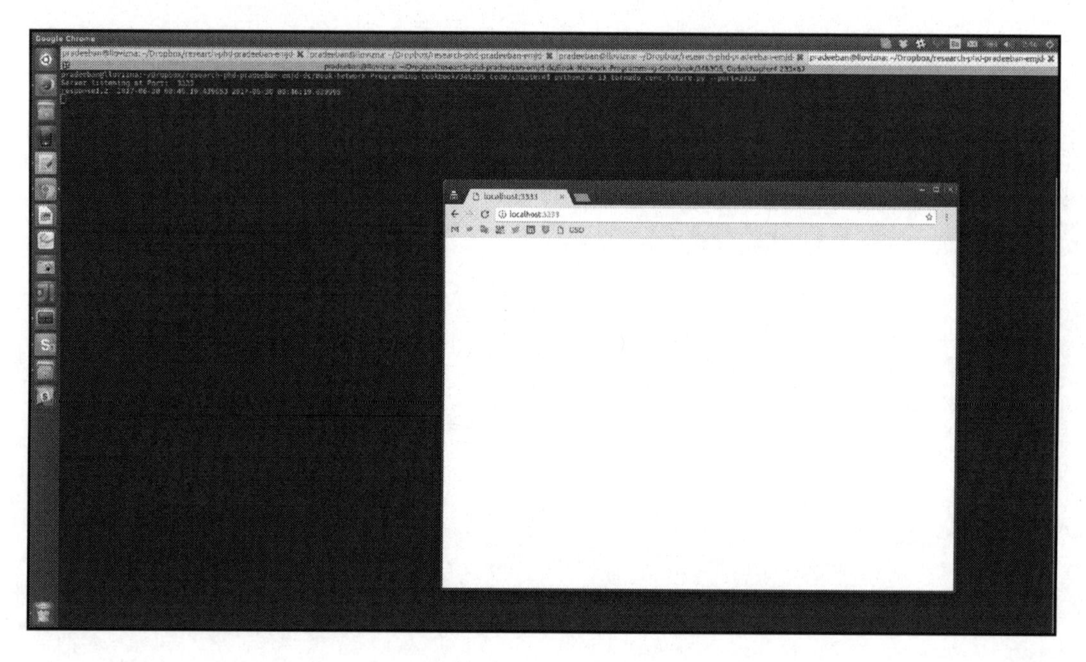

Execution of the Concurrent Application

How it works...

The `concurrent.futures` package is a concurrent programming pattern offered by Python. It consists of the `future` class, which is useful in building concurrent applications in a concise manner.

In the preceding example, `req1` and `req2` represent sample concurrent methods. In place of a workload, we have included small code fraction that waits for a time interval and returns the current time. Either a callback is given to retrieve the execution outcome in a non-blocking manner, or the Future will wait for the function to complete if yield is used (as illustrated by this recipe).

By leveraging the methods and constructs of `concurrent.future` efficiently, we can build concurrent and non-blocking applications.

15
Email Protocols, FTP, and CGI Programming

In this chapter, we will cover the following recipes:

- Listing the files in a remote FTP server
- Uploading a local file to a remote FTP server
- Emailing your current working directory as a compressed ZIP file
- Downloading your Google email with POP3
- Checking your remote email with IMAP
- Sending an email with an attachment via the Gmail SMTP server
- Writing a guest book for your (Python-based) web server with CGI
- Finding the mail server from an email address
- Writing a simple SMTP server
- Writing a secure SMTP client using TLS
- Writing a simple POP3 client

Introduction

This chapter explores the FTP, email, and CGI communications protocol with a Python recipe. Using Python, you can easily code simple FTP actions such as a file download and upload.

There are some interesting recipes in this chapter, such as manipulating your Google email, also known as the Gmail account, from your Python script. You can use these recipes to check, download, and send emails with IMAP, POP3, and SMTP protocols. In another recipe, a web server with CGI also demonstrates the basic CGI action, such as writing a guest comment form in your web application.

Listing the files in a remote FTP server

You would like to list the files available on the official Linux kernel's FTP site, `ftp.kernel.org`. You can select any other FTP site to try this recipe.

Getting ready

If you work on a production/enterprise FTP site with a user account, you need a username and password. However, in this instance, you don't need a username (and password) with the anonymous FTP server at the University of Edinburgh as you can log in anonymously.

How to do it...

We can use the `ftplib` library to fetch files from our selected FTP site. A detailed documentation of this library can be found at `https://docs.python.org/3/library/ftplib.html` for Python 3 and at `http://docs.python.org/2/library/ftplib.html` for Python 2.

`ftplib` is a built-in Python module, and you do not need to install it separately. Let us see how we can fetch some files with `ftplib`.

Listing 5.1 gives a simple FTP connection test as follows:

```
#!/usr/bin/env python
# Python Network Programming Cookbook, Second Edition -- Chapter - 5
# This program is optimized for Python 2.7.12 and Python 3.5.2.
# It may run on any other version with/without modifications.


FTP_SERVER_URL = 'ftp.ed.ac.uk'

import ftplib
from ftplib import FTP
```

```
def test_ftp_connection(path, username, email):
    #Open ftp connection
    ftp = ftplib.FTP(path, username, email)
   #List the files in the /pub directory
    ftp.cwd("/pub")
    print ("File list at %s:" %path)
    files = ftp.dir()
    print (files)

    ftp.quit()

if __name__ == '__main__':
    test_ftp_connection(path=FTP_SERVER_URL, username='anonymous',
                        email='nobody@nourl.com',
                        )
```

This recipe will list the files and folders present in the FTP path, `ftp.kernel.org/pub`. If you run this script, you can see the following output:

```
$ python 15_1_list_files_on_ftp_server.py
File list at ftp.ed.ac.uk:
drwxr-xr-x    4 1005     bin          4096 Oct 11  1999 EMWAC
drwxr-xr-x   13 31763    netserv      4096 May  5  2010 EdLAN
drwxrwxr-x    4 6267     6268         4096 Oct 11  1999 ITFMP
drwxr-xr-x    4 1407     bin          4096 Oct 11  1999 JIPS
drwxr-xr-x    2 root     bin          4096 Oct 11  1999 Mac
drwxr-xr-x    2 10420    7525         4096 Oct  7  2003 PaedTBI
drwxr-xr-x    2 jaw      bin          4096 Oct 11  1999 Printing
drwxr-xr-x    3 root     bin          4096 Oct 11  1999
Student_Societies
drwxr-xr-x    6 root     bin          4096 Feb 19  2014 Unix
drwxr-xr-x    2 root     bin          4096 Oct 11  2016 Unix1
drwxr-xr-x    2 1109     bin          4096 Oct 19  2016 Unix2
drwxr-xr-x    2 2022     bin          4096 Oct 11  1999 X.400
drwxr-xr-x    2 20076    bin          4096 Feb 17  2000 atoz
drwxr-xr-x    2 1403     bin          4096 Aug  9  2001 bill
drwxr-xr-x    2 4414     bin          4096 Oct 11  1999 cartonet
drwxr-xr-x    2 1115     bin          4096 Oct 11  1999 courses
drwxr-xr-x    2 10498    bin          4096 Oct 11  1999 esit04
drwxr-xr-x    2 6314     bin          4096 Oct 11  1999 flp
drwxr-xr-x    2 1400     bin          4096 Nov 19  1999 george
drwxr-xr-x    3 309643   root         4096 Sep 10  2008 geos
drwxr-xr-x    2 1663     root         4096 Apr 23  2013 hssweb
drwxr-xr-x    2 6251     bin          4096 Oct 11  1999 ierm
drwxr-xr-x    2 2126     bin          4096 Nov 12  2004 jbm
drwxr-xr-x    2 1115     bin          4096 Oct 11  1999 kusch
drwxr-xr-x    2 root     bin          4096 Oct 11  1999 lrtt
drwxr-xr-x    7 scott    bin          4096 Nov  9  2015 mail
```

```
drwxr-xr-x    3 1407      bin          4096 Oct 11  1999 maps
drwxr-xr-x    2 2009      bin          4096 Oct 11  1999 mmaccess
drwxr-xr-x    2 2009      bin          4096 Oct 11  1999 mmsurvey
drwx--x--x    3 1943      bin          4096 Dec  1  2000 mww
drwxr-xr-x    2 root      bin          4096 Oct 11  1999 pbowers
drwxr-xr-x    5 7324      bin          4096 Oct 11  1999 rip99
drwxr-xr-x   11 2223      bin          4096 Sep 30  2011 soroti
drwxr-xr-x    2 root      bin          4096 Oct  6  2000 steve
drwxr-xr-x    2 2000      bin          4096 Oct 11  1999 ucsg
drwxr-xr-x    7 20099     bin          4096 Jul 28  2003 unixhelp
drwxr-xr-x    2 root      bin          4096 Oct 11  1999 utopia
drwxr-xr-x    2 2022      bin          4096 Oct 11  1999 whiteosi
None
```

How it works...

This recipe uses `ftplib` to create an FTP client session with `ftp.kernel.org`. The `test_ftp_connection()` function takes the FTP `path`, `username`, and `email` address for connecting to the FTP server.

An FTP client session can be created by calling the `FTP()` function of `ftplib` with the preceding connection's credentials. This returns a client handle, which then can be used to run the usual FTP commands, such as the command to change the working directory or `cwd()`. The `dir()` method returns the directory listing.

It is a good idea to quit the FTP session by calling `ftp.quit()`.

Common error

If you encounter the following error when you run the program, check whether you still can access the `FTP_SERVER_URL`, by pinging to it:

```
Traceback (most recent call last):
  File "15_1_list_files_on_ftp_server.py", line 25, in <module>
    email='nobody@nourl.com',
  File "15_1_list_files_on_ftp_server.py", line 13, in
test_ftp_connection
    ftp = ftplib.FTP(path, username, email)
 File "/usr/lib/python3.5/ftplib.py", line 118, in __init__
    self.connect(host)
  File "/usr/lib/python3.5/ftplib.py", line 153, in connect
    source_address=self.source_address)
  File "/usr/lib/python3.5/socket.py", line 693, in create_connection
   for res in getaddrinfo(host, port, 0, SOCK_STREAM):
```

```
  File "/usr/lib/python3.5/socket.py", line 732, in getaddrinfo
    for res in _socket.getaddrinfo(host, port, family, type, proto,
flags):
socket.gaierror: [Errno -2] Name or service not known
```

Usually, the preceding error means the FTP does not exist anymore, or is not open any more with the anonymous access.

If so, replace the URL with another FTP address that allows anonymous access.

You may verify that the FTP address is valid by trying to open it through your FTP client:

```
$ ftp
ftp> open ftp.ed.ac.uk
Connected to luther.is.ed.ac.uk.
```

Give anonymous and your email address as the username and password when prompted. The outcome is depicted in the following screenshot:

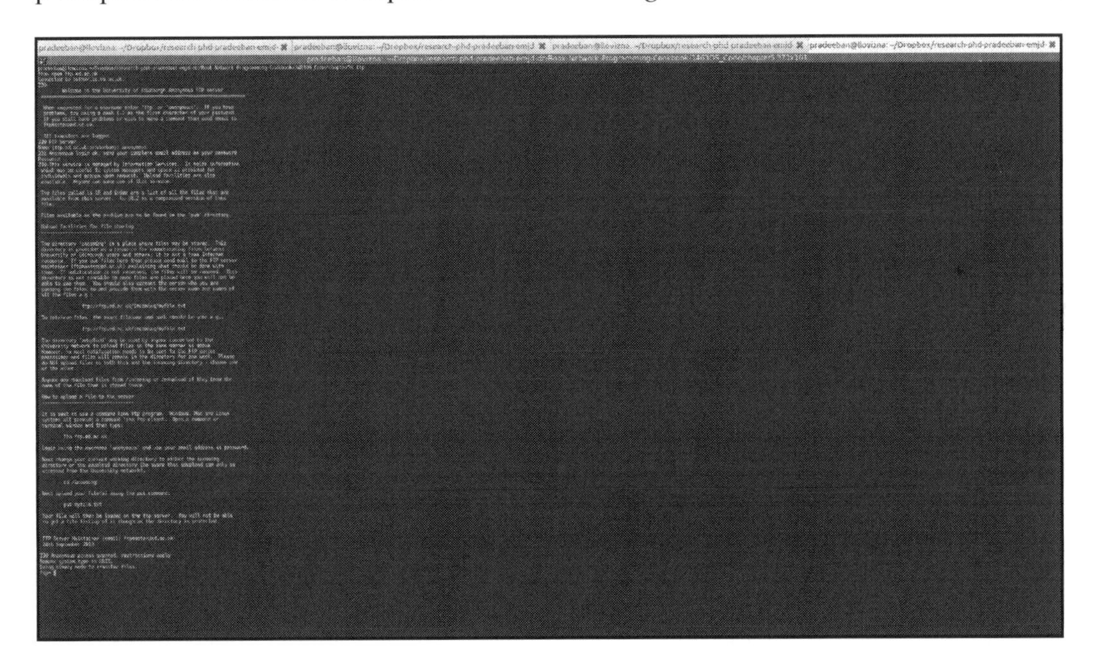

Accessing the FTP Server

Uploading a local file to a remote FTP server

You would like to upload a file to an FTP server.

Getting ready

Let us set up a local FTP server. In Unix/Linux, you can install **VSFTPD** (**Very Secure File Transfer Protocol Daemon**) FTP Server using the following command:

```
$ sudo apt-get install vsftpd
```

On a Windows machine, you can install the FileZilla FTP server, which can be downloaded from `https://filezilla-project.org/download.php?type=server`. FileZilla can also be installed in Linux. For example, in Debian-based Linux distributions such as Ubuntu:

```
$ sudo apt-get install filezilla
```

You should create an FTP user account following the FTP server package's user manual.

You would also like to upload a file to an FTP server. You can specify the server address, login credentials, and filename as the input argument of your script. You should create a local file called `readme.txt` with any text in it.

How to do it...

Using the following script, let's set up a local FTP server. Once you have installed the FTP Server such as VSFTPD or FileZilla, you can upload a file to the logged-in user's `home` directory. You can specify the server address, login credentials, and filename as the input argument of your script.

Listing 5.2 gives the FTP upload example as follows:

```
#!/usr/bin/env python
# Python Network Programming Cookbook, Second Edition -- Chapter - 5
# This program is optimized for Python 2.7.12 and Python 3.5.2.
# It may run on any other version with/without modifications.

import os
```

```
import argparse
import ftplib
import getpass

LOCAL_FTP_SERVER = 'localhost'
LOCAL_FILE = 'readme.txt'

def ftp_upload(ftp_server, username, password, file_name):
    print ("Connecting to FTP server: %s" %ftp_server)
    ftp = ftplib.FTP(ftp_server)
    print ("Login to FTP server: user=%s" %username)
    ftp.login(username, password)
    ext = os.path.splitext(file_name)[1]
    if ext in (".txt", ".htm", ".html"):
        ftp.storlines("STOR " + file_name, open(file_name))
    else:
        ftp.storbinary("STOR " + file_name, open(file_name, "rb"),
1024)
    print ("Uploaded file: %s" %file_name)


if __name__ == '__main__':
    parser = argparse.ArgumentParser(description='FTP Server Upload
Example')
    parser.add_argument('--ftp-server', action="store",
    dest="ftp_server", default=LOCAL_FTP_SERVER)
    parser.add_argument('--file-name', action="store",
    dest="file_name", default=LOCAL_FILE)
    parser.add_argument('--username', action="store",
    dest="username", default=getpass.getuser())
    given_args = parser.parse_args()
    ftp_server, file_name, username = given_args.ftp_server,
     given_args.file_name, given_args.username
    password = getpass.getpass(prompt="Enter you FTP password: ")
    ftp_upload(ftp_server, username, password, file_name)
```

If you set up a local FTP server and run the following script, this script will log in to the FTP server and then will upload a file. If a filename argument is not supplied from the command line by default, it will upload the `readme.txt` file:

```
$ python 15_2_upload_file_to_ftp_server.py
Enter your FTP password:
Connecting to FTP server: localhost
Login to FTP server: user=faruq
Uploaded file: readme.txt
$ cat /home/faruq/readme.txt
This file describes what to do with the .bz2 files you see elsewhere
on this site (ftp.kernel.org).
```

How it works...

In this recipe, we assume that a local FTP server is running. Alternatively, you can connect to a remote FTP server. The `ftp_upload()` method uses the `FTP()` function of Python's `ftplib` to create an FTP connection object. With the `login()` method, it logs in to the server.

After a successful login, the `ftp` object sends the STOR command with either the `storlines()` or `storbinary()` method. The first method is used for sending ASCII text files such as HTML or text files. The latter method is used for binary data such as zipped archive.

It's a good idea to wrap these FTP methods with try-catch error-handling blocks, which is not shown here for the sake of brevity.

Emailing your current working directory as a compressed ZIP file

It might be interesting to send the current working directory contents as a compressed ZIP archive. You can use this recipe to quickly share your files with your friends.

Getting ready

If you don't have any mail server installed on your machine, you need to install a local mail server such as **Postfix**. On a Debian/Ubuntu system, this can be installed with default settings using `apt-get`, as shown in the following command:

```
$ sudo apt-get install postfix
```

How to do it...

Let us first compress the current directory and then create an email message. We can send the email message via an external SMTP host, or we can use a local email server to do this. Like other recipes, let us get the sender and recipient information from parsing the command-line inputs.

Listing 5.3 shows how to convert an `email` folder into a compressed ZIP file as follows:

```
#!/usr/bin/env python
# Python Network Programming Cookbook, Second Edition -- Chapter - 5
# This program is optimized for Python 2.7.12 and Python 3.5.2.
# It may run on any other version with/without modifications.

import os
import argparse
import smtplib
import zipfile
import tempfile
from email import encoders
from email.mime.base import MIMEBase
from email.mime.multipart import MIMEMultipart

def email_dir_zipped(sender, recipient):
    zf = tempfile.TemporaryFile(prefix='mail', suffix='.zip')
    zip = zipfile.ZipFile(zf, 'w')
    print ("Zipping current dir: %s" %os.getcwd())
    for file_name in os.listdir(os.getcwd()):
        zip.write(file_name)
    zip.close()
    zf.seek(0)

    # Create the message
    print ("Creating email message...")
    email_msg = MIMEMultipart()
    email_msg['Subject'] = 'File from path %s' %os.getcwd()
    email_msg['To'] = ', '.join(recipient)
    email_msg['From'] = sender
    email_msg.preamble = 'Testing email from Python.\n'
    msg = MIMEBase('application', 'zip')
    msg.set_payload(zf.read())
    encoders.encode_base64(msg)
    msg.add_header('Content-Disposition', 'attachment',
                   filename=os.getcwd()[-1] + '.zip')
    email_msg.attach(msg)
    email_msg = email_msg.as_string()

    # send the message
    print ("Sending email message...")
    try:
        smtp = smtplib.SMTP('localhost')
        smtp.set_debuglevel(1)
        smtp.sendmail(sender, recipient, email_msg)
    except Exception as e:
```

```
        print ("Error: %s" %str(e))
    finally:
        smtp.close()

if __name__ == '__main__':
    parser = argparse.ArgumentParser(description='Email Example')
    parser.add_argument('--sender', action="store",
    dest="sender", default='you@you.com')
    parser.add_argument('--recipient', action="store",
    dest="recipient")
    given_args = parser.parse_args()
    email_dir_zipped(given_args.sender, given_args.recipient)
```

Running this recipe shows the following output. The extra output is shown because we enabled the email debug level:

```
$ python 15_3_email_current_dir_zipped.py --recipient=faruq@localhost
Zipping current dir: /home/faruq/Dropbox/PacktPub/pynet-
cookbook/pynetcookbook_code/chapter5
Creating email message...
Sending email message...
send: 'ehlo [127.0.0.1]\r\n'
reply: '250-debian6.debian2013.com\r\n'
reply: '250-PIPELINING\r\n'
reply: '250-SIZE 10240000\r\n'
reply: '250-VRFY\r\n'
reply: '250-ETRN\r\n'
reply: '250-STARTTLS\r\n'
reply: '250-ENHANCEDSTATUSCODES\r\n'
reply: '250-8BITMIME\r\n'
reply: '250 DSN\r\n'
reply: retcode (250); Msg: debian6.debian2013.com
PIPELINING
SIZE 10240000
VRFY
ETRN
STARTTLS
ENHANCEDSTATUSCODES
8BITMIME
DSN
send: 'mail FROM:<you@you.com> size=9141\r\n'
reply: '250 2.1.0 Ok\r\n'
reply: retcode (250); Msg: 2.1.0 Ok
send: 'rcpt TO:<faruq@localhost>\r\n'
reply: '250 2.1.5 Ok\r\n'
reply: retcode (250); Msg: 2.1.5 Ok
send: 'data\r\n'
reply: '354 End data with <CR><LF>.<CR><LF>\r\n'
```

```
reply: retcode (354); Msg: End data with <CR><LF>.<CR><LF>
data: (354, 'End data with <CR><LF>.<CR><LF>')
send: 'Content-Type: multipart/mixed;
boundary="===============0388489101==...[TRUNCATED]
reply: '250 2.0.0 Ok: queued as 42D2F34A996\r\n'
reply: retcode (250); Msg: 2.0.0 Ok: queued as 42D2F34A996
data: (250, '2.0.0 Ok: queued as 42D2F34A996')
```

How it works...

We have used Python's `zipfile`, `smtplib`, and an `email` module to achieve our objective of emailing a folder as a zipped archive. This is done using the `email_dir_zipped()` method. This method takes two arguments: the sender and recipient's email addresses to create the email message.

In order to create a ZIP archive, we create a temporary file with the `tempfile` module's `TemporaryFile()` class. We supply a `filename`, `prefix`, `mail`, and `suffix`, `.zip`. Then, we initialize the ZIP archive object with the `ZipFile()` class by passing the temporary file as its argument. Later, we add files of the current directory with the ZIP object's `write()` method call.

To send an email, we create a multipart MIME message with the `MIMEmultipart()` class from the `email.mime.multipart` module. Like our usual email message, the subject, recipient, and sender information is added in the `email` header.

We create the email attachment with the `MIMEBase()` method. Here, we first specify the application/ZIP header and call `set_payload()` on this message object. Then, in order to encode the message correctly, the `encode_base64()` method from encoder's module is used. It is also helpful to use the `add_header()` method to construct the attachment header. Now, our attachment is ready to be included in the main email message with an `attach()` method call.

Sending an email requires you to call the `SMTP()` class instance of `smtplib`. There is a `sendmail()` method that will utilize the routine provided by the OS to actually send the email message correctly. Its details are hidden under the hood. However, you can see a detailed interaction by enabling the debug option as shown in this recipe.

See also

Further information about the Python libraries can be found at:
`http://docs.python.org/3/library/smtplib.html` for Python 3 and
`http://docs.python.org/2/library/smtplib.html` for Python 2.

Downloading your Google email with POP3

You would like to download your Google (or virtually any other email provider's) email via the POP3 protocol.

Getting ready

To run this recipe, you should have an email account with Google or any other service provider.

How to do it...

Here, we attempt to download the first email message from a user's Google email account. The username is supplied from a command line, but the password is kept secret and not passed from the command line. This is rather entered while the script is running and kept hidden from display.

Listing 5.4 shows how to download our Google email via POP3 as follows:

```
#!/usr/bin/env python
# Python Network Programming Cookbook, Second Edition -- Chapter - 5
# This program is optimized for Python 2.7.12 and Python 3.5.2.
# It may run on any other version with/without modifications.

import argparse
import getpass
import poplib

GOOGLE_POP3_SERVER = 'pop.googlemail.com'

def download_email(username):
    mailbox = poplib.POP3_SSL(GOOGLE_POP3_SERVER, '995')
    mailbox.user(username)
```

```
    password = getpass.getpass(prompt="Enter your Google password: ")
    mailbox.pass_(password)
    num_messages = len(mailbox.list()[1])
    print ("Total emails: %s" %num_messages)
    print ("Getting last message")
    for msg in mailbox.retr(num_messages)[1]:
        print (msg)
    mailbox.quit()

if __name__ == '__main__':
    parser = argparse.ArgumentParser(description='Email Download
Example')
    parser.add_argument('--username', action="store",
    dest="username", default=getpass.getuser())
    given_args = parser.parse_args()
    username = given_args.username
    download_email(username)
```

If you run this script, you will see an output similar to the following one. The message is truncated for the sake of privacy:

```
$ python 15_4_download_google_email_via_pop3.py --username=<USERNAME>
Enter your Google password:
Total emails: 333
Getting last message
...[TRUNCATED]
```

How it works...

This recipe downloads a user's first Google message via POP3. The `download_email()` method creates a mailbox object with Python, the `POP3_SSL()` class of `poplib`. We passed the Google POP3 server and port address to the class constructor. The mailbox object then sets up a user account with the `user()` method call. The password is collected from the user securely using the `getpass` module's `getpass()` method and then passed to the `mailbox` object. The mailbox's `list()` method gives us the email messages as a Python list.

This script first displays the number of email messages stored in the mailbox and retrieves the first message with the `retr()` method call. Finally, it's safe to call the `quit()` method on the mailbox to clean up the connection.

Checking your remote email with IMAP

Instead of using POP3, you can also use IMAP to retrieve the email message from your Google account. In this case, the message won't be deleted after retrieval.

Getting ready

To run this recipe, you should have an email account with Google or any other service provider.

How to do it...

Let us connect to your Google email account and read the first email message. If you don't delete it, the first email message would be the welcome message from Google.

Listing 5.5 shows us how to check Google email with IMAP as follows:

```
#!/usr/bin/env python
# Python Network Programming Cookbook, Second Edition -- Chapter - 5
# This program is optimized for Python 2.7.12 and Python 3.5.2.
# It may run on any other version with/without modifications.

import argparse
import getpass
import imaplib

GOOGLE_IMAP_SERVER = 'imap.googlemail.com'

def check_email(username):
    mailbox = imaplib.IMAP4_SSL(GOOGLE_IMAP_SERVER, '993')
    password = getpass.getpass(prompt="Enter your Google password: ")
    mailbox.login(username, password)
    mailbox.select('Inbox')
    typ, data = mailbox.search(None, 'ALL')
    for num in data[0].split():
        typ, data = mailbox.fetch(num, '(RFC822)')
        print ('Message %s\n%s\n' % (num, data[0][1]))
        break
    mailbox.close()
    mailbox.logout()

if __name__ == '__main__':
    parser = argparse.ArgumentParser(description='Email Download
Example')
```

```
parser.add_argument('--username', action="store",
dest="username", default=getpass.getuser())
given_args = parser.parse_args()
username = given_args.username
check_email(username)
```

If you run this script, this will show the following output. In order to remove the private part of the data, we truncated some user data:

```
$ python 15_5_check_remote_email_via_imap.py --username=<USER_NAME>
Enter your Google password:
Message 1
Received: by 10.140.142.16; Sat, 17 Nov 2007 09:26:31 -0800 (PST)
Message-ID: <...>@mail.gmail.com>
Date: Sat, 17 Nov 2007 09:26:31 -0800
From: "Gmail Team" <mail-noreply@google.com>
To: "<User Full Name>" <USER_NAME>@gmail.com>
Subject: Gmail is different. Here's what you need to know.
MIME-Version: 1.0
Content-Type: multipart/alternative;
   boundary="----=_Part_7453_30339499.1195320391988"
------=_Part_7453_30339499.1195320391988
Content-Type: text/plain; charset=ISO-8859-1
Content-Transfer-Encoding: 7bit
Content-Disposition: inline
Messages that are easy to find, an inbox that organizes itself, great
spam-fighting tools and built-in chat. Sound cool? Welcome to Gmail.
To get started, you may want to:
[TRUNCATED]
```

How it works...

The preceding script takes a Google username from the command line and calls the `check_email()` function. This function creates an IMAP mailbox with the `IMAP4_SSL()` class of `imaplib`, which is initialized with Google's IMAP server and default port.

Then, this function logs in to the mailbox with a password, which is captured by the `getpass()` method of the `getpass` module. The `inbox` folder is selected by calling the `select()` method on the mailbox object.

The `mailbox` object has many useful methods. Two of them are `search()` and `fetch()` that are used to get the first email message. Finally, it's safer to call the `close()` and `logout()` method on the `mailbox` object to end the IMAP connection.

Sending an email with an attachment via Gmail SMTP server

You would like to send an email message from your Google email account to another account. You also need to attach a file with this message.

Getting ready

To run this recipe, you should have an email account with Google or any other service provider.

How to do it...

We can create an email message and attach Python's `python-logo.gif` file with the email message. Then, this message is sent from a Google account to a different account.

Listing 4.6 shows us how to send an email from your Google account:

```
#!/usr/bin/env python
# Python Network Programming Cookbook, Second Edition -- Chapter - 5
# This program is optimized for Python 2.7.12 and Python 3.5.2.
# It may run on any other version with/without modifications.

import argparse
import os
import getpass
import re
import sys
import smtplib
from email.mime.image import MIMEImage
from email.mime.multipart import MIMEMultipart
from email.mime.text import MIMEText
SMTP_SERVER = 'smtp.gmail.com'
SMTP_PORT = 587
def send_email(sender, recipient):
    """ Send email message """
    msg = MIMEMultipart()
    msg['Subject'] = 'Python Emaill Test'
    msg['To'] = recipient
    msg['From'] = sender
    subject = 'Python email Test'
```

```
    message = 'Images attached.'
    # attach imgae files
    files = os.listdir(os.getcwd())
    gifsearch = re.compile(".gif", re.IGNORECASE)
    files = filter(gifsearch.search, files)
    for filename in files:
        path = os.path.join(os.getcwd(), filename)
        if not os.path.isfile(path):
            continue
        img = MIMEImage(open(path, 'rb').read(), _subtype="gif")
        img.add_header('Content-Disposition', 'attachment',
        filename=filename)
        msg.attach(img)
    part = MIMEText('text', "plain")
    part.set_payload(message)
    msg.attach(part)
    # create smtp session
    session = smtplib.SMTP(SMTP_SERVER, SMTP_PORT)
    session.ehlo()
    session.starttls()
    session.ehlo
    password = getpass.getpass(prompt="Enter your Google password: ")
    session.login(sender, password)
    session.sendmail(sender, recipient, msg.as_string())
    print ("Email sent.")
    session.quit()
if __name__ == '__main__':
    parser = argparse.ArgumentParser(description='Email Sending
Example')
    parser.add_argument('--sender', action="store", dest="sender")
    parser.add_argument('--recipient', action="store",
dest="recipient")
    given_args = parser.parse_args()
    send_email(given_args.sender, given_args.recipient)
```

Running the following script outputs the success of sending an email to any email address if you provide your Google account details correctly. After running this script, you can check your recipient email account to verify that the email is actually sent:

```
$ python 15_6_send_email_from_gmail.py --sender=<USERNAME>@gmail.com -
recipient=<USER>@<ANOTHER_COMPANY.com>
Enter you Google password:
Email sent.
```

How it works...

In this recipe, an email message is created in the `send_email()` function. This function is supplied with a Google account from where the email message will be sent. The message header object, `msg`, is created by calling the `MIMEMultipart()` class and then subject, recipient, and sender information is added on it.

Python's regular `expression-handling` module is used to filter the `.gif` image on the current path. The image attachment object, `img`, is then created with the `MIMEImage()` method from the `email.mime.image` module. A correct image header is added to this object and finally, the image is attached with the `msg` object created earlier. We can attach multiple image files within a `for` loop as shown in this recipe. We can also attach a plain text attachment in a similar way.

To send the email message, we create an SMTP session. We call some testing method on this session object, such as `ehlo()` or `starttls()`. Then, log in to the Google SMTP server with a username and password and a `sendmail()` method is called to send the email.

Writing a guestbook for your (Python-based) web server with CGI

Common Gateway Interface (**CGI**) is a standard in web programming by which custom scripts can be used to produce web server output. You would like to catch the HTML form input from a user's browser, redirect it to another page, and acknowledge a user action.

Getting ready

To run this recipe, you first need to run a web server that supports CGI scripts.

How to do it...

We placed our Python CGI script inside a `cgi-bin/` subdirectory and then visited the HTML page that contains the feedback form. Upon submitting this form, our web server will send the form data to the CGI script, and we'll see the output produced by this script.

Listing 5.7 shows us how the Python web server supports CGI:

```
#!/usr/bin/env python
# Python Network Programming Cookbook -- Chapter - 5
# This program requires Python 3.5.2 or any later version
# It may run on any other version with/without modifications.
#
# Follow the comments inline to make it run on Python 2.7.x.

import os
import cgi
import argparse

import http.server
# Comment out the above line and uncomment the below for Python 2.7.x.
#import BaseHTTPServer

# Uncomment the below line for Python 2.7.x.
#import CGIHTTPServer

import cgitb
cgitb.enable()  ## enable CGI error reporting


def web_server(port):

    server = http.server.HTTPServer
    # Comment out the above line and uncomment the below for Python
2.7.x.
    #server = BaseHTTPServer.HTTPServer

    handler = http.server.CGIHTTPRequestHandler #RequestsHandler
    # Comment out the above line and uncomment the below for Python
2.7.x.
    #handler = CGIHTTPServer.CGIHTTPRequestHandler #RequestsHandler

    server_address = ("", port)
    handler.cgi_directories = ["/cgi-bin", ]
    httpd = server(server_address, handler)
    print ("Starting web server with CGI support on port: %s ..."
%port)
    httpd.serve_forever()

if __name__ == '__main__':
    parser = argparse.ArgumentParser(description='CGI Server Example')
    parser.add_argument('--port', action="store",
```

```
    dest="port", type=int, required=True)
    given_args = parser.parse_args()
    web_server(given_args.port)
```

The following screenshot shows a CGI enabled web server serving contents:

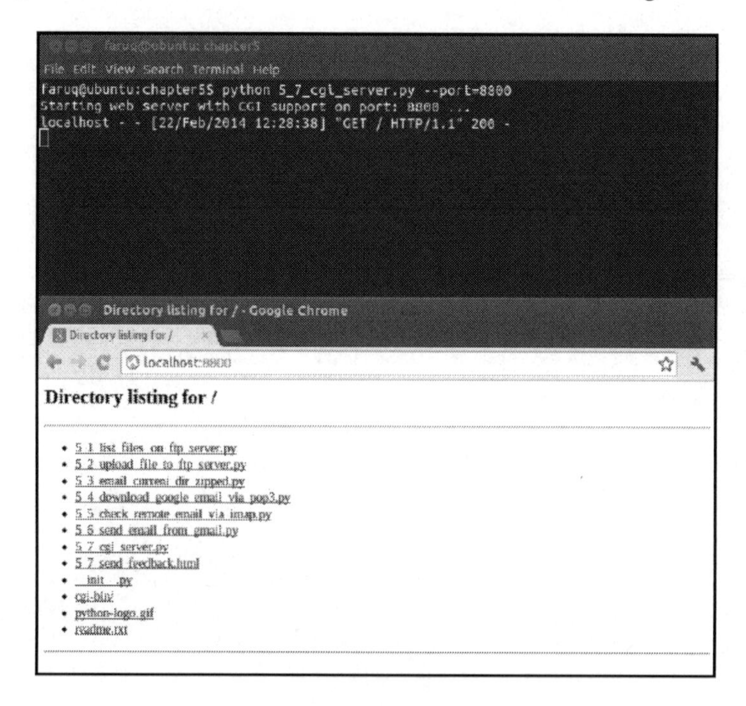

CGI Enabled Web Server

If you run this recipe, you will see the following output:

```
$ python 15_7_cgi_server.py --port=8800
Starting web server with CGI support on port: 8800 ...
localhost - - [19/May/2013 18:40:22] "GET / HTTP/1.1" 200 -
```

Now, you need to visit `http://localhost:8800/15_7_send_feedback.html` from your browser.

You will see an input form. We assume that you provide the following input to this form:

```
Name:  User1
Comment: Comment1
```

The following screenshot shows the entering user comment in a web form:

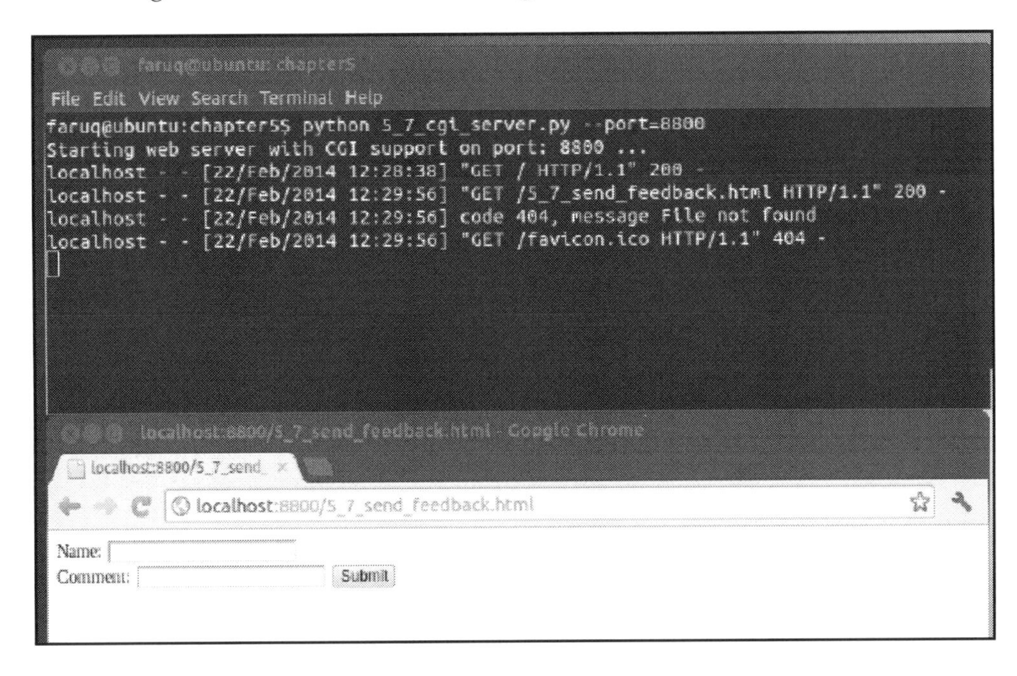

User Comment Input in the Form

Then, your browser will be redirected to `http://localhost:8800/cgi-bin/15_7_get_feedback.py` where you can see the following output:

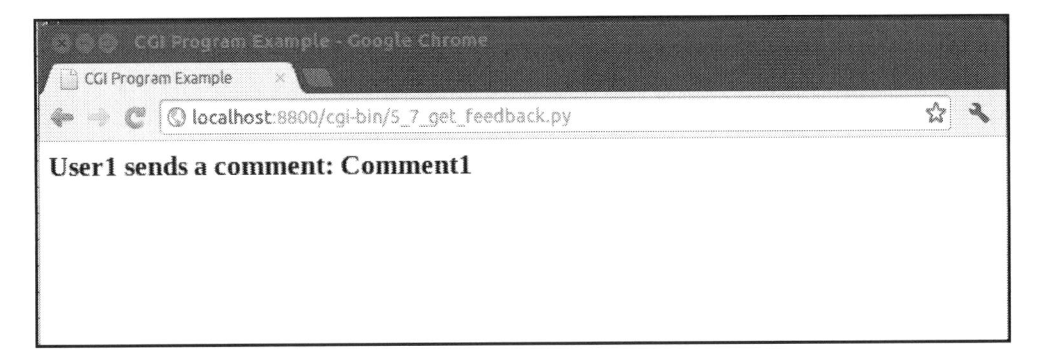

Output from the Browser

How it works...

We have used a basic HTTP server setup that can handle CGI requests. Python 3 provides these interfaces in the `http.server` module. Python 2 had the modules `BaseHTTPServer` and `CGIHTTPserver` to offer the same, which were merged in Python into `http.server`.

The handler is configured to use the `/cgi-bin` path to launch the CGI scripts. No other path can be used to run the CGI scripts.

The HTML feedback form located on `15_7_send_feedback.html` shows a very basic HTML form containing the following code:

```
<html>
   <body>
         <form action="/cgi-bin/15_7_get_feedback.py" method="post">
                Name: <input type="text" name="Name">  <br />
                Comment: <input type="text" name="Comment" />
                <input type="submit" value="Submit" />
         </form>
   </body>
</html>
```

Note that the form method is POST and action is set to the `/cgi-bin/15_7_get_feedback.py` file. The contents of this file are as follows:

```
#!/usr/bin/env python
# Python Network Programming Cookbook, Second Edition -- Chapter - 5
# This program is optimized for Python 2.7.12 and Python 3.5.2.
# It may run on any other version with/without modifications.


#!/usr/bin/python

# Import modules for CGI handling
import cgi
import cgitb

# Create instance of FieldStorage
form = cgi.FieldStorage()

# Get data from fields
name = form.getvalue('Name')
comment  = form.getvalue('Comment')

print ("Content-type:text/html\r\n\r\n")
print ("<html>")
```

```
print ("<head>")
print ("<title>CGI Program Example </title>")
print ("</head>")
print ("<body>")
print ("<h2> %s sends a comment: %s</h2>" % (name, comment))
print ("</body>")
print ("</html>")
```

In this CGI script, the `FieldStorage()` method is called from `cgilib`. This returns a `form` object to process the HTML form inputs. Two inputs are parsed here (`name` and `comment`) using the `getvalue()` method. Finally, the script acknowledges the user input by echoing a line back saying that the user x has sent a comment.

If you encounter any errors as follows:

```
127.0.0.1 - - [22/Jun/2017 00:03:51] code 403, message CGI script is
not executable ('/cgi-bin/15_7_get_feedback.py')
```

Make it executable. It can be done by following the following command in Linux:

```
$ chmod a+x cgi-bin/15_7_get_feedback.py
```

Once it is made executable, you can rerun the program without any issue.

Finding the mail server from an email address

Websites often need to verify an email that is entered by a user for validity. We can verify an email in a few lines of code in Python. First step is to confirm that the email is of the accepted format, to ensure that no random input is accepted as an email. Next is to see whether the email address indeed exists. Due to restrictions in the major email service providers such as Gmail and Hotmail, this code may not work completely. Nevertheless, it gives an overall idea on a given email address.

Getting ready

To run this recipe, you first need to have a from email address that you will use to test the other email addresses (marked as `toaddress`).

How to do it...

Listing 5.8 shows us the code that finds the domain name from the given email address and verifies it:

```
#!/usr/bin/env python
# Python Network Programming Cookbook, Second Edition -- Chapter - 5
# This program is optimized for Python 2.7.12 and Python 3.5.2.
# It may run on any other version with/without modifications.

import re
import smtplib
import dns.resolver
import argparse


def mail_checker(fromAddress, toAddress):

    regex = '^[a-z0-9][a-z0-9._%+-]{0,63}@[a-z0-9-]+
            (\.[a-z0-9-]+)*(\.[a-z]{2,})$'

    addressToVerify = str(toAddress)

    match = re.match(regex, addressToVerify)
    if match == None:
       print('Bad Syntax in the address to verify.
              Re-enter the correct value')
       raise ValueError('Bad Syntax')

    splitAddress = addressToVerify.split('@')
    domain = str(splitAddress[1])

    records = dns.resolver.query(domain, 'MX')
    mxRecord = records[0].exchange
    mxRecord = str(mxRecord)


    server = smtplib.SMTP()
    server.set_debuglevel(1)

    try:
        server.connect(mxRecord)
    except Exception as e:
        print ("Mail Check Failed Due to Error: %s" %str(e))
        return
    server.helo(server.local_hostname)
    server.mail(fromAddress)
    code, message = server.rcpt(str(addressToVerify))
```

```
    server.quit()

    if code == 250:
       print('Successfully verified the email: %s', fromAddress)
    else:
       print('Failed to verify the email: %s', fromAddress)



if __name__ == '__main__':
    parser = argparse.ArgumentParser(description='Mail Server
Example')
    parser.add_argument('--fromAddress', action="store",
    dest="fromAddress", type=str, required=True)
    parser.add_argument('--toAddress', action="store",
    dest="toAddress", type=str, required=True)
    given_args = parser.parse_args()
    mail_checker(given_args.fromAddress, given_args.toAddress)
```

If you run this recipe, you will see the following output:

```
$ python 15_8_verify_email.py --fromAddress=tester@webname.com
--toAddress=test+234@gmail.com
connect: ('alt2.gmail-smtp-in.l.google.com.', 25)
connect: ('alt2.gmail-smtp-in.l.google.com.', 25)
Successfully verified the email: test+234@gmail.com
```

The preceding output is printed when `250` is returned from the mail server. The program may also produce the following output, since mail servers such as Gmail block outside access to port `25`, which is the port of `Simple Mail Transfer Protocol` (`SMTP`) that we are checking:

```
$ python 15_8_verify_email.py --fromAddress=tester@webname.com --
toAddress=test+234@gmail.com
connect: ('alt2.gmail-smtp-in.l.google.com.', 25)
connect: ('alt2.gmail-smtp-in.l.google.com.', 25)
Mail Check Failed Due to Error: [Errno 101] Network is unreachable
```

If you use an invalid domain name as follows, there will be an error message:

```
$ python 15_8_verify_email.py --fromAddress=tester@webname.com --
toAddress=pradeeban@slt.lxx
Traceback (most recent call last):
  File "15_8_verify_email.py", line 57, in <module>
    mail_checker(given_args.fromAddress, given_args.toAddress)
  File "15_8_verify_email.py", line 26, in mail_checker
    records = dns.resolver.query(domain, 'MX')
  File "/usr/local/lib/python2.7/dist-packages/dns/resolver.py", line
```

```
1132, in query
    raise_on_no_answer, source_port)
 File "/usr/local/lib/python2.7/dist-packages/dns/resolver.py", line
1051, in query
   raise NXDOMAIN(qnames=qnames_to_try, responses=nxdomain_responses)
dns.resolver.NXDOMAIN: None of DNS query names exist: slt.lxx.,
slt.lxx.
```

How it works...

We have used a few Python libraries in getting this work. **Regular Expressions (RegEx)** in confirming that the emails belong to the correct format are done by using the `re` library. The library `smtplib` is an SMTP protocol client for Python programs, to execute methods such as sending a message to an SMTP server. You may read more about SMTP at `https://docs.python.org/3/library/smtplib.html`.

Writing a simple SMTP server

In this recipe, we will learn how to build an SMTP server and a client, as a simple mail server and a client. We will use Python's `smtpd` library for this recipe. You may read more about smtpd at `https://docs.python.org/3/library/smtpd.html`.

Getting ready

First, we will write an SMTP server that listens on a particular host and a particular port. Then we will write an SMTP client that connects to the same host and port, with the `fromaddress`, `toaddress`, `subject`, and message passed as the other arguments.

How to do it...

The server receives the messages from the clients and logs them to the console.

Listing 5.9a gives the code for the SMTP server as follows:

```
#!/usr/bin/env python
# Python Network Programming Cookbook, Second Edition -- Chapter - 5
# This program is optimized for Python 2.7.12 and Python 3.5.2.
# It may run on any other version with/without modifications.
```

```
import smtplib
import email.utils
import argparse
from email.mime.text import MIMEText

def mail_client(host, port, fromAddress, toAddress, subject, body):
    msg = MIMEText(body)
    msg['To'] = email.utils.formataddr(('Recipient', toAddress))
    msg['From'] = email.utils.formataddr(('Author', fromAddress))
    msg['Subject'] = subject

    server = smtplib.SMTP(host, port)
    server.set_debuglevel(True)
    try:
        server.sendmail(fromAddress, toAddress, msg.as_string())
    finally:
        server.quit()


if __name__ == '__main__':
    parser = argparse.ArgumentParser(description='Mail Server
Example')
    parser.add_argument('--host', action="store",
    dest="host", type=str, required=True)
    parser.add_argument('--port', action="store",
    dest="port", type=int, required=True)
    parser.add_argument('--fromAddress', action="store",
    dest="fromAddress", type=str, required=True)
    parser.add_argument('--toAddress', action="store",
    dest="toAddress", type=str, required=True)
    parser.add_argument('--subject', action="store",
    dest="subject", type=str, required=True)
    parser.add_argument('--body', action="store",
    dest="body", type=str, required=True)
    given_args = parser.parse_args()
    mail_client(given_args.host, given_args.port,
    given_args.fromAddress, given_args.toAddress,
    given_args.subject, given_args.body)
```

Listing 5.9b gives the code for the SMTP client as follows:

```
#!/usr/bin/env python
# Python Network Programming Cookbook, Second Edition -- Chapter - 5
# This program is optimized for Python 2.7.12 and Python 3.5.2.
# It may run on any other version with/without modifications.

import smtpd
import asyncore
```

```
import argparse

class CustomSMTPServer(smtpd.SMTPServer):
    def process_message(self, peer, mailfrom, rcpttos, data):
        print ('Message Received from:', peer)
        print ('From:', mailfrom)
        print ('To  :', rcpttos)
        print ('Message :', data)
        return

if __name__ == '__main__':
    parser = argparse.ArgumentParser(description='Mail Server
Example')
    parser.add_argument('--host', action="store",
    dest="host", type=str, required=True)
    parser.add_argument('--port', action="store",
    dest="port", type=int, required=True)
    given_args = parser.parse_args()
    server = CustomSMTPServer((given_args.host, given_args.port),
None)
    asyncore.loop()
```

You may run the server and client code. The server handles the emails from the clients, as follows:

```
$ python 15_9a_mail_server.py --host='127.0.0.1' --port=1025
Message Received from the peer: ('127.0.0.1', 47916)
Addressed from: tester@webname.com
Addressed to  : ['test@gmail.com']
Message : Content-Type: text/plain; charset="us-ascii"
MIME-Version: 1.0
Content-Transfer-Encoding: 7bit
To: Recipient <test@gmail.com>
From: Author <tester@webname.com>
Subject: Hi, Hello
$ python 15_9b_mail_client.py --host='127.0.0.1' --port=1025 --
fromAddress=tester@webname.com --toAddress=test@gmail.com --
subject="Hi, Hello" --body="Good to see you all. Keep in touch. Take
Care"
send: 'ehlo [127.0.1.1]\r\n'
reply: b'250-llovizna\r\n'
reply: b'250-SIZE 33554432\r\n'
reply: b'250 HELP\r\n'
reply: retcode (250); Msg: b'llovizna\nSIZE 33554432\nHELP'
send: 'mail FROM:<tester@webname.com> size=232\r\n'
reply: b'250 OK\r\n'
reply: retcode (250); Msg: b'OK'
send: 'rcpt TO:<test@gmail.com>\r\n'
```

```
reply: b'250 OK\r\n'
reply: retcode (250); Msg: b'OK'
send: 'data\r\n'
reply: b'354 End data with <CR><LF>.<CR><LF>\r\n'
reply: retcode (354); Msg: b'End data with <CR><LF>.<CR><LF>'
data: (354, b'End data with <CR><LF>.<CR><LF>')
send: b'Content-Type: text/plain; charset="us-ascii"\r\nMIME-Version:
1.0\r\nContent-Transfer-Encoding: 7bit\r\nTo: Recipient
<test@gmail.com>\r\nFrom: Author <tester@webname.com>\r\nSubject: Hi,
Hello\r\n\r\nGood to see you all. Keep in touch. Take Care\r\n.\r\n'
reply: b'250 OK\r\n'
reply: retcode (250); Msg: b'OK'
data: (250, b'OK')
send: 'quit\r\n'
reply: b'221 Bye\r\n'
reply: retcode (221); Msg: b'Bye'
```

The output is depicted by the following screenshot:

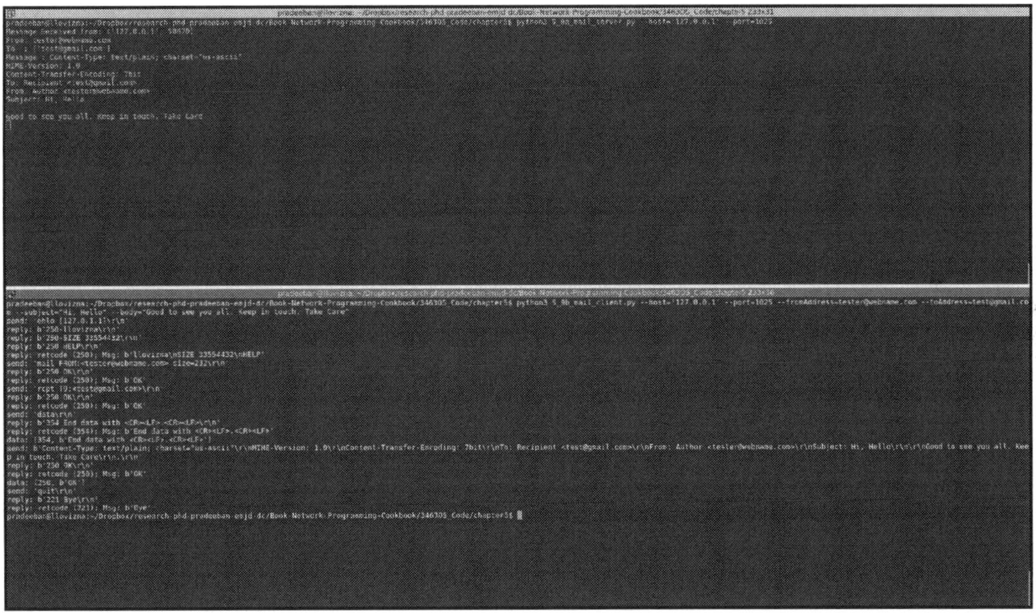

SMTP Server and Client

How it works...

The `email.utils` module offers the utility methods for the email server, such as formatting the to and from addresses. The `smtplib` module lets us create a mail server, while `smtpd` lets us create an email client daemon. The `asyncore` module offers a basic infrastructure to write asynchronous clients and servers.

Writing a secure SMTP client using TLS

Now we will look into how to connect to the mail servers such as Gmail and Yahoo through a simple SMTP client secured with TLS.

Getting ready

This program requires accessing a mail account in a less secured way. Many modern email servers may block your login account. For example, you may have to make sure that *access for less secure apps has been turned on*.

How to do it...

You need to offer a valid email address and password to send an email through this recipe. We pass the email server, SMTP `port`, `fromaddress`, `toaddress`, email `subject`, and email `body` as the arguments, and receive the password to your email (from) address using the `getpass` library (so that your email password is not displayed in plain text).

Listing 5.10 gives the simple email client as follows:

```
#!/usr/bin/env python
# Python Network Programming Cookbook, Second Edition -- Chapter - 5
# This program is optimized for Python 2.7.12 and Python 3.5.2.
# It may run on any other version with/without modifications.

import smtplib
from email.mime.multipart import MIMEMultipart
from email.mime.text import MIMEText
import argparse
import getpass

def mail_client(host, port, fromAddress, password, toAddress, subject,
```

```
body):
    msg = MIMEMultipart()

    msg['From'] = fromAddress
    msg['To'] = toAddress
    msg['Subject'] = subject
    message = body
    msg.attach(MIMEText(message))

    mailserver = smtplib.SMTP(host,port)

    # Identify to the SMTP Gmail Client
    mailserver.ehlo()

    # Secure with TLS Encryption
    mailserver.starttls()

    # Reidentifying as an encrypted connection
    mailserver.ehlo()
    mailserver.login(fromAddress, password)

    mailserver.sendmail(fromAddress,toAddress,msg.as_string())
    print ("Email sent from:", fromAddress)

    mailserver.quit()



if __name__ == '__main__':
    parser = argparse.ArgumentParser(description='Mail Server
Example')
    parser.add_argument('--host', action="store",
    dest="host", type=str, required=True)
    parser.add_argument('--port', action="store",
    dest="port", type=int, required=True)
    parser.add_argument('--fromAddress', action="store",
    dest="fromAddress", type=str, required=True)
    parser.add_argument('--toAddress', action="store",
    dest="toAddress", type=str, required=True)
    parser.add_argument('--subject', action="store",
    dest="subject", type=str, required=True)
    parser.add_argument('--body', action="store",
    dest="body", type=str, required=True)
    password = getpass.getpass("Enter your Password:")
    given_args = parser.parse_args()
    mail_client(given_args.host, given_args.port,
    given_args.fromAddress, password, given_args.toAddress,
    given_args.subject, given_args.body)
```

This recipe logs in as a simple Python-based email client for your email account, and sends a plain-text email to the `toaddress` that you have specified. Running this program gives the following output:

```
$ python 15_10_secure_mail_client.py --host='smtp.gmail.com' --
port=587 --fromAddress=kathiravell@gmail.com --
toAddress=kk.pradeeban@gmail.com -subject="Hi, Hello.." --body="Good
to see you all. Keep in touch. Take Care"
python3 15_10_secure_mail_client.py --host='smtp.gmail.com' --port=587
--fromAddress=kathiravell@gmail.com --toAddress=kk.pradeeban@gmail.com
-subject="Hi, Hello.." --body="Good to see you all. Keep in touch.
Take Care"
Enter your Password:
Email sent from: kathiravell@gmail.com
```

The output is indicated by the following screenshot of the console, as well as the email received:

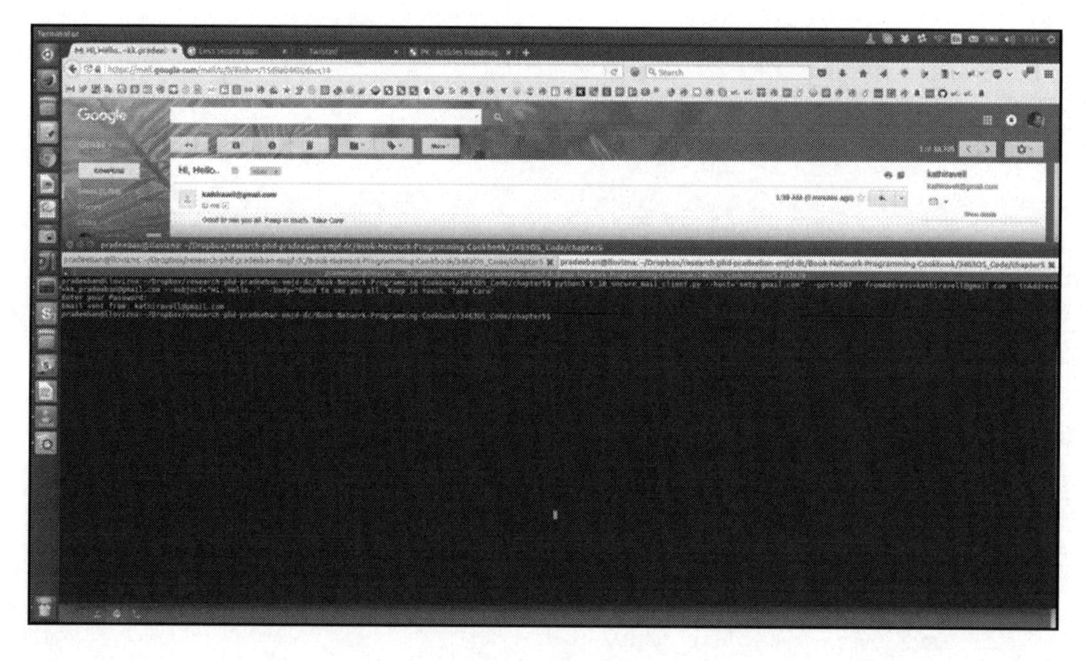

Sending Email from your Email Address

How it works...

If you have not enabled less secure apps to access your email account, it may produce an error message similar to the following:

```
$ python 15_10_secure_mail_client.py
Enter your Password:
Traceback (most recent call last):
  File "15_10_secure_mail_client.py", line 50, in <module>
    mail_client(given_args.host, given_args.port,
given_args.fromAddress, password, given_args.toAddress,
given_args.subject, given_args.body)
  File "15_10_secure_mail_client.py", line 31, in mail_client
    mailserver.login(fromAddress, password)
  File "/usr/lib/python3.5/smtplib.py", line 729, in login
    raise last_exception
  File "/usr/lib/python3.5/smtplib.py", line 720, in login
    initial_response_ok=initial_response_ok)
  File "/usr/lib/python3.5/smtplib.py", line 641, in auth
    raise SMTPAuthenticationError(code, resp)
smtplib.SMTPAuthenticationError: (534, b'5.7.14
<https://accounts.google.com/signin/continue?sarp=1&scc=1&plt=AKgnsbv9
\n5.7.14 d-4CxD9A0qK3z36XteHYOlFaK2-
idda9-3CG5ckc1xi_E1OgaK2aftyHvZvti9jX6fC1kd\n5.7.14
fbTWvC5gKXK_A94zOBm8YQ_myr0uzInTP-
Tf2pTdAZcz3owptTesXllHyXD2SCRHEXRJtk\n5.7.14 nr-
x8QQneko1ZBJCvsbtEmo5EXgETNbESSXmbX7acCZQGukSJJ-5akizNPUrxb6NVMsJwh\n5
.7.14 L-f5XsY1lBjmIlX9GVyQEZQSB-Iis> Please log in via your web
browser and\n5.7.14 then try again.\n5.7.14  Learn more at\n5.7.14
https://support.google.com/mail/answer/78754 o36sm9782398edc.39 -
gsmtp')
```

In addition, your email program would have sent you a warning on this login attempt, advising you on potential compromise of your account, or if the login attempt was indeed you, suggesting you to enable less secure apps.

If the credentials are not correct, it will return a different error:

```
smtplib.SMTPAuthenticationError: (535, b'5.7.8 Username and Password
not accepted. Learn more at\n5.7.8
https://support.google.com/mail/?p=BadCredentials b4sm9037328eda.34 -
gsmtp')
```

Writing an email client with POP3

Now we will look into how to connect to the mail servers with POP3 to fetch an email from the email account.

Getting ready

This program requires accessing a mail account in a less secured way. Many modern email servers may block your login account. For example, you may have to make sure that *access for less secure apps has been turned on*.

How to do it...

You need to offer a valid email address and password to send an email through this recipe. We pass the email server, POP3 `port`, `user` and `password` as the arguments, and receive the password to your email account using the `getpass` library (so that your email password is not displayed in plain text).

Listing 5.11 gives the simple POP3 email client as follows:

```
#!/usr/bin/env python
# Python Network Programming Cookbook, Second Edition -- Chapter - 5
# This program is optimized for Python 2.7.12 and Python 3.5.2.
# It may run on any other version with/without modifications.

import getpass
import poplib
import argparse

def mail_client(host, port, user, password):
    Mailbox = poplib.POP3_SSL(host, port)
    Mailbox.user(user)
    Mailbox.pass_(password)
    numMessages = len(Mailbox.list()[1])
    print (Mailbox.retr(1)[1])
    Mailbox.quit()


if __name__ == '__main__':
    parser = argparse.ArgumentParser(description='Mail Server
Example')
    parser.add_argument('--host', action="store",
    dest="host", type=str, required=True)
```

```
    parser.add_argument('--port', action="store",
    dest="port", type=int, required=True)
    parser.add_argument('--user', action="store",
    dest="user", type=str, required=True)
    password = getpass.getpass("Enter your Password:")
    given_args = parser.parse_args()
    mail_client(given_args.host, given_args.port,
    given_args.user, password)
```

This recipe logs in as a simple Python-based POP3 email client for your email account, and retrieves an email from your email account. Running this program gives the following output:

```
$ python 15_11_pop3_mail_client.py --host='pop.googlemail.com' --
port=995 --user=kathiravell@gmail.com
Enter your Password:
[b'Received: by 10.70.31.12 with HTTP; Mon, 24 Dec 2007 11:48:08 -0800
(PST)', b'Message-ID:
<a80d78ee0712241148v78b4e964u80876a1d6bfdae32@mail.gmail.com>',
b'Date: Tue, 25 Dec 2007 01:18:08 +0530', b'From: "KANAPATHIPILLAI
KATHIRAVELU
....
[Retrieved Email Truncated Here..]
```

How it works...

If you have not enabled less secure apps to access your email account, it may produce an error message.

Once you have enabled access through less secure apps, this recipe can log in as a POP3 client to your email account, retrieve an email from the account, and post it in the console.

16
Programming Across Machine Boundaries

In this chapter, we will cover the following recipes:

- Executing a remote shell command using telnet
- Copying a file to a remote machine by SFTP
- Printing a remote machine's CPU information
- Installing a Python package remotely
- Running a MySQL command remotely
- Transferring files to a remote machine over SSH
- Configuring Apache remotely to host a website

Introduction

This chapter promotes some interesting Python libraries. The recipes are presented aiming at the system administrators and advanced Python programmers who like to write code that connects to remote systems and executes commands. The chapter begins with lightweight recipes with a built-in Python library, `telnetlib`. It then brings `Paramiko`, a well-known remote access library. Finally, the powerful remote system administration library, `fabric`, is presented. The `fabric` library is loved by developers who regularly script for automatic deployments, for example, deploying web applications or building custom application binaries.

Executing a remote shell command using telnet

If you need to connect an old network switch or router via telnet, you can do so from a Python script instead of using a bash script or an interactive shell. This recipe will create a simple telnet session. It will show you how to execute shell commands to the remote host.

Getting ready

You need to install the telnet server on your machine and ensure that it's up and running. You can use a package manager that is specific to your operating system to install the telnet server package. For example, on Debian/Ubuntu, you can use `apt-get` or `aptitude` to install the `telnetd` package, as shown in the following command:

```
$ sudo apt-get install telnetd
$ telnet localhost
```

How to do it...

Let us define a function that will take a user's login credentials from the Command Prompt and connect to a telnet server.

Upon successful connection, it will send the Unix `'ls'` command. Then, it will display the output of the command, for example, listing the contents of a directory.

Listing 6.1 shows the code for a telnet session that executes a Unix command remotely as follows:

```
#!/usr/bin/env python
# Python Network Programming Cookbook, Second Edition -- Chapter - 6
# This program is optimized for Python 3.5.2.
# It may run on any other version with/without modifications.
# To make it run on Python 2.7.x, needs some changes due to API
differences.
# Follow the comments inline to make the program work with Python 2.


import getpass
import sys
```

```
import telnetlib

HOST = "localhost"

def run_telnet_session():

    user = input("Enter your remote account: ")
    # Comment out the above line and uncomment
      the below line for Python 2.7.
    # user = raw_input("Enter your remote account: ")

    password = getpass.getpass()
    session = telnetlib.Telnet(HOST)
    session.read_until(b"login: ")
    session.write(user.encode('ascii') + b"\n")
    if password:
        session.read_until(b"Password: ")
        session.write(password.encode('ascii') + b"\n")
    session.write(b"ls\n")
    session.write(b"exit\n")
    print (session.read_all())

if __name__ == '__main__':
    run_telnet_session()
```

If you run a telnet server on your local machine and run this code, it will ask you for your remote user account and password. The following output shows a telnet session executed on an Ubuntu machine:

```
$ python 16_1_execute_remote_telnet_cmd.py
Enter your remote account: pradeeban
Password:
ls
exit
Last login: Tue Jun  6 22:39:44 CEST 2017 from localhost on pts/20
Welcome to Ubuntu 16.04.2 LTS (GNU/Linux 4.8.0-53-generic x86_64)
* Documentation:  https://help.ubuntu.com
* Management:     https://landscape.canonical.com
* Support:        https://ubuntu.com/advantage
89 packages can be updated.
3 updates are security updates.
pradeeban@llovizna:~$ ls
INESC-ID GSD     openflow
Desktop                   MEOCloud          software
Documents              Downloads        Dropbox
Obidos          floodlight                  OpenDaylight
pradeeban@llovizna:~$ exit
logout
```

How it works...

This recipe relies on Python's built-in `telnetlib` networking library to create a telnet session. The `run_telnet_session()` function takes the username and password from the Command Prompt. The `getpass` module's `getpass()` function is used to get the password as this function won't let you see what is typed on the screen.

In order to create a telnet session, you need to instantiate a `Telnet()` class, which takes a hostname parameter to initialize. In this case, `localhost` is used as the hostname. You can use the `argparse` module to pass a hostname to this script.

The telnet session's remote output can be captured with the `read_until()` method. In the first case, the login prompt is detected using this method. Then, the username with a new line feed is sent to the remote machine by the `write()` method (in this case, the same machine accessed as if it's remote). Similarly, the password was supplied to the remote host.

Then, the `ls` command is sent to be executed. Finally, to disconnect from the remote host, the `exit` command is sent, and all session data received from the remote host is printed on screen using the `read_all()` method.

Copying a file to a remote machine by SFTP

If you want to upload or copy a file from your local machine to a remote machine securely, you can do so via **Secure File Transfer Protocol** (**SFTP**).

Getting ready

This recipe uses a powerful third-party networking library, `Paramiko`, to show you an example of file copying by SFTP, as shown in the following command. You can grab the latest code of `Paramiko` from GitHub (`https://github.com/paramiko/paramiko`) or PyPI:

```
$ pip install paramiko
Make sure to have the SSH server and client installed on the target
host and local host accordingly. In this example, since we are having
localhost also as the target, install SSH locally:
$ sudo apt-get install ssh
```

How to do it...

This recipe takes a few command-line inputs: the remote hostname, server port, source filename, and destination filename. For the sake of simplicity, we can use default or hard-coded values for these input parameters.

In order to connect to the remote host, we need the username and password, which can be obtained from the user from the command line.

Listing 6.2 explains how to copy a file remotely by SFTP, as shown in the following code:

```
#!/usr/bin/env python
# Python Network Programming Cookbook, Second Edition -- Chapter - 6
# This program is optimized for Python 3.5.2.
# It may run on any other version with/without modifications.
# To make it run on Python 2.7.x, needs some changes due to API
differences.
# Follow the comments inline to make the program work with Python 2.


import argparse
import paramiko
import getpass


SOURCE = '16_2_copy_remote_file_over_sftp.py'
DESTINATION ='/tmp/16_2_copy_remote_file_over_sftp.py '


def copy_file(hostname, port, username, password, src, dst):
    client = paramiko.SSHClient()
    client.load_system_host_keys()
    print (" Connecting to %s \n with username=%s...
              \n" %(hostname,username))
    t = paramiko.Transport(hostname, port)
    t.connect(username=username,password=password)
    sftp = paramiko.SFTPClient.from_transport(t)
    print ("Copying file: %s to path: %s" %(src, dst))
    sftp.put(src, dst)
    sftp.close()
    t.close()


if __name__ == '__main__':
    parser = argparse.ArgumentParser(description='Remote file copy')
    parser.add_argument('--host', action="store",
```

```
                        dest="host", default='localhost')
    parser.add_argument('--port', action="store",
                        dest="port", default=22, type=int)
    parser.add_argument('--src', action="store",
                        dest="src", default=SOURCE)
    parser.add_argument('--dst', action="store",
                        dest="dst", default=DESTINATION)
    given_args = parser.parse_args()
    hostname, port =  given_args.host, given_args.port
    src, dst = given_args.src, given_args.dst
    user = input("Enter your remote account: ")
    # Comment out the above line and uncomment the
      below line for Python 2.7.
    # user = raw_input("Enter your remote account: ")

    password = getpass.getpass("Enter password for %s: " %user)
    copy_file(hostname, port, user, password, src, dst)
```

If you run this script, you will see an output similar to the following:

```
$ python3 16_2_copy_remote_file_over_sftp.py
Enter your remote account: pradeeban
Enter password for pradeeban:
 Connecting to localhost
 with username=pradeeban...
Copying file: 16_2_copy_remote_file_over_sftp.py to path:
/tmp/16_2_copy_remote_file_over_sftp.py
```

How it works...

This recipe can take the various inputs for connecting to a remote machine and copying a file over SFTP.

This recipe passes the command-line input to the `copy_file()` function. It then creates an SSH client calling the `SSHClient` class of `paramiko`. The client needs to load the system host keys. It then connects to the remote system, thus creating an instance of the `transport` class. The actual SFTP connection object, `sftp`, is created by calling the `SFTPClient.from_transport()` function of `paramiko`. This takes the `transport` instance as an input.

After the SFTP connection is ready, the local file is copied over this connection to the remote host using the `put()` method.

Finally, it is a good idea to clean up the SFTP connection and underlying objects by calling the `close()` method separately on each object.

Printing a remote machine's CPU information

Sometimes, we need to run a simple command on a remote machine over SSH. For example, we need to query the remote machine's CPU or RAM information. This can be done from a Python script as shown in this recipe.

Getting ready

You need to install the third-party package, `Paramiko`, as shown in the following command, from the source available from GitHub's repository at `https://github.com/paramiko/paramiko`:

```
$ pip install paramiko
```

How to do it...

We can use the `paramiko` module to create a remote session to a Unix machine. Then, from this session, we can read the remote machine's `/proc/cpuinfo` file to extract the CPU information.

Listing 6.3 gives the code for printing a remote machine's CPU information, as follows:

```
#!/usr/bin/env python
# Python Network Programming Cookbook, Second Edition -- Chapter - 6
# This program is optimized for Python 3.5.2.
# It may run on any other version with/without modifications.
# To make it run on Python 2.7.x, needs some changes due to API
differences.
# Follow the comments inline to make the program work with Python 2.


import argparse
import getpass
import paramiko

RECV_BYTES = 4096
COMMAND = 'cat /proc/cpuinfo'

def print_remote_cpu_info(hostname, port, username, password):
    client = paramiko.Transport((hostname, port))
```

```
        client.connect(username=username, password=password)
        stdout_data = []
        stderr_data = []
        session = client.open_channel(kind='session')
        session.exec_command(COMMAND)
        while True:
            if session.recv_ready():
                stdout_data.append(session.recv(RECV_BYTES))
            if session.recv_stderr_ready():
                stderr_data.append(session.recv_stderr(RECV_BYTES))
            if session.exit_status_ready():
                break
        print ('exit status: ', session.recv_exit_status())
        print (b''.join(stdout_data))
        print (b''.join(stderr_data))
        session.close()
        client.close()

if __name__ == '__main__':
    parser = argparse.ArgumentParser(description='Remote file copy')
    parser.add_argument('--host', action="store",
                        dest="host", default='localhost')
    parser.add_argument('--port', action="store",
                        dest="port", default=22, type=int)
    given_args = parser.parse_args()
    hostname, port =  given_args.host, given_args.port
    user = input("Enter your remote account: ")
    # Comment out the above line and uncomment the
      below line for Python 2.7.
    # user = raw_input("Enter your remote account: ")

    password = getpass.getpass("Enter password for %s: " %user)
    print_remote_cpu_info(hostname, port, user, password)
```

Running this script will show the CPU information of a given host, in this case, the local machine. Since my computer is 8 core, it shows the information of all the eight processors as follows (some of the processors are omitted in the following output for brevity):

```
$ python2 16_3_print_remote_cpu_info.py
Enter your remote account: pradeeban
Enter password for pradeeban:
('exit status: ', 0)
processor    : 0
vendor_id    : GenuineIntel
cpu family   : 6
model        : 60
model name   : Intel(R) Core(TM) i7-4700MQ CPU @ 2.40GHz
```

```
stepping	: 3
microcode	: 0x17
cpu MHz		: 2401.171
cache size	: 6144 KB
physical id	: 0
siblings	: 8
core id		: 0
cpu cores	: 4
apicid		: 0
initial apicid	: 0
fpu		: yes
fpu_exception	: yes
cpuid level	: 13
wp		: yes
flags		: fpu vme de pse tsc msr pae mce cx8 apic sep mtrr pge mca
cmov pat pse36 clflush dts acpi mmx fxsr sse sse2 ss ht tm pbe syscall
nx pdpe1gb rdtscp lm constant_tsc arch_perfmon pebs bts rep_good nopl
xtopology nonstop_tsc aperfmperf eagerfpu pni pclmulqdq dtes64 monitor
ds_cpl vmx est tm2 ssse3 sdbg fma cx16 xtpr pdcm pcid sse4_1 sse4_2
movbe popcnt tsc_deadline_timer aes xsave avx f16c rdrand lahf_lm abm
epb tpr_shadow vnmi flexpriority ept vpid fsgsbase tsc_adjust bmi1
avx2 smep bmi2 erms invpcid xsaveopt dtherm ida arat pln pts
bugs		:
bogomips	: 4789.08
clflush size	: 64
cache_alignment	: 64
address sizes	: 39 bits physical, 48 bits virtual
power management:
processor	: 1
vendor_id	: GenuineIntel
cpu family	: 6
model		: 60
model name	: Intel(R) Core(TM) i7-4700MQ CPU @ 2.40GHz
stepping	: 3
microcode	: 0x17
cpu MHz		: 2384.033
cache size	: 6144 KB
physical id	: 0
siblings	: 8
core id		: 0
cpu cores	: 4
apicid		: 1
initial apicid	: 1
fpu		: yes
fpu_exception	: yes
cpuid level	: 13
wp		: yes
flags		: fpu vme de pse tsc msr pae mce cx8 apic sep mtrr pge mca
```

```
cmov pat pse36 clflush dts acpi mmx fxsr sse sse2 ss ht tm pbe syscall
nx pdpe1gb rdtscp lm constant_tsc arch_perfmon pebs bts rep_good nopl
xtopology nonstop_tsc aperfmperf eagerfpu pni pclmulqdq dtes64 monitor
ds_cpl vmx est tm2 ssse3 sdbg fma cx16 xtpr pdcm pcid sse4_1 sse4_2
movbe popcnt tsc_deadline_timer aes xsave avx f16c rdrand lahf_lm abm
epb tpr_shadow vnmi flexpriority ept vpid fsgsbase tsc_adjust bmi1
avx2 smep bmi2 erms invpcid xsaveopt dtherm ida arat pln pts
bugs        :
bogomips    : 4789.08
clflush size      : 64
cache_alignment   : 64
address sizes     : 39 bits physical, 48 bits virtual
power management:
....
...
...
...
...
processor   : 7
vendor_id   : GenuineIntel
cpu family  : 6
model       : 60
model name  : Intel(R) Core(TM) i7-4700MQ CPU @ 2.40GHz
stepping    : 3
microcode   : 0x17
cpu MHz           : 2439.843
cache size  : 6144 KB
physical id : 0
siblings    : 8
core id           : 3
cpu cores   : 4
apicid            : 7
initial apicid    : 7
fpu         : yes
fpu_exception     : yes
cpuid level : 13
wp          : yes
flags       : fpu vme de pse tsc msr pae mce cx8 apic sep mtrr pge mca
cmov pat pse36 clflush dts acpi mmx fxsr sse sse2 ss ht tm pbe syscall
nx pdpe1gb rdtscp lm constant_tsc arch_perfmon pebs bts rep_good nopl
xtopology nonstop_tsc aperfmperf eagerfpu pni pclmulqdq dtes64 monitor
ds_cpl vmx est tm2 ssse3 sdbg fma cx16 xtpr pdcm pcid sse4_1 sse4_2
movbe popcnt tsc_deadline_timer aes xsave avx f16c rdrand lahf_lm abm
epb tpr_shadow vnmi flexpriority ept vpid fsgsbase tsc_adjust bmi1
avx2 smep bmi2 erms invpcid xsaveopt dtherm ida arat pln pts
bugs        :
bogomips    : 4789.08
clflush size      : 64
```

```
cache_alignment   : 64
address sizes     : 39 bits physical, 48 bits virtual
power management:
```

How it works...

First, we collect the connection parameters such as `hostname`, `port`, `username`, and `password`. These parameters are then passed to the `print_remote_cpu_info()` function.

This function creates an SSH client session by calling the `transport` class of `paramiko`. The connection is made thereafter using the supplied username and password. We can create a raw communication session using `open_channel()` on the SSH client. In order to execute a command on the remote host, `exec_command()` can be used.

After sending the command to the remote host, the response from the remote host can be caught by blocking the `recv_ready()` event of the session object. We can create two lists, `stdout_data` and `stderr_data`, and use them to store the remote output and error messages.

When the command exits in the remote machine, it can be detected using the `exit_status_ready()` method, and the remote session data can be concatenated using the `join()` string method.

Finally, the session and client connection can be closed using the `close()` method on each object.

Installing a Python package remotely

While dealing with the remote host in the previous recipes, you may have noticed that we need to do a lot of stuff related to the connection setup. For efficient execution, it is desirable that they become abstract and only the relevant high-level part is exposed to the programmers. It is cumbersome and slow to always explicitly set up connections to execute commands remotely.

Fabric (`http://fabfile.org/`), a third-party Python module, solves this problem. It only exposes as many APIs as can be used to efficiently interact with remote machines.

In this recipe, a simple example of using Fabric will be shown.

Getting ready

We need Fabric to be installed first. You can install Fabric using the Python packing tools, `pip` or `easy_install`, as shown in the following command. Fabric relies on the `paramiko` module, which will be installed automatically:

```
$ pip install fabric
```

Currently the default Fabric does not seem to support Python 3. You may install `fabric3` to fix this:

```
$ sudo pip install fabric3
```

Here, we will connect the remote host using the SSH protocol. So, it's necessary to run the SSH server on the remote end. If you like to test with your local machine (pretending to access as a remote machine), you may install the `openssh` server package locally. On a Debian/Ubuntu machine, this can be done with the package manager, `apt-get`, as shown in the following command:

```
$ sudo apt-get install openssh-server
```

How to do it...

Here's the code for installing a Python package using Fabric.

Listing 6.4 gives the code for installing a Python package remotely as follows:

```
#!/usr/bin/env python
# Python Network Programming Cookbook, Second Edition -- Chapter - 6
# This program is optimized for Python 2.7.12 and Python 3.5.2.
# It may run on any other version with/without modifications.

from getpass import getpass
from fabric.api import settings, run, env, prompt


def remote_server():
    env.hosts = ['127.0.0.1']
    env.user = prompt('Enter user name: ')
    env.password = getpass('Enter password: ')
def install_package():
    run("pip install yolk")
```

Fabric scripts are run in a different way as compared to the normal Python scripts. All functions using the `fabric` library must be referred to a Python script called `fabfile.py`. There's no traditional `__main__` directive in this script. Instead, you can define your method using the Fabric APIs and execute these methods using the command-line tool, `fab`. So, instead of calling `python <script>.py`, you can run a Fabric script, which is defined in a `fabfile.py` script and located under the current directory, by calling `fab one_function_name another_function_name`.

So, let's create a `fabfile.py` script as shown in the following command. For the sake of simplicity, you can create a file shortcut or link from any file to a `fabfile.py` script. First, delete any previously created `fabfile.py` file and create a shortcut to `fabfile`:

```
$ rm -rf fabfile.py
$ ln -s 16_4_install_python_package_remotely.py fabfile.py
```

If you call the `fabfile` now, it will produce the following output after installing the Python package, `yolk`, remotely as follows:

```
$ ln -sfn 16_4_install_python_package_remotely.py fabfile.py
$ fab remote_server install_package
Enter user name: faruq
Enter password:
[127.0.0.1] Executing task 'install_package'
[127.0.0.1] run: pip install yolk
[127.0.0.1] out: Downloading/unpacking yolk
[127.0.0.1] out:   Downloading yolk-0.4.3.tar.gz (86kB):
[127.0.0.1] out:   Downloading yolk-0.4.3.tar.gz (86kB): 100%  86kB
[127.0.0.1] out:   Downloading yolk-0.4.3.tar.gz (86kB):
[127.0.0.1] out:   Downloading yolk-0.4.3.tar.gz (86kB): 86kB
downloaded
[127.0.0.1] out:   Running setup.py egg_info for package yolk
[127.0.0.1] out:     Installing yolk script to /home/faruq/env/bin
[127.0.0.1] out: Successfully installed yolk
[127.0.0.1] out: Cleaning up...
[127.0.0.1] out:
Done.
Disconnecting from 127.0.0.1... done.
```

How it works...

This recipe demonstrates how a system administration task can be done remotely using a Python script. There are two functions present in this script. The `remote_server()` function sets up the Fabric `env` environment variables, for example, the hostname, user, password, and so on.

The other function, `install_package()`, calls the `run()` function. This takes the commands that you usually type in the command line. In this case, the command is `pip install yolk`. This installs the Python package, `yolk`, with `pip`. As compared to the previously described recipes, this method of running a remote command using Fabric is easier and more efficient.

Running a MySQL command remotely

If you ever need to administer a MySQL server remotely, this recipe is for you. It will show you how to send database commands to a remote MySQL server from a Python script. If you need to set up a web application that relies on a backend database, this recipe can be used as a part of your web application setup process.

Getting ready

This recipe also needs Fabric to be installed first. You can install Fabric using the Python packing tools, `pip` or `easy_install`, as shown in the following command. Fabric relies on the `paramiko` module, which will be installed automatically:

```
$ pip install fabric
```

Here, we will connect the remote host using the SSH protocol. So, it's necessary to run the SSH server on the remote end. You also need to run a MySQL server on the remote host. On a Debian/Ubuntu machine, this can be done with the package manager, `apt-get`, as shown in the following command:

```
$ sudo apt-get install openssh-server mysql-server
```

How to do it...

We defined the Fabric environment settings and a few functions for administering MySQL remotely. In these functions, instead of calling the `mysql` executable directly, we send the SQL commands to `mysql` via `echo`. This ensures that arguments are passed properly to the `mysql` executable.

Listing 6.5 gives the code for running MySQL commands remotely, as follows:

```
#!/usr/bin/env python
# Python Network Programming Cookbook, Second Edition -- Chapter - 6
# This program is optimized for Python 2.7.12 and Python 3.5.2.
# It may run on any other version with/without modifications.

from getpass import getpass
from fabric.api import run, env, prompt, cd
def remote_server():
    env.hosts = ['127.0.0.1']
    env.user = prompt('Enter your system username: ')
    env.password = getpass('Enter your system user password: ')
    env.mysqlhost = 'localhost'
    env.mysqluser = prompt('Enter your db username: ')
    env.mysqlpassword = getpass('Enter your db user password: ')
    env.db_name = ''

def show_dbs():
    """ Wraps mysql show databases cmd"""
    q = "show databases"
    run("echo '%s' | mysql -u%s -p%s" %(q, env.mysqluser,
          env.mysqlpassword))


def run_sql(db_name, query):
    """ Generic function to run sql"""
    with cd('/tmp'):
        run("echo '%s' | mysql -u%s -p%s -D %s" %(query,
             env.mysqluser, env.mysqlpassword, db_name))

def create_db():
    """Create a MySQL DB for App version"""
    if not env.db_name:
        db_name = prompt("Enter the DB name:")
    else:
        db_name = env.db_name
    run('echo "CREATE DATABASE %s default character set
         utf8 collate utf8_unicode_ci;"|mysql
         --batch --user=%s --password=%s --host=%s'\
```

```
        % (db_name, env.mysqluser, env.mysqlpassword,
         env.mysqlhost), pty=True)

def ls_db():
    """ List a dbs with size in MB """
    if not env.db_name:
        db_name = prompt("Which DB to ls?")
    else:
        db_name = env.db_name
    query = """SELECT table_schema
                             "DB Name",
       Round(Sum(data_length + index_length) / 1024 / 1024, 1)
        "DB Size in MB"
        FROM   information_schema.tables
        WHERE table_schema = \"%s\"
        GROUP  BY table_schema """ %db_name
    run_sql(db_name, query)


def empty_db():
    """ Empty all tables of a given DB """
    db_name = prompt("Enter DB name to empty:")
    cmd = """
    (echo 'SET foreign_key_checks = 0;';
    (mysqldump -u%s -p%s --add-drop-table --no-data %s |
     grep ^DROP);
     echo 'SET foreign_key_checks = 1;') | \
     mysql -u%s -p%s -b %s
    """ %(env.mysqluser, env.mysqlpassword, db_name,
          env.mysqluser, env.mysqlpassword, db_name)
    run(cmd)
```

In order to run this script, you should create a shortcut, `fabfile.py`. From the command line, you can do this by typing the following command:

```
$ ln -sfn 16_5_run_mysql_command_remotely.py fabfile.py
```

Then, you can call the `fab` executable in various forms.

The following command will show a list of databases (using the SQL query, `show databases`):

```
$ fab remote_server show_dbs
```

The following command will create a new MySQL database. If you haven't defined the Fabric environment variable, `db_name`, a prompt will be shown to enter the target database name. This database will be created using the SQL command, `CREATE DATABASE <database_name> default character set utf8 collate utf8_unicode_ci;`:

```
$ fab remote_server create_db
```

This Fabric command will show the size of a database:

```
$ fab remote_server ls_db()
```

The following Fabric command will use the `mysqldump` and `mysql` executables to empty a database. This behavior of this function is similar to the truncating of a database, except it removes all the tables. The result is as if you created a fresh database without any tables:

```
$ fab remote_server empty_db()
```

The following will be the output:

```
$ fab remote_server show_dbs
[127.0.0.1] Executing task 'show_dbs'
[127.0.0.1] run: echo 'show databases' | mysql -uroot -p<DELETED>
[127.0.0.1] out: Database
[127.0.0.1] out: information_schema
[127.0.0.1] out: mysql
[127.0.0.1] out: phpmyadmin
[127.0.0.1] out:
Done.
Disconnecting from 127.0.0.1... done.
$ fab remote_server create_db
[127.0.0.1] Executing task 'create_db'
Enter the DB name: test123
[127.0.0.1] run: echo "CREATE DATABASE test123 default character set
utf8 collate utf8_unicode_ci;"|mysql --batch --user=root --
password=<DELETED> --host=localhost
Done.
Disconnecting from 127.0.0.1... done.
$ fab remote_server show_dbs
[127.0.0.1] Executing task 'show_dbs'
[127.0.0.1] run: echo 'show databases' | mysql -uroot -p<DELETED>
[127.0.0.1] out: Database
[127.0.0.1] out: information_schema
[127.0.0.1] out: collabtive
[127.0.0.1] out: test123
[127.0.0.1] out: testdb
```

```
[127.0.0.1] out:
Done.
Disconnecting from 127.0.0.1... done.
```

How it works...

This script defines a few functions that are used with Fabric. The first function, `remote_server()`, sets the environment variables. The local loopback IP (`127.0.0.1`) is put to the list of hosts. The local system user and MySQL login credentials are set and collected via `getpass()`.

The other function utilizes the Fabric `run()` function to send MySQL commands to the remote MySQL server by echoing the command to the `mysql` executable.

The `run_sql()` function is a generic function that can be used as a wrapper in other functions. For example, the `empty_db()` function calls it to execute the SQL commands. This can keep your code a bit more organized and cleaner.

Transferring files to a remote machine over SSH

While automating a remote system administration task using Fabric, if you want to transfer files between your local machine and the remote machine with SSH, you can use the Fabric's built-in `get()` and `put()` functions. This recipe shows you how we can create custom functions to transfer files smartly by checking the disk space before and after the transfer.

Getting ready

This recipe also needs Fabric to be installed first. You can install Fabric using Python packing tools, `pip` or `easy_install`, as shown in the following command:

```
$ pip install fabric
```

Here, we will connect the remote host using the SSH protocol. So, it's necessary to install and run the SSH server on the remote host.

How to do it...

Let us first set up the Fabric environment variables and then create two functions, one for downloading files and the other for uploading files.

Listing 6.6 gives the code for transferring files to a remote machine over SSH as follows:

```
#!/usr/bin/env python
# Python Network Programming Cookbook, Second Edition -- Chapter - 6
# This program is optimized for Python 2.7.12 and Python 3.5.2.
# It may run on any other version with/without modifications.


from getpass import getpass
from fabric.api import local, run, env, get, put, prompt, open_shell

def remote_server():
    env.hosts = ['127.0.0.1']
    env.password = getpass('Enter your system password: ')
    env.home_folder = '/tmp'

def login():
    open_shell(command="cd %s" %env.home_folder)


def download_file():
    print ("Checking local disk space...")
    local("df -h")
    remote_path = prompt("Enter the remote file path:")
    local_path = prompt("Enter the local file path:")
    get(remote_path=remote_path, local_path=local_path)
    local("ls %s" %local_path)


def upload_file():
    print ("Checking remote disk space...")
    run("df -h")
    local_path = prompt("Enter the local file path:")
    remote_path = prompt("Enter the remote file path:")
    put(remote_path=remote_path, local_path=local_path)
    run("ls %s" %remote_path)
```

In order to run this script, you should create a shortcut, `fabfile.py`. From the command line, you can do this by typing the following command:

```
$ ln -sfn 16_6_transfer_file_over_ssh.py fabfile.py
```

Then, you can call the `fab` executable in various forms.

First, to log on to a remote server using your script, you can run the following Fabric function:

```
$ fab remote_server login
```

This will give you a minimum shell-like environment. Then, you can download a file from a remote server to your local machine using the following command:

```
$ fab remote_server download_file
```

Similarly, to upload a file, you can use the following command:

```
$ fab remote_server upload_file
```

In this example, the local machine is used via SSH. So, you have to install the SSH server locally to run these scripts. Otherwise, you can modify the `remote_server()` function and point it to a remote server, as follows:

```
$ fab remote_server login
[127.0.0.1] Executing task 'login'
Linux debian6 2.6.32-5-686 #1 SMP Mon Feb 25 01:04:36 UTC 2013 i686
The programs included with the Debian GNU/Linux system are free
software;
the exact distribution terms for each program are described in the
individual files in /usr/share/doc/*/copyright.
Debian GNU/Linux comes with ABSOLUTELY NO WARRANTY, to the extent
permitted by applicable law.
You have new mail.
Last login: Wed Aug 21 15:08:45 2013 from localhost
cd /tmp
faruq@debian6:~$ cd /tmp
faruq@debian6:/tmp$
<CTRL+D>
faruq@debian6:/tmp$ logout
Done.
Disconnecting from 127.0.0.1... done.
$ fab remote_server download_file
[127.0.0.1] Executing task 'download_file'
Checking local disk space...
[localhost] local: df -h
Filesystem            Size  Used Avail Use% Mounted on
```

```
/dev/sda1              62G   47G   12G  81% /
tmpfs                 506M     0  506M   0% /lib/init/rw
udev                  501M  160K  501M   1% /dev
tmpfs                 506M  408K  505M   1% /dev/shm
Z_DRIVE              1012G  944G   69G  94% /media/z
C_DRIVE               466G  248G  218G  54% /media/c
Enter the remote file path: /tmp/op.txt
Enter the local file path: .
[127.0.0.1] download: chapter7/op.txt <- /tmp/op.txt
[localhost] local: ls .
16_1_execute_remote_telnet_cmd.py   16_3_print_remote_cpu_info.py
16_5_run_mysql_command_remotely.py
16_7_configure_Apache_for_hosting_website_remotely.py  fabfile.pyc
__init__.py  test.txt
16_2_copy_remote_file_over_sftp.py
16_4_install_python_package_remotely.py
16_6_transfer_file_over_ssh.py fabfile.py
index.html     op.txt       vhost.conf
Done.
Disconnecting from 127.0.0.1... done.
```

How it works...

In this recipe, we used a few of Fabric's built-in functions to transfer files between local and remote machines. The `local()` function does an action on the local machine, whereas the remote actions are carried out by the `run()` function.

This is useful to check the available disk space on the target machine before uploading a file and vice versa.

This is achieved by using the Unix command, `df`. The source and destination file paths can be specified via the Command Prompt or can be hard coded in the source file in case of an unattended automatic execution.

Configuring Apache remotely to host a website

Fabric functions can be run as both regular and super users. If you need to host a website in a remote Apache web server, you need the administrative user privileges to create configuration files and restart the web server. This recipe introduces the Fabric `sudo()` function that runs commands in the remote machine as a superuser.

Here, we would like to configure the Apache virtual host for running a website.

Getting ready

This recipe needs Fabric to be installed first on your local machine. You can install Fabric using the Python packing tools, `pip` or `easy_install`, as shown in the following command:

```
$ pip install fabric
```

Here, we will connect the remote host using the SSH protocol. So, it's necessary to install and run the SSH server on the remote host. It is also assumed that the Apache web server is installed and running on the remote server. On a Debian/Ubuntu machine, this can be done with the package manager, `apt-get`, as shown in the following command:

```
$ sudo apt-get install openssh-server apache2
```

How to do it...

First, we collect our Apache installation paths and some configuration parameters, such as web server user, group, virtual host configuration path, and initialization scripts. These parameters can be defined as constants.

Then, we set up two functions, `remote_server()` and `setup_vhost()`, to execute the Apache configuration task using Fabric.

Listing 6.7 gives the code for configuring Apache remotely to host a website as follows:

```
#!/usr/bin/env python
# Python Network Programming Cookbook, Second Edition -- Chapter - 6
# This program is optimized for Python 2.7.12 and Python 3.5.2.
# It may run on any other version with/without modifications.

from getpass import getpass
from fabric.api import env, put, sudo, prompt
from fabric.contrib.files import exists

WWW_DOC_ROOT = "/data/apache/test/"
WWW_USER = "www-data"
WWW_GROUP = "www-data"
APACHE_SITES_PATH = "/etc/apache2/sites-enabled/"
```

```
APACHE_INIT_SCRIPT = "/etc/init.d/apache2 "


def remote_server():
    env.hosts = ['127.0.0.1']
    env.user = prompt('Enter user name: ')
    env.password = getpass('Enter your system password: ')


def setup_vhost():
    """ Setup a test website """
    print ("Preparing the Apache vhost setup...")
    print ("Setting up the document root...")
    if exists(WWW_DOC_ROOT):
        sudo("rm -rf %s" %WWW_DOC_ROOT)
    sudo("mkdir -p %s" %WWW_DOC_ROOT)
    sudo("chown -R %s.%s %s" %(env.user, env.user, WWW_DOC_ROOT))
    put(local_path="index.html", remote_path=WWW_DOC_ROOT)
    sudo("chown -R %s.%s %s" %(WWW_USER, WWW_GROUP, WWW_DOC_ROOT))
    print ("Setting up the vhost...")
    sudo("chown -R %s.%s %s" %(env.user, env.user, APACHE_SITES_PATH))
    put(local_path="vhost.conf", remote_path=APACHE_SITES_PATH)
    sudo("chown -R %s.%s %s" %('root', 'root', APACHE_SITES_PATH))
    sudo("%s restart" %APACHE_INIT_SCRIPT)
    print ("Setup complete. Now open the server path
http://abc.remote-server.org/ in your web browser.")
```

In order to run this script, the following line should be appended on your host file, for example, `/etc/hosts`:

```
127.0.0.1 abc.remote-server.org abc
```

You should also create a shortcut, `fabfile.py`. From the command line, you can do this by typing the following command:

```
$ ln -sfn 16_7_configure_Apache_for_hosting_website_remotely.py
fabfile.py
```

Then, you can call the `fab` executable in various forms.

First, to log on to a remote server using your script, you can run the following Fabric function. This will result in the following output:

```
$ fab remote_server setup_vhost
[127.0.0.1] Executing task 'setup_vhost'
Preparing the Apache vhost setup...
Setting up the document root...
[127.0.0.1] sudo: rm -rf /data/apache/test/
```

```
[127.0.0.1] sudo: mkdir -p /data/apache/test/
[127.0.0.1] sudo: chown -R faruq.faruq /data/apache/test/
[127.0.0.1] put: index.html -> /data/apache/test/index.html
[127.0.0.1] sudo: chown -R www-data.www-data /data/apache/test/
Setting up the vhost...
[127.0.0.1] sudo: chown -R faruq.faruq /etc/apache2/sites-enabled/
[127.0.0.1] put: vhost.conf -> /etc/apache2/sites-enabled/vhost.conf
[127.0.0.1] sudo: chown -R root.root /etc/apache2/sites-enabled/
[127.0.0.1] sudo: /etc/init.d/apache2 restart
[127.0.0.1] out: Restarting web server: apache2apache2: Could not
reliably determine the server's fully qualified domain name, using
127.0.0.1 for ServerName
[127.0.0.1] out:  ... waiting apache2: Could not reliably determine
the server's fully qualified domain name, using 127.0.0.1 for
ServerName
[127.0.0.1] out: .
[127.0.0.1] out:
Setup complete. Now open the server path http://abc.remote-server.org/
in your web browser.
Done.
Disconnecting from 127.0.0.1... done.
```

After you execute this recipe, you can open your browser and try to access the path you set up on the host file (for example, /etc/hosts). It should show the following output on your browser:

It works!

This is the default web page for this server.

The web server software is running but no content has been added, yet.

How it works...

This recipe sets up the initial Apache configuration parameters as constants and then defines two functions. In the remote_server() function, the usual Fabric environment parameters, for example, hosts, user, password, and so on, are placed.

The setup_vhost() function executes a series of privileged commands. First, it checks whether the website's document root path is already created using the exists() function. If it exists, it removes that path and creates it in the next step. Using chown, it ensures that the path is owned by the current user.

In the next step, it uploads a bare bone HTML file, `index.html`, to the document root path. After uploading the file, it reverts the permission of the files to the web server user.

After setting up the document root, the `setup_vhost()` function uploads the supplied `vhost.conf` file to the Apache site configuration path. Then, it sets its owner as the root user.

Finally, the script restarts the Apache service so that the configuration is activated. If the configuration is successful, you should see the sample output shown earlier when you open the URL, `http://abc.remote-server.org/`, in your browser.

17
Working with Web Services – SOAP, and REST

In this chapter, we will cover the following recipes:

- Querying a local XML-RPC server
- Writing a multithreaded, multicall XML-RPC server
- Running an XML-RPC server with a basic HTTP authentication
- Collecting some photo information from Flickr using REST
- Searching for SOAP methods from an Amazon S3 web service
- Searching Amazon for books through the product search API
- Creating RESTful web applications with Flask

Introduction

This chapter presents some interesting Python recipes on web services using three different approaches, namely, **XML Remote Procedure Call** (**XML-RPC**), **Simple Object Access Protocol** (**SOAP**), and **Representational State Transfer** (**REST**). The idea behind the web services is to enable an interaction between two software components over the web through a carefully designed protocol. The interface is machine readable. Various protocols are used to facilitate the web services.

Here, we bring examples from three commonly used protocols. XML-RPC uses HTTP as the transport medium, and communication is done using XML contents. A server that implements XML-RPC waits for a call from a suitable client. The client calls that server to execute remote procedures with different parameters. XML-RPC is simpler and comes with a minimum security in mind. On the other hand, SOAP has a rich set of protocols for enhanced remote procedure calls. REST is an architectural style to facilitate web services. It operates with HTTP request methods, namely, `GET()`, `POST()`, `PUT()`, and `DELETE()`. This chapter presents the practical use of these web services protocols and styles to achieve some common tasks.

Querying a local XML-RPC server

If you do a lot of web programming, it's most likely that you will come across this task: to get some information from a website that runs an XML-RPC service. Before we go into the depth of an XML-RPC service, let's launch an XML-RPC server and talk to it first.

Getting ready

In this recipe, we will use the Python Supervisor program that is widely used to launch and manage a bunch of executable programs. Supervisor can be run as a background daemon and can monitor child processes and restart if they die suddenly. We can install Supervisor by simply running the following command:

```
$pip install supervisor
```

Supervisor works on Python 2.x version - 2.4 and later. However, it does not work under Python 3 at the time of writing. So in order to run this example, you need to have Python 2 installed on your computer.

How to do it...

We need to create a configuration file for Supervisor. A sample configuration is given in this recipe. In this example, we define the Unix HTTP server socket and a few other parameters. Note the `rpcinterface:supervisor` section where `rpcinterface_factory` is defined to communicate with clients.

Using Supervisor, we configure a simple server program in the program: `17_2_multithreaded_multicall_xmlrpc_server.py` section by specifying the command and some other parameters.

Listing 7.1a gives the code for a minimal Supervisor configuration, as shown:

```
[unix_http_server]
file=/tmp/supervisor.sock   ; (the path to the socket file)
chmod=0700                 ; socket file mode (default 0700)

[supervisord]
logfile=/tmp/supervisord.log
loglevel=info
pidfile=/tmp/supervisord.pid
nodaemon=true

[rpcinterface:supervisor]
supervisor.rpcinterface_factory =
supervisor.rpcinterface:make_main_rpcinterface

[program:17_2_multithreaded_multicall_xmlrpc_server.py]
command=python 17_2_multithreaded_multicall_xmlrpc_server.py ; the
program (relative uses PATH, can take args)
process_name=%(program_name)s ; process_name expr (default
%(program_name)s)
```

If you create the preceding Supervisor configuration file in your favorite editor, you can run Supervisor by simply calling it.

Now, we can code an XML-RPC client that can act as a Supervisor proxy and give us the information about the running processes.

Listing 7.1b gives the code for querying a local XML-RPC server, as shown:

```
#!/usr/bin/env python
# Python Network Programming Cookbook, Second Edition -- Chapter - 7
# This program is optimized for Python 2.7.12.
# Supervisor requires Python 2.x, and does not run on Python 3.x.


import supervisor.xmlrpc
import xmlrpclib

def query_supervisr(sock):
    transport = supervisor.xmlrpc.SupervisorTransport(None, None,
                'unix://%s' %sock)
    proxy = xmlrpclib.ServerProxy('http://127.0.0.1',
```

```
            transport=transport)
    print ("Getting info about all running processes
            via Supervisord...")
    print (proxy.supervisor.getAllProcessInfo())

if __name__ == '__main__':
    query_supervisr(sock='/tmp/supervisor.sock')
```

If you run the `Supervisor` daemon, it will show output similar to the following:

```
$ supervisord
2013-09-27 16:40:56,861 INFO RPC interface 'supervisor' initialized
2013-09-27 16:40:56,861 CRIT Server 'unix_http_server' running
without any HTTP authentication checking
2013-09-27 16:40:56,861 INFO supervisord started with pid 27436
2013-09-27 16:40:57,864 INFO spawned:
'17_2_multithreaded_multicall_xmlrpc_server.py' with pid 27439
2013-09-27 16:40:58,940 INFO success:
17_2_multithreaded_multicall_xmlrpc_server.py entered RUNNING state,
process has stayed up for > than 1 seconds (startsecs)
```

Note that our child process, `17_2_multithreaded_multicall_xmlrpc_server.py`, has been launched.

Now, if you run the client code, it will query the XML-RPC server interface of Supervisor and list the running processes, as shown:

```
$ python 17_1_query_xmlrpc_server.py
Getting info about all running processes via Supervisord...
[{'now': 1380296807, 'group':
'17_2_multithreaded_multicall_xmlrpc_server.py', 'description': 'pid
27439, uptime 0:05:50', 'pid': 27439, 'stderr_logfile':
'/tmp/17_2_multithreaded_multicall_xmlrpc_server.py-stderr---
supervisor-i_VmKz.log', 'stop': 0, 'statename': 'RUNNING', 'start':
1380296457, 'state': 20, 'stdout_logfile':
'/tmp/17_2_multithreaded_multicall_xmlrpc_server.py-stdout---
supervisor-eMuJqk.log', 'logfile':
'/tmp/17_2_multithreaded_multicall_xmlrpc_server.py-stdout---
supervisor-eMuJqk.log', 'exitstatus': 0, 'spawnerr': '', 'name':
'17_2_multithreaded_multicall_xmlrpc_server.py'}]
```

How it works...

This recipe relies on running the `Supervisor` daemon (configured with `rpcinterface`) in the background. Supervisor launches another XML-RPC server, as follows: `17_2_multithreaded_multicall_xmlrpc_server.py`.

The client code has a `query_supervisr()` method, which takes an argument for the Supervisor socket. In this method, an instance of `SupervisorTransport` is created with the Unix socket path. Then, an XML-RPC server proxy is created by instantiating the `ServerProxy()` class of `xmlrpclib` by passing the server address and previously created transport.

The XML-RPC server proxy then calls the Supervisor's `getAllProcessInfo()` method, which prints the process information of the child process. This process includes `pid`, `statename`, `description`, and so on.

Writing a multithreaded, multicall XML-RPC server

You can make your XML-RPC server accept multiple calls simultaneously. This means that multiple function calls can return a single result. In addition to this, if your server is multithreaded, then you can execute more code after the server is launched in a single thread. The program's main thread will not be blocked in this manner.

How to do it...

We can create a `ServerThread` class inheriting from the threading. Thread class and wrap a `SimpleXMLRPCServer` instance in an attribute of this class. This can be set up to accept multiple calls.

Then, we can create two functions: one launches the multithreaded, multicall XML-RPC server, and the other creates a client to that server.

Listing 7.2 gives the code for writing a multithreaded, multicall XML-RPC server, as shown:

```
#!/usr/bin/env python
# Python Network Programming Cookbook, Second Edition -- Chapter - 7
# This program is optimized for Python 3.5.2.
# To make it work with Python 2.7.12:
#      Follow through the code inline for some changes.
# It may run on any other version with/without modifications.

import argparse
import xmlrpc
```

```
# Comment out the above line and uncomment the below line for Python
2.x.
#import xmlrpclib
import threading

from xmlrpc.server import SimpleXMLRPCServer
# Comment out the above line and uncomment the below line for Python
2.x.
#from SimpleXMLRPCServer import SimpleXMLRPCServer

# some trivial functions
def add(x,y):
    return x+y

def subtract(x, y):
    return x-y

def multiply(x, y):
    return x*y

def divide(x, y):
    return x/y


class ServerThread(threading.Thread):
    def __init__(self, server_addr):
        threading.Thread.__init__(self)
        self.server = SimpleXMLRPCServer(server_addr)
        self.server.register_multicall_functions()
        self.server.register_function(add, 'add')
        self.server.register_function(subtract, 'subtract')
        self.server.register_function(multiply, 'multiply')
        self.server.register_function(divide, 'divide')

    def run(self):
        self.server.serve_forever()
def run_server(host, port):
    # server code
    server_addr = (host, port)
    server = ServerThread(server_addr)
    server.start() # The server is now running
    print ("Server thread started. Testing the server...")

def run_client(host, port):

    # client code
    proxy = xmlrpc.client.ServerProxy("http://%s:%s/" %(host, port))
    # Comment out the above line and uncomment the
```

```
      below line for Python 2.x.
    #proxy = xmlrpclib.ServerProxy("http://%s:%s/" %(host, port))

    multicall = xmlrpc.client.MultiCall(proxy)
    # Comment out the above line and uncomment the
      below line for Python 2.x.
    #multicall = xmlrpclib.MultiCall(proxy)

    multicall.add(7,3)
    multicall.subtract(7,3)
    multicall.multiply(7,3)
    multicall.divide(7,3)
    result = multicall()
    print ("7+3=%d, 7-3=%d, 7*3=%d, 7/3=%d" % tuple(result))

if __name__ == '__main__':
    parser = argparse.ArgumentParser(description='Multithreaded
              multicall XMLRPC Server/Proxy')
    parser.add_argument('--host', action="store", dest="host",
                        default='localhost')
    parser.add_argument('--port', action="store", dest="port",
                        default=8000, type=int)
    # parse arguments
    given_args = parser.parse_args()
    host, port =  given_args.host, given_args.port
    run_server(host, port)
    run_client(host, port)
```

If you run this script, you will see output similar to the following:

```
$ python 17_2_multithreaded_multicall_xmlrpc_server.py --port=8000
Server thread started. Testing the server...
127.0.0.1 - - [13/Jun/2017 23:00:27] "POST / HTTP/1.1" 200 -
7+3=10, 7-3=4, 7*3=21, 7/3=2
```

How it works...

In this recipe, we have created a `ServerThread` subclass inheriting from the Python threading library's `thread` class. This subclass initializes a server attribute that creates an instance of the `SimpleXMLRPC` server. The XML-RPC server address can be given through the command-line input. In order to enable the multicall function, we called the `register_multicall_functions()` method on the server instance.

Then, four trivial functions are registered with this XML-RPC server: `add()`, `subtract()`, `multiply()`, and `divide()`.

These functions do exactly the same operation as their names suggest.

In order to launch the server, we pass a host and port to the `run_server()` function. A server instance is created using the `ServerThread` class discussed earlier. The start() method of this server instance launches the XML-RPC server.

On the client side, the `run_client()` function accepts the same host and port arguments from the command line. It then creates a proxy instance of the XML-RPC server discussed earlier by calling the `ServerProxy()` class from `xmlrpclib`. This proxy instance is then passed onto the `multicall` class instance, multicall. Now, the preceding four trivial RPC methods can be run, for example, add, subtract, multiply, and divide. Finally, we can get the result through a single call, for example, `multicall()`. The result tuple is then printed in a single line.

Running an XML-RPC server with a basic HTTP authentication

Sometimes, you may need to implement authentication with an XML-RPC server. This recipe presents an example of a basic HTTP authentication with an XML-RPC server.

How to do it...

We can create a subclass of `SimpleXMLRPCServer` and override its request handler so that when a request comes, it is verified against given login credentials.

Listing 7.3a gives the code for running an XML-RPC server with a basic HTTP authentication, as shown:

```
#!/usr/bin/env python
# Python Network Programming Cookbook, Second Edition -- Chapter - 7
# This program is optimized for Python 3.5.2.
# To make it work with Python 2.7.12:
#      Follow through the code inline for some changes.
# It may run on any other version with/without modifications.


import argparse
import xmlrpc
# Comment out the above line and uncomment the below line for Python
2.x.
```

```
#import xmlrpclib
from base64 import b64decode

from xmlrpc.server import SimpleXMLRPCServer,
SimpleXMLRPCRequestHandler
# Comment out the above line and uncomment the below line for Python
2.x.
#from SimpleXMLRPCServer  import SimpleXMLRPCServer,
SimpleXMLRPCRequestHandler


class SecureXMLRPCServer(SimpleXMLRPCServer):

    def __init__(self, host, port, username, password, *args,
**kargs):
        self.username = username
        self.password = password
        # authenticate method is called from inner class
        class VerifyingRequestHandler(SimpleXMLRPCRequestHandler):
              # method to override
              def parse_request(request):
                  if SimpleXMLRPCRequestHandler.
                     parse_request(request):
                      # authenticate
                      if self.authenticate(request.headers):
                          return True
                      else:
                          # if authentication fails return 401
                          request.send_error(401, 'Authentication
                           failed, Try agin.')
                  return False
        # initialize
        SimpleXMLRPCServer.__init__(self, (host, port),
        requestHandler=VerifyingRequestHandler, *args, **kargs)

    def authenticate(self, headers):
        headers = headers.get('Authorization').split()
        basic, encoded = headers[0], headers[1]
        if basic != 'Basic':
            print ('Only basic authentication supported')
            return False
        secret = b64decode(encoded).split(b':')
        username, password = secret[0].decode("utf-8"),
                             secret[1].decode("utf-8")
        return True if (username == self.username and
                    password == self.password) else False

def run_server(host, port, username, password):
```

```
    server = SecureXMLRPCServer(host, port, username, password)
    # simple test function
    def echo(msg):
        """Reply client in  uppser case """
        reply = msg.upper()
        print ("Client said: %s. So we echo that in uppercase: %s"
                 %(msg, reply))
        return reply
    server.register_function(echo, 'echo')
    print ("Running a HTTP auth enabled XMLRPC server
             on %s:%s..." %(host, port))
    server.serve_forever()


if __name__ == '__main__':
    parser = argparse.ArgumentParser(description='Multithreaded
              multicall XMLRPC Server/Proxy')
    parser.add_argument('--host', action="store", dest="host",
                         default='localhost')
    parser.add_argument('--port', action="store", dest="port",
                          default=8000, type=int)
    parser.add_argument('--username', action="store",
                         dest="username", default='user')
    parser.add_argument('--password', action="store",
                         dest="password", default='pass')
    # parse arguments
    given_args = parser.parse_args()
    host, port =  given_args.host, given_args.port
    username, password = given_args.username, given_args.password
    run_server(host, port, username, password)
```

If this server is run, then the following output can be seen by default:

```
$ python 17_3a_xmlrpc_server_with_http_auth.py --port=8000
Running a HTTP auth enabled XMLRPC server on localhost:8000...
Client said: hello server.... So we echo that in uppercase: HELLO
SERVER...
127.0.0.1 - - [13/Jun/2017 23:32:14] "POST /RPC2 HTTP/1.1" 200 -
```

Now, let us create a simple client proxy and use the same login credentials as used with the server.

Listing 7.3b gives the code for the XML-RPC client, as shown:

```
#!/usr/bin/env python
# Python Network Programming Cookbook, Second Edition -- Chapter - 7
# This program is optimized for Python 3.5.2.
# To make it work with Python 2.7.12:
```

```
#      Follow through the code inline for some changes.
# It may run on any other version with/without modifications.


import argparse
import xmlrpc
# Comment out the above line and uncomment the below line for Python
2.x.
#import xmlrpclib

from xmlrpc.server import SimpleXMLRPCServer
# Comment out the above line for Python 2.x.

def run_client(host, port, username, password):
    server = xmlrpc.client.ServerProxy('http://%s:%s@%s:%s'
              %(username, password, host, port, ))
    # Comment out the above line and uncomment the
      below line for Python 2.x.
    #server = xmlrpclib.ServerProxy('http://%s:%s@%s:%s'
               %(username, password, host, port, ))
    msg = "hello server..."
    print ("Sending message to server: %s  " %msg)
    print ("Got reply: %s" %server.echo(msg))

if __name__ == '__main__':
    parser = argparse.ArgumentParser(description='Multithreaded
              multicall XMLRPC Server/Proxy')
    parser.add_argument('--host', action="store", dest="host",
                           default='localhost')
    parser.add_argument('--port', action="store", dest="port",
                          default=8000, type=int)
    parser.add_argument('--username', action="store",
                          dest="username", default='user')
    parser.add_argument('--password', action="store",
                          dest="password", default='pass')
    # parse arguments
    given_args = parser.parse_args()
    host, port =  given_args.host, given_args.port
    username, password = given_args.username, given_args.password
    run_client(host, port, username, password)
```

If you run the client, then it shows the following output:

```
$ python 17_3b_xmprpc_client.py --port=8000
Sending message to server: hello server...
Got reply: HELLO SERVER...
```

The following screenshot shows the server and client:

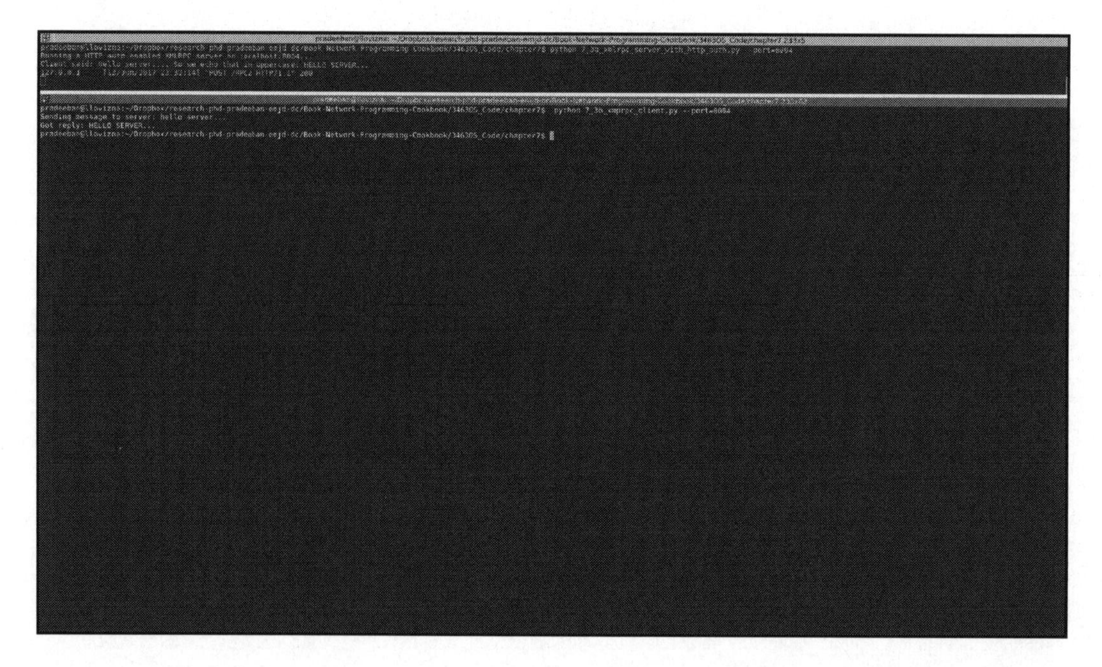

How it works...

In the server script, the `SecureXMLRPCServer` subclass is created by inheriting from `SimpleXMLRPCServer`. In this subclass initialization code, we created the `VerifyingRequestHandler` class that actually intercepts the request and does the basic authentication using the `authenticate()` method.

In the `authenticate()` method, the HTTP request is passed as an argument. This method checks the presence of the value of authorization. If its value is set to basic, it then decodes the encoded password with the `b64decode()` function from the base64 standard module. After extracting the username and password, it then checks that with the server's given credentials set up initially.

In the `run_server()` function, a simple `echo()` sub function is defined and registered with the `SecureXMLRPCServer` instance.

In the client script, run_client() simply takes the server address and login credentials and passes them to the ServerProxy() instance. It then sends a single line message through the echo() method.

Collecting some photo information from Flickr using REST

Many Internet websites provide a web services interface through their REST APIs. Flickr, a famous photo sharing website, has a REST interface. Let's try to gather some photo information to build a specialized database or other photo-related applications.

To run this recipe, you need to install requests using pip:

```
$ sudo pip install requests
```

How to do it...

We need the REST URLs for making the HTTP requests. For simplicity's sake, the URLs are hard coded in this recipe. We can use the third-party requests module to make the REST requests. It has the convenient GET(), POST(), PUT(), and DELETE() methods.

In order to talk to Flickr web services, you need to register yourself and get a secret API key. This API key can be placed in a local_settings.py file or supplied through the command line.

Listing 7.4 gives the code for collecting some photo information from Flickr using REST, as shown:

```
#!/usr/bin/env python
# Python Network Programming Cookbook, Second Edition -- Chapter - 7
# This program is optimized for Python 2.7.12 and Python 3.5.2.
# It may run on any other version with/without modifications.
# Supply Flickr API key via local_settings.py

import argparse
import json
import requests

try:
    from local_settings import flickr_apikey
```

```
except ImportError:
    pass


def collect_photo_info(api_key, tag, max_count):
    """Collects some interesting info about some photos from
Flickr.com for a given tag """
    photo_collection = []
    url =
"http://api.flickr.com/services/rest/?method=flickr.photos.search&tags
=%s&format=json&
       nojsoncallback=1&api_key=%s" %(tag, api_key)
    resp = requests.get(url)
    results = resp.json()
    count  = 0
    for p in results['photos']['photo']:
        if count >= max_count:
            return photo_collection
        print ('Processing photo: "%s"' % p['title'])
        photo = {}
        url = "http://api.flickr.com/services/rest/?
        method=flickr.photos.getInfo&photo_id=" + p['id'] +
        "&format=json&nojsoncallback=1&api_key=" + api_key
        info = requests.get(url).json()
        photo["flickrid"] = p['id']
        photo["title"] = info['photo']['title']['_content']
        photo["description"] = info['photo']['description']
                               ['_content']
        photo["page_url"] = info['photo']['urls']['url'][0]
                            ['_content']
        photo["farm"] = info['photo']['farm']
        photo["server"] = info['photo']['server']
        photo["secret"] = info['photo']['secret']
        # comments
        numcomments = int(info['photo']['comments']['_content'])
        if numcomments:
            #print "   Now reading comments (%d)..." % numcomments
            url = "http://api.flickr.com/services/rest/?
                   method=flickr.photos.comments.
                    getList&photo_id=" + p['id'] +
                    "&format=json&nojsoncallback=1&
                     api_key=" + api_key
            comments = requests.get(url).json()
            photo["comment"] = []
            for c in comments['comments']['comment']:
                comment = {}
                comment["body"] = c['_content']
                comment["authorid"] = c['author']
```

```
                comment["authorname"] = c['authorname']
                photo["comment"].append(comment)
        photo_collection.append(photo)
        count = count + 1
    return photo_collection


if __name__ == '__main__':
    parser = argparse.ArgumentParser(description='Get photo
             info from Flickr')
    parser.add_argument('--api-key', action="store",
             dest="api_key", default=flickr_apikey)
    parser.add_argument('--tag', action="store",
             dest="tag", default='Python')
    parser.add_argument('--max-count', action="store",
             dest="max_count", default=3, type=int)
    # parse arguments
    given_args = parser.parse_args()
    api_key, tag, max_count =  given_args.api_key,
     given_args.tag, given_args.max_count
    photo_info = collect_photo_info(api_key, tag, max_count)
    for photo in photo_info:
        for k,v in photo.iteritems():
            if k == "title":
                print ("Showiing photo info....")
            elif k == "comment":
                "\tPhoto got %s comments." %len(v)
            else:
                print ("\t%s => %s" %(k,v))
```

You can run this recipe with your Flickr API key either by placing it in a `local_settings.py` file or supplying it from the command line (through the `--api-key` argument). In addition to the API key, a search tag and maximum count of the result arguments can be supplied. By default, this recipe will search for the Python tag and restrict the result to three entries, as shown in the following output:

```
$ python 17_4_get_flickr_photo_info.py
Processing photo: "legolas"
Processing photo: ""The Dance of the Hunger of Kaa""
Processing photo: "Rocky"
    description => Stimson Python
Showiing photo info....
    farm => 8
    server => 7402
    secret => 6cbae671b5
    flickrid => 10054626824
    page_url =>
```

```
http://www.flickr.com/photos/102763809@N03/10054626824/
        description => &quot; 'Good. Begins now the dance--the Dance
of the Hunger of Kaa. Sit still and watch.'
    He turned twice or thrice in a big circle, weaving his head from
right to left.
    Then he began making loops and figures of eight with his body, and
soft, oozy triangles that melted into squares and five-sided figures,
and coiled mounds, never resting, never hurrying, and never stopping
his low humming song. It grew darker and darker, till at last the
dragging, shifting coils disappeared, but they could hear the rustle
of the scales.&quot;
    (From &quot;Kaa's Hunting&quot; in &quot;The Jungle Book&quot;
(1893) by Rudyard Kipling)
    These old abandoned temples built around the 12th century belong
to the abandoned city which inspired Kipling's Jungle Book.
    They are rising at the top of a mountain which dominates the
jungle at 811 meters above sea level in the centre of the jungle of
Bandhavgarh located in the Indian state Madhya Pradesh.
    Baghel King Vikramaditya Singh abandoned Bandhavgarh fort in 1617
when Rewa, at a distance of 130 km was established as a capital.
    Abandonment allowed wildlife development in this region.
    When Baghel Kings became aware of it, he declared Bandhavgarh as
their hunting preserve and strictly prohibited tree cutting and
wildlife hunting...
    Join the photographer at <a
href="http://www.facebook.com/laurent.goldstein.photography"
rel="nofollow">www.facebook.com/laurent.goldstein.photography</a>
    © All photographs are copyrighted and all rights reserved.
    Please do not use any photographs without permission (even for
private use).
    The use of any work without consent of the artist is PROHIBITED
and will lead automatically to consequences.
    Showiing photo info....
        farm => 6
        server => 5462
        secret => 6f9c0e7f83
        flickrid => 10051136944
        page_url =>
http://www.flickr.com/photos/designldg/10051136944/
        description => Ball Python
    Showiing photo info....
        farm => 4
        server => 3744
        secret => 529840767f
        flickrid => 10046353675
        page_url =>
    http://www.flickr.com/photos/megzzdollphotos/10046353675/
```

How it works...

This recipe demonstrates how to interact with Flickr using its REST APIs. In this example, the `collect_photo_info()` tag takes three parameters: Flickr API key, a search tag, and the desired number of search results.

We construct the first URL to search for photos. Note that in this URL, the value of the method parameter is `flickr.photos.search` and the desired result format is JSON.

The results of the first `GET()` call are stored in the resp variable and then converted to the JSON format by calling the `json()` method on resp. Now, the JSON data is read in a loop looking into the `['photos']['photo']` iterator. A `photo_collection` list is created to return the result after organizing the information. In this list, each photo's information is represented by a dictionary. The keys of this dictionary are populated by extracting information from the earlier JSON response and another GET request to get the information regarding the specific photo.

Note that to get the comments about a photo, we need to make another `GET()` request and gather comment information from the `['comments']['comment']` elements of the returned JSON. Finally, these comments are appended to a list and attached to the photo dictionary entry.

In the main function, we extract the `photo_collection` dictionary and print some useful information about each photo.

Searching for SOAP methods from an Amazon S3 web service

If you need to interact with a server that implements web services in SOAP, then this recipe can help to get a starting point.

Getting ready

We can use the third-party `SOAPpy` library for this task. This can be installed by running the following command:

```
$ sudo pip install SOAPpy
```

How to do it...

We create a proxy instance and introspect the server methods before we can call them.

In this recipe, let's interact with an Amazon S3 storage service. We have got a test URL for the web services API. An API key is necessary to do this simple task.

Listing 7.5 gives the code for searching for SOAP methods from an Amazon S3 web service, as shown:

```
#!/usr/bin/env python
# Python Network Programming Cookbook -- Chapter - 7
# This program requires Python 2.7 or any later version
# SOAPpy has discontinued its support for Python 3.
# You may find more information and other potential libraries at
https://stackoverflow.com/questions/7817303/what-soap-libraries-exist-
for-python-3-x

import SOAPpy

TEST_URL = 'http://s3.amazonaws.com/ec2-downloads/2009-04-04.ec2.wsdl'


def list_soap_methods(url):
    proxy = SOAPpy.WSDL.Proxy(url)
    print ('%d methods in WSDL:' % len(proxy.methods) + '\n')
    for key in proxy.methods.keys():
        print ("Key Name: %s" %key)
        print ("Key Details:")
        for k,v in proxy.methods[key].__dict__.iteritems():
            print ("%s ==> %s" %(k,v))
        break

if __name__ == '__main__':
    list_soap_methods(TEST_URL)
```

If you run this script, it will print the total number of available methods that support **web services definition language** (**WSDL**) and the details of one arbitrary method, as shown:

```
    $ python 17_5_search_amazonaws_with_SOAP.py
    /home/faruq/env/lib/python2.7/site-
packages/wstools/XMLSchema.py:1280: UserWarning: annotation is
    ignored
      warnings.warn('annotation is ignored')
    43 methods in WSDL:
```

```
Key Name: ReleaseAddress
Key Details:
    encodingStyle ==> None
    style ==> document
    methodName ==> ReleaseAddress
    retval ==> None
    soapAction ==> ReleaseAddress
    namespace ==> None
    use ==> literal
    location ==> https://ec2.amazonaws.com/
    inparams ==> [<wstools.WSDLTools.ParameterInfo instance at
0x8fb9d0c>]
    outheaders ==> []
    inheaders ==> []
    transport ==> http://schemas.xmlsoap.org/soap/http
    outparams ==> [<wstools.WSDLTools.ParameterInfo instance at
0x8fb9d2c>]
```

How it works...

This script defines a method called `list_soap_methods()` that takes a URL and constructs a SOAP proxy object by calling the `WSDL.Proxy()` method of `SOAPpy`. The available SOAP methods are available under this proxy's method attribute.

An iteration over the proxy's method keys are done to introspect the method keys. A for loop just prints the details of a single SOAP method, that is, the name of the key and details about it.

Searching Amazon for books through the product search API

If you like to search for products on Amazon and include some of them in your website or application, this recipe can help you to do that. We can see how to search Amazon for books.

Getting ready

This recipe depends on the third-party Python `bottlenose` library. You can install this library using pip, as shown in the following command:

```
$ pip install  bottlenose
```

First, you need to place your Amazon account's access key, secret key, and affiliate ID into `local_settings.py`. A sample settings file is provided with the book code. You can also edit this script and place it here as well.

How to do it...

We can use the `bottlenose` library that implements the Amazon's product search APIs.

Listing 7.6 gives the code for searching Amazon for books through product search APIs, as shown:

```
#!/usr/bin/env python
# Python Network Programming Cookbook, Second Edition -- Chapter - 7
# This program is optimized for Python 2.7.12 and Python 3.5.2.
# It may run on any other version with/without modifications.
# Supply the Amazon Access and Secret Keys via local_settings.py

import argparse
import bottlenose
from xml.dom import minidom as xml

try:
    from local_settings import amazon_account
except ImportError:
    pass

ACCESS_KEY = amazon_account['access_key']
SECRET_KEY = amazon_account['secret_key']
AFFILIATE_ID = amazon_account['affiliate_id']


def search_for_books(tag, index):
    """Search Amazon for Books """
    amazon = bottlenose.Amazon(ACCESS_KEY, SECRET_KEY, AFFILIATE_ID)
    results = amazon.ItemSearch(
                SearchIndex = index,
                Sort = "relevancerank",
```

```
                Keywords = tag
                )
    parsed_result = xml.parseString(results)

    all_items = []
    attrs = ['Title','Author', 'URL']

    for item in parsed_result.getElementsByTagName('Item'):
        parse_item = {}

        for attr in attrs:
            parse_item[attr] = ""
            try:
                parse_item[attr] = item.getElementsByTagName(attr)
                                   [0].childNodes[0].data
            except:
                pass
        all_items.append(parse_item)
    return all_items

if __name__ == '__main__':
    parser = argparse.ArgumentParser(description='Search
               info from Amazon')
    parser.add_argument('--tag', action="store",
     dest="tag", default='Python')
    parser.add_argument('--index', action="store",
     dest="index", default='Books')
    # parse arguments
    given_args = parser.parse_args()
    books = search_for_books(given_args.tag, given_args.index)
    for book in books:
        for k,v in book.iteritems():
            print ("%s: %s" %(k,v))
        print ("-" * 80)
```

If you run this recipe with a search tag and index, you can see some results similar to the following output:

```
$ python 17_6_search_amazon_for_books.py --tag=Python --index=Books
URL:
http://www.amazon.com/Python-In-Day-Basics-Coding/dp/tech-data/1490475
575%3FSubscriptionId%3DAKIAIPPW3IK76PBRLWBA%26tag%3D7052-6929-7878%261
inkCode%3Dxm2%26camp%3D2025%26creative%3D386001%26creativeASIN%3D14904
75575
Author: Richard Wagstaff
Title: Python In A Day: Learn The Basics, Learn It Quick, Start Coding
Fast (In A Day Books) (Volume 1)
--------------------------------------------------------------------
```

```
URL:
http://www.amazon.com/Learning-Python-Mark-Lutz/dp/tech-data/144935573
0%3FSubscriptionId%3DAKIAIPPW3IK76PBRLWBA%26tag%3D7052-6929-7878%261in
kCode%3Dxm2%26camp%3D2025%26creative%3D386001%26creativeASIN%3D1449355
730
Author: Mark Lutz
Title: Learning Python
---------------------------------------------------------------------
URL:
http://www.amazon.com/Python-Programming-Introduction-Computer-Science
/dp/tech-
data/1590282418%3FSubscriptionId%3DAKIAIPPW3IK76PBRLWBA%26tag%3D7052-6
929-7878%261inkCode%3Dxm2%26camp%3D2025%26creative%3D386001%26creative
ASIN%3D1590282418
Author: John Zelle
Title: Python Programming: An Introduction to Computer Science 2nd
Edition
---------------------------------------------------------------------
```

How it works...

This recipe uses the third-party `bottlenose` library's `Amazon()` class to create an object for searching Amazon through the product search API. This is done by the top-level `search_for_books()` function. The `ItemSearch()` method of this object is invoked with passing values to the `SearchIndex` and `Keywords` keys. It uses the `relevancerank` method to sort the search results.

The search results are processed using the XMLmodule's `minidom` interface, which has a useful `parseString()` method. It returns the parsed XML tree-like data structure. The `getElementsByTagName()` method on this data structure helps to find the item's information. The item attributes are then looked up and placed in a dictionary of parsed items. Finally, all the parsed items are appended in a `all_items()` list and returned to the user.

Creating RESTful web applications with Flask

Creating a simple RESTful web service or a web application with a set of RESTful applications with Python has never been easier. Now you can create a simple web service and make it run in a matter of minutes in Python.

Getting ready

This recipe depends on the third-party Python `Flask` library. If it is not already available in your local Python installation, you can install this library using pip as follows:

```
$ pip install  Flask
```

How to do it...

We can use the `Flask` library to create simple RESTful web services and web applications without having to install any complex web service engines or web application containers.

Listing 7.7 gives the code for a simple web service that gets a number as an input to the RESTful service, and outputs the Fibonacci number and Square of the number:

```
#!/usr/bin/env python
# Python Network Programming Cookbook, Second Edition -- Chapter - 7
# This program is optimized for Python 2.7.12 and Python 3.5.2.
# It may run on any other version with/without modifications.

from flask import Flask
app = Flask(__name__)

@app.route('/<int:num>')
def index(num=1):
    return "Your Python Web Service <hr>Fibonacci("+ str(num) + "):
     "+ str(fibonacci(num))+ "<hr>Square("+ str(num) + "):
     "+ str(square(num))

def fibonacci(n):
    if n == 0:
        return 0
    elif n == 1:
        return 1
    else:
        return fibonacci(n-1) + fibonacci(n-2)


def square(n):
    print ("Calculating for the number %s" %n)
    return n*n
```

```
if __name__ == '__main__':
    app.run(debug=True)
```

If you run this recipe with a search tag and index, you can see some results similar to the following output:

```
$ python 17_7_create_restful_webservice.py
* Running on http://127.0.0.1:5000/ (Press CTRL+C to quit)
* Restarting with stat
* Debugger is active!
* Debugger PIN: 145-461-290
Calculating for the number 25
127.0.0.1 - - [15/Jun/2017 22:16:12] "GET /25 HTTP/1.1" 200 -
127.0.0.1 - - [15/Jun/2017 22:16:12] "GET /favicon.ico HTTP/1.1" 404 -
```

The output is shown in the following screenshot:

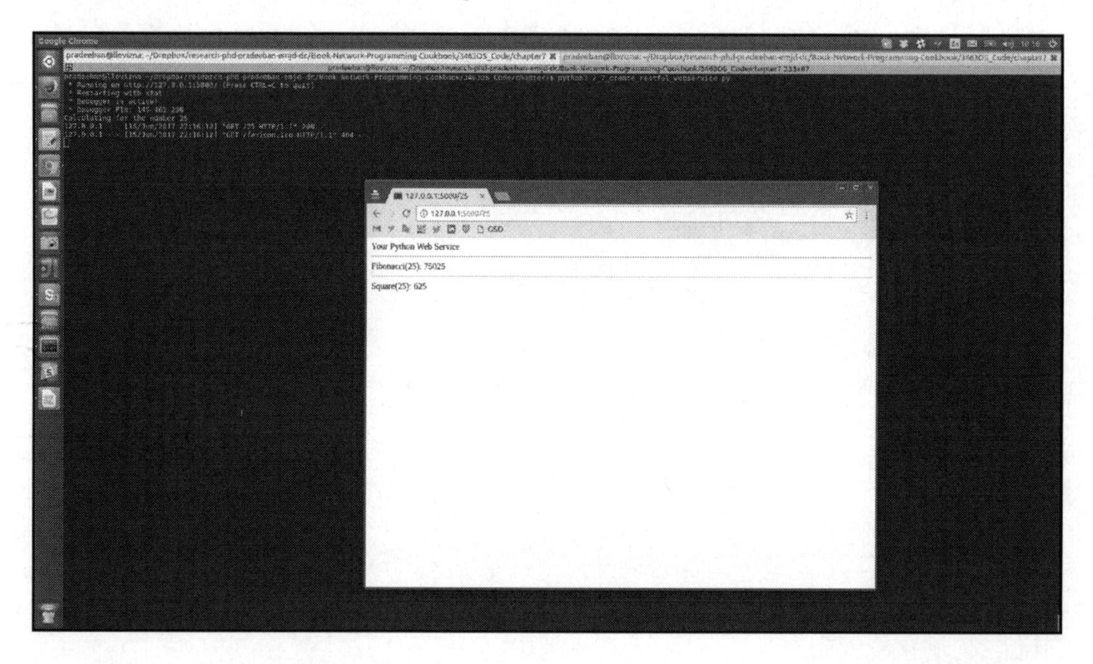

Instead of accessing the web service by the browser, you may also access it through curl.

Curl is very useful for testing RESTful web services. If it is not installed in your computer, you may install it using the following command:

```
$ sudo apt-get install curl
```

Once installed, you may access the RESTful interface of your application using curl:

```
$ curl -i http://127.0.0.1:5000/23
HTTP/1.0 200 OK
Content-Type: text/html; charset=utf-8
Content-Length: 67
Server: Werkzeug/0.12.2 Python/3.5.2
Date: Thu, 15 Jun 2017 21:16:07 GMT
Your Python Web Service <hr>Fibonacci(23): 28657<hr>Square(23): 529
```

The output is displayed in the following screenshot:

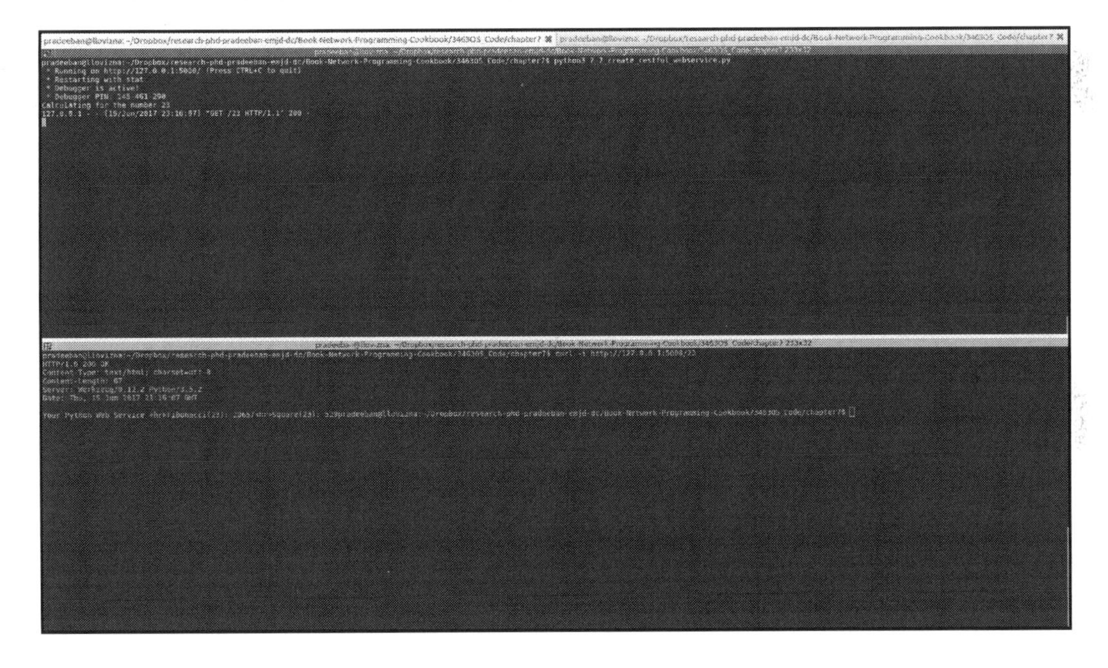

How it works...

This recipe uses the third-party `Flask` library to create a simple RESTful application with the services that we design.

As we designed, the web service accepts the inputs in the formal:

```
http://127.0.0.1:5000/<int>
```

The integer value is taken as the input to both our Fibonacci and Square functions. The computation is done in the Python backend and the output is printed back in the browser—as the output of the web service.

The program can be run with debug mode turned off as well, though in our example we have left it in the debug mode to get more verbose logs.

To learn more about Flask, visit their website at: `http://flask.pocoo.org/`. There are other alternatives to Flask such as Django (`https://docs.djangoproject.com/en/1.11/`) and other frameworks that are built on top of Flask such as Eve (`http://python-eve.org/`) that you may also find useful to build RESTful web services and web applications using Python.

18
Network Monitoring and Security

In this chapter, we will cover the following recipes:

- Sniffing packets on your network
- Saving packets in the pcap format using the pcap dumper
- Adding an extra header in HTTP packets
- Scanning the ports of a remote host
- Customizing the IP address of a packet
- Replaying traffic by reading from a saved pcap file
- Scanning the broadcast of packets

Introduction

This chapter presents some interesting Python recipes for network security monitoring and vulnerability scanning. We begin by sniffing packets on a network using the `pcap` library. Then, we start using `Scapy`, which is a **Swiss knife** type of library that can do many similar tasks. Some common tasks in packet analysis are presented using `Scapy`, such as saving a packet in the `pcap` format, adding an extra header, and modifying the IP address of a packet.

Some other advanced tasks on network intrusion detection are also included in this chapter, for example, replaying traffic from a saved `pcap` file and broadcast scanning.

Sniffing packets on your network

If you are interested in sniffing packets on your local network, this recipe can be used as the starting point. Remember that you may not be able to sniff packets other than what is destined to your machine, as decent network switches will only forward traffic that is designated for your machine.

Getting ready

You need to install the `pylibpcap` library (Version 0.6.4 or greater) for this recipe to work. In Debian-based Linux systems, you may install it using the following command:

```
$ sudo apt-get install python-libpcap
```

It is also available at SourceForge (`http://sourceforge.net/projects/pylibpcap/`).

Python 3 may require you to install `pypcap` using `pip` instead:

```
$ sudo pip install pypcap
```

You also need to install the `construct` library, which can be installed from PyPI via `pip` or `easy_install`, as shown in the following command:

```
$ easy_install construct
```

You may also install `construct` directly from `https://github.com/construct/construct/releases`.

How to do it...

We can supply command-line arguments, for example, the network interface name and TCP port number, for sniffing.

Listing 8.1 gives the code for sniffing packets on your network, as follows:

```
#!/usr/bin/env python
# Python Network Programming Cookbook, Second Edition -- Chapter - 8
# This program is optimized for Python 2.7.12.
# It may run on any other version with/without modifications.
```

```
import argparse
import pcap
from construct.protocols.ipstack import ip_stack


def print_packet(pktlen, data, timestamp):
    """ Callback for priniting the packet payload"""
    if not data:
        return
    stack = ip_stack.parse(data)
    payload = stack.next.next.next
    print (payload)

def main():
    # setup commandline arguments
    parser = argparse.ArgumentParser(description='Packet Sniffer')
    parser.add_argument('--iface', action="store",
     dest="iface", default='eth0')
    parser.add_argument('--port', action="store",
     dest="port", default=80, type=int)
    # parse arguments
    given_args = parser.parse_args()
    iface, port =  given_args.iface, given_args.port
    # start sniffing
    pc = pcap.pcapObject()
    pc.open_live(iface, 1600, 0, 100)
    pc.setfilter('dst port %d' %port, 0, 0)
    print ('Press CTRL+C to end capture')
    try:
        while True:
            pc.dispatch(1, print_packet)
    except KeyboardInterrupt:
        print ('Packet statistics: %d packets received,
                %d packets dropped, %d packets
                dropped by the interface' % pc.stats())

if __name__ == '__main__':
    main()
```

If you run this script by passing the command-line arguments, `--iface=eth0` and `--port=80`, this script will sniff all the HTTP packets from your web browser. So, after running this script, if you access `http://www.google.com` on your browser, you can then see a raw packet output like the following:

```
python 18_1_packet_sniffer.py --iface=eth0 --port=80
Press CTRL+C to end capture
''
0000   47 45 54 20 2f 20 48 54 54 50 2f 31 2e 31 0d 0a   GET /
```

```
HTTP/1.1..
0010   48 6f 73 74 3a 20 77 77 77 2e 67 6f 6f 67 6c 65   Host:
www.google
0020   2e 63 6f 6d 0d 0a 43 6f 6e 6e 65 63 74 69 6f 6e
.com..Connection
0030   3a 20 6b 65 65 70 2d 61 6c 69 76 65 0d 0a 41 63   : keep-
alive..Ac
0040   63 65 70 74 3a 20 74 65 78 74 2f 68 74 6d 6c 2c   cept:
text/html,
0050   61 70 70 6c 69 63 61 74 69 6f 6e 2f 78 68 74 6d
application/xhtm
0060   6c 2b 78 6d 6c 2c 61 70 70 6c 69 63 61 74 69 6f
l+xml,applicatio
0070   6e 2f 78 6d 6c 3b 71 3d 30 2e 39 2c 2a 2f 2a 3b
n/xml;q=0.9,*/*;
0080   71 3d 30 2e 38 0d 0a 55 73 65 72 2d 41 67 65 6e   q=0.8..User-
Agen
0090   74 3a 20 4d 6f 7a 69 6c 6c 61 2f 35 2e 30 20 28   t:
Mozilla/5.0 (
00A0   58 31 31 3b 20 4c 69 6e 75 78 20 69 36 38 36 29   X11; Linux
i686)
00B0   20 41 70 70 6c 65 57 65 62 4b 69 74 2f 35 33 37
AppleWebKit/537
00C0   2e 33 31 20 28 4b 48 54 4d 4c 2c 20 6c 69 6b 65   .31 (KHTML,
like
00D0   20 47 65 63 6b 6f 29 20 43 68 72 6f 6d 65 2f 32    Gecko)
Chrome/2
00E0   36 2e 30 2e 31 34 31 30 2e 34 33 20 53 61 66 61   6.0.1410.43
Safa
00F0   72 69 2f 35 33 37 2e 33 31 0d 0a 58 2d 43 68 72   ri/537.31..X-
Chr
0100   6f 6d 65 2d 56 61 72 69 61 74 69 6f 6e 73 3a 20   ome-
Variations:
0110   43 50 71 31 79 51 45 49 6b 62 62 4a 41 51 69 59
CPq1yQEIkbbJAQiY
0120   74 73 6b 42 43 4b 4f 32 79 51 45 49 70 37 62 4a
tskBCKO2yQEIp7bJ
0130   41 51 69 70 74 73 6b 42 43 4c 65 32 79 51 45 49
AQiptskBCLe2yQEI
0140   2b 6f 50 4b 41 51 3d 3d 0d 0a 44 4e 54 3a 20 31
+oPKAQ==..DNT: 1
0150   0d 0a 41 63 63 65 70 74 2d 45 6e 63 6f 64 69 6e   ..Accept-
Encodin
0160   67 3a 20 67 7a 69 70 2c 64 65 66 6c 61 74 65 2c   g:
gzip,deflate,
0170   73 64 63 68 0d 0a 41 63 63 65 70 74 2d 4c 61 6e   sdch..Accept-
Lan
0180   67 75 61 67 65 3a 20 65 6e 2d 47 42 2c 65 6e 2d   guage: en-
```

```
GB,en-
0190   55 53 3b 71 3d 30 2e 38 2c 65 6e 3b 71 3d 30 2e
US;q=0.8,en;q=0.
01A0   36 0d 0a 41 63 63 65 70 74 2d 43 68 61 72 73 65   6..Accept-
Charse
01B0   74 3a 20 49 53 4f 2d 38 38 35 39 2d 31 2c 75 74   t:
ISO-8859-1,ut
01C0   66 2d 38 3b 71 3d 30 2e 37 2c 2a 3b 71 3d 30 2e
f-8;q=0.7,*;q=0.
01D0   33 0d 0a 43 6f 6f 6b 69 65 3a 20 50 52 45 46 3d   3..Cookie:
PREF=
....
^CPacket statistics: 17 packets received, 0 packets dropped, 0
packets dropped by the interface
```

How it works...

This recipe relies on the `pcapObject()` class from the `pcap` library to create an instance of sniffer. In the `main()` method, an instance of this class is created, and a filter is set using the `setfilter()` method so that only the HTTP packets are captured. Finally, the `dispatch()` method starts sniffing and sends the sniffed packet to the `print_packet()` function for postprocessing.

In the `print_packet()` function, if a packet has data, the payload is extracted using the `ip_stack.parse()` method from the `construct` library. This library is useful for low-level data processing.

Saving packets in the pcap format using the pcap dumper

The `pcap` format, abbreviated from **packet capture**, is a common file format for saving network data. More details on the `pcap` format can be found at `http://wiki.wireshark.org/Development/LibpcapFileFormat`.

If you want to save your captured network packets to a file and later reuse them for further processing, this recipe can be a working example for you.

How to do it...

In this recipe, we use the `Scapy` library to sniff packets and write to a file. All utility functions and definitions of `Scapy` can be imported using the wild card import, as shown in the following command:

```
from scapy.all import *
```

This is only for demonstration purposes and is not recommended for production code.

The `sniff()` function of `Scapy` takes the name of a `callback` function. Let's write a `callback` function that will write the packets onto a file.

Listing 8.2 gives the code for saving packets in the `pcap` format using the `pcap` dumper, as follows:

```
#!/usr/bin/env python
# Python Network Programming Cookbook, Second Edition -- Chapter - 8
# This program is optimized for Python 2.7.12 and Python 3.5.2.
# It may run on any other version with/without modifications.


import os
from scapy.all import *

pkts = []
count = 0
pcapnum = 0

def write_cap(x):
    global pkts
    global count
    global pcapnum
    pkts.append(x)
    count += 1
    if count == 3:
        pcapnum += 1
        pname = "pcap%d.pcap" % pcapnum
        wrpcap(pname, pkts)
        pkts = []
        count = 0

def test_dump_file():
    print ("Testing the dump file...")
    dump_file = "./pcap1.pcap"
    if os.path.exists(dump_file):
```

```
        print ("dump fie %s found." %dump_file)
        pkts = sniff(offline=dump_file)
        count = 0
        while (count <=2):
            print ("----Dumping pkt:%s----" %count)
            print (hexdump(pkts[count]))
            count += 1
    else:
        print ("dump fie %s not found." %dump_file)

if __name__ == '__main__':
    print ("Started packet capturing and dumping... Press
           CTRL+C to exit")
    sniff(prn=write_cap)
    test_dump_file()
```

If you run this script, you will see an output similar to the following:

```
# python 18_2_save_packets_in_pcap_format.py
^CStarted packet capturing and dumping... Press CTRL+C to exit
Testing the dump file...
dump fie ./pcap1.pcap found.
----Dumping pkt:0----
0000   08 00 27 95 0D 1A 52 54  00 12 35 02 08 00 45 00
..'...RT..5...E.
0010   00 DB E2 6D 00 00 40 06  7C 9E 6C A0 A2 62 0A 00
...m..@.|.l..b..
0020   02 0F 00 50 99 55 97 98  2C 84 CE 45 9B 6C 50 18
...P.U..,..E.lP.
0030   FF FF 53 E0 00 00 48 54  54 50 2F 31 2E 31 20 32
..S...HTTP/1.1 2
0040   30 30 20 4F 4B 0D 0A 58  2D 44 42 2D 54 69 6D 65   00 OK..X-DB-
Time
0050   6F 75 74 3A 20 31 32 30  0D 0A 50 72 61 67 6D 61   out:
120..Pragma
0060   3A 20 6E 6F 2D 63 61 63  68 65 0D 0A 43 61 63 68   : no-
cache..Cach
0070   65 2D 43 6F 6E 74 72 6F  6C 3A 20 6E 6F 2D 63 61   e-Control:
no-ca
0080   63 68 65 0D 0A 43 6F 6E  74 65 6E 74 2D 54 79 70
che..Content-Typ
0090   65 3A 20 74 65 78 74 2F  70 6C 61 69 6E 0D 0A 44   e:
text/plain..D
00a0   61 74 65 3A 20 53 75 6E  2C 20 31 35 20 53 65 70   ate: Sun, 15
Sep
00b0   20 32 30 31 33 20 31 35  3A 32 32 3A 33 36 20 47    2013
15:22:36 G
00c0   4D 54 0D 0A 43 6F 6E 74  65 6E 74 2D 4C 65 6E 67   MT..Content-
```

```
Leng
00d0    74 68 3A 20 31 35 0D 0A  0D 0A 7B 22 72 65 74 22    th:
15....{"ret"
00e0    3A 20 22 70 75 6E 74 22  7D                         : "punt"}
None
----Dumping pkt:1----
0000    52 54 00 12 35 02 08 00  27 95 0D 1A 08 00 45 00
RT..5...'.....E.
0010    01 D2 1F 25 40 00 40 06  FE EF 0A 00 02 0F 6C A0
...%@.@.......l.
0020    A2 62 99 55 00 50 CE 45  9B 6C 97 98 2D 37 50 18
.b.U.P.E.l..-7P.
0030    F9 28 1C D6 00 00 47 45  54 20 2F 73 75 62 73 63    .(....GET
/subsc
0040    72 69 62 65 3F 68 6F 73  74 5F 69 6E 74 3D 35 31
ribe?host_int=51
0050    30 35 36 34 37 34 36 26  6E 73 5F 6D 61 70 3D 31
0564746&ns_map=1
0060    36 30 36 39 36 39 39 34  5F 33 30 30 38 30 38 34
60696994_3008084
0070    30 37 37 31 34 2C 31 30  31 39 34 36 31 31 5F 31
07714,10194611_1
0080    31 30 35 33 30 39 38 34  33 38 32 30 32 31 31 2C
105309843820211,
0090    31 34 36 34 32 38 30 35  32 5F 33 32 39 34 33 38
146428052_329438
00a0    36 33 34 34 30 38 34 2C  31 31 36 30 31 35 33 31
6344084,11601531
00b0    5F 32 37 39 31 38 34 34  37 35 37 37 31 2C 31 30
_279184475771,10
00c0    31 39 34 38 32 38 5F 33  30 30 37 34 39 36 35 39
194828_300749659
00d0    30 30 2C 33 33 30 39 39  31 39 38 32 5F 38 31 39
00,330991982_819
00e0    33 35 33 37 30 36 30 36  2C 31 36 33 32 37 38 35
35370606,1632785
00f0    35 5F 31 32 39 30 31 32  32 39 37 34 33 26 75 73
5_12901229743&us
0100    65 72 5F 69 64 3D 36 35  32 30 33 37 32 26 6E 69
er_id=6520372&ni
0110    64 3D 32 26 74 73 3D 31  33 37 39 32 35 38 35 36
d=2&ts=137925856
0120    31 20 48 54 54 50 2F 31  2E 31 0D 0A 48 6F 73 74    1
HTTP/1.1..Host
0130    3A 20 6E 6F 74 69 66 79  33 2E 64 72 6F 70 62 6F    :
notify3.dropbo
0140    78 2E 63 6F 6D 0D 0A 41  63 63 65 70 74 2D 45 6E
x.com..Accept-En
```

```
0150   63 6F 64 69 6E 67 3A 20  69 64 65 6E 74 69 74 79   coding:
identity
0160   0D 0A 43 6F 6E 6E 65 63  74 69 6F 6E 3A 20 6B 65
..Connection: ke
0170   65 70 2D 61 6C 69 76 65  0D 0A 58 2D 44 72 6F 70   ep-alive..X-
Drop
0180   62 6F 78 2D 4C 6F 63 61  6C 65 3A 20 65 6E 5F 55   box-Locale:
en_U
0190   53 0D 0A 55 73 65 72 2D  41 67 65 6E 74 3A 20 44   S..User-
Agent: D
01a0   72 6F 70 62 6F 78 44 65  73 6B 74 6F 70 43 6C 69
ropboxDesktopCli
01b0   65 6E 74 2F 32 2E 30 2E  32 32 20 28 4C 69 6E 75   ent/2.0.22
(Linu
01c0   78 3B 20 32 2E 36 2E 33  32 2D 35 2D 36 38 36 3B   x;
2.6.32-5-686;
01d0   20 69 33 32 3B 20 65 6E  5F 55 53 29 0D 0A 0D 0A    i32;
en_US)....
None
----Dumping pkt:2----
0000   08 00 27 95 0D 1A 52 54  00 12 35 02 08 00 45 00
..'...RT..5...E.
0010   00 28 E2 6E 00 00 40 06  7D 50 6C A0 A2 62 0A 00
.(.n..@.}Pl..b..
0020   02 0F 00 50 99 55 97 98  2D 37 CE 45 9D 16 50 10
...P.U..-7.E..P.
0030   FF FF CA F1 00 00 00 00  00 00 00 00               ............
None
```

You may have to run this program using admin privileges, as otherwise it may produce the `Operation not permitted` error, as follows:

```
$ python 18_2_save_packets_in_pcap_format.py
WARNING: No route found for IPv6 destination :: (no default route?)
Started packet capturing and dumping... Press CTRL+C to exit
Traceback (most recent call last):
  File "18_2_save_packets_in_pcap_format.py", line 43, in <module>
    sniff(prn=write_cap)
  File "/usr/local/lib/python2.7/dist-packages/scapy/sendrecv.py",
line 561, in sniff
    s = L2socket(type=ETH_P_ALL, *arg, **karg)
  File "/usr/local/lib/python2.7/dist-packages/scapy/arch/linux.py",
line 451, in __init__
    self.ins = socket.socket(socket.AF_PACKET, socket.SOCK_RAW,
socket.htons(type))
  File "/usr/lib/python2.7/socket.py", line 191, in __init__
    _sock = _realsocket(family, type, proto)
socket.error: [Errno 1] Operation not permitted
```

How it works...

This recipe uses the `sniff()` and `wrpacp()` utility functions of the `Scapy` library to capture all the network packets and dump them onto a file. After capturing a packet via `sniff()`, the `write_cap()` function is called on that packet. Some global variables are used to work on packets one after another. For example, packets are stored in a `pkts[]` list and packet and variable counts are used. When the value of the count is `3`, the `pkts` list is dumped onto a file named `pcap1.pcap`, the count variable is reset so that we can continue capturing another three packets and dumped onto `pcap2.pcap`, and so on.

In the `test_dump_file()` function, assume the presence of the first dump file, `pcap1.dump`, in the working directory. Now, `sniff()` is used with an offline parameter, which captured packets from the file instead of network. Here, the packets are decoded one after another using the `hexdump()` function. The contents of the packets are then printed on the screen.

Adding an extra header in HTTP packets

Sometimes, you would like to manipulate an application by supplying a custom HTTP header that contains custom information. For example, adding an authorization header can be useful to implement the HTTP basic authentication in your packet capture code. As with the previous recipe, this recipe requires admin privileges to run too.

How to do it...

Let us sniff the packets using the `sniff()` function of `Scapy` and define a callback function, `modify_packet_header()`, which adds an extra header of certain packets.

Listing 8.3 gives the code for adding an extra header in HTTP packets, as follows:

```
#!/usr/bin/env python
# Python Network Programming Cookbook, Second Edition -- Chapter - 8
# This program is optimized for Python 2.7.12 and Python 3.5.2.
# It may run on any other version with/without modifications.


from scapy.all import *

def modify_packet_header(pkt):
```

```
    """ Parse the header and add an extra header"""
    if pkt.haslayer(TCP) and pkt.getlayer(TCP).dport == 80
     and pkt.haslayer(Raw):
        hdr = pkt[TCP].payload.__dict__
        extra_item = {'Extra Header' : ' extra value'}
        hdr.update(extra_item)
        send_hdr = '\r\n'.join(hdr)
        pkt[TCP].payload = send_hdr
        pkt.show()
        del pkt[IP].chksum
        send(pkt)

if __name__ == '__main__':
    # start sniffing
    sniff(filter="tcp and ( port 80 )", prn=modify_packet_header)
```

If you run this script, it will show a captured packet; print the modified version of it and send it to the network, as shown in the following output. This can be verified by other packet capturing tools such as `tcpdump` or `wireshark`:

```
$ python 18_3_add_extra_http_header_in_sniffed_packet.py
###[ Ethernet ]###
  dst       = 52:54:00:12:35:02
  src       = 08:00:27:95:0d:1a
  type      = 0x800
###[ IP ]###
     version   = 4L
     ihl       = 5L
     tos       = 0x0
     len       = 525
     id        = 13419
     flags     = DF
     frag      = 0L
     ttl       = 64
     proto     = tcp
     chksum    = 0x171
     src       = 10.0.2.15
     dst       = 82.94.164.162
     \options   \
###[ TCP ]###
        sport     = 49273
        dport     = www
        seq       = 107715690
        ack       = 216121024
        dataofs   = 5L
        reserved  = 0L
        flags     = PA
        window    = 6432
```

```
        chksum    = 0x50f
        urgptr    = 0
        options   = []
###[ Raw ]###
           load      = 'Extra
Header\r\nsent_time\r\nfields\r\naliastypes\r\npost_transforms\r\nunde
rlayer\r\nfieldtype\r\ntime\r\ninitialized\r\noverloaded_fields\r\npac
ketfields\r\npayload\r\ndefault_fields'
.
Sent 1 packets.
```

How it works...

First, we set up the packet sniffing using the `sniff()` function of `Scapy`, specifying `modify_packet_header()` as the `callback` function for each packet. All TCP packets having TCP and a raw layer that are destined to port `80` (HTTP) are considered for modification. So, the current packet header is extracted from the packet's payload data.

The extra header is then appended to the existing header dictionary. The packet is then printed on screen using the `show()` method, and for avoiding the correctness checking failure, the packet checksum data is removed from the packet. Finally, the packet is sent over the network.

Scanning the ports of a remote host

If you are trying to connect to a remote host using a particular port, sometimes you get a message saying that `Connection is refused`. The reason for this is that, most likely, the server is down on the remote host. In such a situation, you can try to see whether the port is open or in the listening state. You can scan multiple ports to identify the available services in a machine.

How to do it...

Using Python's standard `socket` library, we can accomplish this port-scanning task. We can take three command-line arguments: target `host`, and `start_port` and `end_port` numbers.

Listing 8.4 gives the code for scanning the ports of a remote host, as follows:

```
#!/usr/bin/env python
# Python Network Programming Cookbook, Second Edition -- Chapter - 8
# This program is optimized for Python 2.7.12 and Python 3.5.2.
# It may run on any other version with/without modifications.

import argparse
import socket
import sys
def scan_ports(host, start_port, end_port):
    """ Scan remote hosts """
    #Create socket
    try:
        sock = socket.socket(socket.AF_INET,socket.SOCK_STREAM)
    except socket.error as err_msg:
        print ('Socket creation failed. Error code:
           '+ str(err_msg[0]) + ' Error mesage: ' + err_msg[1])
        sys.exit()
    #Get IP of remote host
    try:
        remote_ip = socket.gethostbyname(host)
    except socket.error as error_msg:
        print (error_msg)
        sys.exit()
    #Scan ports
    end_port += 1
    for port in range(start_port,end_port):
        try:
            sock.connect((remote_ip,port))
            print ('Port ' + str(port) + ' is open')
            sock.close()
            sock = socket.socket(socket.AF_INET,socket.SOCK_STREAM)
        except socket.error:
            pass # skip various socket errors

if __name__ == '__main__':
    # setup commandline arguments
    parser = argparse.ArgumentParser(description='Remote
                                               Port Scanner')
    parser.add_argument('--host', action="store",
                         dest="host", default='localhost')
    parser.add_argument('--start-port', action="store",
                        dest="start_port", default=1, type=int)
    parser.add_argument('--end-port', action="store",
                        dest="end_port", default=100, type=int)
    # parse arguments
    given_args = parser.parse_args()
```

```
host, start_port, end_port =  given_args.host,
given_args.start_port, given_args.end_port
scan_ports(host, start_port, end_port)
```

If you execute this recipe to scan your local machine's port `1` to `100` to detect open ports, you will get an output similar to the following:

```
# python 18_4_scan_port_of_a_remote_host.py --host=localhost --start-
port=1 --end-port=100
Port 21 is open
Port 22 is open
Port 23 is open
Port 25 is open
Port 80 is open
```

How it works...

This recipe demonstrates how to scan open ports of a machine using Python's standard `socket` library. The `scan_port()` function takes three arguments: `host`, `start_port`, and `end_port`. Then, it scans the entire port range in three steps:

1. Create a TCP socket using the `socket()` function.
2. If the socket is created successfully, then resolve the IP address of the remote host using the `gethostbyname()` function.
3. If the target host's IP address is found, try to connect to the IP using the `connect()` function. If that's successful, then it implies that the port is open. Now, close the port with the `close()` function and repeat the first step for the next port.

Customizing the IP address of a packet

If you ever need to create a network packet and customize the source and destination IP or ports, this recipe can serve as the starting point.

How to do it...

We can take all the useful command-line arguments such as network interface name, protocol name, source IP, source port, destination IP, destination port, and optional TCP flags.

We can use the `Scapy` library to create a custom TCP or UDP packet and send it over the network. As with the previous recipes, this recipe requires admin privilege to run.

Listing 8.5 gives the code for customizing the IP address of a packet, as follows:

```
#!/usr/bin/env python
# Python Network Programming Cookbook, Second Edition -- Chapter - 8
# This program is optimized for Python 2.7.12 and Python 3.5.2.
# It may run on any other version with/without modifications.


import argparse
import sys
import re
from random import randint

from scapy.all import IP,TCP,UDP,conf,send


def send_packet(protocol=None, src_ip=None, src_port=None, flags=None,
dst_ip=None, dst_port=None, iface=None):
    """Modify and send an IP packet."""
    if protocol == 'tcp':
        packet = IP(src=src_ip, dst=dst_ip)/TCP(flags=flags,
                    sport=src_port, dport=dst_port)
    elif protocol == 'udp':
        if flags: raise Exception(" Flags are not supported for udp")
        packet = IP(src=src_ip, dst=dst_ip)/UDP(sport=src_port,
                     dport=dst_port)
    else:
        raise Exception("Unknown protocol %s" % protocol)

    send(packet, iface=iface)

if __name__ == '__main__':
    # setup commandline arguments
    parser = argparse.ArgumentParser(description='Packet Modifier')
    parser.add_argument('--iface', action="store",
                        dest="iface", default='eth0')
    parser.add_argument('--protocol', action="store",
                        dest="protocol", default='tcp')
    parser.add_argument('--src-ip', action="store",
                        dest="src_ip", default='1.1.1.1')
    parser.add_argument('--src-port', action="store",
                       dest="src_port", default=randint(0, 65535))
    parser.add_argument('--dst-ip', action="store",
                       dest="dst_ip", default='192.168.1.51')
    parser.add_argument('--dst-port', action="store",
```

```
                        dest="dst_port", default=randint(0, 65535))
    parser.add_argument('--flags', action="store",
                        dest="flags", default=None)
    # parse arguments
    given_args = parser.parse_args()
    iface, protocol, src_ip,  src_port, dst_ip, dst_port,
    flags =  given_args.iface, given_args.protocol,
    given_args.src_ip,\
      given_args.src_port, given_args.dst_ip,
      given_args.dst_port, given_args.flags
    send_packet(protocol, src_ip, src_port, flags,
      dst_ip, dst_port, iface)
```

In order to run this script, enter the following commands:

```
$ sudo tcpdump src 192.168.1.66
tcpdump: verbose output suppressed, use -v or -vv for full protocol
decode
listening on eth0, link-type EN10MB (Ethernet), capture size 65535
bytes
^C18:37:34.309992 IP 192.168.1.66.60698 > 192.168.1.51.666: Flags [S],
seq 0, win 8192, length 0
1 packets captured
1 packets received by filter
0 packets dropped by kernel
$ python 18_5_modify_ip_in_a_packet.py
WARNING: No route found for IPv6 destination :: (no default route?)
.
Sent 1 packets.
```

How it works...

This script defines a `send_packet()` function to construct the IP packet using `Scapy`. The source and destination addresses and ports are supplied to it. Depending on the protocol, for example, TCP or UDP, it constructs the correct type of packet. If the packet is TCP, the `flags` argument is used; if not, an exception is raised.

In order to construct a TCP packet, `Sacpy` supplies the `IP()/TCP()` function. Similarly, in order to create a UDP packet, the `IP()/UDP()` function is used.

Finally, the modified packet is sent using the `send()` function.

Replaying traffic by reading from a saved pcap file

While playing with network packets, you may need to replay traffic by reading from a previously saved `pcap` file. In that case, you'd like to read the `pcap` file and modify the source or destination IP addresses before sending them.

How to do it...

Let us use `Scapy` to read a previously saved `pcap` file. If you don't have a `pcap` file, you can use the *Saving packets in the pcap format using pcap dumper* recipe of this chapter to do that.

Then, parse the arguments from the command line and pass them to a `send_packet()` function along with the parsed raw packets. As with the previous recipes, this recipe requires admin privileges to run.

Listing 8.6 gives the code for replaying traffic by reading from a saved `pcap` file, as follows:

```
#!/usr/bin/env python
# Python Network Programming Cookbook, Second Edition -- Chapter - 8
# This program is optimized for Python 2.7.12 and Python 3.5.2.
# It may run on any other version with/without modifications.


import argparse
from scapy.all import *


def send_packet(recvd_pkt, src_ip, dst_ip, count):
    """ Send modified packets"""
    pkt_cnt = 0
    p_out = []

    for p in recvd_pkt:
        pkt_cnt += 1
        new_pkt = p.payload
        new_pkt[IP].dst = dst_ip
        new_pkt[IP].src = src_ip
        del new_pkt[IP].chksum
        p_out.append(new_pkt)
        if pkt_cnt % count == 0:
```

```
                send(PacketList(p_out))
                p_out = []

        # Send rest of packet
        send(PacketList(p_out))
        print ("Total packets sent: %d" %pkt_cnt)

if __name__ == '__main__':
        # setup commandline arguments
        parser = argparse.ArgumentParser(description='Packet Sniffer')
        parser.add_argument('--infile', action="store", dest="infile",
         default='pcap1.pcap')
        parser.add_argument('--src-ip', action="store", dest="src_ip",
         default='1.1.1.1')
        parser.add_argument('--dst-ip', action="store", dest="dst_ip",
         default='2.2.2.2')
        parser.add_argument('--count', action="store", dest="count",
         default=100, type=int)
        # parse arguments
        given_args = ga = parser.parse_args()
        global src_ip, dst_ip
        infile, src_ip, dst_ip, count =  ga.infile, ga.src_ip,
         ga.dst_ip, ga.count
        try:
            pkt_reader = PcapReader(infile)
            send_packet(pkt_reader, src_ip, dst_ip, count)
        except IOError:
            print ("Failed reading file %s contents" % infile)
            sys.exit(1)
```

If you run this script, it will read the saved `pcap` file, `pcap1.pcap`, by default and send the packet after modifying the source and destination IP addresses to `1.1.1.1` and `2.2.2.2` respectively, as shown in the following output. If you use the `tcpdump` utility, you can see these packet transmissions:

```
# python 18_6_replay_traffic.py
...
Sent 3 packets.
Total packets sent 3
----
# tcpdump src 1.1.1.1
tcpdump: verbose output suppressed, use -v or -vv for full protocol
decode
listening on eth0, link-type EN10MB (Ethernet), capture size 65535
bytes
^C18:44:13.186302 IP 1.1.1.1.www > ARennes-651-1-107-2.w2-
2.abo.wanadoo.fr.39253: Flags [P.], seq 2543332484:2543332663, ack
3460668268, win 65535, length 179
```

```
1 packets captured
3 packets received by filter
0 packets dropped by kernel
```

How it works...

This recipe reads a saved `pcap` file, `pcap1.pcap`, from the disk using the `PcapReader()` function of `Scapy` that returns an iterator of packets. The command-line arguments are parsed if they are supplied. Otherwise, the default value is used as shown in the preceding output.

The command-line arguments and the packet list are passed to the `send_packet()` function. This function places the new packets in the `p_out` list and keeps track of the processed packets. In each packet, the payload is modified, thus changing the source and destination IPs. In addition to this, the `checksum` packet is deleted as it was based on the original IP address.

After processing one of the packets, it is sent over the network immediately. After that, the remaining packets are sent in one go.

As with the previous recipes, this recipe requires admin privileges to run.

Scanning the broadcast of packets

If you encounter the issue of detecting a network broadcast, this recipe is for you. We can learn how to find the information from the broadcast packets.

How to do it...

We can use `Scapy` to sniff the packets arriving to a network interface. After each packet is captured, they can be processed by a callback function to get the useful information from it.

Listing 8.7 gives the code for scanning the broadcast of packets, as follows:

```
#!/usr/bin/env python
# Python Network Programming Cookbook, Second Edition -- Chapter - 8
# This program is optimized for Python 2.7.12 and Python 3.5.2.
# It may run on any other version with/without modifications.
```

```
from scapy.all import *
import os
captured_data = dict()

END_PORT = 1000
def monitor_packet(pkt):
    if IP in pkt:
        if pkt[IP].src not in captured_data:
            captured_data[pkt[IP].src] = []
    if TCP in pkt:
        if pkt[TCP].sport <=  END_PORT:
            if not str(pkt[TCP].sport) in captured_data[pkt[IP].src]:
                captured_data[pkt[IP].src].append(str(pkt[TCP].sport))
    os.system('clear')
    ip_list = sorted(captured_data.keys())
    for key in ip_list:
        ports=', '.join(captured_data[key])
        if len (captured_data[key]) == 0:
            print ('%s' % key)
        else:
            print ('%s (%s)' % (key, ports))

if __name__ == '__main__':
    sniff(prn=monitor_packet, store=0)
```

If you run this script, you can list the broadcast traffic's source IP and ports. The following is a sample output from which the first octet of the IP is replaced:

```
# python 18_7_broadcast_scanning.py
127.0.0.1
127.0.1.1
13.81.252.207 (443)
162.125.17.5 (443)
162.125.18.133 (443)
162.125.65.3 (443)
172.217.17.69 (443)
173.194.69.189 (443)
192.168.137.1
192.168.137.95
216.58.212.174 (443)
34.253.167.3 (443)
40.115.1.44 (443)
40.77.226.194 (443)
52.208.1.170 (443)
52.215.50.173 (443)
54.86.79.27 (443)
68.232.34.200 (443)
```

The following screenshot shows the execution output:

How it works...

This recipe sniffs packets in a network using the `sniff()` function of `Scapy`. It has a `monitor_packet()` callback function that does the postprocessing of packets. Depending on the protocol, for example, IP or TCP, it sorts the packets in a dictionary called `captured_data`.

If an individual IP is not already present in the dictionary, it creates a new entry; otherwise, it updates the dictionary with the port number for that specific IP. Finally, it prints the IP addresses and ports in each line.

19
Network Modeling

In this chapter, we will cover the following recipes:

- Simulating networks with ns-3
- Emulating networks with Mininet
- Distributed network emulation with MaxiNet
- Emulating wireless networks with Mininet-WiFi
- Extending Mininet to emulate containers

Introduction

This chapter explores an early and important aspect of network systems development—network modeling. Specifically, it addresses the simulations and emulations of networks with Python-based projects.

First we will look into network simulations that can model very large systems within a single computer. We will discuss ns-3, a network simulator originally written in C++ with Python bindings, making it easy to simulate networks in Python.

The chapter goes on to network emulation that indeed models resources one-to-one. It discusses Mininet, the most popular network emulator developed in Python. We will further discuss the extensions to Mininet, such as MaxiNet and Mininet-WiFi. The chapter concludes with how to extend existing simulators and emulators and to build a cloud network leveraging these platforms.

Simulating networks with ns-3

Data centers and cloud networks span across a large number of nodes. Network topologies and applications of that scale often can be tested first in simulations to ensure that early results are verified quick before an extensive deployment and testing in a more realistic emulation or a physical test bench. In this recipe, we will learn to simulate network systems with ns-3.

Getting ready

First download ns-3 from `https://www.nsnam.org/ns-3-26/download/`. We are using ns-3.26 in this recipe. Extract the downloaded archive and run from the root directory `ns-allinone-3.26`:

```
$ ./build.py.
```

Since the `allinone` folder contains all the bundles, this build will consume a few minutes.

It shows the following upon the completion of the build:

```
'build' finished successfully (14m22.645s)
Modules built:
antenna                    aodv                       applications
bridge                     buildings                  config-store
core                       csma                       csma-layout
dsdv                       dsr                        energy
fd-net-device              flow-monitor               internet
internet-apps              lr-wpan                    lte
mesh                       mobility                   mpi
netanim (no Python)        network                    nix-vector-routing
olsr                       point-to-point             point-to-point-
layout
propagation                sixlowpan                  spectrum
stats                      tap-bridge                 test (no Python)
topology-read              traffic-control            uan
virtual-net-device         wave                       wifi
wimax
Modules not built (see ns-3 tutorial for explanation):
brite                      click                      openflow
visualizer
Leaving directory `./ns-3.26'
```

In the preceding snippet, you may notice that a few modules including `openflow` are not built when built from the `root` directory. This is the expected behavior.

You may test ns-3 for one of the existing simulations. First go to the `ns-3.26 directory`:

```
$ cd ns-3.26
```

Now, let's test the bench-simulator included in ns-3. We will use `waf`, a Python-based build tool for this:

```
$ ./waf --run bench-simulator
Waf: Entering directory `/home/pradeeban/programs/ns-
allinone-3.26/ns-3.26/build'
Waf: Leaving directory `/home/pradeeban/programs/ns-
allinone-3.26/ns-3.26/build'
Build commands will be stored in build/compile_commands.json
'build' finished successfully (1.473s)
ns3.26-bench-simulator-debug:
ns3.26-bench-simulator-debug: scheduler: ns3::MapScheduler
ns3.26-bench-simulator-debug: population: 100000
ns3.26-bench-simulator-debug: total events: 1000000
ns3.26-bench-simulator-debug: runs: 1
ns3.26-bench-simulator-debug: using default exponential distribution
Run #       Inititialization:                   Simulation:
Time (s)    Rate (ev/s) Per (s/ev)  Time (s)    Rate (ev/s) Per (s/ev)
----------- ----------- ----------- ----------- -----------
(prime)     0.72        138889      7.2e-06     2.84        352113
2.84e-06
0           0.23        434783      2.3e-06     2.94        340136
2.94e-06
```

The screenshot of this simple bench simulation is as follows:

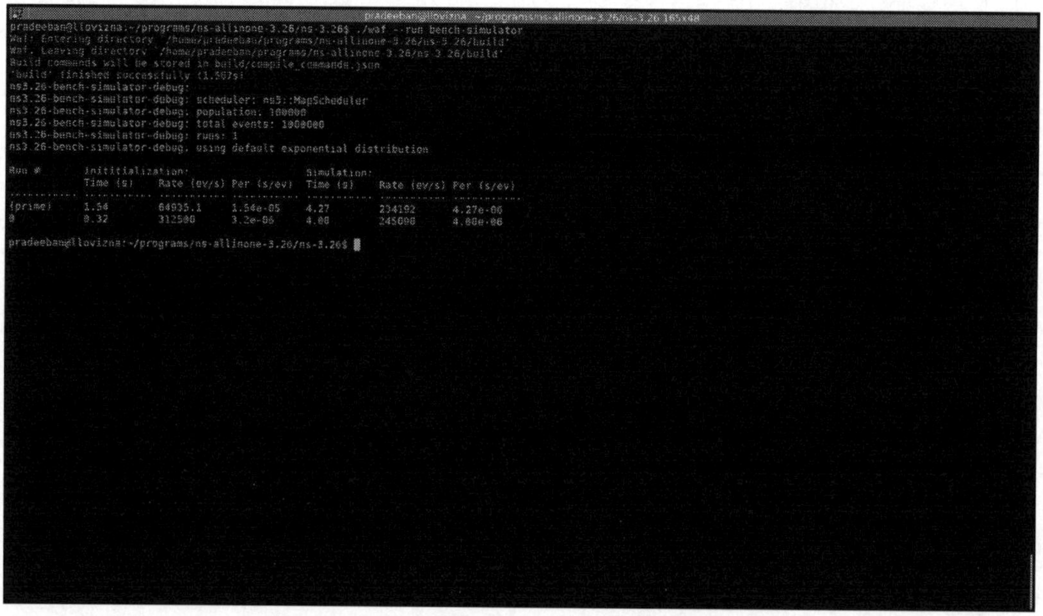

Bench Simulation with ns-3

How to do it...

ns-3 can be used to quickly prototype network protocol implementations and applications. Once you have configured ns-3 correctly, you may start running the Python examples from the folder `ns-allinone-3.26/ns-3.26/examples/tutorial`. More information on this can be found from `https://www.nsnam.org/docs/manual/html/python.html`.

Listing 9.1 simulates a network with two nodes with UDP messages between them:

```
#!/usr/bin/env python
# Python Network Programming Cookbook, Second Edition -- Chapter - 9
# This program is optimized for Python 2.7.12 and Python 3.5.2.
# It may run on any other version with/without modifications.

import ns.applications
import ns.core
import ns.internet
import ns.network
```

```
import ns.point_to_point
import argparse


def simulate(ipv4add, ipv4mask):
    # Enabling logs at INFO level for both the server and the client.
    ns.core.LogComponentEnable("UdpEchoClientApplication",
     ns.core.LOG_LEVEL_INFO)
    ns.core.LogComponentEnable("UdpEchoServerApplication",
     ns.core.LOG_LEVEL_INFO)
    # Create the 2 nodes.
    nodes = ns.network.NodeContainer()
    nodes.Create(2)

    pointToPoint = ns.point_to_point.PointToPointHelper()

    devices = pointToPoint.Install(nodes)

    stack = ns.internet.InternetStackHelper()
    stack.Install(nodes)

    # Set addresses based on the input args.
    address = ns.internet.Ipv4AddressHelper()
    address.SetBase(ns.network.Ipv4Address(ipv4add),
     ns.network.Ipv4Mask(ipv4mask))

    interfaces = address.Assign(devices)

    # Running the echo server
    echoServer = ns.applications.UdpEchoServerHelper(9)
    serverApps = echoServer.Install(nodes.Get(1))

    # Running the echo client
    echoClient = ns.applications.
    UdpEchoClientHelper(interfaces.GetAddress(1), 3)
    clientApps = echoClient.Install(nodes.Get(0))

    # Running the simulator
    ns.core.Simulator.Run()
    ns.core.Simulator.Destroy()


if __name__ == '__main__':
    parser = argparse.ArgumentParser(description='NS-3 Simple
Simulation')
    parser.add_argument('--ipv4add', action="store",
     dest="ipv4add", type=str, required=True)
    parser.add_argument('--ipv4mask', action="store",
```

```
            dest="ipv4mask", type=str, required=True)
        given_args = parser.parse_args()
        simulate(given_args.ipv4add, given_args.ipv4mask)
```

First run the `waf` shell to get the dependencies for the ns-3 simulation before executing the actual simulation:

```
ns-allinone-3.26/ns-3.26$ ./waf shell
```

Next, run the simulation:

```
python 19_1_ns3_simulation.py --ipv4add=100.10.100.0 --
ipv4mask=255.255.255.0
At time 0s client sent 100 bytes to 100.10.100.2 port 3
At time 1s client sent 100 bytes to 100.10.100.2 port 3
At time 2s client sent 100 bytes to 100.10.100.2 port 3
...
At time 97s client sent 100 bytes to 100.10.100.2 port 3
At time 98s client sent 100 bytes to 100.10.100.2 port 3
At time 99s client sent 100 bytes to 100.10.100.2 port 3
```

How it works...

ns-3 simulates the networks including the nodes and the flows. As there is no real emulation of network, complex algorithms and large network systems can be simulated by ns-3. In this recipe, we simulated a simple UDP client-server architecture to pass messages between them, as an echo client. More complex systems can be simulated by following the ns-3 user manuals further.

Emulating networks with Mininet

Emulating networks offer more accurate and realistic results. Therefore, despite the high requirements for resources, emulations are often preferred over simulations in networking systems. Mininet is an enterprise-grade open source network emulator that is widely used in industries and academia. Mininet API and orchestration modules are written in Python, with core emulation performed by compiled C code. You may easily write Python code to emulate networks with Mininet, or to extend it with more capabilities. Mininet is capable of emulating an entire network one-to-one in your laptop. Each node in the network can be represented by a process in Mininet.

Due to its precision, Mininet is extended further for various use cases, including Mininet-WiFi (`https://github.com/intrig-unicamp/mininet-wifi`) to emulate wireless networks, MaxiNet (`https://maxinet.github.io/`) to emulate networks in a cluster, and Containernet (`https://github.com/containernet/containernet`) to have container support to network emulations. In this recipe, we will look into emulating networks with Mininet.

Getting ready

First, install Mininet on your computer. In Debian/Ubuntu based systems, you just need to issue the following command to install Mininet:

```
$ sudo apt-get install mininet
```

Mininet must run as a root, as it should be able to access the programs installed in the host as the processes of the emulated nodes. Thus, this recipe needs to be run as root too, as it has a Mininet emulation.

While it is possible to make Mininet work in Python 3.x, by default it works on Python 2.7.x. Thus, you may need to install Python 2.7.x or later versions of Python 2, if you are using Python 3.x.

How to do it...

Mininet consists of a few network topologies that are predefined. You may define your own topology. In this recipe, we are using tree topology, which is probably the most common and the most basic network topology. We ping one emulated host from another emulated host.

Listing 9.2 emulates a simple network with a tree topology:

```
#!/usr/bin/env python
# Python Network Programming Cookbook, Second Edition -- Chapter - 9
# This program is optimized for Python 2.7.12.
# It may run on any other version with/without modifications.

import argparse
from mininet.net import Mininet
from mininet.topolib import TreeTopo

# Emulate a network with depth of depth_ and fanout of fanout_
def emulate(depth_, fanout_):
```

```
        # Create a network with tree topology
        tree_ = TreeTopo(depth=depth_,fanout=fanout_)
        # Initiating the Mininet instance
        net = Mininet(topo=tree_)
        # Start Execution of the Emulated System.
        net.start()

        # Name two of the instances as h1 and h2.
        h1, h2  = net.hosts[0], net.hosts[depth_]

        # Ping from an instance to another, and print the output.
        print (h1.cmd('ping -c1 %s' % h2.IP()))

        # Stop the Mininet Emulation.
        net.stop()

    if __name__ == '__main__':
        parser = argparse.ArgumentParser(description='Mininet
         Simple Emulation')
        parser.add_argument('--depth', action="store",
         dest="depth", type=int, required=True)
        parser.add_argument('--fanout', action="store",
         dest="fanout", type=int, required=True)
        given_args = parser.parse_args()
        emulate(given_args.depth, given_args.fanout)
```

Tree topology is defined by its `depth` and `fanout`. A network configured to be a complete tree can have (`fanout`) to the power of `depth` number of leaves. As the hosts make the leaves, this leads us to (`fanout`) to the power of `depth` number of hosts in the network. The following figure illustrates a network of tree topology with **Fanout** = 2 and **Depth** = 3:

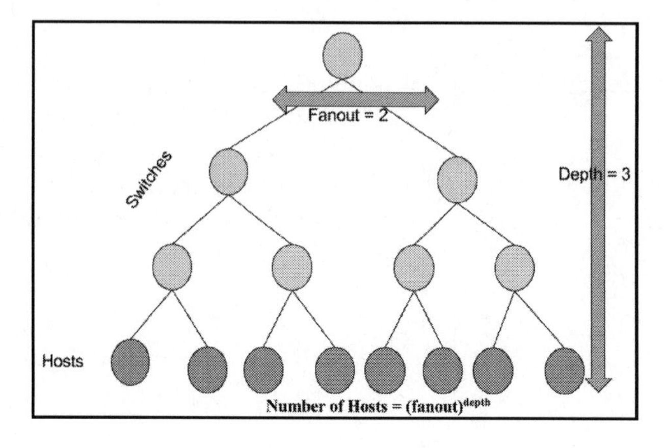

Tree Representation

The following output is printed when the program is executed with the `depth` of `2` and `fanout` of `3` as the arguments:

```
$ sudo python 19_2_mininet_emulation.py --depth=2 --fanout=3
PING 10.0.0.3 (10.0.0.3) 56(84) bytes of data.
64 bytes from 10.0.0.3: icmp_seq=1 ttl=64 time=2.86 ms
--- 10.0.0.3 ping statistics ---
1 packets transmitted, 1 received, 0% packet loss, time 0ms
rtt min/avg/max/mdev = 2.864/2.864/2.864/0.000 ms
```

How it works...

In this recipe, we pinged (`depth`)th host from the 0th host. As (`depth` < the number of hosts), this works well. Note that subsequent executions will give different outcomes as the `ping` statistics. This is because the network is actually emulated with real processes, and hence the `ping` actually occurs between the emulated processes.

You may re-execute the program to see different outcomes to the previous:

```
$ sudo python 19_2_mininet_emulation.py --depth=2 --fanout=3
PING 10.0.0.3 (10.0.0.3) 56(84) bytes of data.
64 bytes from 10.0.0.3: icmp_seq=1 ttl=64 time=3.33 ms
--- 10.0.0.3 ping statistics ---
1 packets transmitted, 1 received, 0% packet loss, time 0ms
rtt min/avg/max/mdev = 3.332/3.332/3.332/0.000 ms
```

Distributed network emulation with MaxiNet

Mininet requires a large amount of resources to emulate large networks. Hence, it is not always feasible to emulate a complex system using Mininet in a single computer or server within a given time. MaxiNet attempts to address this by extending Mininet, and thus enabling an efficient distributed execution on a cluster. In this recipe, we will look into configuring MaxiNet in a cluster and emulating a network in the cluster using MaxiNet.

Getting ready

First, get the MaxiNet installer to all the servers that you would like to install it:

```
$ wget https://github.com/MaxiNet/MaxiNet/raw/v1.0/installer.sh
```

Make sure you can `sudo` without entering a password for the user. In Ubuntu, this can be done by adding the following line to the `/etc/sudoers` file:

```
myusername ALL=(ALL) NOPASSWD: ALL
```

Here, replace `myusername` with your username.

Now if you type:

```
$ sudo su
```

It should not ask for the password.

You will have to install `python-setuptools`, or upgrade it with `pip`, to make the MaxiNet installation work:

```
$ sudo apt-get install python-setuptools
$ pip install --upgrade --user setuptools pip
```

Run the script from all the servers as the user that would run MaxiNet later:

```
$ sh installer.sh
```

Once installed, copy the `MaxiNet.cfg` to `/etc/`:

```
$ sudo cp ~/MaxiNet/share/MaxiNet-cfg-sample /etc/MaxiNet.cfg
```

Modify it to include the two lines:

```
sshuser = yourusername
usesudo = True
```

For example:

```
[all]
...
sshuser = ubuntu
usesudo = True
```

Once you have followed through in all your servers, you have MaxiNet ready in all of them! Alternatively, you may just download the MaxiNet VMs and host them in your servers:

```
$ wget
http://groups.uni-paderborn.de/fg-karl/maxinet/MaxiNet-1.0-rc1.ova
```

Now, from the server that you would like to use as the master instance to run the emulations, run the following:

```
$ screen -d -m -S MaxiNetFrontend MaxiNetFrontendServer
$ screen -d -m -S MaxiNetWorker sudo MaxiNetWorker
```

All your emulations should be executed from this instance. It will communicate and coordinate with the other worker instances on its own.

From the other servers, run the following to make them as worker instances:

```
$ sudo screen -d -m -S MaxiNetWorker MaxiNetWorker
```

For more information on MaxiNet, follow through `https://maxinet.github.io/#quickstart`.

How to do it...

In this recipe, we will rewrite the same recipe of 9.2 for MaxiNet. As you can notice, with minor changes, the code and the API remains compatible with that of Mininet's.

Listing 9.2 adopts the listing 9.1 for MaxiNet, as follows:

```
#!/usr/bin/env python
# Python Network Programming Cookbook, Second Edition -- Chapter - 9
# This program is optimized for Python 2.7.12.
# It may run on any other version with/without modifications.

import sys
import maxinet
from mininet.topolib import TreeTopo

# Emulate a network with depth of depth_ and fanout of fanout_
def emulate(depth_, fanout_):
    # Start the MaxiNet as a Mininet cluster.
    cluster = maxinet.MininetCluster("pc1","pc2","pc3")
    cluster.start()

    # Emulate the network topology.
    emu = maxinet.Emulation(cluster, TreeTopo(depth_,fanout_))
```

```
        # Start Execution of the Emulated System.
        emu.setup()

        # Name two of the instances as h1 and h2.
        h1, h2  = net.hosts[0], net.hosts[depth_]

        # Ping from an instance to another, and print the output.
        print (h1.cmd('ping -c1 %s' % h2.IP()))

        # Stop the MaxiNet Emulation.
        emu.stop()
        cluster.stop()

if __name__ == '__main__':
    parser = argparse.ArgumentParser(description='Maxinet
             Simple Emulation')
    parser.add_argument('--depth', action="store",
     dest="depth", type=int, required=True)
    parser.add_argument('--fanout', action="store",
     dest="fanout", type=int, required=True)
    given_args = parser.parse_args()
    emulate(given_args.depth, given_args.fanout)
```

Now you may run this from the master instance, as you would have run this on a Mininet emulation. The master instance communicates with the other worker instance to distribute the workload:

```
$ sudo python 19_3_maxinet_emulation.py --depth=2 --fanout=3
PING 10.0.0.3 (10.0.0.3) 56(84) bytes of data.
64 bytes from 10.0.0.3: icmp_seq=1 ttl=64 time=1.82 ms
--- 10.0.0.3 ping statistics ---
1 packets transmitted, 1 received, 0% packet loss, time 0ms
rtt min/avg/max/mdev = 1.827/1.827/1.827/0.000 ms
```

How it works...

MaxiNet is Mininet executing in a cluster. It aims to keep the API changes minimal (if any), to be able to offer a quick adoption to the existing Mininet users. Make sure that all the worker instances in MaxiNet can indeed communicate. As you may have noticed, this emulation workload is too little to actually offer any benefits for us to distribute it across a cluster. However, when you start emulating larger networks and complex systems, the advantages become apparent.

Emulating wireless networks with Mininet-WiFi

You may emulate wireless networks and mobile networks through Mininet-WiFi, which was developed as an extension to Mininet. While Mininet enables emulation of Software-Defined Networks, Mininet-WiFi supports emulation of Software-Defined Wireless Networks. Mininet-WiFi emulates mobile terminals efficiently, while also providing a visual graphical user interface of emulated wireless networks.

Getting ready

First install Mininet-WiFi on your computer:

```
$ git clone https://github.com/intrig-unicamp/mininet-wifi
$ cd mininet-wifi
$ sudo util/install.sh -Wnfvl
```

How to do it...

You may emulate **mobile ad hoc network** (**MANET**) and **vehicular ad hoc network** (**VANET**) using Mininet-WiFi, and visualize them in a graphical interface. VANET is a subset of MANET, which can be emulated by sub-classing the generic interfaces of Mininet-WiFi. In this recipe, we will adopt and extend an example from the Mininet-WiFi.

More examples can be found at `https://github.com/intrig-unicamp/mininet-wifi/tree/master/examples`.

Listing 9.4 shows the code to emulate a mobile network:

```
#!/usr/bin/env python
# Python Network Programming Cookbook, Second Edition -- Chapter - 9
# This program is optimized for Python 2.7.12.
# It may run on any other version with/without modifications.

from mininet.net import Mininet
from mininet.node import Controller, OVSKernelAP
from mininet.link import TCLink
from mininet.cli import CLI
```

```
from mininet.log import setLogLevel

def emulate():
    # Setting the position of nodes and providing mobility

    # Create a network.
    net = Mininet(controller=Controller, link=TCLink,
           accessPoint=OVSKernelAP)

    print ("*** Creating nodes")
    # Add the host
    h1 = net.addHost('h1', mac='00:00:00:00:00:01', ip='10.0.0.1/8')

    # Add 3 mobile stations, sta1, sta2, sta3.
    sta1 = net.addStation('sta1', mac='00:00:00:00:00:02',
ip='10.0.0.2/8')
    sta2 = net.addStation('sta2', mac='00:00:00:00:00:03',
ip='10.0.0.3/8')
    sta3 = net.addStation('sta3', mac='00:00:00:00:00:04',
ip='10.0.0.4/8')

    # Add an access point
    ap1 = net.addAccessPoint('ap1', ssid='new-ssid',
           mode='g', channel='1', position='45,40,30')

    # Add a controller
    c1 = net.addController('c1', controller=Controller)

    print ("*** Configuring wifi nodes")
    net.configureWifiNodes()

    print ("*** Associating and Creating links")
    net.addLink(ap1, h1)
    net.addLink(ap1, sta1)
    net.addLink(ap1, sta2)
    net.addLink(ap1, sta3)

    print ("*** Starting network")
    net.build()
    c1.start()
    ap1.start([c1])

    # Plot a 3-dimensional graph.
    net.plotGraph(max_x=100, max_y=100, max_z=200)

    # Start the mobility at the start of the emulation.
    net.startMobility(time=0)
```

```
    # Start the mobile stations from their initial positions.
    net.mobility(sta1, 'start', time=1, position='40.0,30.0,20.0')
    net.mobility(sta2, 'start', time=2, position='40.0,40.0,90.0')
    net.mobility(sta3, 'start', time=3, position='50.0,50.0,160.0')

    # Indicate the final destination of the mobile stations during
      the emulation.
    net.mobility(sta1, 'stop', time=12, position='31.0,10.0,50.0')
    net.mobility(sta2, 'stop', time=22, position='55.0,31.0,30.0')
    net.mobility(sta3, 'stop', time=32, position='75.0,99.0,120.0')

    # Stop the mobility at certain time.
    net.stopMobility(time=33)

    print ("*** Running CLI")
    CLI(net)

    print ("*** Stopping network")
    net.stop()

if __name__ == '__main__':
    setLogLevel('info')
    emulate()
```

In this recipe, we emulate a mobile network with a host, an access point, a controller, and three mobile stations. We start the mobile stations with their initial positions, and let them move to their final positions during the emulation. Once the emulation is done, we stop the mobility and the emulation:

```
$ sudo python 19_4_mininet_wifi_emulation.py
*** Creating nodes
*** Configuring wifi nodes
*** Associating and Creating links
Associating sta1-wlan0 to ap1
Associating sta2-wlan0 to ap1
Associating sta3-wlan0 to ap1
*** Starting network
*** Configuring hosts
Mobility started at 0 second(s)
*** Running CLI
*** Starting CLI:
mininet-wifi> exit
*** Stopping network
*** Stopping 1 controllers
c1
*** Stopping 1 links
.
*** Stopping switches and/or access points
```

```
ap1
*** Stopping hosts and/or stations
h1 sta1 sta2 sta3
*** Done
```

The following screenshots indicate the graph at the start and end of the emulation. The following screenshot shows the positions of the mobile stations at the start of the emulation:

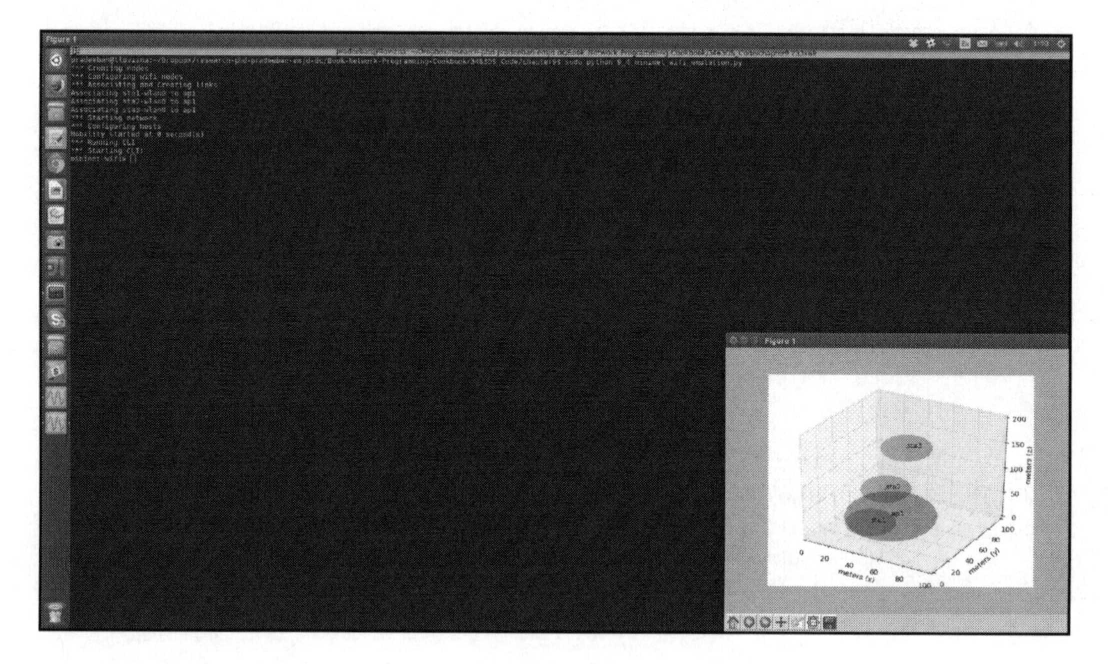

Starting State of the Emulation

The following screenshot shows the position at the end of the emulation:

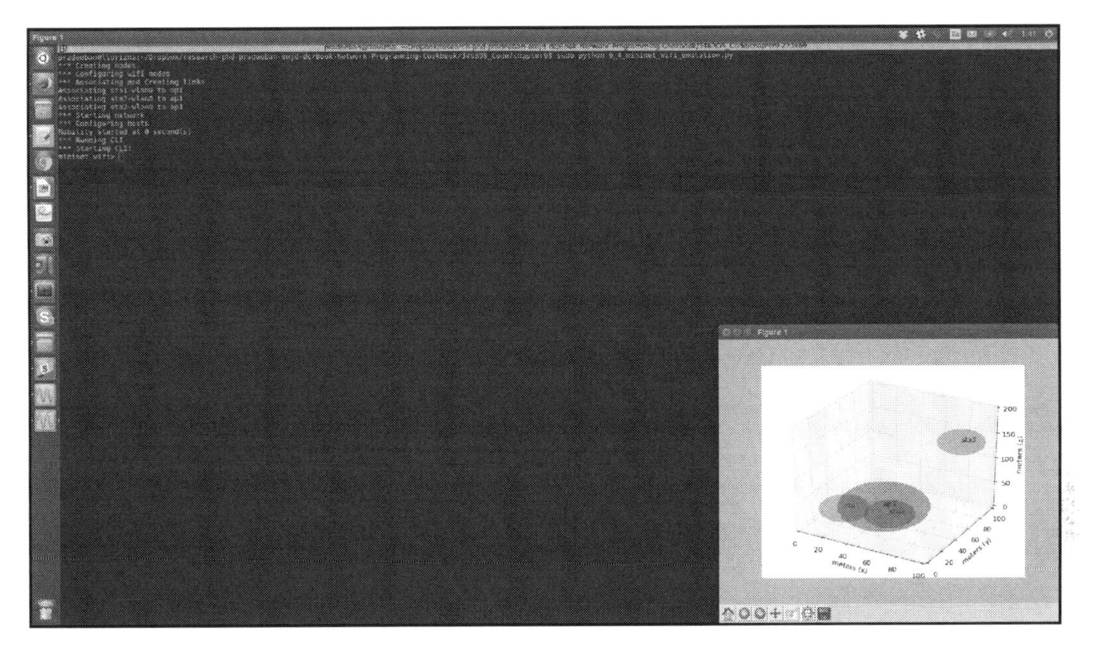

Finishing State of the Emulation

During the course, you may monitor how the mobile stations move between their initial and final positions.

How it works...

Mininet-WiFi extends Mininet for networks that are mobile in nature. In this recipe, we emulated wireless network stations. Following our previous recipe on pinging the hosts, you may easily extend this recipe to let the mobile stations communicate between themselves. You may further model more complex and larger vehicular networks using Mininet-WiFi.

Extending Mininet to emulate containers

Mininet can leverage the applications installed in the server to attach them as processes to the hosts that it emulates. For example, see the following, a `vim` started from a host in Mininet:

```
$ sudo mn
*** Creating network
*** Adding controller
*** Adding hosts and stations:
h1 h2
*** Adding switches and access point(s):
s1
*** Adding link(s):
(h1, s1) (h2, s1)
*** Configuring hosts
*** Starting controller(s)
c0
*** Starting switches and/or access points
s1 ...
*** Starting CLI:
mininet-wifi> h1 vim
```

The preceding command will open a `vim` instance in the Terminal! You may even try other applications such as `gedit`, or even `mininet` itself, to run as a process attached to the emulated host. However, note that these are real processes from the applications that are installed on the server. Not an emulation.

Containernet extends Mininet to use Docker containers as hosts in Mininet emulations, by extending the `host` class of Mininet. Hence, container enables emulation of more interesting and complex functionalities, attaching Docker containers directly as hosts. This allows the programs installed in a container available to the host.

Getting ready

In this recipe, we use Containernet as an example to show how to extend Mininet for more use cases, while using Containernet to show a simple emulation with Docker containers as hosts in Mininet. More complex Mininet algorithms can be run on Containernet, along with its capabilities to run containers as hosts.

First, install Containernet in your computer. Since Containernet uses Ansible for this, you need to install it before:

```
$ sudo apt-get install ansible git aptitude
$ sudo vim /etc/ansible/hosts
```

Add: `localhost ansible_connection=local`

Now, to actually install Containernet:

```
$ git clone https://github.com/containernet/containernet.git
$ cd containernet/ansible
$ sudo ansible-playbook install.yml
```

Alternatively, you may use Vagrant to get Containernet up and running faster, without actually installing it manually. First make sure to have a hypervisor such as Virtualbox installed:

```
$ sudo apt-get install virtualbox
```

Now, you may execute the following to get Vagrant for Containernet:

```
$ cd containernet
$ vagrant up
$ vagrant ssh
```

You may confirm that you have installed Vagrant correctly by running the following from the `containernet` directory:

```
$ sudo py.test -v mininet/test/test_containernet.py
```

The following screenshot indicates the output to the preceding execution in Vagrant:

Emulating Containers

How to do it...

In this recipe, we will attach existing containers to our simple network emulation. To avoid creating Docker images on our own, as it is out of scope for this book, we will use the example included in the Containernet Vagrant image.

Docker containers can be initialized in place of hosts and switches as nodes in constructing the links. Various parameters and the volumes that define the container can be specified.

Listing 9.5 gives a simple emulation of a network with containers as follows:

```
#!/usr/bin/env python
# Python Network Programming Cookbook, Second Edition -- Chapter - 9
# This program is optimized for Python 2.7.12.
# It may run on any other version with/without modifications.

# Adopted from
https://github.com/containernet/containernet/blob/master/examples/dock
erhosts.py
```

```
"""
This example shows how to create a simple network and
how to create docker containers (based on existing images)
to it.
"""

from mininet.net import Containernet
from mininet.node import Controller, Docker, OVSSwitch
from mininet.cli import CLI
from mininet.log import setLogLevel, info
from mininet.link import TCLink, Link


def emulate():

    "Create a network with some docker containers acting as hosts."

    net = Containernet(controller=Controller)

    info('*** Adding controller\n')
    net.addController('c0')

    info('*** Adding hosts\n')
    h1 = net.addHost('h1')
    h2 = net.addHost('h2')

    info('*** Adding docker containers\n')
    d1 = net.addDocker('d1', ip='10.0.0.251', dimage="ubuntu:trusty")
    # A container with more specific params: cpu period and cpu quota
    d2 = net.addDocker('d2', ip='10.0.0.252', dimage="ubuntu:trusty",
          cpu_period=50000, cpu_quota=25000)

    # Add a container as a host, using Docker class option.
    d3 = net.addHost('d3', ip='11.0.0.253', cls=Docker,
          dimage="ubuntu:trusty", cpu_shares=20)

    # Add a container with a specific volume.
    d5 = net.addDocker('d5', dimage="ubuntu:trusty",
          volumes=["/:/mnt/vol1:rw"])

    info('*** Adding switch\n')
    s1 = net.addSwitch('s1')
    s2 = net.addSwitch('s2', cls=OVSSwitch)
    s3 = net.addSwitch('s3')

    info('*** Creating links\n')
    net.addLink(h1, s1)
    net.addLink(s1, d1)
```

```
    net.addLink(h2, s2)
    net.addLink(d2, s2)
    net.addLink(s1, s2)

    # try to add a second interface to a docker container
    net.addLink(d2, s3, params1={"ip": "11.0.0.254/8"})
    net.addLink(d3, s3)

    info('*** Starting network\n')
    net.start()

    # The typical ping example, with two docker instances
       in place of hosts.
    net.ping([d1, d2])

    # our extended ping functionality
    net.ping([d1], manualdestip="10.0.0.252")
    net.ping([d2, d3], manualdestip="11.0.0.254")

    info('*** Dynamically add a container at runtime\n')
    d4 = net.addDocker('d4', dimage="ubuntu:trusty")

    # we have to specify a manual ip when we add a link at runtime
    net.addLink(d4, s1, params1={"ip": "10.0.0.254/8"})

    # Ping docker instance d1.
    net.ping([d1], manualdestip="10.0.0.254")

    info('*** Running CLI\n')
    CLI(net)

    info('*** Stopping network')
    net.stop()

if __name__ == '__main__':
    setLogLevel('info')
    emulate()
```

This is the simple `ping` example that we have been testing in previous recipes, this time with container support. You may extend this to have more container-specific workloads and tasks. You may leverage more processes from the container itself, than from the hosting server (as opposed to the previous situation where we were able to execute applications such as `vim` and `gedit` installed in the server from the hosts emulated in Mininet):

```
$ python 19_5_containernet_emulation.py
*** Adding controller
*** Adding hosts
*** Adding docker containers
d1: update resources {'cpu_quota': -1}
d2: update resources {'cpu_period': 50000, 'cpu_quota': 25000}
d3: update resources {'cpu_quota': -1, 'cpu_shares': 20}
d5: update resources {'cpu_quota': -1}
*** Adding switch
*** Creating links
*** Starting network
*** Configuring hosts
h1 h2 d1 d2 d3 d5 *** defaultIntf: warning: d5 has no interfaces
*** Starting controller
c0
*** Starting 3 switches
s1 s2 s3 ...
d1 -> d2
d2 -> d1
*** Results: 0% dropped (2/2 received)
d1 -> 10.0.0.252
*** Results: 0% dropped (1/1 received)
d2 -> 11.0.0.254
d3 -> 11.0.0.254
*** Results: 0% dropped (2/2 received)
*** Dynamically add a container at runtime
d4: update resources {'cpu_quota': -1}
d1 -> 10.0.0.254
*** Results: 0% dropped (1/1 received)
*** Running CLI
*** Starting CLI:
containernet>
```

How it works...

Containernet extends Mininet with the container support specifically for Docker. It can be installed locally as your Mininet installation, or installed as a Vagrant image.

While MaxiNet aims to increase the scalability and throughput of Mininet, Mininet-WiFi and Containernet aim to offer more features to Mininet. As Mininet offers a Python-based API, it can be extended with Python modules. In the core, you may extend its kernel with C code.

Similar to Mininet-WiFi, Containernet too thrives to maintain backward-compatibility with Mininet. Thus emulations written in Mininet should work in these projects that are started as a fork of Mininet. Moreover, the APIs are maintained to resemble that of Mininet with minimal changes, it is easy to adopt to these emulation platforms.

While these recipes presented the ability to simulate containers in the networks and wireless sensor networks, they also serve the purpose to illustrate the potential to extend Mininet with more capabilities.

20
Authentication, Authorization, and Accounting (AAA)

In this chapter, we will cover the following recipes:

- Finding DNS names of a network
- Finding DNS host information
- Finding DNS resource records
- Making DNS zone transfer
- Querying NTP servers
- Connecting to an LDAP server
- Making LDAP bind
- Reading and writing LDAP
- Authenticating REST APIs with Eve
- Throttling requests with RequestsThrottler

Introduction

Authentication, authorization, and accounting (**AAA**) are the three major pillars of access control. Authentication identifies the user, authorization identifies the roles of the user, and accounting ensures that the user actions are performed within the usage limits (such as throttling). AAA, as they are collectively known, are crucial for networks for proper functioning and security. Hence network projects consider AAA as a crucial factor in their network architecture—remarkably the OpenDaylight's AAA project is considered to be a core project in the SDN controller ecosystem. In this chapter, we will look into the AAA options for networking, and how to configure AAA with Python for the networks. We start the chapter with simpler recipes before going into more complex ones.

Finding DNS names of a network

There are a few libraries in Python for managing the **Domain Name Servers** (**DNS**) of the internet. Each network administrator needs to effectively manage the DNS mappings of their network. In this recipe, we will start by introducing `dnspython`, a simple DNS toolkit developed in Python to manage DNS.

Getting ready

First, install `dnspython` (`https://github.com/rthalley/dnspython`) using the `pip`:

```
$ sudo pip install dnspython
```

How to do it...

We import `dns.name` of `dnspython` to do a simple exercise to find the DNS names from the user inputs of two web URLs, and how these web URLs are related.

Listing 11.1 evaluates the user input of two web URLs for the DNS names as follows:

```
#!/usr/bin/env python
# Python Network Programming Cookbook, Second Edition
  -- Chapter - 11
# This program is optimized for Python 2.7.12 and
  Python 3.5.2.
# It may run on any other version with/without
  modifications.
```

```
import argparse
import dns.name

def main(site1, site2):
    _site1 = dns.name.from_text(site1)
    _site2 = dns.name.from_text(site2)
    print("site1 is subdomain of site2: ",
    _site1.is_subdomain(_site2))
    print("site1 is superdomain of site2: ",
    _site1.is_superdomain(_site2))
    print("site1 labels: ", _site1.labels)
    print("site2 labels: ", _site2.labels)

if __name__ == '__main__':
    parser = argparse.ArgumentParser(description=
                                     'DNS Python')
    parser.add_argument('--site1', action="store",
    dest="site1",  default='www.dnspython.org')
    parser.add_argument('--site2', action="store",
    dest="site2",  default='dnspython.org')
    given_args = parser.parse_args()
    site1 = given_args.site1
    site2 = given_args.site2
    main (site1, site2)
```

The code performs a check to see whether the `site1` is either a subdomain or a superdomain of `site2`, and it finally prints the labels of the sites.

Executing this with two arguments produces the following output:

```
$ python 20_1_dns_names_with_dnspython.py --site1="edition.cnn.com" --
site2="cnn.com"
('site1 is subdomain of site2: ', True)
('site1 is superdomain of site2: ', False)
('site1 labels: ', ('edition', 'cnn', 'com', ''))
('site2 labels: ', ('cnn', 'com', ''))
$ python 20_1_dns_names_with_dnspython.py --site1="edition.cnn.com" --
site2="www.cnn.com"
('site1 is subdomain of site2: ', False)
('site1 is superdomain of site2: ', False)
('site1 labels: ', ('edition', 'cnn', 'com', ''))
('site2 labels: ', ('www', 'cnn', 'com', ''))
$ python 20_1_dns_names_with_dnspython.py --site1="edition.cnn.com" --
site2="edition.cnn.com"
('site1 is subdomain of site2: ', True)
('site1 is superdomain of site2: ', True)
('site1 labels: ', ('edition', 'cnn', 'com', ''))
('site2 labels: ', ('edition', 'cnn', 'com', ''))
```

How it works...

The `dns.name.from_text()` retrieves the DNS name from the Terminal user input. Then it compares the inputs to check whether they are each other's subdomain or superdomain. With `labels` property, we may also retrieve the labels associated with each of the site. These simple methods can be useful in tracing the relationship of two URLs and automating the detection of subdomains and superdomains from the list of URLs.

Finding DNS host information

It may be useful for us to know the domain name of a given IP address. First given an address, we need to know whether it even resolves to a valid address identifiable in the internet. We may use the `dnspython` library for these tasks.

Getting ready

First install `dnspython` (`https://github.com/rthalley/dnspython`) using the `pip`:

```
$ sudo pip install dnspython
```

How to do it...

We import `dns.reversename` of `dnspython` to do a simple exercise of finding the reverse name of an address from the given address. We use `dns.resolver` to find the address that an IP address resolves to be.

Listing 11.2 gives the domain information for a given IP address as follows:

```
#!/usr/bin/env python
# Python Network Programming Cookbook, Second Edition
  -- Chapter - 11
# This program is optimized for Python 2.7.12 and
  Python 3.5.2.
# It may run on any other version with/without
  modifications.


import argparse
import dns.reversename
```

```
import dns.resolver

def main(address):
    n = dns.reversename.from_address(address)
    print(n)
    print(dns.reversename.to_address(n))

    try:
        # Pointer records (PTR) maps a network
          interface (IP) to the host name.
        domain = str(dns.resolver.query(n,"PTR")[0])
        print(domain)
    except Exception as e:
        print ("Error while resolving %s: %s" %(address, e))


if __name__ == '__main__':
    parser = argparse.ArgumentParser(description='DNS Python')
    parser.add_argument('--address', action="store",
    dest="address",  default='127.0.0.1')
    given_args = parser.parse_args()
    address = given_args.address
    main (address)
```

We run this recipe with various inputs for addresses. First with localhost, followed by two valid addresses in the internet, and then an invalid address.

```
$ python 20_2_dns_host_with_dnspython.py --address="127.0.0.1"
1.0.0.127.in-addr.arpa.
b'127.0.0.1'
localhost.
$ python 20_2_dns_host_with_dnspython.py --address="216.58.199.78"
78.199.58.216.in-addr.arpa.
b'216.58.199.78'
syd15s01-in-f78.1e100.net.
$ python 20_2_dns_host_with_dnspython.py --address="172.217.19.193"
193.19.217.172.in-addr.arpa.
b'172.217.19.193'
ams16s31-in-f1.1e100.net.
$ python 20_2_dns_host_with_dnspython.py --address="52.95.3.61"
61.3.95.52.in-addr.arpa.
b'52.95.3.61'
Error while resolving 52.95.3.61: The DNS query name does not exist:
61.3.95.52.in-addr.arpa.
```

How it works...

When we input an invalid IP address, the resolving fails with the message, `The DNS query name does not exist`. It reports the reverse domain name (`{reverse-IP}.in-addr.arpa`) in the message as it could not resolve it to a valid address. If a valid address is found by `dns.resolver.query()`, it is returned. **Pointer records (PTR)** is used in resolving the IP address to its domain, as it maps a network interface (IP) to the host name.

Finding DNS resource records

You may secure your DNS information with **transaction signature (TSIG)**. This ensures a secured authorized update to DNS record. You may receive the **Start of Authority (SOA)** information of a host with the DNS lookup utilities `host` and `dig`. We first look at `host` utility followed by `dig` before looking into the Python code for our current recipe to retrieve the same information:

```
$ host cnn.com
cnn.com has address 151.101.129.67
cnn.com has address 151.101.193.67
cnn.com has address 151.101.1.67
cnn.com has address 151.101.65.67
cnn.com has IPv6 address 2a04:4e42:600::323
cnn.com has IPv6 address 2a04:4e42:400::323
cnn.com has IPv6 address 2a04:4e42:200::323
cnn.com has IPv6 address 2a04:4e42::323
cnn.com mail is handled by 10 mxb-000c6b02.gslb.pphosted.com.
cnn.com mail is handled by 10 mxa-000c6b02.gslb.pphosted.com.
$ host axn.com
axn.com has address 198.212.50.74
axn.com mail is handled by 0 mxa-001d1702.gslb.pphosted.com.
axn.com mail is handled by 0 mxb-001d1702.gslb.pphosted.com.
```

The output indicates that no IPv6 addresses were found for `https://www.axn.com/`.

```
$ host -t soa cnn.com
cnn.com has SOA record ns-47.awsdns-05.com. awsdns-
hostmaster.amazon.com. 1 7200 900 1209600 86400
```

The `-t` flag above indicates the type of the query. The type can also be `cname`, `ns`, `sig`, `key`, or `axfr`. We will look into the name servers of `http://edition.cnn.com/` here:

```
$ host -t ns cnn.com
cnn.com name server ns-47.awsdns-05.com.
cnn.com name server ns-576.awsdns-08.net.
cnn.com name server ns-1086.awsdns-07.org.
cnn.com name server ns-1630.awsdns-11.co.uk.
```

We may receive the `CNAME`, `SIG`, or `KEY` resource records (RR) of the site by using the `cname`, `sig`, and `key` types (`-t`) respectively.

```
$  host -t sig cnn.com
cnn.com has no SIG record
$  host -t key cnn.com
cnn.com has no KEY record
$  host -t cname cnn.com
cnn.com has no CNAME record
```

Outputs of the preceding three operations indicate that no `SIG`, `KEY`, or `CNAME` records were found for `http://cnn.com`. You may also use the `dig` command for further information of the site:

```
$ dig SOA cnn.com
; <<>> DiG 9.10.3-P4-Ubuntu <<>> SOA cnn.com
;; global options: +cmd
;; Got answer:
;; ->>HEADER<<- opcode: QUERY, status: NOERROR, id: 34225
;; flags: qr rd ra; QUERY: 1, ANSWER: 1, AUTHORITY: 4, ADDITIONAL: 1
;; OPT PSEUDOSECTION:
; EDNS: version: 0, flags:; udp: 4096
;; QUESTION SECTION:
;cnn.com.                 IN    SOA
;; ANSWER SECTION:
cnn.com.            285   IN    SOA   ns-47.awsdns-05.com. awsdns-
hostmaster.amazon.com. 1 7200 900 1209600 86400
;; AUTHORITY SECTION:
cnn.com.            1771  IN    NS    ns-1086.awsdns-07.org.
cnn.com.            1771  IN    NS    ns-1630.awsdns-11.co.uk.
cnn.com.            1771  IN    NS    ns-47.awsdns-05.com.
cnn.com.            1771  IN    NS    ns-576.awsdns-08.net.
;; Query time: 9 msec
;; SERVER: 127.0.1.1#53(127.0.1.1)
;; WHEN: Sun Jul 23 18:08:28 CEST 2017
;; MSG SIZE  rcvd: 233
```

Notice that the `ANSWER SECTION` of the output for `dig SOA <domain-name>` matches the output for the `host -t soa <domain-name>` command.

Getting ready

First install the `dnspython` (`https://github.com/rthalley/dnspython`) using the following `pip`:

```
$ sudo pip install dnspython
```

How to do it...

Now we will use `dnspython` to find the same details of a web URL that we earlier found using `dig` and `host` commands.

Listing 11.3 gives a simple, yet verbose code to offer the details of resource records of a given URL:

```
#!/usr/bin/env python
# Python Network Programming Cookbook, Second Edition
  -- Chapter - 11
# This program is optimized for Python 2.7.12 and
  Python 3.5.2.
# It may run on any other version with/without
  modifications.

import argparse
import dns.zone
import dns.resolver
import socket

def main(address):
    # IPv4 DNS Records
    answer = dns.resolver.query(address, 'A')
    for i in xrange(0, len(answer)):
        print("Default: ", answer[i])

    # IPv6 DNS Records
    try:
        answer6 = dns.resolver.query(address, 'AAAA')
        for i in xrange(0, len(answer6)):
            print("Default: ", answer6[i])
    except dns.resolver.NoAnswer as e:
        print("Exception in resolving the IPv6
```

```
                Resource Record:", e)

    # MX (Mail Exchanger) Records
    try:
        mx = dns.resolver.query(address, 'MX')
        for i in xrange(0, len(mx)):
            print("Default: ", mx[i])
    except dns.resolver.NoAnswer as e:
        print("Exception in resolving the MX
                Resource Record:", e)

    try:
        cname_answer = dns.resolver.query(address, 'CNAME')
        print("CNAME: ", cname_answer)
    except dns.resolver.NoAnswer as e:
        print('Exception retrieving CNAME', e)

    try:
        ns_answer = dns.resolver.query(address, 'NS')
        print(ns_answer)
    except dns.resolver.NoAnswer as e:
        print("Exception in resolving the NS Resource Record:", e)

    try:
        sig_answer = dns.resolver.query(address, 'SIG')
        print("SIG: ", sig_answer)
    except dns.resolver.NoAnswer as e:
        print('Exception retrieving SIG', e)

    try:
        key_answer = dns.resolver.query(address, 'KEY')
        print("KEY: ", key_answer)
    except dns.resolver.NoAnswer as e:
        print('Exception retrieving KEY', e)

    soa_answer = dns.resolver.query(address, 'SOA')
    print("SOA Answer: ", soa_answer[0].mname)
    master_answer = dns.resolver.query(soa_answer[0].mname, 'A')
    print("Master Answer: ", master_answer[0].address)


if __name__ == '__main__':
    parser = argparse.ArgumentParser(description='DNS Python')
    parser.add_argument('--address', action="store",
    dest="address",  default='dnspython.org')
    given_args = parser.parse_args()
    address = given_args.address
    main (address)
```

We test the program with a few addresses now.

```
$ python 20_3_find_dns_rr_details.py  --address="cnn.com"
('Default: ', <DNS IN A rdata: 151.101.193.67>)
('Default: ', <DNS IN A rdata: 151.101.1.67>)
('Default: ', <DNS IN A rdata: 151.101.65.67>)
('Default: ', <DNS IN A rdata: 151.101.129.67>)
('Default: ', <DNS IN AAAA rdata: 2a04:4e42::323>)
('Default: ', <DNS IN AAAA rdata: 2a04:4e42:200::323>)
('Default: ', <DNS IN AAAA rdata: 2a04:4e42:600::323>)
('Default: ', <DNS IN AAAA rdata: 2a04:4e42:400::323>)
('Default: ', <DNS IN MX rdata: 10 mxa-000c6b02.gslb.pphosted.com.>)
('Default: ', <DNS IN MX rdata: 10 mxb-000c6b02.gslb.pphosted.com.>)
('Exception retrieving CNAME', NoAnswer('The DNS response does not
contain an answer to the question: cnn.com. IN CNAME',))
<dns.resolver.Answer object at 0x7fb88ef23f90>
('Exception retrieving SIG', NoAnswer('The DNS response does not
contain an answer to the question: cnn.com. IN SIG',))
('Exception retrieving KEY', NoAnswer('The DNS response does not
contain an answer to the question: cnn.com. IN KEY',))
('SOA Answer: ', <DNS name ns-47.awsdns-05.com.>)
('Master Answer: ', u'205.251.192.47')
$ python 20_3_find_dns_rr_details.py  --address="google.com"
('Default: ', <DNS IN A rdata: 216.58.212.174>)
('Default: ', <DNS IN AAAA rdata: 2a00:1450:400e:801::200e>)
('Default: ', <DNS IN MX rdata: 50 alt4.aspmx.l.google.com.>)
('Default: ', <DNS IN MX rdata: 30 alt2.aspmx.l.google.com.>)
('Default: ', <DNS IN MX rdata: 10 aspmx.l.google.com.>)
('Default: ', <DNS IN MX rdata: 40 alt3.aspmx.l.google.com.>)
('Default: ', <DNS IN MX rdata: 20 alt1.aspmx.l.google.com.>)
('Exception retrieving CNAME', NoAnswer('The DNS response does not
contain an answer to the question: google.com. IN CNAME',))
<dns.resolver.Answer object at 0x7f30308b6f50>
('Exception retrieving SIG', NoAnswer('The DNS response does not
contain an answer to the question: google.com. IN SIG',))
('Exception retrieving KEY', NoAnswer('The DNS response does not
contain an answer to the question: google.com. IN KEY',))
('SOA Answer: ', <DNS name ns3.google.com.>)
('Master Answer: ', u'216.239.36.10')
$ python 20_3_find_dns_rr_details.py  --address="axn.com"
('Default: ', <DNS IN A rdata: 198.212.50.74>)
('Exception in resolving the IPv6 DNS Record:', NoAnswer('The DNS
response does not contain an answer to the question: axn.com. IN
AAAA',))
('Default: ', <DNS IN MX rdata: 0 mxb-001d1702.gslb.pphosted.com.>)
('Default: ', <DNS IN MX rdata: 0 mxa-001d1702.gslb.pphosted.com.>)
('Exception retrieving CNAME', NoAnswer('The DNS response does not
contain an answer to the question: axn.com. IN CNAME',))
```

```
<dns.resolver.Answer object at 0x7fb085878f50>
('Exception retrieving SIG', NoAnswer('The DNS response does not
contain an answer to the question: axn.com. IN SIG',))
('Exception retrieving KEY', NoAnswer('The DNS response does not
contain an answer to the question: axn.com. IN KEY',))
('SOA Answer: ', <DNS name udns1.ultradns.net.>)
('Master Answer: ', u'204.69.234.1')
$ python 20_3_find_dns_rr_details.py --address="zonetransfer.me"
('Default: ', <DNS IN A rdata: 217.147.177.157>)
('Exception in resolving the IPv6 Resource Record:', NoAnswer('The DNS
response does not contain an answer to the question: zonetransfer.me.
IN AAAA',))
('Default: ', <DNS IN MX rdata: 0 ASPMX.L.GOOGLE.COM.>)
('Default: ', <DNS IN MX rdata: 20 ASPMX3.GOOGLEMAIL.COM.>)
('Default: ', <DNS IN MX rdata: 20 ASPMX4.GOOGLEMAIL.COM.>)
('Default: ', <DNS IN MX rdata: 20 ASPMX5.GOOGLEMAIL.COM.>)
('Default: ', <DNS IN MX rdata: 10 ALT2.ASPMX.L.GOOGLE.COM.>)
('Default: ', <DNS IN MX rdata: 20 ASPMX2.GOOGLEMAIL.COM.>)
('Default: ', <DNS IN MX rdata: 10 ALT1.ASPMX.L.GOOGLE.COM.>)
('Exception retrieving CNAME', NoAnswer('The DNS response does not
contain an answer to the question: zonetransfer.me. IN CNAME',))
<dns.resolver.Answer object at 0x7f3184ba2cd0>
('Exception retrieving SIG', NoAnswer('The DNS response does not
contain an answer to the question: zonetransfer.me. IN SIG',))
('Exception retrieving KEY', NoAnswer('The DNS response does not
contain an answer to the question: zonetransfer.me. IN KEY',))
('SOA Answer: ', <DNS name nsztm1.digi.ninja.>)
('Master Answer: ', u'81.4.108.41')
```

How it works...

The `dns.resolver.query(address, <type>)` resolves the address for the query type. The command `host` looks for `A` (IPv4 address), `AAAA` (IPv6 address), and `MX` resource records when the type is not specified. We specify `A`, `AAAA`, `MX`, `SOA`, `CNAME`, `NS`, `SIG`, and `KEY` as the resource record types to resolve the addresses in our recipe. The output indicates that some of these records are not set for the sites that we tested.

The websites that we tested do not contain a `SIG`, `KEY`, or `CNAME` record as we found before with the `host -t` command. Since we do not have the authorization or the key to actually perform the zone transfer for these sites, this will fail with the message `Failed to perform zone transfer`. Also note that `http://axn.com` notes that, there was no answer for the `AAAA`, thus pointing that no IPv6 DNS record found for the website.

Making DNS zone transfer

We may transfer the DNS zone with the `dnspython` bundle. SOA record consists of crucial information for a zone transfer. Our recipe attempts the DNS zone transfer and compares the output with that from the `dig` utility. While zone transfer is not something that is performed by website users, we used `zonetransfer.me` test website to test our recipe and show the zone transfer output. Thanks to `https://digi.ninja/projects/zonetransferme.php` for setting this site up and running for educational purposes. You may read more on zone transfer and the test website `zonetransfer.me` from the site.

Getting ready

First install `dnspython` (`https://github.com/rthalley/dnspython`) using the following `pip`:

```
$ sudo pip install dnspython
```

How to do it...

We will use `dnspython` for the DNS zone transfer.

Listing 11.4 gives a simple code for a zone transfer as follows:

```
#!/usr/bin/env python
# Python Network Programming Cookbook, Second Edition
  -- Chapter - 11
# This program is optimized for Python 2.7.12 and
  Python 3.5.2.
# It may run on any other version with/without
  modifications.

import argparse
import dns.zone
import dns.resolver
import socket

def main(address):
    soa_answer = dns.resolver.query(address, 'SOA')
    master_answer = dns.resolver.query(soa_answer[0].mname, 'A')
    try:
        z = dns.zone.from_xfr(dns.query.
```

```
            xfr(master_answer[0].address, address))
        names = z.nodes.keys()
        names.sort()
        for n in names:
            print(z[n].to_text(n))
    except socket.error as e:
        print('Failed to perform zone transfer:', e)
    except dns.exception.FormError as e:
        print('Failed to perform zone transfer:', e)


if __name__ == '__main__':
    parser = argparse.ArgumentParser(description='DNS Python')
    parser.add_argument('--address', action="store",
    dest="address",  default='dnspython.org')
    given_args = parser.parse_args()
    address = given_args.address
    main (address)
```

We test the program with a few addresses now:

```
$ python 20_4_dns_zone_transfer.py --address="cnn.com"
('Failed to perform zone transfer:', error(104, 'Connection reset by
peer'))
$ python 20_4_dns_zone_transfer.py --address="google.com"
('Failed to perform zone transfer:', FormError('No answer or RRset not
for qname',))
$ python 20_4_dns_zone_transfer.py --address="axn.com"
('Failed to perform zone transfer:', FormError('No answer or RRset not
for qname',))
```

DNS zone transfer is a transaction where a copy of the database of the DNS server known as the **zone file**, is passed to another DNS server. As the zone file consists of server information that is sensitive and may open up avenues for attacks, zone servers are often restricted to the site administrators. Luckily for us, `zonetransfer.me` is a website set up solely for the purpose of testing zone transfers. Let's test our recipe again with this.

```
$ python 20_4_dns_zone_transfer.py --address="zonetransfer.me"
@ 7200 IN SOA nsztm1.digi.ninja. robin.digi.ninja. 2014101603 172800
900 1209600 3600
@ 7200 IN RRSIG SOA 8 2 7200 20160330133700 20160229123700 44244 @
GzQojkYAP8zuTOB9UAx66mTDiEGJ26hV IIP2ifk2DpbQLrEAPg4M77i4M0yFWHpN
fMJIuuJ8nMxQgFVCU3yTOeT/EMbN98FY C8lVYwEZeWHtbMmS88jVlF+cOz2WarjC
dyV0+UJCTdGtBJriIczC52EXKkw2RCkv 3gtdKKVafBE=
@ 7200 IN NS nsztm1.digi.ninja.
@ 7200 IN NS nsztm2.digi.ninja.
```

```
@ 7200 IN RRSIG NS 8 2 7200 20160330133700 20160229123700 44244 @
TyFngBk2PMWxgJc6RtgCE/RhE0kqeWfw hYSBxFxezupFLeiDjHeVXo+SWZxP54Xv
wfk7jlFClNZ9lRNkL5qHyxRElhlH1JJI 1hjvod0fycqLqCnxXIqkOzUCkm2Mxr8O
cGf2jVNDUcLPDO5XjHgOXCK9tRbVVKIp B92f4Qalulw=
@ 7200 IN A 217.147.177.157
@ 7200 IN RRSIG A 8 2 7200 20160330133700 20160229123700 44244 @
unoMaEPiyoAr0yAWg/coPbAFNznaAlUJ W3/QrvJleer50VvGLW/cK+VEDcZLfCu6
paQhgJHVddG4p145vVQe3QRvp7EJpUh+ SU7dX0I3gngmOa4Hk190S4utcXY5FhaN
7xBKHVWBlavQaSHTg61g/iuLSB0lS1gp /DAMUpC+WzE=
@ 300 IN HINFO "Casio fx-700G" "Windows XP"
@ 300 IN RRSIG HINFO 8 2 300 20160330133700 20160229123700 44244 @
Xebvrpv8nCGn/+iHqok1rcItTPqcskV6 jpJ1pCo4WYbnqByLultzygWxJlyVzz+w
JHEqRQYDjqGbl0dyUgKn2FFnqb1O92kK ghcHHvoMEh+Jf5i70trtucpRs3AtlneL
j2vauOCIEdbjma4IxgdwPahKIhgtgWcU InVFh3RrSwM=
@ 7200 IN MX 0 ASPMX.L.GOOGLE.COM.
@ 7200 IN MX 10 ALT1.ASPMX.L.GOOGLE.COM.
@ 7200 IN MX 10 ALT2.ASPMX.L.GOOGLE.COM.
.........
.........
www 3600 IN RRSIG NSEC 8 3 3600 20160330133700 20160229123700 44244 @
0xCqc6tWcT11ACD24Ap68hc7HRyAcCf7 MrkDqe2HyYMGuGS9YSwosiF3QzffhuY5
qagIFbpI3f7xVGxykngThTk37/JO2Srf I7Z5kvqLHdEd6GD9sogsLqTfHE9UToOY
YfuasO+IsJLyPALh89yk3bY+NipvpEPn gSnxN6ehIkc=
xss 300 IN TXT "'><script>alert('Boo')</script>"
xss 300 IN RRSIG TXT 8 3 300 20160330133700 20160229123700 44244 @
yvLf2kmOIKO22VT7Ml7/zuz7GbO2Ugvs O/VxLwXrGx+ewE12g2VCwsElYg/eMtsp
jJ38g7CbUltYLc5YydsdtFV3jzDAYbaw zFvugx0zmtN6kwpDa5LHs4BBSsjBBMM0
69IeD15ko5DLi+FWmPKoy5/CBNLlvwv8 a1S58MlHpU0=
xss 3600 IN NSEC @ TXT RRSIG NSEC
xss 3600 IN RRSIG NSEC 8 3 3600 20160330133700 20160229123700 44244 @
a7tFtY1bsTwztv/khjV/NEgaOQyiI8t2 R0xgQUp9ANKmAPqu83119rpIrwKpBF88
atlvQYTv9bRTjA/Y58WxsBYw+SOe3j3C UmHlQVbj8CJQpfJKcW1w7DoX8O1PYbWu
CAhciUyh1CV4Y5a8pcPBiZBM6225h4eA dE6Ahx3SXGY=
```

The following screenshot shows the verbose outcome of the zone transfer of `zonetransfer.me` site with our Python program. You may use `zonetransfer.me` for further testing:

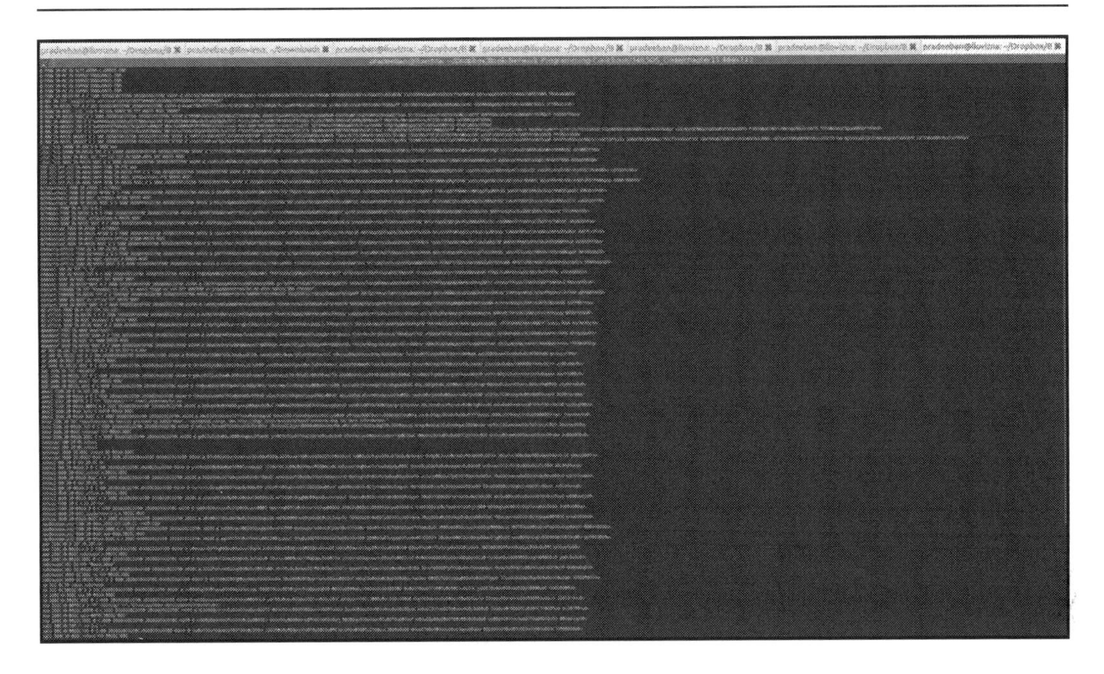

DNS Zone Transfer

You may confirm the output of the preceding DNS zone transfer by using the `dig` utility to perform the zone transfer as well, it is as shown following:

```
$ dig axfr @nsztm1.digi.ninja zonetransfer.me
; <<>> DiG 9.10.3-P4-Ubuntu <<>> axfr @nsztm1.digi.ninja
zonetransfer.me
; (1 server found)
;; global options: +cmd
zonetransfer.me.  7200  IN    SOA   nsztm1.digi.ninja.
robin.digi.ninja. 2014101603 172800 900 1209600 3600
......
xss.zonetransfer.me.    3600  IN    NSEC  zonetransfer.me. TXT RRSIG
NSEC
xss.zonetransfer.me.    3600  IN    RRSIG NSEC 8 3 3600 20160330133700
20160229123700 44244 zonetransfer.me.
a7tFtY1bsTwztv/khjV/NEgaOQyiI8t2R0xgQUp9ANKmAPqu831l9rpI
rwKpBF88atlvQYTv9bRTjA/Y58WxsBYw+SOe3j3CUmHlQVbj8CJQpfJK
cW1w7DoX8O1PYbWuCAhciUyh1CV4Y5a8pcPBiZBM6225h4eAdE6Ahx3S XGY=
zonetransfer.me.  7200  IN    SOA   nsztm1.digi.ninja.
robin.digi.ninja. 2014101603 172800 900 1209600 3600
;; Query time: 55 msec
;; SERVER: 81.4.108.41#53(81.4.108.41)
;; WHEN: Sun Jul 23 22:06:38 CEST 2017
;; XFR size: 153 records (messages 1, bytes 16183)
```

How it works...

The `dns.query.xfr()` takes two inputs similar to the `dig` utility (`dig axfr @nsztm1.digi.ninja zonetransfer.me`). It gets the first input parameter (in the case of `zonetransfer.me`, it is `nsztm1.digi.ninja`), by processing `master_answer[0].address`, which is essentially retrieved from the single command-line argument (and also the second input parameter), address. We print the sorted names after the zone transfer.

Querying NTP servers

Network Time Protocol (NTP): `http://www.ntp.org/ntpfaq/NTP-s-def.htm` is a protocol that is used to query and synchronize the clocks of the computers connected to the internet. In this recipe, we will be using `ntplib` (`https://pypi.python.org/pypi/ntplib/`), a Python module that offers an interface to query the NTP servers, to learn about the NTP servers, you may use `http://www.pool.ntp.org/en/use.html` which finds the closest NTP server for you to synchronize your server clock. It also gives guidelines on contributing your computing resources as an NTP server.

Getting ready

First install `ntplib` in your computer.

```
$ sudo apt-get install python-ntplib
```

`ntplib` works on Python 2. You may install `python3-ntplib` that works for Python 3 from `https://launchpad.net/ubuntu/yakkety/amd64/python3-ntplib/0.3.3-1`, or by following the succeeding commands:

```
$ wget
http://launchpadlibrarian.net/260811286/python3-ntplib_0.3.3-1_all.deb
$ sudo dpkg -i python3-ntplib_0.3.3-1_all.deb
```

How to do it...

Synchronizing your time is crucial accounting task. While it is not ideal to depend on the time from the internet for mission-critical systems, the NTP time is sufficiently accurate for most of the computing requirements.

Listing 11.5 gives a simple NTP server connection test as follows:

```
#!/usr/bin/env python
# Python Network Programming Cookbook, Second Edition
  -- Chapter - 11
# This program is optimized for Python 2.7.12 and
  Python 3.5.2.
# It may run on any other version with/without
  modifications.

import argparse
import ntplib
from time import ctime


def main(address, v):
    c = ntplib.NTPClient()
    response = c.request(address, version=v)
    print("Response Offset: ", response.offset)
    print("Version: ", response.version)
    print("Response (Time): ", ctime(response.tx_time))
    print("Leap: ", ntplib.leap_to_text(response.leap))
    print("Root Delay: ", response.root_delay)
    print(ntplib.ref_id_to_text(response.ref_id))


if __name__ == '__main__':
    parser = argparse.ArgumentParser(description='Query NTP Server')
    parser.add_argument('--address', action="store",
    dest="address",  default='pool.ntp.org')
    parser.add_argument('--version', action="store",
    dest="version",  type=int, default=3)
    given_args = parser.parse_args()
    address = given_args.address
    version = given_args.version
    main (address, version)
```

In this recipe, we provide an NTP server to query the time. Running this program provides the following outcome:

```
$  python 20_5_query_ntp_server.py --address=europe.pool.ntp.org --
version=3
('Response Offset: ', -0.002687215805053711)
('Version: ', 3)
('Response (Time): ', 'Mon Jul 24 23:06:10 2017')
('Leap: ', 'no warning')
('Root Delay: ', 0.00372314453125)
10.176.63.115
```

```
This recipe is similar to the  standard NTP query program ntpq.
$ ntpq -pn
remote           refid      st t when poll reach   delay   offset
jitter
==============================================================
0.ubuntu.pool.n .POOL.          16 p    -   64    0    0.000    0.000
0.000
1.ubuntu.pool.n .POOL.          16 p    -   64    0    0.000    0.000
0.000
2.ubuntu.pool.n .POOL.          16 p    -   64    0    0.000    0.000
0.000
3.ubuntu.pool.n .POOL.          16 p    -   64    0    0.000    0.000
0.000
ntp.ubuntu.com  .POOL.          16 p    -   64    0    0.000    0.000
0.000
-91.189.91.157   132.246.11.231   2 u  257  512  377   94.363   -3.998
13.016
+193.190.147.153 193.190.230.65   2 u  184  512  377   10.327   -2.246
1.235
+91.189.89.198   17.253.52.125    2 u  169  512  377   14.206   -2.744
1.414
*94.143.184.140   .GPS.           1 u  279  512  377   14.208   -2.743
2.453
+213.189.188.3   193.190.230.65   2 u    1  512  377   11.015   -2.192
1.569
```

How it works...

We query and print the time from a remote NTP server using `ctime(response.tx_time)`. We can pass the address of an NTP server and version (1-7) as the arguments to the program. When a generic address such as `pool.ntp.org` is used, the closest server is picked based on the requesting server's location. Hence, you receive a response with minimal latency.

Connecting to an LDAP server

Lightweight Directory Access Protocol (**LDAP**) is an identity management protocol organizing individuals, organizations, resources, and the roles and access of those entities, organized locally, in the intranet or in the internet. Many LDAP servers are available for download and install and are free and open source, including the OpenLDAP and Apache Directory.

Getting ready

For those who like to try an LDAP instance without actually going through the hassle of installing the server, there are a few open and public LDAP servers available online. Some of them offer write access, for example, FreeIPA (`https://www.freeipa.org/page/Main_Page`). FreeIPA is an integrated security information management solution that offers an online demo installation for testing purposes at `https://ipa.demo1.freeipa.org/ipa/ui/`. We will use it for our recipes. As with any public server with write access, FreeIPA server needs to be cleaned up daily. During these hours, it goes offline. The FreeIPA web interface is shown as follows:

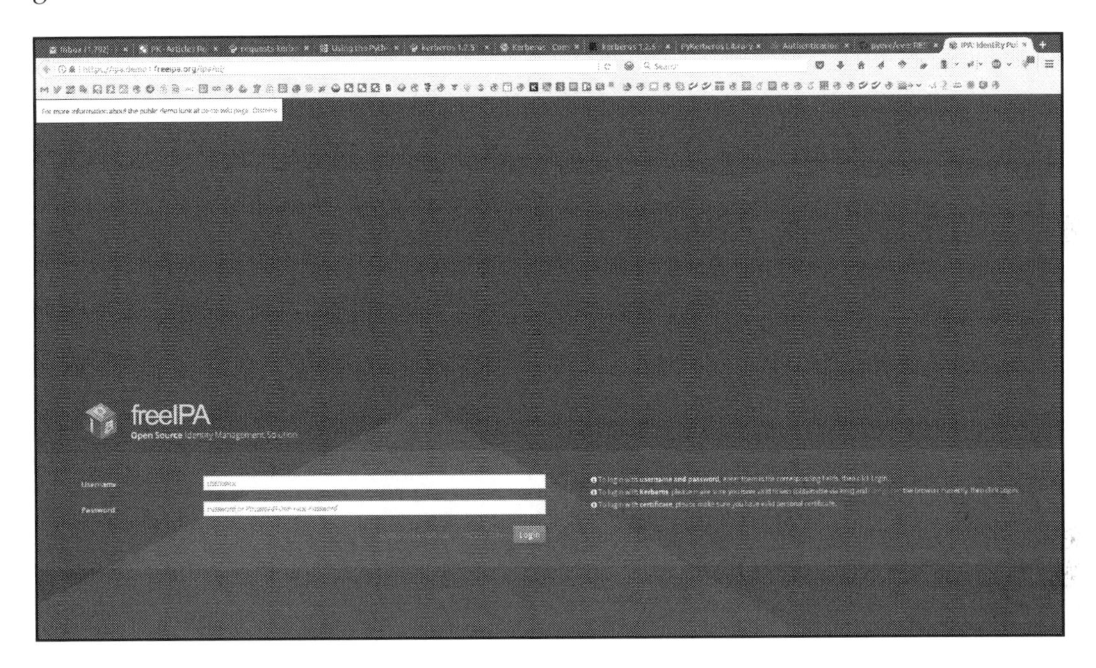

FreeIPA Log in Screen

You may also use `ldap.forumsys.com`, another public LDAP server with read-only access to test our recipes. You may find more LDAP servers accessible online with read-only and write accesses, or you may even configure your own LDAP server to have full control. In this recipe, we will connect to the LDAP server and receive information from it through our Python program.

First, install the `python-ldap3` (`http://ldap3.readthedocs.io/tutorial_intro.html`) package as a prerequisite for this recipe using the following command:

```
$ sudo pip install ldap3
```

How to do it...

We will use the `ldap3` library and import `Server`, `Connection`, and `ALL` modules from it. `ldap3` offers an object-oriented access to the directory servers of LDAP.

Listing 11.6 connects to a remote LDAP server and retrieves the server information and schema as follows:

```
#!/usr/bin/env python
# Python Network Programming Cookbook, Second Edition
  -- Chapter - 11
# This program is optimized for Python 2.7.12 and
  Python 3.5.2.
# It may run on any other version with/without
  modifications.

import argparse
from ldap3 import Server, Connection, ALL


def main(address):
    # Create the Server object with the given address.
    # Get ALL information.
    server = Server(address, get_info=ALL)
    #Create a connection object, and bind with auto
     bind set to true.
    conn = Connection(server, auto_bind=True)
    # Print the LDAP Server Information.
    print('******************Server Info**************')
    print(server.info)

    # Print the LDAP Server Detailed Schema.
    print('******************Server Schema**************')
    print(server.schema)

if __name__ == '__main__':
    parser = argparse.ArgumentParser(description=
                                    'Query LDAP Server')
    parser.add_argument('--address', action="store",
    dest="address",  default='ipa.demo1.freeipa.org')
    given_args = parser.parse_args()
```

```
    address = given_args.address
    main (address)
```

Here we pass the address to the LDAP server as a command-line argument to print a detailed information of it shown as following:

```
$ python 20_6_connect_ldap_server.py --address=ldap.forumsys.com
******************Server Info**************
DSA info (from DSE):
Supported LDAP versions: 3
Naming contexts:
dc=example,dc=com
Supported controls:
1.2.826.0.1.3344810.2.3 - Matched Values - Control - RFC3876
1.2.840.113556.1.4.319 - LDAP Simple Paged Results - Control - RFC2696
1.3.6.1.1.12 - Assertion - Control - RFC4528
1.3.6.1.1.13.1 - LDAP Pre-read - Control - RFC4527
1.3.6.1.1.13.2 - LDAP Post-read - Control - RFC4527
1.3.6.1.4.1.4203.1.10.1 - Subentries - Control - RFC3672
2.16.840.1.113730.3.4.18 - Proxy Authorization Control - Control -
RFC6171
2.16.840.1.113730.3.4.2 - ManageDsaIT - Control - RFC3296
Supported extensions:
1.3.6.1.1.8 - Cancel Operation - Extension - RFC3909
1.3.6.1.4.1.1466.20037 - StartTLS - Extension - RFC4511-RFC4513
1.3.6.1.4.1.4203.1.11.1 - Modify Password - Extension - RFC3062
1.3.6.1.4.1.4203.1.11.3 - Who am I - Extension - RFC4532
Supported features:
1.3.6.1.1.14 - Modify-Increment - Feature - RFC4525
1.3.6.1.4.1.4203.1.5.1 - All Op Attrs - Feature - RFC3673
1.3.6.1.4.1.4203.1.5.2 - OC AD Lists - Feature - RFC4529
1.3.6.1.4.1.4203.1.5.3 - True/False filters - Feature - RFC4526
1.3.6.1.4.1.4203.1.5.4 - Language Tag Options - Feature - RFC3866
1.3.6.1.4.1.4203.1.5.5 - language Range Options - Feature - RFC3866
Schema entry:
cn=Subschema
Vendor name: []
Vendor version: []
Other:
objectClass:
top
OpenLDAProotDSE
structuralObjectClass:
OpenLDAProotDSE
entryDN:
configContext:
cn=config
******************Server Schema**************
```

```
DSA Schema from: cn=Subschema
Attribute types:{'olcAuthIDRewrite': Attribute type:
1.3.6.1.4.1.4203.1.12.2.3.0.6
Short name: olcAuthIDRewrite
Single value: False
Equality rule: caseIgnoreMatch
Syntax: 1.3.6.1.4.1.1466.115.121.1.15
[('1.3.6.1.4.1.1466.115.121.1.15', 'LDAP_SYNTAX', 'Directory String',
'RFC4517')]
Optional in: olcGlobal
Extensions:
X-ORDERED: VALUES
, 'olcUpdateDN': Attribute type: 1.3.6.1.4.1.4203.1.12.2.3.2.0.12
Short name: olcUpdateDN
Single value: True
Syntax: 1.3.6.1.4.1.1466.115.121.1.12
[('1.3.6.1.4.1.1466.115.121.1.12', 'LDAP_SYNTAX', 'DN', 'RFC4517')]
Optional in: olcDatabaseConfig
, 'namingContexts': Attribute type: 1.3.6.1.4.1.1466.101.120.5
Short name: namingContexts
Description: RFC4512: naming contexts
Single value: False
Usage: unknown
Syntax: 1.3.6.1.4.1.1466.115.121.1.12
[('1.3.6.1.4.1.1466.115.121.1.12', 'LDAP_SYNTAX', 'DN', 'RFC4517')]
OidInfo: ('1.3.6.1.4.1.1466.101.120.5', 'ATTRIBUTE_TYPE',
'namingContexts', 'RFC4512')
, 'olcAccess': Attribute type: 1.3.6.1.4.1.4203.1.12.2.3.0.1
Short name: olcAccess
Description: Access Control List
Single value: False
Equality rule: caseIgnoreMatch
Syntax: 1.3.6.1.4.1.1466.115.121.1.15
[('1.3.6.1.4.1.1466.115.121.1.15', 'LDAP_SYNTAX', 'Directory String',
'RFC4517')]
Optional in: olcDatabaseConfig
Extensions:
X-ORDERED: VALUES
, 'businessCategory': Attribute type: 2.5.4.15
Short name: businessCategory
........
......
```

The complete output of the execution for the address `https://ipa.demo1.freeipa.org/ipa/ui/` and `ldap.forumsys.com` are stored in the files `20_6_output_with_ipa.demo1.freeipa.org.txt` and `20_6_output_with_ldap.forumsys.com.txt` respectively.

Following is a screenshot of the execution, indicating the detailed output of the execution:

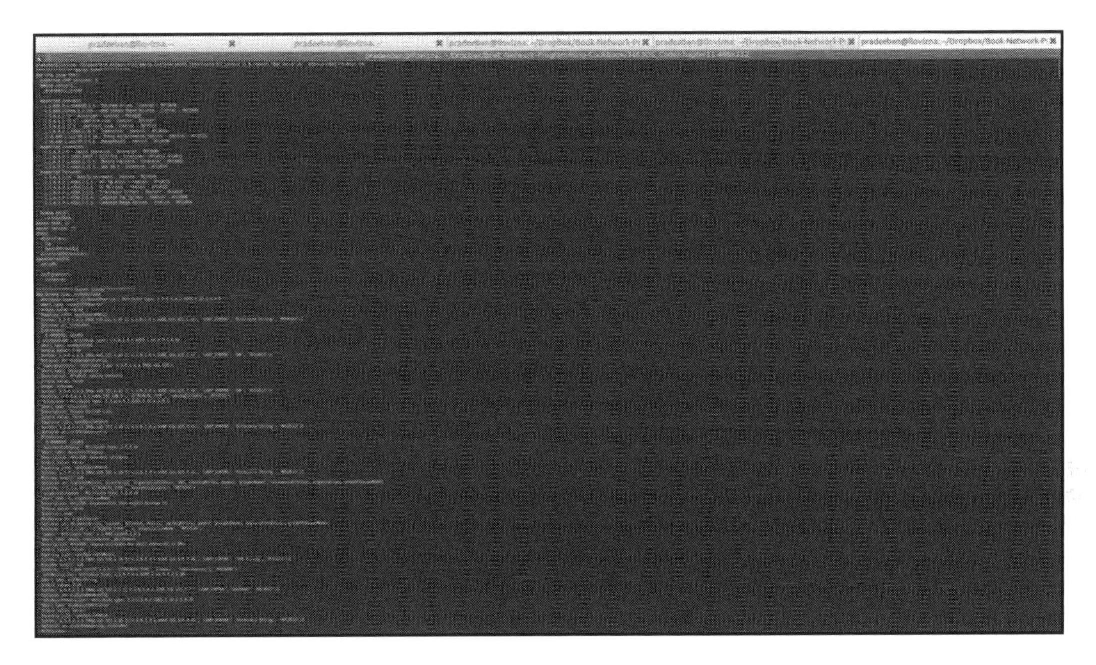

Connect to the LDAP Server

How it works...

In the server information, we receive details such as supported controls, extensions, and features. Moreover, we also get the schema entry and configuration context. In the LDAP server schema, we retrieve information on the various attributes as shown as follows:

```
'memberUid': Attribute type: 1.3.6.1.1.1.1.12
  Short name: memberUid
  Single value: False
  Equality rule: caseExactIA5Match
  Syntax: 1.3.6.1.4.1.1466.115.121.1.26
[('1.3.6.1.4.1.1466.115.121.1.26', 'LDAP_SYNTAX', 'IA5 String',
'RFC4517')]
  Optional in: posixGroup
```

Making LDAP bind

We need to authenticate an LDAP user with their password for accessing more information relevant for their role. In this recipe, we will attempt to make an LDAP bind with the correct password and an invalid one.

Getting ready

Install `ldap3` Python client, the prerequisite for this recipe:

```
$ sudo pip install ldap3
```

How to do it...

We will provide the bind `dn` and `password` in addition to the `address` of the LDAP server address, as the input arguments.

Listing 11.7 elaborates how to make an LDAP bind:

```
#!/usr/bin/env python
# Python Network Programming Cookbook, Second Edition
  -- Chapter - 11
# This program is optimized for Python 2.7.12 and
  Python 3.5.2.
# It may run on any other version with/without
  modifications.

import argparse
from ldap3 import Server, Connection, ALL, core


def main(address, dn, password):
    # Create the Server object with the given address.
    server = Server(address, get_info=ALL)
    #Create a connection object, and bind with the
     given DN and password.
    try:
        conn = Connection(server, dn, password, auto_bind=True)
        print('LDAP Bind Successful.')
        print(conn)
    except core.exceptions.LDAPBindError as e:
        # If the LDAP bind failed for reasons such
          as authentication failure.
        print('LDAP Bind Failed: ', e)
```

```
if __name__ == '__main__':
    parser = argparse.ArgumentParser(description='Query LDAP Server')
    parser.add_argument('--address', action="store",
    dest="address",  default='ldap.forumsys.com')
    parser.add_argument('--dn', action="store",
    dest="dn",  default='cn=read-only-admin,dc=example,dc=com')
    parser.add_argument('--password', action="store",
    dest="password",  default='password')
    given_args = parser.parse_args()
    address = given_args.address
    dn = given_args.dn
    password = given_args.password
    main (address, dn, password)
```

We will first test the recipe with a correct `dn` and `password`:

```
$ python 20_7_query_ldap_server.py --address=ldap.forumsys.com --
dn=cn=read-only-admin,dc=example,dc=com --password=password
LDAP Bind Successful.
ldap://ldap.forumsys.com:389 - cleartext - user: cn=read-only-
admin,dc=example,dc=com - not lazy - bound - open - <local:
109.141.39.196:60340 - remote: 54.196.176.103:389> - tls not started -
listening - SyncStrategy - internal decoder
```

Now again with a wrong combination of `dn` and `password`:

```
$ python 20_7_query_ldap_server.py --address=ldap.forumsys.com --
dn=ou=mathematicians,dc=example,dc=com --password=password1
LDAP Bind Failed:  automatic bind not successful - invalidCredentials
```

The LDAP bind will fail with the `invalidCredentials` error if the `dn` does not exist, or if the `password` is incorrect. The authentication error message does not differentiate these two cases, as a security best practice, thus not letting an attacker narrow down on their attacks.

To actually query the entries, we need to perform a search. We slightly modify our recipe as listed in `20_7_query_ldap_server_b.py` for this. The following segment elaborates the changes in Listing 11.7:

```
    try:
        conn = Connection(server, dn, password, auto_bind=True)
        print('LDAP Bind Successful.')
        # Perform a search for a pre-defined criteria.
        # Mention the search filter / filter type and attributes.
        conn.search('dc=example,dc=com', '(&(uid=euler))' ,
        attributes=['sn'])
        # Print the resulting entries.
```

```
        print(conn.entries[0])
    except core.exceptions.LDAPBindError as e:
        # If the LDAP bind failed for reasons such
          as authentication failure.
        print('LDAP Bind Failed: ', e)
```

We run the modified recipe to produce the following output:

```
$ python3 20_7_query_ldap_server_b.py --address=ldap.forumsys.com --
dn=cn=read-only-admin,dc=example,dc=com --password=password
LDAP Bind Successful.
DN: uid=euler,dc=example,dc=com - STATUS: Read - READ TIME:
2017-07-26T22:57:48.011791
    sn: Euler
```

Here we elaborated how the LDAP can be queried by providing the filter type and the attributes. Providing an invalid attribute type will result in an error. For example, seeking invalid attribute type of `krbLastPwdChange` in place of `sn` in the preceding code produces the following error message:

```
ldap3.core.exceptions.LDAPAttributeError: invalid attribute type
krbLastPwdChange
```

Similarly, an invalid filter throws the following error:

```
ldap3.core.exceptions.LDAPInvalidFilterError: invalid filter
```

How it works...

The LDAP bind succeeds with the correct credentials. Then you may define your search criteria with a relevant filter type and attributes. Once you have performed the search, you may iterate and print the resultant entries.

Reading and writing LDAP

In this recipe, we will read and write from the FreeIPA LDAP demo server.

Getting ready

Install `ldap3` Python client, the prerequisite for this recipe:

```
$ sudo pip install ldap3
```

How to do it...

First we will read LDAP with a `Reader` object as shown by Listing 11.8 as follows:

```
#!/usr/bin/env python
# Python Network Programming Cookbook, Second Edition
  -- Chapter - 11
# This program is optimized for Python 2.7.12 and
  Python 3.5.2.
# It may run on any other version with/without
  modifications.
# Adopted from
http://ldap3.readthedocs.io/tutorial_abstraction_basic.html

from ldap3 import Server, Connection, ObjectDef, AttrDef, Reader,
Writer, ALL


def main():
    server = Server('ipa.demo1.freeipa.org', get_info=ALL)
    conn = Connection(server,
'uid=admin,cn=users,cn=accounts,dc=demo1,dc=freeipa,dc=org',
'Secret123', auto_bind=True)
    person = ObjectDef('person', conn)
    r = Reader(conn, person, 'ou=ldap3-
                tutorial,dc=demo1,dc=freeipa,dc=org')
    print(r)
    print('************')
    person+='uid'
    print(r)

if __name__ == '__main__':
    main ()
```

This recipe performs an implicit creation of a new attribute definition by the following line:

```
    person+='uid'
```

By running this recipe, you may observe the following output:

```
$ python 20_8_read_ldap_server.py
CURSOR : Reader
CONN   : ldap://ipa.demo1.freeipa.org:389 - cleartext - user:
uid=admin,cn=users,cn=accounts,dc=demo1,dc=freeipa,dc=org - not lazy -
bound - open - <local: 192.168.137.95:44860 - remote:
52.57.162.88:389> - tls not started - listening - SyncStrategy -
internal decoder
```

```
DEFS    : [u'person'] [cn, description, objectClass, seeAlso, sn,
telephoneNumber, userPassword]
ATTRS   : [u'cn', u'description', u'objectClass', u'seeAlso', u'sn',
u'telephoneNumber', u'userPassword']
BASE    : 'ou=ldap3-tutorial,dc=demo1,dc=freeipa,dc=org' [SUB]
FILTER : u'(objectClass=person)'
************
CURSOR : Reader
CONN    : ldap://ipa.demo1.freeipa.org:389 - cleartext - user:
uid=admin,cn=users,cn=accounts,dc=demo1,dc=freeipa,dc=org - not lazy -
bound - open - <local: 192.168.137.95:44860 - remote:
52.57.162.88:389> - tls not started - listening - SyncStrategy -
internal decoder
DEFS    : [u'person'] [cn, description, objectClass, seeAlso, sn,
telephoneNumber, uid, userPassword]
ATTRS   : [u'cn', u'description', u'objectClass', u'seeAlso', u'sn',
u'telephoneNumber', u'userPassword']
BASE    : 'ou=ldap3-tutorial,dc=demo1,dc=freeipa,dc=org' [SUB]
FILTER : u'(objectClass=person)'
```

As highlighted in the preceding recipe, after the attribute definition `uid` is added to the `person` object, it is reflected in the DEFS after the line: `person+='uid'`. However, if you re-execute the recipe, you will notice that the previous changes to the `person` object are not present. This is because the changes are not written with the `Reader` cursor. For that, you will need a `Writer`. You may initiate a `Writer` from the `Reader` cursor as shown here:

```
w = Writer.from_cursor(r)
w[0].sn += 'Smyth'
w.commit()
```

Make sure you have the write access to the LDAP server with the correct `dn` and `password` for the commit to succeed. It is recommended to try this in a private LDAP server that gives you complete admin access.

How it works...

We define the object in the line:

```
person = ObjectDef('person', conn)
```

Then we define a `Reader` cursor and read it by:

```
r = Reader(conn, person, 'ou=ldap3-
tutorial,dc=demo1,dc=freeipa,dc=org')
```

Authenticating REST APIs with Eve

Eve is a REST API server built in Python. We will test how to use Eve REST API framework with `BasicAuth`, global authentication. Eve can also be started without any authentication at all, as a simple REST API server. This recipe is a simple demonstration of serving the entire web server. However, Eve provides more sophisticated and more role-based access control that protects certain APIs with roles for the users.

The server is started with a username and password, and the client passes on the `base64` encode of the format `username:password` to the server to get authenticated.

Getting ready

First install Eve using Python:

```
$ sudo pip install eve
```

This will install Eve, along with its dependencies, `cerberus-0.9.2`, `eve-0.7.4`, `events-0.2.2`, `flask-0.12`, `flask-pymongo-0.5.1`, `pymongo-3.4.0`, `simplejson-3.11.1`, `werkzeug-0.11.15`.

In this recipe, we will start a simple server with a username and password as the basic authentication.

How to do it...

First make sure that you have the domain configurations saved as a Python file named `settings.py` in the same folder as your program. In this recipe, we have included a simple `settings.py` with the following content as a sample:

```
DOMAIN = {'people': {}}
```

If `settings.py` is not found, the program will halt with the following error:

```
eve.exceptions.ConfigException: DOMAIN dictionary missing or wrong.
```

Listing 11.9 gives a REST server with `BasicAuth` as follows:

```
#!/usr/bin/env python
# Python Network Programming Cookbook, Second Edition
  -- Chapter - 11
# This program is optimized for Python 2.7.12 and
  Python 3.5.2.
# It may run on any other version with/without
  modifications.

from eve import Eve
from eve.auth import BasicAuth

class MyBasicAuth(BasicAuth):
    def check_auth(self, username, password, allowed_roles,
   resource,
                   method):
        return username == 'admin' and password == 'secret'

def run_server():
    app = Eve(auth=MyBasicAuth)
    app.run()
if __name__ == '__main__':
    run_server()
```

We run the server with the username `admin` and password `secret`.

```
$ python 20_9_eve_basic_auth.py
  * Running on http://127.0.0.1:5000/ (Press CTRL+C to quit)
```

Assuming username `admin` and password `secret`, to retrieve the `base64` encoded string of this credentials, you may use the following command:

```
$ echo -n admin:secret | base64
YWRtaW46c2VjcmV0
```

Now we run the client with the correct `base64` encoded `secret`:

```
$ curl -H "Authorization: Basic YWRtaW46c2VjcmV0" -i
http://127.0.0.1:5000
$ curl -H "Authorization: Basic YWRtaW46c2VjcmV0" -i
http://127.0.0.1:5000
HTTP/1.0 200 OK
Content-Type: application/json
Content-Length: 62
Server: Eve/0.7.4 Werkzeug/0.11.15 Python/2.7.12
Date: Sat, 29 Jul 2017 12:10:04 GMT
{"_links": {"child": [{"href": "people", "title": "people"}]}}
```

If you run `curl` with no credentials, the following output will be produced:

```
$ curl -i http://127.0.0.1:5000
HTTP/1.0 401 UNAUTHORIZED
Content-Type: application/json
Content-Length: 91
WWW-Authenticate: Basic realm="eve"
Server: Eve/0.7.4 Werkzeug/0.11.15 Python/2.7.12
Date: Sat, 29 Jul 2017 12:09:02 GMT
{"_status": "ERR", "_error": {"message": "Please provide proper
credentials", "code": 401}}
```

The server will bring the following log to indicate the failed attempt:

```
127.0.0.1 - - [29/Jul/2017 14:09:02] "GET / HTTP/1.1" 401 -
```

The output for an attempt with wrong credentials would be similar to the preceding ones with no credentials:

```
curl -H "Authorization: Basic YV1" -i http://127.0.0.1:5000
```

How it works...

Eve can be initialized with custom authentication. We created our class as a simple basic authentication, with a given username and password (which can easily be extended to receive the credentials as command-line arguments). The `check_auth()` returns `true` if both the client provided username and password (as a `base64` encoded string) matches the ones that the server is started with.

Throttling requests with RequestsThrottler

Networks need to have accounting in addition to authorization and authentication. Accounting ensures proper use of the resources, this means that everyone gets to use the services in a fair manner. Network throttling enables accounting in the web services. This is a simple recipe that offers a throttling service to the web requests.

Getting ready

We use `requests_throttler` Python module to throttle the web requests. First, install the module and configure our recipe using the following script:

```
$ sh 20_10_requests_throttling.sh
#!/bin/bash
##############################################################
# Python Network Programming Cookbook, Second Edition --
Chapter - 11
##############################################################
# Download and extract RequestsThrottler
wget
https://pypi.python.org/packages/d5/db/fc7558a14efa163cd2d3e4515cdfbbf
c2daccld2c4285b095104c58065c7/RequestsThrottler-0.1.0.tar.gz
tar -xvf RequestsThrottler-0.1.0.tar.gz
cd RequestsThrottler-0.1.0
# Copy our recipe into the folder
cp ../20_10_requests_throttling.py requests_throttler
# Configure and Install RequestsThrottling
python setup.py build
sudo python setup.py install
```

How to do it...

Now, you may execute your recipe by going to the folder, `RequestsThrottler-0.1.0/requests_throttler`.

```
$ cd RequestsThrottler-0.1.0/requests_throttler
```

Make sure to give the full addresses as the command-line argument. For example, provide `http://cnn.com`. Not `cnn.com`. Otherwise, you will receive an error message similar to the one shown following:

```
requests.exceptions.MissingSchema: Invalid URL 'cnn.com': No schema
supplied. Perhaps you meant http://cnn.com?
```

Run the recipe using the following command:

```
$  python 20_10_requests_throttling.py --address="http://cnn.com"
^[[1~[Thread=MainThread - 2017-07-29 19:34:08,897 - INFO]: Starting
base throttler 'base-throttler'...
[Thread=MainThread - 2017-07-29 19:34:08,897 - INFO]: Submitting
request to base throttler (url: http://cnn.com)...
[Thread=Thread-1 - 2017-07-29 19:34:08,897 - INFO]: Starting main
loop...
[Thread=MainThread - 2017-07-29 19:34:08,900 - INFO]: Submitting
request to base throttler (url: http://cnn.com)...
[Thread=Thread-1 - 2017-07-29 19:34:08,900 - INFO]: Sending request
(url: http://cnn.com/)...
[Thread=MainThread - 2017-07-29 19:34:08,900 - INFO]: Submitting
request to base throttler (url: http://cnn.com)...
[Thread=MainThread - 2017-07-29 19:34:08,901 - INFO]: Submitting
request to base throttler (url: http://cnn.com)...
[Thread=MainThread - 2017-07-29 19:34:08,901 - INFO]: Submitting
request to base throttler (url: http://cnn.com)...
.............
[Thread=Thread-1 - 2017-07-29 19:34:09,184 - INFO]: Request sent!
(url: http://cnn.com/)
[Thread=Thread-1 - 2017-07-29 19:34:09,184 - INFO]: Sending request
(url: http://cnn.com/)...
<Response [200]>
[Thread=Thread-1 - 2017-07-29 19:34:09,343 - INFO]: Request sent!
(url: http://www.cnn.com/)
<Response [200]>
[Thread=Thread-1 - 2017-07-29 19:34:10,401 - INFO]: Sending request
(url: http://cnn.com/)...
[Thread=Thread-1 - 2017-07-29 19:34:10,545 - INFO]: Request sent!
(url: http://www.cnn.com/)
<Response [200]>
.......
Success: 10, Failures: 0
[Thread=Thread-1 - 2017-07-29 19:34:22,412 - INFO]: Exited from main
loop.
```

The following screenshot shows the output of our recipe:

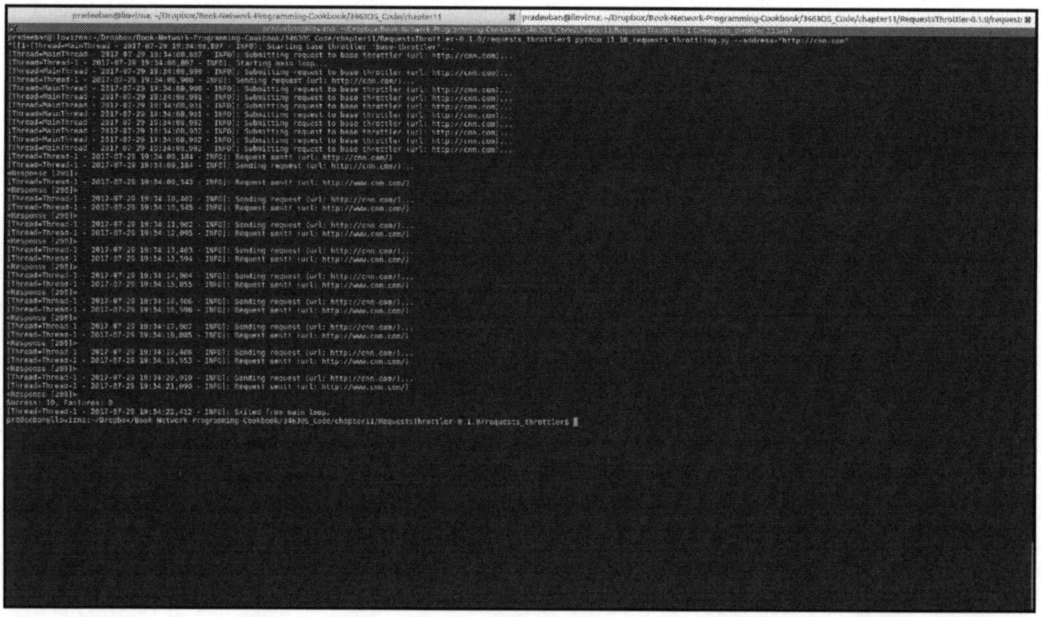

Throttled Requests to a Web Server

Listing 11.10 shows our recipe, that sends requests to the website provided as the command-line input, in a throttled manner:

```
#!/usr/bin/env python
# Python Network Programming Cookbook, Second Edition
  -- Chapter - 11
# This program is optimized for Python 2.7.12.
# It may run on any other version with/without
  modifications.

import argparse
import requests
from throttler.base_throttler import BaseThrottler


def main(address):

    # Throttle the requests with the BaseThrottler, delaying 1.5s.
    bt = BaseThrottler(name='base-throttler', delay=1.5)

    # Visit the address provided by the user. Complete URL only.
```

```
    r = requests.Request(method='GET', url=address)

    # 10 requests.
    reqs = [r for i in range(0, 10)]

    # Submit the requests with the required throttling.
    with bt:
        throttled_requests = bt.submit(reqs)

    # Print the response for each of the requests.
    for r in throttled_requests:
        print (r.response)

    # Final status of the requests.
    print ("Success: {s}, Failures: {f}".format(s=bt.successes,
            f=bt.failures))


if __name__ == '__main__':
    parser = argparse.ArgumentParser(description=
                                     'Requests Throttling')
    parser.add_argument('--address', action="store",
    dest="address",  default='http://www.google.com')
    given_args = parser.parse_args()
    address = given_args.address
    main (address)
```

This recipe performs the accounting action, by making sure each request are sent only after a certain delay. Here we use `BaseThrottler`, this ensures that each request is started with a 1.5 second delay in between.

How it works...

The `requests_throttler` Python module supports throttling requests to the web servers. There are more throttling implementations based in Python, for example, throttle (`https://pypi.python.org/pypi/throttle`) is an implementation based on token bucket algorithm.

Throttling can ensure that only a given number of requests are satisfied for a given user in a given time interval. Thus, it protects the server from attackers who try to flood the server with the requests, as in **denial-of-service** (**DoS**) attacks.

21
Open and Proprietary Networking Solutions

In this chapter, we will cover the following recipes:

- Configuring Red PNDA
- Configuring VMware NSX for vSphere 6.3.2
- Configuring Juniper Contrail Server Manager
- Configuring OpenContrail controller
- Configuring OpenContrail cluster
- Interacting with devices running Cisco IOS XR
- Collaborating with Cisco Spark API

Introduction

We discussed Open SDN projects such as OpenDaylight and ONOS from the Linux Foundation and other open source efforts such as Floodlight in the previous chapters. In this chapter, we will look more into advanced open and vendor-specific SDN programming, and configure various networking projects. Cisco **Application Centric Infrastructure** (**ACI**) is an SDN solution from Cisco. Its building blocks include the hardware switches of Cisco Nexus 7000 and 9000 Series and Cisco **Application Policy Infrastructure Controller** (**APIC**). Juniper Contrail, which was later open sourced as **OpenContrail** is another example for a vendor-specific SDN. VMware NSX a proprietary SDN solution, also has its open source versions available for public download. This chapter will serve as an introduction to a wide range of enterprise options available for SDN and networking architecture. While we introduce many solutions, we will restrict our detailed discussions to the solutions that are available for free.

Configuring Red PNDA

PNDA is an open source platform for network data analytics. It is horizontally scalable and complex to deploy on a single computer. To be able to test smaller scale applications in the developer computers, a smaller downsized version of PNDA known as Red PNDA (`https://github.com/pndaproject/red-pnda`) is also available. In this recipe, we will configure Red PNDA, the minimal version of PNDA in a laptop.

Getting ready

You need to have a minimum of 4GB memory, 2 VCPUs, and 8GB hard disk to install Red PNDA. It requires up to an hour to configure and install, this also depends on how fast your internet connection is.

How to do it...

You may configure Red PNDA by following the succeeding commands. First clone the project code base:

```
$ git clone https://github.com/pndaproject/red-pnda.git
$ cd red-pnda
```

Build it as a super user.

```
$ sudo su
$ bash scripts/install-dependencies.sh wlo1
```

In the preceding command, replace `wlo1` with one of your active network interfaces. You may find it by using the `ifconfig` command in Linux and `ipcofig` in Windows.

The build requires an internet connection as it downloads the required dependencies. You may monitor the status of the build from the logs, as the build logs are verbose. Sample configuration logs (as observed in my laptop during the build) are provided in the `file 21_1_configure_red_pnda_output` for your reference. After an hour or so, the following message will be printed upon a successful installation:

```
....
Adding platformlibs 0.6.8 to easy-install.pth file
Installed /usr/local/lib/python3.5/dist-packages/platformlibs-0.6.8-
py2.7.egg
```

```
Processing dependencies for platformlibs==0.6.8
Searching for platformlibs==0.6.8
Reading https://pypi.python.org/simple/platformlibs/
Couldn't find index page for 'platformlibs' (maybe misspelled?)
Scanning index of all packages (this may take a while)
Reading https://pypi.python.org/simple/
No local packages or working download links found for
platformlibs==0.6.8
error: Could not find suitable distribution for
Requirement.parse('platformlibs==0.6.8')
Failed to restart data-manager.service: Unit data-manager.service not
found.
#####################################################
Your Red-PNDA is successfully installed. Go to http://109.141.41.113
on your browser to view the console!
```

In the log you may find some error messages. Some of them are due to the fact that PNDA is written for Python 2 and hence producing error or warning messages when built with Python 3 environment. If a few libraries failed to download or configure properly, you may manually resume and fix them accordingly. The last logs indicate the admin console URL of Red PNDA. Open the URL in your browser to access it. Red PNDA can be accessed from `http://localhost` or `http://<your-ip-address>` as shown here in the following screenshot:

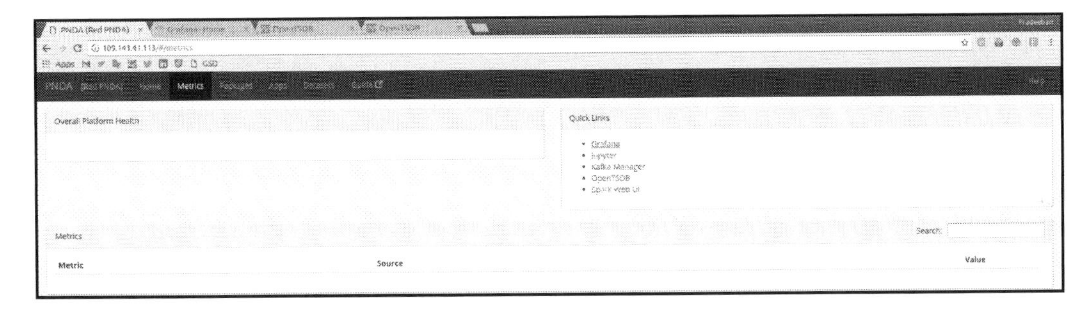

RED PNDA Admin Console

Grafana (`https://grafana.com/`) is a platform for data analytics and monitoring that is used in PNDA and Red PNDA. You may access Grafana from the Red PNDA web console. You may register yourself as a PNDA user with an email address and password using the Grafana's **Log In** page or sign up if you haven't already registered.

Grafana can be accessed from `http://localhost:3000` or `http://<your-ip-address>:3000` as shown in the following screenshot:

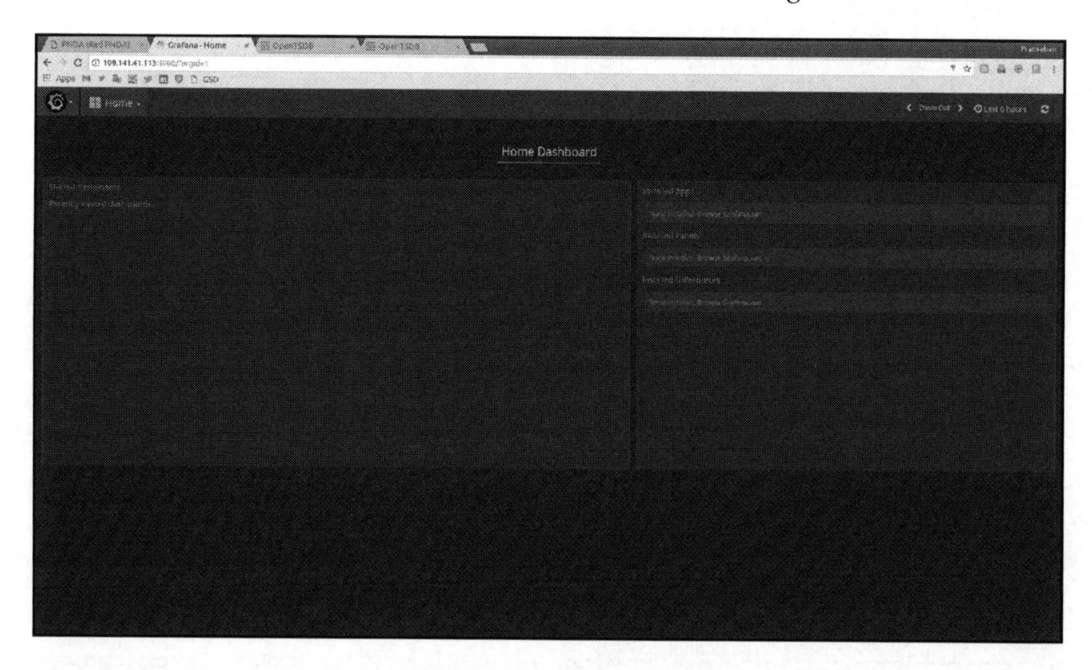

Grafana Admin Console

OpenTSDB (`http://opentsdb.net/`) is a scalable time series database used by PNDA. It stores and serves time series data and its admin interface can be accessed from the Red PNDA web console as well. OpenTSTB can be accessed from `http://localhost:4242/` or `http://<your-ip-address>:4242/` as shown here in the following screenshot:

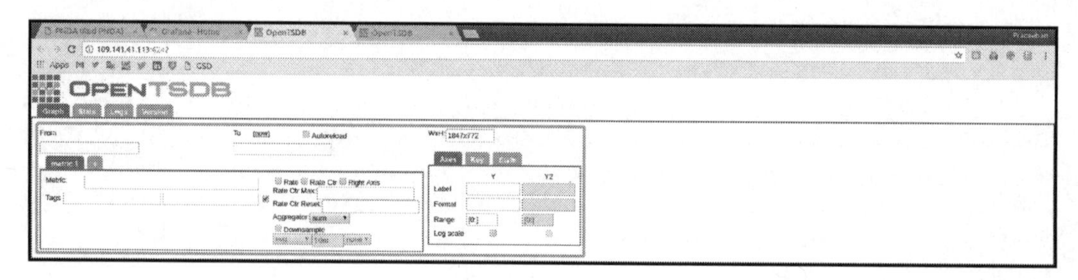

OpenTSTB Admin Console

Red PNDA consists of a few scripts that are important to configure the networking data analytics platform. Your Python knowledge comes in handy when extending and executing these Python programs.

You may find four Python programs in the folder, `red-pnda/scripts/files`. `producer.py` and `consumer.py` function which is a Kafka producer and a consumer. You need a Kafka broker running to make these producer and consumer communicate to each other. `hbase_spark_metric.py` connects to the HBase and Spark to store the status of the network. Finally, `create_or_update_ds.py` creates a data source in OpenTSTB, or updates an existing data source.

You may use the Python script with the username and password that you have created using Grafana before. The addresses indicate the URLs of the Grafana console and the OpenTSTB console.

```
$ python create_or_update_ds.py kk.pradeeban@gmail.com password
http://localhost:3000 '{ "name": "PNDA OpenTSDB", "type": "opentsdb",
"url": "http://localhost:4243", "access": "proxy", "basicAuth": false,
"isDefault": true }'
```

If the credentials are not correct, you will receive this error message:

```
requests.exceptions.HTTPError: 401 Client Error: Unauthorized for url:
http://localhost:3000/api/datasources
```

If the credentials are correct but the data source or OpenTSTB is not configured properly during the Red PNDA configuration, you will receive the following error message:

```
requests.exceptions.HTTPError: 403 Client Error: Forbidden for url:
http://localhost:3000/api/datasources
```

How it works...

Red PNDA is a minimalist version of PNDA networking data analytics platform. Unlike PNDA, Red PNDA is configured to be run in a single computer and should not be used as a production solution due to its limited horizontal scalability.

In addition to the software bundles that we discussed before in this recipe (such as Spark, Hbase, Kafka, OpenTSTB, and Grafana), Red PNDA also depends on the below additional software: PNDA console frontend (https://github.com/pndaproject/platform-console-frontend), PNDA console backend (https://github.com/pndaproject/platform-console-backend), PNDA platform testing (https://github.com/pndaproject/platform-testing), PNDA platform libraries (https://github.com/pndaproject/platform-libraries), Jupyter Notebook (http://jupyter.org), Kafka Manager (https://github.com/yahoo/kafka-manager), PNDA's example Kafka clients (https://github.com/pndaproject/example-kafka-clients), and JMXProxy 3.2.0 (https://github.com/mk23/jmxproxy).

Configuring VMware NSX for vSphere 6.3.2

NSX is a network virtualization and security platform offered by VMware in its effort towards creating a Software-Defined Data Center. You may download tarballs of NSX controller and NSX for vSphere 6.3.2 hypervisor at https://my.vmware.com/group/vmware/details?downloadGroup=NSXV_632_OSSproductId=417. With the server virtualization offered by vSphere and the network virtualization offered by NSX, VMware virtualizes an entire data center. The NSX controller functions as a control point for the logical switches and overlay transport tunnels. In this recipe, we will learn to use pynsxv (https://github.com/vmware/pynsxv), a Python-based library and CLI tool, to control NSX for vSphere.

Getting ready

First install pynsxv using pip:

```
$ sudo pip install pynsxv
```

You may confirm that the installation was successful by executing the following commands:

```
$ pynsxv -h
usage: pynsxv [-h] [-i INI] [-v] [-d]
{lswitch,dlr,esg,dhcp,lb,dfw,usage} ...
PyNSXv Command Line Client for NSX for vSphere
positional arguments:
{lswitch,dlr,esg,dhcp,lb,dfw,usage}
lswitch             Functions for logical switches
```

```
dlr                   Functions for distributed logical routers
esg                   Functions for edge services gateways
dhcp                  Functions for Edge DHCP
lb                    Functions for Edge Load Balancer
dfw                   Functions for distributed firewall
usage                 Functions to retrieve NSX-v usage statistics
optional arguments:
-h, --help              show this help message and exit
-i INI, --ini INI       nsx configuration file
-v, --verbose           increase output verbosity
-d, --debug             print low level debug of http transactions
```

You may encounter the following error due to some version mismatching:

```
pkg_resources.DistributionNotFound: The 'urllib3<1.22,>=1.21.1'
distribution was not found and is required by requests
```

By repeating with the version explicitly specified for `pip`, this issue can be fixed:

```
$ sudo pip2 install pynsxv
$ pynsxv lswitch -h
usage: pynsxv lswitch [-h] [-t TRANSPORT_ZONE] [-n NAME] command
Functions for logical switches
positional arguments:
command
                                create: create a new logical switch
                                read:   return the virtual wire id of
a logical switch
                                delete: delete a logical switch"
                                list:   return a list of all logical
switches
optional arguments:
-h, --help            show this help message and exit
-t TRANSPORT_ZONE, --transport_zone TRANSPORT_ZONE
                           nsx transport zone
-n NAME, --name NAME  logical switch name, needed for create, read and
delete
```

A Python code to use the RESTful API of NSX Manager can be downloaded from `https://code.vmware.com/samples/1988/python-code-to-use-the-nsx-manager-rest-api-interface`, and can be executed using the following command:

```
$ python snippet.py
```

Optionally, you may also install the Python `nsx` library for OpenStack using the following command:

```
$ sudo pip install vmware-nsx
```

How to do it...

PyNSXv is a Python project to configure and control NSX based Software-Defined Data Centers. First configure `nsx.ini` to point to the correct values for the parameters:

```
[nsxv]
nsx_manager = <nsx_manager_IP>
nsx_username = admin
nsx_password = <nsx_manager_password>
[vcenter]
vcenter = <VC_IP_or_Hostname>
vcenter_user = administrator@domain.local
vcenter_passwd = <vc_password>
[defaults]
transport_zone = <transport_zone_name>
datacenter_name = <vcenter datacenter name>
edge_datastore = <datastore name to deploy edges in>
edge_cluster = <vcenter cluster for edge gateways>
```

Then `pynsxv` can offer a global view of the data center network to configure and control it as shown by the following output:

```
$ pynsxv lswitch list
+---------------------+----------------+
| LS name             | LS ID          |
|---------------------+----------------|
| edge_ls             | virtualwire-63 |
| dlr_ls              | virtualwire-64 |
+---------------------+----------------+
```

How it works...

PyNSXv offers a Python-based API and interface to control NSX. You just need to offer the NSX Manager and the vCenter IP and credentials as well as names for the vCenter data center, edge data store, and edge cluster for the gateways. A complete *NSX API Guide* can be found at `https://pubs.vmware.com/NSX-6/topic/com.vmware.ICbase/PDF/nsx_604_api.pdf` and *NSX for vSphere API Guide* can be found at `https://docs.vmware.com/en/Vmware-NSX-for-vSphere/6.3/nsx_63_api.pdf`.

Configuring Juniper Contrail Server Manager

Juniper Networks (`http://www.juniper.net/us/en/`) offer a set of products aimed at network performance and security. It also provides Python-based open source projects (`https://github.com/Juniper`) to manage its platform. Contrail offers an SDN-enabled management solution and service delivery for wide area networks, thus supporting **Software-Defined Wide Area Networks** (**SD-WANs**).

Contrail Server Manager is a platform to manage the servers in a Contrail cluster. In this recipe, first we will set up Juniper Contrail Server Manager (`https://github.com/Juniper/contrail-server-manager`). You may learn more about configuring Contrail Server Manager and other Contrail bundles from `http://www.juniper.net/documentation/en_US/contrail4.0/information-products/pathway-pages/getting-started-pwp.pdf`.

Juniper is open sourcing many of its networking solutions under OpenContrail project. We will look into the open source scripts available to manage and configure Contrail. Written in Python 2, these scripts do not support Python 3.

Getting ready

You may download the relevant software bundle of Juniper Contrail Server Manager from `http://www.juniper.net/support/downloads/?p=contrail#sw` and install the Contrail Server Manager or Server Manager Lite directly from the command (after replacing with the relevant file number):

```
$ sudo dpkg -i contrail-server-manager-installer_2.22~juno_all.deb
```

More installation instructions can be found at `https://www.juniper.net/documentation/en_US/contrail4.0/topics/concept/install-containers-smlite.html`.

You may also seek a slot to test Juniper Contrail cloud automation platform and AppFormix cloud operations optimization tool in a sandbox environment from `http://www.juniper.net/us/en/cloud-software/trial/` for free as shown here in the following screenshot:

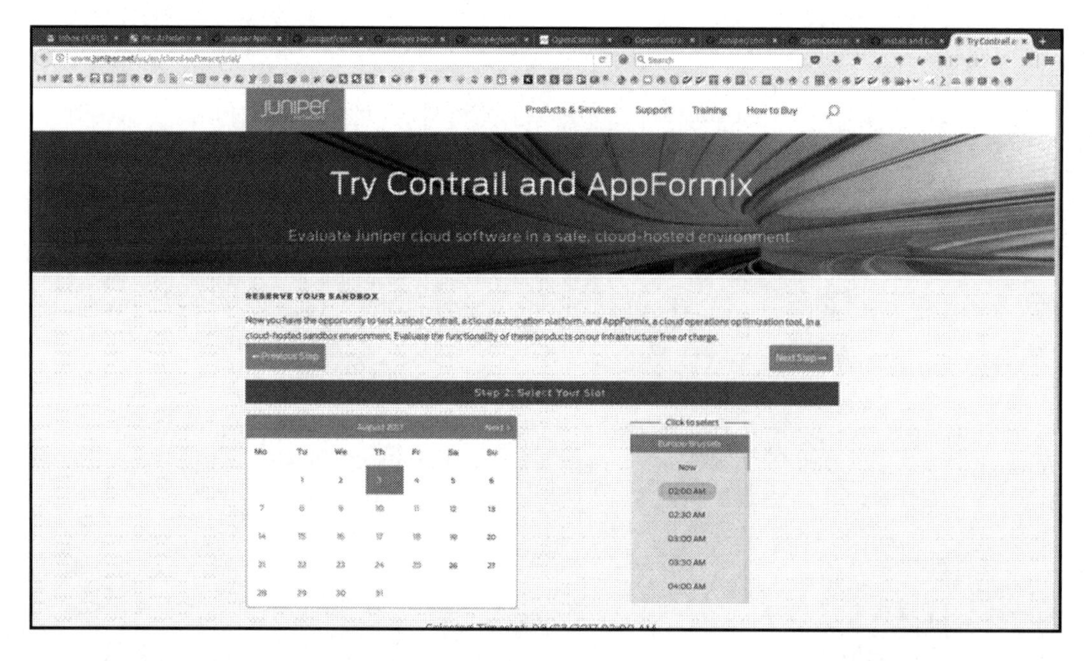

Reserve Your Slot at Juniper!

A sandbox user guide can be found at `http://www.juniper.net/documentation/cloud-software/ContrailSandbox-UserGuide.pdf`.

In this recipe, we will look deep into the Python source code repository of the server manager. You may configure the Contrail Server Manager through the following commands.

First checkout the source code from the code repository:

```
$ git clone https://github.com/Juniper/contrail-server-manager.git
```

Now build and install it through the setup script:

```
$ cd contrail-server-manager/
$ python setup.py build
$ sudo python setup.py install
```

You may receive help by using the following command:

```
$ sudo python setup.py -help
```

You may receive instruction specific help using the `--help` flag following a command. For example, to receive installation specific commands, use the following command:

```
$ python setup.py install --help
/usr/local/lib/python2.7/dist-packages/setuptools/dist.py:333:
UserWarning: Normalizing '0.1dev' to '0.1.dev0'
normalized_version,
Common commands: (see '--help-commands' for more)
setup.py build      will build the package underneath 'build/'
setup.py install    will install the package
Global options:
--verbose (-v)  run verbosely (default)
--quiet (-q)    run quietly (turns verbosity off)
--dry-run (-n)  don't actually do anything
--help (-h)     show detailed help message
--no-user-cfg   ignore pydistutils.cfg in your home directory
Options for 'install' command:
--prefix                     installation prefix
--exec-prefix                (Unix only) prefix for
                             platform-specific files
--home                       (Unix only) home directory
                             to install under
--user                       install in user site-package

'/home/pradeeban/.local/lib/python2.7/site-packages'
--install-base                         base installation directory
(instead of --prefix or --home)
--install-platbase                     base installation directory for
platform-specific files (instead of --exec-prefix or --home)
--root                                 install everything relative to
this alternate root directory
--install-purelib                      installation directory for pure
Python module distributions
--install-platlib                      installation directory for non-
pure module distributions
--install-lib                          installation directory for all
module distributions (overrides --install-purelib and --install-
```

```
platlib)
--install-headers                     installation directory for C/C++
headers
 --install-scripts                     installation directory for
Python scripts
--install-data                        installation directory for data
files
--compile (-c)                        compile .py to .pyc [default]
--no-compile                          don't compile .py files
--optimize (-O)                       also compile with optimization: -
O1 for "python -O", -O2 for "python -OO", and
 -O0 to disable [default: -O0]
--force (-f)                          force installation (overwrite any
existing files)
--skip-build                          skip rebuilding everything (for
testing/debugging)
--record                              filename in which to record list
of installed files
--install-layout                      installation layout to choose
(known values: deb, unix)
--old-and-unmanageable                Try not to use this!
--single-version-externally-managed  used by system package builders
to create 'flat' eggs
usage: setup.py [global_opts] cmd1 [cmd1_opts] [cmd2 [cmd2_opts] ...]
or: setup.py --help [cmd1 cmd2 ...]
or: setup.py --help-commands
or: setup.py cmd --help
```

How to do it...

Let's install Contrail Server Manager in our current directory.

```
$ sudo python setup.py install --root install
```

This will set up the server manager inside a directory called `install` which is inside the current directory.

Now you will be able to see a bunch of Python scripts of the server manager inside the folder `install/usr/local/lib/python2.7/dist-packages/src`:

```
$ cd  install/usr/local/lib/python2.7/dist-packages/src
$ ls
contrail_defaults.py         __init__.pyc
server_mgr_db_convert.py
server_mgr_disk_filesystem_view.pyc  server_mgr_ipmi_monitoring.py
server_mgr_mon_base_plugin.pyc  server_mgr_utils.py
```

```
contrail_defaults.pyc       inplace_upgrade.py
server_mgr_db_convert.pyc           server_mgr_docker.py
server_mgr_ipmi_monitoring.pyc  server_mgr_puppet.py
server_mgr_utils.pyc
create_vm.py                inplace_upgrade.pyc
server_mgr_db.py                    server_mgr_docker.pyc
server_mgr_issu.py              server_mgr_puppet.pyc
server_mgr_validations.py
create_vm.pyc               server_mgr_certs.py
server_mgr_db.pyc                   server_mgr_err.py
server_mgr_issu.pyc             server_mgr_ssh_client.py
server_mgr_validations.pyc
generate_dhcp_template.py   server_mgr_certs.pyc
server_mgr_defaults.py              server_mgr_err.pyc
server_mgr_logger.py            server_mgr_ssh_client.pyc
smgr_dhcp_event.py
generate_dhcp_template.pyc  server_mgr_cert_utils.py
server_mgr_defaults.pyc             server_mgr_exception.py
server_mgr_logger.pyc           server_mgr_status.py
smgr_dhcp_event.pyc
generate_openssl_cfg.py     server_mgr_cert_utils.pyc
server_mgr_discovery.py             server_mgr_exception.pyc
server_mgr_main.py              server_mgr_status.pyc
generate_openssl_cfg.pyc    server_mgr_cobbler.py
server_mgr_discovery.pyc            server_mgr_inventory.py
server_mgr_main.pyc             server_mgr_storage.py
__init__.py                 server_mgr_cobbler.pyc
server_mgr_disk_filesystem_view.py  server_mgr_inventory.pyc
server_mgr_mon_base_plugin.py   server_mgr_storage.pyc
```

How it works...

While Juniper Contrail is a proprietary solution that needs a login to download and use the Contrail Server Manager and other products, these open source python scripts can be used to manage the Juniper Contrail networking cluster.

Configuring OpenContrail controller

OpenContrail (`http://www.opencontrail.org/`) is an open source network virtualization platform for the cloud from Juniper Networks. In this recipe, we will learn to configure OpenContrail controller, also known as the OpenContrail core project (`https://github.com/Juniper/contrail-controller`). This project is developed in C++ and Python.

Getting ready

In this recipe we will configure OpenContrail. We will offer complementary information to the configuration instructions that can be found in `https://github.com/Juniper/contrail-controller/wiki/OpenContrail-bring-up-and-provisioning`. OpenContrail can be executed in a distributed environment consisting of multiple servers for configuration node, analytics node, a control node, and compute node. Each node serves their purpose and they all can be virtualized and installed inside fewer nodes. However, due to their hardware requirements (memory and CPU), it is recommended to run them in individual servers in a cluster, if possible.

How to do it...

You may configure the control node by using the script (`21_4_open_contrail_control_node.sh`):

```
#!/bin/bash
##############################################################################
########
# Python Network Programming Cookbook, Second Edition -- Chapter - 12
# Adopted from
https://github.com/Juniper/contrail-controller/wiki/Install-and-Config
ure-OpenContrail-1.06
##############################################################################
########

# Configue the Ubuntu repositories.
echo "deb http://ppa.launchpad.net/opencontrail/ppa/ubuntu precise
main" | sudo tee -a /etc/apt/sources.list.d/opencontrail.list
sudo apt-key adv --keyserver keyserver.ubuntu.com --recv-keys
16BD83506839FE77
sudo apt-get update

# Install Contrail Control
sudo apt-get install contrail-control
```

You may execute the script to configure a node as the control node as shown here:

```
$ sh 21_4_open_contrail_control_node.sh
```

Update /etc/contrail/control-node.conf:

```
[DISCOVERY]
port=5998
server=127.0.0.1 # discovery_server IP address

[IFMAP]
password=control
user=control
```

Restart control:

```
$ sudo service contrail-control restart
```

How it works...

The control node orchestrates the OpenContrail cluster. You may receive the registration of control in discovery using the following command:

```
$ curl http://127.0.0.1:5998/services
```

The following command shows the control as a generator in the analytics API:

```
$ curl http://127.0.0.1:8081/analytics/uves/generators | python -
mjson.tool
```

Configuring OpenContrail cluster

The OpenContrail cluster requires configuration of an analytics node, configuration node, and a compute node in addition to the controller node that we configured in the previous recipe. In this recipe, we will configure OpenContrail cluster, which is composed of many components and sub-projects. Many of the platform tools and projects of OpenContrail are built in Python.

Important!

The following scripts need to be run in different servers than the controller (each on its own), otherwise they will add the same repository to the sources list multiple times, which may break your Ubuntu update manager. It is highly recommended to test these in virtual machines, unless you are confident of breaking and fixing.

How to do it...

First you need to download and configure the below services for the configuration node:

- Apache ZooKeeper, an open source server for a highly reliable distributed coordination: `https://zookeeper.apache.org/`
- Apache Cassandra, a distributed open source NoSQL database management system: `http://cassandra.apache.org/`
- RabbitMQ message broker: `https://www.rabbitmq.com/`
- **network time protocol** (**NTP**) for time synchronization: `http://www.ntp.org/`

The following script (`21_5_open_contrail_configuration_node.sh`) configures a server as the configuration node:

```
#!/bin/bash
##############################################################################
########
# Python Network Programming Cookbook, Second Edition -- Chapter - 12
# Adopted from
https://github.com/Juniper/contrail-controller/wiki/Install-and-Config
ure-OpenContrail-1.06
##############################################################################
########

# Download and manually install python-support, as it is dropped from
Ubuntu 16.04.
wget
http://launchpadlibrarian.net/109052632/python-support_1.0.15_all.deb
sudo dpkg -i python-support_1.0.15_all.deb

# Configuring the package list.
echo "deb http://ppa.launchpad.net/opencontrail/ppa/ubuntu precise
main" | sudo tee -a /etc/apt/sources.list.d/opencontrail.list
sudo apt-key adv --keyserver keyserver.ubuntu.com --recv-keys
16BD83506839FE77
echo "deb http://debian.datastax.com/community stable main" | sudo tee
-a /etc/apt/sources.list.d/cassandra.sources.list
curl -L http://debian.datastax.com/debian/repo_key | sudo apt-key add
-

# Run update
sudo apt-get update

# Install dependencies
```

```
sudo apt-get install cassandra=1.2.18 zookeeperd rabbitmq-server
ifmap-server

# Install Contrail Config
sudo apt-get install contrail-config

# Configre ifmap-server
echo "control:control" | sudo tee -a /etc/ifmap-
server/basicauthusers.properties
sudo service ifmap-server restart
```

Execute the script on a server to configure it as the configuration node:

```
$ sh 21_5_open_contrail_configuration_node.sh
```

The updates may leave you with the warnings similar to the following ones:

```
W:
https://archive.cloudera.com/cm5/ubuntu/trusty/amd64/cm/dists/trusty-c
m5.9.0/InRelease: Signature by key
F36A89E33CC1BD0F71079007327574EE02A818DD uses weak digest algorithm
(SHA1)
W:
http://repo.saltstack.com/apt/ubuntu/14.04/amd64/archive/2015.8.11/dis
ts/trusty/InRelease: Signature by key
754A1A7AE731F165D5E6D4BD0E08A149DE57BFBE uses weak digest algorithm
(SHA1)
```

This is because of the weak digest algorithm used by the *Cloudera* and *SaltStack* repositories.

Now we will configure the analytics node with the following script (`21_5_open_contrail_analytics_node.sh`):

```
#!/bin/bash
##########################################################################
########
# Python Network Programming Cookbook, Second Edition -- Chapter - 12
# Adopted from
https://github.com/Juniper/contrail-controller/wiki/Install-and-Config
ure-OpenContrail-1.06
##########################################################################
########

# Get the redis server binary from
http://ftp.ksu.edu.tw/FTP/Linux/ubuntu/ubuntu/pool/universe/r/redis/
# You may use any other working mirror as well.
wget
```

```
http://ftp.ksu.edu.tw/FTP/Linux/ubuntu/ubuntu/pool/universe/r/redis/re
dis-server_2.6.13-1_amd64.deb
sudo apt-get install libjemalloc1

# Install redis server
sudo dpkg -i redis-server_2.6.13-1_amd64.deb

echo "deb http://ppa.launchpad.net/opencontrail/ppa/ubuntu precise
main" | sudo tee -a /etc/apt/sources.list.d/opencontrail.list
sudo apt-key adv --keyserver keyserver.ubuntu.com --recv-keys
16BD83506839FE77
sudo apt-get update

# Install Contrail Analytics
sudo apt-get install contrail-analytics
```

You may execute the following script to configure a node as the analytics node:

```
$ sh 21_5_open_contrail_analytics_node.sh
```

Update the port in `/etc/redis/redis.conf` from `6379` to `6381` and restart the Redis server:

```
$ sudo service redis-server restart
```

Update discovery and Redis settings in `/etc/contrail/contrail-collector.conf` with that from `etc/contrail/contrail-collector.conf` in the accompanying source:

```
[DISCOVERY]
port=5998
server=127.0.0.1
[REDIS]
port=6381
server=127.0.0.1
```

Restart the collector.

```
$ sudo service contrail-collector restart
```

Update discovery and Redis settings in `/etc/contrail/contrail-query-engine.conf` shown as follows:

```
[DISCOVERY]
port=5998
server=127.0.0.1
[REDIS]
port=6381
```

```
    server=127.0.0.1
```

Restart the query engine:

```
$ sudo service contrail-query-engine restart
```

Update Redis settings in /etc/contrail/contrail-analytics-api.conf:

```
    [REDIS]
    server=127.0.0.1
    redis_server_port=6381
    redis_query_port=6381
```

Restart the analytics API server:

```
$ sudo service contrail-analytics-api restart
```

Finally, you may configure the compute node by using the script (21_5_open_contrail_compute_node.sh):

```
#!/bin/bash
##############################################################################
########
# Python Network Programming Cookbook, Second Edition -- Chapter - 12
# Adopted from
https://github.com/Juniper/contrail-controller/wiki/Install-and-Config
ure-OpenContrail-1.06
##############################################################################
########

# Configue the Ubuntu repositories.
echo "deb http://ppa.launchpad.net/opencontrail/ppa/ubuntu precise
main" | sudo tee -a /etc/apt/sources.list.d/opencontrail.list
sudo apt-key adv --keyserver keyserver.ubuntu.com --recv-keys
16BD83506839FE77
sudo apt-get update

# Install Contrail Virtual Rouer Agent
sudo apt-get install contrail-vrouter-agent

sudo modprobe vrouter
echo "vrouter" | sudo tee -a /etc/modules
```

You may run it as follows:

```
$ sh 21_5_open_contrail_compute_node.sh
```

Update `/etc/contrail/contrail-vrouter-agent.conf`:

```
# IP address of discovery server
server=10.8.1.10

[VIRTUAL-HOST-INTERFACE]
# Everything in this section is mandatory

# name of virtual host interface
name=vhost0

# IP address and prefix in ip/prefix_len format
ip=10.8.1.11/24

# Gateway IP address for virtual host
gateway=10.8.1.254

# Physical interface name to which virtual host interface maps to
physical_interface=eth1
```

Update `/etc/network/interfaces`:

```
auto eth1
iface eth1 inet static
        address 0.0.0.0
        up ifconfig $IFACE up
        down ifconfig $IFACE down

auto vhost0
iface vhost0 inet static
        pre-up vif --create vhost0 --mac $(cat
/sys/class/net/eth1/address)
        pre-up vif --add vhost0 --mac $(cat
/sys/class/net/eth1/address) --vrf 0
        --mode x --type vhost
        pre-up vif --add eth1 --mac $(cat /sys/class/net/eth1/address)
--vrf 0
        --mode x --type physical
        address 10.8.1.11
        netmask 255.255.255.0
        #network 10.8.1.0
        #broadcast 10.8.1.255
        #gateway 10.8.1.254
        # dns-* options are implemented by the resolvconf package, if
installed
        dns-nameservers 8.8.8.8
```

Restart the networking and vRouter agents, and finally restart the compute node:

```
$ sudo service networking restart
$ sudo service contrail-vrouter-agent restart
$ sudo reboot now
```

How it works...

Make sure to set the host names correctly in `/etc/hosts` as you start configuring OpenContrail nodes. Once you have configured the configuration node consisting of the API server, you may receive the list of tenants or projects by querying using the following command:

```
$ curl http://127.0.0.1:8082/projects | python -mjson.tool
```

You may receive the list of services and clients respectively that are consuming the services by the using the following RESTful invocations:

```
$ curl http://127.0.0.1:5998/services
$ curl http://127.0.0.1:5998/clients
```

The analytics node provides the analytics API server. List of Contrail's generators can be found using the following command:

```
$ curl http://127.0.0.1:8081/analytics/generators | python -mjson.tool
```

Compute nodes perform the underlying computations of the Contrail cluster.

Interacting with devices running Cisco IOS XR

Cisco IOS XR (`http://www.cisco.com/c/en/us/products/ios-nx-os-software/ios-xr-software/index.html`) is a distributed network operating system for service providers. It supports many devices to provide a cloud scale networking. It is known as a self-healing distributed networking operating system.

`PyIOSXR` (`https://github.com/fooelisa/pyiosxr`) is a Python library used to manage the devices that are running IOS XR. In this recipe, we will install `pyIOSXR`, mock a network, and coordinate it with a Python program based on `pyIOSXR`.

Getting ready

First install `pyIOSXR`:

```
$ sudo pip install pyIOSXR
```

How to do it...

Now you may connect to your device using Python as shown by the following code segment:

```
from pyIOSXR import IOSXR
device = IOSXR(hostname='lab001', username='ejasinska',
password='passwd',
 port=22, timeout=120)
device.open()
```

You may test `pyIOSXR` without an IOS XR device using the mock scripts provided by the project.

Checkout the source code from the source repository:

```
$ git clone https://github.com/fooelisa/pyiosxr.git
$ cd test
```

Now you may run `test.py` to test the installation:

```
$ python test.py
............................................
----------------------------------------------
Ran 44 tests in 0.043s
OK
```

How it works...

The `test.py` script gets the mock scripts consisting of `xml` and `cfg` files from the mock folder. `from pyIOSXR import IOSXR` imports the relevant bundles for the management of IOS XR devices from the project. The mock files are converted by the test script to emulate the Cisco IOS XR devices.

Collaborating with Cisco Spark API

Cisco Spark (`https://www.ciscospark.com/products/overview.html`) is a cloud-based collaboration platform from Cisco. It supports communication and collaboration from multiple devices for meetings, messages, and calls.

`ciscosparkapi` (`https://github.com/CiscoDevNet/ciscosparkapi`) is an open source project that offers a simple and compact Python-based API to Cisco Spark where all the operations can easily be performed with simple Python calls. In this recipe, we will configure `ciscosparkapi`.

Cisco Spark is available as a mobile, desktop, and web-based application (`https://web.ciscospark.com/signin?mid=22237844097353833060667005765798180584`). Following is the web interface of Cisco Spark after signing in:

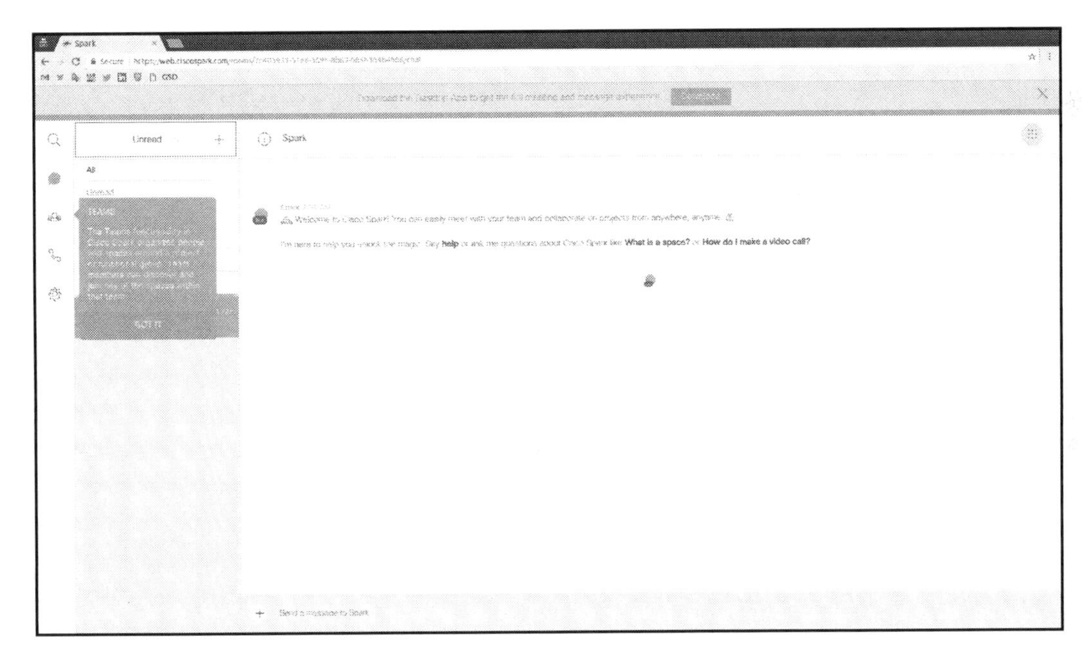

Cisco Spark Dashboard

Getting ready

Install Spark API:

```
$ sudo pip install ciscosparkapi
```

Make sure to export your Spark access token before running this recipe:

```
$ export SPARK_ACCESS_TOKEN="XXXX"
```

If your access token is incorrect, you will receive the following error message:

```
ciscosparkapi.exceptions.SparkApiError: Response Code [401] -
Authentication credentials were missing or incorrect.
```

If you have not set the access token, the following message will be reported:

```
ciscosparkapi.exceptions.ciscosparkapiException: You must provide an
Spark access token to interact with the Cisco Spark APIs, either via a
SPARK_ACCESS_TOKEN environment variable or via the access_token
argument.
```

You may copy your access token from the developer portal of Cisco Spark (`https://developer.ciscospark.com/#`).

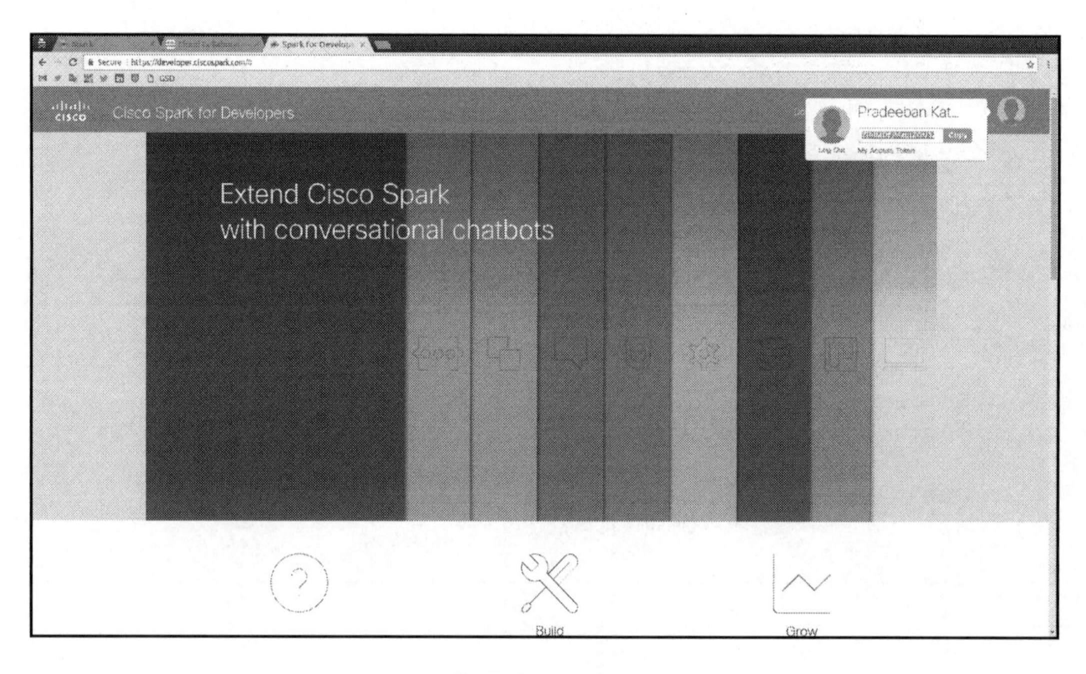

Cisco Spark Developer Portal

How to do it...

Execute the below recipe to create a new room and post a photo to it.

Listing 12.7 gives a simple program that connects to the Cisco Spark cloud, creates a room, shares a textual message as well as a photo as follows:

```
#!/usr/bin/env python
# Python Network Programming Cookbook, Second Edition -- Chapter - 12
# This program is optimized for Python 3.5.2 and Python 2.7.12.
# It may run on any other version with/without modifications.


from ciscosparkapi import CiscoSparkAPI

api = CiscoSparkAPI()

# Create a new demo room
demo_room = api.rooms.create('ciscosparkapi Demonstration')
print('Successfully Created the Room')

# Post a message to the new room, and upload an image from a web url.
api.messages.create(demo_room.id, text="Welcome to the room!",
files=["https://3.bp.blogspot.com/-wWHD9LVAI7c/WVeyurRmeDI/AAAAAAAADXc
/CDY17VfYBdAMbI4GS6dGm2Tc4pHBvmpngCLcBGAs/
s1600/IMG_4469.JPG"])
print('Successfully Posted the Message and the Image to the Room')
```

This program creates a room called `ciscosparkapi Desmonstration` and posts the message `Welcome to the room!`.

Running the recipe produces the following output in the console and in the Cisco Spark as shown by the following screenshot:

```
$ python 21_7_cisco_spark_api.py
Successfully Created the Room
Successfully Posted the Message and the Image to the Room
```

The output is shown as follows:

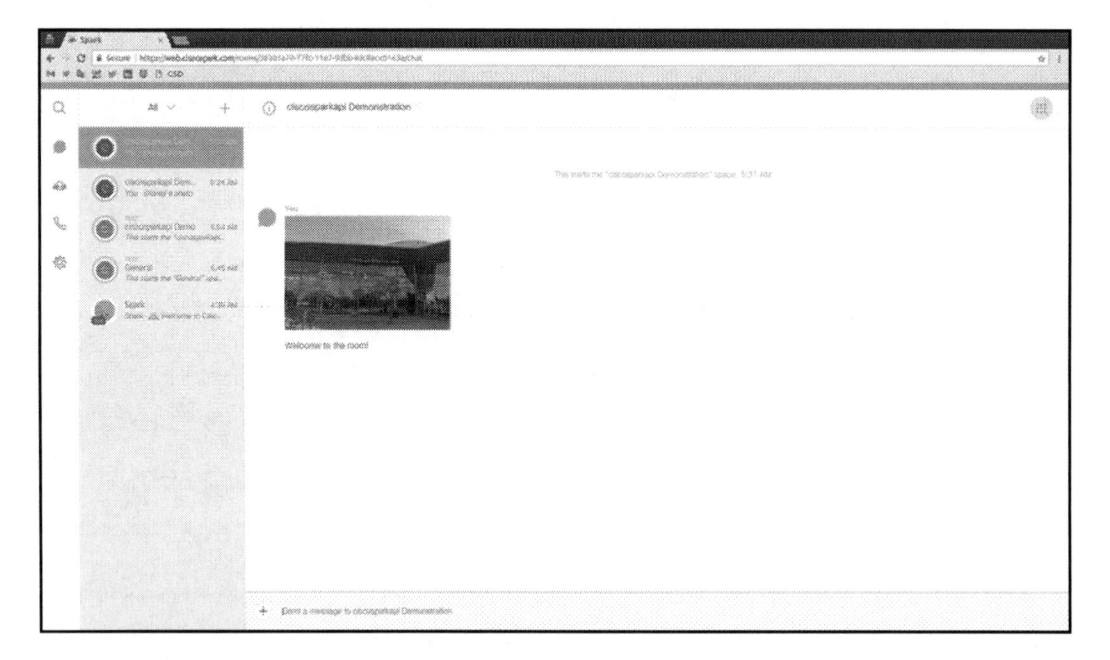

Post an Image to the Room

How it works...

`ciscosparkapi` wraps the public API of Spark communication platform to offer a Python-based interface to control and manage it. With the Spark access token, we may create rooms in our channel, delete existing rooms, post to the rooms, add colleagues to the room, and perform more activities—all from the Python program.

22
NFV and Orchestration – A Larger Ecosystem

–In this chapter, we will cover the following recipes:

- Building VNFs with OPNFV
- Packet processing with DPDK
- Parsing BMP messages with SNAS.io
- Controlling drones with a wireless network
- Creating PNDA clusters

Introduction

Network softwarization brings software development aspects to networking. We discussed how SDN enables a logically centralized control to the data plane in previous chapters. In this chapter, we will look into the larger ecosystem of **Network Function Virtualization** (**NFV**) and orchestration.

The Linux Foundation leads many open source networking and orchestration projects such as OPNFV, ONAP, PNDA, DPDK, SNAS, ODPi, and FD.io. We will look into how to use Python to extend these projects, and leverage them to build and orchestrate enterprise network solutions. While many of these are built with multiple languages, Python plays an important role in most of these projects as a tool for building and testing, if not as the coding language. We will look into how Python is used in configuring and installing these projects, while addressing common issues faced in configuring these enterprise-grade projects.

The Linux Foundation has a large community bonding effort on bringing various companies and organizations together for a set of open source projects. We looked at a few remarkable projects for NFV and orchestration in the previous recipes of the chapter. In fact, there are many more projects from the Linux Foundation that are worth looking at, and this list keeps growing. You can find a list of active Linux Foundation projects from its website: `https://www.linuxfoundation.org/projects`.

Building VNFs with OPNFV

Open Platform for NFV (**OPNFV**) (`http://docs.opnfv.org/en/stable-danube/index.html`) is an open platform from the Linux Foundation to facilitate **Network Functions Virtualization** (**NFV**) across various projects. Various network functions are virtualized and deployed as **Virtual Network Functions** (**VNFs**), with the support of NFV platforms such as OPNFV. OPNFV consists of many projects and features for **Network Function Virtualization Infrastructure** (**NFVI**).

OPNFV can be installed using various installation tools: Compass, Fuel, TripleO from Apex, and Juju. More details on the installation alternatives can be found at `https://www.opnfv.org/software/downloads/release-archives/danube-2-0`. In this recipe, we will look in to installing OPNFV with Compass in detail. As a large-scale cross-layer project with many components, OPNFV is developed in multiple languages. Python is used in OPNFV for many scripts including configuration and installation actions. As we will learn from this recipe, installing and troubleshooting OPNFV requires a Python development environment and extensive experience in Python.

Getting ready

This recipe involves setting up the OPNFV Platform in bare-metal to build VNFs. We have slightly modified the `quickstart` provided by OPNFV for it to work in a single script. This recipe requires downloading a few GB of image files. If you cannot download 20-30 GB in your current data plan, stop executing this recipe. If your disk space is running low, this may exhaust your remaining space with the configuration of OPNFV as well.

This recipe requires around 1 TB of free hard disk space and 64 GB of RAM. Smaller disks may cause issues such as out of space error when the script sets up five hosts for the NFV. Similarly, if you do not have enough memory, starting the domain will fail. This recipe requires you to have the latest version of Python 2 (tested with Python 2.7). OPNFV projects are not yet compatible with Python 3 as a few libraries are incompatible to work with Python 3.

The installation will take around an hour. So be prepared to wait. Make sure to have at least 30 GB hard disk to be spent for this exercise and a stable internet connection for the script to download and configure the repositories. More details on configuring OPNFV can be found at `http://docs.opnfv.org/en/stable-danube/submodules/compass4nfv/docs/release/installation/vmdeploy.html`. The details given here are supplementary information to the installation guides of OPNFV. A complete offline installation is also possible, as described at `http://docs.opnfv.org/en/stable-danube/submodules/compass4nfv/docs/release/installation/offline-deploy.html`.

How to do it...

Install OPNFV in your computer by using the following script:

```
$  sh 22_1_quickstart.sh
```

Listing 13.1 is a script that invokes other commands to build and install OPNFV as follows:

```
#!/bin/bash
##################################################
# Python Network Programming Cookbook, Second Edition
  -- Chapter - 13
##################################################

sudo apt-get update
sudo apt-get install -y git
# To offer the capability for sys-admins to
  restrict program capabilities
#   with per-program profiles.
sudo apt-get install -y apparmor

# Pyyaml is a required package for the
  configuration scripts.
sudo pip2 install pyyaml
```

```
# Cheetah is a required package for the templates and code generation.
sudo pip2 install cheetah

git clone https://gerrit.opnfv.org/gerrit/compass4nfv

cd compass4nfv

CURRENT_DIR=$PWD
SCENARIO=${SCENARIO:-os-nosdn-nofeature-ha.yml}

# The build script builds the iso file.
# You could also have downloaded the iso file: such as,
# $ wget http://artifacts.opnfv.org/compass4nfv/danube/
    opnfv-2017-07-19_08-55-09.iso
./build.sh

export TAR_URL=file://$CURRENT_DIR/work/building/compass.tar.gz

# Export the below locations.
export DHA=$CURRENT_DIR/deploy/conf/vm_environment/
$SCENARIO
export NETWORK=$CURRENT_DIR/deploy/conf/vm_environment/
network.yml
# Otherwise, your installation will fail with an error
  message similar to the below:
#    + check_input_para
#    + python /home/pradeeban/programs/opnfv/util/
     check_valid.py '' ''
#    DHA file doesn't exist
#    + '[' 1 -ne 0 ']'
#    + exit 1


# If you were following the offline installation, you also
  need to download a jumpshot environment bundle.
# It consists of the dependencies.
# $ wget http://artifacts.opnfv.org/compass4nfv/package/master/
    jh_env_package.tar.gz
# Now export the absolute path for these directions
   (following the below example):
# export ISO_URL=file:///home/compass/compass4nfv.iso
# export JHPKG_URL=file:///home/compass/jh_env_package.tar.gz

# This is the command that is common for both online and
  offline installations.
./deploy.sh
```

This script downloads the *OPNFV Compass* installer project to configure OPNFV. It builds OPNFV through the installer, and deploys it. You may observe the installation progress through the logs.

```
pradeeban@llovizna: ~/compass 165x48
generating PXE menu structure
copying files for distro: CentOS-7-Minimal-1611-x86_64
trying hardlink /var/www/cobbler/ks_mirror/CentOS-7-Minimal-1611-x86_64/images/pxeboot/vmlinuz -> /var/www/cobbler/images/CentOS-7-Minimal-1611-x86_64/vmlinuz
trying hardlink /var/www/cobbler/ks_mirror/CentOS-7-Minimal-1611-x86_64/images/pxeboot/initrd.img -> /var/www/cobbler/images/CentOS-7-Minimal-1611-x86_64/initrd.img
writing template files for CentOS-7-Minimal-1611-x86_64
copying files for distro: ubuntu-16.04-server-x86_64
trying hardlink /var/www/cobbler/ks_mirror/ubuntu-16.04-server-x86_64/install/netboot/ubuntu-installer/amd64/linux -> /var/www/cobbler/images/ubuntu-16.04-server-x86
_64/linux
trying hardlink /var/www/cobbler/ks_mirror/ubuntu-16.04-server-x86_64/install/netboot/ubuntu-installer/amd64/initrd.gz -> /var/www/cobbler/images/ubuntu-16.04-server
-x86_64/initrd.gz
writing template files for ubuntu-16.04-server-x86_64
rendering DHCP files
generating /etc/dhcp/dhcpd.conf
rendering DNS files
generating /etc/named.conf
generating /etc/secondary.conf
generating (forward) /var/named/ods.com
rendering TFTPD files
generating /etc/xinetd.d/tftp
processing boot files for distro: CentOS-7-Minimal-1611-x86_64
processing boot_files for distro: ubuntu-16.04-server-x86_64
cleaning link caches
running: find /var/lib/tftpboot/images/.link_cache -maxdepth 1 -type f -links 1 -exec rm -f '{}' ';'
received on stdout:
received on stderr:
running post-sync triggers
running python triggers from /var/lib/cobbler/triggers/sync/post/*
running python trigger cobbler.modules.sync_post_restart_services
running: dhcpd -t -q
received on stdout:
received on stderr:
running: service dhcpd restart
received on stdout:
received on stderr: Redirecting to /bin/systemctl restart  dhcpd.service

running: service named restart
received on stdout:
received on stderr: Redirecting to /bin/systemctl restart  named.service

running shell triggers from /var/lib/cobbler/triggers/sync/post/*
running shell trigger /var/lib/cobbler/triggers/sync/post/migrate_ks.py
running: ['/var/lib/cobbler/triggers/sync/post/migrate_ks.py']
received on stdout:
received on stderr:
running python triggers from /var/lib/cobbler/triggers/change/*
running python trigger cobbler.modules.scm_track
running shell triggers from /var/lib/cobbler/triggers/change/*
*** TASK COMPLETE ***
```

Install OPNFV

How it works...

If the computer that you run this recipe does not have enough memory, it will produce these following logs during the last few steps:

```
+ sudo virsh start host4
error: Failed to start domain host4
error: internal error: early end of file from monitor,
possible problem: 2017-07-18T16:29:50.376832Z
qemu-system-x86_64: cannot set up guest memory
'pc.ram': Cannot allocate memory
```

This can be confirmed by examining `compass4nfv/work/deploy/vm/hostN/libvirt.xml`, where `N = [1, 6]`. You will find the following lines in these files:

```
<memory unit='MiB'>16384</memory>
<currentMemory unit='MiB'>16384</currentMemory>
```

These lines indicate that 16 GB of memory is required for these virtual machines.

Make sure that both your `python` and `pip` commands point to a Python 2 installation. If both Python 2 and Python 3 are installed, it is likely to have `pip` referring to Python 3 while python referring to Python 2. For example, see the following scenario:

```
$ pip --version
pip 9.0.1 from /home/pradeeban/.local/lib/python3.5/site-packages
(python 3.5)
$ python --version
Python 2.7.12
$ python3 --version
Python 3.5.2
$ pip2 --version
pip 8.1.1 from /usr/lib/python2.7/dist-packages (python 2.7)
```

Here it is obvious that the `pip` and `python` commands are pointing to two different versions—Python 3 and Python 2. To fix this:

```
$ sudo python3 -m pip install -U --force-reinstall pip
$ sudo python -m pip install -U --force-reinstall pip
```

The preceding commands will ensure that `pip` points to `pip2`, the Python 2 version. You may confirm this by running the command again:

```
$ pip2 --version
pip 8.1.1 from /usr/lib/python2.7/dist-packages (python 2.7)
$ pip --version
pip 8.1.1 from /usr/lib/python2.7/dist-packages (python 2.7)
$ pip3 --version
pip 9.0.1 from /usr/local/lib/python3.5/dist-packages (python 3.5)
```

If you encounter errors such as the following during the installation:

```
OSError: [Errno 13] Permission denied:
'/home/pradeeban/.ansible/tmp/ansible-local-24931HCfLEe'
+ log_error 'launch_compass failed'
+ echo -e 'launch_compass failed'
launch_compass failed
```

Check the permissions to confirm that the root folder `.ansible` can be updated by the current user. If not, change the permissions or delete the folder.

The installation of Python that bundles through `pip` may fail if the locales are not configured properly. You may confirm this through the following command:

```
$ pip2 show virtualenv
Traceback (most recent call last):
  File "/usr/bin/pip2", line 9, in <module>
  load_entry_point('pip==8.1.1', 'console_scripts', 'pip2')()
  File "/usr/lib/python2.7/dist-packages/pip/__init__.py",
  line 215, in main
    locale.setlocale(locale.LC_ALL, '')
  File "/usr/lib/python2.7/locale.py", line 581, in setlocale
    return _setlocale(category, locale)
locale.Error: unsupported locale setting
```

If the output is an error as shown, set the locale through the following commands:

```
export LC_ALL="en_US.UTF-8"
export LC_CTYPE="en_US.UTF-8"
sudo dpkg-reconfigure locales
```

You may of course replace the locale of `en_US.UTF-8` with the language and locale of your preference.

If you run out of space during the final stages of configuration by OPNFV Compass, it will fail with a message similar to the following:

```
changed: [localhost] => (item=compass4nfv/compass-deck)
failed: [localhost] (item=compass4nfv/compass-tasks-osa) =>
{"changed": true, "cmd": "docker load -i
\"/dev/opnfv/compass4nfv/work/deploy/installer/compass_dists/compass-
tasks-osa.tar\"", "delta": "0:00:14.055573", "end": "2017-07-19
17:19:13.758734", "failed": true, "item": "compass4nfv/compass-tasks-
osa", "rc": 1, "start": "2017-07-19 17:18:59.703161", "stderr": "Error
processing tar file(exit status 1): write
/df21d65fec8fc853792311af3739a78e018b098a5aa3b1f6ff67f44b330423b8/laye
r.tar: no space left on device", "stderr_lines": ["Error processing
tar file(exit status 1): write
/df21d65fec8fc853792311af3739a78e018b098a5aa3b1f6ff67f44b330423b8/laye
r.tar: no space left on device"], "stdout": "", "stdout_lines": []}
```

If your computer does not have the memory or disk space to run this recipe, you may run this in an optimized spot instance such as `r4.8xlarge` in Amazon `Elastic Compute Cloud` (`EC2`). Before launching the instance, increase the storage of the default EBS volume from 8 GB to 1000 GB, so that you won't run out of disk space during the installation of OPNFV.

Many Python extensions have been built around OPNFV. One example is the SDNVPN (`https://wiki.opnfv.org/display/sdnvpn/SDNVPN+project+main+page`) project that seeks to integrate the virtual networking components to provide layer 2/3 **virtual private network** (**VPN**) functionalities in OPNFV. You may clone the source code of SDNVPN from the source code repository to build it with Python:

```
$ git clone https://github.com/opnfv/sdnvpn.git
$ cd sdnvpn/
$ python setup.py build
$ sudo python setup.py install
```

While OPNFV is a complex networking project with clusters of computers involved, we can configure useful and interesting scenarios efficiently using Python on OPNFV.

Packet processing with DPDK

Data Plane Development Kit (**DPDK**) is a Linux Foundation project aimed to offer libraries and drivers for past packet processing for any processor. DPDK libraries can be used to implement `tcpdump`—like packet capture algorithms, and send and receive packets fast and efficiently with usually less than 80 CPU cycles.

True to its name, DPDK limits its focus to the data plane, and does not aim to provide a stack consisting of network functions. Thus, network middlebox actions such as security and firewalls as well as the layer 3 forwarding are not offered by DPDK by design. In this recipe, we will configure DPDK for a fast and efficient packet processing.

DPDK is developed in C language though Python applications have been built on top of it. In this recipe, we will install DPDK and look into a simple Python application built with DPDK.

Getting ready

You may install DPDK in your computer by using the following script:

```
$ sh 22_2_quickstart.sh
```

This script will take a few minutes to configure and install DPDK, and produce the following lines when it completes its successful installation:

```
..
Installation in /usr/local/ complete
DPDK Installation Complete.
```

The content of the script is described in detail in the following steps.

Install `pcap` dependencies, as DPDK depends on `pcap` for the user level packet capture:

```
$ sudo apt-get install libpcap-dev
Failure to have pcap in your system will fail the build with the error
message "dpdk-stable-17.05.1/drivers/net/pcap/rte_eth_pcap.c:39:18:
fatal error: pcap.h: No such file or directory"
```

Download DPDK's latest stable version from `http://dpdk.org/download`:

```
$ wget http://fast.dpdk.org/rel/dpdk-17.05.1.tar.xz
```

Extract and configure DPDK:

```
$ tar -xvf dpdk-17.05.1.tar.xz
$ cd dpdk-stable-17.05.1
$ make config T=x86_64-native-linuxapp-gcc DESTDIR=install
Configuration done
```

Enable `pcap` as the `pcap` headers are required for the capture file format:

```
$ sed -ri 's,(PMD_PCAP=).*,\1y,' build/.config
```

You have two options to build. Option 1 is to build manually using make (which we also have used in our script), and option 2 is to build using the provided `dpdk-setup.sh` script:

- **Option 1**:

```
$ make
..
== Build app/test-crypto-perf
  CC main.o
```

```
  CC cperf_ops.o
  CC cperf_options_parsing.o
  CC cperf_test_vectors.o
  CC cperf_test_throughput.o
  CC cperf_test_latency.o
  CC cperf_test_verify.o
  CC cperf_test_vector_parsing.o
  LD dpdk-test-crypto-perf
  INSTALL-APP dpdk-test-crypto-perf
  INSTALL-MAP dpdk-test-crypto-perf.map
Build complete [x86_64-native-linuxapp-gcc]
```

- **Option 2**:

```
$ cd usertools
$ ./dpdk-setup.sh
------------------------------------------------
 Step 1: Select the DPDK environment to build
------------------------------------------------
[1] arm64-armv8a-linuxapp-gcc
[2] arm64-dpaa2-linuxapp-gcc
[3] arm64-thunderx-linuxapp-gcc
[4] arm64-xgene1-linuxapp-gcc
[5] arm-armv7a-linuxapp-gcc
[6] i686-native-linuxapp-gcc
[7] i686-native-linuxapp-icc
[8] ppc_64-power8-linuxapp-gcc
[9] x86_64-native-bsdapp-clang
[10] x86_64-native-bsdapp-gcc
[11] x86_64-native-linuxapp-clang
[12] x86_64-native-linuxapp-gcc
[13] x86_64-native-linuxapp-icc
[14] x86_x32-native-linuxapp-gcc
...
```

Choose one of the preceding fourteen options to build. I have used option `12` for my build. You may set up huge page mappings using options `18` or `19` in the setup script, or use the following commands:

```
$ sudo mkdir -p /mnt/huge
$ sudo mount -t hugetlbfs nodev /mnt/huge
$ sudo su
$ echo 64 >
/sys/devices/system/node/node0/hugepages/hugepages-2048kB/nr_hugepages
```

Now you may install DPDK using the following command:

```
$ sudo make install
```

How to do it...

After the installation, you may test DPDK with the sample applications following the following command:

```
$ make -C examples RTE_SDK=$(pwd) RTE_TARGET=build
O=$(pwd)/build/examples
```

`usertools` consists of a few utility bundles written in Python. For example, running `cpu_layout.py` produces the following output in my computer:

```
$ cd usertools
$ python cpu_layout.py
======================================================
Core and Socket Information (as reported by '/sys/devices/system/cpu')
======================================================
cores =  [0, 1, 2, 3]
sockets =  [0]
        Socket 0
        --------
Core 0 [0, 1]
Core 1 [2, 3]
Core 2 [4, 5]
Core 3 [6, 7]
```

This reports the layout of the quad cores of my laptop. You may receive similar output based on your system.

More networking examples or utility tools can be found inside the folder `build/examples`. More products are built extending or leveraging DPDK. Cisco TRex is a traffic generator developed in C and Python, on top of DPDK. You may configure it locally using the following commands:

```
$ wget http://trex-tgn.cisco.com/trex/release/latest
$ tar -xvf latest
$ cd v2.27/
```

Inside the `v2.27` folder, you will find the Python scripts to execute TRex based on DPDK. For example, you may start the master daemon using Python as follows:

```
$ sudo python master_daemon.py start
Master daemon is started
$ sudo python master_daemon.py show
Master daemon is running
```

How it works...

DPDK is a set of libraries and modules for developing the data plane. It exploits many popular tools and projects such as `pcap` to capture the packets. Many of its user tools and configuration scripts are written in Python, and a few libraries written in Python to extend DPDK. The DPDK example applications found in `build/examples` leverage the core of DPDK to program the data plane.

The bundled example applications are (as named by DPDK) `bond`, `ethtool`, `ip_pipeline`, `kni`, `l2fwd-jobstats`, `l3fwd-acl`, `link_status_interrupt`, `netmap_compat`, `qos_meter`, `rxtx_callbacks`, `tep_termination`, `vmdq`, `cmdline`, `exception_path`, `ipsec-secgw`, `l2fwd`, `l2fwd-keepalive`, `l3fwd-power`, `load_balancer`, `packet_ordering`, `qos_sched`, `server_node_efd`, `timer`, `vmdq_dcb`, `distributor`, `helloworld`, `ipv4_multicast`, `l2fwd-crypto`, `l3fwd`, `l3fwd-vf`, `multi_process`, `performance-thread`, `quota_watermark`, `skeleton`, `vhost`, and `vm_power_manager`.

Parsing BMP messages with SNAS.io

Streaming Network Analytics System (**SNAS**) or commonly known as SNAS.io is a Linux Foundation project that consists of a framework and libraries to track and access a large number of routing objects including routers, peers, and prefixes in real time. Formerly known as OpenBMP, SNAS implements BMP message bus specification. BMP refers to BGP monitoring protocol and by implementing the BMP protocol, SNAS communicates with the BMP devices such as routers.

SNAS has a Python API that lets you develop Python applications on top of SNAS for BMP messages. SNAS also consists of an `mrt2bmp` converter developed in Python, which reads the routers' **MRT** (**Multi-threaded Routing Toolkit**) files and sends BMP messages simultaneously. This SNAS conversion workflow is: **Router** | **MRT** | **MRT2BMP** | **OpenBMP collector** | **Kafka message bus** | **MySQL consumer**. You may find more information on these projects at `https://github.com/OpenBMP`.

Getting ready

First install and configure the Apache Kafka and SNAS library for parsing OpenBMP Kafka messages:

```
$ sh 22_3_install.sh
#!/bin/bash
##############################################################
# Python Network Programming Cookbook, Second Edition -- Chapter - 13
##############################################################
# Install Dependencies
sudo apt-get install python-dev python-pip libsnappy-dev
sudo pip install python-snappy kafka-python pyyaml
# Install SNAS Python API
git clone https://github.com/OpenBMP/openbmp-python-api-message.git
cd openbmp-python-api-message
sudo pip install .
# Go back to the root directory.
cd ..
# Download Apache Kafka
wget http://apache.belnet.be/kafka/0.11.0.0/kafka_2.11-0.11.0.0.tgz
tar -xzf kafka_2.11-0.11.0.0.tgz
```

Follow the preceding installation script once to download the dependencies, SNAS, and Kafka. Use the following script to quick-start Kafka Server:

```
$ sh 22_3 quickstart.sh
#!/bin/bash
###############################################
# Python Network Programming Cookbook, Second Edition
  -- Chapter - 13
###############################################

# Start Zookeeper. To view the logs real time,
  in a terminal: "tail -f zk-server.out".

nohup kafka_2.11-0.11.0.0/bin/zookeeper-server-start.sh
kafka_2.11-0.11.0.0/config/zookeeper.properties >
zk-server.out &
# Start Kafka-Server. To view the logs real time, in a
terminal: "tail -f kafka-server.out".
nohup kafka_2.11-0.11.0.0/bin/kafka-server-start.sh
kafka_2.11-0.11.0.0/config/server.properties >
kafka-server.out &
```

As this script starts Kafka and ZooKeeper as `nohup`, you need to find and kill these processes when you want to stop them. You may find them by:

```
$ ps -xa | grep java
```

Then kill the process using the following command for the relevant Kafka and ZooKeeper processes:

```
$ kill {process-id}
```

How to do it...

Once you have installed the SNAS BMP message API and started ZooKeeper server and Kafka server as shown previously, you are ready to run a simple listener for the BMP messages.

First, start the Python client of the SNAS message API:

```
$ python 22_3_log_consumer.py
Connecting to kafka... takes a minute to load offsets and topics,
please wait
Now consuming/waiting for messages...

22_3_snas_log_consumer.py is adopted from openbmp-python-api-
message/examples/log_consumer.py.
```

Now, if you run the following from another Terminal and send an empty message using the *Enter* key in your keyboard:

```
$ kafka_2.11-0.11.0.0/bin/kafka-console-producer.sh --broker-list
localhost:9092 --topic openbmp.parsed.router
>
>
```

You will receive the following message:

```
$ python 22_3_snas_log_consumer.py --conf="config.yaml"
Connecting to kafka... takes a minute to load offsets and topics,
please wait
Now consuming/waiting for messages...
Received Message (2017-07-21 12:17:53.536705) : ROUTER(V: 0.0)
[]
```

If you run the following command, you will see a list of topics created for BMP by the 22_3_snas_log_consumer.py:

```
$ kafka_2.11-0.11.0.0/bin/kafka-topics.sh --list --zookeeper
localhost:2181
__consumer_offsets
openbmp.parsed.bmp_stat
openbmp.parsed.collector
openbmp.parsed.l3vpn
openbmp.parsed.ls_link
openbmp.parsed.ls_node
openbmp.parsed.ls_prefix
openbmp.parsed.peer
openbmp.parsed.router
openbmp.parsed.unicast_prefix
```

Listing 13.3 gives the simple BMP log consumer, adopted from the SNAS examples. This listing omits a few lines of code for brevity. Check the full code at 22_3_snas_log_consumer.py:

```
#!/usr/bin/env python
# Python Network Programming Cookbook, Second Edition
 -- Chapter - 13
# This program is optimized for Python 2.7.12.
# SNAS Message API Requires Python 2.7 to Run.
# This program may run on any other version with/without
 modifications.
# Adopted from openbmp-python-api-message/examples/
log_consumer.py

import argparse
import yaml
import datetime
import time
import kafka

from openbmp.api.parsed.message import Message
from openbmp.api.parsed.message import BmpStat
from openbmp.api.parsed.message import Collector
from openbmp.api.parsed.message import LsLink
from openbmp.api.parsed.message import LsNode
from openbmp.api.parsed.message import LsPrefix
from openbmp.api.parsed.message import Peer
from openbmp.api.parsed.message import Router
from openbmp.api.parsed.message import UnicastPrefix
from openbmp.api.parsed.message import L3VpnPrefix

def process_message(msg):
```

```
    m = Message(msg.value)  # Gets body of kafka message.
    t = msg.topic  # Gets topic of kafka message.
    m_tag = t.split('.')[2].upper()
    t_stamp = str(datetime.datetime.now())

    # For various cases of BMP message topics. Omitted
      logs for the sake of space.
    if t == "openbmp.parsed.router":
        router = Router(m)
        print ('\n' + 'Received Message (' + t_stamp + ')
         : ' + m_tag + '(V: ' + str(m.version) + ')')
        print (router.to_json_pretty())

    elif t == "openbmp.parsed.peer":
        peer = Peer(m)

    elif t == "openbmp.parsed.collector":
        collector = Collector(m)

    elif t == "openbmp.parsed.bmp_stat":
        bmp_stat = BmpStat(m)

    elif t == "openbmp.parsed.unicast_prefix":
        unicast_prefix = UnicastPrefix(m)

    elif t == "openbmp.parsed.l3vpn":
        l3vpn_prefix = L3VpnPrefix(m)

    elif t == "openbmp.parsed.ls_node":
        ls_node = LsNode(m)

    elif t == "openbmp.parsed.ls_link":
        ls_link = LsLink(m)

    elif t == "openbmp.parsed.ls_prefix":
        ls_prefix = LsPrefix(m)

def main(conf):
    # Enable to topics/feeds
    topics = [
        'openbmp.parsed.router', 'openbmp.parsed.peer',
        'openbmp.parsed.collector',
        'openbmp.parsed.bmp_stat', 'openbmp.parsed.
         unicast_prefix', 'openbmp.parsed.ls_node',
        'openbmp.parsed.ls_link',
       'openbmp.parsed.ls_prefix',
       'openbmp.parsed.l3vpn'
    ]
```

```
    # Read config file
    with open(conf, 'r') as f:
        config_content = yaml.load(f)

    bootstrap_server = config_content['bootstrap_servers']

    try:
        # connect and bind to topics
        print ("Connecting to kafka... takes a minute to
        load offsets and topics, please wait")
        consumer = kafka.KafkaConsumer(
            *topics,
            bootstrap_servers=bootstrap_server,
            client_id="dev-testing" + str(time.time()),
            group_id="dev-testing" + str(time.time()),
            enable_auto_commit=True,
            auto_commit_interval_ms=1000,
            auto_offset_reset="largest"
        )
        for m in consumer:
            process_message(m)

    except kafka.common.KafkaUnavailableError as err:
        print ("Kafka Error: %s" % str(err))

    except KeyboardInterrupt:
        print ("User stop requested")

if __name__ == '__main__':
    parser = argparse.ArgumentParser(description='SNAS
                                        Log Consumer')
    parser.add_argument('--conf', action="store",
    dest="conf",  default="config.yaml")
    given_args = parser.parse_args()
    conf = given_args.conf
    main (conf)
```

A configuration file can be passed by the `--conf` parameter. Default is `config.yaml`, which just points to the default Kafka server location:

```
bootstrap_servers: localhost:9092
```

The following screenshot shows the output of the Python program of the SNAS message API and the Kafka broker, along with the list of topics created by the Python program:

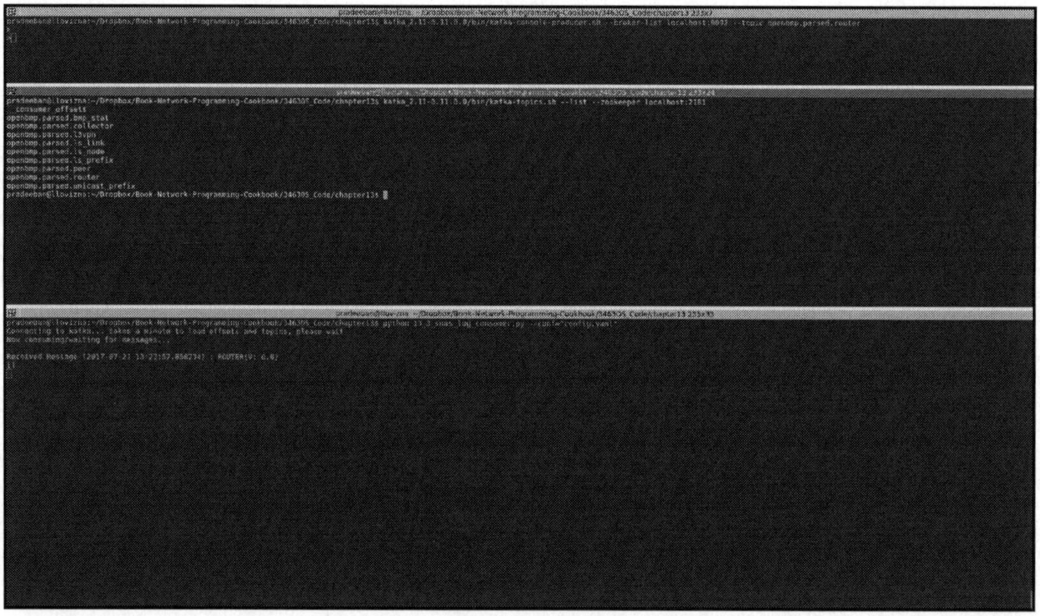

SNAS Message API and Kafka Broker

How it works...

First the nine topics of BMP messages are defined and the SNAS log consumer program subscribes to them through the Kafka broker. The BMP parsed messages include notifications of `router`, `peer`, `collector`, `bmp_stat`, `unicast_prefix`, `l3vpn`, `ls_node`, `ls_link`, and `ls_prefix`. Once started, the log consumer waits for messages on one of these nine topics. When you connect `kafka-console-producer.sh`, you may send messages to the broker. However, the messages will not reach the log consumer unless they are of one of the nine topics. You may emulate the BMP messages by starting the `kafka-console-producer.sh` with one of the topics, as we did in the example with `--topic openbmp.parsed.router` flag. The received messages for these subscribed topics are pretty printed using `to_json_pretty()` in an if-else loop for each of these topics.

Controlling drones with a wireless network

Drones are used more ubiquitously these days with controllers capable to control them from ground through TCP or UDP messages in a wireless network. **Dronecode** offers a platform to control and program drones, with a simulation environment to sandbox the developments. Developed in Python, Dronecode is managed by the Linux Foundation. In this recipe, we will run a simplest of drone simulation. More interesting recipes can be learned by following their website (`https://www.dronecode.org`).

Getting ready

Dronekit requires Python 2.7 to run. Install the Dronekit and Dronekit **Software in the Loop** (**SITL**) Simulator using Python `pip`:

```
$ pip install dronekit
$ pip install dronekit-sitl
```

How to do it...

In this recipe, we will simulate a simple drone with `dronekit-sitl`. The simulator API is compatible with the Dronekit API that actually controls the drones. Hence, you may develop once and run in simulation and production very easily, as with our previous recipes on Mininet emulation.

First, run the `dronekit-sitl` in a Terminal before running `22_4_dronekit_sitl_simulation.py`:

```
$ dronekit-sitl copter-3.3 --home=-45.12,149.22,544.55,343.55
os: linux, apm: copter, release: 3.3
SITL already Downloaded and Extracted.
Ready to boot.
Execute: /home/pradeeban/.dronekit/sitl/copter-3.3/apm --
home=-45.12,149.22,544.55,343.55 --model=quad
Started model quad at -45.12,149.22,544.55,343.55 at speed 1.0
bind port 5760 for 0
Starting sketch 'ArduCopter'
Serial port 0 on TCP port 5760
Starting SITL input
Waiting for connection ....
```

Listing 13.4 provides a simple simulation of a drone, which can connect to the drone or in our case, a simulation running, through a TCP network connection:

```
#!/usr/bin/env python
# Python Network Programming Cookbook, Second Edition -- Chapter - 13
# This program is optimized for Python 2.7.12.
# It may run on any other version with/without modifications.

import dronekit_sitl
from dronekit import connect, VehicleMode

# Connect to the default sitl, if not one running.
sitl = dronekit_sitl.start_default()
connection_string = sitl.connection_string()

# Connect to the Vehicle.
print("Connected: %s" % (connection_string))
vehicle = connect(connection_string, wait_ready=True)

print ("GPS: %s" % vehicle.gps_0)
print ("Battery: %s" % vehicle.battery)
print ("Last Heartbeat: %s" % vehicle.last_heartbeat)
print ("Is Armable?: %s" % vehicle.is_armable)
print ("System status: %s" % vehicle.system_status.state)
print ("Mode: %s" % vehicle.mode.name)

# Close vehicle object before exiting script
vehicle.close()

print("Completed")
```

The following code shows the execution of Dronekit:

```
$ python 22_4_dronekit_sitl_simulation.py
Starting copter simulator (SITL)
SITL already Downloaded and Extracted.
Ready to boot.
Connected: tcp:127.0.0.1:5760
>>> APM:Copter V3.3 (d6053245)
>>> Frame: QUAD
>>> Calibrating barometer
>>> Initialising APM...
>>> barometer calibration complete
>>> GROUND START
GPS: GPSInfo:fix=3,num_sat=10
Battery: Battery:voltage=12.587,current=0.0,level=100
Last Heartbeat: 0.862903219997
Is Armable?: False
```

```
System status: STANDBY
Mode: STABILIZE
Completed
```

The following screenshot shows the execution of both the Dronekit and the simulator:

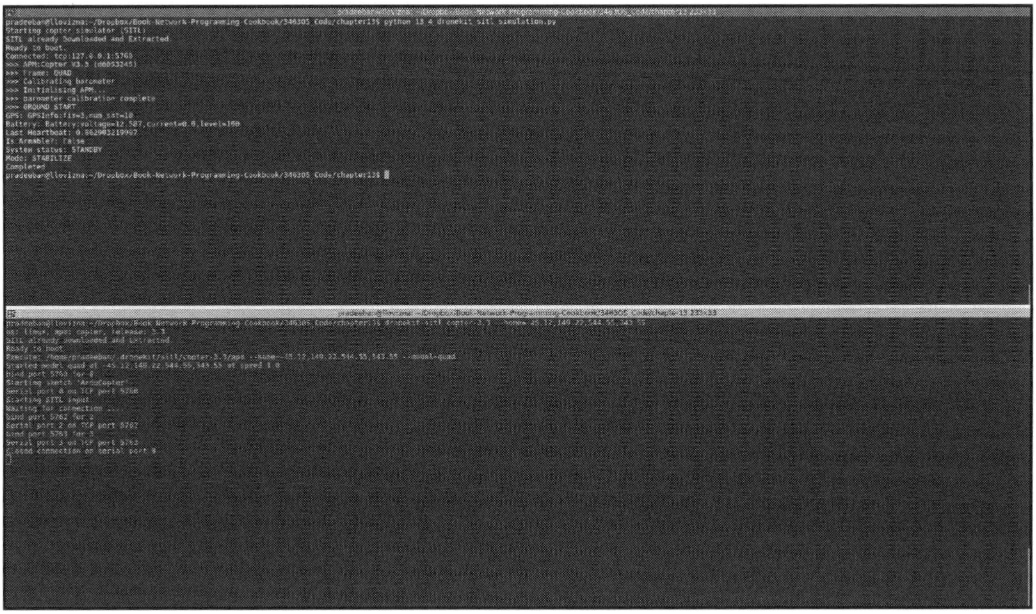

DroneKit and the Simulation

The following lines are printed in the SITL Terminal window, indicating the TCP connection:

```
bind port 5762 for 2
Serial port 2 on TCP port 5762
bind port 5763 for 3
Serial port 3 on TCP port 5763
Closed connection on serial port 0
```

This recipe shows the simulated default values and connects to the SITL with the ports, and closes the execution on its own when it completes.

How it works...

This recipe initializes a simple drone and prints its status. You may execute it to set its parameters and modify its values dynamically. More examples on Dronekit can be found at `http://python.dronekit.io/examples/`.

Creating PNDA clusters

PNDA (`http://pnda.io/`) is a scalable big data analytics platform for networks and services from the Linux Foundation. PNDA requires a cluster to run efficiently. PNDA offers Python scripts (`https://github.com/pndaproject/pnda-aws-templates`) to deploy it over Amazon EC2.

Getting ready

Create an S3 bucket from `https://s3.console.aws.amazon.com/s3/home?region=eu-west-1`. We are using **EU (Ireland)** as our default region for this recipe. PNDA applications will be hosted in this bucket. Replace the `pnda-apps` with the name of your S3 bucket. Since the bucket names are shared across all the users in the region, you may not be able to use `pnda-apps` as your `Bucket name` as it would already have been used by someone:

```
# S3 container to use for PNDA application packages
PNDA_APPS_CONTAINER: pnda-apps
```

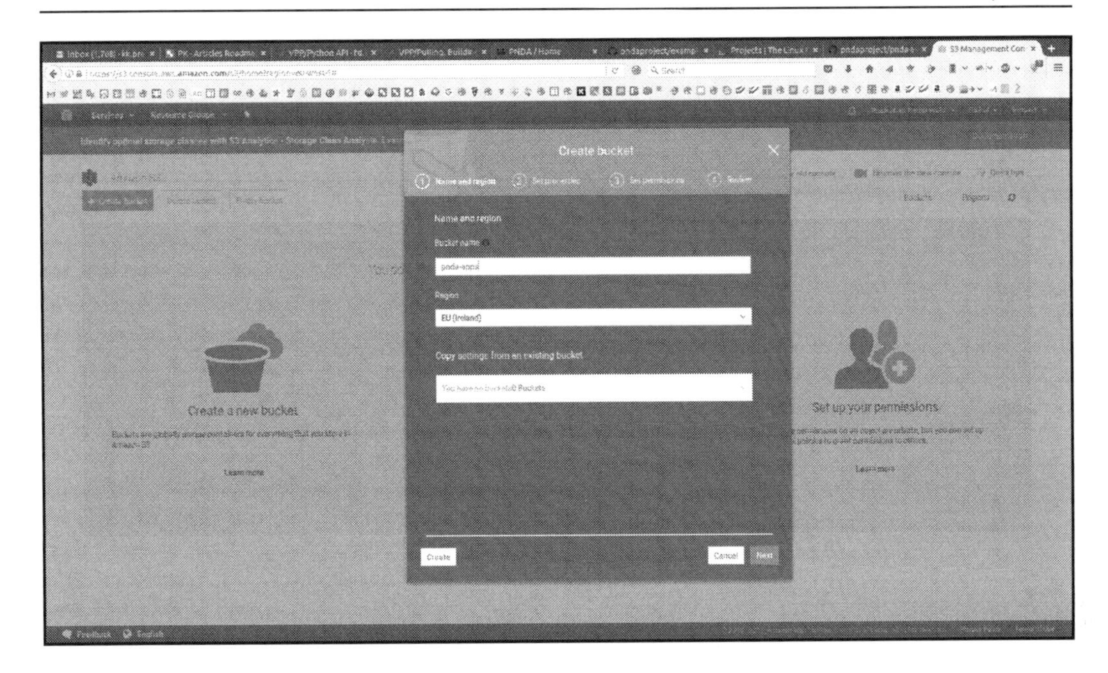

Creating an S3 Bucket for PNDA

Create a key from
`https://console.aws.amazon.com/iam/home?#/security_credential`.

Don't forget to download the key (`rootkey.csv`):

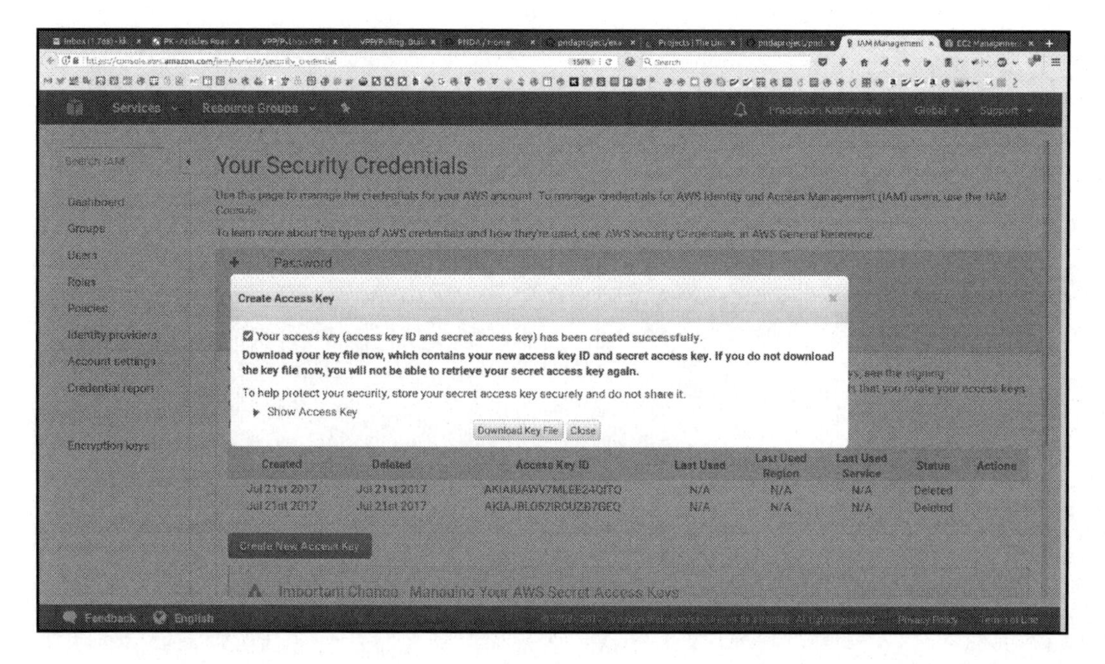

Creating Access Key

Open the `rootkey.csv` and replace the following values in `pnda_env.yaml`. These values appear three times. Make sure to replace all of them accordingly:

```
AWS_ACCESS_KEY_ID: xxxx
AWS_SECRET_ACCESS_KEY: xxxx
```

Replace the value of `PNDA_ARCHIVE_CONTAINER` to something else (more representative and long enough to be unique). However, this bucket will be auto-created.

Create an SSH **Key pair name** named `key` (`https://eu-west-1.console.aws.amazon.com/ec2/v2/home?region=eu-west-1#KeyPairs:sort=keyName`). Download and save the private key, `key.pem`.

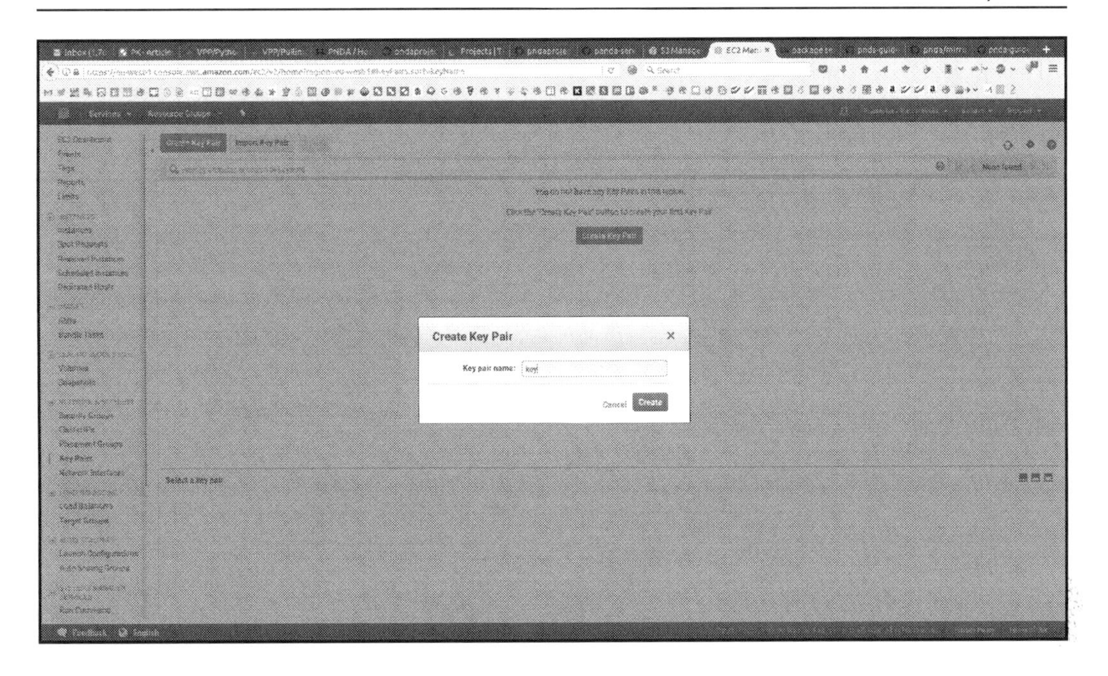

Create and Download the Private Key

Configure the dependencies and AWS templates:

```
$ sh 22_5_pnda_aws_setup.sh
#!/bin/bash
###############################################
# Python Network Programming Cookbook, Second Edition -- Chapter - 13
###############################################
# Clone the Platform Salt
git clone https://github.com/pndaproject/platform-salt.git
cd platform-salt
git checkout release/3.4.1
cd ..
# Clone the PNDA AWS Template latest release tag
git clone git@github.com:pndaproject/pnda-aws-templates.git
cd pnda-aws-templates
git checkout release/3.4.1
# Copy the sample pnda_env.yaml to the project after modifying as in
the recipe.
cp ../pnda_env.yaml pnda_env.yaml
# Install Dependencies
cd cli
sudo pip install -r requirements.txt
```

Now you can create PNDA distribution from the PNDA repository by following the scripts in the `mirror` directory. Execute these commands from your web server:

```
$ git clone git@github.com:pndaproject/pnda.git
$ sudo su
$ cd pnda/mirror
$ ./create_mirror.sh
```

Once the mirror build is complete, move the built folders inside the `mirror-dist` folder (`mirror_anaconda`, `mirror_cloudera`, and `mirror_misc`) to a folder of your choice (we assume the folder name to be `packages`). Now you have mirrored PNDA to your web server location. Change the following URI to indicate this publicly accessible mirror from your site:

```
pnda_component_packages:
  # HTTP server containing the compiled binary packages for
    the components
  # required to provision PNDA
  PACKAGES_SERVER_URI: http://x.x.x.x/packages
```

You may even host this inside an EC2 instance after installing a web server such as Apache2. In that case, you will have a packages server URI similar to, `http://ec2-34-253-229-120.eu-west-1.compute.amazonaws.com/packages/`.

How to do it...

Now you may create a PNDA cluster with the commands:

```
$ cd cli
$ python pnda-cli.py create -e <cluster_name> -s <key_name> -f
standard -o {no-of-tsdb-instances} -n {no-of-hadoop-data-nodes} -k
{no-of-kafka-brokers} -z {no-of-zookeeper-nodes}
```

Replace the names accordingly. For example:

```
$ python pnda-cli.py create -e pnda -s key -f standard -o 2 -n 3 -k 2
-z 3
```

Or with just one instance for each:

```
$ python pnda-cli.py create -e pnda -s key -f standard -o 1 -n 1 -k 1
-z 1
```

Currently `pnda-cli.py` and the other Python scripts in PNDA do not support Python 3, as they are written for Python 2. It is recommended to use Python 2.7. This will be verbose during the setup, and produce the elapsed time at the end of execution.

How it works...

In this recipe, `pnda-cli.py` first checks whether the `pnda_env.yaml` file exists, and reads the parameters from it. It uses boto's EC2 interface (`http://boto.cloudhackers.com/en/latest/ec2_tut.html`) to run many tasks such as connecting to the region, initializing the EC2 instances, and configuring them. Expect this to take a few minutes, also depending on the connectivity between your mirror and the EC2 instance. Thus it might be a good idea to actually create your PNDA cluster in a region that is closest to you to minimize the latency.

In this recipe, we learned how to configure PNDA in AWS. In this process, we also learned how useful Python can be for such complex configuration tasks as we used it to read the `.yaml` configuration file and configure an AWS cluster based on our configurations.

23
Programming the Internet

In this chapter, we will cover the following recipes:

- Checking a website status
- Benchmarking BGP implementations with bgperf
- BGP with ExaBGP
- Looking glass implementations with Python
- Understanding the internet ecosystem with Python
- Establishing BGP connections with yabgp

Introduction

Autonomous Systems (**ASes**) make the internet. Communications between the ASes are handled through implementations of protocols known as **Exterior Gateway Protocols** (**EGP**). **Border Gateway Protocol** (**BGP**) is a standardized EGP, designed for exchanging routing and reachability information between the ASes. In this chapter, we will look into Python libraries for BGP such as `exabgp` and `yabgp`, and how to program the internet with Python.

Checking a website status

A website may be down as its connectivity to the rest of the internet is broken in some way. We start this chapter by checking the status of a website. Though this is a very simple exercise done with just Python, this can be extended as a health monitor application for more complex scenarios on the internet.

Getting ready

This function tests the connectivity of a website by a given address or a **fully qualified domain name** (**FQDN**) and port (default `80` assumed). When a domain name is passed as an address, the `socket.connect()` method resolves it.

How to do it...

Here we will look into a simple recipe that performs this action, as indicated by listing 14.1:

```
#!/usr/bin/env python
# Python Network Programming Cookbook, Second Edition
  -- Chapter - 14
# This program is optimized for Python 2.7.12 and
  Python 3.5.2.
# It may run on any other version with/without modifications.
import socket
from sys import stdout
from time import sleep
import argparse
def is_alive(address, port):
    # Create a socket object to connect with
    s = socket.socket()
    # Now try connecting, passing in a tuple with
      address & port
    try:
        s.connect((address, port))
        return True
    except socket.error:
        return False
    finally:
        s.close()

def confirm(addres, port):
    while True:
        if is_alive(address, port):
            stdout.write(address + ":" +
            str(port) + ' is alive\n')
            stdout.flush()
        else:
            stdout.write(address + ":" +
            str(port) + ' is dead\n')
            stdout.flush()
        sleep(10)
```

```
if __name__ == '__main__':
    # setup commandline arguments
    parser = argparse.ArgumentParser
            (description='Health Checker')
    parser.add_argument('--address', action="store",
    dest="address")
    parser.add_argument('--port', action="store",
    dest="port", default=80, type=int)
    # parse arguments
    given_args = parser.parse_args()
    address, port =  given_args.address,
                     given_args.port
    confirm(address, port)
```

The following is the sample output of the program:

```
$ python 23_1_healthcheck.py --address=google.com --port=80
google.com:80 is alive
google.com:80 is alive
```

How it works...

This program checks the website periodically to see if it is up, and prints the log accordingly. If the website is down, it will notify the same, in the time intervals.

Benchmarking BGP implementations with bgperf

In this recipe, we aim to introduce BGP implementations with Python through a simple benchmarking project, as a simple exercise. We will benchmark a few BGP implementations with `bgpert`, a Python-based benchmarking tool for BGP implementations.

Getting ready

To install `bgperf`, clone the source code from its source repository:

```
$ git clone https://github.com/pradeeban/bgperf.git
```

For this recipe, we forked `bgperf` and did some minor fixes to make it work with Python 3. The parent project is at `https://github.com/osrg/bgperf`, which is aimed to work with Python 2, and at the time of writing does not support Python 3. A copy of the `pradeeban/bgperf` repository as of now has also been included in the source code bundle of this book in the folder `23_2_benchmark_with_bgperf` for your ease of reference.

Once you have cloned our `bgperf` fork, go to the parent directory of `bgperf`:

```
$ cd bgperf
```

The following command installs the listed requirements. This includes Docker and `pyyaml`:

```
$ sudo pip install -r pip-requirements.txt
```

Now your `bgperf` is ready to benchmark the BGP implementations! Confirm it by running the following command:

```
$ sudo python3 bgperf.py -help
```

Now prepare `bgperf` for benchmarks:

```
$ sudo python3 bgperf.py prepare
```

During this command, `bgperf` downloads the BGP implementations locally. You will be able to observe this from the logs displayed:

```
Removing intermediate container 782c2b5dcecf
Step 5/6 : RUN git clone https://github.com/Exa-Networks/exabgp && (cd
exabgp && git checkout HEAD && pip install six && pip install -r
requirements.txt && python setup.py install)
---> Running in 833e710df9df
Cloning into 'exabgp'...
```

As this command actually downloads and installs many of the BGP implementations, it will take more than an hour to complete. On my laptop, it took me 90 minutes! Nevertheless, the logs will keep you informed and entertained. So you may keep an eye on the logs once in a while, as this progresses.

Eventually, it will succeed with these logs:

```
...
if test -n "birdc" ; then
\
      /usr/bin/install -c ../birdc //usr/local/sbin/birdc ; \
fi
```

```
if ! test -f //usr/local/etc/bird.conf ; then
\
     /usr/bin/install -c -m 644 ../doc/bird.conf.example
//usr/local/etc/bird.conf ;      \
else                             \
      echo "Not overwriting old bird.conf" ;
\
fi
make[1]: Leaving directory '/root/bird/obj'
---> ad49f9e6f4f0
Removing intermediate container 488a2f8827eb
Successfully built ad49f9e6f4f0
Successfully tagged bgperf/bird:latest
```

Now it is time to finalize the installation of `bgperf` with the following command:

```
$ sudo python3 bgperf.py doctor
[sudo] password for pradeeban:
docker version ... ok (17.06.0-ce)
bgperf image
... ok
gobgp image
... ok
bird image
... ok
quagga image
... ok
/proc/sys/net/ipv4/neigh/default/gc_thresh3 ... 1024
```

You have `bgperf` ready in your system now, to benchmark the BGP implementations.

How to do it...

Once you have configured `bgperf`, you will be able to benchmark the BGP implementations.

For example:

```
$ sudo python3 bgperf.py bench
run tester
tester booting.. (100/100)
run gobgp
elapsed: 16sec, cpu: 0.20%, mem: 580.90MB
elapsed time: 11sec
```

The execution stops only when `100` BGP peers are successfully booted. Further benchmarks can be executed by following the project page.

How it works...

This recipe looks into the common BGP implementations and benchmarks them through the `bgperf` open source project. In the rest of the chapters, we will look at some BGP implementations.

BGP with ExaBGP

ExaBGP (`https://github.com/Exa-Networks/exabgp`) facilitates convenient implementation of SDN by converting BGP messages into plain text or JSON formats.

Getting ready

Install ExaBGP using `pip`:

```
$ sudo pip install exabgp
```

Generate the environment file by using the following command:

```
$ sudo su
$ mkdir /etc/exabgp
$ exabgp --fi >/etc/exabgp/exabgp.env
```

How to do it...

Now you have installed ExaBGP in your computer. You may explore its command using its `help` flag:

```
$ exabgp -help
```

Looking glass implementations with Python

Internet Exchange Points (IXPs) are the backbones of the internet, as they offer easy connectivity between the **Autonomous Systems (ASes)** of the internet. The **looking glass (lg)** implementation is a commonly deployed software in the IXPs. They can be used to trace how an IXP can reach any given IP address on the internet. The lg implementations are made public such that anyone can use it to trace how to connect to a given IP address, thus offering an emulation environment to test the connectivity and performance of an IXP for the service providers before committing to use an IXP for their own connectivity needs.

BIX is an IXP based in Bulgaria. You may access the lg of **Bulgarian Internet Exchange (BIX)** at `http://lg.bix.bg/`. For example, see the output of the query from your browser: `http://lg.bix.bg/?query=summaryaddr=216.146.35.35router=rs1.bix.bg+%28IPv6%29` for the IP (IPv6) BGP summary of `216.146.35.35` (`http://dyn.com/labs/dyn-internet-guide/`). The output of this query is shown in the following screenshot:

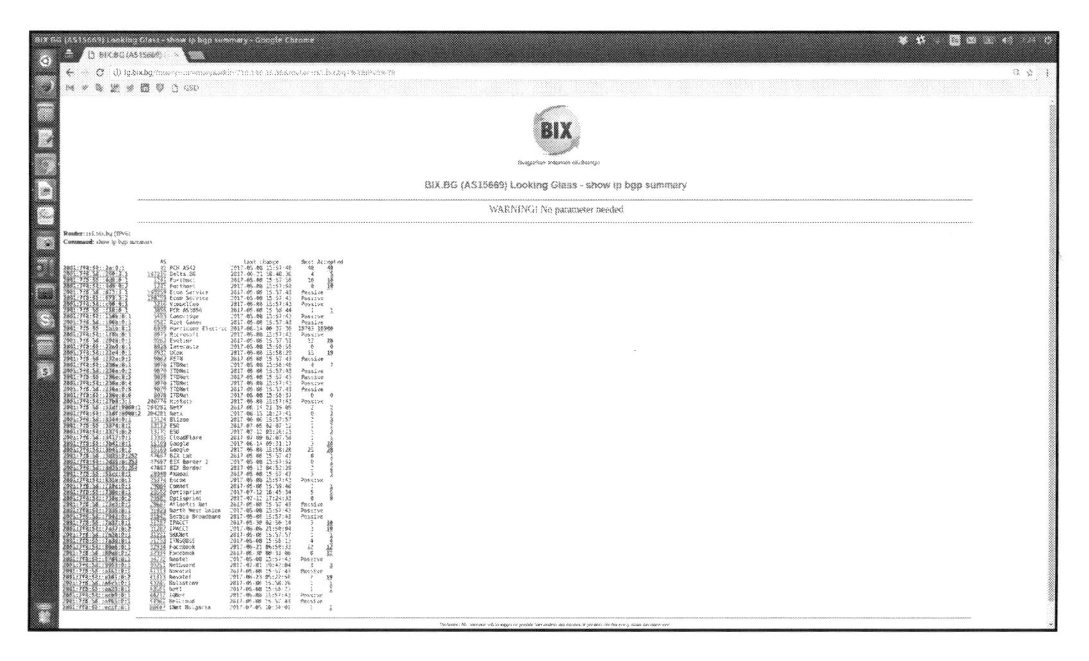

Looking Glass of BIX.bg

You may also run a `traceroute` from the lg (using the web service APIs of the browser) to observe how a given IP is connected through the IXP.

For example, access `http://lg.bix.bg/?query=traceaddr=216.146.35.35router=rs1.bix.bg+%28IPv6%29` from your browser.

It will produce the following output in the browser window:

Router: rs1.bix.bg (IPv6)
Command: traceroute -w 3 216.146.35.35

```
traceroute to 216.146.35.35 (216.146.35.35), 30 hops max, 60 byte packets
 1  router.bix.bg (193.169.199.254)  3.600 ms  3.760 ms  3.576 ms
 2  xe-0-2-0--br2.sof.ITDNet.net (212.116.129.29)  0.516 ms  0.532 ms  0.523 ms
 3  br1.sof.ITDNet.net (212.116.133.17)  0.742 ms  0.749 ms  0.747 ms
 4  10ge5-1.core1.sof1.he.net (216.66.85.129)  0.838 ms  0.737 ms  0.926 ms
 5  100ge10-2.core1.buh1.he.net (184.105.65.50)  8.798 ms  8.817 ms  8.843 ms
 6  buca-b1-link.telia.net (62.115.49.165)  26.499 ms  27.758 ms  27.716 ms
 7  ffm-bb3-link.telia.net (62.115.135.250)  40.182 ms ffm-bb3-link.telia.net (62.115.135.242)  39.069 ms ffm-bb3-link.telia.net (62.115.135.234)  39.315 ms
 8  ffm-b1-link.telia.net (62.115.116.160)  32.201 ms ffm-b1-link.telia.net (62.115.121.7)  35.001 ms ffm-b1-link.telia.net (62.115.137.165)  36.025 ms
 9  tata-ic-321348-ffm-b1.c.telia.net (213.248.82.41)  39.816 ms  39.941 ms  44.285 ms
10  if-ae-4-2.tcore1.FR0-Frankfurt.as6453.net (195.219.87.18)  40.336 ms  40.452 ms  44.162 ms
11  195.219.50.186 (195.219.50.186)  40.025 ms  39.887 ms  39.989 ms
12  resolver1.dyndnsinternetguide.com (216.146.35.35)  44.719 ms  40.042 ms  44.152 ms
```

You may notice that the output is different from the same command run from your console, as it will produce the hops from your local network (while the one from the lg produced the output of `traceroute` as seen from the routers of BIX).

The lg can be implemented in Python, and `py-lookingglass` is such an implementation.

You may `install py-lookingglass` through `pip`:

```
$ sudo pip install py-lookingglass
```

Once installed, you may execute the following command to show the options:

```
$ python -m lg -h
usage: lg.py [-h] [-n NAME] [-c [COMMANDS [COMMANDS ...]]]
             [-H [HOSTS [HOSTS ...]]] [-b BIND] [-p PORT]
optional arguments:
  -h, --help            show this help message and exit
  -n NAME, --name NAME  Header name for pages
  -c [COMMANDS [COMMANDS ...]], --commands [COMMANDS [COMMANDS ...]]
Json array for profiles where key is profile name, use %ARG% for
substition of IP/hostname argument. Key in command is display friendly
version.
Example:
{
"cisco": {
```

```
"Ping": "ping %ARG%",
"BGP Advertised _ARGUMENT_ to Neighbor": "sh ip bgp neighbor %ARG%
advertised",
"BGP Summary": "sh ip bgp summary",
"Traceroute": "traceroute %ARG%"
},
"juniper": {
"Ping": "ping -c 4 %ARG%",
"BGP Advertised _ARGUMENT_ to Neighbor": "cli -c \"show route
advertising-protocol bgp %ARG%\"",
"BGP Summary": "cli -c \"sh bgp sum\"",
"Traceroute": "traceroute %ARG%"
}
}
-H [HOSTS [HOSTS ...]], --hosts [HOSTS [HOSTS ...]]
 Comma separated profile for router
'password','host_address',port_number,type_of_connection(1 for ssh and
0 for telnet),name,command_profile separated by space.
Example

"password1","192.168.0.1",23,0,"Cisco","cisco"
"login:password2","192.168.1.1",22,0,"Juniper","juniper"
-b BIND, --bind BIND  IP to bind
-p PORT, --port PORT  port to bind
```

Getting ready

There are more Python-based applications that offer a complete DNS looking glass solution. Dyn `dns_lg` (`https://github.com/dyninc/dns_lg`) is a DNS looking glass solution that depends on `ldns` (`http://www.linuxfromscratch.org/blfs/view/cvs/basicnet/ldns.html`), a fast and efficient DNS library and `ldns-python` package. `ldns` depends on SWIG interface compiler (`http://www.swig.org`) to connect its core modules developed in C and Python code used. Make sure you have SWIG installed on your computer:

1. You may install it using the following command in Ubuntu/Debian-based systems:

   ```
   $ sudo apt-get install swig
   ```

2. Download the source of `ldns` using the following command:

   ```
   $ wget -nc http://www.nlnetlabs.nl/downloads/
     ldns/ldns-1.7.0.tar.gz
   ```

3. Unzip the archive:

```
$ tar -xzf ldns-1.7.0.tar.gz
```

4. Move to the `ldns` directory:

```
$ cd ldns-1.7.0/
```

5. Now you may install `ldns`:

```
$ ./configure --prefix=/usr          \
            --sysconfdir=/etc        \
            --disable-static         \
            --disable-dane-ta-usage \
            --with-drill \
      --with-pyldns            &&
make
$ sudo make install
```

How to do it...

As you have installed `ldns`, now you may check out the Dyn's `dns_lg` source code from its source code repository:

```
git clone git@github.com:dyninc/dns_lg.git
cd dns_lg/
```

Now, you may run the application simply by executing `api.py`. Running it produces the following output:

```
$ python api.py
* Running on http://0.0.0.0:8185/
 (Press CTRL+C to quit)
```

Now open another console window to run a `curl`:

```
curl http://0.0.0.0:8185/cnn.com/
```

This will output a line to the preceding `api.py` console:

```
127.0.0.1 - - [15/Jul/2017 23:33:40]
"GET /cnn.com/ HTTP/1.1" 200 -
```

The `curl` command produces the following output with the detailed DNS information from the looking glass implementation:

```
$ curl http://0.0.0.0:8185/cnn.com/
{
  "AdditionalSection": [
    {
      "Address": "205.251.192.47",
      "Class": "IN",
      "Name": "ns-47.awsdns-05.com.",
      "TTL": "20545",
      "Type": "A"
    },
    {
      "Address": "205.251.194.64",
      "Class": "IN",
      "Name": "ns-576.awsdns-08.net.",
      "TTL": "20545",
      "Type": "A"
    }
  ],
  "AnswerSection": [],
  "AuthoritySection": [
    {
      "Class": "IN",
      "Name": "cnn.com.",
      "TTL": "20545",
      "Target": "ns-47.awsdns-05.com.",
      "Type": "NS"
    },
    {
      "Class": "IN",
      "Name": "cnn.com.",
      "TTL": "20545",
      "Target": "ns-1086.awsdns-07.org.",
      "Type": "NS"
    },
    {
      "Class": "IN",
      "Name": "cnn.com.",
      "TTL": "20545",
      "Target": "ns-576.awsdns-08.net.",
      "Type": "NS"
    },
    {
      "Class": "IN",
      "Name": "cnn.com.",
      "TTL": "20545",
```

```
        "Target": "ns-1630.awsdns-11.co.uk.",
        "Type": "NS"
      }
    ],
    "None": "true",
    "Query": {
      "Duration": 118,
      "Server": "",
      "ServerIP": "127.0.1.1",
      "Versions": "Dyn DNS Looking Glass 1.0.0"
    },
    "QuestionSection": {
      "Qclass": "IN",
      "Qname": "cnn.com.",
      "Qtype": "A"
    },
    "ReturnCode": "NOERROR"
  }
```

The preceding output shows Dyn's `dns_lg` and `curl` in action. Please note that currently Dyn's `dns_lg` works only in Python 2.x. However, with some minor fixes, this can easily be ported to Python 3.x. As we ported `bgperf` to Python 3.x in a previous recipe, this is left as an exercise for those who like to port this to Python 3.x.

How it works...

Looking glass offers you an opportunity to see how you can connect to another part of the internet through the routers of any given IXP. Similar to the functionality of `traceroute`, lg implementations show you the connectivity in the internet scale. They are deployed by the IXPs to demonstrate the IXP performance to the potential customers.

Understanding the internet ecosystem with Python

When network traffic is sent to the internet, it passes through various ASes and IXPs. Tools such as `traceroute` and `tcptraceroute` can be used to trace how a particular network node in the internet can be accessed from your computer through your internet provider. Various tools developed in Python can be used to understand the nature of the internet. traIXroute (`https://pypi.python.org/pypi/traixroute`) is a tool developed on Python 3, which identifies the IXPs on the `traceroute` path.

Getting ready

You may install traIXroute through `pip`:

```
$ sudo pip install traixroute
```

To measure the performance and topologies of the internet, you also need to install scamper (`https://www.caida.org/tools/measurement/scamper/`), a parallel measurement utility for the internet:

```
$ sudo scamper-install
```

Your traIXroute is now ready to analyze the internet connectivity through the IXPs. You may confirm your successful install by running the `--help` command, which will produce the output as follows:

```
$ traixroute --help
usage: traixroute [-h] [-dns] [-asn] [-db] [-rule] [-u] [-m] [-o
OUTPUT] [-v]
                 {probe,ripe,import} ...
positional arguments:
  {probe,ripe,import}
    probe                probe --help
    ripe                 ripe --help
    import               import --help
optional arguments:
  -h, --help                 show this help message and exit
  -dns, --enable-dns-print
                             Enables printing the domain name
 of each IP hop in the traceroute path.
  -asn, --enable-asn-print
                             Enables printing the ASN of
 each IP hop in the traceroute path.
      -db, --store-database
                             Enables printing the database information.
      -rule, --enable-rule-print
                             Enables printing the hit IXP detection
rule(s) in the traceroute path.
      -u, --update           Updates the database with up-to-date
datasets.
      -m, --merge            Exports the database to distinct files,
the ixp_prefixes.txt and ixp_membership.txt.
      -o OUTPUT, --output OUTPUT
                             Specifies the output file name to redirect
the traIXroute results.
      -v, --version          show program's version number and exit
```

How to do it...

Now you may run `traixroute` to see the IXPs in your path. Running `traixroute` for the first time takes a few minutes, as it has to perform a few initialization actions, downloading the datasets:

```
$ traixroute probe -dest cnn.com -s="-m 12"
Dataset files are missing.
Updating the database...
Started downloading PDB dataset.
Started downloading PCH dataset.
Started downloading RouteViews dataset.
Routeviews has been updated successfully.
PDB dataset has been updated successfully.
PCH dataset has been updated successfully.
Database has been updated successfully.
Imported 13 IXP Detection Rules from /configuration/rules.txt.
Loading from PCH, PDB, Routeviews and additional_info.txt.
traIXroute using scamper with "-m 12" options.
[15:08:06:001] scamper_privsep_init: could not mkdir /var/empty:
Permission denied
Scamper failed. Trying to run with sudo..
[sudo] password for pradeeban:
traIXroute to cnn.com (151.101.1.67).
1)      (62.4.224.1) 15.465 ms
2)      (91.183.241.176) 18.642 ms
3)      (91.183.246.112) 12.178 ms
4)      (62.115.40.97) 20.216 ms
5)      (213.155.136.216) 20.027 ms
6)      (80.91.253.163) 12.127 ms
7)      (*) -
8)      (*) -
9)      (*) -
10)     (*) -
11)     (*) -
```

This did not indicate any IXP in the path between my network and `http://edition.cnn.com/`. Let's try once more towards `register.bg`:

```
$ sudo traixroute probe -dest register.bg -s="-m 12"
Imported 13 IXP Detection Rules from /configuration/rules.txt.
Loading from Database.
traIXroute using scamper with "-m 12" options.
traIXroute to register.bg (192.92.129.35).
1)      (62.4.224.1) 21.699 ms
2)      (91.183.241.176) 7.769 ms
3)      (91.183.246.114) 8.056 ms
```

```
4)     (BNIX)->AS9002     (194.53.172.71) 7.417 ms
5)      (87.245.234.130) 51.538 ms
6)      (87.245.240.146) 51.324 ms
7)      (178.132.82.126) 44.711 ms
8)      (193.68.0.150) 46.406 ms
9)      (193.68.0.181) 44.492 ms
10)     (192.92.129.35) 44.777 ms
IXP hops:
3) 91.183.246.114 <--- BNIX (BE,Brussels) ---> 4) 194.53.172.71
```

This shows that my request had an `IXP hops` (`BNIX` in `Brussels`) in between. If you repeat the request, you may notice that the `IXP hops` most certainly remained the same while other hops may have changed. You may repeat with other websites to see which IXPs that your network traffic passes through.

How it works...

The `-m` flag indicates the maximum **time-to-live** (**TTL**) between the hops. The `*` in the output logs indicates failure to trace a node within the given TTL, as no response was received. The `-m` flag dictates the maximum number of hops to be traced. It can be a value between 1 and 255, with 1 producing just 1 hop in between, where 255 produces up to 255 hops towards the end point. However, note that it is unlikely to have such a long path in the internet, and if exists, it is even more unlikely to retrieve the exact IP addresses through `traceroute` or `traixroute` (you will more likely receive `*` for the latter hops).

Establishing BGP connections with yabgp

Yabgp is a Python implementation for BGP protocol that supports establishing BGP connections from various routers. It can be used for various advanced use cases such as future analysis. In this recipe, we will install `yabgp` using `virtualenv` virtual environment for Python programs.

Getting ready

First, get the sources of `yabgp`:

```
$ git clone https://github.com/smartbgp/yabgp
```

Now to build `yabgp`:

```
$ cd yabgp
```

Install the requirements following this command, and observe the following logs:

```
$ pip install -r requirements.txt
..
Successfully installed Twisted Flask Flask-HTTPAuth netaddr
zope.interface Werkzeug Jinja2 itsdangerous MarkupSafe
Cleaning up...
```

Now you may confirm the correct installation of `yabgpd` by using the following command:

```
$ cd bin
$ python yabgpd -h
```

This will output detailed help information on `yabgpd`.

How to do it...

`yabgpd` is a BGP agent that can orchestrate the BGP routers. You may start the agent as a Python application. Make sure to update the correct values for the BGP local and remote addresses, and the local and remote BGP autonomous system values. The program will print a set of log lines as follows:

```
$ python yabgpd --bgp-local_addr=172.31.0.232 --bgp-local_as=23650 \
--bgp-remote_addr=52.58.130.47 --bgp-remote_as=23650
2017-07-16 16:19:05,837.837 78465 INFO yabgp.agent [-] Log (Re)opened.
2017-07-16 16:19:05,837.837 78465 INFO yabgp.agent [-] Configuration:
2017-07-16 16:19:05,837.837 78465 INFO yabgp.agent [-]
*****************************************************
2017-07-16 16:19:05,837.837 78465 INFO yabgp.agent [-] Configuration
options gathered from:
2017-07-16 16:19:05,837.837 78465 INFO yabgp.agent [-] command line
args: ['--bgp-local_addr=172.31.0.232', '--bgp-local_as=23650', '--
bgp-remote_addr=10.124.1.245', '--bgp-remote_as=23650']
2017-07-16 16:19:05,837.837 78465 INFO yabgp.agent [-] config files:
[]
```

```
2017-07-16 16:19:05,837.837 78465 INFO yabgp.agent [-]
=======================================================
....
...
2017-07-16 16:19:05,840.840 78465 INFO yabgp.agent [-] ---remote_as =
23650
2017-07-16 16:19:05,840.840 78465 INFO yabgp.agent [-] ---remote_addr
= 10.124.1.245
2017-07-16 16:19:05,840.840 78465 INFO yabgp.agent [-] ---local_as =
23650
2017-07-16 16:19:05,840.840 78465 INFO yabgp.agent [-] ---local_addr =
172.31.0.232
2017-07-16 16:19:05,840.840 78465 INFO yabgp.agent [-] ---capability =
{'remote': {}, 'local': {'cisco_route_refresh': True, 'route_refresh':
True, 'graceful_restart': True, 'cisco_multi_session': True,
'four_bytes_as': True, 'enhanced_route_refresh': True, 'add_path':
None}}
2017-07-16 16:19:05,840.840 78465 INFO yabgp.agent [-] ---afi_safi =
['ipv4']
2017-07-16 16:19:05,840.840 78465 INFO yabgp.agent [-] ---md5 = None
2017-07-16 16:19:05,840.840 78465 INFO yabgp.handler.default_handler
[-] Create dir /home/ubuntu/data/bgp/10.124.1.245 for peer
10.124.1.245
2017-07-16 16:19:05,840.840 78465 INFO yabgp.handler.default_handler
[-] BGP message file path is /home/ubuntu/data/bgp/10.124.1.245
2017-07-16 16:19:05,840.840 78465 INFO yabgp.handler.default_handler
[-] get the last bgp message seq for this peer
2017-07-16 16:19:05,840.840 78465 INFO yabgp.handler.default_handler
[-] BGP message file 1500221945.84.msg
2017-07-16 16:19:05,840.840 78465 INFO yabgp.handler.default_handler
[-] The last bgp message seq number is 0
2017-07-16 16:19:05,841.841 78465 INFO yabgp.agent [-] Create
BGPPeering twsited instance
2017-07-16 16:19:05,841.841 78465 INFO yabgp.core.factory [-] Init
BGPPeering for peer 10.124.1.245
2017-07-16 16:19:05,841.841 78465 INFO yabgp.agent [-] Prepare RESTAPI
service
2017-07-16 16:19:05,842.842 78465 INFO yabgp.agent [-] serving RESTAPI
on http://0.0.0.0:8801
2017-07-16 16:19:05,842.842 78465 INFO yabgp.agent [-] Starting
BGPPeering twsited instance
2017-07-16 16:19:05,842.842 78465 INFO yabgp.core.fsm [-] Automatic
start
2017-07-16 16:19:05,842.842 78465 INFO yabgp.core.fsm [-] Do not need
Idle Hold, start right now.
2017-07-16 16:19:05,842.842 78465 INFO yabgp.core.fsm [-] Connect
retry counter: 0
2017-07-16 16:19:05,843.843 78465 INFO yabgp.core.fsm [-] Connect
```

```
retry timer, time=30
2017-07-16 16:19:05,843.843 78465 INFO yabgp.core.fsm [-]
[10.124.1.245]State is now:CONNECT
2017-07-16 16:19:05,843.843 78465 INFO yabgp.core.factory [-]
(Re)connect to 10.124.1.245
....
```

As can be seen from the logs, the BGP message file is created in the folder, `/home/ubuntu/data/bgp/10.124.1.245`.

By analyzing the logs, you may notice logs are stored from both the remote and local BGP addresses:

```
$ tree /home/ubuntu/data/bgp
/home/ubuntu/data/bgp
├── 10.124.1.245
│   └── msg
│       └── 1500221945.84.msg
└── 52.58.130.47
    └── msg
        └── 1500221444.73.msg
```

How it works...

`yabgpd` is a BGP agent that can establish BGP connections with various routers. The agent receives the BGP messages and is capable of using them for further uses, such as future analysis. Running these applications require access to BGP routers to route traffic between the autonomous systems. These recipes illustrate the capability of Python to build large-scale complex network applications in the internet scale.

Other Books You May Enjoy

If you enjoyed this book, you may be interested in these other books by Packt:

Network Analysis using Wireshark 2 Cookbook - Second Edition
Nagendra Kumar Nainar, Yogesh Ramdoss, Yoram Orzach

ISBN: 978-1-78646-167-4

- Configure Wireshark 2 for effective network analysis and troubleshooting
- Set up various display and capture filters
- Understand networking layers, including IPv4 and IPv6 analysis
- Explore performance issues in TCP/IP
- Get to know about Wi-Fi testing and how to resolve problems related to wireless LANs
- Get information about network phenomena, events, and errors
- Locate faults in detecting security failures and breaches in networks

Practical Network Scanning
Ajay Singh Chauhan

ISBN: 978-1-78883-923-5

- Achieve an effective security posture to design security architectures
- Learn vital security aspects before moving to the Cloud
- Launch secure applications with Web Application Security and SQL Injection
- Explore the basics of threat detection/response/ mitigation with important use cases
- Learn all about integration principles for PKI and tips to secure it
- Design a WAN infrastructure and ensure security over a public WAN

Leave a review - let other readers know what you think

Please share your thoughts on this book with others by leaving a review on the site that you bought it from. If you purchased the book from Amazon, please leave us an honest review on this book's Amazon page. This is vital so that other potential readers can see and use your unbiased opinion to make purchasing decisions, we can understand what our customers think about our products, and our authors can see your feedback on the title that they have worked with Packt to create. It will only take a few minutes of your time, but is valuable to other potential customers, our authors, and Packt. Thank you!

Index

A

B

C

D

E

F

G

H

I

J

K

L

M

R

S

T

U

V

W

X

Y

Made in the USA
Columbia, SC
12 May 2020